SPRINGER SERIES IN NEUROPSYCHOLOGY

Harry A. Whitaker, Series Editor

Springer Series in Neuropsychology

Harry A. Whitaker, Series Editor

Keith Rayner
Editor

Eye Movements and Visual Cognition

Scene Perception and Reading

With 100 Illustrations

Springer-Verlag
New York Berlin Heidelberg London Paris
Tokyo Hong Kong Barcelona Budapest

Keith Rayner
Department of Psychology
University of Massachusetts at Amherst
Amherst, MA 01003
USA

Library of Congress Cataloging-in-Publication Data
Eye movements and visual cognition: scene perception and reading/
    edited by Keith Rayner.
        p.   cm.
    Based on a conference held at the University of Massachusetts
sponsored by the U.S. Air Force Office of Scientific Research (grant
AFOSR 90-0073).
    Includes bibliographical references and index.
    ISBN 0-387-97711-2.—ISBN 3-540-97711-2
    1. Eye—Movements—Congresses.   2. Visual perception—Congresses.
3. Cognition—Congresses.   4. Reading—congresses.   I. Rayner,
Keith.   II. United States. Air Force. Office of Scientific
Research.
    [DNLM: 1. Cognition—congresses.   2. Eye Movements—congresses.
3. Visual Perception—congresses.   WW 400 E976]
QP477.5.E943   1992
612.8'46—dc20
DNLM/DLC
for Library of Congress   91-33689

Printed on acid-free paper.

Production managed by Christin R. Ciresi; Manufacturing supervised by Jacqui Ashri.
Typeset by Best-set Typesetter Ltd., Hong Kong.
Printed and bound by Edwards Brothers, Inc., Ann Arbor, MI.
Printed in the United States of America.

9 8 7 6 5 4 3 2 1

ISBN 0-387-97711-2 Springer-Verlag New York Berlin Heidelberg
ISBN 3-540-97711-2 Springer-Verlag Berlin Heidelberg New York

Preface

This volume is intended as a follow-up to an earlier volume on the topic of eye movements and reading that appeared in 1983. The present volume documents the considerable growth of the eye movement industry in experimental psychology over the past 10 years. Eye movement data are now used to study a number of topics related to visual cognition; the present volume emphasizes research on scene perception and reading.

The chapters in this volume were originally presented at a conference held at the University of Massachusetts sponsored by the United States Air Force Office of Scientific Research (Grant AFOSR 90-0073). Because all of the participants at the conference wrote chapters, the volume represents the structure and content of the conference. It is intended as an up-to-date overview of the topics relevant to understanding the relationship between eye movements and visual cognition, particularly in relation to scene perception and reading. The conference itself was vigorous and stimulating. The discussions at the end of each session were extremely interesting. I hope that much of the excitement that was present at the meeting is captured in the pages of this volume.

The book is divided into five sections. Each section deals with a specific topic and concludes with some comments by a discussant. These comments serve to place the chapters in proper perspective and to tie together the chapters that are presented in each section.

There are many people that I would like to thank for their assistance in making this volume come to fruition. First, I would like to thank all of the authors for the care that they took in preparing their chapters. I would also like to thank my friends and colleagues at the University of Massachusetts for their assistance in organizing the conference and putting the volume together. In particular, I thank Sandy Pollatsek, Chuck Clifton, Robin Morris, and Sara Sereno. I also appreciate the advice of Harry Whitaker, the series editor, and the editorial staff at Springer-Verlag. Jeanie Sullivan provided expert secretarial assistance and I thank her for her help. I also greatly appreciate the support of Al Fregly and John Jonides (in conjunction with their assignments at the Air Force

Office of Scientific Research) for their support in organizing the conference and producing the volume; the financial support for both endeavors that I received from the Air Force Office of Scientific Research is greatly appreciated. My final appreciation goes to Susan Rayner for her continued support and assistance.

Contents

Section 2   Visual Search and Integration

Section 3   Scene Perception

Section 4   Reading

Section 5   Reading and Pictures

Contributors

RICHARD A. ABRAMS Department of Psychology, Washington University, St. Louis, MO 63130, USA

GREGORY BOHEMIER Department of Psychology, SUNY-Binghamton, Binghamton, NY 13901, USA

SUSAN J. BOYCE AT&T, Room 2D-6222, Crawsford Corner Road, Holmdel, NJ 07733, USA

DEBORAH BRIIHL Department of Psychology, SUNY-Binghamton, Binghamton, NY 13901, USA

PATRICK J. CARROLL Department of Psychology, University of Texas, Austin, TX 78712, USA

CHARLES CLIFTON, JR. Department of Psychology, University of Massachusetts, Amherst, MA 01003, USA

PETER DE GRAEF Faculteit Psychologie, Tiensestraat 102, 3000 Leuven, Belgium

SUSAN A. DUFFY Department of Psychology, Amherst College, Amherst, MA 01002, USA

GÉRY D'YDEWALLE Faculteit Psychologie, Tiensestraat 102, 3000 Leuven, Belgium

JOHN M. FINDLAY Department of Psychology, University of Durham, Science Laboratories, South Road, Durham, England DH1 3LE

BURKHART FISCHER Department of Neurology and Neurophysiology, University of Freiburg, D-7800 Freiburg, Germany

DONALD L. FISHER   Department of Industrial Engineering, University of Massachusetts, Amherst, MA 01003, USA

INGRID GIELEN   Laboratory of Experimental Psychology, Department of Psychology, University of Leuven, B-3000 Leuven, Belgium

MICHAEL S. GUERTIN   Department of Psychology, University of Texas, Austin, TX 78712, USA

MARY HEGARTY   Department of Psychology, University of California, Santa Barbara, CA 93117, USA

JOHN M. HENDERSON   Department of Psychology, Michigan State University, East Lansing, MI 48824, USA

MARY M. HAYHOE   Center for Visual Science, University of Rochester, Rochester, NY 14627, USA

ALBRECHT WERNER INHOFF   Department of Psychology, SUNY-Binghamton, Binghamton, NY 13901, USA

DAVID E. IRWIN   Department of Psychology, University of Illinois at Urbana-Champaign, Champaign, IL 61820, USA

LEAH KAUFMAN   Department of Psychology, University of Washington, Seattle, WA 98195, USA

ALAN KENNEDY   Department of Psychology, University of Dundee, Dundee, Scotland

ALAN KINGSTONE   Department of Psychology, Dalhousie University, Halifax, Nova Scotia B3H 4JI, Canada

RAYMOND KLEIN   Department of Psychology, Dalhousie University, Halifax, Nova Scotia B3H 4JI, Canada

JUDITH F. KROLL   Department of Psychology, Mount Holyoke College, South Hadley, MA 01075, USA

JOEL LACHTER   Center for Visual Science, University of Rochester, Rochester, NY 14627, USA

GEOFFREY R. LOFTUS   Department of Psychology, University of Washington, Seattle, WA 98195, USA

GEORGE W. MCCONKIE   Center for Study of Reading, University of Illinosis at Urbana-Champaign, Champaign, IL 61820, USA

ROBIN K. MORRIS   Department of Psychology, University of South Carolina, Columbia, SC 29208, USA

PER MOELLER   Center for Visual Science, University of Rochester, Rochester, NY 14627, USA

DIETER NATTKEMPER   Max-Planck-Institute for Psychological Research, Postfach 44 01 09, D-8000 München 44, Germany

TAKEHIKO NISHIMOTO   Department of Psychology, Washeda University, Tokyo, Japan

J. KEVIN O'REGAN   Groupe Regard, Lab. de Psych. Experimentale, CNRS, EHESS, EPHE, Université René Descartes, 28 Rue Serpente, 75006 Paris, France

ALEXANDER POLLATSEK   Department of Psychology, University of Massachusetts, Amherst, MA 01003, USA

AMANDA PONTEFRACT   Department of Psychology, Dalhousie University, Halifax, Nova Scotia B3H 4JI, Canada

WOLFGANG PRINZ   Max-Planck-Institut for Psychological Research, Postfach 44 01 09, D-8000 München 44, Germany

KEITH RAYNER   Department of Psychology, University of Massachusetts, Amherst, MA 01003, USA

MICHAEL D. REDDIX   Center for the Study of Reading, University of Illinois at Urbona-Champaign, Champaign, IL 61820, USA

ERIC RUTHRUFF   Department of Psychology, University of California–San Diego, San Diego, CA, USA

A. RENÉ SCHMAUDER   Department of Psychology, University of Massachusetts, Amherst, MA 01003, USA

ANNE B. SERENO   Department of Psychology, Harvard University, Cambridge, MA 02138, USA

SARA C. SERENO   Department of Psychology, University of Massachusetts, Amherst, MA 01003, USA

THOMAS ULLMANN   Department of Psychology, University of Bielefield, Bielefield, Germany

JASON R. YOUNG   Department of Psychology, Hunter College, City University of New York, New York, NY, USA

DAVID ZOLA   Center for the Study of Reading, University of Illinois at Urbana-Champaign, Champaign, IL 61820, USA

1
Eye Movements and Visual Cognition: Introduction

KEITH RAYNER

When we read or look at a scene or search for an object in our environment, we do so by moving our eyes over the visual field. Limitations of visual acuity necessitate these eye movements; we move our eyes so that the fovea (or center of vision) is directed toward what we wish to process in detail. Our eyes do not move smoothly over the stimulus; rather, we make a series of fixations and saccades. Fixations, the period of time when our eyes are relatively still, typically last for approximately 150 to 350 ms. Following a fixation, our eyes make a saccade (or jump) to a new location. Although it has been known for some time that we can dissociate our attention from the point of fixation, most of the time our attention and our eyes are directed at the same part of the stimulus field.

The fact that eye movements occur so frequently in various visual cognition tasks (like reading and scene perception) has led a number of research investigators to utilize the eye movement record to infer something about the cognitive processes involved in such tasks. We are now into the third generation of eye movement research and the current volume deals with work in this third generation (for a discussion of the first two generations of eye movement research, see Rayner, 1978).

A review relating eye movements to cognitive processes written nearly 15 years ago (Rayner, 1978) concluded that the future success of eye movement research depended on the degree to which researchers utilizing eye movement records were able to design interesting and informative experiments. As we look back over the past 15 years, it is clear that eye movement research has been quite influential across several domains. Research on the reading process has benefited significantly from insights obtained from eye movement data (see Just & Carpenter, 1987; O'Regan, 1990; Rayner & Pollatsek, 1989); such data have become particularly important in adjudicating among alternative accounts of the processes associated with skilled reading. In addition to reading, work on scene perception, visual search, and other perceptual and cognitive processes has advanced because of research utilizing various types of eye movement data.

Although understanding eye movement behavior in tasks like reading and scene perception is important, much of the recent success of eye movement research has been due to inferences researchers make about underlying cognitive processes. The eyes are sometimes referred to as a "window to the mind." Over the past decade, however, it has become evident that eye movements are not a perfect reflection of cognitive processes. Nevertheless, they remain a rather good index of the moment-to-moment on-line processing activities that accompany visual cognition tasks like reading and scene perception.

The present volume categorizes and summarizes current state-of-the-art work on eye movements and visual cognition. Before outlining the various sections of this volume, I would like to briefly comment on some of the factors that have led to the recent successes of eye movement research in dealing with various cognitive processes. However, this is done with the full realization that advances in understanding oculomotor behavior per se have also had an important impact on the growth of the field.

Reasons for Recent Successes in Eye Movement Research

One important factor involved in the recent success of eye movement research has been the development of eye-contingent display change techniques that have given experimenters considerable control over various stimulus input and timing variables. In the early 1970s, the eye movement–contingent display change technique was developed by McConkie and Rayner (1975) and Reder (1973). The work by McConkie and Rayner, conducted at the Massachusetts Institute of Technology, and the work by Reder, at Rockefeller University, were independently initiated at the same time. Reder's article, which appeared in *Behavior Research Methods and Instrumentation*, outlined the basic rationale. McConkie and Rayner's article, which appeared in *Perception & Psychophysics*, also outlined the rationale and presented data from an experiment in which the amount of information that a reader could process on each eye fixation was manipulated.

The technique developed by McConkie and Rayner and by Reder, called the *moving window paradigm*, has had a major impact on research on reading. Although some studies have used the technique to study scene perception (e.g., Saida & Ikeda, 1979), to date it has not had as much impact. My guess is that this will change in the near future as interest increases in eye movements and scene perception. The moving window paradigm (described in more detail in the chapters by Pollatsek and Rayner; Henderson; and Inhoff, Bohemier, and Briihl in this volume) involves interfacing a computer system with an eye-tracking system so that an experimenter can control the amount of information available to the subject on each eye fixation. Wherever the reader looks, normal text is presented around the fixation point; outside of this *window* area, the text is mutilated in some way.

Another technique, the *boundary* paradigm developed by Rayner (1975), allows the experimenter to be more diagnostic about what kind of information is acquired at different distances from fixation. In this technique, a word or nonword letter string is initially presented in a target location. However, when the reader's eye movement crosses an invisible boundary location, the initially presented stimulus is replaced by the target word. The amount of time that the subject looks at the target word is influenced by the relationship between the initially presented stimulus and the target word and the distance from the launch site to the target location. The fixation time on the target word thus allows the experimenter to make inferences about the type of information acquired from the target location when it was in parafoveal vision.

A variation of the boundary technique (see Rayner, McConkie, & Ehrlich, 1978) has also been used to investigate basic reading processes. In this variation, a word or letter string is presented in parafoveal vision and subjects are instructed to name a target word following an eye movement to the target location. During the eye movement, the initially presented stimulus is replaced by the target word. This paradigm has also been used to investigate object perception (see Pollatsek, Rayner, & Collins, 1984). Two other very recent variations of the boundary technique are described in the current volume in the chapters by S. Sereno and by Boyce and Pollatsek.

As indicated above, the various types of eye-contingent display change techniques have had a major impact on research on reading and scene perception because they allow the experimenter to control the information available to the subject at any point in time. Certain types of information can be presented (or masked) at specified intervals during an eye fixation (see Morris, Rayner, & Pollatsek, 1990; Rayner, Inhoff, Morrison, Slowiaczek, & Bertera, 1981). Such experimental control over the nature of timing of the available information has enabled researchers to draw interesting conclusions about on-line aspects of reading and scene perception.

Fortuitously, it has also turned out to be the case that much recent theoretical discussion concerning reading and scene perception has focused on moment-to-moment processing. A great deal of earlier research on reading and scene perception relied upon either very global measures of processing time (such as the amount of time it takes a subject to read a sentence) or very microscopic measures (such as very brief tachistoscopic exposures of stimuli). Data from such research have not been very diagnostic concerning how it is that readers understand text on a moment-to-moment basis. Interestingly, in the last 10 years, theories of language processing have become much more concerned with on-line processing issues (see Just & Carpenter, 1987; Rayner & Pollatsek, 1989). Eye movement data have turned out to be very informative in choosing among various alternative theoretical accounts of moment-to-moment processing (see Rayner, Sereno, Morris, Schmauder, & Clifton, 1989; also Clifton's chapter in this volume).

Finally, much of the recent success of eye movement research has been due to the development of computer-based data collection and analysis routines. Eye movement recording techniques make available to an experimenter a vast array of data. How to analyze such a large amount of data has often been a major problem for eye movement researchers. However, the capability of interfacing eye-tracking systems with high-speed computers has made data collection much easier than it used to be. Likewise, the use of computers has made the analysis of the resulting data considerably more manageable than used to be the case.

Overview of the Volume

The present volume consists of chapters by researchers interested in various aspects of the relationship between eye movements and visual cognition. Section 1 deals largely with issues related to programming eye movements, eye movement latencies, and the role of attention in moving one's eyes. Although these chapters do not directly deal with more complex cognitive activities such as reading and scene perception, anyone interested in the relationship between eye movements and visual cognition must take into account the kind of data and theorizing represented in the various chapters of Section 1. The neurophysiological basis for the programming of eye movements has been extensively studied over the past 20 years and the chapters in Section 1 provide important information concerning what has been learned.

Section 2 deals with the role of eye movements in visual search and the extent to which different types of information are integrated across eye movements. One of the chapters in the section deals with visual search, whereas the others deal primarily with integration across fixations. Of course, the issues of what is integrated across eye movements and how that information is integrated are unique to the field of eye movement research. Many issues dealing with reading and scene perception can be addressed quite independently of eye movements. Nonetheless, questions of integration are theoretically very interesting. How exactly does the brain smooth out the discrete inputs of eye fixations separated by rapid saccadic eye movements? Most of the chapters in Section 2 deal with this question.

Section 3 deals primarily with the topic of scene perception, although some of the chapters also discuss the reading process. Recently, a great many experiments using either tachistoscopic presentations (see Biederman, Mezzanotte, & Rabinowitz, 1982) or eye movement recordings (see Loftus & Mackworth, 1978) have concluded that subjects get the gist of a scene very early in the process of looking, sometimes even from a single brief exposure. The idea that has been advocated relative to eye movements in scene perception, therefore, has been that the gist of the scene is abstracted on the first couple of fixations and the remainder of the eye fixations on the scene are then used to fill in details. Given these findings, one may question the value of information likely to be gleaned from experiments relying on detailed eye movement analyses as people look at scenes. Although this is a reasonable question, it basically assumes that the conclusions reached in the types of studies mentioned are valid. However, it remains to be conclusively demonstrated that the tachistoscopic studies are revealing a perceptual effect rather than the outcome of memory processes or guessing strategies. Likewise, with eye movement studies that have supported the idea that the gist is abstracted very quickly from a scene, there are concerns that can be generated. One finding is that the eyes are quickly drawn to informative regions of a picture (Antes, 1974; Mackworth & Morandi, 1967). Another prominent finding is that the eyes quickly move to an object that is out of place in a scene (Friedman, 1979; Loftus & Mackworth, 1978). This has been taken as evidence that subjects quickly get the gist of the scene and move their eyes to the object that does not fit. However, it may be that the eyes are quickly drawn to informative areas because such areas are physically distinctive in pictures; the definition of what is informative in these studies often corresponds to the definition of what is distinctive. And, in the studies in which the eyes quickly move to an out-of-place object, it is also possible that such objects are physically distinct from the surroundings. In large part, the chapters in Section 3 deal with the issue of how scene contexts influence scene perception and eye movement characteristics.

Sections 4 and 5 both deal with eye movements and reading. In the domain of reading, as noted above, eye movement studies have had notable success in influencing theories of the reading process and in explaining the moment-to-moment processing activities involved in the task. The chapters in these two sections are representative of the various types of issues that have been addressed using eye movement data. The research described in these chapters ranges from studies dealing with low-level perceptual processing during reading to studies in which eye movements are used to infer higher order processes. Section 5, in particular, includes some chapters in which the interplay between reading text and looking at pictures is discussed. The chapters in both sections exemplify the benefits to eye movement research arising from advances in technology and theorizing.

Central Theme of the Volume

The present volume is intended as an update of a book (Rayner, 1983) published 9 years ago. The earlier volume dealt solely with the topic of reading. The present volume is more general in that it deals more broadly with visual cognition exemplified in scene perception and reading. Although there are some differences of opinion among the authors of the various chapters concerning important theoretical principles, the central theme running through the different chapters is that eye movement data can profitably be used to examine on-line visual cognition. The range of questions addressed and the clever nature of the experimental procedures in the volume serve as testimony to the success of the third generation of eye movement research.

References

Antes, J.R. (1974). The time course of picture viewing. *Journal of Experimental Psychology*, *103*, 62–70.

Biederman, I., Mezzanotte, R.J., & Rabinowitz, J.C. (1982). Scene perception: Detecting and judging objects undergoing relational violations. *Cognitive Psychology*, *14*, 143–177.

Friedman, A. (1979). Framing pictures: The role of knowledge in automatized encoding and memory for gist. *Journal of Experimental Psychology: General*, *108*, 316–355.

Just, M.A., & Carpenter, P.A. (1987). *The psychology of reading and language comprehension*. Newton, MA: Allyn and Bacon.

Loftus, G.R., & Mackworth, N.H. (1978). Cognitive determinants of fixation location during picture viewing. *Journal of Experimental Psychology: Human Perception and Performance*, *4*, 565–572.

Mackworth, N.H., & Morandi, A.J. (1967). The gaze selects informative details within pictures. *Perception & Psychophysics*, *2*, 547–552.

McConkie, G.W., & Rayner, K. (1975). The span of the effective stimulus during a fixation in reading. *Perception & Psychophysics*, *17*, 578–586.

Morris, R.K., Rayner, K., & Pollatsek, A. (1990). Eye movement guidance in reading: The role of parafoveal letter and space information. *Journal of Experimental Psychology: Human Perception and Performance*, *16*, 268–281.

O'Regan, J.K. (1990). Eye movements and reading. In E. Kowler (Ed.), *Eye movements and their role in visual and cognitive processes*. Amsterdam: Elsevier.

Pollatsek, A., Rayner, K., & Collins, W.E. (1984). Integrating pictorial information across eye movements. *Journal of Experimental Psychology: General*, *113*, 426–442.

Rayner, K. (1975). The perceptual span and peripheral cues in reading. *Cognitive Psychology*, *7*, 65–81.

Rayner, K. (1978). Eye movements in reading and information processing. *Psychological Bulletin*, *85*, 618–660.

Rayner, K. (1983). *Eye movements in reading: Perceptual and language processes*. New York: Academic Press.

Rayner, K., Inhoff, A.W., Morrison, R.E., Slowiaczek, M.L., & Bertera, J.H. (1981). Masking of foveal and parafoveal vision during eye fixations in reading. *Journal of Experimental Psychology: Human Perception and Performance*, *7*, 167–179.

Rayner, K., McConkie, G.W., & Ehrlich, S. (1978). Eye movements and integrating information across eye movements. *Journal of Experimental Psychology: Human Perception and Performance*, *4*, 529–544.

Rayner, K., & Pollatsek, A. (1989). *The psychology of reading*. Englewood Cliffs, NJ: Prentice Hall.

Rayner, K., Sereno, S.C., Morris, R.K., Schmauder, A.R., & Clifton, C. (1989). Eye movements and on-line comprehension processes. *Language and Cognitive Processes*, *4*, SI21–50.

Reder, S.M. (1973). On-line monitoring of eye position signals in contingent and noncontingent paradigms. *Behavior Research Methods and Instrumentation*, *5*, 218–228.

Saida, S., & Ikeda, M. (1979). Useful visual field for pattern perception. *Perception & Psychophysics*, *25*, 119–125.

2
Programming of Stimulus-Elicited Saccadic Eye Movements

JOHN M. FINDLAY

Eye movements and visual cognition have in the past seemed like two separate continents separated by an enormous and ill-charted ocean. As the chapters in this volume show, many navigators are now successfully venturing on this ocean. However, the strategy of the work described here is somewhat more modest and may be likened to that of the early explorers who kept well within sight of the coastline. The coastline is the target-elicited saccadic eye movement, where a subject orients to a well-defined target that appears suddenly in the visual periphery. This is a piece of behavior that has been extensively studied and is reasonably well understood. It is argued that it can provide a good point of departure for examining cognitive influences.

Saccades and their Characteristics

One of the most amazing features of the human eye is its effortless mobility. The ability to redirect the gaze within a fraction of a second to any part of the visual field ranks high among the significant features of vision. It results in what might with some justification be termed the most powerful visual illusion of all—the impression that the visual world has a detailed, immediate, picture-like quality. We know this is an illusion from consideration of the way acuity varies over the retina. High-resolution vision is only available for a small central region around the fovea. Moving away from this region, resolution deteriorates progressively (Virsu & Rovamo, 1979; Wertheim, 1894) and lateral interference effects contribute further to the degradation of vision (Bouma, 1978). Nevertheless, since we can direct our eyes with a saccadic eye movement to any desired region of the visual field, and obtain high-resolution information as soon as the gaze is so directed, the limitations of parafoveal and peripheral vision are rarely noticeable and it is easy to overlook the essential role played by the eye muscles in the visual process.

Saccadic eye movements are sometimes classified into voluntary and reflexive (e.g., Walls, 1962). Although both the terminology and the dichotomy will be questioned at a later point in the chapter, let us accept them for the moment. The target-elicited eye movement is then held to fall in the reflexive category. It is certainly the case that orienting to a novel visual target in the periphery is a very simple and natural response. Such orienting responses have in consequence been intensively studied in humans and, because training is relatively easy, in nonhuman primates also. The most common task for investigating target-elicited saccades requires the subject to fixate one display point initially and to change fixation as rapidly as possible when a target appears. If the target falls within approximately the central 15° of vision, then humans generally orient to it with saccadic eye movements alone; orienting to targets at greater eccentricities will normally involve head movements also (Sanders, 1962).

Two generalizations about saccades were established in early work: notably that saccades appeared ballistic and stereotyped. Ballistic implies that once a saccade has been initiated, the moving eye cannot be influenced in any way. Stereotyped implies that for a saccadic eye rotation of a particular size, the same trajectory is reproduced each time the movement is made. The trajectory can be characterized by the duration of the movement and the maximum velocity attained by the eye during the movement. These properties depend in a systematic way on the size of the movement; saccade duration for a small saccade is about 20 ms and increases to about 100 ms for very large movements. Use of an imaginative analogy from astrophysics has resulted in the term *main sequence* to describe saccades showing these stereotyped properties (Bahill, Clark, & Stark, 1975).

Although this is an adequate characterization for many purposes, it is now clear that saccades are neither completely ballistic nor totally stereotyped. Saccadic trajectories seem insensitive to new visual information appearing after the saccade has started. However, if the target appears and then changes position about 100 ms before the saccade starts, this may result in a change of trajectory in a manner to compensate for this position change. Figure 2.1 shows some particularly dramatic demonstrations of this phenomenon. These occur when the target position change alters the direction of the saccade to give a markedly curved trajectory (Findlay & Harris, 1984; Van Gisbergen, Van Opstal, & Roebroek, 1987). These demonstrations provide support for a model of saccade programming in which internal feedback plays a part in determining the saccade goal (Robinson, 1975).

Further support for this suggestion comes from detailed analysis of departures from the stereotyped main sequence (Findlay & Crawford, 1986; Jürgens, Becker, & Kornhuber, 1981). Considering saccades to targets at a particular position, it turns out that there is statistically a

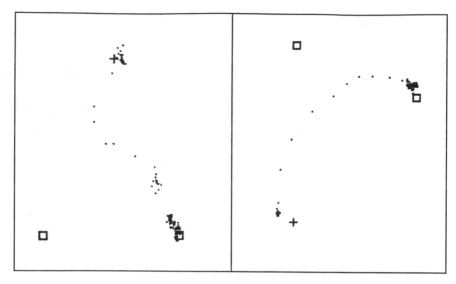

FIGURE 2.1. Two examples of saccadic trajectories showing pronounced curvature. The saccades were recorded in the double-step paradigm. The cross shows the initial fixation point and the two squares the successive positions of the target. The small dots represent successive visual axis positions, sampled every 10 ms. The saccades are initially directed at the first target position. The target stepped between the two positions about 100 ms before the saccade started. Reprinted by permission, from Findlay and Harris (1984).

greater variability in the duration or velocity of saccades than would be expected from the variability in saccade amplitude. This may be interpreted as meaning that if a saccade starts with a slower eye velocity than normal, it will proceed for longer than normal to compensate (and vice versa for saccades starting faster than normal).

A variety of other factors (fatigue, drugs, etc.) influences saccade characteristics, generally leading to slower saccade trajectories than expected on the main sequence basis (Galley, 1989). Voluntary reduction of velocity by means of biofeedback-like training can occur (Crawford, 1984; Findlay & Crawford, 1986). Saccades are slower in the dark, and in general target-elicited saccades are faster than non–target-elicited (e.g., anticipatory) saccades (Smit & Van Gisbergen, 1989).

Separation of Spatial and Temporal Factors

Notwithstanding the findings of the previous section, for many purposes the detailed characteristics of saccades are of little concern and the issue of saccade programming revolves around two measures relating to space and to time. The *size* of the saccade is usually expressed in terms of the amplitude of rotation together with the direction of rotation relative to horizontal and vertical axes. The time of initiation, for target-elicited saccades, is generally measured as the *latency* from the appearance of the target to the start of the eye movement.

A classic paper by Becker and Jürgens (1979; see also Becker, 1989) has considerably influenced modern thinking about saccade programming. These authors studied target-elicited saccades generated in the *double-step paradigm*. In this paradigm, on some trials the target, following its appearance, would make a further step movement subsequently. Becker and Jürgens carried out a series of experiments with this paradigm and expressed their results in terms of a model.

The chief experimental finding, which has proved easy to replicate (Findlay & Harris, 1984; Ottes, Van Gisbergen, & Eggermont, 1984), is the *amplitude transition function*. If the target appears initially at a position denoted *P1* and makes a subsequent jump to a position denoted *P2*, the first saccade made by a subject will be one of three types. Using the terminology introduced by Becker and Jürgens (1979), these are *initial angle responses*, *final angle responses*, and *transitional responses*. Initial angle responses are identical to saccades when a single target is presented at *P1*, final angle responses are equivalent to those when a single target is presented at *P2*, and transitional responses are ones that arrive at an intermediate position between *P1* and *P2*. The variability inherent in the saccadic system means that individual responses cannot always be assigned unambiguously to one of these categories. However, the analysis is supported by the amplitude transition function (ATF). Over a series of double-step trials, saccade amplitude is plotted against a time variable designated *D*. *D* measures the time from the second jump of the target to the first saccade; it can be thought of as measuring the time available for the second target jump to perturb the saccade that is in preparation to the first target. *D* is influenced by two factors: the interval between the two target jumps, which may be varied by the experimenter, and the intrinsic variability in the saccade initiation process.

For small values of *D*, initial angle responses occur. In other words, a certain minimum time must elapse before any effect of the second, perturbing, target step is manifest. Typically the minimum is 70 to 80 ms. This figure gives the absolute minimum time required to modify a saccade in course of preparation by visual stimulation. The time is in fact quite similar to the delays estimated in the peripheral retinal (Parker & Salzen, 1977) and oculomotor (Keller, 1974) systems.

For values of *D* greater than some value (usually about 200 ms), final angle responses occur: the system seems to ignore the appearance of the target in the first position and the eye moves directly to the second target. For intermediate values of *D*, the transition responses occur in which saccades are aimed at intermediate positions. There is an approximately linear relation between the actual position between *P1* and *P2* and the position, earlier or later, within the transition region.

Becker and Jürgens (1979) accounted for the results with a model postulating two stages of processing. The *decision mechanism* is a process that operates as a trigger-like device to initiate the saccadic process. It receives input from the visual signal but does not program the detailed metrics of the saccade. This is the function of the second mechanism, the *amplitude computation process*. The amplitude computation process is envisaged to be automatic, making reference to the visual stimulation and operating through a process of temporal and spatial integration. The model postulates a point in the course of saccade generation at which a decision has been taken irrevocably to initiate the movement, but the exact metrics still await specification. It is thus possible for the perturbing second step to exert an influence on the saccade amplitude at a comparatively late stage. This amplitude computation process involves *spatial and temporal integration*. Rather than using the visual stimulation at a particular point in time and in space, the system integrates stimulation over a broad spatial window and over a temporal window whose duration is similar to that of the transition function. The integration processes are assumed to be inherent in the neural processing. This model predicts quantitatively the presence of intermediate saccades and the time course of the ATF.

The idea that the temporal and spatial components of saccades are programmed separately, in some important sense, has been a theme of workers studying saccades from a more physiologically oriented viewpoint; sometimes the terminology of a "WHEN" system and a "WHERE" system is used to indicate the functions of the two postulated sub-systems (Van Gisbergen, Gielen, Cox, Bruijns, & Kleine Schaars, 1981). One factor influencing such thinking is that such a separation is found at the level of brain stem oculomotor neurophysiology. One type of neuron, the "omnipauser" neurons, are found to have the property of

---

FIGURE 2.2. Saccades in the double-step paradigm. The top diagram shows the stimulus display. The subject fixated a target at the central point and followed it when it made a jump to one of the eight possible peripheral positions (denoted *P1*). On double-step trials the target made a further jump after a brief interval to a second position (denoted *P2*), either clockwise or counterclockwise. In the plots, the amplitudes of the first saccades and their direction relative to the target directions are plotted. The abscissa shows the time in milliseconds between the second step and the commencement of the first, i.e., the time available for the *second* step to perturb the saccade, which is in preparation to the *first* step. Each dot shows one saccade and the solid line joins the median points in successive 10-ms bins (20 ms when the data are sparse). Reprinted by permission, from Findlay and Harris (1984).

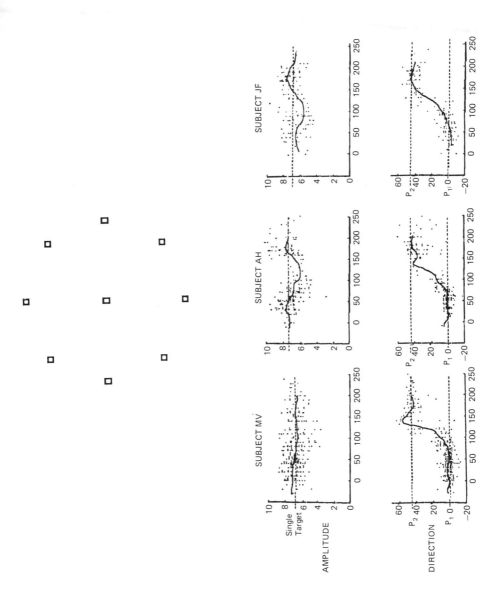

being normally active, but this activity ceases abruptly whenever any saccade is made. Another type of neuron, the burst cell, codes the spatial properties of the movement. In at least one major review (Gouras, 1985), an explicit correspondence is drawn between the burst cell/pause cell system of the brain stem and the control of saccades at a behavioral level.

An issue still to be resolved concerns whether direction and amplitude are separately programmed. The Becker and Jürgens (1979) model includes in the first (decision) stage the process of establishing the direction of the saccade. However, their experimental results concerned horizontal saccades only. Experimental work on oblique saccades demonstrates that the components of the movement are *not* independently planned and executed (Van Gisbergen, Van Opstal, & Schoenmakers, 1985) suggesting an overall spatial framework rather than one in which direction and amplitude are separate. Work on the double step paradigm has not yet resolved the issue. Hou and Fender (1979) argued from their data that there was a stage at which the direction of a saccade could not be altered, whereas the amplitude could be reduced. Findlay and Harris (1984) used the analysis methods of Becker and Jürgens (1979) in a two-step experiment where the second step changed the required direction for the saccade. They found an angle transition function (Figure 2.2) whose time course was very similar to that reported for the amplitude transition function. They suggested that the two functions were produced by a single process. Aslin and Shea (1987), however, on the basis of small, but consistent, differences in timing between the transition functions for amplitude and for angle, argued once again for two separate processes. Another approach to this question is that of Abrams and Jonides (1988) who determined the benefits (saccade latency reduction) of precuing amplitude or direction of saccades (see chapter by Abrams in this volume).

Spatial Programming of Target-Elicited Saccades

In the case of saccades to single visual targets, the spatial aspect of saccade programming might appear straightforward because the position of the target on the retina provides a unique code for the position of the target in space and the eye rotation equired to fixate the target. Indeed, many models of saccadic programming contain an input labeled "retinal error."

This simple approach to spatial coding turns out to be inadequate, however. Evidence has accumulated to show that target position is not encoded in a point-to-point form as just suggested but rather in a highly distributed form. On the basis of physiological studies in the superior colliculus, McIlwain (1976) made the farsighted suggestion that there might be a remapping of retinal space into a representation involving very large, overlapping, receptive fields. He further suggested that this type of recoding could provide a way in which the spatial signal from the retina could generate a signal appropriate to the oculomotor command cells. More recent work has confirmed the validity of this idea. A particularly neat study was that of Lee, Rohrer, and Sparks (1988) using a technique that reversibly deactivated a subset of neurons in the colliculus. Exactly the effects predicted on the basis of population coding were obtained.

This distributed coding is of considerable theoretical significance for vision. At first sight, distributed coding appears to sacrifice resolution. However, theoretical arguments have been advanced that this is not the case and indeed distributed coding can allow finer discriminations to be possible in the location of a single target than point-to-point mapping (Hinton, McClelland, & Rumelhart, 1986). The price that is paid is in terms of interference between adjacent stimuli. Interference of this type has indeed long been recognized as a feature of peripheral vision generally (Bouma, 1978) and is also observed in the saccadic control system under certain conditions (see below). Several other advantages of distributed coding have been suggested (Findlay, 1987). For example, a distributed representation allows ready modification of the relationship between location of stimulation on the retina and saccade size. It is known that such plasticity exists (Deubel, 1987; McLoughlin, 1967; see also chapter by Abrams, this volume) and is of benefit in clinical conditions such as muscular weakness (Optican, Zee, & Chu, 1987).

A result at the behavioral level that is attributable to distributed coding is the *global effect*. The term describes the finding than when an orienting response is made to a target pair consisting of two neighboring but separated elements, the first saccade lands in between the two elements. This result, first reported by Coren and Hoenig (1972) has been the subject of considerable recent investigation (Deubel, Wolf, & Hauske, 1984; Findlay, 1982, 1985; Ottes et al., 1984). Coren and Hoenig used the term *center of gravity* to describe the tendency of the eye to aim at the central position. The validity of this term has been established by recording saccades made to target pairs when the two elements differ in their visual properties. If one member of the pair is larger (Findlay, 1982), more intense (Deubel et al., 1984), presented with higher contrast (Deubel & Hauske, 1988) or higher dot density (Menz & Groner, 1987), then the first orienting saccade lands relatively closer to that target in comparison with the condition where the two target elements are identical. These findings make clear that the global averaging takes place in the visual pathways (rather than, for example, at a stage where the locations of each target have been extracted separately prior to averaging). It seems very probable that the averaging process is the same as the spatiotemporal averaging described in the previous section in connection with double-step responses.

The averaging process operates on a nonlinear representation of the signal. If one target is of positive contrast and the other of negative

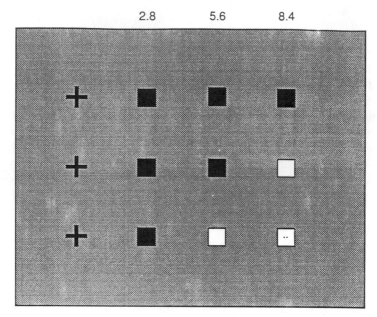

FIGURE 2.3. Target configurations used in the "grouping" experiment. On each trial the subject was presented with either a single square at 2.8°, 5.6°, or 8.4° eccentricity, or else one of six triple-square configurations. These six comprised the three shown and a further three with black and white squares interchanged. The targets could be on the right or on the left. The task was to detect a small dot or dot pair that could appear in any of the three squares on triple-target trials (example shown on lowest right square).

contrast (i.e., a black and a white target on a midluminance background), the saccade still lands at a midway position (Deubel, Findlay, Jacobs, & Brogan, 1988; Zetzsche, Deubel, & Elsner, 1984). This shows that it is not mediated by low spatial frequency channels in the way that such channels are normally defined. A further finding is that edges are particularly important. Boundaries between regions of different texture provide a signal of high salience in the spatiotemporal integration process (Deubel et al., 1988).

Furthermore, the signal seems to emphasize information at very coarse spatial scales. A striking illustration of this comes from a recent experiment carried out with M. Wenban-Smith at Durham. We studied saccades to target triples, as shown in Figure 2.3, where the individual targets were either white or black squares on a midluminance gray background. Our original hypothesis was that, even though black and white targets had been shown to be of equal salience in the center-of-gravity computation (Deubel et al., 1988), some grouping process might result in differential salience for pairs of identical targets. In fact, we found such differential salience but in the opposite direction to the one we expected. As shown in Figure 2.4, it emerges that the configuration with the odd target in the far position elicits larger saccades than the other configurations.

A plausible interpretation of this finding is that the discontinuity between the two types of target constitutes one salient feature to enter into the center-of-gravity calculation. Figure 2.3 shows how such a discontinuity can form a prominent boundary between regions. The global edge at the black/white boundary seems to dominate perceptually over the local edges of the individual squares constituting the pattern. The result we obtained suggests that global edges are emphasized also in the spatial signal for target-elicited saccades.

Relationships with Visual Processing

In his well-known model of vision, Marr (1982) argued that edge detection was a vital early process of visual perception. Subsequent work has supported this view in general and many studies show that certain primitive visual properties are processed in parallel across the visual field. These can make a target "pop out," allowing rapid and effortless search (Treisman, 1985), and can lead to rapid and effortless texture segregation (Bergen & Julesz, 1983). Marr's theory of vision suggested that parallel visual processing continued through to the highest levels and offered no role for scanning eye movements. However, more recent work (e.g., Nakayama, 1990) has attempted to combine parallel and serial processes.

The work described in the previous section has also demonstrated the salience of edges in the signal controlling target-elicited saccadic eye movements. It is tempting to suggest that the convergence on visual edges is not coincidental and that the signal that is demonstrated in the saccade paradigm is the same as that used in visual perception (Deubel et al., 1988). This gets quite close to the suggestion of Strong and Whitehead (1989) that the spatial location of features is "tagged" with reference to the pattern of salience vis-à-vis eye movement elicitation and that this salience signal operates in parallel but separately from more feature-analytic processes concerned with perceptual recognition.

Figure 2.4 shows another characteristic of the global effect, its time-dependent nature. Short latency saccades are directed close to the geometric center of the target configuration but with increasing latency a reduction in the extent of the global effect occurs. This has been found in other studies (Findlay, 1981b) and seems in part to be a reflection of automatic visual processing. Other findings and theoretical approaches in vision suggest that global processes operate more rapidly than local ones (Earhard & Walker, 1985; Watt, 1987).

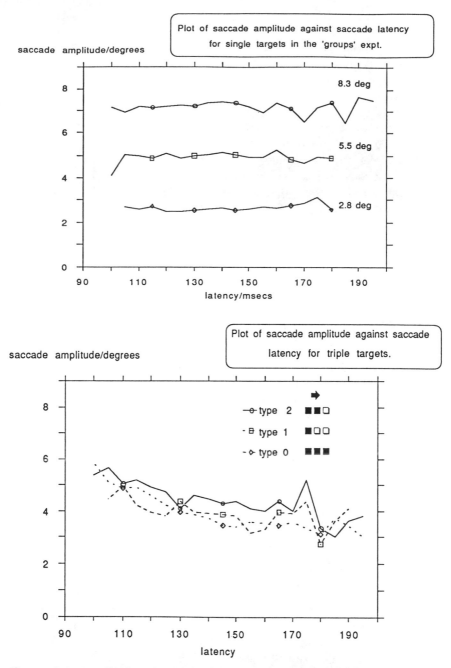

FIGURE 2.4. Amplitudes of saccades in the "grouping" experiment, plotted as a function of saccade latency. The top plot shows saccades to single-square targets and the lower plot saccades to triple-square targets. The shortest latency saccades to triple-square targets are directed at the center of the configuration, but with increasing latency become directed toward the nearest target. At all latencies, the configuration with an odd target in the furthest position produces larger saccades than the other two configurations.

Spatial Frameworks

Orienting responses are not exclusively the province of the visual modality. Saccades can be made readily to localized auditory targets (Zahn, Abel, & Dell'Osso, 1978; Zambarbieri, Schmid, Magenes, & Prablanc, 1982). Moreover, Lueck, Crawford, Savage, and Kennard (1990) have shown that integrative effects between targets in two separate positions can occur when one target is visual and one is auditory. This suggests that some common framework is used to encode spatial stimulation in different modalities. A question then raised is whether this framework is in an eye-centered, head-centered, or some other spatial coordinate frame.

A very influential paper of Robinson (1975) argued that all saccades were planned in a coordinate frame that was fixed relative to the head rather than relative to the eye. A head-centered framework appears necessary to allow saccades to be made to remembered targets, nonvisual targets, and auditory targets. For visually elicited saccades it is logically sufficient to use a retinocentric programming frame (the movement required to foveate a visual target is the same whatever position the eye had originally). Nevertheless, Robinson argued that even for visually elicited saccades, the head-centered frame was involved through a double transformation. First, the retinal signal was converted to head-centered coordinates, and then at a subsequent stage another equal transformation in the opposite direction occurred to generate the oculomotor signal.

Several results appeared to support Robinson's viewpoint. Hallett and Lightstone (1976) showed that when a target was flashed briefly during the course of a saccade in darkness, subjects could make a second saccade back to the target position in space, a task that could not be accomplished on the basis of retinal stimulation alone. Working with monkeys, Mays and Sparks (1980) stimulated the superior colliculus electrically during the preparatory period of saccades elicited to a visual target. The effect of the electrical stimulation was to generate an immediate rapid eye movement. They found that when the target-elicited saccade occurred, it was in a direction that compensated for the electrically stimulated movement. Again, such a result could not occur if the saccade was planned in a retinocentric framework.

However, the idea that the brain maintains a spatial map in head-centered or body-centered coordinates has not been without problems, one of which is that no direct physiological evidence for such a map has been found (but see Andersen, Essick, & Siegel, 1985). An alternative viewpoint has been advocated by Sparks (1986). He suggests that, at least in the superior colliculus of the brain, spatial location may be encoded solely in terms of the eye muscle activation necessary to fixate the location (the motor error signal). Support for this position comes from the physiological work of Jay and Sparks (1987). They found, again in the superior colliculus, cells sensitive to localized auditory stimulation, whose optimal stimulation location is changed when the animal fixates a different location. In other words, auditory mapping in this center shifts every time a saccade is made. Honda (1989) has also repeated the experiments of Hallett and Lightstone (1976) and has shown that a somewhat different interpretation is possible.

Cognitive Influences

In contrast to what might be expected by the use of term *reflexive* to describe target-elicited saccades, the sizes of such saccades are not entirely determined by the location of the target stimulation. Kapoula (1985) showed that saccades to single targets showed a small but consistent "range effect." In an experiment during the course of which targets at a range of different eccentricities are presented, saccades to the nearest targets show a relative overshoot and saccades to the furthest target show a relative undershoot. The subject's knowledge and expectations of the range over which the targets will occur is reflected in this effect on saccade amplitude, although it must be emphasized that the effect is quite small.

A somewhat similar effect has recently been reported with saccades to double targets (He & Kowler, 1989). Here the two targets were visually different, and the subject was instructed to search for one type. In different experimental blocks, the probability that the sought-for target would be in a particular position varied. In this situation, the landing position of the eye was affected by the probability manipulation. If the target was, for example, most likely to occur in a rightward position, the subject's saccades were directed further right. He and Kowler wish to argue from this result that high-level plans, rather than a sensorimotor averaging mechanism, can account for the effects of nontargets on saccade metrics. It is difficult to see how such an extreme conclusion is warranted. Their results have shown that high-level plans can influence the saccade landing position, not that such plans determine the landing position.

The results just described seem to show a central influence that operates in a relatively automatic manner. Other forms of central influence can also be shown. One study (carried out with L. Harris and Z. Kapoula) was concerned with the ability to pay attention to detail. Introspectively, it seems that we possess the capacity either to scan material in a casual way or alternatively to give it close scrutiny. We presented subjects with displays consisting of one or more squares (Figure 2.5) and their task was to count the total number of spots in the squares to compare with a prememorized number. In one condition (normal scanning), each square contained either one or two spots. This provides a relatively easy task. The second condition (accuracy) was much more demanding. Each square contained either three or four spots. The second condition re-

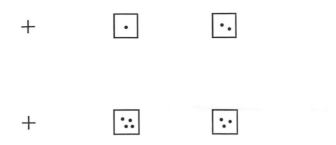

FIGURE 2.5. Design of the spot-counting task. One each trial, following initial fixation on the cross, the subject was presented with a combination of one, two, or three squares at various positions. The task was to count the number of spots inside the squares and check this against a figure presented at the start of the trial. In the "normal" condition, each square contained either one or two spots. In the more demanding "accuracy" condition, each square contained three or four spots.

quires close scrutiny because the discrimination can only be made if the fovea is positioned within about half a degree of the center of the square (Findlay & Crawford, 1983).

The amplitudes and latencies of the first saccades in this study are shown in Figure 2.6. There is no effect of task on the latencies of the first saccade, although subsequent fixation durations are considerably longer in the scrutiny condition. The results suggest that the initial, target-elicited saccade is triggered in the same way whatever are the subject's intentions. Intention to scrutinize has little effect on the global effect when the targets are close (2° and 4°) but the influence of the more eccentric target is progressively reduced as the target separation increases. Indeed for the 2° and 8° pairing, it appears that the effect actually reverses (four out of five subjects showed saccades in this condition that were of smaller amplitude than saccades to the control single 2° target, and the fifth showed saccades of identical size). Current work on spatial attention suggests that attention can operate like a spotlight or zoom lens (Eriksen & St James, 1986; Posner, 1980). It is possible that scrutiny involves active exclusion of material outside the spotlight beam, leading to the occurrence of the opposite type of influence to the usual one. Such reversed attentional effects have been noted elsewhere (Driver & Tipper, 1989).

Chronometry

Many factors influence the latency of target-elicited saccades. In an earlier review (Findlay, 1983), the suggestion was made that visual characteristics of the target produce rather weak effects, whereas general effects relating to the preparatory state of the subject was much more

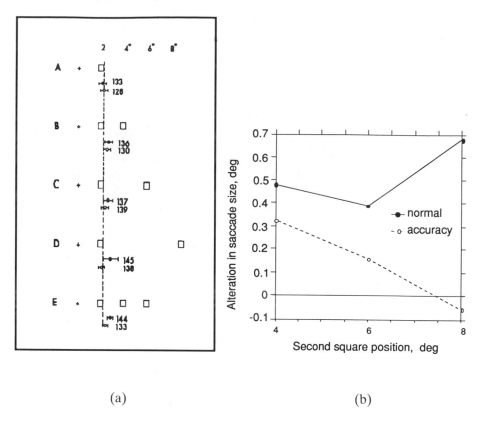

(a)   (b)

FIGURE 2.6. (a) Amplitude of saccade to various target configurations in the spot-counting experiment. Filled symbols show the normal condition and open circles show the accuracy condition. (b) Influence of the more distant target in two-square configurations.

significant. These findings were used to support the WHEN/WHERE distinction already referred to. The idea is that the saccade triggering the "WHEN" process only requires some minimal signal from the target and this signal is processed equally readily wherever the target occurs. This view still seems useful as a generality. The thorough studies of Doma and Hallett (1988) show that properties of the visual target affect latencies, but these effects are large (i.e., more than 10 to 20 ms) only in the scotopic and near-threshold regions for target-elicited saccades. Similarly, the eccentricity of the target seems to exert no systematic effect within the range of 1° to 15°, although targets outside this region are associated with increased latencies. However, a puzzling exception to these general finding of minimal effects of target properties occurs when direction in the visual field is varied. When targets can occur in all visual field positions, latencies to targets along the horizontal axis and in the upper visual field do not differ systematically but latencies of saccades to targets

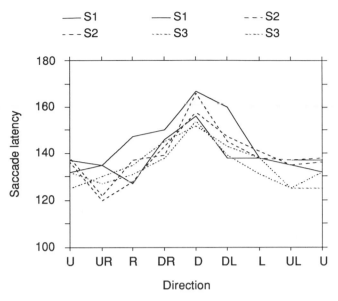

FIGURE 2.7. Variation of saccade latency with visual field direction. Three subjects made saccades to targets appearing at unpredictable positions around a clock face. Each point represents the mean of eight trials. Two blocks were recorded for each subject.

in the lower visual field have been reported on several occasions to be systematically increased (Honda & Findlay, in press; Hackman, 1940; Heywood & Churcher, 1980) (Figure 2.7). The reasons for this effect are unknown, although it might possibly be related to visual ecology (Previc, 1990).

In the task where a subject has to move from a fixation point to a peripheral target, Saslow (1967) showed that a substantial reduction in latency occurs when the fixation point disappears shortly (up to 200 ms) before the appearance of the target. This happens whether or not the target position is predictable and suggests once again that the programming of the spatial characteristics of the saccade may represent a rather late stage in the programming process. The latency reduction in the "gap" condition, in which the fixation point disappears before target onset, was investigated thoroughly by Ross and Ross (1980, 1981). In part, the speeding up relates to the temporal warning provided by the fixation point offset. However, visual offset is more effective than a neutral (auditory) cue, which in turn is more effective than onset of visual stimulation at the fixation point. This suggests that some process that may be termed *relinquishing of attention* is involved in the saccade.

Interest in these results has intensified recently because of the suggestion that a separate category of saccades with extremely short latencies may occur (see Fischer, this volume). Fischer and Boch (1983) used the "gap" paradigm in rhesus monkeys and demonstrated such short latency saccades, which they termed *express saccades*. The distribution of saccade latencies was clearly bimodal, providing evidence for the two categories of saccades. Fischer and Ramsperger (1984) have also reported similar bimodal distributions in saccades recorded from human subjects and suggested that express saccades also occur in humans. However, the bimodality of the distributions shown in the data from human subjects has been less convincing. Recent work has carefully examined the latency distributions of saccades elicited with a range of gap durations (Wenban-Smith, 1990; Wenban-Smith & Findlay, 1991). As the gap duration is increased, there is no evidence of any increase in the variance of the latency distribution. Such a change would be expected if an increasing contribution from a separate population was occurring.

Cognitive Influences on Chronometry

The logic of the WHERE/WHEN separation might imply that fore-knowledge of target position would not influence saccade latency. When this has been investigated, such an extreme result has not been found, in general. However, the reported effects of spatial predictability on saccade latencies have not been large (Abrams & Jonides, 1988; Heywood & Churcher, 1980; Posner, Nissen, & Ogden, 1978; Rayner, Slowiaczek, Clifton, & Bertera, 1983), except when complete position information is given and anticipatory saccades become possible. Michard, Têtard, and Lévy-Schoen (1974) showed that spatial predictability effects did not interact with temporal predictability effects.

Because saccades are generally voluntary and target-elicited saccades can be readily suppressed, it should occasion no surprise that cognitive factors can be shown to influence saccade latencies. So, for example, Gould (1973) showed an effect of memory load on saccade latencies and fixation durations in a search task and recent studies by Inhoff (1986) and by Zingale and Kowler (1987) have shown that under some circumstances, latencies increase when a number of saccades are planned in a sequence. These results are only surprising if a rigid reflexive/voluntary distinction is adhered to. It is argued in the next section that such a dichotomy is best abandoned.

Is the Reflexive/Voluntary Distinction a Valid One?

Several recent papers have been critical of work on target-elicited saccades as being unrealistic and inappropriate for building an understanding of saccades in scanning situations. Lemij and Collewijn (1989) compared the accuracy of saccades under target-elicited conditions and saccades when the targets were two steadily illuminated light-emitting diodes (LEDs) and the subject made saccades between them. Accuracy was considerably greater in the second condition. It should be noted, however, that the saccade rate (50 steps per minute) was considerably slower than that of normal scanning. This work, together with that of Zingale and Kowler (1987) and He and Kowler (1989) already mentioned, is critical of an approach that treats saccades as reflex-like movements. This criticism provides a valuable corrective to the view that saccades are under the control of stimulus factors alone, although it is not clear that such a view is widely held. However, the polemic nature of the arguments may serve to obscure the fact that few workers believe the distinction between reflexive and voluntary saccades is an absolute one. Cooperation ought to be possible between a worker studying attentional influences on target-elicited saccades and one studying voluntary saccades to different types of targets.

Are there good grounds for regarding the reflexive/voluntary distinction as dichotomous rather than as a continuum? Walls (1962) in his classic paper on the evolution of eye movements, argues that saccades evolved as "voluntary" eye movements and that the stimulus-elicited saccade, the "psycho-optic" reflex, was a late evolutionary development. However, it has been demonstrated in this chapter that even the simplest reflex-like saccades are subject to higher influences. Another way in which the distinction is brought into question is through the phenomenon of anticipatory saccades. Although anticipatory and target-elicited saccades can be separated because the former show a slightly slower trajectory (Bronstein & Kennard, 1987; Smit & Van Gisbergen, 1989), this difference only emerges for large saccades (Findlay, 1981a) and is possibly an effect that occurs after the saccade is triggered. A more profitable position might be to avoid attempting to give complete credit for the production of the saccade either uniquely to the stimulus or the observer and instead to regard the saccade as a key to unlock the interface between environment and cognition.

References

Abrams, R.A., & Jonides, J. (1988). Programming saccadic eye movements. *Journal of Experimental Psychology: Human Perception and Performance, 14,* 428–443.

Andersen, R.A., Essick, G.K., & Siegel, R.M. (1985). Encoding of spatial location by posterior parietal neurons. *Science, 230,* 456–458.

Aslin, R.N., & Shea, S.L. (1987). The amplitude and angle of saccades to double-step target displacements. *Vision Research, 27,* 1925–1942.

Bahill, A.T., Clark, M.R., & Stark, L. (1975). The main sequence: a tool for studying eye movements. *Mathematical Biosciences, 24,* 191–204.

Becker, W. (1989). Metrics. In R.H. Wurtz and M.E. Goldberg (Eds.), *The neurobiology of saccadic eye movements* (pp. 13–67). Amsterdam: Elsevier.

Becker, W., & Jürgens, R. (1979). An analysis of the saccadic system by means of double step stimuli. *Vision Research*, *19*, 967–983.

Bergen, J.R., & Julesz, B. (1983). Parallel versus serial visual processing in rapid pattern discrimination. *Nature*, *343*, 696–698.

Bouma, H. (1978). Visual search and reading: eye movements and functional visual field. A tutorial review. *Attention and Performance*, *11*, 115–147.

Bronstein, A.M., & Kennard, C. (1987). Predictive saccades are different from visually triggered saccades. Vision Research, *27*, 517–520.

Coren, S., & Hoenig, P. (1972). Effect of non-target stimuli on the length of voluntary saccades. *Perceptual and Motor Skills*, *34*, 499–508.

Crawford, T.J. (1984). The plasticity of human saccadic eye movements. PhD Thesis, University of Durham.

Deubel, H. (1987). Adaptivity of gain and direction in oblique saccades. In J.K. O'Regan & A. Lévy-Schoen (Eds.), *Eye movements: from physiology to cognition* (pp. 181–190). Amsterdam: Elsevier, North Holland.

Deubel, H., Findlay, J., Jacobs, A., & Brogan, D. (1988). Saccadic eye movements to targets defined by structure differences. In G. Lüer, U. Lass, & J. Shallo-Hoffman (Eds.), *Eye movement research: Physiological and psychological aspects* (pp. 107–145). Toronto S.J. Hogrefe, 1988.

Deubel, H., & Hauske, G. (1988). The programming of visually guided saccades. In H. Marko, G. Hauske, & A. Struppler (Eds.), *Processing structures for perception and action* (pp. 67–74). Weinheim Germany: Verlag Chemie.

Deubel, H., Wolf, W., & Hauske, G. (1984). The evaluation of the oculomotor error signal. In A.G. Gale & F.W. Johnson (Eds.), *Theoretical and applied aspects of oculomotor research*. Amsterdam: North-Holland.

Doma, H., & Hallett, P.E. (1988). Dependence of saccadic eye-movement on stimulus luminance and an effect of task. *Vision Research*, *28*, 915–924.

Driver, J., & Tipper, S.P. (1989). On the nonselectivity of "selective" seeing: contrasts between interference and priming in selective attention. *Journal of Experimental Psychology: Human Perception and Performance*, *15*, 304–314.

Earhard, B., & Walker, H. (1985). An "outside-in" processing strategy for the perception of form. *Perception and Psychophysics*, *38*, 249–260.

Eriksen, C.W., & St James, J.D. (1986). Visual attention within and around the field of focal attention: a zoom lens model. *Perception and Psychophysics*, *40*, 225–240.

Findlay, J.M. (1981a). Spatial and temporal factors in the predictive generation of saccadic eye movements. *Vision Research*, *21*, 347–354.

Findlay, J.M. (1981b). Local and global influences on saccadic eye movements. In D.F. Fisher, R.A. Monty, & J.W. Senders (Eds.), *Eye movements, cognition and visual perception*. Hillsdale, NJ: Lawrence Erlbaum.

Findlay, J.M. (1982). Global processing for saccadic eye movements. *Vision Research*, *22*, 1033–1045.

Findlay, J.M. (1983). Visual information for saccadic eye movements. In A. Hein & M. Jeannerod (Eds.), *Spatially oriented behavior* (pp. 281–303). New York: Springer-Verlag.

Findlay, J.M. (1985). Eye movements and visual cognition. *L'Année Psychologique*, *85*, 101–136.

Findlay, J.M. (1987). Visual computation and saccadic eye movements. *Spatial Vision*, *2*, 175–189.

Findlay, J.M., & Crawford, T.J. (1983). The visual control of saccadic eye movements: evidence for limited plasticity. In R. Groner, C. Menz, D.F. Fisher, & R.A. Monty (Eds.), *Eye movements and psychological processes: international perspectives* (pp. 115–127). Hillsdale, NJ: Lawrence Erlbaum.

Findlay, J.M., & Crawford, T.J. (1986). Plasticity in the control of the spatial characteristic of saccadic eye movements. In S. Ron, R. Schmid, & M. Jeannerod (Eds.), *Sensorimotor plasticity: theoretical, experimental and clinical aspects*. Paris, INSERM.

Findlay, J.M., & Harris, L.R. (1984). Small saccades to double stepped targets moving in two dimensions. In A.G. Gale & F.W. Johnson (Eds.), *Theoretical and applied aspects of oculomotor research* (pp. 71–77). Amsterdam: Elsevier.

Fischer, B., & Boch, R. (1983). Saccadic eye movements after extremely short reaction times in the monkey. *Brain Research, 260,* 21–26.

Fischer, B., & Ramsperger, E. (1984). Human express saccades: extremely short reaction times of goal directed eye movements. *Experimental Brain Research, 57,* 191–195.

Galley, N. (1989). Saccadic eye movement velocity as an indicator of (de)activation. A review and some speculations. *Journal of Psychophysiology, 3,* 229–244.

Gould, J.D. (1973). Eye movements during visual search and memory search. *Journal of Experimental Psychology, 98,* 184–195.

Gouras, P. (1985). The oculomotor system. In E.R. Kandel & J.H. Schwartz (Eds.), *Principles of neural science* (2nd ed. Chap. 43). Amsterdam: Elsevier.

Hackman, R. (1940). An experimental study of the variability in ocular latency *Journal of Experimental Psychology, 27,* 546–558.

Hallett, P.E., & Lightstone, A.D. (1976). Saccadic eye movements to flashed targets. *Vision Research, 16,* 107–114.

He, P., & Kowler, E. (1989). The role of location probability in the programming of saccades: implications for "center-of-gravity" tendencies. Vision Research, 29, 1165–1181.

Heywood, S., & Churcher, J. (1980). Structure of the visual array and saccadic latency: implications for oculomotor control. *Quarterly Journal of Experimental Psychology, 32,* 335–341.

Hinton, G.E., McClelland, J.L., & Rumelhart, D.E. (1986). Distributed representations. In D.E. Rumelhart, J.L. McClelland, & the PDP Research Group (Eds.), *Explorations in the microstructure of cognition* (pp. 77–109). Cambridge: MIT Press.

Honda, H. (1989). Perceptual localization of stimuli flashed during saccades. *Perception and Psychophysics, 45,* 162–174.

Honda, H., & Findlay, J.M. (in press). Saccades to targets in three-dimensional space: dependence of saccadic latency on target position. Perception and Psychophysics.

Hou, R.L., & Fender, D.H. (1979). Processing of direction and magnitude information by the saccadic system. *Vision Research, 19,* 1421–1426.

Inhoff, A.W. (1986). Preparing sequences of saccades. *Acta Psychologica, 61,* 211–228.

Jay, M.F., & Sparks, D.L. (1987). Sensorimotor integration in the primate superior colliculus. II. Co-ordinates of auditory signals. J Neurophysiology, 57, 35–54.

Jürgens, R., Becker, W., & Kornhuber, H.H. (1981). Natural and drug-induced variations of velocity and duration of human saccadic eye movements: evidence for a control of the neural pulse generator by local feedback. *Biological Cybernetics*, *39*, 87–96.

Kapoula, Z. (1985). Evidence for a range effect in the saccadic system. *Vision Research*, *25*, 1155–1157.

Keller, E.L. (1974). Participation of medial pontine reticular formation in eye movement generation in the monkey. *Journal of Neurophysiology*, *37*, 316–322.

Lee, C., Rohrer, W.H., & Sparks, D.L. (1988). Population coding of saccadic eye movements by the superior colliculus. *Nature*, *332*, 357–359.

Lemij, H.G., & Collewijn, H. (1989). Differences in accuracy of human saccades between stationary and jumping targets. Vision Research, *29*, 1737–1748.

Lueck, C.J., Crawford, T.J., Savage, C.J., & Kennard, C. (1990). Auditory-visual interaction in the generation of saccades in man. *Experimental Brain Research*, *82*, 149–157.

Marr, D. (1982). *Vision*. San Francisco: W.H. Freeman.

Mays, L.E., & Sparks, D.L. (1980). Saccades are spatially, not retinotopically, coded. *Science*, *208*, 1163–1165.

McIlwain, J.T. (1976). Large receptive fields and spatial transformations in the visual system. In R. Porter (Ed.), *International review of physiology, Volume 10: Neurophysiology II* (pp. 223–248). Baltimore: University Park Press.

McLoughlin, S. (1967). Parametric adjustment in saccadic eye movements. *Perception and Psychophysics*, *2*, 359–362.

Menz, C., & Groner, R. (1987). Saccadic programming with multiple targets under different task conditions. In J.K. O'Regan & A. Lévy-Schoen (Eds.), *Eye movements: from physiology to cognition*. Amsterdam: North-Holland.

Michard, A., Têtard, C., & Lévy-Schoen, A. (1974). Attente du signal et temps de réaction oculomoteur. *L'Année Psychologique*, *74*, 387–402.

Nakayama, K. (1990). The iconic bottleneck and the tenuous link between early visual processing and perception. In C. Blakemore (Ed.), *Vision: coding and efficiency*, Cambridge University Press.

Optican, L.M., Zee, D.S., & Chu, F.C. (1987). Adaptive response to ocular muscle weakness in human pursuit and saccadic eye movements. *Journal of Neurophysiology*, *54*, 110–122.

Ottes, F.P., van Gisbergen, J.A.M., & Eggermont, J.J. (1984). Metrics of saccadic responses to double stimuli: two different modes. *Vision Research*, *24*, 1169–1179.

Parker, D.M., & Salzen, E. (1977). Latency changes in the human visual evoked response to sinusoidal gratings. *Vision Research*, *17*, 1201–1204.

Posner, M.I. (1980). Orienting of attention. Quarterly Journal of Experimental Psychology, *32*, 3–25.

Posner, M.I., Nissen, M.J., & Ogden, M.C. (1978). Attended and unattended processing modes: the role of set for spatial location. In H.L. Pick & I.J. Saltzman (Eds.), *Modes of perceiving and processing information* (pp. 137–157). Hillsdale: Lawrence Erlbaum.

Previc, F.H. (1990). Functional specialization in the lower and upper visual fields in humans: its ecological origins and neurophysiological implications. *Behavioral and Brain Sciences*, *13*, 519–575.

Rayner, K., Slowiaczek, M.L., Clifton, C.Jr., & Bertera, J.H. (1983). Latency of sequential eye movements: implications for reading. *Journal of Experimental Psychology Human Perception and Performance*, 9, 912–922.

Robinson, D.A. (1975). Oculomotor control signals. In P. Bach-y-Rita & G. Lennestrand (Eds.), *Basic mechanisms of ocular motility and their clinical applications*. Oxford: Pergamon Press.

Ross, L.E., & Ross, S.M. (1980). Saccade latency and warning signals: stimulus onset, offset and change as warning events. *Perception and Psychophysics*, 27, 251–257.

Ross, S.M., & Ross, L.E. (1981). Saccade latency and warning signals: effects of auditory and visual offset and onset. *Perception and Psychophysics*, 29, 429–437.

Sanders, A.F. (1962). *The selective process in the functional visual field*. Report IZF22, Institute for Perception RVO-TNO Soesterberg, The Netherlands.

Saslow, M.G. (1967). Effects of components of displacement-step stimuli upon latency for saccadic eye movement. *Journal of the Optical Society of America*, 57, 1024–1029.

Smit, A.C., & Van Gisbergen, J.A.M. (1989). A short-latency transition in saccade dynamics during square-wave tracking and its significance for the differentiation of visually guided and predictive saccades. *Experimental Brain Research*, 76, 64–94.

Sparks, D.L. (1986). The neural translation of sensory signals into commands for the control of saccadic eye movements: the role of the superior colliculus. *Physiological Review*, 66, 118–171.

Strong, G.W., & Whitehead, B.A. (1989). A solution to the tag-assignment problem for neural networks. *Behavioral and Brain Sciences*, 12, 381–433.

Treisman, A. (1985). Preattentive processing in vision. *Computer Vision, Graphics and Image Processing*, 31, 156–177.

Van Gisbergen, J.A.M., Gielen, S., Cox, H., Bruijns, J., & Kleine Schaars, H. (1981). Relation between metrics of saccades and stimulus trajectory in target tracking: implications for models of the saccadic system. In A.F. Fuchs & W. Becker (Eds.), *Progress in oculomotor research* (pp. 17–27). Amsterdam: Elsevier.

Van Gisbergen, J.A.M., Van Opstal, A.J., & Roebroek, J.G.H. (1987). Stimulus induced midflight modification of saccade trajectories. In J.K. O'Regan & A. Levy-Schoen (Eds.), *Eye movements: from physiology to cognition* (pp. 27–36). Amsterdam: North-Holland.

Van Gisbergen, J.A.M., Van Opstal, A.J., & Schoenmakers, J.J.M. (1985). Experimental test of two models for the generation of oblique saccades. *Experimental Brain Research*, 57, 321–336.

Virsu, V., & Rovamo, J. (1979). Visual resolution, contrast sensitivity, and the cortical magnification factor. *Experimental Brain Research*, 37, 475–494.

Walls, G. (1962). The evolutionary history of eye movements. *Vision Research*, 2, 69–80.

Watt, R.J. (1987). Scanning from coarse to fine spatial scales in the visual system after the onset of a stimulus. *Journal of the Optical Society of America*, A4, 2006–2021.

Wenban-Smith, M.G. (1990). *The latency of target elicited saccadic eye movements*. M Sc Thesis, University of Durham.

Wenban-Smith, M.G., & Findlay, J.M. (1991). Express saccades: is there a separate population in humans. *Experimental Brain Research*, *87*, 218–222.

Wertheim, T. (1894). Über die indirekte Sehschärfe. *Zeitschrift fur Psychologie Physiologie, des Sinnesorgane*, *7*, 121–187.

Zahn, J.R., Abel, L.A., & Dell'Osso, L.F. (1978). The audio-ocular response characteristics. *Sensory Processes*, *2*, 32–37.

Zambarbieri, D., Schmid, R., Magenes, C., & Prablanc, C. (1982). Saccadic responses evoked by presentation of visual and auditory targets. *Experimental Brain Research*, *47*, 417–427.

Zetzsche, C., Deubel, H., & Elsner, T. (1984). Similar mechanisms of visual processing in perception and oculomotor control. *Perception*, *13*, A16.

Zingale, C.M., & Kowler, E. (1987). Planning sequences of saccades. *Vision Research*, *27*, 1327–1341.

3
Saccadic Reaction Time: Implications for Reading, Dyslexia, and Visual Cognition

Burkhart Fischer

Visual perception in man and higher vertebrates with a specialized fovea requires scanning of the field of view. Within the central 20° of the visual field this scanning is accomplished by saccadic eye movements. The neural structures of the central visual system involved in the analysis of "what" and "where" are required to take into account these eye movements. They also must contribute to the preparation of the saccades, as these are preprogrammed movements and the information "where" the eyes should move next must be delivered at the oculomotor centers before the movement starts.

In sequences of saccades (three to four per second, about 2° to 5° each) the processes that follow one saccade and the ones that precede the next are identical. In our studies we have investigated the time from an external "go" command to the beginning of the eye movement—the saccadic reaction time (SRT)—as an index for one or the other process involved in vision and in the generation of this particular saccade. We have used detailed and extensive manipulations of the physical (external) and psychological (internal) experimental conditions of saccade generation in monkeys and in human subjects categorized as adults (above age 20), children (ages 7 to 10), and dyslexic children.

Express Saccades

The basic observation that stimulated our further reaction time studies was made first in the monkey (Fischer & Boch, 1983) and later in humans (Fischer & Ramsperger, 1984): when the sudden appearance of a visual stimulus is delayed by about 200 to 300 ms after the offset of a fixation point (gap paradigm, Figure 3.1, upper left) the reaction times of saccades to that stimulus form a bimodal distribution.

Figure 3.1 shows such a distribution as obtained from a human subject. A first peak occurs just above 100 ms and a second one just above 150 ms. Saccades contributing to the first peak are called *express saccades*,

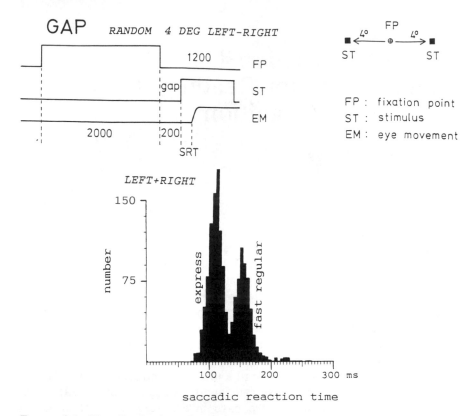

FIGURE 3.1. The distribution of saccadic reaction times obtained from a single highly trained human subject. The gap paradigm (upper left) was used, the target stimulus occurred randomly 4° to the right or left of the fixation point. The distribution clearly exhibits two distinct peaks, one labeled *express saccades* at about 100 ms and the other labeled *regular saccades* at about 150 ms.

those forming the second peak *fast regular saccades*. In the monkey, saccadic reaction times are about 30 ms shorter: 70 ms for express, and 140 ms for fast regular saccades. A small third peak occurring sometimes above 200 ms is made up of the so-called slow regular saccades. Some subjects show a very clear bimodality, others need some amount of practice. Sometimes the two peaks are apparently fused. Highly trained subjects may produce a single peak of express saccades. Another example of a typical multimodal SRT distribution is shown in the upper panel of Figure 3.2.

Our second basic observation confirmed earlier results of Saslow (1967): if the fixation point remains visible (overlap paradigm) instead of being extinguished before target onset, saccadic reaction times are considerably prolonged to values of around 220 ms in humans and 190 ms in

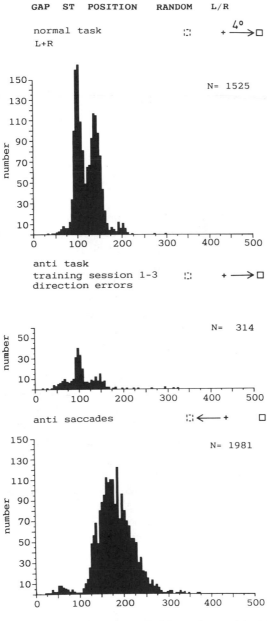

FIGURE 3.2. Saccadic reaction times (sampled from three subjects) collected using a gap paradigm. Normal saccades (to the target), antisaccades (to the side opposite to the target), and direction errors in the antisaccade task are shown. At 100 ms, where the express peak occurs in the normal saccade task there are almost no values in the antisaccade task. The direction errors form a distribution similar to that obtained in the normal task.

monkeys, making up a large peak of slow regular saccades (Boch & Fischer, 1986; Saslow, 1967). These two basic experimental results lead to a number of questions and experiments. The main results of our experiments and other relevant findings are briefly summarized below. The physical and psychological conditions for express saccades are considered first. Second, the neurophysiological findings are described and the anatomical structures for express saccades are discussed. Finally, we consider a functional concept of saccade generation and its implications for reading and dyslexia.

The Physical Conditions for Express Saccades

With respect to the fixation point we have found the following. First, in total darkness express saccades are absent. Instead of express saccades, slow regular saccades are obtained in response to a suddenly appearing light stimulus. Second, if the temporal gap between fixation point offset and target onset is too short (<80 ms) or too long (>800 ms) express saccades cannot be obtained unless other (psychological) conditions are fulfilled (see below). Third, if the luminance of the fixation point is gradually decreased, the number of express saccades decreases to zero (Mayfrank, Mobashery, Kimmig, & Fischer, 1986).

With respect to the visual target the results are as follows. First, varying the luminance, size, and eccentricity of the target over wide ranges does not change the number of express saccades but only their reaction time (Boch, Fischer, & Ramsperger, 1984). Second, express saccades are unchanged in reaction time and frequency if isoluminant, pure-color contrast targets (e.g., red stimulus, green background) are used (Weber, Fischer, Bock, & Aiple, 1991). Third, express saccades can be made to targets that are flashed for only a few milliseconds such that the saccade begins when the stimulus has already disappeared. Fourth, express saccades are absent if the subject is asked to look to the side opposite to that where the stimulus occurs (antisaccade task) even when the gap paradigm is used. This is demonstrated by the data of Figure 3.2 showing the distribution of normal saccades (upper panel) and those of antisaccades (lower panel), both obtained in the gap paradigm. The panel in the middle shows the distribution of reaction times of those saccades that the subject involuntarily made to the stimulus rather than to the opposite side. These direction errors in the context of the antisaccade task clearly show express and fast regular reaction times as they are obtained in the normal task. One also sees a few saccades with reaction times below 75 ms. These are anticipatory saccades, which fail to reach the target and have slower peak velocities. Fifth, express saccades are absent if the target position must be remembered or if the target is visible all the time.

In conclusion, neither the presence or absence of a fixation point nor the physical parameters of the target can uniquely determine the occurrence of express saccades. The sudden appearance of just any well-visible target seems to be the only physical condition that is necessary (but not sufficient) to obtain express saccades.

The Psychological Conditions for Express Saccades

First, if subjects are asked not to pay attention to the fixation point but only keep their eyes on it, express saccades occur in the overlap paradigm, where they are usually absent in normal adult subjects (Mayfrank et al., 1986), but not in young dyslexics (see below). Second, the instruction to pay attention to any peripheral stimulus suppresses the occurrence of express saccades. This is also true if the attended stimulus is positioned at the same location where the saccade target will appear (Mayfrank et al., 1986) such that the subject knows the direction and size of the saccade he/she will have to make within the next second. Third, human subjects as well as monkeys learn by daily practice to increase the number of their express saccades in the gap as well as in the overlap paradigm (Fischer, Boch, and Ramsperger, 1984; Fischer & Ramsperger, 1986). The training effects are spatially selective for the target positions used. Fourth, the gain of monkey express saccades (ratio of saccade size and target eccentricity) can be changed, if the target is displaced at the beginning of the saccade (Weber & Fischer, unpublished observation). This adaptive gain change seems to be the same for express as for regular saccades in man (Deubel, Wolf, & Hauske, 1986) as well as in monkeys (Albano & King, 1989) (Figure 3.3). Fifth, children (ages 9 to 10) have more express saccades than adults, and dyslexic children have more than normal readers of the same age (Fischer & Weber, 1990).

In conclusion; internal rather than external factors determine the occurrence of express saccades. The gap paradigm facilitates the establishment of the internal condition that fosters express saccades as a prompt and quick response to a suddenly appearing stimulus. Directed visual attention inhibits the occurrence of express saccades.

Neurophysiological Findings

The fact that some visual stimuli lead to saccades and others do not implies that somewhere in the visual and/or oculomotor brain structures neural activity changes before a visually guided saccade. Similarly one predicts changes of neural activity in cases where the saccade is suppressed but visual attention changes its direction. It is well known that the visual on-responses of neurons in several brain structures (superior col-

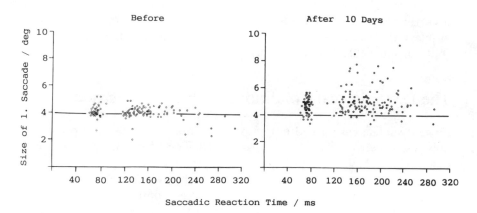

FIGURE 3.3. Scatter plot of saccadic reaction times (horizontal) versus size of the first saccade (vertical) of the monkey in a double-step saccade task before (left) and after (right) the animal has adapted to the task. (Anticipatory saccades with latencies below 60 ms are removed from the plot.) The first group of saccades (between 65 and 80 ms) represents the express saccades in each plot. Both express as well as regular saccades (latencies above 100 ms) are increased in size "after" as compared to "before" adaptation.

liculus, frontal eye fields, parietal cortex, prelunate cortex) can be enhanced if the receptive field stimulus is the target of a saccade (for review see Fischer & Boch, 1990).

However, these studies alone do not allow us to differentiate between premotor aspects and attentional aspects of the enhancement. The use of a peripheral attention task (without saccades) has revealed that the enhancement of frontal eye field and superior colliculus neurons is closely related to the saccade rather than to visual attention as such (Goldberg & Bushnell, 1981; Wurtz & Mohler, 1976). On the other hand, parietal cells exhibit the enhancement effect irrespective of the type of movement (eye or reach) or even in the absence of any motor reaction to the stimulus (Bushnell, Goldberg, & Robinson, 1981).

A special neural activity particularly related to fixation and attention has been reported for cells in the striate cortex (Boch, 1986), in the cortex of the prelunate gyrus (Fischer & Boch, 1985), in the parietal cortex (Boch, 1989b), and in the prefrontal cortex (Boch & Goldberg, 1989): the activity of these cells is increased if the monkey suppresses the eye movement when it is left without a fixation point in the presence of a receptive field stimulus. It is not clear, however, from these studies whether this state of increased cortical activity must be attributed to visual attention being engaged to the peripheral stimulus or to visual attention being disengaged from the fixation point.

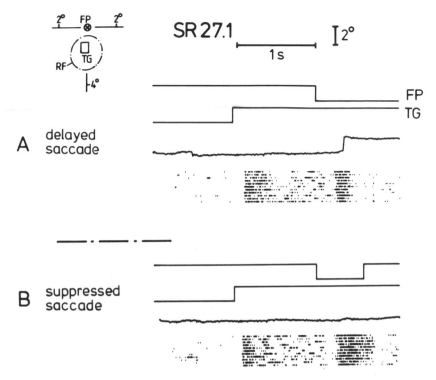

FIGURE 3.4. Raster display of the discharges of a prelunate cortical cell of the monkey in a delayed saccade task and a suppressed saccade task. The second increase of impulse activity occurs when the fixation point disappears regardless of whether the animal makes a saccade (A) or not (B).

Figure 3.4 shows an example of a prelunate cortical cell of a monkey that was trained to fixate a spot of light. When a new stimulus appeared in its field of view (i.e., in the receptive field of the cell being recorded) the monkey maintained fixation. But when, later in the trial, the fixation point was switched off, the animal was free to look at the new stimulus or not. Part A of Figure 3.4 shows data we collected in trials in which the monkey made saccades. Part B shows data when the direction of gaze is maintained straight ahead, always recording from the same cell. In both groups of trials one clearly sees the visual on-response of the cell following the onset of the receptive field stimulus (upper left inset of the figure). One also sees a second activation following the offset of the fixation point irrespective of whether the monkey made the saccade or not. This activity presumably reflects a change in the animal's attentional system. We will see below how the attentional system may control the eye movement system, permitting or inhibiting saccades.

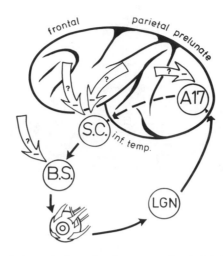

FIGURE 3.5. Schematic lateral view of a rhesus monkey's left hemisphere with the different cortical areas that may exhibit, directly or indirectly, control over the pathway for the reflex-like express saccades containing the lateral geniculate nucleus (LGN), the primary visual cortex (A17), the superior colliculus (S.C.), and the brain stem (B.S.). The exact sites and mechanisms of the control process are still not clear.

Anatomical Structures for Express Saccades

The extremely short reaction times of expess saccades suggest that only a few structures can be involved in their generation. All structures containing neurons with long latency visual on-responses must be excluded. From this point of view cortical areas beyond the striate cortex should be not necessary for express saccades, because the latencies exceed 70 ms. Additional findings from lesion studies include the following: First, express saccades are abolished if the superior colliculus is destroyed, but they survive lesions of the frontal eye fields in the monkey (Schiller, Sandell, & Maunsell, 1987). Second, express saccades are absent to target positions that are affected by a local lesion of the striate cortex, regular saccades remaining intact (Boch, 1989a). Third, local chemical lesions of the visual association cortex (V4) in the prelunate gyrus increase the number of express saccades reversibly (Weber & Fischer, 1990). Fourth, neither destruction of the parvo- or magnocellular layers of the lateral geniculate nucleus, nor lesions of the cortical areas V4 or MT lead to any substantial deficit in the generation of express saccades (Schiller, Logethetis, Charles, & Kyoungmin, 1990).

In conclusion, the pathway for express saccades, besides the retina, the lateral geniculate nucleus, and the brain stem, includes the primary visual cortex and the superior colliculus.

Figure 3.5 schematically illustrates the neuroanatomical connections that are involved in the generation of the express saccade and their cortical control. Retinal ganglion cells project to striate cortex via both the parvo- and magnocellular layers of the lateral geniculate nucleus. Neurons in layer VI of striate cortex activate the superficial layer cells of the superior colliculus, which in turn feed the intermediate and deep layer collicular cells. These project to the brain stem structures of the paramedian pontine and mesencephalic reticular formation that finally activate the oculomotor nuclei. This pathway, however, must be under control of other brain structures, probably cortical, which, at least in healthy adult subjects, inhibit the express way during fixation and during times of peripherally directed attention. Otherwise any suddenly occurring light would automatically lead to a saccade. In order to generate a saccade this inhibition must be terminated, which takes extra time, accounting for the longer reaction times of the regular saccades. If the subject can terminate this inhibition before the visual stimulus appears, for example because the offset of the fixation point facilitates this disinhibition, the following saccade is initiated like a reflex, has the minimal reaction time, and is of the express type.

The details of the control mechanism and its anatomical sites are still unknown as is the functional significance of the projections from the monkey retina directly to the superior colliculus (Hubel, LeVay, & Wiesel, 1975; Perry & Cowey, 1984), and from striate cortex to the brain stem (Glickstein et al., 1980) (not shown in Figure 3.5). One control mechanism certainly originates from the frontal cortex, especially from the frontal eye fields, taking the route through the caudate nucleus and the substantia nigra and ending in the superior colliculus. Parietal and prelunate cortex, so intimately related to visual attention and eye movements (Fischer & Boch, 1985; Mountcastle, Andersen, & Motter, 1981) may also directly or indirectly control the express way.

A Visuomotor Reflex and its Control

The idea of a reflex-like mechanism for the generation of express saccades is further substantiated by the following facts: First, patients with frontal lobe lesion cannot suppress saccades to a suddenly appearing visual stimulus, even though they were instructed to look to the opposite side in an antisaccade task. These saccades have latencies of about 100 ms (Guitton, Buchtel, & Douglas 1985). In these patients the express way seems to be almost permanently disinhibited. Second, patients with parietal lesions sometimes are unable to break fixation and to look away from whatever they are looking at. The saccade system appears to be almost permanently inhibited (Pierrot-Deseilligny, Rivaud, Penet, & Rigolet, 1987). Third, normal adult subjects make a substantial number of saccades to the target side in the antisaccade task if the gap paradigm is used, whereas these saccades are absent in the antisaccade overlap paradigm. Most of these direction errors (in the sense of the anti task) have express latencies (Figure 3.2, middle panel). This means that normal adults in the gap situation show a phenomenon very similar if not identical to the "symptom" of patients with frontal lobe lesions. Fourth, infants under 1 year of age have many intersaccadic intervals around 80 to 100 ms (Bronson, 1981; Harris, et al., 1988). Fifth, normal children, ages 8 to 10, have more express saccades than adults above age 20 (Fischer & Weber, 1990).

These latter findings suggest that early in life there exists a visuo-oculomotor reflex that during development is subjected more and more to the control of a higher mechanism, which is necessary for solving the problems of increasing difficulty in visual perception and cognition (such as reading) that requires proper sequences of attentive fixation and saccades, not just eye rests and eye movements.

The fact that express saccades are abolished when visual attention is directed to a certain position in the visual field regardless of where this position is in relation to the saccade target suggests that the saccade system is under the control of the attentional system and furthermore that the attentional system has two states: engaged (or directed or focused) and disengaged (or not directed or defocused). During engaged attention saccades are inhibited; during disengaged attention saccades are permitted. It should be noted that "disengaged" does not mean "inattentive."

The functional aspects of visual attention—engaged or disengaged— and its control over the movements of the eyes are illustrated by the scheme of Figure 3.6. It shows, schematically, an eye movement trace (in the middle part) with a first period of no movement (fixation) followed by a saccade and by the next fixation. Below, the attentional system with its two possible states—engaged and disengaged—is shown. In the engaged state the saccade system is inhibited, providing stable eye position during attentive fixation. Once in the disengaged state the saccade system is disinhibited and may or may not generate an eye movement. Therefore, the period of no eye movement consists internally of two different periods: one of attentive fixation (engaged attention) as indicated by the heavy line and one of disengaged attention. The evidence for this relationship as revealed by eye movement studies has been summarized earlier (Fischer & Breitmeyer, 1987).

Mishkin proposed two cortical systems, one for analyzing "what" and the other for analysing "where" something is (Mishkin, Ungerleider, & Macko, 1983). To this idea we want to add a temporal aspect: while attention is engaged, visual information arriving mainly from the striate cortex is fed into an "identification" system (the ventral route) probably including the inferotemporal cortex. During disengaged attention, visual information is fed to a "localization" system (the dorsal route), which

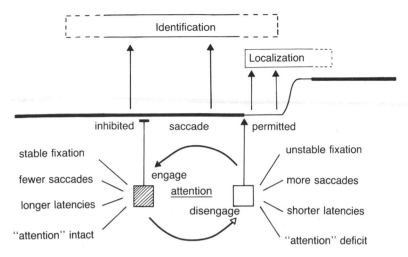

FIGURE 3.6. Schematic illustration of the attentional control over the saccade generating system and the possible symptoms caused by deficits. (Details in the text.)

provides the spatial parameters to initiate not only eye movements but also other goal-directed movements such as reach movements. The latter system probably includes the parietal cortex (Andersen, 1989).

Implications for Reading and Dyslexia

The concept of a reflex-like visuo-oculomotor pathway and its control by visual attention is fairly simple and clearly oversimplifies the rather complex processes taking place in the brain. Yet it allows for an explanation of many findings, most of them listed above. Moreover, it leads to at least qualitative predictions of symptoms as consequences of one or the other defect in the attentional system and/or in its control over the oculomotor system.

Suppose, that the development of the attentional system is delayed behind the development of the visual and the oculomotor system; infants and children will perform poorly in tasks requiring visual attention in the first place and they will exhibit many more express saccades as compared to adults because they react to light stimuli via the still uncontrolled reflex pathway. They will have difficulties in tasks that require coordinated visual attention and eye movements, but they will learn to handle such tasks as they become older and by practice when the attentional system develops and takes control over the saccade generating system.

If this development for one reason or another does not take place or is delayed, several symptoms will occur depending on the exact nature of the defect. Suppose that the attentional system stays in the disengaged state for longer (than normal) periods of time, i.e., the subject has difficulties switching to the engaged state. As indicated in the lower right part of Figure 3.6, a subject with this kind of defect will have a rather unstable fixation with a tendency to make more saccades. He will exhibit saccades with short reaction times and an increased amount of express saccades. Moreover, he will be impaired on any task that requires proper engagement of visual attention and in tasks that require, in addition, sequencing of eye movements, as, for example, reading. In other words such a subject represents a more or less severe case of dyslexia with an additional defect of visual attention.

If, on the other hand, the attentional system stays in the engaged state for longer periods of time (Figure 3.6, lower left), the subject will show rather stable fixation with smaller amounts of saccades. His saccadic reaction times will be longer or he will exhibit a preponderance of long latency saccades. But he will have no difficulties with tasks that require engaged visual attention. Yet his reading abilities will be impaired mostly with respect to speed. In other words, such a subject will appear as a slow reader with no attentional deficit.

Finally one can think of a case in which the attentional system is completely intact in switching back and forth between the engaged and the disengaged state, but the control signal does not arrive properly at the oculomotor structures or the subject has no control over the switching mechanism. The first case is a poor reader without attentional deficits; the second case is a dyslexic reader who performs inconsistently in attention tasks.

Depending on the exact nature of the defect and its quantitative aspects the simple concept of Figure 3.6 predicts a whole spectrum of combinations of attentional and reading problems, some reflected in the eye movement patterns as such, others evident only in the distribution of the saccadic reaction times. In any of these cases the eye movements system as such is assumed to be intact. Nevertheless, the disturbance in its control may cause faulty eye movements, which in addition impede fluent reading without being the cause of dyslexia (Rayner, 1985).

Figure 3.7 shows a distribution of saccadic reaction times in a 9-year-old dyslexic boy. His saccadic reaction times are almost exclusively of the express type regardless of the paradigm (overlap or gap) used. In the context of Figure 3.6 one can say that this child was unable to engage his attention to the fixation point.

All of the dyslexic children we have seen so far showed more express saccades than the age-matched control group of normal readers. We are presently working on the possibility of using noncognitive eye movement tests to analyze the difficulties of subjects with reading problems. The contradictory results of Pavlidis (1981) on the one hand and Olson, Kliegl, and Davidson (1983) on the other make such a study the more

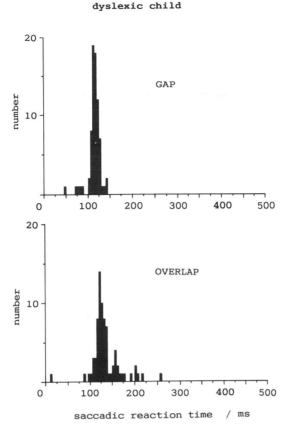

FIGURE 3.7. Distribution of saccadic reaction times of a dyslexic child in gap (above) and overlap trials. Long latency saccades, so common in normal subjects, are completely missing in overlap trials of this subject.

interesting. Pavlidis claims that about 80 to 90% of dyslexic subjects can be identified on the basis of their eye movement pattern in a "light test" whereas Olson et al. completely failed to replicate Pavlidis's results, even though they tried to use exactly the same methods. The additional analysis of saccadic reaction times in gap and overlap trials may help to resolve this obvious contradiction.

References

Albano, J.E., & King, W.M. (1989). Rapid adaptation of saccadic amplitude in humans and monkeys. *Investigative Ophthalmology and Visual Sciences*, *30*, 1883–1893.

Andersen, R.A. (1989). Visual and eye movement functions of the posterior parietal cortex. *Annual Review of Neurosciences*, *12*, 377–403.

Boch, R. (1986). Behavioral modulation of neuronal activity in monkey striate cortex: excitation in the absence of active central fixation. *Experimental Brain Research*, *64*, 610–614.

Boch, R. (1989a). Saccadic reaction times after chemical lesions in striate and prestriate cortex of the rhesus monkey. *Investigative Ophthalmology and Visual Sciences*, *30*, 184.

Boch, R. (1989b). Behavioral modulation of neuronal activity in the posterior parietal cortex of the rhesus monkey. *Behavioural Brain Research*, *33*, 318.

Boch, R., & Fischer, B. (1986). Further observations on the occurrence of express-saccades in the monkey. *Experimental Brain Research*, *63*, 487–494.

Boch, R., Fischer, B., & Ramsperger, E. (1984). Express-saccades of the monkey: reaction times versus intensity, size, duration, and eccentricity of their targets. Experimental Brain Research, *55*, 223–231.

Boch, R.A., & Goldberg, M.E. (1989). Participation of prefrontal neurons in the preparation of visually guided eye movements in the rhesus monkey. *Journal of Neurophysiology*, *61*, 1064–1084.

Bronson, G.W. (1981). The scanning patterns of human infants: implication for visual learning. In L.P. Lipsitt (Ed.), *Monographs on infancy*. Norwood, NJ: Ablex.

Bushnell, M.C., Goldberg, M.E., & Robinson, D.L. (1981). Behavioral enhancement of visual responses in monkey cerebral cortex. I. Modulation in posterior parietal cortex related to selective visual attention. *Journal of Neurophysiology*, *46*, 755–772.

Deubel, H., Wolf, W., & Hauske, G. (1986). Adaptive gain control of saccadic eye movements. *Human Neurobiology*, *5*, 245–253.

Fischer, B., & Boch, R. (1983). Saccadic eye movements after extremely short reaction times in the monkey. *Brain Research*, *260*, 21–26.

Fischer, B., & Boch, R. (1985). Peripheral attention versus central fixation: modulation of the visual activity of prelunate cortical cells of the rhesus monkey. *Brain Research*, *345*, 111–123.

Fischer, B., & Boch R. (1990). Cerebral cortex. In R. Carpenter (Ed.), *Vision and visual dysfunction*. Macmillan.

Fischer, B., Boch, R., & Ramsperger, E. (1984). Express-saccades of the monkey: effect of daily training on probability of occurrence and reaction time. *Experimental Brain Research*, *55*, 232–242.

Fischer, B., & Breitmeyer, B. (1987). Mechanisms of visual attention revealed by saccadic eye movements. *Neuropsychology*, *25*, 73–83.

Fischer, B., & Ramsperger, E. (1984). Human express saccades: extremely short reaction times of goal directed eye movements. *Experimental Brain Research*, *57*, 191–195.

Fischer, B., & Ramsperger, E. (1986). Human express saccades: effects of randomization and daily practice. *Experimental Brain Research*, *64*, 569–578.

Fischer, B., & Weber, H. (1990). Saccadic reaction times of dyslexic and age-matched normal subjects. *Perception*, *19*, 805–818.

Glickstein, M., Cohen, J.L., Dixon, B., Gibson, A., Hollins, M., LaBossiere, E., & Robinson, F. (1980). Corticopontine visual projections in macaque monkeys. *Journal of Comparative Neurology*, *190*, 209–229.

Goldberg, M.E., & Bushnell, M.C. (1981). Behavioral enhancement of visual responses in monkey cerebral cortex. II. Modulation in frontal eye fields specifically related to saccades. *Journal of Neurophysiology*, *46*, 773–787.

Guitton, D., Buchtel, H.A., & Douglas, R.M. (1985). Frontal lobe lesions in man cause difficulties in suppressing reflexive glances and in generating goal-directed saccades. *Experimental Brain Research, 58*, 455–472.

Harris, C.M., Hainline, L., Abramov, I., Lemerise, E., & Camenzuli, C. (1988). The distribution of fixation durations in infants and naive adults. *Vision Research, 28*, 419–432.

Hubel, D.II., LeVay, S., & Wiesel, T.N. (1975). Mode of termination of retinotectal fibers in the macaque monkey. *Brain Research, 96*, 25–40.

Mayfrank, L., Mobashery, M., Kimmig, H., & Fischer, B. (1986). The role of fixation and visual attention in the occurrence of express saccades in man. *European Archive of Psychiatry and Neurological Sciences, 235*, 269–275.

Mishkin, M., Ungerleider, L.G., & Macko, K.A. (1983). Object vision and spatial vision: two cortical pathways. *Trends in Neurosciences, 6*, 414–417.

Mountcastle, V.B., Andersen, R.A., & Motter, B.C. (1981). The influence of attentive fixation upon the excitability of the light-sensitive neurons of the posterior parietal cortex. *Journal of Neuroscience, 1*, 1218–1225.

Olson, R.K., Kliegl, R., & Davidson, B.J. (1983). Dyslexic and normal readers' eye movements. *Journal of Experimental Psychology: Human Perception and Performance, 9*, 816–825.

Pavlidis, G.T. (1981). Do eye movements hold the key to dyslexia? *Neuropsychologia, 19*, 57–64.

Perry, V.H., & Cowey, A. (1984). Retinal ganglion cells that project to the superior colliculus and pretectum in the macaque monkey. *Neuroscience, 12*, 1125–1137.

Pierrot-Deseilligny, C., Rivaud, S., Penet, C., & Rigolet, M.-H. (1987). Latencies of visually guided saccades in unilateral hemispheric cerebral lesions. *Annual Neurology, 21*, 138–148.

Rayner, K. (1985). Do faulty eye movements cause dyslexia? *Developmental Neuropsychology, 1*, 3–15.

Saslow, M.G. (1967). Effects of components of displacement-step stimuli upon latency for saccadic eye movement. *Journal of the Optical Society of America, 57*, 1024–1029.

Schiller, P., Logethetis, N., Charles, E., & Kyoungmin, L. (1990). The effects of LGN, V4 and MT lesions on visually guided eye movements to stationary targets. *Investigative Ophthalmology and Visual Sciences, 31*, 399.

Schiller, P.H., Sandell, J.H., & Maunsell, J.H. (1987). The effect of frontal eye field and superior colliculus lesions on saccadic latencies in the rhesus monkey. *Journal of Neurophysiology, 57*, 1033–1049.

Weber, H., & Fischer, B. (1990). Effect of a local ibotenic acid lesion in the visual association area on the prelunate gyrus (area V4) on saccadic reaction times in trained rhesus monkeys. *Experimental Brain Research, 81*, 134–139.

Weber, H., Fischer, B., Bach, M., & Aiple, F. (1991). Occurrence of express saccades under isoluminance and low contrast luminance conditions. *Visual Neuroscience, 7*, 505–510.

Wurtz, R.H., & Mohler, C.W. (1976). Organization of monkey superior colliculus: enhanced visual response of superficial layer cells. *Journal of Neurophysiology, 39*, 745–765.

4
Orienting of Visual Attention

RAYMOND KLEIN, ALAN KINGSTONE, and
AMANDA PONTEFRACT

Spatial selectivity, which is essential in the perception of any visual scene or display, can be accomplished in two quite distinct ways. First, *overt* adjustments of gaze direction can be made to control which regions of the visual scene are processed by the sensitive fovea and its associated neural machinery. Second, *covert* adjustments can be made to determine which specific objects or regions are selected (in the absence of gaze changes) for preferential treatment. Overt orienting can be directly observed in the form of eye movements; convert orienting involves an internal adjustment and must be inferred from performance patterns. James (1890) probably had a distinction of this sort in mind when he contrasted adjustment of the sensory organs with an internal "anticipatory preparation."

Another important distinction concerns whether orienting (overt or covert) is controlled exogenously or endogenously. *Exogenous* control depends upon factors, outside the observer, such as the pattern of sensory stimulation. In contrast, *endogenous* control depends upon the observer's intentions and expectancies. In its pure form, this contrast can be traced back to Descartes who distinguished between voluntary, willful control of behavior by the mind and reflexive, automatic control by sensory stimulation.

These two distinctions suggest a 2×2 classification scheme (Figure 4.1). Oculomotor responses may be controlled either exogenously or endogenously. Exogenous control is associated with sensory stimulation—sudden changes in the periphery, particularly abrupt onsets, tend to elicit saccadic eye movements. For example, the lightning flash we detect in peripheral vision is usually quickly foveated by a coordinated movement of the eyes and head. In contrast, endogenous control can be observed when the same stimulus pattern elicits quite different oculomotor behavior depending on the observer's interest and intensions. Studies of Yarbus (1967) nicely illustrate this point. He showed observers the same complex painting (*The Unexpected Visitor*), asking different questions (e.g., Are they happy to see him? Are they well off?). Monitoring of eye position revealed quite different scan paths depending on the nature of the ques-

	Overt	Covert
Exogenous		
Endogenous		

FIGURE 4.1. A 2 × 2 classification of visual orienting.

tion to be answered. Admittedly this example is not pure (involving both exogenous and endogenous components), but it does nicely illustrate how endogenous factors can modulate overt orienting. A similar interplay between endogenous and exogenous control of overt orienting takes place in reading (cf. Rayner & Pollatsek, 1989).

As with overt attentional shifts, covert shifts may also be controlled exogenously or endogenously. Peripheral visual events, like a brief flash of light, can "pull" our attention covertly to the stimulated location. Because this pull of attention appears to be reflexive and automatic (Jonides, 1981), we refer to this attention shift as exogenous covert orienting. That attention is reliably and often unintentionally drawn to changes in the periphery is one factor that allows the magician's skill to deceive and surprise us. In contrast, endogenous covert orienting involves voluntary control of the region of space to receive preferential treatment in the absence of eye movements. The experiments of Helmholtz and Wundt, which depended rather too heavily on introspective evidence, sought to demonstrate this ability. Helmholtz (1925), for example, found that he reported more items from an attended region of a briefly flashed display than from equivalent unattended regions. In recent years more objective methods for exploring endogenous covert orienting have been developed (Posner, Snyder, & Davidson, 1980; Sperling, 1960). In these paradigms the observer is given a symbolic cue indicating which item(s) to report in a multi-item display, or indicating the likely location of a prespecified target in a single or multi-item display. Selection in the former case and performance differences between cued and uncued locations in the latter case—in the absence of shifts in gaze direction— provide objective and converging evidence that attention is "pushed" endogenously and covertly to the cued location.

In the real world pure examples of endogenous and exogenous orienting are not common because we usually "want" to inspect objects and events that reflexively attract our attention. Similarly, because the fovea and its associated neural machinery is usually brought to bear on objects and events that are the (covert) focus of attention, pure examples of overt and covert orienting are also uncommon outside the laboratory. To some, this state of affairs might suggest ecologically valid studies of visual orienting in the real world. We do not dispute the value of such studies. It is our strategy, however, to conduct laboratory studies to reveal the nature of the mechanisms associated with the individual cells of the matrix in Figure 4.1 and to reveal the nature of the interrelationships among these mechanisms.

Research Questions

Research in our laboratory has been aimed at achieving a better understanding of the individual cells of this matrix, as well as of the interrelationships among the cells. Our research has emphasized, like much of the literature during the past 10 years, endogenous control of covert orienting. In this chapter we will pose three questions about visual orienting. Each question explores the relationship between the lower right cell of Figure 4.1 (covert endogenous orienting) and one of the other cells. We will draw on our own conducted research, proposed experiments, and the published work of others to develop answers to these questions.

Are the Same Attentional Mechanisms Involved in Endogenous and Exogenous Covert Orienting?

To address this question requires a paradigm for studying *covert* visual orienting in which both endogenous and exogenous control can be implemented. A cuing or cost/benefit (cf. Posner & Snyder, 1975) paradigm is well suited for this purpose. In a typical version of this paradigm the task might be simple detection of a luminance increment. Changes in fixation are discouraged and because observers have poor introspective awareness of where they are looking (Kauffman & Richards, 1969), eye position monitoring to ensure fixation is a necessity.

To explore endogenous control, explicit information is provided concerning the likely target location in the form of a cue, such as an arrow presented at fixation. The cue is valid on most trials but on some trials the cue is invalid and the target appears at the uncued location. A neutral cue, e.g., a plus sign, might be used instead of an arrow on some trials. Following the neutral cue the target is equally likely to occur at any of the possible locations. It is typically observed that detection latencies are faster in the valid condition (when the target occurs at the cued location) than in the invalid condition (when the target occurs at the uncued location) with the neutral condition usually falling between these extremes (Posner, 1978, 1980). A similar pattern of benefits (valid vs. neutral) and costs (invalid vs. neutral) is observed when accuracy is the dependent variable (Downing, 1988; Hawkins et al., 1990). Evidence gathered with this paradigm led Posner to describe visual attention as a spotlight "that enhances the efficiency of detection of events within its beam" (Posner et

TABLE 4.1. Comparison of endogenous and exogenous orienting (Jonides).

	Endogenous	Exogenous
Time to orient	Slow	Fast
Effect of load	Eliminates	No effect
Instruction to ignore	Eliminates	No effect

al., 1980). This metaphor guided much of the research on visual orienting during the 1980s.

To explore exogenous covert orienting, a noninformative spatial cue is presented in the region of a target location. The terms *valid* and *invalid* are somewhat inappropriately carried over from the endogenous situation referring to whether the cue and target are in the same location (valid) or different locations (invalid). It would be more accurate to use the terms *cued* and *uncued* to refer to the match versus mismatch between cue and target location, and to reserve the terms *valid* and *invalid* to refer to situations in which the cue carries probabilistic information that is confirmed (valid) or disconfirmed (invalid) when the target appears. Of course, if it were the case that endogenous and exogenous covert orienting involved identical mechanisms, this distinction would not be important. However, as we shall see, although both endogenous and exogenous orienting usually produce roughly symmetric costs and benefits, they behave quite differently in several important ways.

Jonides (1976, 1981) was one of the first investigators to directly compare endogenous and exogenous covert orienting. Some of his findings are summarized in Table 4.1. Jonides's results demonstrated that exogenous orienting is fast and automatic, whereas endogenous orienting is slow and under strategic control. But is the difference merely one of "transportation" as assumed by Jonides and other investigators? In other words, do endogenous and exogenous orienting involve different ways of getting the same attentional resources to a cued location? Or are there differences in the nature of the attentional resources or processes recruited through these two different methods?

Briand and Klein (1987) asked whether "Posner's beam is the same as Treisman's glue," or does the visual attention that is shifted in response to visual cues perform the functions attributed to attention within Treisman's feature integration theory (FIT) (Treisman & Gelade, 1980; Treisman & Schmidt, 1982)? According to Treisman's theory targets that can be distinguished by a unique feature (R, in a background of Ps and Bs, which can be distinguished by the slanted line) can be detected preattentively, whereas targets defined by a conjunction of features (R, in a background of Ps and Qs) require focused attention in order to "glue" the separate features into a single object. The basic result Briand and Klein expected to obtain, if this question were to be answered in the

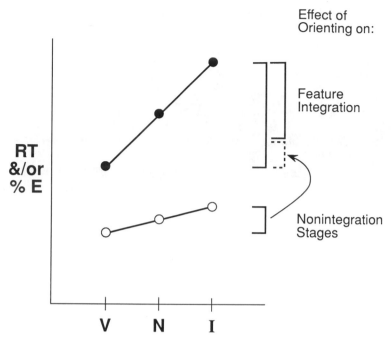

FIGURE 4.2. Pattern of interaction between cue condition (valid [V], neutral [N], and invalid [I]) and distractor type (target defined by a feature or conjunction of features) predicted by the view that orienting of attention affects feature integration.

affirmative, was a larger effect of attentional allocation (costs plus benefits) for targets requiring feature integration than for targets that could be distinguished by a single feature (Figure 4.2). Precisely this pattern was obtained when peripheral cues were used to elicit exogenous orienting, a finding that has also been obtained by Treisman (1985) and Prinzmetal, Presti, and Posner (1986). However, when central arrow cues were used to endogenously orient attention, the effect of orienting was the same for feature and conjunction sets. This additivity implies that endogenously oriented attention plays no role in feature integration stages. The implication of this pattern of results is that exogenously controlled resources perform the functions attributed to attention within Treisman's FIT, whereas endogenously controlled resources do not.

Klein and Hansen (1990) asked whether attending a spatial location is like generating any other expectancy (see also Kingstone & Klein, 1991). If not (i.e., if attending space is special), then attending to location and expecting a particular stimulus/response should produce additive effects on reaction time (RT). On the other hand, if the same stage of processing is involved in generation of these expectancies, then there should be an

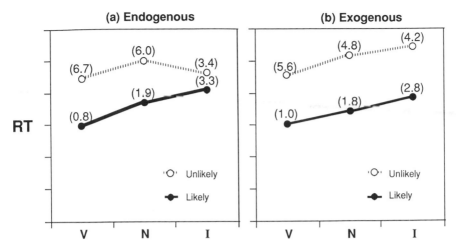

FIGURE 4.3. Reaction time (RT) and accuracy (in parentheses) as a function of cue condition (valid, neutral, and invalid) and stimulus/response likelihood (likely event occurred 80% of the time; unlikely event occurred 20% of the time). (a) Endogenous orienting with central cues; (b) Exogenous orienting with peripheral cues. (Because these cues had the same validity as the central ones, this represents a mixed case with both endogenous and exogenous components.) In both endogenous and exogenous orienting the cues were uninformative about the location of the unlikely events.

interactive pattern. In Klein and Hansen's experiments central cues were used to allocate attention in the direction of the likely target location. In one pair of experiments the subject's task was to determine if a luminance change was an increment or decrement, and make a choice response. One of these changes was much more likely than the other. Interestingly, reaction time to the unlikely event (type of luminance change) showed little or no effect of attentional allocation, even though the likely event showed a large cuing effect. This absence of cuing was accompanied by an error pattern suggesting that subjects were biased to miscategorize the unlikely event at the cued location as the likely event, and it was proposed that this bias might have "masked" an underlying cuing effect. This experiment was modified to permit comparison of endogenous and exogenous orienting: the targets were changed from brightening versus dimming to expansion versus contraction of one of two peripheral squares. "Spotlight masking" and response bias effects were observed with endogenous orienting (Figure 4.3a) but with exogenous orienting the likely and unlikely events showed identical performance patterns as a function of cue condition (i.e., near-perfect additivity) (Figure 4.3b).

These patterns might be explained by assuming that separate attentional systems are involved in endogenous and exogenous orienting, as if

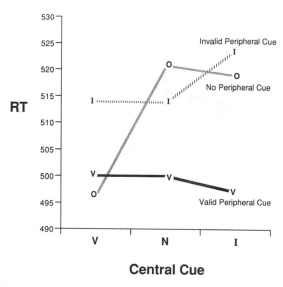

Central Cue

FIGURE 4.4. Combining exogenous and endogenous covert orienting. Reaction time to targets preceded by both centrally (SOA = 600) and peripherally (SOA = 100) presented cues.

two separate "flashlights" were involved. The one you point intentionally does not perform feature integration and is used to generate nonspatial expectancies. The one that is reflexively attracted to a peripheral event, does perform feature integration and is not involved in nonspatial expectancies. If two separate "beams" are involved, then endogenous and exogenous orienting should have additive effects when they are combined orthogonally. To test this, spatial expectancies were pitted against an uninformative abrupt onset (see also Müller & Rabbitt, 1989; Yantis & Jonides, 1990). On each trial a central cue (endogenous control) was presented that was either a plus sign (neutral) or an arrow, which was a valid indicator of the target location on about 80% of the trials (and invalid on the remaining 20%). The target stimulus occurred 600 ms following onset of the central cue. On two-thirds of the trials, a brief flash near one of the possible target locations occurred 100 ms before the target. This peripheral cue conveyed no information about the impending target's location. The results are shown in Figure 4.4. Endogenous orienting was observed when there was no peripheral cue. However, when there was a peripheral cue, RT was fast when the cue and target were in the same region and slow when they were not, regardless of the nature of the central cue. Thus, with this task and choice of cue-target stimulus onset asynchrony (SOA), exogenous orienting overrides endogenous orienting.

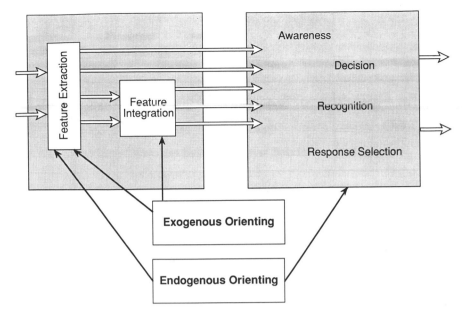

FIGURE 4.5. Tentative model of the possible loci of attentional effects associated with endogenous and exogenous control of visual orienting (see text for explanation).

We can think of no *simple* model that can accommodate our results, and at the same time be consistent with the major findings in the literature. What we speculate might be going on is presented in Figure 4.5. Endogenous and exogenous orienting involve enhancement of feature extraction from the attended location (spotlight); exogenous orienting involves the additional role of feature integration as described in Treisman's theory; exogenous control of the "spotlight" overrides endogenous control when they are in conflict; finally, specific event expectancies (brightening, expansion on the left) are dealt with by a pigeonholing (cf. Broadbent, 1971) mechanism at the decision/response-selection stage. The answer to the question we posed earlier is that there is some overlap between endogenous and exogenous covert orienting, but each control system has its own singularities. While trying to answer our second question we will add support to this conclusion.

Does Overt Orienting (Oculomotor Programming) Play a Mediating Role in Covert Endogenous Orienting? (Or, in Other Words, is Covert Orienting Unexecuted Overt Orienting?)

Klein (1980) proposed an explicit oculomotor readiness hypothesis for endogenous covert orienting. According to this proposal, endogenous covert orienting of attention is accomplished by preparing to move the eyes to the to-be-attended location. It was pointed out that there was a plausible neural substrate for such a mechanism, and that it was quite consistent with several findings in the area of eye movements and attention (e.g., Bryden, 1961; Crovitz & Daves, 1962; Rayner, McConkie, & Ehrlich, 1978). Nevertheless, these previous findings involved attention shifts in response to peripherally presented information and/or involved overt orienting, so a direct test of the hypothesis was warranted. The proposal made two distinct predictions, each of which was tested in a dual-task situation. First, if the subject is preparing to move his/her eyes to a particular location, the detection of events presented there should be facilitated. Second, if the subject is attending to a location, eye movements to that location should be facilitated. Neither of these predictions was confirmed, and it was concluded that endogenous covert orienting is independent of the oculomotor system.

Klein (1980) was careful to point out that this conclusion did not necessarily apply to overt orienting or to exogenous control. Indeed, data from Posner's laboratory (e.g., Posner, 1980) strongly suggested (a) that peripheral events attract both attention and saccades, (b) that attention shifts before the eyes, and (c) that the presaccadic attentional effect is larger when subjects shift gaze than when they maintain fixation.[1] Shepherd, Findlay, and Hockey (1986) used central arrow cues both as signals for saccadic eye movements and to provide information about the location of an upcoming target requiring a manual response. They found that an attention shift in the direction of the ensuing saccade precedes that saccade even when target probabilities indicate that attention should be directed toward the opposite location. That attention shifts before an endogenously generated saccade is consistent with the oculomotor readiness proposal, but as with the Bryden (1961) and Crovitz and Daves (1962) experiments, the Shepherd et al. (1986) finding relates attention shifts to actual saccades. Together with my own findings, these results suggest that there is a tight linkage between attention and saccade *execution*. In the absence of execution, attention is strongly activated by stimuli that normally elicit eye movements and which presumably activate saccadic programming exogenously; *but*, attention is not linked to endogenously generated saccade *programming*.

A recent paper by Rafal, Calabresi, Brennan, and Sciolto (1989) provides converging evidence for this conclusion. They used endogenous and

---

[1] This finding has rather disastrous implications for investigators who hope to avoid the necessity of eye position monitoring by combining peripheral cues with short cue-target SOAs. Although under these circumstances the displays may terminate before peripheral targets might be foveated, saccades may nevertheless be frequently elicited, and Posner's results suggest that different mechanisms may be brought to bear on trials when they are.

exogenous cues to direct or prepare eye movements or attention shifts. On some trials the eyes or attention were drawn back to fixation or the saccade preparation was "canceled" and a simple detection target was presented at the previously cued or uncued location. They found that an inhibitory effect (inhibition of return, cf. Maylor & Hockey, 1985; Posner & Cohen, 1984) accrues to locations that subjects had either planned to fixate or actually had just fixated. This effect was independent of the nature of the cue. When the pre-cues were used to direct attention, and the subjects were instructed to keep their eyes fixed, the inhibitory effect was observed following peripheral cues which elicit orienting exogenously, but it was *not* observed following central cues which elicit endogenous orienting. (This harkens back to our first question, and provides an additional and quite important difference between exogenous and endogenous control of visual attention.) The set of conditions that produces inhibition of return suggests that it is a consequence of prior saccadic programming. That inhibition of return does not accompany endogenous orienting suggests that such orienting is accomplished without any saccadic programming.

In recent years the oculomotor readiness hypothesis for endogenous covert orienting has experienced something of a revival. Rizzolatti, Riggio, Dascolo, and Umilta (1987), in particular, have argued in favor of such a proposal (which they refer to as a "premotor" theory). They provide a rather poor platform from which to mount a resurrection of the oculomotor readiness proposal. First, they only address one of Klein's (1980) two experiments; second, their criticism of that experiment (a "flaw" in the logic) depends on the controversial assumption that "detection of a stimulus required orienting of attention" (orienting may accompany detection, and may facilitate it, but there is no data we are aware of that demonstrate that it *must* precede it); third, their experiment does not test the occulomotor readiness proposal, but merely generates data that might be consistent with that proposal (increased costs due to crossing the vertical or horizontal meridian). Although Klein's original experiments provided negative evidence for such a mechanism, we would be quite satisfied if some flaws in the experiments were elaborated, and positive evidence for the original proposal was reported. Indeed, recent work in our laboratory by Pontefract starts from the premise that it is possible to rescue the oculomotor readiness hypothesis from the implications of Klein's (1980) original experiments by resorting to alternative explanations for the findings.

Klein's (1980) first experiment required an eye movement to a set location in response to an asterisk on 80% of the trials, or a simple manual detection response to a dot brightening (luminance increment) on 20% of the trials. Results showed that manual detection latency was not facilitated when a luminance increment occurred at the prespecified eye movement location. This null result suggests that the presumed oculomotor readiness was not accompanied by an attentional shift to the eye movement location. An alternative explanation is that subjects were not actually preparing to make an eye movement, due to lack of incentive or the blocked manipulation of eye movement direction (cf. Posner et al., 1980). The design of the experiment did not permit an independent assessment of this.

Pontefract (1991), in her follow-up to this experiment, used trial-by-trial cuing of the saccadic response most likely to be required, with occasional luminance increment probes presented at one of the two possible target locations. The eye movement directional cues and imperative signals were the auditorily presented words "left" and "right," whereas the manual detection task was a luminance increment. Because the auditory command signals are not expected to reflexively elicit eye movement programming and because the auditory/visual discrimination is simpler than the visual/visual one, subjects may have greater incentive to prepare the movements than in Klein's study where all the signals are visual. Moreover, cost-benefit analysis can be applied to the eye movement data to determine if saccades are actually prepared. As in Klein's original study, the purpose is to see if detection of the luminance increment is facilitated at the location the eye movement system is prepared to fixate. A significant cuing effect (84.5 ms) was obtained for the primary eye movement task, showing that subjects were preparing eye movements in the cued direction. A much smaller (13.5 ms), but nevertheless significant, effect of the cues was observed for the detection probes. Two aspects of the probe data are not consistent with the oculomotor readiness proposal. First the cuing effect for eye movements was the same whether subjects prepared leftward (87 ms) or rightward (82 ms) movements. But the corresponding detection probes only showed a significant cuing effect when rightward movements were prepared (24 ms vs. 3 ms). If oculomotor preparation produces an attentional shift then one would not expect equal degrees of preparation to be associated with such unequal evidence for attentional shifts. Second, the magnitudes of the saccadic and detection cuing effects following rightward preparation were not significantly correlated ($r10 = .18$, ns).

In Klein's second experiment, arrow cues directed the subject's attention for a highly likely luminance target, and the less likely appearance of an asterisk called for a compatible or incompatible eye movement (i.e., normal vs. antisaccade). It was assumed that if covert orienting was accomplished by preparing an eye movement to the attended location then eye movements to that location would be faster than to nonattended locations. The direction of attention had no effect on saccadic latencies, so it was concluded that covert orienting was not accomplished by oculomotor preparation. However, it is possible that the appearance of a salient visual event such as an asterisk triggers the rapid and reflexive computation of a saccadic program to fixate the event. Such a program might "overwrite" a preprogrammed eye movement, thus destroying any evidence that a saccade had been prepared to produce the attentional shift.

In Pontefract's second experiment each trial began with a visual cue at fixation indicating the location likely to contain a luminance increment requiring a manual response. On occasional probe trials (20%) there was an auditory cue informing the subject to move his eyes "left" or "right." As in Klein (1980) the premise was to get subjects to attend to the cued location, and then measure if eye movement latencies are quicker in the attended, rather than unattended, directions. The use of auditory/verbal signals to indicate which saccade is required should overcome the objection that in Klein (1980) any saccade preparation (used to elicit orienting) might have been "overwritten" when a new saccade program was reflexively computed in response to the visually presented target. A significant cuing effect was observed for the manual detection task (38.5 ms) but there was no evidence that eye movements were faster in the attended direction. On the contrary, saccadic reaction time in the cued (attended) direction was significantly slower (14 ms) than in the uncued (unattended) direction.

These findings provide no support for the oculomotor readiness hypothesis as originally proposed by Klein (1980) and subsequently endorsed by others (Rizzolatti et al., 1987). On the contrary, Pontefract's (1991) findings provide strong support for the conclusion reached by Klein (1980) and others (Posner, 1980; Remington, 1980) that endogenous covert orienting is independent of eye-movement programming.

Is the Predisengagement of Attention (viz., the Cancellation of Covert Endogenous Orienting) Necessary for Rapid Overt Exogenous Orienting (Express Saccades)?

So far we have focused on covert orienting, emphasizing the possible role that might be played by oculomotor programming. Let us now shift gears to overt orienting. That our expectancies and intentions play an important role in endogenous control of overt orienting is shown by the effect of instructions in Yarbus's visual scanning experiments. Presumably, strategic control of the eye movement system is used to direct it to the locations containing the pertinent information.

Exogenous control of the eye movement system can be explored by giving the observer a simple task: shift gaze in the direction of a luminance target. Klein (1978) described some experiments in which the appearance of a target was accompanied by the simultaneous offset of the fixation point on half the trials. Turning the fixation point off produced a 40-ms improvement in saccadic choice reaction time. Saslow (1967) had previously parametrically manipulated the interval between target onset and fixation offset, demonstrating that with a 200-ms "gap" mean RTs of about 140 ms were obtained, an 80-ms reduction (see also Ross & Ross, 1980, 1981 for a similar latency reduction). Later, in the hands of Fischer and his colleagues (e.g., Fischer & Breitmeyer, 1987; Fischer & Ramsperger, 1984, 1986; see also Fischer, this volume) these rapid saccades would be called "express saccades." Introspectively speaking, the conditions that elicit express saccades exert a powerful exogenous influence on orienting mechanisms.

Klein (1978) proposed two interpretations of his finding. One was that offset of the fixation point turns on stimulus-seeking mechanisms that speed the detection of the target; the other was that removing fixation eliminates response competition. Fischer and Breitmeyer (1987), using a framework for visual orienting developed by Posner (Posner, Walker, Friedrich, & Rafal, 1984), and drawing on the empirical work of Mayfrank, Mobashery, Kimmig, and Fisher (1986), proposed a third explanation for the speeded saccades following fixation offset: saccade initiation requires the prior disengagement of attention and so the "gap" condition, fixation offset, accomplishes disengagement before target onset. Referring to Figure 4.1, this notion might be construed in terms of an inhibitory connection from endogenous covert orienting upon exogenous overt orienting. (These three mechanisms are not mutually exclusive.) We thought the "predisengagement" hypothesis was an intriguing idea, but we were not convinced by the evidence marshaled in its favor. In particular, in the Mayfrank et al. (1986) study the manipulation of attentional allocation was weak, and there was no objective measure of attentional allocation. We designed a test of this proposal, but before conducting it we thought it advisable to first demonstrate that we could obtain express saccades using a 200-ms "gap."

We eliminated some of the methodological weaknesses that we felt characterized the earlier work, and we started out by looking for bimodal RT distributions with one peak between 100 and 130 ms, which is how Fischer defined express saccades. Our preliminary experiments demonstrated the importance of using catch trials or choice reactions. When subjects knew when and where they would be required to shift their gaze, their mean RT approached 0 ms, and there were many anticipatory movements. Introspectively, this did not seem to be intentional "jumping the gun," but rather a more automatic process of matching behavior to environmental conditions. In any event, in subsequent experiments we used only the choice procedure, which keeps anticipations to a minimum. Because we were not getting latencies in the desired range we decided to add a no-gap condition so we could determine if the subjects were benefiting from the gap. There are several noteworthy aspects to the data from this experiment: (a) the 200-ms; gap produces a 40-ms improvement in speed of response (no gap, 236 ms; gap, 195 ms); (b) there were few saccades less than 140 ms; (c) the distributions were rarely bimodal.

Although our procedure was producing a gap/no gap difference we felt that possibly express saccades did not exist because we were not seeing latencies in the desired range. We subsequently learned[2] that saccadic latencies in the 100 to 120 ms range could be achieved if bright light-emitting diodes (LED)s were used as targets. When we repeated our experiment with LEDs all our latencies were more rapid, and in the gap condition we now had many saccades that would be considered "express" by the latency criterion. Latency distributions from the oscilloscope and LED conditions are shown in Figure 4.6. All but one subject show a substantial latency improvement in the gap condition. It must be noted that the effect of the gap was roughly the same magnitude as with the oscilloscopic stimuli (no gap 186 ms, gap 139 ms) and that in the gap condition we rarely observed bimodality. We subsequently demonstrated, by dimming the LEDs and brightening the oscilloscope stimuli, that the only important difference between these two situations was luminance, and that luminance was additive with gap versus no gap (consistent with Hughes, personal communication). This suggests that the gap that allows express saccades does not operate by enhancing stimulus detection.

Does the saccadic RT advantage in the gap condition occur because removal of the attended fixation stimulus eliminates one operation from the set of those required to program and initiate a saccade, viz., disengagement of attention? We recently addressed this question in two dual-task RT experiments (Kingstone & Klein, 1990).

One experiment controlled visual attention endogenously using central arrow cues. When the arrow pointed up, a target demanding a manual response was likely to appear at a cross positioned above fixation (valid) and unlikely to appear at a cross below (invalid). The converse was true if the arrow pointed down. Cue validity was 87%. When the cue was a plus sign the manual response target was equally likely to appear above or below fixation (neutral). The second experiment controlled visual attention exogenously by brightening one of the peripheral crosses where a manual target might appear or by brightening a cross at fixation (neutral). These cues were uninformative about target location (cue validity was 50%). In both experiments, on half of all the trials, there was no manual target. Instead, a circular eye movement target was presented to the left or right of fixation. In the gap condition, the central fixation cue or one of the two peripheral crosses were extinguished when a manual target was due to appear, and 200 ms later the eye movement target appeared. In

---

[2] At Psychonomics (November, 1989) we learned from Bruno Breitmeyer, Howard Hughes, and Jon Vaughan, all of whom had been working in this area, that whether the stimuli are little dim dots on an oscilloscope or big bright red LEDs makes a big difference.

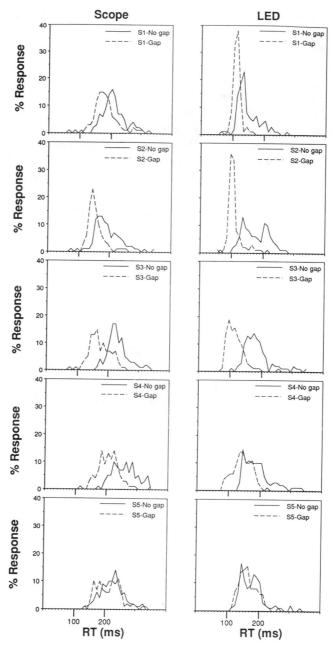

FIGURE 4.6. Saccadic latency distributions when fixation remains present during the trial (solid curve) and when it disappears 200 ms before the appearance of the target (dashed curve). For the left panel stimuli were single pixels on a Tektronix 604 display monitor; for the right panel stimuli were red LEDs.

TABLE 4.2. Reaction times (ms) for manual and saccadic responses following endogenous and exogenous orienting. Peripheral gap, fixation gap, and no gap refer to trials when the offset stimulus is a peripheral cross, a cue at fixation, or when there is no offset stimulus, respectively. The manual target could occur at the cued (V) or uncued (I) locations or following a neutral (N) cue. Similarly, the peripheral-gap condition involved offset of the cross at a cued (V) or uncued (I) location or following a neutral cue (N). Saccadic targets in the fixation-gap and no-gap conditions could occur following neutral (N) or nonneutral (NN) cues.

| | Manual task | | | Saccadic task | | | | | | |
| | | | | Peripheral gap | | | Fixation gap | | No gap | |
	V	N	I	V	N	I	N	NN	N	NN
Endogenous	394	473	509	281	275	275	245	237	345	326
Exogenous	467	526	521	259	243	267	243	211	297	262

the no-gap condition, the central cue and the peripheral crosses remained present for the duration of the trial.

Manual and saccadic response times are shown in Table 4.2. Whether attention was controlled endogenously or exogenously, manual responses to targets occurring at the cued location (valid) were faster than to those at uncued locations (neutral and invalid). This pattern of results provides objective evidence that attention was indeed engaged at the cued locations. The eye movement data reveal a large and significant gap effect (see for example the fixation-gap vs. no-gap data). If the gap effect is due to a predisengagement of attention, we would expect to find faster saccadic latencies when the attended cross was extinguished than when the unattended cross was extinguished. However, whether attention was manipulated endogenously or exogenously there was no difference between these two conditions (see peripheral-gap cued vs. peripheral-gap uncued). This result clearly disconfirms the hypothesis that express saccades the enabled by the predisengagement of attention.

Summary and Conclusions

Are the same attentional mechanisms involved in endogenous and exogenous covert orienting? Based on our results and analysis of the literature, we suggest that it should not be assumed that exogenous and endogenous orienting will necessarily involve identical mechanisms. This view recommends a particular research strategy in which spatial, temporal, and other properties of visual attention are measured in the context of both endogenous and exogenous control (cf. Kingstone & Klein, 1990; Klein, Briand & Hansen, 1987; Müller & Rabbitt, 1989).

Is endogenously controlled covert orienting mediated by endogenous programming of overt orienting? On the basis of Klein's (1980) & Pontefract's (1991) findings, we think not. Although we feel that endogenous covert orienting is independent of the programming of saccades, we also believe that with exogenous control there is a tight coupling between the covert (attentional) and overt (saccadic) systems, and that execution of a saccadic program may involve an obligatory attentional shift.

Is disengaging attention a prerequisite for express saccades, or, in other words, does endogenously engaged attention inhibit overt orienting? This intriguing idea has received some support (Mayfrank et al., 1986). However, our experiments using endogenous and exogenous control of covert orienting and objective measures to ensure attentional allocation provide no evidence to support this hypothesis. Our findings suggest instead that the mechanism(s) responsible for rapid saccades in the context of fixation offset are independent of visual attention.

We have tried to illustrate, through our review of the literature and our own findings, that the distinctions between overt and covert orienting and between exogenous and endogenous control are important ones. We hope to stimulate clever and creative experimental work that will illuminate the mechanisms underlying these aspects of visual orienting as well as their interrelationships.

References

Briand, K., & Klein, R.M. (1987). Is Posner's "beam" the same as Treisman's "glue": On the relationship between visual orienting and feature integration theory. *Journal of Experimental Psychology: Human Perception and Performance*, *13*, 228–241.

Broadbent, D.E. (1971). *Decision and stress*. London: Academic Press.

Bryden, M.P. (1961). The role of post-exposural eye movements in tachistoscopic perception. *Canadian Journal of Psychology*, *15*, 220–225.

Crovitz, H.F., & Daves, W. (1962). Tendencies to eye movement and perceptual accuracy. *Journal of Experimental Psychology*, *63*, 496–498.

Downing, C. (1988). Expectancy and visual-spacial attention: Effects on perceptual quality. *Journal of Experimental Psychology: Human Perception and Performance*, *14*, 188–202.

Fischer, B., & Breitmeyer, B. (1987). Mechanisms of visual attention revealed by saccadic eye movements. *Neuropsychologia*, *25*, 73–83.

Fischer, B., & Ramsperger, E. (1984). Human express-saccades: Extremely short reaction times of goal directed eye movements: *Experimental Brain Research*, *57*, 191–195.

Fischer, B., & Ramsperger, E. (1986). Human express-saccades: Effects of randomization and daily practice. *Experimental Brain Research*, *64*, 569–578.

Hawkins, H.L., Hillyard, S.A., Luck, S.J., Mouloua, M., Downing, C.J., & Woodward, D.P. (1990). Visual attention modulates signal detectability. *Journal of Experimental Psychology: Human Perception and Performance*, *16*(4), 802–811.

Helmholtz, H. von. (1925). *Hondbuch der Physiologischen optik* (J.P.C. Southall, Trans.).

James, W. (1890). *Principles of psychology* (Vols. 1 & 2). New York: Holt.

Jonides, J. (1976, June). *Voluntary versus reflexive control of the mind's eye's movement.* Paper presented at Psychonomics, St. Louis.

Jonides, J. (1981). Voluntary versus automatic control over the mind's eye's movement. In J. Long & A. Baddeley (Eds.), *Attention and performance IX.* Hillsdale, NJ: Erlbaum.

Kauffman, L., & Richards, W. (1969). Spontaneous fixation tendencies for visual forms. *Perception and Psychophysics, 5,* 85–88.

Kingstone, A., & Klein, R.M. (1990, November). Attention and express saccades. Paper presented at Psychonomics, New Orleans.

Kingstone, A., & Klein, R.M. (1991). Combining shape and position expectancies: Hierarchical processing and selective inhibition. *Journal of Experimental Psychology: Human Perception and Performance, 17*(2), 512–519.

Klein, R.M. (1978). Chronometric analysis of saccadic eye movements: Reflexive and cognitive control. In D. Landers & R. Christina (Eds.), *Psychology of motor behaviour and sport 1977.* Champaign, IL: Human Kinetics.

Klein, R.M. (1980). Does oculomotor readiness mediate cognitive control of visual attention? In Nickerson (Ed.), *Attention and performance VIII.* Hillsdale, NJ: Erlbaum.

Klein, R., Briand, K., & Hansen, E. (1987, July). *Covert visual orienting: Endogenous and exogenous attentional mechanisms.* Paper presented at a joint meeting of the Experimental Psychology Society and the Canadian Psychological Association. Oxford.

Klein, R.M., & Hansen, E. (1990). Chronometric analysis of spotlight failure in endogenous visual orienting. *Journal of Experimental Psychology: Human Perception and Performance, 16*(4), 790–801.

Mayfrank, L., Mobashery, M., Kimmig, H., & Fisher, B. (1986). The role of fixation and visual attention on the occurrence of express saccades in man. *European Journal of Psychiatry Neurological Science, 235,* 269–275.

Maylor, E.A., & Hockey, R. (1985). Inhibitory component of externally controlled covert orienting in visual space. *Journal of Experimental Psychology: Human Perception and Performance, 11,* 777–787.

Müller, H.J., & Rabbitt, P.M.A. (1989). Reflexive and voluntary orienting of visual attention: Time course of activation and resistance to interruption. *Journal of Experimental Psychology: Human Perception and Performance, 15,* 315–330.

Pontefract, A.J. (1991). The relationship between endogenous covert orienting and oculomotor preparation. Unpublished masters thesis, Dalhousie University.

Posner, M.I. (1978). Chronometric explorations of mind. Hillsdale, NJ: Erlbaum.

Posner, M.I. (1980). Orienting of attention. *Quarterly Journal of Experimental Psychology, 32,* 3–25.

Posner, M.I., & Cohen, Y. (1984). Components of visual orienting. In H. Bouma & D.G. Bouwhuis (Eds.), *Attention and performance X. Control of language processes.* Hillsdale, NJ: Erlbaum.

Posner, M.I., & Snyder, C.R.R. (1975). Attention and cognitive control. In R.L. Solso (Ed.), *Information processing and cognition: The Loyola symposium.* Hillsdale, NJ: Erlbaum.

Posner, M.I., Snyder, C.R.R., & Davidson, B.J. (1980). Attention and the detection of signals. *Journal of Experimental Psychology: General, 109,* 160–174.

Posner, M.I., Walker, J.A., Friedrich, F.J., & Rafal, R.D. (1984). Effects of parietal injury on covert orienting of attention. *Journal of Neuroscience, 4,* 1863–1874.

Prinzmetal, W., Presti, D.E., & Posner, M.I. (1986). Does attention affect visual feature integration. *Journal of Experimental Psychology: Human Perception & Performance, 12,* 361–369.

Rafal, R.D., Calabresi, P.A., Brennan, C.W., & Sciolto, T.K. (1989). Saccade preparation inhibits reorienting to recently attended locations. *Journal of Experimental Psychology: Human Perception and Performance, 15,* 673–685.

Rayner, K., McConkie, G.W., & Ehrlich, S. (1978). Eye movements and integrating information across fixations. *Journal of Experimental Psychology: Human Perception and Performance, 4,* 529–544.

Rayner, K., & Pollatsek, A. (1989). *The psychology of reading.* Englewood Cliffs, NJ: Prentice Hall.

Remington, R.W. (1980). Attention and saccadic eye movements. *Journal of Experimental Psychology: Human Perception and Performance, 6,* 726–744.

Rizzolatti, G., Riggio, L., Dascolo, I., & Umilta, C. (1987). Reorienting attention across the horizontal and vertical meridians: Evidence in favor of a premotor theory of attention. *Neuropsychologia, 25,* 31–40.

Ross, L.E., & Ross, S.M. (1980). Saccade latency and warning signals: Stimulus onset, offset, and change as warning events. *Perception and Psychophysics, 27,* 251–257.

Ross, S.M., & Ross, L.E. (1981). Saccade latency and warning signals: Effects of auditory and visual stimulus onset and offset. *Perception and Psychophysics, 29,* 429–437.

Saslow, M.G. (1967). Effects of components of displacement-step stimuli upon latency of saccadic eye movements. *Journal of the Optical Society of America, 57,* 1024–1029.

Shepherd, M., Findlay, J.M., & Hockey, R.J. (1986). The relationship between eye movements and spatial attention. *Quarterly Journal of Experimental Psychology, 38A,* 475–491.

Sperling, G. (1960). The information available in brief visual displays. *Psychological Monographs, 74* (11, Whole No. 498).

Treisman, A. (1985). Preattentive processing in vision. *Computer Processing, Graphics, and Image Processing, 31,* 156–177.

Treisman, A., & Gelade, G. (1980). A feature-integration theory of attention. *Cognitive Psychology, 12,* 97–136.

Treisman, A., & Schmidt, H. (1982). Illusory conjunctions in the perception of objects. *Cognitive Psychology, 14,* 107–141.

Yantis, S., & Jonides, J. (1990). Abrupt visual onsets and selective attention: Voluntary versus automatic allocation. *Journal of Experimental Psychology: Human Perception and Performance, 16,* 121–134.

Yarbus, A.L. (1967). *Eye movements and vision* (B. Haigh, Trans.). New York: Plenum Press.

5
Planning and Producing Saccadic Eye Movements

RICHARD A. ABRAMS

Each day, as people explore their visual worlds, they produce more than 150,000 saccadic eye movements (Robinson, 1981a). Saccades serve the important role of bringing a new array of stimuli onto the fovea, allowing an observer to inspect some previously uninspected part of their environment. In order to learn more about the processes involved in perception in general, researchers have turned to learning more about details of the mechanisms that underlie the production of saccades. The belief is that a better understanding of the processes involved in guiding movements of the eyes might lead to insight into the other psychological mechanisms underlying perception and visual cognition.

This chapter focuses on the kinds of decisions and computations that people must make in order to move their eyes from one location to another. Several experiments are described that were conducted in collaboration with a number of other researchers. The framework that we have adopted assumes that a saccade arises as the result of the specification of a number of different parameters. People must make decisions about the values of these parameters before a saccade can be produced. Given this framework, the questions upon which we have focused our research can be expressed as follows: What are the parameters that must be specified prior to a saccade? When are the parameters specified? Are the parameters specified in a particular order? Do values of one parameter constrain the values of others? What is the nature of the noise, if any, in the specification and implementation of the parameters? Can a single parameter be changed at the last minute?

Overview

Four interrelated areas of research are discussed. The first deals with the way that people prepare the motor commands that ultimately lead to saccades. Of particular concern is whether people make individual decisions about separate parameters that define the spatial goal for the saccade. The second addresses questions about the principles underlying the production of force pulses that move the eye from one location to another, and focuses explicitly on stochastic variability in those pulses. The third area focuses on the response of the oculomotor system to a rearrangement of the visual feedback that is typically available after a saccade. Finally, we describe some research on the ability of people to cancel and reprogram a saccade shortly before it is produced. Taken together, these lines of inquiry lead to a view of the saccadic system as one in which a number of separate decisions must be made in order to move the eyes from one location to another. The separate decisions are at least partially independent of one another, they need not be made in a rigid order, and they can be changed quite quickly, shortly before the eyes begin to move.

Programming Saccades

Because saccades are so brief, it is believed that the motor commands that move the eye must usually be completely prepared prior to the onset of any movement. Such *programming* of the motor commands for saccades has received considerable attention recently. One of the most common ways to study the programming process is by measuring the amount of time that people need to program and initiate saccades in various situations. A better understanding of the construction of the motor commands for saccades could eventually lead to new knowledge about visual perception more generally.

Direction and Amplitude Parameters

Following the lead of other researchers, we characterized a saccade in terms of the spatial coordinates of the direction and amplitude of the new, desired fixation location relative to the current position of gaze. Thus, programming a saccade involves the specification of values for two parameters: the *direction* in which the eye is to more, and the *amplitude* through which the eye must move. Given this perspective, we were interested in distinguishing between a number of alternative ways in which people might program the two parameters (Abrams & Jonides, 1988).

The issue that we were primarily concerned with was whether the direction and amplitude parameters are computed and processed separately prior to a saccade or whether they are specified jointly in a unitary fashion. There is some evidence to suggest that decisions about direction and amplitude can be made separately. Indeed, several researchers have suggested that the specification of direction must be completed before amplitude can be programmed (e.g., Becker & Jurgens, 1979; Hou &

Fender, 1979). However, there are some reasons to questions these conclusions (for a discussion, see Abrams & Jonides, 1988). If indeed direction and amplitude are programmed separately, we are interested in details of the programming processes: Must one value be specified before another? Does each take the same amount of time to program?

There is also some evidence that people do not separately compute values for direction and amplitude parameters. Rather, saccades may be programmed more "holistically," with values for direction and amplitude essentially being specified simultaneously. According to this view, there might not even be any distinct computation of direction and amplitude values at all; instead, subjects may specify only the desired final location of the eye in the orbit, without regard to the direction and amplitude relative to the current eye position. Support for this possibility comes from studies in which subjects produced accurate saccades to briefly flashed targets despite undetected (experimenter-induced) perturbations of their eyes shortly before the saccade was emitted (Mays & Sparks, 1980; additional evidence consistent with this possibility has been reported by Hallett & Lightstone, 1976, and Zee, Optican, Cook, Robinson, & Engel, 1976). Such a result could only occur if the motor commands for the saccades included, at some level, a specification of the final desired position of the eye irrespective of the direction and amplitude of the vector between the current and desired positions.

The distinction between separate and simultaneous specification of direction and amplitude parameters has also received some attention in work on aimed limb movements. There, the issue is whether subjects program the final *location* of a movement without regard to the distance to be moved (simultaneous specification), or whether they compute a specific value for an *amplitude* parameter, which must take into account both the initial and final, desired limb positions (Abrams & Landgraf, 1990; Abrams, Meyer, & Kornblum, 1990). Some evidence suggests that limb movements may be programmed only in terms of the final desired location (Polit & Bizzi, 1979), but other evidence suggests that movements are better characterized in terms of the amplitude and duration of the forces that produce the movement (Meyer, Abrams, Kornblum, Wright, & Smith, 1988), suggesting that people do compute a value for an amplitude parameter. There is even some evidence that both types of programming may be used to guide some rapid limb movements (Abrams et al., 1990).

To study these issues, we used a reaction-time method similar to one that had been initially applied to the study of limb movements (Rosenbaum, 1980). The method, called the *movement precuing technique*, involves presenting subjects initially with a precue that partially specifies the spatial location of the target for a saccade. The subject presumably tries to use this information to partially program the saccade. Next, a reaction signal is presented that completely specifies the required movement, and the subject is to produce the appropriate saccade as soon as possible. The latency to begin moving the eye includes the time needed to prepare the parameters of the saccade that could not be prepared before the reaction signal. If indeed people separately specify direction and amplitude parameters, and if they are able to program some parameters of a saccade in advance, then the latency would reflect the time needed to program the parameters that were not contained in the precue. With the appropriate selection of precues, the technique can be used to make inferences about the preparation of parameters for saccades.

On each trial of the experiment, subjects made a saccade to one of four locations: 3° or 6° to the left or right of fixation. Precues presented before the reaction signal provided the subject with no, partial, or complete information about the saccade that would be required: on *one-alternative* trials, subjects were completely informed about which saccade would be called for; on *two-alternative* trials one of two specified locations would be the target for the saccade; and on *four-alternative* trials the target for the saccade could be any of the four possible target locations. The trials of most interest involve those with the *two-alternative* precues. There were three different types of two-alternative precues: (a) *direction* precues informed the subject of the direction of the required saccade (e.g., to the right), but did not specify the amplitude of the saccade; (b) *amplitude* precues informed the subject of the required saccade amplitude (e.g., 3°), but did not specify whether the target would be to the left or the right; and (c) *mixed* precue trials informed the subject of neither the direction nor the amplitude in advance, although only two locations would be possible saccade targets (e.g., 3° left and 6° right).[1]

The two alternative ways of programming saccades make different predictions about what might happen on the various two-alternative trials. If subjects do separately specify values for direction and amplitude parameters, and if they can partially program a saccade in advance, then the latency on direction precue trials would reflect the time needed to program saccade amplitude. This is because subjects would presumably have already programmed the direction of the saccade in advance of the reaction signal on those trials. Similarly, the latency to begin the eye movement on amplitude precue trials should reflect the time needed to program saccade direction because subjects would be able to program the

---

[1] The precues and reaction signals were presented by filling in one or more of four small circles that were arranged with two on each side of the fixation point. The stimulus-response mapping was such that circles on the left represented targets to the right of fixation. This was done to avoid difficulties in interpreting reaction times when subjects are able to produce saccades in the direction of sudden-onset stimuli. Seveal experiments were conducted to demonstrate that our results could not be attributed to unnatural stimulus-response translation processes caused by our stimuli. These are discussed elsewhere (Abrams & Jonides, 1988).

TABLE 5.1. Saccade latency (in milliseconds) as a function of the type of precue.

One alternative	Type of precue			Four alternatives
	Two alternatives			
	Direction	Amplitude	Mixed	
165.8	216.6	218.6	230.8	251.6

amplitude in advance of the reaction signal. Finally, the latency on mixed precue trials should include the time needed to program both amplitude and direction because neither of these parameters were known in advance on those trials despite the fact that, like the amplitude and direction-precue trials, there were only two potential saccade targets. Alternatively, if people specify direction and amplitude parameters simultaneously, then advance knowledge of one parameter without knowledge of the other should not help them reduce their saccade latencies.

The results are shown in Table 5.1. First note that latencies decreased dramatically as the information provided by the precue increased: one-alternative trials had the shortest latencies and four-alternative trials had the longest latencies. This shows that subjects were attending to the information in the precue. The results of most interest involve the latencies on the different types of two-alternative trials. As seen in the table, subjects were faster to initiate saccades when they knew the direction or amplitude of the saccade to be made in advance. When neither parameter was known until the reaction signal (mixed-precue trials), subjects were on the average 13 ms slower to begin moving the eye.

Conclusions

The results have several important implications for the processes involved in programming saccades. First, the fact that any partial advance preparation occurred suggests that saccades need not be specified holistically, with decisions about direction and amplitude made simultaneously. Rather, it seems that the specification of direction and of amplitude for a saccade can be performed separately. Second, the observation that advance knowledge of either direction or amplitude was useful without knowledge of the other parameter suggests that the two parameters need not be programmed in a fixed order. Subjects appear to have been able to program the amplitude (or direction) for a saccade before knowing in which direction (or how far) the eye was to move. This contrasts with claims by others that direction must be specified before computations about amplitude can be performed. Finally, advance knowledge of either direction or amplitude reduced saccade latencies by equal amounts relative to mixed-precue trials. This suggests that the times needed to specify direction and amplitude are equivalent.

These results may shed some light on the sometimes very short intervals observed between one eye movement and the next during reading. Apparently, if a subject has some partial information about the direction or amplitude of the movement to the next desired fixation location, then some of the saccade programming can be performed in advance. The subject need only finish construction of the motor program and initiate it when he or she is ready to move on to the next fixation.

Programming Saccade Amplitude: Force and Time Parameters

The experiment described above suggests that people program saccades by separately specifying values for direction and amplitude parameters. To learn more about the production of saccades, we turned next to questions about details of the specification of the amplitude parameter (Abrams, Meyer, & Kornblum, 1989). In particular, we were concerned with the way in which the oculomotor system specifies the forces that move the eyes. Regardless of the manner in which saccades are programmed (i.e., individual vs. simultaneous specification of direction and amplitude parameters), the oculomotor system must eventually implement the motor commands by transforming them into appropriate forces. The specification and implementation of the motor commands, however, is subject to noise in the motor system. This neuromotor noise causes saccades to exhibit some variability in their spatial and temporal properties over repeated attempts to produce nominally equivalent eye movements. Presumably, the oculomotor system is designed in such a way so as to minimize the potential impact of this noise on movements of the eye. It is of considerable interest to study properties of the noise in order to learn more about the way in which the oculomotor system deals with it.

As with most simple movements, saccades can be described in terms of the application of a pulse of force to the eye of a specific magnitude for a particular amount of time. Thus, two parameters can be identified that define the forces involved in a saccade: a *force parameter*, which specifies the magnitude of the force pulse, and a *time parameter*, which specifies the duration of the pulse. One goal of the present work was to obtain estimates of the values of the force and time parameters in saccades of various sizes, and to determine the extent to which variability in the parameters can account for variability in saccadic eye movements.

Details of the force pulses and neuromotor noise of saccades are also of interest to researchers interested in motor control mechanisms more generally. This is because several models of movement control have been developed that focus explicitly on stochastic variability in the forces that produce aimed limb movements (e.g., Meyer, Smith, & Wright, 1982;

Schmidt, Zelaznik, Hawkins, Frank, & Quinn, 1979). Evaluation of these models has been hampered, in part, by the relative complexity of limb movements and the difficulty of obtaining accurate recordings of limb movement trajectories. Saccades, however, involve fairly simple sets of muscles, and the oculomotor system has the virtue of allowing saccade trajectories to directly reflect details of the underlying neurological control signals (Robinson, 1981b). Thus, saccades may provide an ideal opportunity to test some of the assumptions upon which these models are based. Such an endeavor may also help to strengthen ties between research on eye movements and research on limb movements.

The Symmetric Impulse-Variability Model and the Linear Speed-Accuracy Trade-off

One model of the class described above that has receive some attention is the symmetric impulse-variability model (Meyer et al., 1982). This model makes several assumptions about the shape of the force-time curves that underlie movement, and about the effects of neuromotor noise on the force-time curves. In theory, these assumptions might apply to eye movements as well as limb movements. The major assumptions of the model are summarized below.

FORCE-TIME RESCALABILITY

The model assumes that the production of a movement involves selecting a force-time function that specifies the net amount of force applied to a body part as a function of time. The force-time function is assumed to come from a family of similar force-time functions, all with the same general shape. The selection of the particular function for a movement is based on the values of a force parameter and a time parameter, which are applied to the prototype of the family of force-time functions. Changes in the values of the parameters would yield force-time functions that are rescaled from the prototype in the force and time domains.

SHAPE OF FORCE-TIME FUNCTIONS

The model also makes some assumptions about the general shape of the force-time functions: The net force operating on the body part should be positive during the first half of the movement and negative during the second half. Furthermore, the force-time function during the second half of movement is assumed to be a mirror image of the first half.

VARIABILITY OF PARAMETER VALUES

Additionally, the model makes assumptions about a person's ability to select values for the force and time parameters. The force and time parameters are assumed to be random variables whose standard deviations increase proportionally with their means, as in Weber's law from sensory psychophysics. Because these parameters determine the amplitude and duration of the force-time function used to produce a movement, variability of these parameters from movement to movement produces variability in the force-time functions, and hence variability in the movements' distance and duration.

PREDICTION OF LINEAR SPEED-ACCURACY TRADE-OFF

Taken together, the assumptions outlined above, along with a few other ancillary ones, predict that movements that obey the model should exhibit a trade-off between their speed and their spatial precision. For a set of movements, all of which are intended to travel the same distance and have the same duration, the standard deviation of the movements' endpoints in space should be a linear function of the movements' average velocity. This linear speed-accuracy trade-off can be expressed as follows:

$$SD = K_1 + K_2V,$$

where SD is the standard deviation of the movements' endpoints in space, V is the average movement velocity (total movement distance divided by movement duration), and K_1 and K_2 are nonnegative constants. (For more information about the model and its predictions, see Meyer et al., 1982, and Abrams, Meyer, & Kornblum 1989). This prediction has been verified in a number of experiments on limb movements (Schmidt et al., 1979; Meyer et al., 1988; Wright & Meyer, 1983; Zelaznik, Shapiro, & McColsky, 1981).

Our goal was to determine the extent to which the assumptions and predictions of the symmetric impulse variability model apply to saccades. One reason for doing this was to provide a more direct test of the model than has been possible based on evaluation of limb movements. Another reason for the present study was to learn more about the oculomotor system.

To address these issues we had subjects produce small horizontal saccades of several different amplitudes to visible targets. Subjects were not pressured to minimize their latencies, but they were continually encouraged to produce saccades that landed as close to the target as possible. (Additional methodological details are included in Abrams, Meyer, & Kornblum, 1989.)

For each target distance we computed the means and standard deviations of the saccade distances and durations, and various other kinematic features of the saccades such as the time to peak velocity and the peak force attained. Data that show the form of the speed-accuracy trade-off are presented in Figure 5.1. Here the standard deviations of the spatial endpoints of the saccades are plotted as a function of the saccades'

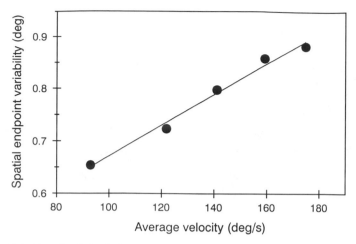

FIGURE 5.1. Standard deviation of saccade spatial endpoints as a function of saccade average velocity. (The line is the best-fitting regression function). Adapted by permission from R.A. Abrams, D.E. Meyer, and S. Kornblum, 1989. Copyright 1989 by the American Psychological Association.

average velocities, separately for each target distance studied. A linear trend accounted for nearly 99% of the variance in the saccade endpoints, demonstrating that saccades, like limb movements, obey the form of trade-off predicted by the symmetric impulse-variability model.

Saccades also provide an opportunity to test some of the assumptions that allow the symmetric impulse-variability model to predict a linear speed-accuracy trade-off. One assumption was that the variability in the force and time parameters would be proportional to their mean values. A good estimate of the magnitude of the time parameter for a saccade is provided by the time of peak velocity. An estimate of the value of the force parameter is provided by the peak force (acceleration) attained. Figure 5.2 shows the standard deviation of these measures as a function of their mean, for each of the saccade amplitudes studied. As can be seen the standard deviations of the force and time parameters increased approximately linearly with their means, consistent with the symmetric impulse-variability model.

Finally, we also obtained data regarding the shape of the force-time functions and force-time rescalability of saccades. The force-time (acceleration-time) functions are shown in Figure 5.3. These were obtained by plotting the mean accelerations and times associated with five events in the saccades: movement onset, peak positive acceleration, peak velocity, peak negative acceleration, and the movement end. These functions match the shape assumed by the symmetric impulse-variability model quite well: the curves are reasonably symmetric, the peak velocity (transition from positive to negative force) occurred close to the midpoint of the movement, and the deceleration phase was approximately a mirror image of the acceleration phase, consistent with predictions of the model. In addition to having the predicted shape, the force-time curves for larger saccades appear to be rescaled versions of those from the smaller saccades in both force and time. Thus, these data support the notion that saccades of different amplitudes are derived from a common prototypical force-time function.[2]

Conclusions

The results of the present experiment reveal a number of important features of saccadic eye movements and the oculomotor system. Standard deviations of certain kinematic features of saccades increased proportionally with their means, indicating the presence of neuromotor noise in the oculomotor system. Comparison of the acceleration-time functions from saccades of different amplitudes suggests that saccades may result from rescaling a prototypical force-time function in force and time. This implies that saccades arise from the adjustment of a few key parameters, an argument that has been made by others (Abrams & Jonides, 1988; Reinhart & Zuber, 1971). Most important, the processes associated with parameter selection, force-time rescaling, and noise in the motor system lead directly to a linear trade-off between the average speed of a saccadic eye movement and its spatial accuracy. In addition to providing support for impulse variability models of movement production (e.g., Meyer et al., 1982; Schmidt et al., 1979), these results suggests that a single theoretical framework may eventually describe the processes underlying a wide range of motor behaviors.

The presence of neuromotor noise in the oculomotor system may also lead to a better understanding of some perceptual processes. For example, a number of researchers have proposed that our perceptions of the sizes and locations of visible objects is based, at least in part, on knowledge that we have about the eye movements that we must make to scan those objects (e.g., Coren, 1986). Depending on how the perceptual system monitors the eye movements that we make, it is possible that variability in the eye movements could contribute to variability in perception. Detailed studies of variability in saccades may help inform these and other issues about perception and visual cognition.

---

[2] Some quantitative aspects of the saccade trajectories departed in small, but significant ways from the model's predictions. Most notably, larger amplitude saccades had peak velocities that occurred relatively early in the movement (compared to shorter saccades), suggesting that the model does not capture all aspects of saccade production. See Abrams, Meyer, and Kornblum, (1989) for further discussion.

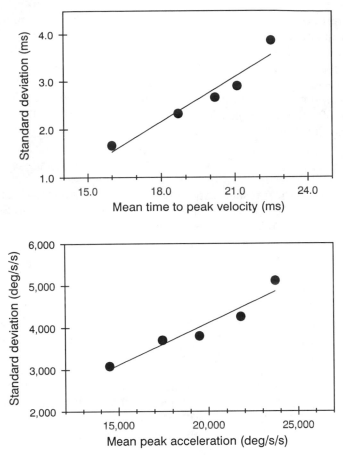

FIGURE 5.2. Top panel: Standard deviation of the time to peak velocity as a function of the mean time to peak velocity. Bottom panel: Standard deviation of the peak acceleration as a function of the mean peak acceleration. (The lines are the best-fitting regression functions.) Adapted by permission from R.A. Abrams, D.E. Meyer, and S. Kornblum, 1989. Copyright 1989 by the American Psychological Association.

Parametric Adaptation: Dissociating the Force and Time Parameters

One of the most interesting features of saccades, and one that distinguishes saccadic eye movements from rapid movements of other body parts, is the highly stereotyped relation between saccade amplitude and kinematic features of the saccades such as their duration and force magnitude (e.g., see Figure 5.3). In theory, an infinite number of force-parameter/time-parameter pairs could produce a movement of a given size. Lower force magnitudes (force parameter) would simply need to be

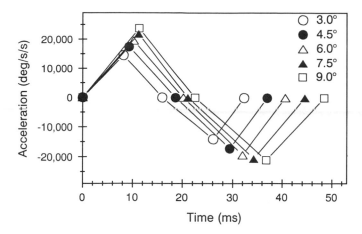

FIGURE 5.3. Mean force-time functions for saccades of different amplitudes. Adapted by permission from R.A. Abrams, D.E. Meyer, and S. Kornblum, 1989. Copyright 1989 by the American Psychological Association.

applied for longer durations (time parameter). Nevertheless, although people can easily move their limbs through a specified distance over a wide range of velocities, saccades of a given size exhibit relatively little variability in speed. One question about this relation that we were interested in is whether the tight link between saccade amplitude and saccade kinematics is a feature of the "hardware" of the oculomotor system or of the "software" of the system. In other words, is it possible for the oculomotor system to separately adjust values of the force and time parameters, or must the force and time parameters covary nearly perfectly? (Of course, as seen above, neuromotor noise will introduce random variation into the values of the parameters.)

Despite the fact that the majority of saccades do exhibit a tight link between amplitude and duration, there are a number of situations where saccades with nonnormal kinematic features have been observed. For example, saccades of a given size are slower than normal when produced in darkness (Becker & Fuchs, 1969; Henriksson, Pyykko, Schalen, & Wennmo, 1980), and when present in certain pathologies (Zee et al., 1976). These results suggest that the mechanisms involved in the specification of the force and time parameters for saccades are at least partially independent of each other.[3] Despite these possibilities, most normal

---

[3] It should also be noted that the symmetric impulse-variability model assumes that the force and time parameters are not perfectly correlated. If they were perfectly correlated then the model would fail to predict the observed linear speed-accuracy trade-off. Thus, we would expect the two parameters to be separable to the extent that the symmetric impulse-variability model explains saccades.

saccades made to visible targets exhibit the stereotypical relation between amplitude and duration.

Saccade Adaptation

To examine the possibility that the force and time parameters might be separately modulated, we sought a situation that might cause subjects to modify one parameter but not another (Abrams, Scharf, & Dobkin, 1989). We reasoned that subjects might do so if they were confronted with a situation in which their saccades appeared to be inaccurate. An abnormally large fixation error after a saccade might cause subjects to believe that their selection of force and/or time parameters was incorrect, and they might modify the parameter selection process accordingly. Of course there is no guarantee that the error will lead to a change in only one parameter. But, if it did, then that would be evidence that the parameters are separately modulated. To explore this possibility, we distorted the retinal feedback available to subjects after a saccade by displacing the target for the saccade during the eye movement toward it. When the target is displaced only a small distance, subjects typically do not notice the displacement. As several researchers have shown, the result of this *adaptive modification* procedure is that subjects alter the amplitudes of subsequent saccades to compensate for the saccade-contingent displacement of the target (e.g., McLaughlin, 1967; McLaughlin, Kelly, Anderson, & Wenz, 1968; Miller, Anstis, & Templeton, 1981).

To learn about the modulation of saccadic force and time parameters, we compared the saccades after adaptation with normal saccades of the same amplitude. If the adaptation caused subjects to alter only the force parameter or only the time parameter then there should be systematic differences in kinematic features of the adapted and equal-size normal saccades.

Along with our interest in the independence of saccadic force and time parameters we also had an interest in details of the process by which the oculomotor system adapts to rearranged retinal feedback. Several explanations have been proposed to account for the adaptation, but they have not all received a strong test. Through an examination of saccade kinematics, however, such a test is possible. For example, one possible explanation of the adaptive behavior is that subjects modify some *spatial map* to compensate for the distortion introduced by the adaptive technique (Semmlow, Gauthier, & Vercher, 1989; cf. Abrams, Dobkin, & Helfrich, in press). According to this explanation, a given retinal target after adaptation would become associated with a saccade of a different amplitude from what would have been produced to the same target before adaptation. This possibility predicts that saccades after adaptation should be indistinguishable from nonadapted saccades of the same size. The present experiment allowed us to test this possibility directly.

TABLE 5.2. Mean amplitudes (in degrees) and durations (in milliseconds) of baseline, adapted, and control saccades.

	Condition		
	Baseline	Adapted	Control
Amplitude	7.69	6.91	6.94
Duration	49.4	48.3	46.8

To study these issues we obtained three different classes of saccades, in different phases of an experiment (baseline, adapt, and control). After an initial warmup block, *baseline* saccades were obtained by having subjects look to a target that was 8° to the right of fixation. Next, subjects produced a number of saccades to a target that was initially at 8°, but then jumped 2° closer to fixation at the onset of eye movement. These served as adaptation-training trials. After the training trials, subjects produced *adapted* saccades by looking once again to a stationary 8° target. Finally, several hours after the adaptation, we obtained *control* saccades. The target for the control saccades was varied from trial to trial by an algorithm designed to yield saccade amplitudes that converged on the mean amplitude of the adapted saccades. All of the baseline, adapted, and control saccades were directed at targets that disappeared shortly after the onset of eye movement. Thus, because the experiment was conducted in a completely dark room, subjects had no retinal feedback regarding the accuracy of these movements.[4]

We first compared the amplitudes of the three types of saccades to determine the success of our manipulations. These are shown in the top row of Table 5.2. As can be seen, adapted saccades were shorter than baseline saccades. This difference is presumably due to the adaptation-training trials in which the saccade target was displaced closer to fixation during the saccade. Next, as expected, the control saccades did not differ in amplitude from the adapted saccades. Thus, we successfully produced adaptive modification of saccades, and obtained normal nonadapted saccades of the same size as the adapted ones.

Next, we examined the saccade durations, which are shown in the bottom row of Table 5.2. The adapted saccades were somewhat shorter in duration than the baseline saccades, which might be expected given that they were also much shorter in amplitude. More importantly, the adapted saccades were longer in duration than the equal-size control saccades. This shows that the adaptive modification caused subjects to

---

[4] The adaptation-training trials and the adapted trials were interspersed throughout a block. Additional methodological details are in Abrams, Dobkin, and Helfrich (in press).

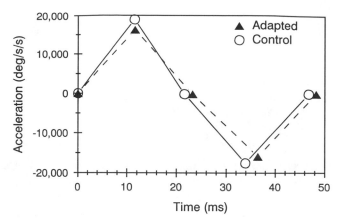

FIGURE 5.4. Force-time curves for adapted and equal-size control saccades.

produce saccades that were not merely shorter in amplitude than the baseline saccades. Rather, some changes occurred in kinematic features of the saccades beyond what would be expected if subjects were simply producing shorter, but normal, eye movements.

This conclusion is further supported by an examination of kinematic features of the saccades. Acceleration-time curves from the adapted and control saccades are shown in Figure 5.4. Adapted saccades had smaller peak positive and negative accelerations than the control saccades. Additionally, the times of peak positive and negative acceleration and peak velocity were all later in the adapted saccades, as compared to the control saccades.[5]

Conclusions

The present results show that it is possible for people to separately modulate the force and time parameters for saccades. Adaptive modification of saccade amplitude in response to saccade-contingent target steps caused subjects not only to produce shorter eye movements, but also to

---

[5] The baseline saccades had force-time functions with longer durations and larger peak forces than the adapted saccades, as would be expected. Examination of the velocity profiles (velocity as a function of time) for the baseline, adapted, and control movements confirm the observations made on the acceleration profiles: velocities of the adapted saccades at the peak positive and negative accelerations and peak velocity were lower than those for the larger baseline saccades. Differences in instantaneous velocities were also apparent between the equal-size control and adapted saccades: adapted saccades were traveling slower than the control saccades at the peak positive acceleration and at peak velocity even though the times were somewhat later relative to saccade onset.

produce movements with kinematic features that differed from those of normal saccades of the same size. The adapted movements had durations that were inappropriately long and forces that were inappropriately small, compared to normal saccades of the same size. This suggests that the adaptation caused subjects to adjust primarily the force parameter for the saccades, not the time parameter. As a result, the saccade durations were too long—more appropriate to the longer baseline saccades. Thus, it seems possible that the usual relation between saccade amplitude and duration may reflect an optimization strategy used by the oculomotor system to produce movements that are relatively fast, yet still reasonably accurate. Similar suggestions have been made for the control of limb movements (Meyer et al., 1988).

The present results also bear on models of the oculomotor control mechanisms involved in the adaptive behavior. Because the adapted saccades had nonnormal kinematics, it is possible to rule out any explanation that attributes the adaptation to a remapping of saccade amplitudes with retinal target locations. This is because any such remapping would presumably yield normal saccades that differed from baseline saccades only in amplitude (and in other amplitude-dependent ways). Instead, the results suggest that the adaptation causes subjects to modify the *gain* of the saccadic system (others have made similar suggestions: Miller et al., 1981; Semmlow et al., 1989). What is interesting about the present findings is that the change in gain is accomplished mainly through a change in the force parameter for the saccades, not the time parameter.[6]

Reprogramming Saccades

One question asked by researchers interested in both eye and limb movements is the extent to which a motor program is modifiable once it has been partially or completely prepared (e.g., for eye movements: Becker & Jurgens, 1979; Hou & Fender, 1979; Wheeless, Boynton, & Cohen, 1966; for limb movements: Larish & Frekany, 1985). When an actor decides to modify an already planned movement must the entire motor program be discarded, or can some time (and processing resources) be saved by using some components of the initial motor program? Under-

---

[6] There is some reason to expect the change to occur in the force parameter and not the time parameter. The timing of movement is believed to be controlled by a central timing generator that is accessible to a number of different movement systems. Ideally, such a central timing generator should be unaffected by a potentially peripheral disturbance in only a single movement system (e.g., the disturbance introduced by the present method). Thus, force magnitude would be more likely to be modified than force duration when inappropriate movements are detected, consistent with the present results.

TABLE 5.3. Percent of successfully reprogrammed saccades as a function of the nature of the change and the interval between target steps.

Condition	Interstep interval (ms)		
	60	100	160
Shorten	86.4	73.2	37.0
Change direction	78.4	40.0	12.8
Lengthen	32.2	17.8	6.4

standing the dynamics of this *reprogramming* of the motor commands could lead to insights into the programming process. Additionally, such last-moment changes in the plan of action might actually occur quite often in situations where observers are actively engaged in extracting information from various parts of a complex display, for example, during reading (Morrison, 1984; Rayner, Slowiaczek, Clifton, & Bertera, 1983). Thus, an understanding of reprogramming might be informative regarding visual perception and cognition more generally.

In our first experiment, the subject was to follow by eye, as quickly as possible, a dot that stepped from a central fixation location to a peripheral target location 5° or 10° to the right or left of fixation. On half of the trials the target also stepped a second time after a short delay. There were three types of such "double-step" trials, depending on the location of the target steps: (a) on *lengthen* trials, the target stepped from 5° (the end of the first step) to 10°, requiring the subject, if possible, to lengthen the saccade that they had been preparing; (b) on *shorten* trials, the target first stepped 10°, and it then was displaced 5° closer to fixation, requiring the subject to shorten the saccade that had been undergoing preparation; and (c) on *change-direction* trials, the target ended either 5° or 10° on the opposite side of fixation from the initial step, requiring that the subject modify the direction parameter for the saccade. Each type of double-step trial was presented under one of three interstep intervals: either 60, 100, or 160 ms elapsed between the first and second target steps.

Table 5.3 shows the probability that subjects canceled or modified the initial motor program and looked directly to the final target location.[7] As others have shown, regardless of the type of reprogramming required, people are less likely to successfully inhibit the initial saccade as the time interval between the two target steps increases (e.g., Hou & Fender, 1979; Wheeless et al., 1966). Apparently, as more and more motor programming has been completed, it becomes more difficult to halt the

---

[7] We defined a successfully reprogrammed saccade as one that landed more than two standard deviations away from the mean end location of saccades to each target on single-step trials.

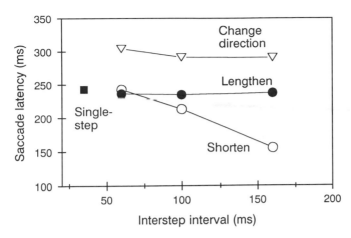

FIGURE 5.5. Latency between second target step and onset of saccade as a function of the interval between target steps, for the saccades described in Table 5.3.

execution of the program. We also found differences in people's ability to reprogram the saccades that depended on the nature of the change required in the program. Subjects were able to shorten a saccade relatively easily; they were less likely to change the direction of a saccade and even less likely to lengthen it.

Figure 5.5 shows the latencies of the successfully reprogrammed saccades. These latencies are measured from the time of the second target step until the onset of the saccade, so they include the time needed to perceive the second step as well as the time needed to cancel or modify the motor program. Also shown on the figure is the mean latency of saccades on single-step trials. Latencies on the change-direction trials were longest, and they were about 60 ms longer than latencies to single-step targets, suggesting that some additional time may be needed to cancel the initial motor program when the direction must be changed. Latencies on lengthen trials were almost exactly equal to the single-step latencies, showing that there was no cost for reprogramming the saccades on these trials, nor was there a benefit of having already prepared a partial saccade motor program. Finally, latencies on shorten trials were shortest overall, and they decreased as the time between steps increased, such that they were well below the single-step latencies at the longer interstep intervals. This suggests that subjects were able to benefit from the partially prepared motor program, and they reaped a greater benefit the further along they were with the initial program.

Results such as these have been used to argue that the direction parameter for saccades is specified prior to the amplitude parameter (e.g., Becker & Jurgens, 1979; Hou & Fender, 1979). Presumably, once

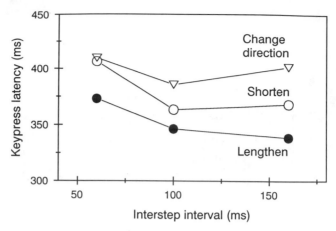

FIGURE 5.6. Latency of key-press responses to the second target step as a function of the interval between target steps.

subjects have specified a saccade direction, the entire saccade motor program must be erased or canceled. This cancellation takes time; hence, the latency of successful direction-change trials was longer than the mean latency of single-step trials. If the new motor program shares the same direction as the original one, as in the case of shorten or lengthen trials, then there may be some savings and the reprogramming may actually take less time than programming a saccade anew.

Nevertheless, there is some reason to question the implications that these results have for the *motor programming* processes that precede the onset of typical voluntary saccades. This is because the latency interval on double-step trials includes not only the time needed to cancel and reprogram the saccade, but also the time needed to detect the second target step. However, it has been well documented that the ability to detect visual stimuli changes around the time of a saccade: even before the eye moves, there is an advantage to detecting stimuli at locations close to the saccade target (Bryden, 1961). Thus, at least some of the latency differences may be due to differences in the time needed to perceive the stimulus, and not differences in the time needed to cancel and reprogram the saccade.

To estimate the possible contribution of differential stimulus-detection times to the latencies from the previous experiment, we conducted another experiment. Here subjects viewed exactly the same stimuli under exactly the same conditions as in the previous experiment. Subjects were instructed to follow the stimulus, but we did not monitor eye movements. Instead, subjects were to push one of two keys with their index fingers on trials on which the target stepped twice. The task was simply to judge whether the final location of the target was to the right or the left of fixation.

Latencies of key presses measured from the second target step are shown in Figure 5.6. As can be seen, it took longer for subjects to detect the second step when it was in the opposite direction from the first step, compared to when it was to the same side of fixation as the first step. Furthermore, subjects detected second steps indicating a lengthening more rapidly than those signaling a shortening.

When these results are considered along with the results of the previous experiment (Figure 5.5), a different picture of saccade programming and reprogramming emerges. First, at least part of the apparent "cost" associated with changing the direction of a saccade can be attributed to the time needed to perceive the second step when it calls for a direction change: it simply takes subjects more time to perceive the stimulus when it jumps to the opposite side of fixation. Second, the relative savings realized when an in-preparation saccade must be shortened as opposed to lengthened may be even greater than that revealed by the results of the previous experiment (Figure 5.5). This is because it actually took longer for subjects to perceive the second step when it called for a shorter saccade than when it called for a longer one.

Conclusions

Several tentative conclusions about the preparation of saccades are possible from the results of the experiments on reprogramming. First, changing the direction of a saccade may not require any more time than changing its amplitude. Instead, much of the apparent "cost" of a direction change may be attributable to additional time needed to perceive the target. Second, changing the amplitude of a saccade does not seem to be as simple as substituting a new value for an amplitude parameter. Rather, there are some important differences in the time needed to increase the amplitude parameter as opposed to decrease it. Similar conclusions have been made for changes in ongoing rapid limb movements (Carlton & Carlton, 1987). Work is presently underway to confirm and extend these findings.

Summary

The research described above has provided some new insights into details of the processes involved in the preparation and production of saccades. Saccades appear to arise from separate specification of the amplitude and direction between the current eye position and the desired final position. Decisions about amplitude and direction take the same amount of time and can be made in a flexible order. Programming saccade amplitude involves the specification of a force parameter (force magnitude) and a time parameter (force duration). The parameter values are determined at least partially independently of one another: adaptation to saccade-contingent target steps influences primarily the force parameter. Variability in the parameters leads to a linear trade-off between saccadic accuracy and saccade average velocity. Additionally, saccades obey the predictions of a model initially developed to describe aimed limb movements, suggesting that common principles may underlie the production of both types of movement. Finally, direction and amplitude parameters for an upcoming saccade can be changed shortly before the saccade is produced. Important differences exist in the time needed to perform such reprogramming, depending on the nature of the change that is required.

It is hoped that a better understanding of the processes involved in the planning and control of saccadic eye movements can lead to new insights into some of the behaviors (such as reading and scanning complex scenes) discussed elsewhere in this volume that depend so crucially on them.

Acknowledgment. Preparation of this chapter was supported by grant R29-MH45145 from the National Institute of Mental Health.

References

Abrams, R.A., Dobkin, R.S., & Helfrich, M.K. (in press). Adaptive modification of saccadic eye movements. *Journal of Experimental Psychology: Human Perception and Performance*.

Abrams, R.A., & Jonides, J. (1988). Programming saccadic eye movements. *Journal of Experimental Psychology: Human Perception and Performance*, *14*, 428–443.

Abrams, R.A., & Landgraf, J.Z. (1990). Differential use of distance and location information for spatial localization. *Perception and Psychophysics*, *47*, 349–359.

Abrams, R.A., Meyer, D.E., & Kornblum, S. (1989). Speed and accuracy of saccadic eye movements: Characteristics of impulse variability in the oculomotor system. *Journal of Experimental Psychology: Human Perception and Performance*, *15*, 529–543.

Abrams, R.A., Meyer, D.E., & Kornblum, S. (1990). Eye-hand coordination: Oculomotor control in rapid aimed limb movements. *Journal of Experimental Psychology: Human Perception and Performance*, *16*, 248–267.

Abrams, R.A., Scharf, M.K., & Dobkin, R.S. (1989, November). Adaptation and aftereffect in the oculomotor system. Poster presented at the meeting of the Psychonomic Society, Atlanta, GA.

Becker, W., & Fuchs, A.F. (1969). Further properties of the human saccadic system: Eye movements and correction saccades with and without visual fixation points. *Vision Research*, *9*, 1247–1258.

Becker, W., & Jurgens, R. (1979). An analysis of the saccadic system by means of double step stimuli. *Vision Research*, *19*, 967–983.

Bryden, M.P. (1961). The role of post-exposural eye movements in tachistoscopic perception. *Canadian Journal of Psychology*, *15*, 220–225.

Carlton, L.G., & Carlton M.J. (1987). Response amendment latencies during discrete arm movements. *Journal of Motor Behavior*, *19*, 227–239.

Coren, S. (1986). An efferent component in the visual perception of direction and extent. *Psychological Review*, *93*, 391–410.

Hallett, P.E., & Lightstone, A.D. (1976). Saccadic eye movements to flashed targets. *Vision Research*, *16*, 107–114.

Henriksson, N.G., Pyykko, I., Schalen, L., & Wennmo, C. (1980). Velocity patterns of rapid eye movements. *Acta Oto-Laryngologica*, *89*, 504–512.

Hou, R.L., & Fender, D.H. (1979). Processing of direction and magnitude by the saccadic eye-movement system. *Vision Research*, *19*, 1421–1426.

Larish, D.D., & Frekany, G.A. (1985). Planning and preparing expected and unexpected movements: Reexamining the relationships of arm, direction, and extent of movement. *Journal of Motor Behavior*, *17*, 168–189.

Mays, L.E., & Sparks, D.L. (1980). Saccades are spatially, not retinotopically coded. *Science*, *208*, 1163–1164.

McLaughlin, S. (1967). Parametric adjustment in saccadic eye movements. *Perception and Psychophysics*, *2*, 359–362.

McLaughlin, S., Kelly, M., Anderson, R., & Wenz, T. (1968). Localization of a peripheral target during parametric adaptation of saccadic eye movements. *Perception and Psychophysics*, *4*, 45–48.

Meyer, D.E., Abrams, R.A., Kornblum, S., Wright, C.E., & Smith, J.E.K. (1988). Optimality in human motor performance: Ideal control of rapid aimed movements. *Psychological Review*, *95*, 340–370.

Meyer, D.E., Smith, J.E.K., & Wright, C.E. (1982). Models for the speed and accuracy of aimed movements. *Psychological Review*, *89*, 449–482.

Miller, J.M., Anstis, T., & Templeton, W. (1981). Saccadic plasticity: Parametric adaptive control by retinal feedback. *Journal of Experimental Psychology: Human Perception and Performance*, *7*, 356–366.

Morrison, R.E. (1984). Manipulation of stimulus onset delay in reading: Evidence for parallel programming of saccades. *Journal of Experimental Psychology: Human Perception and Performance*, *10*, 667–682.

Polit, A., & Bizzi, E. (1979). Characteristics of motor programs underlying arm movements in monkeys. *Journal of Neurophysiology*, *42*, 183–194.

Rayner, K., Slowiaczek, M.L., Clifton, C., Jr., & Bertera, J.H. (1983). Latency of sequential eye movements: Implications for reading. *Journal of Experimental Psychology: Human Perception and Performance*, *9*, 912–922.

Reinhart, R.J., & Zuber, B.L. (1971). Parameters of the control signals for saccadic eye movement: Electrical stimulation and modeling. *Experimental Neurology*, *30*, 148–161.

Robinson, D.A. (1981a), Control of eye movements. In *Handbook of Physiology, Section I: The nervous system, 2*. Bethesda, MD: American Physiological Society.

Robinson, D.A. (1981b). The use of control systems analysis in the neurophysiology of eye movements. *Annual Review of Neuroscience*, *4*, 463–503.

Rosenbaum, D.A. (1980). Human movement initiation: Specification of arm, direction, and extent. *Journal of Experimental Psychology: General*, *109*, 444–474.

Schmidt, R.A., Zelaznik, H., Hawkins, B., Frank, J.S., & Quinn, J. (1979). Motor output variability: A theory for the accuracy of rapid motor acts. *Psychological Review*, *86*, 415–451.

Semmlow, J.L., Gauthier, G.M., & Vercher, J. (1989). Mechanisms of short-term saccadic adaptation. *Journal of Experimental Psychology: Human Perception and Performance*, *15*, 249–258.

Wheeless, L.L., Boynton, R.M., & Cohen, G.H. (1966). Eye-movement responses to step and pulse-step stimuli. *Journal of the Optical Society of America*, *56*, 956–960.

Wright, C.E., & Meyer, D.E. (1983). Conditions for a linear speed-accuracy trade-off in aimed movements. *Quarterly Journal of Experimental Psychology*, *35A*, 279–296.

Zee, D.S., Optican, L.M., Cook, J. D., Robinson, D.A., & Engel, W.K. (1976). Slow saccades in spinocerebellar degeneration. *Archives of Neurology*, *33*, 243–251.

Zelaznik, H.N., Shapiro, D.C., & McColsky, D. (1981). Effects of a secondary task on the accuracy of single aiming movements. *Journal of Experimental Psychology: Human Perception and Performance*, *7*, 1007–1018.

6
Programming Saccades: The Role of Attention

ANNE B. SERENO

Many different lines of research have attempted to answer questions about how the brain produces a saccadic eye movement. Often visual attention is an important factor in the findings of eye movement research. For this reason, it should prove useful to review some basic issues in eye movement research and the role attention plays.

One point of controversy in the saccadic programming literature (also discussed in the chapters by Findlay and by Abrams, this volume), involves specifying exactly how a saccade is programmed. Many researchers have chosen to characterize a saccade in terms of the direction and amplitude of a new fixation position relative to the current position of gaze. That is, they define a saccade in terms of the direction in which the eyes move and the distance or amplitude through which they must move. Thus, programming a saccade involves the specification of values for these two parameters which together can unambiguously distinguish one saccade from all others (given a common starting point).

Much research has focused on questions about when or how these parameters are specified: (a) Are the parameters computed in a serial or a parallel fashion? (b) If they are computed serially, is this done in a fixed or variable order? (c) Are the computation times different for the two parameters (in particular, which one takes longer)? (d) In fact, are they even computed separately at all? The results of experiments dealing with these issues have been mixed. I will focus on two paradigms and some related attentional problems that caution against easy answers to these difficult issues.

One method for studying these questions uses a precuing paradigm. In this paradigm, subjects are first presented a precue that partially specifies the spatial location of the saccade target; next, they are presented a reaction signal that completely specifies the required movement; finally, they are required to make the appropriate saccade as quickly as possible (see Abrams's chapter in this volume). Such studies have examined the separate effects of advance knowledge about either direction or amplitude upon the latency of the following saccade. Some studies suggest that advance information about amplitude results in reduced latencies (e.g., Viviani & Swensson, 1982). Others, however, report that saccade latencies are reduced by direction precuing, but are not affected by amplitude precuing (e.g., Megaw & Armstrong, 1973). Abrams and Jonides (1988) outlined several difficulties with the precuing paradigm. In particular, they questioned whether advance information about target location really helped the motor programming of the saccade or merely facilitated the detection of the stimulus. In other words, was the latency of the saccade reduced because of advance preparation of a component of the saccadic response or simply because advance information about target location led to faster detection of the target? Abrams and Jonides attempted to control for this possible confound by using a central cue both to precue and direct the saccade. They found that, under these conditions, saccade latencies were reduced, not only when subjects were provided with advance information about the direction, but also when they were provided with advance information about the amplitude of the upcoming saccade.

Another paradigm that has been used to investigate the question of whether or not direction and amplitude are separately programmed is the double-step paradigm (see, e.g., Komoda, Festinger, Phillips, Duckman, & Young, 1973; Lisberger, Fuchs, King, & Evinger, 1975; Wheeless, Boynton, & Cohen, 1966; for a review, see Findlay's chapter, this volume). In this paradigm, subjects are instructed to make an eye movement to the target as soon as it appears. However, on some trials the target moves to a second position—after the target's initial appearance but before the subject is able to make an eye movement. The subject must then try to modify or cancel the program for the first saccade in order to reach the final position of the target. Sometimes, subjects are able to suppress the saccade to the first target and move their eyes directly to the final position of the target. When that happens, the time required to reprogram a saccade (measured from the time of onset of the second step) depends on the type of displacement—that is, whether the displacement is one of direction or amplitude. When the second target position calls for a saccade in a different direction from the initial target position, some studies have shown that saccade latencies are elevated relative to the latency on a single-target trial (e.g., Hou & Fender, 1979; Komoda et al., 1973). However, when the second target position requires only a change in amplitude, some studies have shown that latencies are somewhat shorter (e.g., Becker & Jürgens, 1979; Komoda et al., 1973). Together, these studies suggest that modifying the direction of a saccade takes more time than programming the saccade from scratch, whereas modifying the amplitude of a saccade benefits from initial preparation for the first saccade. These results imply that direction and amplitude are computed separately and, in particular, that direction is specified before amplitude.

As Abrams and others (Abrams & Jonides, 1988; also see Abrams's chapter in this volume) have pointed out, however, there are attentional confounds in the double-step paradigm that limit hard-and-fast conclusions. Many researchers have shown that the onset of a peripheral stimulus automatically attracts attention to the region of the stimulus and, consequently, detection or discrimination is subsequently facilitated in this region (e.g., Jonides, 1981; Posner, Snyder, & Davidson, 1980). Such facilitation is often described in terms of a gradient in which facilitation falls off with distance from the location of the stimulus (Downing & Pinker, 1985; Erikson & Yeh, 1985; LaBerge, 1983). In addition, some researchers have noted an increased cost upon crossing the vertical meridian, so that when attention is drawn to one hemifield, the responses to stimuli appearing in the other hemifield are slower (Hughes & Zimba, 1985; Rizzolatti, Riggio, Dascola, & Ulmita, 1987).

These demonstrated attentional effects can complicate the findings obtained in the double-step paradigm. For example, when there is a change in direction, the second target position is often further from the original target position (and thus further from the attentional focus) than when there is a change in amplitude. This could explain reduced latencies following a change in amplitude. In addition, when the second target position differs in direction from the first position, it often falls in the opposite hemifield from the first position, incurring an additional attentional cost. Such is not the case when there is a change in amplitude because the second target position always occurs in the same visual hemifield as the original target position. This might explain longer latencies when there is a change in direction.

It is important to note that studies involving the double-step paradigm do not all contain an attentional confound of field (i.e., some have direction changes within the same hemifield) and they attempt in most instances to control for an attentional confound of distance (e.g., by maintaining an equal distance between the first and second step targets across conditions; see Aslin & Shea, 1987). However, as Abrams and Jonides (1988) point out, the possible effects of attention should be kept in mind when considering the results of eye movement experiments.

O'Regan's "optimal viewing position" phenomenon (see O'Regan's chapter in this volume) is another example of an attentional effect that may confound eye movement research. Although his aim is to investigate how this phenomenon is related to the behavior of the eye in normal reading, the phenomenon itself is likely to be an attentional effect due to the particular task used. When a set of words of a given length is presented at different initial positions relative to a fixation mark, a spatial expectancy about where the information will appear is generated. Specifically, there is certainty that some part of the word will appear in the vicinity of the fixation mark, with smaller probabilities that parts of the word will appear to the left or to the right of fixation. As many have shown, the gradient of facilitation (or the size of the spotlight of attention) depends on the demands of the task (Erikson & Yeh, 1985; LaBerge, 1983; LaBerge & Brown, 1986; Treisman & Gelade, 1980). Thus, the longer latency obtained for fixations at the beginning or at the end of words may simply be the result of a less than optimal attentional facilitation due to the fact that a part of the word falls beyond the optimal region of attention created by task demands. One way to get around this problem would be to block trials so that the fixation always occurs in a given position of the word. Another method would be to provide a string of nonsense characters (e.g., asterisks) as a warning signal indicating where the word will appear relative to the fixation mark while the subject maintains fixation. Although both these suggestions seem good controls for removing attentional effects, it is clear that such an imposed task is not a good model for understanding how the eye behaves in normal reading, given that there are quite specific and robust attentional effects in reading (see Henderson's chapter, this volume). It is not surprising, then, that the optimal landing position effect is very small (as measured by refixation probability) and disappears completely (as measured by gaze duration) in a text-reading situation (Vitu, O'Regan, & Mittau, 1990).

Another area where attention has played a role in eye movement research is in the classification of saccadic eye movements. Saccadic eye movements are often categorized as either reflexive or voluntary. Reflexive saccades are target-elicited saccades, whereas voluntary saccades can be obtained, for example, by instructing a subject to look to the left or to the right. An extreme example of a voluntary saccade is demonstrated in the anti-saccade task, in which the subject is instructed to look to the visual hemifield opposite to the one in which a peripheral target appears. Fischer and colleagues (Fischer & Boch, 1983; Fischer & Breitmeyer, 1987; Fischer & Ramsperger, 1984, 1986) most recently have suggested that a separate category of saccades with a very short latency exists. These very short latency reflexive saccades, which they call "express" saccades, were first described by Saslow (1967) and Ross and Ross (1980, 1981); for reviews, see Klein, Kingstone, and Pontefract's and Findlay's chapters, this volume. These saccades are obtained in the so-called gap task—the fixation point is turned off and a temporal gap precedes the presentation of the peripheral target. Fischer claims that in order to make an eye movement, attention needs to be disengaged from its current focus in the visual field. In the gap paradigm, the removal of the fixation point disengages attention and thus allows a faster eye movement. In addition, Fischer and Breitmeyer (1987) have shown that attention directed to the target position provides no advantage over attention directed to the fixation point when a saccadic eye movement to a peripheral target is required. Other findings, however, suggest that attention to the target position does reduce saccadic latency. Shepherd, Findlay, and Hockey (1986) demonstrated that saccadic latencies were shortened if a probe stimulus appeared at the target position. An important difference between the two paradigms might explain the apparent contradiction: in Fischer and Breitmeyer's experiment, attention was cued endogenously, whereas, in Shepherd et al.'s experiment, attention was cued exogenously (see Klein et al., this volume). More specifically, in Fischer and Breitmeyer's experiment, subjects were instructed to fixate the center of a screen while attending to a spot above the saccade target. In this overlap paradigm, the attention spot stayed on throughout the trial, requiring sustained or endogenous attention. However, in Shepherd et al.'s experiment, there was a sudden onset of a probe in the target position, resulting in transient or exogenous attention. To see how this difference could affect the results, it might help to use a classification of orienting that has been adapted from Klein et al. (this volume).

As illustrated in Figure 6.1, orienting is divided into four cells. Possible physiological underpinnings are listed underneath each type of orienting. It is suggested here that exogenous orienting may involve the superior colliculus and other related brain stem nuclei, whereas endogenous orienting may involve the prefrontal cortex, specifically the frontal eye fields (FEFs) and area 46 (the principal sulcus). The frontal eye fields project directly (Lynch & Graybiel, 1983) and indirectly to the superior colliculus. Recent work has suggested that an indirect projection from the frontal eye fields via the substantia nigra may be responsible for tonic inhibition of the superior colliculus (Fischer, 1987; Hikosaka & Wurtz, 1985a, 1985b). Such a finding would support the inhibition of exogenous processes by endogenous processes as shown in the diagram. Much behavioral work in frontal brain-damaged patients and lesion work in monkeys support the idea that the frontal eye fields play a controlling and often inhibitory role with respect to the superior colliculus (see, e.g., Guitton, Buchtel, & Douglas, 1982, 1985; Schiller, Sandell, & Maunsell, 1987). The diagram also makes explicit a mutual facilitation between covert (attentional) and overt (saccadic eye movement) mechanisms within the same structures.

Figure 6.2 illustrates the model in greater detail and incorporates several underlying assumptions. It is assumed that there are two general orienting systems—"exogenous" and "endogenous"—that operate in parallel in the sense that both systems receive visual inputs and both can produce a similar behavioral output. More than a century ago, Hughlings Jackson articulated the idea that the central nervous system is organized hierarchically with specific reference to the motor system. Critical to this formulation is the idea that higher centers act upon lower centers and that they merely represent in greater complexity the very same impressions and movements as the lower centers represent. Although perhaps not explicit in the diagram, a similar assumption of hierarchy is present: the cortical (endogenous) system acts upon and sometimes through the subcortical (exogenous) system. In the case of overt orienting, both outputs

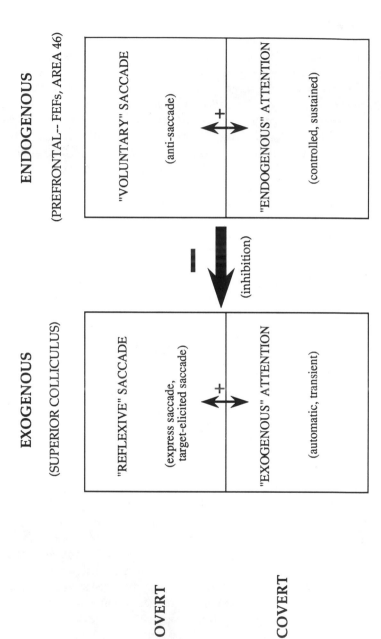

FIGURE 6.1. Classification of orienting, adapted from Klein, Kingstone, and Pontefract (this volume). FEFs, frontal eye fields; Area 46 = the principal sulcus.

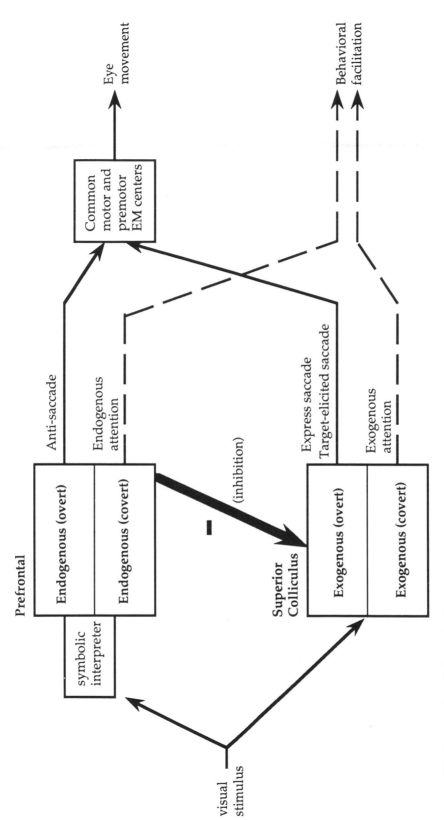

FIGURE 6.2. Proposed model of orienting.

eventually pass through the same motor and premotor centers (which may include the superior colliculus itself). In the case of covert orienting, both outputs produce a facilitation of response due to an attentional enhancement. Temporal characteristics are important, but difficult to indicate in the figure. There is much evidence suggesting that exogenous orienting is fast, transient, and relatively automatic, whereas endogenous orienting is slow, sustained, and under voluntary control (Jonides, 1981; Nakayama & Mackeben, 1989; see also Klein et al.'s chapter, this volume). Endogenous orienting often requires an extra stage of symbolic interpretation. The symbolic interpreter merely represents the extra processing steps required to interpret an endogenous cue or the instruction "look to the field opposite to the target," in the case of the anti-saccade task. Note that, although endogenous covert orienting is slower, the model permits situations where endogenous instructions can eliminate benefits of an exogenous cue by increasing the inhibitory role of the endogenous system. Such a situation may explain why Warner, Juola, and Koshino (1990) come to their conclusion that attentional capture by abrupt-onset stimuli is not strongly automatic.

The present model may account for apparent contradictions in the literature, for example, whether attention facilitates or inhibits an eye movement (see discussion above with reference to Shepherd et al., 1986 and Fischer & Breitmeyer, 1987). In Fischer and Breitmeyer's experiment, endogenous attention inhibits exogenous mechanisms, including target-elicited saccades. In Shepherd et al.'s experiment, exogenous attention facilitates eye movement production (within common motor or premotor centers), and thus facilitates endogenous or voluntary saccades. One possible prediction of the model is that endogenous attention can facilitate an endogenous saccadic eye movement. A simple test of such a prediction would be to show whether or not an endogenous cue facilitates saccadic response time in an anti-saccade task.

Such a model can also explain difficulties arising in Henderson's sequential attention model (this volume). Specifically, the present model of orienting would argue that each particular type of attention (exogenous or endogenous) is automatically coincident with its respective eye movement preparation because, within a system, attention and eye movements may share the same structures (or at least activate similar neural networks). However, eye movement preparation, like attention, does not necessarily lead to an eye movement. Explaining how the difficulty of foveal processing can affect extrafoveal processing (see Henderson's chapter, this volume) does not require one to assume that eye movement programming begins prior to a shift of attention. If foveal processing is easy, then attention can precede the final eye movement programming, and the preview benefit will be maximal. If foveal processing is difficult, then the attention shift will coincide with the beginning of eye movement programming, reducing the amount of extrafoveal attentive processing and thus the preview benefit.

Much evidence agrees with the proposed orienting model (Figure 6.2). Patients with frontal lesions are often unable to make voluntary saccades; they also exhibit more short latency saccades (Guitton et al., 1982, 1985). Inhibition of return is an inhibitory effect occurring about 300 ms after a visual event as long as attention is not maintained at the location of the event (Posner & Cohen, 1984). Rafal, Calabresi, Brennan, and Sciolto (1989) have shown that inhibition of return is intimately connected to exogenous orienting but not to endogenous orienting. In agreement with the tentative physiology of the model, it has been demonstrated that patients with peritectal degeneration show inhibition of return only for the same directions in which their eye movements are intact (Posner, Rafal, Choate, & Vaughn, 1985). Schiller et al. (1987) have reported supporting evidence for overt orienting in the monkey. Monkeys with frontal eye field lesions make more express saccades, whereas monkeys with superior colliculus lesions are unable to generate express saccades.

This model is the underlying framework for some work I am currently doing on attention and oculomotor function with schizophrenic patients (Sereno, 1991). Holzman and colleagues have previously established that although 60 to 80% of schizophrenic patients have disturbed smooth pursuit eye movements, less than 10% of normal subjects show similar abnormalities (Holzman & Levy, 1977; Holzman, Proctor, & Hughes, 1973; Holzman et al., 1974). A frequent interruption that occurs in the abnormal smooth pursuit trackings of schizophrenic patients is a saccadic intrusion. Saccadic intrusion is a generic term that has been used to describe several classes of saccadic events occurring during smooth pursuit tracking or fixation which are disruptive rather than corrective. In addition to this disinhibition of the saccadic system, schizophrenic patients often have low gain during smooth pursuit (Levin et al., 1988). The deficit in schizophrenic patients probably involves both the saccadic and smooth pursuit systems.

The most often cited behavioral deficit in schizophrenia has been an attentional disorder. The hypothesis that an attentional dysfunction is a central aspect of schizophrenic psychopathology is as old as the recognition of schizophrenia as a psychiatric disorder (Kraepelin, 1919). Taken together, the pattern of deficits in eye movements and attention in schizophrenic patients might help elucidate how the brain programs an eye movement.

In schizophrenic patients who exhibit smooth pursuit eye movement deficits, several studies have shown that the generation of slow eye movements (i.e., smooth pursuit-like eye movements) in these patients is normal and free of intrusive saccades when their eye movements are based on vestibular signals or full-field visual signals (Latham, Holzman, Manschreck, & Tole, 1981; Levy, Holzman, & Proctor, 1978; Levin, Jones, Stark, Merrin, & Holzman, 1982). These results argue against the presence of a deficit or lesion in motor or premotor eye movement centers, where the separate neural pathways generating the various types

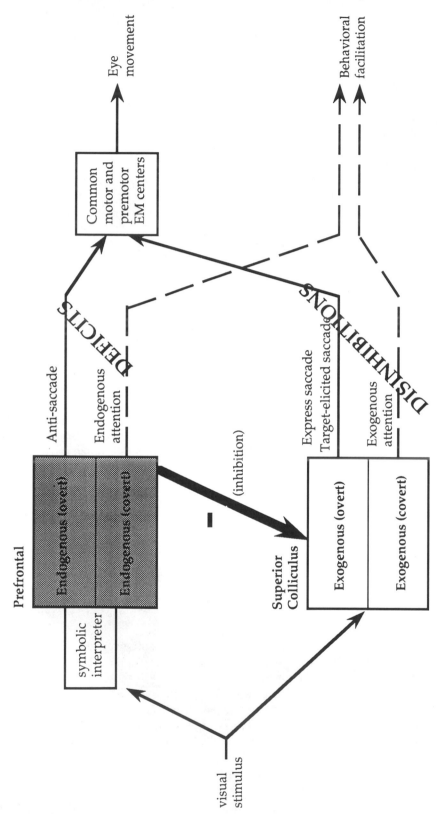

FIGURE 6.3. Proposed model of schizophrenic orienting. It is suggested that a prefrontal dysfunction in schizophrenic patients leads to deficits in their endogenous orienting system and disinhibitions in their exogenous orienting system.

of eye movements converge. In addition, these findings suggest that the subcortical pathways responsible for optokinetic nystagmus (OKN) and the vestibulo-ocular reflex (VOR) are intact in schizophrenic patients with smooth pursuit eye movement deficits.

There is also much evidence suggesting a possible relation between schizophrenia and prefrontal cortex dysfunction. Specifically, several blood-flow studies of brain activity (using positron emission tomography and xenon-133 techniques) have shown reduced activity in the prefrontal cortex of schizophrenic patients (Berman, Zec, & Weinberger, 1986; Buchsbaum et al., 1984; DeLisi et al., 1985; Franzen & Ingvar, 1975a, 1975b; Ingvar & Franzen, 1974a, 1974b; Weinberger, Berman, & Zec, 1986; see Buchsbaum & Haier, 1987, for a recent review). Schizophrenic patients are impaired on both the spatial delayed response tasks (Malmo, 1974) and the Wisconsin Card Sort (Weinberger et al., 1986); these tests are diagnostic of prefrontal cortex injury (Milner, 1963, 1964, 1982; Stuss & Benson, 1984). There is also some neuroanatomical evidence that schizophrenic patients have reduced numbers of neurons in certain layers of prefrontal cortex (Layers II, III, VI) (Benes, Davidson, & Bird, 1986). A deficit in prefrontal cortex could lead to problems in both the pursuit and saccadic systems. Neurophysiological and lesion studies (see, e.g., Bruce, Goldberg, Bushnell, & Stanton, 1985; Lynch, 1987; Schiller, True, & Conway, 1980) suggest that the prefrontal cortex plays a role in both systems.

The basic hypothesis about attention and oculomotor function in schizophrenic patients suggested here is that these patients differ from normal subjects because they have a dysfunction in prefrontal cortex and thus in endogenous orienting (Figure 6.3). This dysfunction leads to two behavioral changes: (a) loss of proper function of endogenous orienting, and (b) disinhibition of exogenous orienting. Because schizophrenia may not be a unitary disorder with a single underlying pathology, it is expected that only schizophrenic patients with smooth pursuit eye movement deficits will show these changes. Abnormal smooth pursuit eye movements may possibly be a marker for a subpopulation of schizophrenic patients who have a prefrontal deficit.

The present model makes clear predictions. Schizophrenic patients with smooth pursuit eye movement deficits should show deficits on tasks of both overt and covert endogenous orienting. That is, they should have problems with the antisaccade task (longer latencies, more errors) and show less facilitation than normal subjects when cued endogenously. In addition, schizophrenic patients with smooth pursuit eye movement deficits should show disinhibition on tasks of both overt and covert exogenous orienting. That is, they should exhibit greater benefits than normals in the gap paradigm (more express saccades, faster mean saccadic response time) and more facilitation than normal subjects when cued exogenously.

Thirteen schizophrenic patients, 13 patients with affective disorder, and 14 normal controls were tested on a series of tasks examining attention, saccadic eye movements, and smooth pursuit eye movements. There was no significant difference between groups with regard to age, gender, years of education, and handedness. In addition, patient groups did not differ on age of onset or duration of illness.

To test covert orienting, a spatially directed visual attention task was used. A horizontal bar was briefly (33 ms) presented as a cue to indicate the position of the following target. After a brief interval, the target appeared for 150 ms with an 80% probability of occurring in the position opposite to the position of the cue (valid trial) and a 20% probability of occurring in the position of the cue (invalid trial). The interstimulus interval (ISI) between the cue and target was either 67 or 500 ms, as illustrated in Figure 6.4. Subjects were balanced so that half of them first performed the short then long ISI version of the task and vice versa. It was expected in the short ISI version that normal subjects would show facilitation of response times when the target appeared in the same position as the preceding cue, despite the fact that subjects knew this was not where the target was most likely to appear. This expectation was based on the well-documented finding that a peripheral cue automatically captures attention (see, e.g., Jonides, 1981; Nakayama & Mackeben, 1989). With the long ISI version, normal subjects were expected to be faster when the target appeared in its most likely position (opposite the cue). This expectation was based on the finding that a symbolic cue, which indicates where the target is to appear, summons an attentional effect beginning about 200 ms after the onset of the cue and peaking around 350 ms (see, e.g., Posner, 1980; Shulman, Remington, & McLean, 1979). In addition to these tests of covert orienting, there were three saccadic eye movement tasks: (a) a saccade task where there was simultaneous onset of the target and offset of the fixation point, (b) a gap task where the offset of the fixation point preceded the onset of the target by 150 ms, and (c) an antisaccade task where the fixation overlapped the presentation of the target and subjects were required to look to the field opposite to the target as quickly as possible. Finally, subjects were instructed to track a horizontally moving target while their smooth pursuit eye movements were recorded.

Preliminary results on the covert orienting tasks indicate that no group (normal, schizophrenic, or affective disorder) showed facilitation on invalid trials at the short ISI. This agrees with the recent findings of Warner et al. (1990) who demonstrate in a similar paradigm that the exogenous component of attention can be reduced by task demands. However, only schizophrenic patients showed a significant difference in the effect of validity across the two different ISI intervals. It appeared that some factor reduced the validity effect at the short ISI interval in schizophrenic patients. These results agree with the idea that schizophrenic

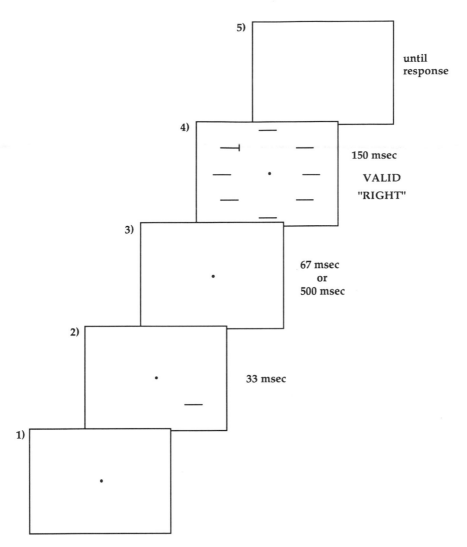

FIGURE 6.4. A sample trial from the attention tasks. Each trial was composed of 5 events: 1) A fixation point screen that was present before the initiation of the trial until 550 ms after the initiation of the trial. 2) A cue that appeared briefly (33 ms) indicating where the target was most likely to appear. 3) The interstimulus interval (ISI), which consisted of a fixation point screen having a duration of either 67 ms in the "exogenous" attention task or 500 ms in the "endogenous" attention task. 4) A target screen, which was presented for 150 ms and consisted of the target and seven distractors. 5) A blank screen, which was presented until the subject responded by pressing a key. Eye position was monitored through-out the trial, and the trial was automatically aborted and rerun later if the subject moved his/her eyes away from the fixation point during the cue, ISI, or target screens. Valid trials were trials in which the target appeared in the position opposite to the cued position; 80% of the trials were valid trials. Invalid trials were trials in which the target appeared in the same position as the cue; 20% of the trials were invalid trials. The correct response for the valid trial pictured was "right" (versus "left").

patients have an enhanced component of exogenous attention that can facilitate response on the invalid trials at the short ISI. The error rate data did not show any speed-accuracy trade-offs for these effects.

All subjects had fastest mean saccadic response times on the gap task and slowest mean saccadic response times on the antisaccade task. Schizophrenic patients showed a greater benefit than normals in the gap task compared to the saccade task. Normal subjects were only 10 ms faster in the gap task compared to the saccade task, whereas schizophrenic patients were 25 ms faster. The error rate data also supported this finding. In addition, schizophrenic patients showed a greater slowing in mean saccadic response time than normals on the antisaccade task compared to the saccade task. Normal subjects were 42 ms slower in the antisaccade task compared to the saccade task, but schizophrenic patients were 187 ms slower. The error rate data again supported this finding. Normals made slightly more errors on the antisaccade task (7.1%) compared to the saccade task (2.3%), whereas schizophrenic patients made many more errors on the antisaccade task (21.5%) compared to the saccade task (3.5%). This same pattern of performance on the antisaccade task was also true for affective disorder patients who showed a greater slowing in response time and higher number of errors than normals in the anti-saccade task.

Subjects' smooth pursuit eye movement data was qualitatively scored by raters as showing normal or impaired pursuit. Smooth pursuit eye movement recordings of some subjects were not included in the analysis because they were not available, contained too much noise to be scored, or were classified as borderline. Affective disorder patients were not included because many were treated with lithium which has been shown to affect smooth pursuit eye movements (Holzman, O'Brian, & Waternaux, 1991). All 11 normal subjects showed normal pursuit; 5 schizophrenic patients demonstrated normal pursuit and 5, impaired pursuit. These 21 subjects were then divided into two groups: those with normal pursuit ($N = 16$) and those with impaired pursuit ($N = 5$).

There was a trend toward an interaction between smooth pursuit eye movement performance and the attention tasks in response latency, such that subjects with impaired pursuit showed a larger difference in the validity effect at the two different intervals and subjects with normal pursuit showed less difference in the validity effect at the two different intervals. Subjects with impaired pursuit showed larger benefits in mean saccadic response times on the gap task compared to the saccade task than did subjects with normal pursuit. Subjects with impaired pursuit made significantly more errors on the antisaccade task compared to the saccade task than did subjects with normal pursuit. There was also some indication that subjects with impaired pursuit had slower saccadic response times on the antisaccade task compared to the saccade task than did subjects with normal pursuit. Preliminary analysis thus suggests that impaired smooth pursuit eye movements are related to a specific pattern of attention and saccadic eye movement results. It is possible therefore that a study of attention and saccadic eye movements in schizophrenic patients could help in understanding the underlying mechanisms involved in these processes.

In conclusion, it seems that there are still many avenues to explore in the study of eye movements and the role of attention. It is likely that only with the help of all of these approaches will we achieve a more complete understanding of how one programs a saccade.

Acknowledgments. This work was supported in part by US Public Service Grants R01 MH31340, MH31154, and P50 MH44866, and by the Stanley Foundation Research Awards Program.

The author would like to thank Keith Rayner and Philip Holzman for comments on earlier versions of this manuscript.

References

Abrams, R.A., & Jonides, J. (1988). Programming saccadic eye movements. *Journal of Experimental Psychology: Human Perception and Performance, 14,* 428–443.

Aslin, R.N., & Shea, S.L. (1987). The amplitude and angle of saccades to double-step target displacements. *Vision Research, 27,* 1925–1942.

Becker, W., & Jürgens, R. (1979). An analysis of the saccadic system by means of double step stimuli. *Vision Research, 19,* 967–983.

Benes, F.M., Davidson, J., & Bird, E.D. (1986). Quantitative cytoarchitectural studies of the cerebral cortex of schizophrenics. *Archives of General Psychiatry, 43,* 31–35.

Berman, K.F., Zec, R.F., & Weinberger, D.R. (1986). Physiologic dysfunction of dorsolateral prefrontal cortex in schizophrenia: II. Role of neuroleptic treatment, attention and mental effort. *Archives of General Psychiatry, 43,* 126–134.

Bruce, C.J., Goldberg, M.E., Bushnell, M.C., & Stanton, G.B. (1985). Primate frontal eye fields. II. Physiological and anatomical correlates of electrically evoked eye movements. *Journal of Neurophysiology, 54,* 714–734.

Buchsbaum, M.S., DeLisi, L.E., Holcomb, H.H., Cappelletti, J., King, A.C., Johnson, J., Hazlett, E., Dowling-Zimmerman, S., Post, R.M., Morihisa, J., Carpenter, W., Cohen, R., Pickar, D., Weinberger, D.R., Margolin, R., & Kessler, R.M. (1984). Anteroposterior gradients in cerebral glucose use in schizophrenia and affective disorders. *Archives of General Psychiatry, 41,* 1159–1165.

Buchsbaum, M.S., & Haier, R.J. (1987). Functional and anatomical brain imaging: Impact on schizophrenia research. *Schizophrenia Bulletin, 13,* 115–132.

DeLisi, L.E., Buchsbaum, M.S., Holcomb, H.H., Dowling-Zimmerman, S., Pickar, D., Boronow, J., Morihisa, J.M., van Kammen, D.P., Carpenter, W.T., Kessler, R., & Cohen, R.M. (1985). Clinical correlates of decreased anteroposterior metabolic gradients in positron emission tomography (PET) of schizophrenic patients. *American Journal of Psychiatry, 142,* 78–81.

Downing, C.J., & Pinker, S. (1985). The spatial structure of visual attention. In M.I. Posner & O.S.M. Marin (Eds.), *Attention and performance XI* (pp. 171–187). Hillsdale, NJ: Erlbaum.

Erikson, C.W., & Yeh, Y. (1985). Allocation of attention in the visual field. *Journal of Experimental Psychology: Human Perception and Performance, 11,* 583–597.

Fischer, B. (1987). The preparation of visually guided saccades. *Reviews of Physiology, Biochemistry, and Pharmacology, 106,* 1–35.

Fischer, B., & Boch, B. (1983). Saccadic eye movements after extremely short reaction times in the monkey. *Brain Research, 260,* 21–26.

Fischer, B., & Breitmeyer, B. (1987). Mechanisms of visual attention revealed by saccadic eye movements. *Neuropsychologia, 25,* 73–83.

Fischer, B., & Ramsperger, E. (1984). Human express-saccades: extremely short reaction times of goal directed eye movements. *Experimental Brain Research, 57,* 191–195.

Fischer, B., & Ramsperger, E. (1986) Human express-saccades: effects of randomization and daily practice. *Experimental Brain Research, 64,* 569–578.

Franzen, G., & Ingvar, D.H. (1975a). Abnormal distribution of cerebral activity in chronic schizophrenia. *Journal of Psychiatric Research, 12,* 199–214.

Franzen, G., & Ingvar, D.H. (1975b). Absence of activation in frontal structures during psychological testing in chronic schizophrenia. *Journal of Neurology, Neurosurgery, and Psychiatry, 38,* 1027–1032.

Guitton, D., Buchtel, H.A., & Douglas, R.M. (1982). Disturbances of voluntary saccadic eye movements mechanisms following discrete unilateral frontal lobe removals. In G. Lennerstrand, D.S. Zee, & E. Keller (Eds.), *Functional basis of ocular motility disorders* (pp. 497–499). Oxford, UK: Pergamon Press.

Guitton, D., Buchtel, H.A., & Douglas, R.M. (1985). Frontal lobe lesions in man cause difficulties in suppressing reflexive glances and in generating goal-directed saccades. *Experimental Brain Research, 58,* 455–472.

Hikosaka, O., & Wurtz, R.H. (1985a). Modification of saccadic eye movements by GABA-related substances. I. Effect of muscimol and bicuculline in monkey superior colliculus. *Journal of Neurophysiology, 53,* 266–291.

Hikosaka, O., & Wurtz, R.H. (1985b). Modification of saccadic eye movements by GABA-related substances. II. Effects of muscimol in monkey substantia nigra pars reticulata. *Journal of Neurophysiology, 53,* 292–308.

Holzman, P., & Levy, D. (1977). Smooth pursuit eye movements and functional psychoses: A review. *Schizophrenia Bulletin, 3,* 15–27.

Holzman, P.S., O'Brian, C., & Waternaux, C. (1991). Effects of lithium treatment on eye movements. *Biological Psychiatry, 29,* 1001–1015.

Holzman, P., Proctor, L., & Hughes, D. (1973). Eye-tracking patterns in schizophrenia. *Science, 181,* 179–181.

Holzman, P., Proctor, L., Levy, D., Yasillo, N., Meltzer, H., & Hurt, S. (1974). Eye-tracking dysfunctions in schizophrenic patients and their relatives. *Archives of General Psychiatry, 31,* 143–51.

Hou, R.L., & Fender, D.H. (1979). Processing of direction and magnitude by the saccadic eye-movement system. *Vision Research, 19,* 1421–1426.

Hughes, H.C., & Zimba, L.D. (1985). Spatial maps of directed visual attention. *Journal of Experimental Psychology: Human Perception and Performance, 11,* 409–430.

Ingvar, D.H., & Franzen, G. (1974a). Abnormalities of cerebral blood flow distribution in patients with chronic schizophrenia. *Acta Psychiatrica Scandinavica*, *50*, 425–462.

Ingvar, D.H., & Franzen, G. (1974b). Distribution of cerebral activity in chronic schizophrenia. *Lancet*, *ii*, 1481–1485.

Jonides, J. (1981). Voluntary versus automatic control over the mind's eye's movement. In J. Long & A. Baddeley (Eds.), *Attention and performance IX*. Hillsdale, NJ: Erlbaum.

Komoda, M.K., Festinger, L., Phillips, L.J., Duckman, R.H., & Young, R.A. (1973). Some observations concerning saccadic eye movements. *Vision Research*, *13*, 1009–1020.

Kraepelin, E. (1919). *Dementia praecox* (R.M. Barclay, Trans., 1971). Edinburgh: Livingstone.

LaBerge, D. (1983). Spatial extent of attention to letters and words. *Journal of Experimental Psychology: Human Perception and Performance*, *9*, 371–379.

LaBerge, D., & Brown, V. (1986). Variations in size of the visual field in which targets are presented: An attentional range effect. *Perception and Psychophysics*, *40*, 188–200.

Latham, C., Holzman, P., Manschreck, T.C., & Tole, J. (1981). Optokinetic nystagmus and pursuit eye movements in schizophrenia. *Archives of General Psychology*, *38*, 997–1003.

Levin, S., Jones, A., Stark, L., Merrin, E.L., & Holzman, P.S. (1982). Identification of abnormal patterns in eye movements of schizophrenic patients measured by reflected light technique. *Archives of General Psychology*, *39*, 1125–1130.

Levin, S., Luebke, A., Zee D.S., Hain, T.C., Robinson, D.A., & Holzman, P.S. (1988). Smooth pursuit eye movements in schizophrenics: Quantitative measurements with the search-coil technique. *Journal of Psychiatric Research*, *22*, 195–206.

Levy, D.L., Holzman, P.S., & Proctor, L.R. (1978). Vestibular responses in schizophrenia. *Archives of General Psychology*, *35*, 972–981.

Lisberger, S.G., Fuchs, A.F., King, W.M., & Evinger, L.C. (1975). Effect of mean reaction time on saccadic responses to two-step stimuli with horizontal and vertical components. *Vision Research*, *15*, 1021–1025.

Lynch, J.C. (1987). Frontal eye field lesions in monkeys disrupt visual pursuit. *Experimental Brain Research*, *68*, 437–441.

Lynch, J.C., & Graybiel, A.M. (1983). Comparison of afferents traced to the superior colliculus from the frontal eye fields and from two subregions of area 7 of the rhesus monkey. *Neuroscience Abstracts*, *220.5*, 750.

Malmo, H.P. (1974). On frontal lobe functions: psychiatric patient controls. *Cortex*, *10*, 231–237.

Megaw, E.D., & Armstrong, W. (1973). Individual and simultaneous tracking of a step input by the horizontal saccadic eye movement and manual control systems. *Journal of Experimental Psychology*, *100*, 18–28.

Milner, B. (1963). Effects of different brain lesions on card sorting. *Archives of Neurology*, *9*, 100–110.

Milner, B. (1964). Some effects of frontal lobectomy in man. In J.M. Warren & K. Akert (Eds.), *The frontal granular cortex and behavior* (pp. 313–334). New York: McGraw-Hill.

Milner, B. (1982). Some cognitive effects of frontal-lobe lesions in man. *Philosophical Transactions of the Royal Society in London* (B), *298*, 211–226.

Nakayama, K. & Mackeben, M. (1989). Sustained and transient components of focal visual attention. *Vision Research*, *29*, 1631–1647.

Posner, M.I. (1980). Orienting of attention. *Quarterly Journal of Experimental Psychology*, *32*, 3–25.

Posner, M.I., & Cohen, Y. (1984). Components of visual orienting. In H. Bouma & D.G. Bouwhuis (Eds.), *Attention and performance X* (pp. 531–556). Hillsdale, NJ: LEA.

Posner, M.I., Rafal, R.D., Choate, L.S., & Vaughn, L. (1985). Inhibition of return: neural basis and function. *Cognitive Neuropsychology*, *2*, 211–228.

Posner, M.I., Snyder, C.R.R., & Davidson, B.J. (1980). Attention and the detection of signals. *Journal of Experimental Psychology: General*, *109*, 160–174.

Rafal, R.D., Calabresi, P.A., Brennan, C.W., & Sciolto, T.K. (1989). Saccade preparation inhibits reorienting to recently attended locations. *Journal of Experimental Psychology: Human Perception and Performance*, *15*, 673–685.

Rizzolatti, G., Riggio, L., Dascola, I., & Ulmita, C. (1987). Reorienting attention across the horizontal and vertical meridians: Evidence in favor of a premotor theory of attention. *Neuropsychologia*, *25*(1A), 31–40.

Ross, L.E., & Ross, S.M. (1980). Saccade latency and warning signals: Stimulus onset, offset, and change as warning events. *Perception and Psychophysics*, *27*, 251–257.

Ross, S.M., & Ross, L.E. (1981). Saccade latency a warning signals: Effects of auditory and visual stimulus onset and offset. *Perception and Psychophysics*, *29*, 429–437.

Saslow, K. (1967). Effects of components of displacement-step stimuli upon latency of saccadic eye movements. *Journal of the Optical Society of America*, *57*, 1024–1029.

Schiller, P.H., Sandell, J.H., & Maunsell, J.H.R. (1987). The effect of frontal eye field and superior colliculus lesions on saccadic latencies in the rhesus monkey. *Journal of Neurophysiology*, *57*, 1033–1049.

Schiller, P.H., True, S.D., & Conway, J.L. (1980). Deficits in eye movements following frontal eye-field and superior colliculus ablations. *Journal of Neurophysiology*, *44*, 1175–1189.

Sereno, A. (1991). *Attention and eye movements in schizophrenic, affective disorder, and normal subjects*. Unpublished doctoral dissertation, Harvard University.

Shepherd, M., Findlay, J.M., & Hockey, R.J. (1986). The relationship between eye movements and spatial attention. *Quarterly Journal of Experimental Psychology*, *38A*, 475–491.

Shulman, G.L., Remington, R.W., & McLean, J.P. (1979). Moving attention through visual space. *Journal of Experimental Psychology: Human Perception and Perfromance*, *5*, 522–526.

Stuss, D.T. & Benson, D.F. (1984). Neuropsychological studies of the frontal lobes. *Psychological Bulletin*, *95*, 3–28.

Treisman, A., & Gelade, G. (1980). A feature-integration theory of attention. *Cognitive Psychology*, *12*, 97–136.

Vitu, F., O'Regan, J.K., & Mittau, M. (1990). Optimal landing position in reading isolated words and continuous text. *Perception and Psychophysics*, *47*, 583–600.

Viviani, P., & Swensson, R.G. (1982). Saccadic eye movements to peripherally discriminated visual targets. *Journal of Experimental Psychology: Human Perception and Performance*, *8*, 113–126.

Warner, C.B., Juola, J.F., & Koshino, H. (1990). Voluntary allocation versus automatic capture of visual attention. *Perception and Psychophysics*, *48*, 243–251.

Weinberger, D.R., Berman, K.F., & Zec, R.F. (1986). Physiological dysfunction of dorsolateral prefrontal cortex in schizophrenia. I. Regional cerebral blood flow (rCBF) evidence. *Archives of General Psychiatry*, *43*, 114–125.

Wheeless, L., Boynton, R., & Cohen, G. (1966). Eye-movement responses to step and pulse-step stimuli. *Journal of the Optical Society of America*, *56*, 956–960.

7
Moment-to-Moment Control of Saccadic Eye Movements: Evidence from Continuous Search

Wolfgang Prinz, Dieter Nattkemper, and Thomas Ullmann

Global Versus Local Control of Saccadic Eye Movements

This chapter is concerned with understanding the mechanisms underlying the control of temporal and spatial properties of the eyes' scanning pattern in visual monitoring tasks. Basically, three types of models have been distinguished that differ with respect to the assumed relationship between the ongoing processing and the temporal and spatial decisions of the control system (cf. McConkie, 1983; Rayner, 1984).

At the one extreme, *global control* models view the temporal and spatial parameters of eye movements as having almost no relationship to the ongoing processing in a given visual task. By contrast, models of *local control* assume that the control system's decisions of how long to fixate and where to move next are fairly closely linked to the ongoing processing.

Under this view, a further issue can be raised that refers to the level of local control. On the one hand, models of *direct*, or *moment-to-moment*, *control* suggest that temporal and spatial parameters of eye movements are so closely linked to the ongoing processing that the control system's decisions of how long to remain at fixation and where to send the eyes next are based on information processed on the current fixation (Carpenter & Just, 1983; Hochberg, 1976; Just & Carpenter, 1980; McConkie, 1979; Rayner, 1977; Rayner & McConkie, 1975). These may be considered models of low-level control. On the other hand, models of *indirect control* assume that the control of fixation durations and saccade amplitudes is shifted to a somewhat higher level where the quality of immediately preceding processing is evaluated and where the parameters of these variables get fixed for some time on the basis of the results of this evaluation. Obviously, with a model like this, the scanning pattern of the eyes can only gradually be adjusted to changes in processing demands (Bouma & de Voogd, 1974; Buswell, 1935; Kolers, 1976; Shebilske,

```
TMNUMKFML TVKLNHVTNUHMHTTXHNHTNVHFNTNT
HMTHMTXMNUTTNMFMTMMMUFVVFHLNXMKMFULLN
MXVLXVMHKKNFNVTNKFNXKTXNXVHHUTFHHVUUH
VLXFVNNVMLLVFMFLTHFUHVLXMUUFMVKHTNKKU
LHNTUMNVHLNFXFNXHNNVHMFHKNTHFLLKNHMXV
LHHKKUXNTXTVKHMMXXTFUFNLVKKHLKXMTHKUT
KLVLNNFUFMXNKTUKUHFKFUKLVXFUVTUXFKKNU
VHFLVXVHTNXXFUFTFKNVXFHMXMTVXHVHVLLUF
HTTVTHVKTKUFMFUNNUXUTTXTTXHXXHMHUNTFM
MFTTKNLXTKXHTKKTNXKHVNXNKHUUHMMHTMLFK
MFKHTXVVLUTHXXVMXHHNNUNUNHUFNLMVUTHMU
KHHKMLMUFVMFHKVXNKFXMMDUNUTLXXXVLLKUL
VTLTLNNFXKVLTFMXMXLXUFULNHTFTFFVLNHLU
VXVKHNTTNUTFXLNVVFFLKKKFUMHHFUFTUMMUN
VVMHTVTHHVHLLHVVKLFFXXHUUXKLUVNVKFTVM
MTFTLVHXFHXUVNTHFHKMMMFKVLHTNTFNMKFFF
KKLFXKKFUXHXLMMUHKVUMTNLHVTHTKVVNMXMM
KXVUKXUVVLKVLHTNKLNKNTULXFXFVKVXMKLVU
TNMKHMHMTLTLLFTLLTLKHHXLTFXHMFVKXNFTX
FKLNKNUNNHUUUMMKHNNULHTLTLNLTLNNKUNKT
```

FIGURE 7.1. Search list as used in the continuous search task (see text for details of the task).

1975). These may be considered high-level models of local eye movement control.

In this chapter we shall examine some evidence from the continuous visual search paradigm with respect to the issue how direct versus indirect the control of saccadic eye movements is (see also Jacobs, 1986; Rayner & Fisher, 1987). The continuous visual search task requires the subject to scan through lists made up of random strings of letters and to look for a predefined target. Sometimes the instructions require subjects to search for one out of several possible targets (disjunctive search), but in all cases only one of the possible targets would appear once in each list, and the subject would be instructed to press a button and to stop the search after detecting the target.

In our experiments lists were arranged in horizontal lines of equal length (Figure 7.1) and the subject was instructed to scan them "as in reading," e.g., line by line and from left to right within lines, and to do so as fast as possible. During the scan the horizontal component of the EOG was recorded in order to identify saccades and fixations.

We shall examine three lines of pertinent evidence. First, we will consider data that reflect the normal scan through nontarget strings in search lists. As will be seen, these data seem to support the notion of local control of the scan, though the evidence is not unequivocal. Moreover, the data from these studies do not speak to the issue of the level of local control (i.e., high vs. low level).

Second, we will turn to data that reflect interruptions of the normal scanning routine, e.g., backward saccades and saccades that precede the detection of targets. These data are more clearly indicative of local control, and they seem to suggest that rather direct, low-level forms of control are involved.

Third, we will discuss the results of an experiment where the subject had to adjust his/her scan to a sudden change in the structure of the background. It will be seen that the results of this experiment are quite unequivocally supportive of the notion that a low-level mechanism of direct moment-to-moment control is involved.

It should be pointed out that the three pieces of evidence differ in their methodological status. The illustrations that refer to normal scanning and to interruptions of the scan are selectively taken from a couple of previous experiments that were conducted mainly for different purposes. This does not apply to the experiment on adjusting the scan, which was conducted as a direct test of the notion of moment-to-moment control.

Evidence from Continuous Search

Scanning Through Nontarget Strings

AMPLITUDES AND FIXATION TIMES

A first line of evidence that may be considered to be at least suggestive of the operation of a low-level, moment-to-moment control mechanism comes from a study where we looked for correlations between saccade amplitudes and fixation durations. What we found in this study was a moderate positive correlation between the amplitudes of saccades and the durations of subsequent fixations: the larger saccade amplitudes were the longer were the durations of the fixations that immediately followed these saccades (Nattkemper & Prinz, 1986).

Three things should be noted with respect to this finding: (a) The correlations were generally rather low, ranging somewhere between zero and +.40, depending on the subject. (b) The relationship was more or less linear in the range of small and medium-size saccades; it tended to flatten out in the range of the (less frequent) large saccades. (c) It is noteworthy that no such relationship holds in the reverse direction, i.e., no correlation whatsoever was observed between fixation durations and the amplitudes of subsequent saccades.

An account of this finding can be based on the notion of preprocessing. If one assumes that partial information from noncentral vision (for the distinction between a central and a more eccentric region of processing, see Rayner & Fisher, 1987) is integrated across saccades, one should expect that the amplitude of the saccade that takes the eye to a given fixation location determines the degree to which information to be processed on that fixation has already been preprocessed on the fixation before (i.e., the one from where the saccade started). The larger the amplitude the smaller, on average, the amount of information will be that has been preprocessed before. This leads to an increase in the time needed to identify the elements encountered on a fixation after a long saccade.

If this account is correct the results of this study can be taken to suggest low-level control. Yet, an account in terms of high-level (or even global) control is possible as well. For this one would simply have to assume that the system operates in a way where three classes of parameters are fixed for each trial (or even for each group of trials):

1. parameters of the distribution of fixation durations,
2. parameters of the distribution of saccade amplitudes,
3. a parameter for the regression of fixation durations on preceding saccade amplitudes.

With this view, a mild degree of positive correlation between fixation duration and saccade amplitudes could be considered to indicate the wisdom of Mother Nature who has furnished the control system with the built-in feature of some trade-off between spatial and temporal properties of the scan. If so, there is no need for low-level, moment-to-moment control because high-level control has arranged for some complementarity between these two properties of the scan.

RANDOM AND REDUNDANT STRINGS

We now consider a further piece of evidence that also refers to the normal scanning through nontarget strings. Consider again what a simple model of global control would have to assume for each trial. According to this view one would assume that the system fixes the parameters of the relevant distributions of the spatial and the temporal properties of the

fixation time

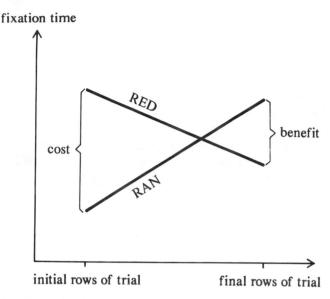

initial rows of trial   final rows of trial

FIGURE 7.2. Schematic sketch of the course of within-trial development of performance in random and predictable lists (after Nattkemper & Prinz, 1984; Prinz & Prinz, 1985).

scan only once, either prior to or immediately after the onset of each trial, and then scans through the list with this routine, more or less independent of what it encounters there. The setting of the parameters might depend on such general factors as training, visual acuity, search strategy, perhaps also on some raw stimulus factors such as context complexity or ease of target/nontarget discrimination, etc. According to this view, variations of the temporal and/or the spatial properties of the scan within trials (i.e., within search lists) could merely reflect random fluctuations around preset parameter values.

Yet, there is an interesting observation suggesting that at least the temporal parameter of the scan (fixation duration) is more closely related to the ongoing processing within trials. This observation has emerged in a couple of experiments that were run in order to assess the effects of sequential redundancy on search performance (Prinz, 1983; Prinz & Nattkemper, 1987). In most of these studies performance was compared for two types of search lists, random and predictable. In random lists the nontarget background consisted of a random sequence of letters. In predictable lists, the letter string was constructed according to certain arbitrary rules, thereby introducing some degree of predictability across subsequent items in the list (for details see Nattkemper & Prinz, 1984; Prinz, 1979, 1983; Prinz & Nattkemper, 1987).

In these experiments we observed a difference in the course of the within-trial development of performance between predictable and random lists. In the random condition, average fixation duration tended to increase in the course of the trial, whereas it tended to decrease in the predictable condition. Sometimes, the scan of predictable lists would even start with longer average fixation durations and end up with shorter fixation durations as compared to random lists (Figure 7.2) (Nattkemper & Prinz, 1984; Prinz & Prinz, 1985).

In an attempt to explain this pattern of results we assumed that, with predictable lists, an internal model of the particular pattern of predictability is assembled in each trial. To assemble this model, the system first has to invest some costs for the acquisition of this pattern before it can benefit from the internal model later in the course of the trial. This results in (relatively) long fixation durations at the onset and (relatively) short fixation durations at the end of each trial. According to this account the parameters of the fixation time distribution are not constant over a given trial, but undergo gradual change instead, depending on the information encountered, which implies some degree of local control.

Note, however, that a global control model could handle these data as well. For this one would have to assume that immediately after the onset of each trial, perhaps on the basis of the information encountered during the very first fixations, pertinent parameters get fixed at two levels:

1. a first-order parameter that characterizes the initial distribution of fixation durations
2. a second-order parameter that controls the change of the first-order parameter over the trial.

In conclusion, the evidence can be considered to be suggestive of local control, but it is certainly not unequivocal. In both cases global control models could account for the data as well. Though these accounts are basically ad hoc, it seems that further evidence is needed before final conclusions can be drawn.

Interrupting the Scan

In the present task there are two basic ways that the normal scan can get interrupted: by regressive eye movements and by eye movements in close vicinity to the target. A look at the details of the eye movement patterns in both of these cases of interruptions seems to suggest that direct, low-level control is involved in the control of the scan.

JUMPING BACKWARD

In some of our previous experiments we looked in detail at backward saccades or, more precisely, at the pattern of forward saccades and

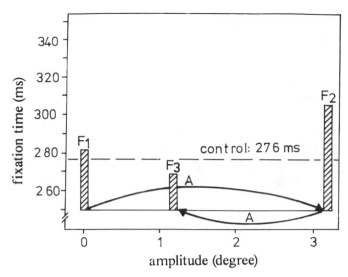

FIGURE 7.3. Saccades and fixations preceding backward saccades. Shown are the mean amplitudes of the last two forward saccades (A_1, A_2) that precede the backward saccade (A_3). F_1, F_2, and F_3 give the average fixation durations of the three fixations following the three saccades. The broken line indicates the average fixation duration obtained in other portions of the list (control).

fixations that immediately preceded the incidence of backward saccades (Nattkemper, 1990; Nattkemper & Prinz, 1987, 1989). A summary of findings from one of these experiments is shown in Figure 7.3 (Prinz & Nattkemper, 1985, 1987). It is fairly typical of the overall results we observed in a couple of other experiments as well. The main purpose of this experiment was to assess the effects of sequential redundancy on search performance. In the analysis of its results we considered all backward saccades that were at least preceded by two forward saccades in the same line.

As can be seen from the summary of the results in Figure 7.3, there is one conspicuous feature in which the pattern of events that immediately precede a backward saccade differs markedly from the standard pattern of events in the forward scan: the fixation that immediately precedes the backward saccade (F_2) was, on the average, considerably longer than the mean fixation duration of standard fixations in the forward scan.

It is obvious what this finding might suggest: regressive eye movements are triggered on the basis of locally emerging processing problems, i.e., problems with processing the stimulus elements encountered during the fixation preceding the backward saccade (F_2). Yet, unfortunately, an entirely different and no less obvious account is possible as well. This account starts from the fact that a backward saccade implies a change in the eyes' preferred movement direction. If one assumes that such a change of direction requires additional costs of reprogramming, a simple explanation for the prolongation prior to the backward saccade offers itself. One might then suspect that the additional time is needed for the reversal of the scanning direction. This explanation leaves entirely open what causes and what triggers the backward saccade. It merely offers an alternative explanation for the prolongation of F_2.

To examine the reprogramming account, we entered into a more detailed analysis of the data for random and redundant lists. One of the standard observations in redundancy experiments is that fixation durations are, on the average, shorter for redundant as compared to random lists (Nattkemper & Prinz, 1984; Prinz & Nattkemper, 1985, 1987). This observation can be used to test the motor programming explanation. This hypothesis leads one to expect that the prolongation of the fixation that precedes the regression is constant, i.e., independent of the redundancy condition. This is because, under this view, the additional time needed is exclusively due to the reprogramming and should thus be completely independent of list type. By contrast, any effect of list type on the prolongation of the fixation prior to the backward saccade would speak against the reprogramming hypothesis.

The results are summarized in Figure 7.4. As can be seen the fixation that immediately precedes the backward saccade (F_2) was in both conditions clearly prolonged (as compared to the respective control fixation durations indicated by the broken lines). More importantly, however, the amount of this prolongation was different in the two conditions: when scanning random letter strings, F_2 was on the average 53 ms longer than control fixations. In redundant letter strings this difference was smaller and insignificant (26 ms as compared to average control fixation duration after forward saccades in redundant lists).

These data do not speak in favor of an explanation that relates the prolongation of F_2 to an additional load arising in the programming activity of the oculomotor system. Rather, the increase of fixation time seems to reflect some additional processing of the stimulus items. We may conclude, therefore, that backward saccades are triggered on a local basis. Our observations suggest that the eye movement control system responds to occasionally emerging processing problems in two steps (whatever the nature of these problems may be): First, it increases fixation time, presumably in order to provide additional time for further processing. Second, if the first step does not help (and if the problem refers to items on the left-hand side of the fixation point), it interrupts the scan and takes the eye back, presumably in order to provide an additional opportunity to process these items.

APPROACHING THE TARGET

A further piece of evidence that demonstrates how temporal and spatial characteristics of eye movements depend on local stimulus properties and

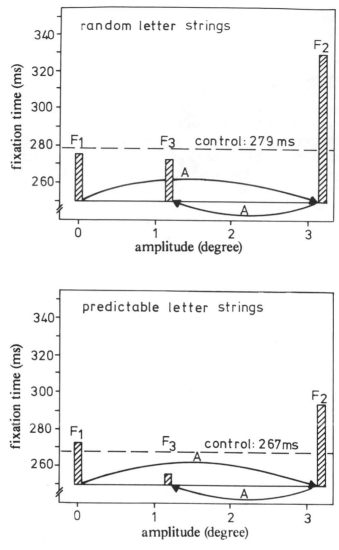

FIGURE 7.4. Saccades and fixations preceding backward saccades in random and predictable letter strings. For details see Figure 7.3 (see text for explanation).

local information processing demands has emerged from the analysis of the pattern of eye movements observed when the eye approaches a target in search (Nattkemper & Prinz, 1988, 1990).

How do the eyes move when they approach a target? In an attempt to answer this question we examined the data from an experiment planned to assess the effects of stimulus density on search performance (Nattkemper, 1988). In this experiment, the targets were D and Z,

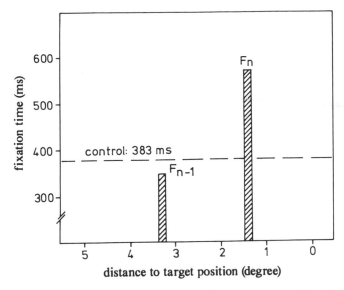

FIGURE 7.5. Average duration and average distance-to-target for the last two fixations preceding target detection. The location of the target is at position 0. (See text for further details.)

(disjunctive search) and they had to be detected in a background made up of angular letters (W T N M H K V F X L). With this background, target D could be separated from the nontargets in terms of simple features (e.g., roundness) that were easy to detect, whereas the angular target Z required some deeper and more detailed analysis.

We took a closer look at the pattern of eye movements in those rows where the subjects indicated the detection of the target by the button press that terminates the scan. The results we discuss are taken from trials where at least two fixations could be identified as being left of the location of the target in that line (in addition to the very first fixation after the big return sweep). For these two fixations (F_n; F_{n-1}) average fixation durations and the mean amplitude of the saccade between them were obtained. Furthermore, we obtained the average horizontal distances between the locations of these two fixations and the location of the target.

The main results are shown in Figure 7.5 in terms of means over seven subjects. In addition to the experimental data, which come from the line where the target was detected, control data for average fixation duration are also given. These control data are taken from the line immediately above the one in which the target was detected.

Two features of this result are worth mentioning. First, the fixation next to the target (F_n) was much longer than the mean fixation duration from the control line. Second, the preceding fixation (F_{n-1}) was slightly

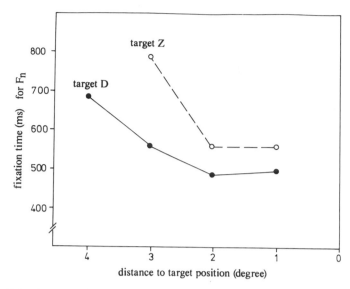

FIGURE 7.6. Average duration of fixation F_n over distance to target for targets D and Z.

shorter than average control fixation time. Both of these effects were significant.

As far as F_n is concerned one might suspect that the prolongation of fixation F_n is related to the processing of the identity of the target. Evidence that bears on this can be expected from a closer look at the data. As mentioned above, subjects had to search for two targes, D and Z, which could be more or less easily separated from the background. If F_n indeed reflects processing that is related to the identity of the target, its duration should be different for the two targets.

The results are presented in Figure 7.6. As can be seen, fixation times for F_n were clearly dependent on target identity. F_n was shorter for the "easy" target, D, than for the more difficult target, Z. In addition, there was a pronounced distance effect. The duration of F_n was a function of the distance to the target. The larger this distance was the longer was the duration of F_n. This pattern of results is well in line with the notion that F_n reflects processing that refers to the identity of the target.

There is an interesting further observation about the preceding fixation F_{n-1}. If one plots the amplitude of the saccade between F_{n-1} and F_n as a function of the distance between the location of F_{n-1} and the location of the target, a monotonic positive relationship is obtained (Figure 7.7): the larger the distance to target the larger is the amplitude of the saccade. This seems to be well in line with the notion that the processing during this "early" fixation, F_{n-1}, reflects operations of detecting and localizing the target and, presumably, of computing a saccade that takes the eyes to

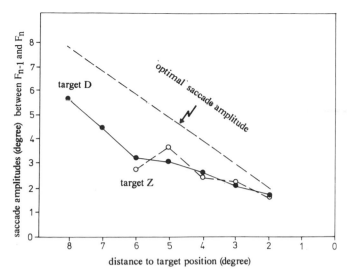

FIGURE 7.7. Mean amplitude of the forward saccade between F_{n-1} and F_n as a function of distance to target (i.e., the distance between fixation F_{n-1} and the target location) for the two targets, D and Z.

the target's vicinity. Interestingly, the function relating saccade amplitude to the distance to target is virtually identical for the two targets. This is in clear contrast to the pronounced target effect in fixation F_n (Figure 7.6) and seems to support the notion that processing at fixation F_{n-1} does not refer to target identity.

A simple (and presumably oversimplified) summary account would then be that two fixations will, on the average, be involved when the eyes approach a target in the list. The first of them, which is relatively short, detects and localizes a critical location in the list and sends the eyes close to this location; the second, which is relatively long, checks and identifies the information encountered there. If this account is true, it seems that in this task *where* processing comes first and *what* processing comes second and that these two operations tend to be neatly divided across two successive saccades.

Note that this view implies direct, or moment-to-moment control of the scan. First, it is assumed that the amplitude of a saccade can be determined during the fixation preceding it, and second, it is assumed that the duration of a fixation can be determined by the discriminability of the information encountered on that fixation.

Adjusting the Scan

One of the problems with the illustrations discussed so far is that they do not lend themselves to an unambiguous interpretation. This is because two variables covarying (say, fixation duration and target identity, or saccade amplitude and distance to target) may be suggestive of moment-to-moment control, but certainly not in the sense that other explanations are excluded. For instance, it is always possible that the correlation between the two variables is not due to the fact that one affects the other, but rather to the operation of some third factor that affects both of them simultaneously. This third factor might be related to information acquired in parafoveal vision on a still earlier occasion, for instance during the scan of the immediately preceding line. A similar point has been raised by McConkie (1983).

Thus, if one wants to establish unequivocal evidence in favor of low-level, moment-to-moment control one has to design the task in a way that excludes the possibility that preliminary information has been acquired on earlier fixations. This was done in an experiment that had the following two major features (for details see Nattkemper, Ullmann, & Prinz, 1991). The first feature was that processing demands were manipulated within trials. This was done by way of altering the complexity of the nontarget strings across two consecutive rows within search lists. The basic question then was how fast the pattern of fixations and saccades would adjust to the new structure: immediately (i.e., on the first fixation and in the first saccade after the change) or delayed (somewhat later).

The second feature was that in this experiment search lists were presented *row by row*, i.e., one row after another, and not in the form of a simultaneously visible matrix of several rows. Accordingly, the processing of a given row could never be affected by information acquired in parafoveal vision during the scan of the preceding rows. This would exclude parafoveal interactions across rows. Moreover, because the alteration of list structure would always commence at the very beginning (i.e., the left end) of a new row, any parafoveal interactions *within* rows were excluded as well.

The structure of the nontarget strings was varied in three steps: low, medium, and high complexity. String complexity was manipulated by way of fixing the number of different letters that could, on average, occur within a given number of horizontally adjacent locations. For example, low-complexity strings would, on the average, contain three different symbols within any sample of six adjacent locations. In medium- and high-complexity strings, any sample of that size would, on average, contain four and six different symbols, respectively. Within each sample, symbols were randomly assigned to locations, with the restriction that repetitions of symbols in immediately adjacent locations were not permitted to occur (for details Nattkemper et al., 1991).

On each trial a list was presented row by row. The presentation of rows was contingent on the subject's eye movements: a new row would replace the old one during the eyes' big return sweep from the end of the row to its beginning. The technical details of this procedure were arranged such

FIGURE 7.8. Example of a search list with low complexity strings in rows 1 to 4 and high-complexity strings in individual rows. Note that subjects would see one row after another. (See text for further details.) (This list is a photo taken from the display when the consecutive rows were arranged in a rectangular matrix for the purpose of demonstration.)

that the exchange itself was not visible for the subject. He/she would always encounter the new row when his/her eyes landed at its leftmost end.

Search lists were assembled from the three-string complexity conditions in the following way. The first four or five rows that formed the initial section of each list would consist of four or five consecutive rows from one of the three complexity conditions. The final section (which started with row 5 or 6) would contain a couple of strings from either the same or one of the two other complexity conditions. When string complexity was the same in both sections there was no change in list structure. There was a change, however, when strings of different complexity were used in the two sections. In this case two directions of the change could be distinguished: an increase or a decrease in complexity. In the experiment we realized each of the nine possible conditions resulting from the combination of 3 (initial complexity) × 3 (final complexity) conditions. An example is shown in Figure 7.8.

TABLE 7.1. Mean saccade amplitude and mean fixation duration for the three string complexity conditions.

	String complexity		
	Low	Medium	High
Saccade amplitude (degree)	2.65	2.38	2.23
Fixation duration (ms)	262	267	271

TABLE 7.2. Saccade amplitude and fixation duration in initial and final list sections for the three complexity alteration conditions.

	Complexity alteration					
	Unchanged (CU) List section		Reduced (CR) List section		Increased (CI) List section	
	Initial	Final	Initial	Final	Initial	Final
Saccade amplitude (degree)	2.38	2.52	2.20	2.60	2.49	2.30
Fixation duration (ms)	263	266	267	264	267	275

There were six subjects participating in four experimental sessions. In each session there were nine blocks of five trials each for each of the nine list conditions. The sequence of the nine blocks was randomized over sessions and subjects. The task was to search for two targets disjunctively (D or Z). The nontarget background was made up of random strings drawn from a set of nine nontarget letters (*WTNMHKVFX*).

Before we look at the eyes' reaction to the alteration itself, we must first make sure whether or not the manipulation of string complexity was effective at all.

The relevant results are given in Table 7.1. This table summarizes mean saccade amplitudes and mean fixation durations for the three string complexity conditions (irrespective of list section, viz., initial vs. final). It can be seen that both saccade amplitude and fixation duration do indeed respond to the complexity manipulation. Saccade amplitudes are smaller for high as compared to low complexity, and fixation durations are longer for high as compared to low complexity. Though the effect is more pronounced in the amplitudes it seems to be present in the fixation durations as well (significant linear trend in both cases).

Table 7.2 gives a first and rough idea of how the eyes responded to the alteration of string structure within lists. For this summary table, the nine experimental conditions have been combined to form three basic conditions of complexity alteration: complexity unchanged (CU), complexity reduced (CR), and complexity increased (CI). The data for the complexity unchanged conditions give an indication of the development of the scanning pattern within trials in standard lists (i.e., unaltered lists).

It can be seen that in these lists saccade amplitudes tend to become somewhat larger in the course of the trial, whereas fixation durations remain basically unchanged. The increase in saccade amplitudes is also observed in the complexity reduced list conditions (CR), and as one would expect it is still somewhat (though not significantly) larger than in the control condition. More interestingly, the effect is completely reversed in the complexity increased condition (CI). In this condition saccade amplitudes become smaller in the final section. A similar picture emerges with respect to fixation durations. When complexity is reduced, fixation durations tend to become slightly shorter in the final section, whereas when complexity is increased they clearly become longer. From these data we may conclude that the complexity manipulation was effective both between and within lists. Saccade amplitudes were clearly affected by string complexity and there was a tendency for fixation durations to be weakly affected as well.

We can now take a closer look at the details of the adjustment of the scan. For this we first consider the within-trial development of saccade amplitudes and fixation durations for the three string complexity alteration conditions. In Figure 7.9 within-trial development is summarized in terms of means for each of the last three rows before and the first three rows after the alteration.

As far as saccade amplitude is concerned there seems to be an immediate adjustment to the alteration. There was a sudden increase of mean saccade amplitude when scanning the very first row where complexity was reduced, and, correspondingly, a sudden decrease of amplitude when complexity was increased. Again, the result is less clear-cut for fixation durations. When string complexity was reduced during the trial there was no indication of an immediate adjustment. When complexity was increased there was a slight increase of fixation duration in the first new row, which then continued monotonically in the two consecutive rows.

Before we draw conclusions from this we should take a somewhat stronger magnifying glass and look in still greater detail at the very first fixations and saccades in the first row of the final list section. Figure 7.10 shows the results for the first two fixations and the first two saccades in terms of costs and benefits observed in the first new row (final section) relative to the last old row (initial section).

As far as fixation duration is concerned, consider first the black bars, which reflect the results for the control condition where complexity was not altered between these two lines. The black bars then reflect the difference in fixation time for the first and second fixation in these two lines. Positive values indicate fixation time costs (i.e., fixation duration gets longer across the two lines); negative values indicate fixation time benefits (i.e., fixation duration getting shorter). For the CU condition, the picture indicates that the first fixation in the first new line is, on the

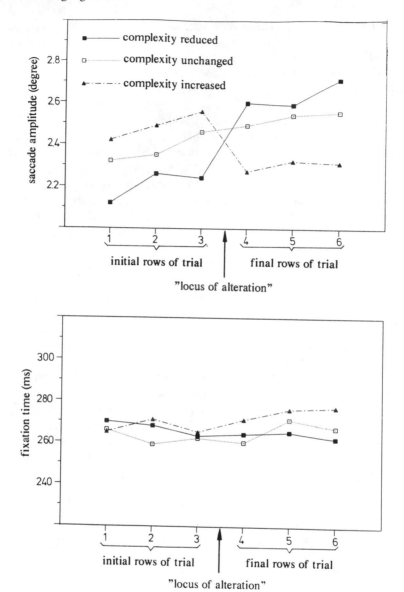

FIGURE 7.9. Mean saccade amplitudes (top) and mean fixation duration (bottom) for the last three rows from the initial section and the first three rows from the final section of search lists for the three complexity alteration conditions.

average, about 17 ms shorter than the corresponding first fixation in the last old line. The black bar can thus be considered to provide a reference for the fixation durations observed for the other two complexity alteration conditions. When complexity is altered it seems that fixation times

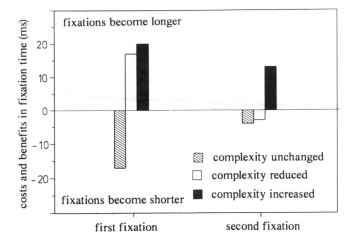

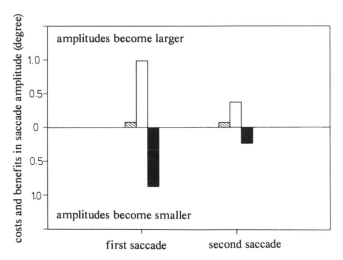

FIGURE 7.10. Costs and benefits for fixation durations and saccades amplitudes observed for the first two fixations (first two saccades) in the first row of the final section as compared to the last row of the initial section.

become longer on the very first fixation. Interestingly, this effect seems not to depend on whether the change is a decrease or an increase in complexity. Yet, there is no such effect in the second fixation, and the effect for the first fixation is insignificant on the basis of the data collected so far. Therefore, it seems that this part of the results is disappointing with respect to the moment-to-moment control hypothesis.

A much neater picture emerges for the saccade amplitudes. Note, that in this panel costs and benefits are reversed. Negative values indicate that amplitudes become smaller after the change (costs); positive values indicate that they become larger (benefits). When complexity is increased we observe a strong immediate effect in the very first saccade in the row that contains the new structure: saccade amplitude is reduced by about 0.8°, and this effect gradually decreased over the next two saccades (only one of which is shown in the figure). The same applies when complexity is reduced: amplitude is increased for the very first saccade by approximately 1°, and this effect is then gradually reduced as well. These effects are not only substantial in size but also robust in terms of their statistical reliability.

At first glance these results seem to suggest that there is no specific response to the complexity alteration on the very first fixation in the first row that exhibits the new string structure. If there is a response at all it is an unspecific prolongation of this fixation, perhaps an unspecific response to the novelty of the stimulus structure encountered there. At second glance, however, it becomes clear that this does not imply that the direction of the alteration is not recognized during the first fixation. Quite the contrary, we have to assume that the new structure is identified and that the scanning pattern is immediately adjusted to it. This is borne out by the specific response of the saccade that takes the eye from the first to the second fixation and that must have been programmed (or, at least, adjusted to the new string structure) on the basis of the information encountered on the first fixation. This saccade is relatively large when string structure is less complex and relatively small when it is more complex that it used to be before.

In summary, then, at least two (and perhaps three) processing components can be identified that must be included in the processing of the information encountered on the first fixation that refers to the altered structure:

1. identifying the new string structure
2. programming (or, adjusting) saccades in accordance with the new string structure
3. perhaps, responding to stimulus novelty.

Though it is clear that these operations (at least the first two of them) must be performed during the first fixation it is still an open question on the basis of the present results whether or not they are associated with fixation time costs.[1]

---

[1] This open question is one of the reasons why an extended replication of the experiment is worthwhile. Another independent point is that this replication should be run with a slight modification of the design. In this modification the nine experimental conditions should be randomized within blocks rather than assigned to blocks. This is because it could be argued that when conditions are assigned to blocks, subjects could learn within the blocks to prepare themselves for the alteration of structure between the initial and the final list section.

Conclusion

To summarize, the evidence suggests that we have reasons to believe that the spatial and perhaps also the temporal parameters of the search scan can be controlled in a moment-to-moment fashion. Yet, these observations do not necessarily imply that the decision of how long to fixate and where to go next are always and exclusively controlled by information encountered on the current fixation. It is certainly reasonable to assume that, in addition to this rather direct, low-level mode of control, more indirect, high-level modes of control come into play as well.

A more complete and more realistic picture of the whole story could then be that, in a monitoring task like continuous search, high-level control would usually guide the scan unless a local singularity (such as a target or a change in nontarget structure) requires a modification. This modification can then be performed right on the spot in a moment-to-moment fashion.[2]

---

[2] A view like this might lead one to expect some asymmetry of the effects of complexity increase versus decrease. In the case of a sudden *increase* of string complexity the system must instantaneously adjust its scanning routine if it wants to avoid errors. However, in the case of a sudden *decrease* of complexity it could afford to continue the old routine for some time and only gradually adjust it to the new requirements. Some of this may perhaps be seen in the asymmetry of the response of fixation durations to string structure alteration (cf. Figure 7.9). When complexity is decreased, fixation durations do not respond at all (perhaps with the exception of the very first fixation in the first line of alteration), whereas they do respond when complexity is increased.

Acknowledgment. The major part of the experiments described in this chapter was supported by Deutsche Forschungsgemeinschaft (grants Pr 118/5–9 to the first author).

References

Bouma, H., & de Voogd, A.H. (1974). On the control of eye saccades in reading. *Vision Research*, *14*, 273–284.

Buswell, G.T. (1935). *How people look at pictures*. Chicago: University of Chicago Press.

Carpenter, P.A., & Just, M.A. (1983). What your eyes do while your mind is reading. In K. Rayner (Ed.), *Eye movements in reading. Perceptual and language processes* (pp. 275–305). New York: Academic Press.

Hochberg, J. (1976). Toward a speech-plan eye-movement model of reading. In R.A. Monty & J.W. Senders (Eds.), *Eye movements and psychological processes* (pp. 397–416). Hillsdale, NJ: Erlbaum.

Jacobs, A.M. (1986). Eye-movement control in visual search: How direct is visual span control? *Perception & Psychophysics*, *39*(1), 47–58.

Just, M.A., & Carpenter, P.A. (1980). A theory of reading: From eye fixations to comprehension. *Psychological Review, 87*, 329–354.

Kolers, P.A. (1976). Buswell's discoveries. In R.A. Monty & J.W. Senders (Eds.), *Eye movements and psychological processes* (pp. 373–395). Hillsdale, NJ: Erlbaum.

McConkie, G.W. (1979). On the role and control of eye movements in reading. In P.A. Kolers, M.E. Wrolstad, & H. Bouma (Eds.), *Processing of visible language* (pp. 37–48). New York: Plenum Press.

McConkie, G.W. (1983). Eye movements and perception during reading. In K. Rayner (Ed.), *Eye movements in reading. Perceptual and language processes* (pp. 65–96). New York: Academic Press.

Nattkemper, D. (1988). *Zeichendichte und Kontrollbereiche bei visueller Suche*. Unpublished doctoral dissertation, University of Bielefeld, Germany.

Nattkemper, D. (1990). Mechanismen der Steuerung sakkadischer Augenbewegungen—Neue Funde beim Suchen. In C. Meinecke & L. Kehrer (Eds.), *Bielefelder Beiträge zur Kognitionspsychologie* (pp. 1–26). Göttingen, Toronto, Zürich: Hogrefe Verlag für Psychologie.

Nattkemper, D., & Prinz, W. (1984). Costs and benefits of redundancy in visual search. In A.G. Gale & F. Johnson (Eds.), *Theoretical and applied aspects of eye movement research* (pp. 343–351). Amsterdam: North-Holland.

Nattkemper, D., & Prinz, W. (1986). Saccade amplitude determines fixation duration: Evidence from continuous search. In J.K. O'Regan & A. Levy-Schoen (Eds.), *Eye movements: From physiology to cognition* (pp. 285–292). Amsterdam: North-Holland.

Nattkemper, D., & Prinz, W. (1987). Zum Mechanismus der Steuerung sakkadischer Augenbewegungen. In H.G. Geißler & K. Reschke (Eds.), *Psychophysische Grundlagen mentaler Prozesse—in memoriam G.Th. Fechner (1801–1887)* (pp. 182–202). Leipzig: Karl-Marx-Universität.

Nattkemper, D., & Prinz, W. (1988). *Target-Entdeckung bei visueller Suche*. Paper read at the 30. Teap in Marburg, Germany.

Nattkemper, D., & Prinz, W. (1989). *The basis for regressive eye movements—evidence from continuous search*. Paper read at the 5th European Conference on Eye Movements, Pavia, Italy.

Nattkemper, D., & Prinz, W. (1990). *Target selection in continuous search—localization before identification*. Paper read at the 4th Conference of the European Society for Cognitive Psychology, Como, Italy.

Nattkemper, D., Ullmann, T., & Prinz, W. (1991). Adjusting saccadic eye movements to variations of stimulus complexilty—evidence from continuous search. Paper read at the 14th European Conference on Visual Perception, Vilnins, Lithuania.

Prinz, W. (1979). Integration of information in visual search. *Quarterly Journal of Experimental Psychology, 31*, 287–304.

Prinz, W. (1983). Redundanzausnutzung bei kontinuierlicher Suchtätigkeit. *Psychologische Beiträge, 25*, 12–56.

Prinz, W., & Nattkemper, D. (1985). *Utilization of sequential redundancy in continuous search: Evidence for two modes of information integration*. Report No. 47, ZiF Research Group Perception and Action, University of Bielefeld, Germany.

Prinz, W., & Nattkemper, D. (1987). *Integrating non-target information in continuous search*. Report No. 155, ZiF Research Group Perception and Action, University of Bielefeld, Germany.

Prinz, W., & Prinz, U. (1985). Verarbeitung redundanter Zeichensequenzen durch Kinder im Grundschulalter. *Zeitschrift für Entwicklungspsychologie und Pädagogische Psychologie, 177*, 210–222.

Rayner, K. (1977). Visual attention in reading: Eye movements reflect cognitive processing. *Memory and Cognition, 4*, 443–448.

Rayner, K. (1984). Visual selection in reading, picture perception and visual search—A tutorial review. In H. Bouma & D.G. Bowhuis (Eds.), *Attention and performance X: Control of language processes* (pp. 67–96). London: Erlbaum.

Rayner, K., & Fisher, D.L. (1987). Letter processing during eye fixations in visual search. *Perception & Psychophysics, 42*(1), 87–100.

Rayner, K., & McConkie, G.W. (1976). What guides a reader's eye movements? *Vision Research, 16*, 829–839.

Shebilske, W. (1975). Reading eye movements from an information-processing point of view. In D. Massaro (Ed.), *Understanding language*. New York: Academic Press.

8
Spatial Memory and Integration Across Saccadic Eye Movements

Mary M. Hayhoe, Joel Lachter, and Per Moeller

Many aspects of visual perception can be treated in terms of the information available in a single fixation, or frame. However, the eyes, head, and body are constantly moving, and from this time-varying input on the retina we must construct a representation of a scene in coordinates that are fixed to the world and not to the body. Most research on this problem has focused on the consequences of saccadic eye movements. These high-velocity movements, which occur several times a second, move the high-acuity foveal region around the scene and impose a frame-like structure on the visual input. That is, we can think of the visual input as a sequence of stationary frames sampling different parts of the scene, interposed by brief periods of blur. To explain our perception of a stable world it is generally assumed that the perceptual system constructs a representation of the scene that is integrated across these successive views in an external coordinate frame. If this is so, we can identify three aspects of the problem, as follows:

1. What is the nature of the information retained from previous views? One explicit suggestion, made originally by McConkie and Rayner (1976), is that information retained from previous views is rather like an iconic image, and that the current view is simply added to the previous one (see also Breitmeyer, Kropfl, & Julesz, 1982; Jonides, Irwin, & Yantis, 1982). This idea has little empirical support. As discussed in the chapters by Irwin and by Pollatsek and Rayner in this volume, numerous attempts to show some "fusion" or addition of images from different fixations have been unsuccessful (Irwin, Brown, & Sun, 1988; Irwin, Yantis, & Jonides, 1983; Irwin, Zacks, & Brown, 1990; O'Regan & Levy-Schoen, 1983; Rayner & Pollatsek, 1983). For example, Irwin and colleagues used a task requiring subjects to find the missing dot in an array of 25 dots when half the dots were presented before a saccade, and the rest after the saccade. If this task were possible to do, it would mean that the information retained in the previous view was something like an image, and that the images were

added in a point-by-point fashion. However, the task is found to be impossible over a range of conditions (Irwin et al., 1988, 1990). This implies that the information retained is not in the form of an image, or if it is, the combination is not like a simple addition (see item 3, below). There are, however, a range of other possibilities. We return to this question below.

2. An independent aspect of the problem arises from the question of visual stability and concerns how the frames are aligned in the appropriate spatial arrangement. The usual assumption, for which there is substantial evidence, is that an eye position signal indicating how far the eye has moved, is subtracted from the retinal image displacement to yield spatial location. This is sometimes referred to as "cancellation theory," and it appears that both efferent and proprioceptive signals are used (see review by Matin, 1986). However, additional information is available in the images themselves. Successive frames could be aligned by some sort of visual correspondence or matching mechanism. The nature of such a mechanism would depend on the nature of the signals remaining from the previous view. For example, if low-level information is retained, alignment could be done by a cross-correlation of low frequency information. If it is high level, it might involve the matching of identified objects. Whether this information is in fact used for aligning frames for visual stability is not at all clear, nor is the nature of the mechanism.

3. Once the frames are aligned, what is the nature of the interaction of the information in a given spatial location? Again, the nature of the interaction depends to some extent on the nature of the residual information. The hypothesis described above, which has received the most attention, was that there might be some kind of image from the previous view that was added in a point-by-point fashion to the current retinal input. Alternatively, high-quality foveal information might overwrite or augment peripheral information, or there may be no influence of prior information as long as it is consistent with the new information. A number of investigators have looked for some sort of facilitation of perception (e.g., of a word or picture) by presenting a stimulus in a peripheral location before the saccade. Although substantial priming effects are found, they do not appear to be linked tightly to spatial location nor to the particular visual features of the peripheral stimulus in the previous view (McConkie & Zola, 1979; McConkie, Zola, Blanchard, & Wolverton, 1982; Pollatsek, Rayner, & Collins, 1984; Pollatsek, Rayner, & Hendersen, 1990; Rayner, McConkie, & Zola, 1980). For example, changing the case of the letters in a word has no effect on naming times or reading. These studies are reviewed in more detail by Pollatsek and Rayner in this volume, and like those in item 1 above, they clearly demonstrate both that the information from the previous view is not in the form of an

image, and that the process of information combination is not like a simple addition.

Because this simplest hypothesis is ruled out, we must turn once again to the question raised in item 1, about the nature of the information retained from the previous view or views. It is possible that very little information is retained, perhaps only a sparse semantic description of the objects in a scene and their approximate locations, as O'Regan and Levy-Schoen (1983) have suggested. To get some sense of what to look for, it is useful to consider the possible functions an integrative process might subserve. The first and most obvious is visual stability, because we clearly have some ability to compare the locations of objects in subsequent frames. A second is that certain perceptual tasks, such as fusing random dot stereograms or perceiving structure from motion, appear to require information accrued over periods longer than the duration of a single fixation and so must be independent of eye position. In the case of structure from motion, with a display of moving dots that define a rotating cylinder, information accumulated over a period of close to a second may be required to perceive the cylinder, even though the lifetime of individual moving dots in the stimulus display is only about 100 ms (Husain, Treue, & Andersen, 1989; Treue, Husain, & Andersen, 1991). This suggests a process that integrates across time to generate a surface representation in a nonretinotopic frame. A third possible function may be the building of a representation that combines information from prior foveal views to produce a more complete scene description than is available from a single view. Both long-term and short-term spatial memory require a representation like this. For example, actions like orienting toward an object not currently in view, crossing a busy street, or judging the shape of a large building require integration in this sense. For these purposes we need a fairly precise representation of spatial location. However, we know very little about the precision with which we can perform such tasks. Perception of form, for example, is generally thought to be based on the retinal image information available in a single fixation. We do not know how well a simple shape judgment can be made when only part of the shape information is available in one fixation. Some ability to do this would be expected on the basis of the fact that subjects are able to make judgments about the visual direction of a point of light in the dark and detect changes in its position that occur during a saccadic eye movement. However, it is not clear from these experiments how well subjects would do in extracting form information, because the magnitude of displacement required for detection of a change is somewhat variable, and thresholds ranging between 7 and 30% of the saccade magnitude have been reported (see, e.g., Bridgeman, Hendry, & Stark, 1975; Bridgeman & Stark, 1979; Li & Matin, 1990).

Time-integrated Stimulus

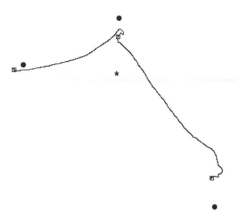

Sequence of Events

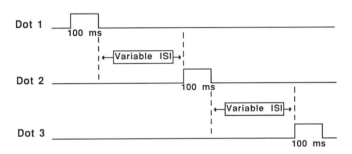

FIGURE 8.1. The stimulus, integrated over time. The points were presented in order from left to right, and the top angle of the triangle was judged acute or obtuse. When the fixed reference point was present it was located as shown by the asterisk. A typical eye movement trace during the eye movement conditions is shown. The squares show the location of the eye when the spot was presented.

Integration of Form

In an experiment in collaboration with Feldman (Hayhoe, Lachter, & Feldman, 1991) we investigated the precision with which subjects can judge the angle defined by three points. The points were presented in succession, and subjects tried to judge whether the top angle in the triangle defined by the time-integrated view was acute or obtuse. This is illustrated in Figure 8.1. The question of interest is how well subjects can do this when the eyes move in between the dot presentations, because in this case the location of the dots must be retained in a frame independent of eye position if the task is to be performed accurately. There were three conditions. In the first, subjects fixated a fixed reference point while the three points were flashed in sequence. This task simply measures the ability to integrate over time and provides a baseline by which to judge performance in the other conditions. In the other two conditions subjects were asked to move their eyes to the approximate anticipated location of each dot, so that all the dots fell in roughly the same retinal region, close to the fovea. In one case the fixation point remained present, allowing alignment of successive frames relative to this point. In the other case the fixation point was removed, so eye position information was required to compute the location of the dots. This allows us to address the issue raised in item 2 above about the mechanism by which successive retinal frames are aligned in the correct spatial relationship. These two conditions allow a comparison of the roles of visual and eye position cues in relating successive views.

As shown in Figure 8.1, the duration of each was 100 ms, and the interval between the dots was varied from simultaneous presentation to 800 ms. Because of the brief duration, no eye movements were possible for simultaneous presentation. The largest side of the triangles subtended approximately 15° of visual angle. Subjects made acute/obtuse judgments for angles ranging from 79° to 101° in 2° steps. The different angles were generated by displacement of all three dots. The triangles were randomly rotated by ±15° and translated by ±1° from trial to trial to decorrelate position of individual dots from the angle to be judged. (For one subject, MH, the rotations were ±6°, with no translations.) Subjects' heads were not fixed except when eye position was recorded, as described below. Point stimuli were displayed on an oscilloscope with P31 phosphor, and were viewed binocularly through a red cutoff filter. This roughly equated rod and cone sensitivity and reduced the visibility of phosphor persistence. Stimuli were presented at approximately 1 log unit above threshold. In a separate experiment, screen persistence was measured by opening a shutter at varying time intervals following the offset of the stimulus. Detectability measured by d' fell to zero by 7 ms. All experiments were run in the dark. Feedback was given after each trial.

Figure 8.2 shows thresholds (75% correct) for discriminating the angle from 90° as a function of interstimulus interval. The data indicate that the task is quite an easy one, with thresholds ranging from 2° to 4° for simultaneous presentation, to about twice that value at an interstimulus interval of 800 ms. Overall, the loss of position information over time is quite slow. The best performance was obtained when there was a reference point (filled circles and open triangles). There appears to be little systematic difference between these two conditions. There is some indication of a systematic elevation of thresholds for subjects KK and JL. Some small elevation of threshold might be expected because subjects

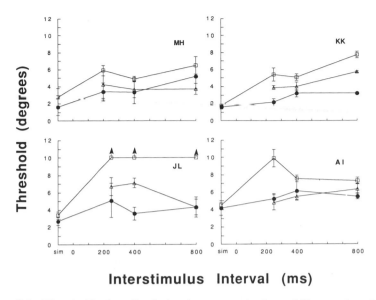

Interstimulus Interval (ms)

FIGURE 8.2. Thresholds for discriminating an angle from 90° as a function of interstimulus interval. Data for four subjects are shown for each of the three conditions. The filled circles show thresholds for the condition where subjects fixated a continuously present point. The triangles indicate the condition where the fixed reference point remained visible, but subjects moved their eyes before each point was presented, to its anticipated location. The open squares show performance when similar eye movements were made, but the reference point was removed. (No eye movements were attempted during simultaneous presentations in this condition.) The arrows for subject JL indicate failure to reach 75% criterion at the largest deviations from a right angle that were used (±11°). Standard errors are ±1 SEM between sessions.

may occasionally fail to reach the anticipated location of the dot during the interstimulus interval, so the eye will be in motion during the presentation of a dot. On the whole, when a reference point is visible it makes little difference whether or not saccades are made. Thus, there does not appear to be much added cost to integrating over saccades beyond a slow decay over time. When the reference point is removed (shown by the filled squares), subjects must use eye position information to compute the location of the dots. In this case accurate judgments are still possible, although performance declines for all subjects. There is considerable variability among subjects in this condition. Performance declines substantially for subject JL, who could not perform the task to 75% criterion level even at 11° deviations from a right angle, which were the largest ones we explored. For MH, however, thresholds are elevated only slightly. Subjects can clearly use eye position information to integrate in an external reference frame, although performance is improved with a fixed reference point.

It is difficult to specify exactly how these angle thresholds translate into the spatial precision with which each point is known, but we can get some idea of how they are related. If all of the error were in the estimated position of only one of the points (that is, the other two were known exactly), and if the direction of the error was in the direction from the true location that maximized the change in angle, then a threshold of 2° in this experiment would correspond to only a 14-min arc positional error. This value increases proportionately to the threshold, so that a 6° threshold, for example, would correspond to a 42-min arc displacement in one of the points. In actuality, however, this error will be dependent on the direction of error in each of the points on a particular trial, so this value is a lower bound to the total error in the three points. Also, the error will in fact be distributed roughly equally between the three points. Given the retinal eccentricities and the magnitude of the eye movements involved, this performance is remarkably good.

An important question here is whether subjects were moving their eyes as instructed. To investigate this we monitored eye position in a separate set of trials for each of the subjects using an SRI Dual Purkinje Image eye tracker (Generation V). Subjects performed as expected with little difficulty. A typical eye movement trace during a trial is shown in Figure 8.1. The squares show the location of the eye when the spot was presented. Although we cannot guarantee that this reflects performance in the trials in which the data in Figure 8.2 were collected, major deviations would be surprising, as the appearance of the dots provided subjects with feedback as to whether they were moving their eyes approximately to the correct locations.

We also ran control trials to investigate whether subjects were basing their performance on all three dots. On these trials only the first two dots were presented. Despite the random rotations and translations, the slope of the line defined by these two dots is partly correlated with the size of the angle to be judged, so above-chance performance would be expected if judgments are based on this information alone. Although subjects responded above chance with two dots, as expected, performance was substantially better with three dots.

It is clear from this experiment that quite precise judgments of form can be made from information gathered from separate fixations. The representation used to make these judgments appears to be similar to that underlying ordinary perceptual judgments, because there is only a slow falloff in performance with time. Whether this representation is best described as a perceptual or memory representation is not clear. In this experiment the offset of each of the dots is apparent, but the subject has a clear "sense" of a triangle. However, because of its precision it is not well described as semantic or propositional as suggested most explicitly by

O'Regan and Levy-Schoen (1983), and it seems more likely that the integration is performed at some intermediate level of visual representation. It is hard to form more definitive conclusions than this from a single experiment. The form information in this experiment does not emerge until after integration, so our results are consistent with integration at a precategorical level, perhaps at a level like Feldman's stable feature frame (Feldman, 1985). However, it may be the case that the task is only possible when the subject uses attention to encode the location of each of the dots, and experiments are currently under way by Lachter to investigate this possibility. This would be consistent with Irwin's suggestion that visual memory across saccades is capacity limited (Irwin, 1991; see also Irwin's chapter, ths volume). Just how limited is not clear at this point, and may require investigation of extended, complex scenes.

The sort of visual memory revealed here, which integrates information from different locations in an extended spatial representation, seems most closely related to that revealed in aperture-viewing experiments. When subjects track an aperture moving across a figure the form can be perceived (Rock & Halper, 1969; Rock & Sigman, 1973). This demonstrates integration in a spatial frame for the pursuit system, resembling ours with saccades. This suggests that fundamentally similar processes operate during both pursuit and saccadic eye movements to construct a world-centered representation, despite the fact that different neural mechanisms control the two types of movement. Form perception is also possible when the aperture is fixed and the object moves behind it (Hochberg, 1968; Parks, 1965). Although this is partly due to painting of the image on the retina by pursuit eye movements (e.g., Anstis & Atkinson, 1967; Haber & Nathanson, 1968; Morgan, Findlay, & Watt, 1982), form judgments are clearly still possible when the eye is stationary (Hochberg, 1968; Morgan et al., 1982).

Our results also have implications for the mechanisms of visual stability. The potential role of purely visual cues, in addition to eye position information, has long been recognized (Gibson, 1966; MacKay, 1973). The importance of visual reference frames has been demonstrated in judgments of visual direction, where visual information dominates over eye-position signals when the two are in conflict (Bridgeman & Fishman, 1985; Matin, et al., 1982; Stark & Bridgeman, 1983). Visual stability requires that the appropriate relation between frames is achieved as well as preserving the relation between the scene and the observer, which is reflected in visual direction judgments. When the relation between successive frames is not consistent with the corollary discharge signal, as when the eyes are partially paralyzed, transient instabilities result (Stark & Bridgeman, 1983; Stevens et al., 1976). This indicates that the eye movement signal is actively operating even in a normally lighted environment to relate successive views. However, the results of the present experiment clearly indicate a visual matching strategy in relating successive views, because subjects do better when successive frames can be aligned with respect to the fixed reference point. The variability between subjects without a reference point indicates wide variability in the fidelity of the eye position signal or in the ability to use it. This subject variability essentially disappears in the reference point condition. This, together with the superior performance in this condition, suggests that the visual reference information is used to refine eye position information, and that spatial locations of objects in successive frames are assigned with respect to objects common to the frames. In the next experiment we explore further the relationship between these two sorts of information.

Saccades to Remembered Visual Targets

As discussed above, it is clearly necessary to retain sufficient visual information from previous views to allow one to construct the spatially extended representations underlying both long- and short-term spatial memory, in order to subserve behaviors such as finding one's way around a large building, or orienting toward an object not currently in view—for example, when we look up from the computer terminal to reach for a book from the shelves, or turn around to answer a knock at the door. Recently, Hayhoe, Moeller, Ballard, and Albano (1990) investigated the reference frames that determine eye movements to remembered locations in space, and in this context we can make some conclusions about how visual relationships and knowledge of eye position are combined to determine the perception of spatial position.

To make an eye movement toward a remembered object we must have some record of the location of the object in memory. What is the nature of that record? There are two ways we can encode the location of an object: As described above, the classical idea is that its location on the retina is combined with an efference copy signal of eye position to compute spatial location. The other way we can encode location is in relation to other objects. In the case of targets that are not currently in view it seems almost inevitable that the locations are remembered in terms of their relationship to other objects—for example, my telephone is to the right of my computer terminal. Storing the positions of objects this way means that one does not need to take into account changes in eye or body position. In this experiment we attempted to see how these two sources of information are combined. We did this by putting the visual relationship information in conflict with the position of the target relative to the observer.

Observers viewed a cathode ray tube (CRT) screen in complete darkness with their heads stabilized by a bite bar. As shown in Figure 8.3, there were two conditions: sequential and simultaneous. In the sequential

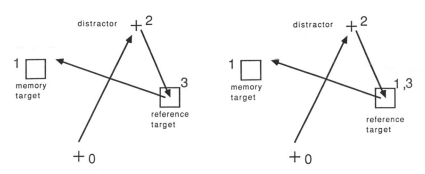

FIGURE 8.3. The sequence of events in the simultaneous and sequential conditions, as described in the text. The numbers beside the stimuli indicate their order in the sequence of events. Note that in the simultaneous condition the reference target appears twice. The solid lines with arrows indicate saccades.

condition the sequence of events was as follows: At the beginning of a trial, a fixation point was presented until the observer directed his gaze at it. This point was then extinguished and the observer maintained his gaze in this direction during a dark interval of 500 ms. The target to be remembered was then presented for 500 ms. This was followed by another dark interval. Then a distractor stimulus was presented for 250 ms and the subject was required to make a saccade to this target. After another dark interval, yet another visual target was presented, called the reference target. This target was the signal for the subject to make a saccade first to the center of the box and then to the location of the memory target. The target boxes were about 0.8° on a side, and the subject was instructed to saccade to the center of the box. The reference target remained visible during both these movements. The subject was instructed to return to the reference box following the saccade to the remembered location. In this condition no more than one visual stimulus is present at any one time. In order to make the eye movement to the memory target, the visuomotor system must take into account the two intervening eye movements to the distractor and reference targets.

Trials for the simultaneous condition were intermixed with the sequential trials. The only difference in these trials was that the reference box was presented at the same time as the memory target so that the observer could encode the position of the target relative to the reference box. The reference target was then presented a second time following the eye movement to the distractor. There was also one other difference: the reference box was sometimes shifted up or down by a small amount on the second presentation without the subject's knowledge. The question is,

Does the subject simply go to the actual location of the memory target, or does he use the remembered relationship between the boxes to guide him? In this case he would go to a location that was shifted up or down by the amount that the reference target was shifted. Because we did not want subjects using conscious strategies we made the displacement quite small ($\pm 1°$), and the distractor target served to make the displacement less detectable. Three naive subjects were used. Two of the three were unaware that the shifts were being made; the third spontaneously reported occasional shifts. However, these reports were unreliable, because apparent shifts also occurred when none were in fact made. In a subsequent experiment we examined whether or not the shifts were detectable by explicitly asking subjects to detect the displacement. In this experiment we found that detectability as measured by d' was about 0.5 so we can assume that for the most part subjects were not using conscious strategies and that the displacement was only barely detectable.

To prevent subjects from learning target locations, targets appeared in a range of locations across trials. No feedback about performance was given. The relationship between memory and reference targets was also varied. The distance between memory and reference targets varied between 5° and 10°, and the angle of the line connecting the two targets varied between $-40°$ and $+40°$. Eye positions were recorded by means of an SRI eye tracker.

The landing points of the saccades to the memory target were determined and from these points we computed two statistics: the mean landing point, which indicates if there is any overall bias in targeting, and the standard deviation of the landing points, which is a measure of precision, measuring how close to the target the landing points generally fall.

The mean landing points for one subject are shown in Figure 8.4. Zero on this plot indicates the location of the target. The x axis is roughly in the direction of the saccade and the y axis is roughly perpendicular to the saccade. The circle shows the mean landing point in the sequential condition. The upward triangle shows mean landing point for the simultaneous condition when the reference box was shifted up by 1°, and the downward triangle shows the mean landing point when the reference box was shifted down by 1°. The error bars are between-session standard errors of the mean. Shifting the reference point clearly biased the mean landing points in the direction of the shift. However, the bias is only about half the amount by which the reference box was shifted. A similar result was found on two other subjects. The results are summarized in Figure 8.5, which shows the difference in mean landing points for the two simultaneous conditions for each subject. This difference was divided by two, so this represents the effects of the shift in just one direction. That is, a difference of 1° would mean the landing point shifted by the same amount as the reference box. Zero would mean that subjects went to the actual location of the target and were unaffected by the shift in the

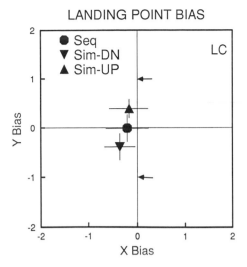

FIGURE 8.4. Mean landing points for one subject in the sequential condition (circle) and the simultaneous condition with the reference target shifted up (upward triangle) or down (downward triangle.) The point (0,0) is the actual target position, and the x axis is in the direction of the saccade. The error bars are ±1 SEM between sessions. The arrows show the extent of the shift of the reference target.

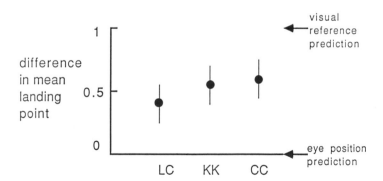

FIGURE 8.5. Shift in mean landing point for the simultaneous condition, averaged over the upward and downward shift trials, for three subjects. Zero indicates the actual memory target location. One indicates the extent of the shift of the reference target, in degrees.

reference. In fact, the landing points are displaced by about half that of the shift in the reference box. This indicates that information about the visual relationship and information about position relative to the body are being given about equal weight.

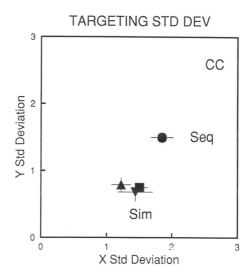

FIGURE 8.6. Standard deviations of the landing points for the sequential condition (circle) and the three simultaneous conditions: no shift (square), shifted up (upward triangle), and shifted down (downward triangle). Error bars are between-sessions standard errors of the estimates.

One not very interesting way that we could obtain this result would be if subjects detected the shift on some trials and consciously based their eye movements on the relationship on those trials, whereas on other trials they simply ignored the relationship information and based their saccades on the memory of position relative to the body. We can rule out this possibility by examining the variability in the landing points. This is shown in Figure 8.6, which plots the standard deviation of the landing points in the x direction (i.e., along the trajectory of the saccade) against the standard deviation in the y direction, perpendicular to the saccade. The variability in the landing points is greatest in the sequential condition (filled circle), when eye position information alone must be used to compute the location of the target. When the reference point is available, the variability is reduced by about 50%. The square is for the simultaneous condition, with no shift, and the triangles for the simultaneous condition with the reference shifted up or down. The variability is very similar whether or not the reference box has been shifted. That is, shifting the reference box simply shifts the landing points up or down without increasing their variance. This rules out the hypothesis where subjects shift conscious strategies from trial to trial, as this would lead to greatest variance in the shift conditions. This result was also observed with the other two subjects.

Instead, the data suggest the more interesting possibility that eye position and visual context signals are averaged to determine spatial location, and neither one alone is given priority. Eye position information is not suppressed or ignored when relational information is present. Rather, there is some internal average of the two sorts of information. It is also interesting to note that in a recent experiment Matin and Fox (1989) found a similar averaging of the effects of visual context and eye and head position signals on judgments of eye level horizontal. It seems likely that the relative weights of the two sorts of information in the present situation may depend on the complexity of the context. In judgments of egocentric visual direction Bridgeman & Graziano (1989) found the greatest influence, or "capture," by the visual context with a complex scene. A random dot texture had less influence. The visual context we have provided in the present experiment is a rather minimal one, and it may be that the visual relationship information gets progressively more weight as the context is made more complex.

Conclusions

To return to the question of integration across saccades, the picture that emerges from previous work is that nothing like an iconic image is retained from the previous view, but we still have only limited understanding of just what is retained. Experiments by Irwin (1991) suggest rather strict capacity limits on memory for visual patterns across eye movements. A series of studies by Pollatsek and Rayner, reviewed in their chapter in this volume, suggests limited interaction between the pre- and postsaccadic stimuli. The interactions that are observed appear to be in a representation that is independent of spatial location and this suggests that what is retained is at a level involved in location-independent pattern recognition. It may be important to consider the tasks involved, however. The above tasks involve same-different judgments of patterns, and pattern naming, tasks that need to be accomplished by the visual system independent of spatial location. In the present experiments, however, a different domain is explored, that of spatial memory where there is a clear need, and ability, to relate locations in successive views. The performance demonstrated in these tasks reveals a precise and slowly decaying representation of spatial location that is integrated across eye movements. This may be a consequence of the separate processing of pattern and location information in ventral and dorsal streams in the extrastriate visual cortex.

Acknowledgments. This work was supported by NIH grant EY05729 to Mary Hayhoe, EY01319 to the Center for Visual Science, and an NSF predoctoral fellowship to Joel Lachter.

References

Anstis, S.M., & Atkinson, J. (1967). Distortions in moving figures viewed through a stationary slit. *American Journal of Psychology*, *80*, 572–585.

Breitmeyer, B.G., Kropfl, W., & Julesz, B. (1982). The existence and role of retinotopic and spatiotopic forms of visual persistence. *Acta Psychologica*, *52*, 175–196.

Bridgeman, B., & Fishman, R. (1985). Dissociation of corollary discharge from gaze direction does not induce a straight-ahead shift. *Perception and Psychophysics*, *37*, 523–528.

Bridgeman, B., & Graziano, J.A. (1989). Effect of context and efference copy on visual straight ahead. *Vision Research*, *29*, 1729–1736.

Bridgeman, B., Hendry, D., & Stark, L. (1975). Failure to detect displacement of the visual world during saccadic eye movements. *Vision Research*, *15*, 719–722.

Bridgeman, B., & Stark, L. (1979). Omnidirectional increase in threshold for image shifts during saccadic eye movements. *Perception and Psychophysics*, *25*, 241–243.

Feldman, J.A. (1985). Four frames suffice: A provisional model of vision and space. *Behavioral and Brain Sciences*, *8*, 265–289.

Gibson, J.J. (1966). *The senses considered as perceptual systems*. Boston: Houghton Mifflin.

Haber, R.N., & Nathanson, L.S. (1968). Post-retinal storage? Some further observations on Parks' camel as seen through the eye of a needle. *Perception and Psychophysics*, *3*, 349–355.

Hayhoe, M.M., Lachter, J., & Feldman, J.A. (1991). Integration of form across saccadic eye movements. *Perception*, *20*, 393–402.

Hayhoe, M.M., Moeller, P., Ballard, D., & Albano, J.E. (1990). Guidance of saccades to remembered targets and the perception of spatial position. *Investigative Ophthalmology and Visual Science (Suppl.)*, *31*, 603.

Hochberg, J. (1968). In the mind's eye. In R.N. Haber (Ed.), *Contemporary theory and research in visual perception*. New York: Appleton-Century-Crofts.

Husain, M., Treue, S., & Andersen, R.A., (1989). Surface interpolation in three-dimensional structure-from-motion perception. *Neural Computation*, *1*, 324–333.

Irwin, D.E. (1991). Information integration across saccadic eye movements. *Cognitive Psychology*, *23*, 420–456.

Irwin, D.E., Brown, J.S., & Sun, J.S. (1988). Visual masking and visual integration across saccadic eye movements. *Journal of Experimental Psychology: General*, *117*, 276–287.

Irwin, D.E., Yantis, S., & Jonides, J. (1983). Evidence against visual integration across saccadic eye movements. *Perception and Psychophysics*, *34*, 49–57.

Irwin, D.E., Zacks, J.L., & Brown, J.S. (1990). Visual memory and the perception of a stable visual environment. *Perception and Psychophysics*, *47*, 35–46.

Jonides, J., Irwin, D.E., & Yantis, S. (1982). Integrating visual information from successive fixations. *Science*, *215*, 192–194.

Li, W., & Matin, L. (1990). Saccadic suppression of displacement: influence of postsaccadic exposure duration and of saccadic stimulus elimination. *Vision Research*, *30*(6), 945–955.

MacKay, D.M. (1973). Visual stability and voluntary eye movements. In R. Jung (Ed.), *Handbook of sensory physiology*. Berlin: Springer.

Matin, L. (1986). Visual localization and eye movements. In K.R. Boff, L. Kaufman, & J.P. Thomas (Eds.), *Handbook of perception and human performance, Vol. 1: Sensory processes and perception*. New York: John Wiley.

Matin, L., & Fox, C.R. (1989). Visually perceived eye level and perceived elevation of objects: Linearly additive influences from visual field pitch and from gravity. *Vision Research, 29*, 315–324.

Matin, L., Picoult, E., Stevens, J.K., Edwards, M.W. Jr., Young, D., & MacArthur, R. (1982). Oculoparalytic illusion: Visual-field dependent spatial mislocalizations by humans partially paralyzed with curare. *Science, 26*, 198–201.

McConkie, G.W., & Rayner, K. (1976). Identifying the span of the effective stimulus in reading: Literature review and theories of reading. In H. Singer & R.B. Ruddell (Eds.), *Theoretical models and processes of reading* (pp. 137–162). Newark, DE: International Reading Association.

McConkie, G.W., & Zola, D. (1979). Is visual information integrated across successive fixations in reading? *Perception and Psychophysics, 25*, 221–224.

Morgan, M.J., Findlay, J.M., & Watt, R.J. (1982). Aperture viewing: a review and a synthesis. *Quarterly Journal of Experimental Psychology, 34*, 211–233.

O'Regan, J.K., & Levy-Schoen, A. (1983). Integrating visual information from successive fixations: Does trans-saccadic fusion exist? *Vision Research, 23*, 765–768.

Parks, T.E. (1965). Post-retinal visual storage. *American Journal of Psychology, 78*, 145–147.

Pollatsek, A., Rayner, K., & Collins, W.E. (1984). Integrating pictorial information across eye movements. *Journal of Experimental Psychology: General, 113*, 426–442.

Pollatsek, A., Rayner, K., & Henderson, J.M. (1990). Role of spatial location in integration of pictorial information across saccades. *Journal of Experimental Psychology: Human Perception and Performance, 16*, 199–210.

Rayner, K., McConkie, G.W., & Zola, D. (1980). Integrating information across eye movements. *Cognitive Psychology, 12*, 206–226.

Rayner, K., & Pollatsek, A. (1983). Is visual information integrated across saccades? *Perception and Psychophysics, 34*, 39–48.

Rock, I., & Halper, F. (1969). Form perception without a retinal image. *American Journal of Psychology, 82*, 425–440.

Rock, I., & Sigman, E. (1973). Intelligence factors in perception of form through a moving slit. *Perception, 2*, 357–369.

Stark, L., & Bridgeman, B. (1983). Role of corollary discharge in space constancy. *Perception and Psychophysics, 34*, 371–380.

Stevens, J.K., Emerson, R.C., Gerstein, G.L., Kallos, T., Neufeld, G.R., Nichols, C.W., & Rosenquist, A.C. (1976). Paralysis of the awake human: visual perceptions. *Vision Research, 16*, 93–98.

Treue, S., Husain, M., & Andersen, R.A. (1991). Human perception of structure from motion *Vision Research, 31*, 59–75.

9
Visual Memory Within and Across Fixations

DAVID E. IRWIN

A single eye fixation encompasses approximately 25,000 square degrees of the visual world, roughly 180° horizontally by 130° vertically (Harrington, 1981). The quality of the visual information that is available in this total area is quite variable, however. The area that is seen most clearly, with the highest resolution, corresponds to that part of the world that falls on the fovea, but this includes only 3 or 4 square degrees out of the 25,000 that are available. Visual acuity drops off very rapidly with increasing retinal eccentricity, being reduced by 50% at a distance of 5° from the fovea and by 90% at 40° (Hochberg, 1978). Because of these acuity limitations, humans make eye, head, and body movements to fixate objects of interest in the world; somehow the contents of these successive fixations must be combined across movements to produce a coherent representation of the visual environment. How this combination is accomplished has puzzled psychologists and vision researchers for over a century.

Research in my laboratory has addressed two aspects of this puzzle: memory for the contents of individual fixations, and information integration from successive fixations. One goal of my research has been to uncover the characteristics of the memory or memories that preserve position and identity information from a single glance at a scene, based on the assumption that an understanding of how the contents of individual fixations are analyzed and coded is necessary before one can understand how information is combined across eye movements; a second goal has been to determine what role, if any, these memories might play in integrating information across eye movements. In this chapter I will summarize the progress I have made toward achieving these goals and discuss what my findings reveal about the mechanisms that underlie our perception of a coherent visual environment.

Memory for the Contents of a Single Fixation

"Iconic" Memory

It has been known for centuries that visual sensation persists after stimulus offset; the writings of Aristotle (384 322 B.C.) reportedly contain the first known reference to this phenomenon (Allen, 1926). Sperling (1960) is most responsible for reviving contemporary interest in this property of the visual system. In Sperling's experiments, subjects were presented an array of letters for a brief time. Following stimulus offset, a subset of the information in the array was cued for report. Sperling found that subjects' recall performance for cued information was very high if the cue was presented immediately after stimulus offset, but recall accuracy decreased as the time between stimulus offset and cue presentation increased. These results contrasted with performance when subjects were asked to report the entire array of letters. Under these circumstances, recall performance was limited to only a few items from the array. Taken together, these results suggested that immediately following stimulus offset there was more information available about the array than could be normally reported, but this information disappeared quickly with the passage of time. Subsequent experiments showed that the visual characteristics of the exposure fields presented before and after the stimulus array had a sizable effect on performance, indicating that the persisting information was indeed visual. The method of sampling a subset of the total information present in an array has been called the *partial report technique*, and the superior recall performance under these conditions (relative to full report) the *partial report superiority effect*.

Other, more "direct" methods of investigating visual persistence were developed soon after (see Coltheart, 1980, and Long, 1980, for comprehensive reviews). Sperling (1967), for example, introduced a technique for measuring the phenomenal duration of a stimulus by adjusting the occurrence of a probe so that its onset and offset appeared to be synchronous with stimulus onset and offset. Estimates of persistence duration obtained with this method were similar to those obtained from partial report (e.g., Haber & Standing, 1970). Eriksen and Collins (1967, 1968) introduced a technique in which two random dot patterns were presented sequentially in time, separated by an interstimulus interval. When superimposed, these patterns formed a nonsense syllable. They found that subjects could temporally integrate the two dot patterns to perceive the nonsense syllable over intervals as long as 100 ms, yielding an estimate of persistence duration similar to that obtained from partial report.

As a result of studies like these, almost all contemporary models of visual information processing now assume the existence of a very short-term visual memory that stores the contents of a visual scene for some period of time after its offset. Until fairly recently, the characteristics of this memory (usually called "iconic memory" after Neisser, 1967) were thought to be well known; based on the results of hundreds of partial-report and "direct measurement" studies, the consensus view of iconic memory was that it was a visible, precategorical, high capacity, quickly decaying memory whose purpose was to register incoming visual information and hold it for further processing by other components of the information processing system (Coltheart, Lea, & Thompson, 1974; Dick, 1974; von Wright, 1972). This simple, one-store view of iconic memory appears to be wrong, however. Rather, there appear to be several different kinds of early visual memory. Coltheart (1980) has convincingly argued that visible persistence (the phenomenal lingering trace of an extinguished stimulus measured by "direct" persistence methods) and informational persistence (knowledge about the visual properties of an extinguished stimulus, measured by partial report) are separate forms of visual memory; this argument is based on the fact that direct persistence tasks and partial report tasks are affected differently by stimulus variables such as intensity and duration. Visible persistence duration decreases as stimulus duration and stimulus intensity increase (e.g., Bowen, Pola, & Matin, 1974; Di Lollo, 1980; Efron, 1970), but duration and intensity have little or no effect on informational persistence (Adelson & Jonides, 1980; Irwin & Yeomans, 1986; Loftus, 1985; Yeomans & Irwin, 1985). If visible persistence and informational persistence rely on the same unitary memory, they should be affected in the same way by the same stimulus variables.

Another problem for the unitary view of iconic memory is that partial report performance appears to rely on more than just raw stimulus persistence. Several investigators have found that most errors in partial report tasks are location errors rather than identification errors; in other words, errors tend to be reports of noncued letters in the array rather than reports of letters that were not presented (Dick, 1969; Townsend, 1973). Furthermore, increasing the familiarity of the stimulus array increases accuracy by reducing identification errors (Mewhort, Campbell, Marchetti, & Campbell, 1981). These results suggest that partial report performance relies, at least in part, on a postcategorical store that contains identity codes for the displayed items.

Based on these findings, Coltheart (1980) argued that "iconic memory" is actually a conflation of at least three kinds of stimulus persistence: neural persistence, or residual activity in the visual pathway; visible persistence, or the phenomenal impression that the stimulus is still visibly present; and informational persistence, knowledge about the visual properties of the stimulus. Coltheart argued that visible persistence is merely a by-product of neural persistence, whereas informational persistence might have a postcategorical basis.

Based on Coltheart's arguments, Irwin and Yeomans (1986) and Irwin and Brown (1987) attempted to better define the characteristics of informational persistence. Irwin and Yeomans (1986) conducted three experiments in which 3 × 3 letter arrays were presented for exposure durations ranging from 50 to 500 ms. Some time after array offset, a single-character mask was presented at one of the letter locations; this mask cued the subject to report the entire row of the array containing the mask. Of interest was the effect of exposure duration and cue delay on report of the masked letter in the cued row relative to report of the nonmasked letters in that row. Irwin and Yeomans (1986) found that report of the masked letter was significantly worse than report of the nonmasked letters for cue delays of 0 to 150 ms, after which time masked and nonmasked letter report was no different. This was true for every exposure duration tested, although overall accuracy increased and identification errors decreased as exposure duration increased. These results indicate that partial-report performance is based on at least two memory components: a relatively brief, visual (i.e., maskable) component whose duration is independent of stimulus exposure duration, and a long-lasting, nonmaskable, postcategorical component. Irwin and Brown (1987) replicated these findings and further discovered that the first component was precategorical, and the second had a limited capacity of about five stimulus items. The first memory component differs from visible persistence in that its duration is independent of stimulus exposure duration; it differs from the traditional conception of short-term memory in that it has a brief duration and is maskable. The second component, on the other hand, is not discriminable from short-term memory—both are long-lasting, limited-capacity, postcategorical memories. In sum, partial report performance appears to rely on short-term memory and on a brief, precategorical, visual memory that is nonvisible but maintains form and structure information about the contents of a display for a constant period of time after stimulus offset. I'll use the term *informational persistence* to refer to this latter memory.

Visual Matching

The "iconic memory" studies reviewed above suggest the existence of three kinds of memory for individual fixations: visible persistence, a highly detailed, phenomenal trace of the fixation; informational persistence, a nonvisible but maskable representation that maintains form and structure information about the contents of the fixation; and visual short-term memory, which holds a more abstract description of the display. Additional evidence for the existence of these three memory components is provided by an unpublished set of same-different matching experiments from my laboratory. These studies were based on the work of Phillips (1974). On each experimental trial a random-dot pattern (usually 12 dots randomly chosen from a 5 × 5 dot matrix) was presented for some duration in the center of an oscilloscopic display. Some time after the

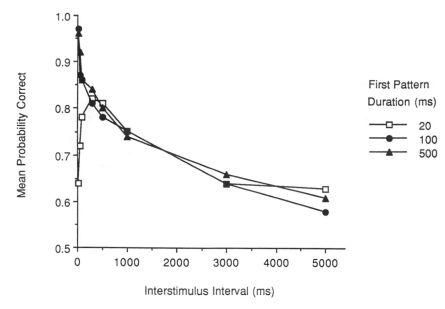

FIGURE 9.1. Same-different judgments of random dot patterns viewed within fixations. Mean probability correct is a function of ISI and first pattern duration.

offset of this pattern, a second pattern of 12 dots was presented; this second pattern was either identical to the first or different by the displacement of one dot. Subjects indicated whether the two patterns were identical or different, and accuracy was the dependent variable. The experimental chamber was illuminated to eliminate visible phosphor persistence.

Figure 9.1 shows the results of one such experiment. In this experiment the first pattern was presented for either 20, 100, or 500 ms, and the second pattern was presented (for 20 ms) either 10, 50, 100, 300, 500, 1,000, 3,000, or 5,000 ms after the offset of the first pattern. For short exposure durations (20 ms), accuracy increased as the interstimulus interval (ISI) between the two patterns increased from 10 to 300 ms. Accuracy then remained fairly constant and quite high for ISIs of 300 to 500 ms, then declined (but remained above chance) as ISI increased from 500 to 5,000 ms. For long exposure durations (100 and 500 ms) a similar pattern of performance was found, except there was no decrement in performance at the shortest ISIs. A second experiment showed that shifting the second pattern, so that it occupied different retinal and spatial coordinates from the first pattern, disrupted accuracy for both short- and long-exposure displays for ISIs as long as 300 ms, but shifts after this time had no effect on accuracy. A third experiment found that interposing a masking stimulus between the two patterns interfered with both short- and long-exposure displays for ISIs as long as 250 ms. A fourth experiment found that pattern complexity had no effect at ISIs below 1 second, but at longer intervals accuracy was higher for simple displays than for complex displays.

These results provide some additional support for the existence of three distinct forms of visual memory for individual fixations. As noted earlier, visible persistence causes temporal integration of successive visual displays whose onsets occur during a 100-ms window of time (e.g., Di Lollo, 1980; Eriksen & Collins, 1967). Thus, visible persistence would cause a decrement in same-different matching accuracy when brief stimulus exposures were separated by a short ISI because the two patterns would fuse into a single perceptual composite and subjects would be unable to tell whether the two patterns were identical or different. Because visible persistence duration decreases with increasing stimulus duration and is negligible for stimulus exposures exceeding 100 ms, long-exposure displays would not suffer any accuracy decrement at the shortest ISIs.

The second form of memory suggested by these results appears to operate at ISIs between 0 and 500 ms, and it corresponds to informational persistence. Some of its characteristics are revealed by the 100 ms- and 500 ms-duration curves in Figure 9.1. It appears to hold a well-defined but nonvisible representation of the array, allowing subjects to respond with a high degree of accuracy. Furthermore, it is unaffected by stimulus duration. The second and thrid experiments indicate that it is maskable and it is disrupted by pattern displacement, however. The fourth experiment shows that stimulus complexity has no effect on informational persistence, so it appears to have a high capacity.

The third form of memory revealed by these visual matching experiments appears to have a long duration and to hold only an abstract, schematic representation of the array, with little detail. This memory has a limited capacity, as shown by its sensitivity to stimulus complexity. This memory presumably corresponds to visual short-term memory.

Summary

The results of several partial report, visible persistence, and visual matching studies from my laboratory converge in defining three levels of visual memory for the contents of individual fixations.[1] These memories appear to have the following characteristics: The first level, visible persistence, is a phenomenal trace of an extinguished display that fuses with successive visual displays if display onsets are separated by less than 100 ms or so.

---

[1] Of course, there are undoubtedly other forms of memory for the contents of individual fixations as well, such as short-term conceptual memory (Intraub, 1980, 1984; Loftus & Ginn, 1984; Potter, 1976, 1983) and long-term memory (e.g., Friedman, 1979; Nelson & Loftus, 1980; Pezdek et al., 1988), but their role in information integration across eye movements is unclear.

The studies reported above do not specify whether visible persistence is coded in retinotopic or spatiotopic (i.e., environmental) coordinates (or both); visible persistence might play a role in information integration across eye movements if persistence is coded in spatiotopic coordinates. The second level of memory, informational persistence, appears to be a high-capacity, maskable representation that is precategorical, with a duration that is independent of stimulus exposure duration, capable of coding form and location information in a precise way. These characteristics make it a plausible candidate for mediating information integration across eye movements. The third level of memory, visual short-term memory, is an abstract, postcategorical memory that is nonmaskable, has a limited capacity, and a long duration. It too may play a role in information integration across saccades, though its limited capacity would be restricting. The eye movement studies described below have begun to investigate what role these visual memories might play in the integration of information from successive flxations.

Integration of Information from Successive Fixations

Spatiotopic Visible Persistence

Much of the research that I have conducted on this topic has concerned the role that visible persistence might play in integration across eye movements. The reason for this is that many investigators have hypothesized that a spatiotopically coded level of visible persistence could explain in an intuitively satisfying way human perception of a stable and continuous visual world across changes in eye position (e.g., Banks, 1983; Breitmeyer, 1984; Breitmeyer, Kropfl, & Julesz, 1982; Jonides, Irwin, & Yantis, 1982; McConkie & Rayner, 1976; Trehub, 1977). According to this hypothesis, at some level in the perceptual system there exists a visible representation of the fixation that is coded in environmental or spatiotopic coordinates, rather than retinotopic coordinates; when the eyes move, the contents of the new fixation are simply fused with the contents of the old fixation at this spatiotopic level, yielding an integrated, composite image of the visual environment. Despite the intuitive appeal of this hypothesis, substantial empirical evidence suggests that spatiotopic visible persistence does not exist, and that information integration across saccades does not depend on spatiotopic "fusion" of visual information (see Irwin, in press, for a detailed review). Below I will describe the results of two studies that support this conclusion.

To test for the existence of spatiotopic visible persistence, Irwin, Brown, and Sun (1988) used a temporal integration task that Jonides, Irwin, and Yantis (1982) had used to study integration across eye movements. This task was based on a paradigm developed by Di Lollo (1977,

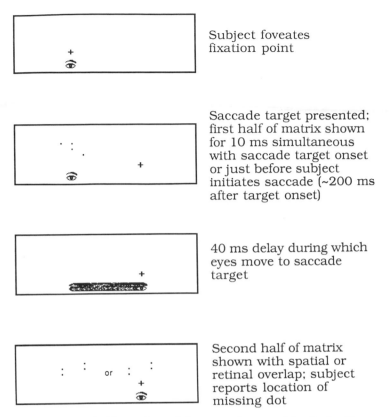

Subject foveates
fixation point

Saccade target presented;
first half of matrix shown
for 10 ms simultaneous
with saccade target onset
or just before subject
initiates saccade (~200 ms
after target onset)

40 ms delay during which
eyes move to saccade
target

Second half of matrix
shown with spatial or
retinal overlap; subject
reports location of
missing dot

FIGURE 9.2. Schematic illustration of the procedure used by Irwin, Brown, and Sun (1988) to investigate retinotopic and spatiotopic integration across saccades.

1980) to study retinotopic visible persistence. Di Lollo's procedure was very similar to that used by Eriksen and Collins (1967) in their studies of visible persistence that were described earlier. In Di Lollo's experiments two halves of a dot matrix, minus one dot, were presented in two frames of time, and the subject had to report the location of the missing dot. Performing this task accurately is quite difficult unless the subject can integrate the persisting image of the first frame of dots with the second frame of dots to perceive a single composite representation. Di Lollo found that when the two frames of dots were presented to the fixating eye, integration accuracy and the perception of a fused composite image decreased as the temporal interval between the two frames increased. These results provide evidence for a short-lived retinotopic visible persistence, consistent with Eriksen and Collins (1967). To determine whether retinotopic and/or spatiotopic visible persistence survives an eye movement, Irwin et al. presented the first frame of dots during one fixation and the second frame of dots during a second fixation, after a saccade had been made (Figure 9.2). Sometimes the second frame of dots was presented in the same spatial area as the first frame, and sometimes in the same retinal area, so that the two halves of the matrix overlapped either spatially but not retinally (thereby measuring spatiotopic visible persistence), or retinally but not spatially (measuring retinotopic visible persistence). The temporal interval between the two frames of dots was varied by presenting the first frame either just before, or well before, the saccade occurred. In the Irwin et al. experiment, interframe intervals averaged 69 ms in the short-interval condition and 246 ms in the long-interval condition. Eye position was monitored throughout the experiment. The stimuli were presented on an oscilloscope that subjects viewed through filters that eliminated visible phosphor persistence (this was true of all the eye movement experiments conducted in my laboratory reported in this chapter).

In addition to these saccade trials, Irwin et al. (1988) collected data from two no-saccade control conditions. In one condition, both frames of dots were presented foveally while the subject maintained fixation at one location; thus, the two halves of the matrix overlapped retinally and spatially, as in Di Lollo's experiments. In the other control condition, the first frame was presented foveally and the second frame was presented peripherally, so that the two halves of the matrix overlapped neither retinally nor spatially; this control allowed for an assessment of task performance when no persistence-based integration was possible. Also note that the first control mimicked the retinal layout of the retinal overlap saccade trials, whereas the second control mimicked the retinal layout of the spatial overlap saccade trials. Short and long interframe intervals were used in these no-saccade control conditions so that they could serve as reference points for performance in the saccade conditions.

The results of this experiment are shown in Figure 9.3. When a short interval separated the two frames of dots, integration accuracy exceeded that of the no-overlap control only in the retinal overlap and retinal + spatial overlap conditions. When a long interval separated the two frames of dots, performance in no condition exceeded that of the no-overlap control. The results of the retinal + spatial overlap condition agree with those of Di Lollo (1980): integration accuracy decreased as the interval between the two dot frames increased when the frames were viewed foveally during maintained fixation. The results of the retinal overlap saccade condition reveal that retinotopic integration across saccades is possible when short temporal intervals separate the onsets of successive visual displays. Of course, this situation rarely occurs under ordinary viewing conditions because typical fixation durations approximate 250 ms; that is why people do not experience overlapping visual images when they move their eyes. Most importantly, there was no evidence for spatiotopic integration across saccades at either short or long temporal intervals. In sum, these results provide evidence for the existence of retinotopic visible

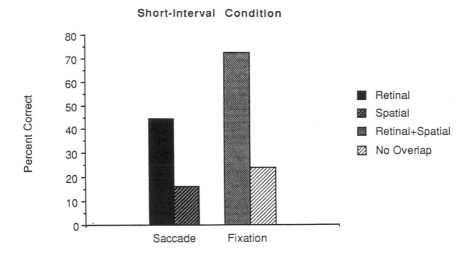

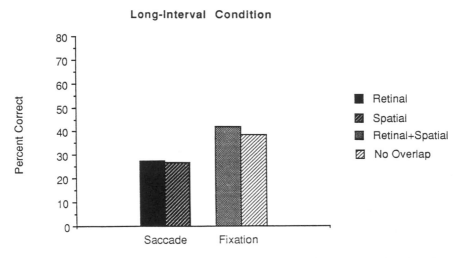

FIGURE 9.3. Results of the Irwin, Brown, and Sun (1988) retinotopic/spatiotopic integration experiment.

persistence, but no evidence for the existence of spatiotopic visible persistence. Several other investigators have also failed to find evidence for spatiotopic fusion across saccades using variants of the eye movement paradigm described above, adding further strength to this conclusion (e.g., Bridgeman & Mayer, 1983; Irwin, Yantis, & Jonides, 1983; Jonides, Irwin, & Yantis, 1983; O'Regan & Levy-Schoen, 1983; Rayner & Pollatsek, 1983).

Another study providing evidence against the existence of spatiotopic visible persistence was reported by Irwin, Zacks, and Brown (1990).

Instead of requiring subjects to integrate material that changed during a saccade (i.e., two different frames of dots), Irwin et al. (1990) tried to determine whether subjects could summate information about the same stimulus viewed in successive fixations. Specifically, they investigated whether one's ability to detect a stimulus (a sine wave grating) presented after a saccade is affected by presenting the same stimulus in the same place in space before the saccade. Wolf, Hauske, and Lupp (1978, 1980) reported that the detection threshold for the post saccadic stimulus was lowered under these conditions, but Irwin et al. suggested that the Wolf et al. results may have been due to phosphor persistence or to retinal overlap between the pre- and post saccadic stimuli. Thus, Irwin et al. attempted to replicate the Wolf et al. results under conditions in which phosphor persistence and retinal overlap were eliminated; this was accomplished by using shutters and an optical system to eliminate visible phosphor persistence, and by presenting the prime and the target to nonoverlapping regions of the retina.

In the Irwin et al. (1990) experiments, a "prime" grating was presented in the visual periphery while the subject fixated a central point. When the subject initiated a saccade to this grating, it disappeared and a new stimulus was presented; this stimulus was either a grating of 3 cycles per degree (cpd) or a blank field with the same luminance as the grating. The subject was required to discriminate between these two stimuli and the contrast of the target grating was varied across trials to determine its discrimination threshold. Thresholds were calculated for three different priming conditions: in one the prime had the same spatial frequency as the target grating (3 cpd); in a second, the prime had a spatial frequency of 8 cpd; and in a third, the prime had a spatial frequency of 0 cpd (i.e., it was a blank field). The question of interest was whether the contrast threshold for the target grating would differ when the prime had the same spatial frequency as the target compared to when it did not. For purposes of comparison, data from two no-saccade control conditions were also collected. In one, the subject maintained fixation and the prime and the target were presented foveally; in the other, the subject maintained fixation and the prime and the target were presented peripherally.

In the foveal control condition, the contrast threshold for the target grating was 2.5 to 5 times higher when the prime had the same spatial frequency as the target compared to when it had a different spatial frequency. In other words, the prime with the same spatial frequency as the target caused masking; masking occurred because the prime persisted in the visual system, so that even when the blank field was presented the subject still "saw" the prime, making the discrimination of target and blank more difficult. The peripheral control condition provided similar results.

These controls demonstrated that the prime grating could be resolved in the periphery, and that at the very least the prime had an effect at a retinotopic level of representation. The critical question, however, was whether the prime would affect contrast threshold across a saccade, when the prime and the target overlapped only spatially. The answer was no. Contrast threshold for the target grating was the same regardless of the prime's spatial frequency. Irwin et al. (1990) concluded that the Wolf et al. (1978, 1980) results were probably artifactual. It appears that even when one uses a task that requires the subject to integrate the same stimulus across a saccade no evidence for spatiotopic fusion is found.

In sum, spatiotopic visible persistence appears not to exist. Accordingly, recent research in my laboratory has examined what role other visual memories might play in information integration across eye movements.

Informational Persistence and Visual Short-Term Memory

Several studies have investigated masking and partial report across eye movements in an effort to determine if informational persistence is involved in the integration of successive fixations. One study examined masking and integration during pursuit eye movements. This study was motivated by previous research by White (1976). White reported that presentation of a masking stimulus during a pursuit eye movement interfered with the perception of a target stimulus that shared the same spatial, rather than retinal, coordinates as the mask. This finding had been interpreted as evidence for spatiotopic visual (visible and/or informational) persistence. White's results were questionable, however, because subjects' eye position was not monitored; if White's subjects did not make continuous pursuit eye movements, it might appear that masking was spatial when in fact it was retinal. In particular, if subjects' eyes stopped moving when the target stimulus was presented, the "spatial" mask would actually be a retinal mask and the "retinal" mask would appear adjacent to the stimulus and have little effect on its perceptibility. Sun and Irwin (1987) attempted to replicate White's results and found that when eye position was monitored to ensure that subjects made continuous pursuit eye movements, masking was retinal rather than spatial. Subjects' phenomenal judgments of the locations of two successive stimuli briefly flashed during pursuit movements indicated that integration, as well as masking, operated on the basis of retinotopic rather than spatiotopic coordinates. Sun and Irwin concluded that White's (1976) work does not constitute good evidence for spatiotopic visual persistence.

Another study investigated masking and integration across saccades, based on work by Davidson, Fox, and Dick (1973). Davidson et al. presented a letter array just prior to a saccade and a mask at one of the letter positions just after the saccade and found that the mask inhibited report of the letter that shared its retinal coordinates but appeared to occupy the same position as the letter that shared its spatial coordinates. This pattern of results has been interpreted as evidence for the existence of a retinotopic visual persistence that is maskable and a spatiotopic visual persistence that supports integration across saccades. Using a similar procedure, Irwin, Brown, & Sun (1988) found that both masking and integration across saccades appeared to occur on the basis of retinotopic coordinates; in other words, the mask appeared to cover the letter whose report it interfered with. In a second experiment, instead of a mask Irwin et al. presented a bar marker over one of the letter positions, and subjects reported which letter appeared to be underneath the bar. The expectation was that this partial report procedure would access spatiotopic informational persistence and subjects would report the letter with the same spatial coordinates as the bar marker. Instead, subjects usually reported the letter with the same retinal coordinates as the bar marker, again indicating retinotopic rather than spatiotopic integration across saccades. Even though integration was retinotopic, however, subjects were still able to accurately specify the spatial location of the bar marker; so, in a sense, Irwin et al. did replicate the finding that a postsaccadic stimulus (a mask or bar marker, in this case) could have an effect at a retinotopic level while appearing to maintain its actual spatial location. Irwin et al. argued that subjects' ability to report the spatial location of the bar marker was based on retinal (visual) "landmarks" that were present in the second fixation only, however, rather than on spatiotopic integration. They concluded that the results of Davidson et al. could be explained solely in retinotopic terms, and thus provide no convincing evidence for spatiotopic informational persistence (see also Van der Heijden, Bridgeman, & Mewhort, 1986).

During the course of these experiments, however, Irwin et al. (1988) noticed that the exposure parameters that they and Davidson et al. (1973) had used were biased in favor of retinotopic, rather than spatiotopic, coding: the letter array was presented very briefly just before the saccade, and spatial coding is poor under these conditions (e.g., Matin, 1972). Thus, Irwin et al. conducted an additional experiment in which the letter array was presented approximately 250 ms before the saccade occurred, so that there would be ample time for spatiotopic coding. Under these conditions, they found evidence for spatiotopic integration: when the bar marker was presented after the saccade above one of the previously occupied letter positions, subjects usually reported the letter that occupied the same spatial position as the bar marker. Unfortunately, it is not clear whether these reports were based on informational persistence or on short-term memory because only five letters were contained in the letter array and the interval between the letter array and the bar marker was not manipulated. Additional research with this paradigm is required to determine whether the memory involved has the properties of informational persistence (precategorical, high-capacity, short-lived, vulnerable to masking) or of visual short-term memory (postcategorical, limited-capacity, long-lived, nonmaskable).

The possible role of informational persistence and visual short-term memory (as well as visible persistence) has been studied using an eye movement version of the Phillips (1974) paradigm described earlier, however. Irwin (1991) presented two random-dot patterns and asked people to judge whether they were identical or not. The patterns were presented in separate fixations, separated by a saccade. Recognition accuracy was moderately high (about 70% for 8-dot patterns) and declined only slightly as the interpattern interval increased from 1 to 5,000 ms. Furthermore, accuracy was the same regardless of whether the patterns appeared in the same or different spatial locations across the saccade, suggesting that the underlying memory is insensitive to stimulus displacements from one fixation to the next. Pattern complexity had a large effect on accuracy, however; simple patterns were recognized much more accurately than complex patterns, regardless of interpattern interval. In sum, subjects were relying on a long-lasting, limited-capacity memory that is not strictly tied to absolute spatial position to compare the contents of successive fixations. These are the characteristics of visual short-term memory, rather than visible or informational persistence.

Summary and Conclusions

The eye movement studies conducted in my laboratory indicate that visible persistence plays little or no role in normal information integration across eye movements. Retinotopic visible persistence exists, but its time course is such that it does not ordinarily interact with new information experienced after a saccade; this is advantageous, because retinotopic fusion across saccades would produce a chaotic collage of conflicting images. Spatiotopic visible persistence, hypothesized by many people to underlie the fusion of information across saccades, appears not to exist. Similarly, there is little compelling evidence that informational persistence plays any role in information integration across eye movements, though it is premature to rule out this possibility until further experiments investigating partial report across eye movements have been conducted. Some suggestive evidence has been provided by McRae, Butler, and Popiel (1987), who found evidene for spatiotopic masking across saccades. Furthermore, recent research by Palmer and Ames (1989) and by Hayhoe, Lachter, and Feldman (1991; see also, Hayhoe, Lachter, and Moeller, this volume) suggests that some precategorical visual information may be retained across saccades. Palmer and Ames (1989) found that subjects could make very precise discriminations of line length across fixations, and Hayhoe et al. found that subjects could integrate the spatial positions of single dots viewed in successive fixations to judge whether or not they formed a right triangle. Little is known about the capacity and time course of the memory used to make these judgments, however, so it is unclear at present whether subjects were relying on informational persistence or on visual short-term memory. The role of informational persistence in integration across saccades requires further investigation.

Whatever the role of informational persistence might be, it is clear from the research of Irwin (1991) that visual short-term memory is used to combine information from successive fixations. This study showed that the representation of the visual environment that is built up across eye movements is long-lived, not tied to absolute spatial position, and limited in capacity. Supporting evidence for this conclusion comes from experiments examining integration across eye movements during reading and picture viewing. Rayner, McConkie, and Zola (1980) found that a word presented in the visual periphery of one fixation facilitated naming latency for a word viewed in a subsequent fixation if the two words shared the same beginning letters; this was true regardless of whether the case of the letters stayed the same across fixations. Rayner et al. found a similar pattern of facilitation when the first word was presented peripherally and the second word was presented foveally, with no intervening eye movement. These results indicate that a postcategorical memory not tied to absolute spatial position was used to combine information from successive views. Pollatsek, Rayner, and Collins (1984) and Pollatsek, Rayner, and Henderson (1990) found similar results using pictures as stimuli. These results may have been due to priming of long-term memory representations, rather than to visual short-term memory, however (see Pollatsek and Rayner, this volume).

Closing Arguments

One of the classic questions in perception concerns how people perceive the world as unified, stable, and continuous across changes in eye position. My approach to this question has been to consider what role visual memory plays in this perception. The research reviewed above suggests that integration across eye movements relies largely on a general purpose memory, visual short-term memory, that operates to combine information both within and across fixations. This conclusion is surprising, given the characteristics of our perceptual experience—how could a limited-capacity, abstract memory explain why the world appears stable and continuous across eye movements? Intuitively, this perception would seem to require a detailed memory for the contents of the presaccadic fixation that could be combined with the contents of the postsaccadic fixation to render an integrated, composite representation of the visual environment. It is possible, however, that this intuition is exactly backward; the world may seem stable and continuous across eye movements not because integration occurs, but because very little is remembered

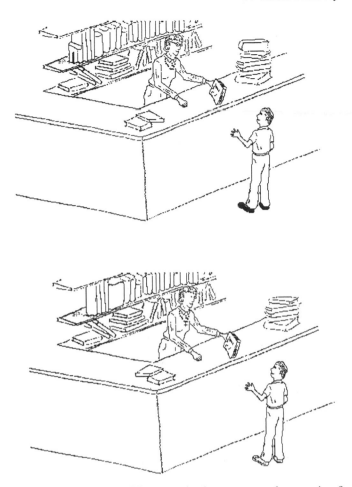

FIGURE 9.4. Demonstration that differences in the contents of successive fixations are difficult to detect. The top drawing is different from the bottom drawing in several details, but the differences are not noticeable unless specific objects are attended to and encoded into memory. *Note.* From "Information Integration Across Saccadic Eye Movements" by D.E. Irwin, 1991, *Cognitive Psychology*, *23*, p. 452. Copyright 1991 by Academic Press, Inc. Reprinted by permission.

from one fixation to the next. Support for this hypothesis is provided by an inspection of Figure 9.4. The top and bottom drawings in this figure differ in several ways, but these differences are not immediately apparent as one shifts fixation between the two drawings; instead, the differences are noticeable only if one carefully attends to and encodes a piece of one drawing and compares it to the other. Similarly, unless an object in the world is attended to and encoded into short-term memory, its fate from one fixation to the next may be unknown. Our perceptual systems may treat successive fixations individually, and simply assume the world remains stable across saccades (MacKay, 1973). Consequently, we may rely more on the visible contents of the current fixation for information about the state of the world, rather than on some representation of previous fixations built up in memory (O'Regan & Levy-Schoen, 1983). This conclusion makes sense given that fixation durations are roughly 10 times longer than saccade durations; 90% of our perceptual experience is spent in a state in which the eye is relatively stable and an image of the world is continuously present on the retina. The representation that is built up across eye movements may be nothing more than an abstract description of the environment, no more detailed than the representation of the world that we have when we close our eyes.

Acknowledgment. Preparation of this chapter was supported by grant BNS 89-08699 from the National Science Foundation to the author.

References

Adelson, E.H., & Jonides, J. (1980). The psychophysics of iconic storage. *Journal of Experimental Psychology: Human Perception and Performance, 6,* 486–493.

Allen, F. (1926). The persistence of vision. *American Journal of Physiological Optics, 7,* 439–457.

Banks, W.P. (1983). On the decay of the icon. *Behavioral and Brain Sciences, 6,* 14.

Bowen, R.W., Pola, J., & Matin, L. (1974). Visual persistence: Effects of flash luminance, duration, and energy. *Vision Research, 14,* 295–303.

Breitmeyer, B.G. (1984). *Visual masking: An integrative approach.* New York: Oxford University Press.

Breitmeyer, B.G., Kropfl, W., & Julesz, B. (1982). The existence and role of retinotopic and spatiotopic forms of visual persistence. *Acta Psychologica, 52,* 175–196.

Bridgeman, B., & Mayer, M. (1983). Failure to integrate visual information from successive fixations. *Bulletin of the Psychonomic Society, 21,* 285–286.

Coltheart, M. (1980). Iconic memory and visible persistence. *Perception & Psychophysics, 27,* 183–228.

Coltheart, M., Lea, C.D., & Thompson, K. (1974). In defence of iconic memory. *Quarterly Journal of Experimental Psychology, 26,* 633–641.

Davidson, M.L., Fox, M.J., & Dick, A.O. (1973). Effect of eye movements on backward masking and perceived location. *Perception & Psychophysics, 14,* 110–116.

Dick, A.O. (1969). Relations between the sensory register and short-term storage in tachistoscopic recognition. *Journal of Experimental Psychology, 82,* 279–284.

Dick, A.O. (1974). Iconic memory and its relation to perceptual processes and other mechanisms. *Perception & Psychophysics, 16,* 575–596.

Di Lollo, V. (1977). Temporal characteristics of iconic memory. *Nature, 267,* 241–243.

Di Lollo, V. (1980). Temporal integration in visual memory. *Journal of Experimental Psychology: General, 109,* 75–97.

Efron, R. (1970). Effect of stimulus duration on perceptual onset and offset latencies. *Perception & Psychophysics, 8,* 231–234.

Eriksen, C.W., & Collins, J.F. (1967). Some temporal characteristics of visual pattern perception. *Journal of Experimental Psychology, 74,* 476–484.

Eriksen, C.W., & Collins, J.F. (1968). Sensory traces versus the psychological moment in the temporal organization of form. *Journal of Experimental Psychology, 77,* 376–382.

Friedman, A. (1979). Framing pictures: The role of knowledge in automatized encoding and memory for gist. *Journal of Experimental Psychology: General, 108,* 316–355.

Haber, R.N., & Standing, L. (1970). Direct estimates of the apparent duration of a flash. *Canadian Journal of Psychology, 24,* 216–229.

Harrington, D.O. (1981). *The visual fields: A textbook and atlas of clinical perimetry.* St. Louis, MO: Mosby.

Hayhoe, M., Lachter, J., & Feldman, J. (1991). Integration of form across saccadic eye movements. *Perception, 20,* 393–402.

Hochberg, J. (1978). *Perception.* Englewood Cliffs, NJ: Prentice-Hall.

Intraub, H. (1980). Presentation rate and the representation of briefly glimpsed pictures in memory. *Journal of Experimental Psychology: Human Learning and Memory, 6,* 1–12.

Intraub, H. (1984). Conceptual masking: The effects of subsequent visual events on memory for pictures. *Journal of Experimental Psychology: Learning, Memory, and Cognition, 10,* 115–125.

Irwin, D.E. (1991). Information integration across saccadic eye movements. *Cognitive Psychology, 23,* 420–456.

Irwin, D.E. (in press). Perceiving an integrated visual world. In D.E. Meyer and S. Kornblum (Eds.), *Attention and performance Vol. XIV: A silver jubilee.* Cambridge, MA: MIT Press.

Irwin, D.E., & Brown, J.S. (1987). Tests of a model of informational persistence. *Canadian Journal of Psychology, 41,* 317–338.

Irwin, D.E., Brown, J.S., & Sun, J.S. (1988). Visual masking and visual integration across saccadic eye movements. *Journal of Experimental Psychology: General, 117,* 276–287.

Irwin, D.E., Yantis, S., & Jonides, J. (1983). Evidence against visual integration across saccadic eye movements. *Perception & Psychophysics, 34,* 49–57.

Irwin, D.E., & Yeomans, J.M. (1986). Sensory registration and informational persistence. *Journal of Experimental Psychology: Human Perception and Performance, 12,* 343–360.

Irwin, D.E., Zacks, J.L., & Brown, J.S. (1990). Visual memory and the perception of a stable visual environment. *Perception & Psychophysics, 47,* 35–46.

Jonides, J., Irwin, D.E., & Yantis, S. (1982). Integrating visual information from successive fixations. *Science, 215,* 192–194.

Jonides, J., Irwin, D.E., & Yantis, S. (1983). Failure to integrate information from successive fixations. *Science, 222,* 188.

Loftus, G. (1985). On worthwhile icons: Reply to Di Lollo and Haber. *Journal of Experimental Psychology: Human Perception and Performance, 11,* 384–388.

Loftus, G., & Ginn, M. (1984). Perceptual and conceptual masking of pictures. *Journal of Experimental Psychology: Learning, Memory, and Cognition, 10,* 435–441.

Long, G.M. (1980). Iconic memory: A review and critique of study of short-term storage. *Psychological Bulletin, 88,* 785–820.

MacKay, D. (1973). Visual stability and voluntary eye movements. In R. Jung (Ed.), *Handbook of sensory physiology.* (Vol. 7, No. 3, pp. 307–332). Berlin: Springer-Verlag.

Matin, L. (1972). Eye movements and perceived visual direction. In D. Jameson & L.M. Hurvich (Eds.), *Handbook of sensory physiology* (Vol. 7, No. 4, pp. 331–379). Berlin: Springer-Verlag.

McConkie, G.W., & Rayner, K. (1976). Identifying the span of the effective stimulus in reading: Literature review and theories of reading. In H. Singer & R.B. Ruddell (Eds.), *Theoretical models and processes of reading* (pp. 137–162). Newark, DE: International Reading Association.

McRae, K., Butler, B.E., & Popiel, S.J. (1987). Spatiotopic and retinotopic components of iconic memory. *Psychological Research, 49,* 221–227.

Mewhort, D.J.K., Campbell, A.J., Marchetti, F.M., & Campbell, J.I.D. (1981). Identification, localization, and "iconic" memory: An evaluation of the bar-probe task. *Memory & Cogniton, 9,* 50–67.

Neisser, U. (1967). *Cognitive psychology.* New York: Appleton-Century-Crofts.

Nelson, W., & Loftus, G. (1980). The functional visual field during picture viewing. *Journal of Experimental Psychology: Human Learning and Memory, 6,* 391–399.

O'Regan, J.K., & Levy-Schoen, A. (1983). Integrating visual information from successive fixations: Does trans-saccadic fusion exist? *Vision Research, 23,* 765–768.

Palmer, J., & Ames, C.T. (1989). Measuring the effect of multiple eye fixations on size and shape discrimination. *Investigative Ophthalmology and Visual Science (Supplement), 30,* 159.

Pezdek, K., Maki, R., Valencia-Laver, D., Whetstone, T., Stoeckert, J., & Dougherty, T. (1988). Picture memory: Recognizing added and deleted details. *Journal of Experimental Psychology: Learning, Memory, and Cognition, 14,* 468–476.

Phillips, W.A. (1974). On the distinction between sensory storage and short-term visual memory. *Perception & Psychophysics, 16,* 283–290.

Pollatsek, A., Rayner, K., & Collins, W.E. (1984). Integrating pictorial information across eye movements. *Journal of Experimental Psychology: General, 113,* 426–442.

Pollatsek, A., Rayner, K., & Henderson, J.M. (1990). Role of spatial location in integration of pictorial information across saccades. *Journal of Experimental Psychology: Human Perception and Performance, 16,* 199–210.

Potter, M.C. (1976). Short-term conceptual memory for pictures. *Journal of Experimental Psychology: Human Learning and Memory, 2,* 509–522.

Potter, M.C. (1983). Representational buffers: The eye-mind hypothesis in picture perception, reading, and visual search. In K. Rayner (Ed.), *Eye movements in reading* (pp. 413–437). New York: Academic Press.

Rayner, K., McConkie, G.W., & Zola, D. (1980). Integrating information across eye movements. *Cognitive Psychology, 12,* 206–226.

Rayner, K., & Pollatsek, A. (1983). Is visual information integrated across saccades? *Perception & Psychophysics*, *34*, 39–48.

Sperling, G. (1960). The information available in brief visual presentations. *Psychological Monographs*, *74*(11, Whole No. 498).

Sperling, G. (1967). Successive approximations to a model for short-term memory. *Acta Psychologica*, *27*, 285–292.

Sun, J.S., & Irwin, D.E. (1987). Retinal masking during pursuit eye movements: Implications for spatiotopic visual persistence. *Journal of Experimental Psychology: Human Perception and Performance*, *13*, 140–145.

Townsend, V.M. (1973). Loss of spatial and identity information following a tachistoscopic exposure. *Journal of Experimental Psychology*, *98*, 113–118.

Trehub, A. (1977). Neuronal models for cognitive processes: Networks for learning, perception, and imagination. *Journal of Theoretical Biology*, *65*, 141–169.

Van der Heijden, A.H.C., Bridgeman, B., & Mewhort, D.J.K. (1986). Is stimulus persistence affected by eye movements? A critique of Davidson, Fox, and Dick (1973). *Psychological Research*, *48*, 179–181.

von Wright, J.M. (1972). On the problem of selection in iconic memory. *Scandinavian Journal of Psychology*, *13*, 159–171.

White, C.W. (1976). Visual masking during pursuit eye movements. *Journal of Experimental Psychology: Human Perception and Performance*, *2*, 469–478.

Wolf, W., Hauske, G., & Lupp, U. (1978). How pre-saccadic gratings modify post-saccadic modulation transfer functions. *Vision Research*, *18*, 1173–1179.

Wolf, W., Hauske, G., & Lupp, U. (1980). Interactions of pre- and post-saccadic patterns having the same coordinates in space. *Vision Research*, *20*, 117–125.

Yeomans, J.M., & Irwin, D.E. (1985). Stimulus duration and partial report performance. *Perception & Psychophysics*, *37*, 163–169.

10
What Is Integrated Across Fixations?

ALEXANDER POLLATSEK and KEITH RAYNER

Our strongest introspection in perception is of a stable world. However, the visual system obtains an input that is far from stable. In normal viewing conditions—when the eye is not tracking a moving object—the eyes stay relatively immobile for periods of only a fraction of a second. In between these periods of rest (called *fixations*), there are rapid ballistic eye movements (called *saccades*) in which the retinal image is merely a smear. Thus, vision usually consists of the following sequence of events: an interval of a sixth to about a half a second in which there is a stable retinal image followed by a brief interval of a smear, an interval with a different stable retinal image, another smear, and so on (Rayner, 1978a). A central question of visual perception is how the percept of a stable world emerges from all this chaos.

One reason for this chaos is the limitations of the eye. When one looks at a stable real-world scene or a painting, or reads a book, the detail of only a small part of the scene can be apprehended, because acuity drops off rapidly from around the *fovea* (the area of central vision). Although the area in which meaningful detail can be extracted varies across different viewing situations (see below), the eyes have to be active for many acts of identification to take place. Many objects in a scene or most words on a page have to be fixated in order to be reliably identified (McConkie & Rayner, 1975; Nelson & Loftus, 1980).

The central question that we will concern ourselves with in this chapter is how the human visual system integrates the information received on the various fixations. That is, on each fixation, the system receives a "snapshot" from the retina. Presumably, the current percept is some sort of integration of the information received on the current fixation and some residue of the snapshots taken on prior fixations. But what sort of integration is it? As we will see, the experimental data do not elucidate any of the details of the mechanism of integration. Instead, the question that has been focused on is, What codes remain from the memory of prior fixations that are of use on the current fixation to the integration process?

Let us make clear that the above description of the chaos is somewhat oversimplified. In addition to eye movements, there are head and body movements in normal viewing conditions as well. Moreover, the eyes are not really still during a fixation; there are very small movements (called *nystagmus*) and larger movements—slow *drifts* from a fixation point with faster *microsaccades* that attempt to bring them back to the original position. The problem of integration of retinal information is complicated enough without having to worry about all of that. In addition, we will assume that the visual information that comes in during saccades is ignored in normal viewing conditions. Currently, it appears that the primary mechanism that allows the information to be ignored, *backward masking*, is relatively peripheral and simple (Matin, 1974). In sum, we will assume the snapshot model stated in the prior paragraph, with blank intervals between the snapshots while the eye is executing a saccade. We will also not concern ourselves with how the perceptual system "fills in" the time during the saccade so that the discontinuities are not noticed.

An important point should be made at the outset. The stability of the perceptual world suggests that the process of integration is merely one of the visual system taking the prior snapshots, figuring out how far the eye (and/or head) has moved, and aligning the visual representations in some sort of two-dimensional spatiotopic representation in which the local information is summed pixel by pixel. Such a representation has been proposed under several different names: "integrative visual buffer" (McConkie & Rayner, 1976a), "retinoid" (Trehub, 1977), and "stable feature frame" (Feldman, 1985). In fact, such a representation appears to be tacitly assumed by many people in machine vision, although the elements integrated may be more complex than pixels (such as the feature information contained in Marr's, 1982, "primal sketch"). (We should add that not all these theorists have tackled the integration process in their models.) It is tempting to posit that such a representation is a primary locus of the integration process across fixations. However, we wish to argue that the bulk of the evidence indicates that this model is in error and that there is little evidence that visual information (in the form of pixel by pixel information) from prior fixations survives. Instead, the codes that seem to survive are more abstract: name codes, meaning codes, and some sort of more abstract visual codes.

Because this conclusion is quite counterintuitive to most people, we will devote much of the chapter to trying to document it. At the end, we will discuss ways to think about vision in which the finding is not so counterintuitive. Before we discuss possible situations in which information might be integrated across fixations, however, we need to provide some background on the acuity of the eye and the region from which meaningful visual information can be extracted.

Limitations on Vision

It is well known that visual acuity decreases as one gets further from fixation. The density of photoreceptors decreases markedly when one gets beyond the 2° of foveal vision (Pirenne, 1967), mirrored by a rapid decrease in acuity, measured psychophysically (Alpern, 1962). The implication of these findings for normal visual computations, however, is far from clear. For example, isolated letters can be perceived quite well fairly far into the periphery, whereas the legibility of letters with Xs flanking them falls off quite precipitously (Bouma, 1973; Estes, Allmeyer, & Reder, 1976; Mackworth, 1965). The usual explanation for this finding is that some sort of "lateral inhibition" mechanism causes the Xs to interfere with perceptibility of letters. However, the actual mechanism is not well understood.

We do not wish to get into a detailed discussion of acuity issues here. Our main point is that the perceptibility of objects or features in a visual display is complex, and is not a trivial consequence of either the physiology of the retina or the psychophysics of grating acuity. As a result, it is of interest to determine what visual information is actually extracted on a fixation that is used in real-life perceptual acts. In particular, we are interested in a region in which meaningful information is extracted, but where more information is needed from a later fixation in order to complete the perceptual act.

We will first discuss reading, because that situation has been most studied. Mindful of the fact that reading is an atypical visual situation, we will also discuss what is known about scene perception and other non-reading situations. The picture that emerges is that limitations of information extraction are due not only to limitations on acuity (such as distance from the center of vision and lateral masking considerations) but to covert visual attention as well.

Limits of Visual Information Extracted During Reading

The visual stimulus in reading, though artificial, is well defined and easy to characterize. The major technique for exploring the limitation of useful vision during reading is the *moving window technique* (McConkie & Rayner, 1975). In this paradigm, a subject is asked to read text on a cathode ray tube (CRT) while his or her eye movements are monitored. The current information on eye position is sent to a computer and, as a result, the display on the screen can be changed contingent on the reader's current eye position (see Figure 10.1). For example, the reader might see text in which the letter being fixated and 14 letters to the left and right of fixation are normal, and the remainder of the line of text is replaced by Xs. With each new fixation, the reader sees a new "window"

```
By far the single most abundant substance in the biosphere


                  *
By far the single most abundXXXXXXXXXXXXXXXXXXXXXXXXXXXXXXX    (1)
                   *
XXXXXr the single most abundant suXXXXXXXXXXXXXXXXXXXXXXXX    (2)
                    *
XXXXXXXXXXXsingle most abundant substanceXXXXXXXXXXXXXXXXX    (3)
                          *
XXXXXXXXXXXXXXXXXXXXXXXXXbundant substance in the biosXXXXX    (4)
                              *
XXXXXXXXXXXXXXXXXXXXXXXXXXXXXXXXXXXXtance in the biosphere    (5)
```

FIGURE 10.1. Illustration of a moving window. The top line represents a normal line of text. Lines 1–5 represent windows that a reader might see on five consecutive fixations in reading the line of text. In this figure, the window area extends from 14 letter spaces to the left of fixation (indicated by the *) to 14 letter spaces to the right of fixation. Under these conditions, reading rate and comprehension would be the same as if the text were presented without any window restrictions (see text).

of text of 29 letters, centered around the current fixation point, regardless of whether the reader moves forward or backward in the text.

The key question in the experiments is what size of window is sufficient to enable normal reading to occur (i.e., at normal speed and comprehension). For example, if subjects could read normally with the above 29-character window, then one could conclude that they were extracting no useful information beyond that window. In fact, several experiments (Den Buurman, Boersema & Gerrisen, 1981; McConkie & Rayner, 1975; Rayner & Bertera, 1979; Rayner, Inhoff, Morrison, Slowiaczek, & Bertera, 1981) have shown that readers extract no useful information beyond this point. (Although most of the experiments have been conducted with three characters of text equaling 1° of visual angle, similar results have been obtained with somewhat different sizes of text indicating that, within limits, describing the window in terms of characters is the appropriate metric.)

This finding raises several questions. First, is the limitation due to lower level factors such as distance from fovea, size of print, and density of the visual display, or is it merely due to the fact that reading does not require more information to be used on a fixation? The answer is that the limit of about 14 characters to the right of fixation is almost certainly due to low-level factors such as acuity. (We will discuss processing to the left of fixation later.) First, a *moving mask* experiment, in which central vision was blocked out but peripheral vision remained (the inverse of the moving window conditions), found that little information could be extracted beyond 12 characters to the right of fixation (Rayner & Bertera, 1979). That is, in conditions when subjects were forced to rely on visual information beyond 12 characters, they were virtually unable to extract any meaningful letter information.

A second paradigm, which we will describe in more detail later, reveals a similar picture. In this *parafoveal preview* experiment (Rayner, 1978b), the subject sees a single word in the parafovea, shifts fixation to it, and names the word as rapidly as possible. The usefulness of the parafoveal preview of the word is assessed by comparing the time to name the word when there is a preview to naming time when there is no preview (e.g., a row of Xs is presented in the parafovea instead of the word to be named). We will term this difference in times, the parafoveal *preview benefit*. It was found (Rayner, McConkie, & Ehrlich, 1978) that when the parafoveal word was 5° from fixation (i.e., 15 character spaces), that there was no preview benefit, whereas at distances up to 3° from the fovea there was significant benefit from the preview.

To summarize, with text or text-like displays, there appears to be a limit in the extraction of useful visual information at about 14 characters from the fixation point. This limit is one of acuity. When textual information is further from fixation, the features needed to identify letters are too small to be seen. Although the result probably depends to some extent on the distance the text is from the screen, within limits there is probably an approximate trade-off: if the text is moved nearer the eye, the individual letters would be bigger and hence easier to process, but they would also be farther from fixation and hence harder to process (Morrison & Rayner, 1981).

The above data do not imply that visual information is extracted no further than 14 characters from fixation. If the printed page beyond 14 characters were replaced by a blinding light, a void, or an elephant, it would obviously be detectable to the reader. However, the visual confirmation of the knowledge that there is a book beyond 14 characters (and print on it) is apparently of no use to the reader.

The above data also do not reveal anything directly about how far from fixation various kinds of information can be extracted. That is, it is possible that certain kinds of information useful to reading can be extracted further than others. For example, perhaps information about where spaces between words are (which might be of use to the eye-guidance system) might be extracted further from fixation than information about the identities of letters. This conjecture has been confirmed by experiments varying the type of information outside the window (Figure 10.2), because manipulating the presence and absence of spaces affected reading out to 14 to 15 character positions, whereas manipulating the presence and absence of letter information affected reading only within a narrower region (McConkie & Rayner, 1975). The extreme limit

```
By far the single most abundant substance in the biosphere


                            *
XXXXXXXXXX single most abundant substanXXXXXXXXXXXXXXXXXXXX  (1)


                            *
XXXXXXXXXXXXXXXXXXXXXXst abundaXXXXXXXXXXXXXXXXXXXXXXXXXXXXXX  (2)


                            *
XXXXXXXXXXXXXXXXXXXXXXst abundant substanXXXXXXXXXXXXXXXXXXXX  (3)


                            *
XX XXX XXX XXXXXX XXst abundant substanXXXXX XXX XXXXXXXXX  (4)


                            *
Nw oqm kxe cbwpnd ewst abundant substanqm vr upq copzmwlhg  (5)


                            *
XX XXX XXX XXXXXX XXXX abundant XXXXXXXXX XX XXX XXXXXXXXX  (6)


                            *
XX XXX XXX XXXXXX XXXX abundant substance XX XXX XXXXXXXXX  (7)


                            *
XX XXX XXX XXXXXX XXXX abundant subXXXXXX XX XXX XXXXXXXXX  (8)
```

FIGURE 10.2. Examples of various kinds of window restrictions. The top line depicts a line of text and lines 1–5 illustrate alternative types of windows that have been used. In all cases, the fixation point is on the "b" in "abundant." Lines 1–3 depict different possible modifications of the extent of the window region. In line 1, the region extends 14 character spaces on either side of the fixated letter, whereas in line 2, the region extends only 4 character spaces on either side. In line 3, the region is asymmetric, extending 4 character spaces to the left and 14 to the right. Reading is normal for conditions represented by lines 1 and 3, but considerably slower than normal for conditions represented by line 2. Lines 3–5 illustrate several alternatives for material outside the window region. In line 3, only Xs are outside the window region, whereas in line 4, the spaces between words are preserved. In line 5, the letters are replaced by random letters and the spaces are preserved as well. Lines 6–8 illustrate windows defined by words rather than character spaces. Line 6 is a one-word window, line 7 is a two-word window, and line 8 is a hybrid one-word + three-letter window. The fact that reading in the latter condition is substantially better than in a one-word window condition indicates that information is integrated across fixations (see text).

```
                              *    |
Fixation N:        the baker rushed the wedding bomb to the reception.

                                   |    *
Fixation N+1:      the baker rushed the wedding cake to the reception.
```

FIGURE 10.3. An example of the boundary technique. On fixation N, the reader is fixated on the letter "e" in wedding. However, as soon as the eye movement crosses over the boundary location (in this case, the letter "n" in "wedding"), the computer replaces "bomb" with the target word "cake." The asterisks mark the location of the fixations, and the bar marks the location of the boundary. (The boundary location is invisible to the subject.) Besides the visually dissimilar and semantically anomalous preview "bomb," other previews for "cake" that could appear on fixation N are "cake" (identical), "cahc" (visually similar), "pies" or "picz" (visually dissimilar).

of the region from which letter information can be extracted has not been precisely determined; however, it is at least nine characters from fixation (Pollatsek, Rayner, & Balota, 1986).

In this regard, it is worth mentioning that the *boundary technique* (which is a variant of the moving window technique) has been useful for diagnosing the regions from which various types of information are extracted (Rayner, 1975). In the boundary technique, only a single region (usually a word) is changed contingent on the position of the eyes. That is, there is a single target word that, when fixated, is normal. However, before the subject's eyes cross a certain *boundary* location, a preview word (or nonword) appears in the target word location (Figure 10.3). The type of preview and the location of the boundary can be varied and the subject's performance is assessed by measuring fixation times on the target word and the succeeding word and the lengths and direction of saccades off of the target word (see also McConkie, Underwood, Zola, & Wolverton, 1985). The logic is thus basically the same as the moving window: one can measure how changes of different sorts at different eccentricities from fixation affect reading. The difference is that there is only a single display change so that a more detailed assessment of the effects of a display change can be made. Results from experiments using the boundary technique indicate that the word identification span is smaller than the total perceptual span (Rayner, 1975).

The work on reading indicates that attentional factors also help to define the area from which useful information is extracted. The window of useful viewing is actually asymmetric (McConkie & Rayner, 1976b), with information to the left of fixation extracted from a narrower region (4 characters) than from the right of fixation (14 characters). In fact, readers do not appear to be extracting any useful information from words to the left of the fixated word (Rayner, Well, & Pollatsek, 1980). This asymmetry is due to the direction of eye movements and attention, rather than to the right visual field being more directly connected to the language-specialized left hemisphere. When readers of Hebrew—which runs across the page from right to left—were tested, their perceptual spans were the opposite of English readers; they extracted little information to the right of fixation (Pollatsek, Bolozky, Well, & Rayner, 1981).

Work employing the parafoveal naming paradigm also implicates attentional factors. When two preview words were presented symmetrically around the fixation point, there was no preview benefit from a word identical to the fixated word unless the eye movement went to the same location as the previewed word (Rayner et al., 1978). That is, it appeared that subjects only attended to the previewed word that was in the same location that they would move their eyes to. We will return to this point later.

To summarize, the window of useful information in reading is narrow, including a region of about 4 characters to the left of fixation and 14 characters to the right of fixation (for English readers). The window appears to be determined by both acuity and attentional considerations. Furthermore, the window is not all-or-none. Full identification of words may be possible within a relatively narrow region, but other kinds of information may be extracted from a broader region. We will elaborate on this point below.

Before moving on to scene perception, we should make a comment about reading in nonalphabetic languages such as Chinese and Japanese. There, the window has been determined to be about two or three characters from fixation (Ikeda & Saida, 1978), but the asymmetry has not been tested. In visual terms, this is somewhat narrower than in English, but in informational terms, the window is at least as great (about 1.5 to 2 words ahead). It is not clear whether the somewhat different-sized window in other languages is due to higher level factors related to linguistic differences among the languages or to differing visual features that define the logographic and syllabic characters. Certainly, one cannot rule out the hypothesis that the features defining Chinese logographs are smaller and harder to see and hence the window in Chinese and Japanese, like English, is limited by purely visual factors.

Limits on Information Extraction During Scene Perception

The size of the window of useful information in scene perception is still a matter of considerable controversy. There are claims, for example, that subjects can extract huge amounts of information from a single fixation when viewing scenes represented by line drawings or photographs (e.g., Biederman, Mezzanotte, & Rabinowitz, 1982). When we get to pictures, however, the kinds of useful information are more varied and harder to classify than in reading. When we discussed text, we tacitly assumed that the letter and word boundary information were essentially the only relevant information sources on the page. In contrast, when people look at pictures (or the actual three-dimensional world), it is clear that they can extract some useful information very far from fixation (most noticeably motion). Furthermore, it is likely that extremely gross features of a scene (such as those that allow discrimination between a uniform region and a nonuniform region with an object of interest in it) can likely be extracted from great distances. Thus, the question in scene perception cannot be How far from fixation is useful information extracted? but rather How far can a certain kind of information be extracted? We will focus on information that is useful in object identification.

Several procedures have been used to understand the window of useful information in scene perception. One is recognition memory. That is, one relates the eccentricity from fixation of certain types of information to recognition memory performance on those scenes. In one example, Nelson and Loftus (1980) manipulated the eccentricity of a "significant detail" (i.e., a relatively small object in the scene) and analyzed the subjects' ability to judge whether the object was in the scene (vis-à-vis another plausible object in that location). The results of several experiments indicated that recognition memory for these objects was only a bit better than chance (although significantly so) when they were more than about 3° from fixation. Thus, for the purposes of recognition memory, it appears that for these particular scenes, only a little information is getting in farther than 3° that enables the viewer to identify individual objects.

A related technique used by Loftus and Mackworth (1978) involved putting an anomalous object in a scene (e.g., an octopus in a farm scene). They compared the subjects' eye movement pattern to that when viewing the same scene with a normal object in the same location (e.g., a tractor). Loftus and Mackworth found that subjects tended to fixate the anomalous object sooner than the matched normal object. This finding indicates that the subject extracts some meaningful information before fixating the object. However, given the analyses done in the experiment, it is not clear how far from fixation this effect holds. Moreover, although the conclusion was that the object is fixated "early" because it is semantically anomalous, the authors could not rule out the hypothesis that at least part of the effect was due to the anomalous object having had distinctive physical features.

A third paradigm employed the moving window technique (Saida & Ikeda, 1979). Subjects viewed a sequence of pictures and then were given a recognition memory test on the pictures. Performance on the memory test was analyzed as a function of the size of the window restriction imposed when the subject originally viewed the picture. Saida and Ikeda concluded that the size of the window was about half of the total area of the picture viewed for each of the two sizes of pictures that they employed. There are problems that arise in interpreting these experiments, however. First, the display was completely blank outside the window, so that one can only conclude that some aspect of the information outside the window was of value. Similarly, because one does not know exactly what information is used to achieve above-chance performance in the recognition memory task, one does not know how performance in the recognition memory task relates to what is perceived on a fixation. In particular, it is possible that finer detail was needed for good recognition memory performance in the smaller pictures than in the larger pictures.

To summarize, the above experiments indicate that some information can be extracted relatively far from fixation in viewing scenes. However, it appears that some, but not much, of the detail needed to identify objects is usually extracted in scene viewing from more than about 3°. In contrast, experiments with isolated line drawings of objects indicate that object identification can go on quite far from fixation. In one experiment, subjects could identify line drawings (that were 2° across) 95% of the time when they were 5° from fixation and 85% of the time when they were 10° from fixation (Pollatsek, Rayner, & Collins, 1984). This discrepancy suggests that the relatively limited amount of information extracted from extrafoveal objects in scene viewing is probably not due to simple acuity limitations. Part may be due to the background of the scene producing lateral inhibition (or camouflaging the object in some other way), and part may be due to attentional factors.

Integration of Information

We see that objects can be identified to some extent at relatively large eccentricities in normal scene viewing. However, the typical finding is that subjects usually fixate most objects that they want to identify. For example, Parker (1978) found that if subjects had to judge whether a line drawing was the same or different from a well-memorized standard scene, they had to fixate each object in turn to determine whether it was the same or different from the object in the memorized standard. (They did not need to fixate, however, to determine that an object was "missing.") Similarly, Henderson, Pollatsek, and Rayner (1989) found that when subjects viewed arrays of four line drawings of objects and answered an immediate memory test (e.g., "Was there a dog in the array?") they fixated each object in turn, skipping over objects only about 1% of the time.

In reading, the area in which meaningful information is extracted that can be used to identify words is more limited; however, it goes beyond the fixated word. One piece of evidence for this is that predictable words are skipped in reading more often than less predictable words. That is, if a word is predictable, the reader is more likely to identify it when it is to the right of the fixated word and skip over it. Part of this effect may be due to guessing that the predictable word is present (without actually doing visual processing of the letters). However, at least some of the increased skipping is due to actually processing the word to the right of fixation, because readers skip over a predictable word in a sentence more frequently than a less predictable word of the same length that is in the same location in the sentence (Balota, Pollatsek, & Rayner, 1985; Ehrlich & Rayner, 1981).

It thus appears that some meaningful information can be extracted beyond the word or object fixated. An important question is whether there is meaningful information that can be extracted that is less than full identification of the word or object but that would facilitate identification of the word when it is later fixated. A corollary question that is central to our discussion is what we can say about the processes of integration. Because we know more about reading, we will start there.

Integration of Information Across Saccades in Processing Text

The three paradigms we have discussed have all been employed in studying this question: the two involving reading text (the moving window technique and the boundary technique) and the (single word) parafoveal preview technique. We will focus on the results from the latter technique, because it is easier to interpret and discuss. However, we will argue below that the results from the three are in virtually complete agreement. As explained earlier, subjects in the parafoveal preview technique are given a string of letters in the parafovea. They then execute a saccade to that location and name the word that they are fixating. Because the display is often changed during the saccade, the string of letters in the parafovea may not be the same as the fixated word (Figure 10.4). The primary question is how much faster subjects are in naming a word, given a "good" preview of it in the parafovea than if given a preview that contains no meaningful visual information except where the stimulus is (e.g., a string of Xs). This *preview benefit* will be interpreted as a measure of integration of information across the two fixations.

Of primary interest is the preview benefit when the preview is similar, but not identical, to the fixated word. There have been many experiments (Balota & Rayner, 1983; McClelland & O'Regan, 1981; Rayner, 1978b; Rayner et al., 1978; Rayner, McConkie, & Zola, 1980), so we will summarize only the most relevant findings. First, there is a significant benefit when there is only a partial overlap; if only the first two or three letters of the preview and target match (e.g., "TRASH"–"TRAIN"), one gets a preview benefit that is close to that when the preview and target are identical. A second finding of major importance is that changing the case of the letters does not matter, so that a full preview benefit is obtained when "trash" is the preview and "TRASH" is the target (or vice

```
Fixation 1:        +         chest     (Preview)
                   *

Fixation 2:        +         chart     (Target)
                                *
```

FIGURE 10.4. Illustration of the single word parafoveal preview paradigm. The asterisk represents the fixation point. On the first fixation, the preview word "chest" is presented, and when the eye crosses a boundary about 0.5° from the fixation point, "chest" is replaced by "chart"; thus, the word "chart" is present for the entire second fixation. The condition depicted above is a visually similar preview condition. In addition, other previews could be "dense" or "xxxxx" (visually dissimilar control conditions), "chart" (identical preview), or "CHART" (case change). An important finding is that "CHART" is as good a preview as "chart" and that "chest" is almost as good a preview as "chart" (see text).

versa). Third, the beginnings of words matter more than the ends of words, so that there is little benefit when the last four letters overlap but the first letters do not (e.g., "CRASH"–"TRASH"). Moreover, the importance of the initial letters obtains even when the words are presented to the left of fixation, indicating that the effect is due to the importance of beginning letters in lexical processing rather than acuity (Rayner et al., 1980).

These findings indicate that information of some sort is retained on the first fixation that aids in naming the word on the second fixation. Moreover, partial information is facilitating, because a visually similar word markedly facilitates naming time. Most importantly, the finding that case change produces no effect indicates that the information retained is neither pixel by pixel information nor some sort of visual feature or form information, because the change of case should produce significant disruption as the forms of the letters change.

Before going on, a few general comments about the methodology are in order. First, many of the findings above were replicated with tasks that do not require explicit naming (e.g., lexical decision), so that they are not merely findings about naming (see also below). Second, the subject is rarely aware of what the first stimulus is (this is a surprising and still poorly understood phenomenon). In fact, subjects are not much above chance in determining if a change has taken place as long as there are the same number of letters in the preview and the target (Rayner, 1978b). Thus, the disruption in naming caused by changing letters is not due to a superficial disruption in the response system, but to the change of the letter information.

Before discussing nonverbal stimuli, we wish to show that similar findings are obtained in a more ecologically valid task, namely reading text. In these experiments, as indicated in the prior section, the information outside a window of normal text is degraded in various ways and the size of the window can also be varied. To set the stage, the reading rate is about 200 words per minute (wpm) if the right boundary of the window stops at the end of the fixated word (word n) but is about 300 wpm if it stops at the end of the following word (word $n+1$). (Reading rate is about 330 wpm in these experiments for normal text.) Thus, readers are extracting significant information from the word to the right of fixation in normal reading.

One issue of interest is what would happen if only parts of word $n+1$ are visible. In two experiments, we exposed the beginning two or three letters of word $n+1$ and found that reading was markedly improved over situations in which word $n+1$ was not visible and close to that when all of word $n+1$ was visible (Rayner, Well, Pollatsek, & Bertera, 1982). In addition, McConkie and Zola (1979) changed the case of text on each fixation (e.g., "MaNgRoVe" changed to "mAnGrOvE" and back to "MaNgRoVe") and found no effect of the case changing on reading rate or comprehension. Thus, as with naming isolated words, subjects reading text use partial information (primarily the beginnings of words) to help them read more rapidly, but it appears that visual features are not used in the process, as the case change manipulation had no effect. The text manipulations in the moving window experiments (including changes of case) are almost never noticed by the readers.

Other experiments employing naming and moving window techniques have tried to pin down the locus of the integration effect. To date, there is no evidence that partial meaning of the preview is processed. Several experiments (Inhoff, 1989; Lima, 1987) have failed to find any morphemic involvement, and Rayner, Balota, and Pollatsek (1986) failed to find any benefit from a semantically related word. In contrast, there is now clear evidence that phonological codes are involved in the integration process. Pollatsek, Lesch, Morris and Rayner (1992) demonstrated that a homophone provided greater preview benefit (in both a naming and reading task) than did a visually matched control (e.g., "CITE" was a better preview for "SITE" than "SAKE" was for "CAKE").

There is another line of evidence that indicates that the integration process is not visual: it does not depend on the preview and target stimuli being in the same location (Rayner et al., 1978). First, if the subject is required to maintain fixation while a parafoveal preview and a foveal target are presented (see Figure 10.4), the same parafoveal preview benefit obtains as in the experiments described above. That is, the two snapshots are as easily integrated when they are in different locations as when they are in the same location. Second, if the text is moved a character or two during the saccade in reading, readers are unaware of this and their reading rate and comprehension are unaltered (McConkie, Zola, & Wolverton, 1980; O'Regan, 1981). (Occasionally, small corrective saccades are made, which could merely reflect the fact that the fixation point is occasionally too far from the intended target.)

To summarize, there is no evidence that "raw" visual information that aids in the identification of words is maintained across fixations, even though a visually related stimulus presented on a prior fixation does aid in its later identification. One model that is consistent with the data is a parallel processing model of the form of McClelland and Rumelhart (1981) or Paap, Newsome, McDonald, & Schvaneveldt (1982). In these models, at early stages of word processing, a "candidate set" of lexical items that are similar to (i.e., have significant letter overlap with) the input are activated. As visual input continues, the excitation of the lexical entry for the actual stimulus would usually get significantly stronger than any of the other candidates and the word would be identified. (Occasionally, especially with poor or brief visual input, another lexical entry in the candidate set might be the most strongly activated and thus the word would be misidentified.) With the additional assumption that beginning letters are weighted most strongly in the activation of words, such a model makes sense of the constellation of findings. When a word such as "TRASH" is presented parafoveally, it will excite a neighborhood of lexical entries including "trash," "train," "trail," "treat," "threw," and "crash." However, the words that have the same beginning letters will be excited most strongly and will prime activation of those entries if they are presented on the succeeding fixation. That is, if "TRAIN" is presented on the first fixation, it will significantly activate the lexical entry "trash." When the subject then fixates "TRASH," this activation will significantly speed identification of "TRASH."

Whether or not this account is true in detail, it captures the essence of the findings, namely that there is no strong evidence that any visual feature information is retained across fixations and that the improved performance produced by the preview is produced primarily by activated lexical information. (Our homophone result suggests that the story might be a bit more complex than this, and that one might need to include an "auditory lexicon" in the explanation as well.)

Integration of Information in Object Identification

It would clearly be hazardous to generalize from processing of text to visual processing in general, both because reading involves language in ways that other visual processing tasks do not and because of the special symbolic nature of the stimuli. To try to bridge the gap, we have conducted a series of experiments involving pictures (Henderson, Pollatsek, & Rayner, 1987; Pollatsek et al., 1984; Pollatsek, Rayner, & Henderson, 1990). The results are somewhat different from those with words, but do not support an integrated visual beffer model.

The basic paradigm was the same as the naming task with words. A picture was presented extrafoveally and the subject moved his or her eyes to the picture and named the picture that appeared there after the eye movement. As in the word experiments, the picture could either be the same as the extrafoveal one or different from it. Unsurprisingly, there was a significant advantage in naming time (preview benefit) when an identical stimulus was presented extrafoveally (compared to a neutral baseline of a square frame presented extrafoveally).

As with the word experiments, it did not appear that the integration process was a summing of pixel information, because a size change in the picture made no difference. However, changing the form of the preview but preserving the meaning did alter the preview benefit. That is, the benefit was significantly smaller when one picture of a dog was the preview picture and a picture of a different dog was the target than when the preview and target were identical. Thus, integration is taking place at a level less abstract than the "basic level concept." Another finding that indicated that something less abstract than the meaning was involved in the integration process was that a visually similar preview was facilitory (such as a carrot preview for a baseball bat), whereas a semantically similar preview was not (such as a baseball preview for a baseball bat).

These findings indicate that visual form (in some sense) is mediating the integration across saccades. Whether visual features are preserved, however, is an open question. It is possible that the parafoveal visual form activates a neighborhood of stored entries visually similar to itself (as in the word identification models sketched earlier), so that a carrot presented parafoveally would excite the stored entries for carrot, pencil, baseball bat, etc. Thus, it is possible that the integration process might not be that different for words and pictures.

Another result that indicates that the integration process is different from that of an integrative buffer (a pixel-by-pixel summation process) is the fact that switching locations of pictures produces only a small change in the size of the facilitation effect (Pollatsek et al., 1990). Two extrafoveal pictures were presented side by side. When a saccade was made to the pictures, a single picture was presented foveally in the same location as one of the pictures. In fact, the preview benefit was only slightly less when the preview of the target was in the other location as when it was in the same location. Thus, it does not appear that anything resembling precise spatial alignment is needed for combining information across saccades. In addition, as with words, virtually the same preview benefit can be obtained if the preview is presented parafoveally, the target presented foveally with the subject maintaining fixation throughout (Pollatsek et al., 1990). Thus, although there is some nonabstract aspect to the integration of pictorial information, the integration process does not depend on spatial alignment of the two images.

Summary of Word and Object Identification

We started out with a model of integration across fixations that corresponded to naive intuition, namely that one integrated snapshots of the world on each fixation in a point-by-point manner. We then examined situations in which meaningful information was gathered extrafoveally with words and with line drawings of objects. With words, meaningful information about letters can be obtained somewhat beyond 3° of visual angle, because preview of letter information at this eccentricity can aid later foveal word identification. However, the information that is retained from the parafoveal input appears to be relatively abstract in that case changes do not affect the process. In addition, spatial alignment of the two images is unimportant. With pictures, neither precise spatial alignment nor preservation of size mattered. However, the integration appeared to depend more on the similarities of the forms.

We suggested that both sets of phenomena could be accounted for by a model in which "lexical entries" that represented objects that were similar to the visual input were excited on the first fixation, and if one of these entries matched the input on the second fixation, identification of the stimulus would be facilitated. In the case of pictures, the model clearly involves a lot of "hand waving," as it is far from clear what a lexicon of stored visual representations would be. The important point is that both sets of results suggest that the arena in which the integration process takes place is considerably removed from a point-by-point spatial buffer or even a feature-by-feature buffer if those features are indexed by spatial location.

Other Possible Integration Phenomena

The above discussion indicates that the visual system does not use anything like an integrative visual buffer for identifying objects. Perhaps, however, there are other perceptual acts that use such a mechanism. Over the years, there have been reports of such integration. Unfortunately, there were artifacts in most of them. Let us discuss these situations in some detail as they provide more negative evidence against such a buffer.

There have been several attempts to show that fragments of figures can be integrated across fixations into a unified perceptual whole. The strongest apparent such demonstration was by Jonides, Irwin, and Yantis (1982). They presented subjects a parafoveal display of 12 dots that were located in a 5 × 5 matrix. When the subjects fixated that location, the original 12 dots were removed and a different 12 dots were presented. The subjects' task was to report the location of the dot in the array that was not illuminated, an easy task if subjects can integrate the visual information across fixations and an easy task if both displays are presented on the same fixation (Di Lollo, 1977). The original report was that subjects did quite well on the task and scored much higher than in a control condition where the retinal events were duplicated but the arrays were not spatially aligned (i.e., the subject maintained fixation while the parafoveal and foveal stimuli were presented).

Unfortunately, this result has subsequently been shown to be the result of an artifact. The stimuli were presented on a CRT screen, and although phosphor decays rapidly in the first few milliseconds to about 1% of its former luminance, decay is gradual after that (even for "fast" phosphors). Thus, the integration reported could have been the integration of the information presented on the second fixation and the remaining phosphor excitation from the first fixation. When this artifact was controlled, there was no longer any evidence of integration beyond the little that could be done when the images were not spatially aligned (Bridgeman & Mayer, 1983; Irwin, Yantis, & Jonides, 1983; Jonides, Irwin, & Yantis, 1983; O'Regan & Levy-Schoen, 1983; Rayner & Pollatsek, 1983).

Another report of integration across saccades has also been shown to be a result of the phosphor artifact. Wolf, Hauske, and Lupp (1978, 1980) reported that a square-wave grating of a certain frequency presented parafoveally facilitated perception of a grating seen foveally on the next fixation if the two were spatially aligned. However, Irwin, Zacks, and Brown (1989) have demonstrated that this facilitation disappears when phosphor persistence is controlled for.

Another phenomenon that would be consistent with an integrated visual buffer model is if "backward masking" occurred across fixations. That is, if a stimulus appeared in a spatial location and a "mask" appeared in the same spatial location on the subsequent fixation, would the mask affect the visibility of the stimulus? Davidson, Fox, and Dick (1973) reported that there was an cross-saccadic effect of retinotopic masking (i.e., that a later mask in the same retinal location inhibited identification of a stimulus) and that a mask in the same spatial location as the target appeared phenomenally to cover it but did not actually degrade the information. Later work by Irwin, Brown, and Sun (1988) indicates that the retinal masking phenomenon can be replicated. However, there is little evidence that the mask in the same spatial location has any effect either informationally or phenomenally on the visibility of the target stimulus (see also Van der Heijden, Bridgeman, & Mewhort, 1986).

IT IS REASONABLE THAT VISUAL INFORMATION IS NOT INTEGRATED ACROSS FIXATIONS

In sum, there is little evidence supporting the notion that *visual* information processed on one fixation is retained after that fixation. The only data that we presented that could be interpreted in that light is the visual similarity result in object identification. In that case, however, there is an alternative explanation: a family of object detectors is excited. Moreover, even that effect did not depend on any spatial alignment, so that the integration process would not appear to be done in anything like an integrative visual buffer.

Although these negative findings might seem surprising at first, further reflection indicates that they might make sense. Consider what would be involved in integrating visual information across saccades. One obstacle would be the different resolution of the information processed foveally compared to that processed extrafoveally. One image would be clear and the other "fuzzy." Although such integration is possible, it is not clear whether the use of the preview would increase or decrease the signal-to-noise ratio of the information obtained foveally, whether it be pixels, edge detectors, or whatever. Second, the scale of the visual images may not be the same. That is, there may be significant distortions of scale as one moves out from the fovea to the periphery. Third, there are changes in the image from fixation to fixation produced by the optics of the visual system that may not easily be compensated for by the neural hardware. For example, lines that are parallel on one fixation may not be parallel on a subsequent fixation. Fourth, precise alignment of the "corresponding" visual information may be difficult because there is variability in the eye movement system: eye movements only go approximately to the intended target. Although it is possible that the visual system monitors the amount of movement of the eye (and/or head) and automatically compensates for it, it seems implausible and is contraindicated by the available data. For example, as indicated earlier, McConkie et al. (1980) moved the line of text by small amounts horizontally when the eye was in a saccade and it neither affected the speed of reading nor were subjects aware of this movement. If alignment of information depended on precise calibration of the actual movement of the eye, one would expect that these movements would have been detectable.

Thus, given the fact that the extrafoveal and foveal images are different, given that the extrafoveal one is relatively noisy, and given that precise alignment is difficult, integration of relatively raw information is unlikely to be a benefit to object identification or to perception of any other kind of detail that can be obtained adequately from the fovea. In contrast, it does make sense that information is meaningfully combined at a somewhat more abstract level. Even fuzzy information can alter the odds as to what an object is (motion and gross real-world size information would be particularly helpful as would some information about overall shape). In other words, in the constrained set of real-world objects, it would make sense to retain and use the noisy data obtained from the parafovea and even the periphery.

We hasten to point out, though, that our results with pictures indicate that the "object" for which evidence is accumulating across fixations is more concrete than a basic-level concept (e.g., "dog"). Instead, it appears to be something like a representation of the particular dog, perhaps an excitation of stored memory exemplars that are visually similar to that dog. Or, rather than the lexical metaphor that we have used for pictures, consider an alternative distributed representation metaphor. In such a model, the visual information would be expressed as the pattern of excitation on a set of n input "feature" vectors and the identification of the visual form would be expressed as a pattern of excitation on a set of m output vectors, with a matrix of nm weights transforming the input into the outputs. Moreover, as is standard in these models, the weights would be conditioned by past experience so that output patterns that matched prior input patterns were "better" in terms of some criterion. It might make sense to postulate that the transformation from extrafoveal information to output pattern would be different for extrafoveal information, because certain information is missing or less diagnostic (e.g., color, high spatial-frequency information). Thus, by saying that the integration of information is not "visual" but more "abstract," we are supposing that after the eye movement is made, the excitation of the input vectors from the prior fixation is lost, and all that remains is the excitation from the output vectors.

Thus, in essence, all that is left after a fixation is the excitation of some sort of memory representation (be it a set of vectors in "object space" or a set of lexical entries) and not anything one would call "visual features." To put it differently, all that is left of the visual image of a dog after a saccade (assuming the dog is removed) is no different in kind from the information that would be used if you were told to form an image of the dog 5 minutes later. Moreover, the work cited earlier indicates that this memory representation is not tightly bound to location information.

Can it really be true that all visual feature information from the prior fixation is flushed away from the system once a new fixation begins? Our introspection suggests otherwise, but our introspection may be misleading, because each new fixation presents some information about the entire visual display and thus we are perceiving something at each spatial location on each fixation. Although we clearly have more information than the current visual information from locations that have been previously fixated—not only about the identity of objects, but about their location, depth, orientation, etc.—that information may be maintained in a more abstract form than our intuition suggests.

Positive Evidence for Visual Integration?

One phenomenon that we noticed when setting up our picture experiments is that if there were large changes in size in the picture from parafovea to fovea (more than about 30%) one noticed looming or receding effects. Although we have not done appropriate controls either for phosphor persistence or for whether such effects would still obtain if the two images were not spatially aligned, we suspect that there is a real effect there. On one level the phenomenon makes sense, because retinal image size can probably be computed fairly accurately even from a fuzzy image and even a rough calculation would allow a veridical computation to be made of whether an object was coming toward you or going away from you. On another level it does not make sense, because it is not clear why one would need to do such a computation across saccades; in most real-world situations, sufficient information should occur within fixations to make the computation. The explanation may be that although organisms could survive even if such computations are not done, it may be easier to leave whatever is computing this kind of motion running at all times rather than turning it off and on during a saccade. Perhaps computations of the speed and direction of such motions are aided by being left on at all times. (Of course, the retinal information during the saccade would have to be filtered out in such computations.)

There is a second piece of evidence that suggests that visual information is integrated across saccades (this is also cited in this context by Feldman, 1985). When viewing one of Kanisza's figures, one sees illusory edges that are presumably formed from the local information of the wedges. However, when one forces oneself to maintain fixation in the center, the edges seem to disappear. In contrast, when one consciously fixates the wedges in turn, the edges appear as clear as in normal viewing (i.e., when one is not aware of what he or she is doing). This suggests that the illusory contours are the product of integrating detailed visual information about the edges of the wedges from fixation to fixation. If so, this would be an interesting example of integration of low-level featural information across fixations. We plan to investigate this phenomenon using a moving window technique in order to determine if the contour information can be integrated across fixations.

Another piece of evidence suggestive of integration of visual information across saccades has been presented by Palmer and Ames (1989). Their task was to compare the lengths of two line segments. In one condition, the lines were seen foveally on different fixations and in a control condition one line was only seen extrafoveally. They took the superiority in the former condition to reflect a more accurate comparison enabled by examining the lines in the fovea and assumed that the comparison process was across visual representations. Although the former assumption is clearly true, the latter is not compelling, as subjects could code the length information more abstractly (e.g., into numerals). Thus, this result is only suggestive; a better criterion is needed to determine if the comparison process is visual.

These results suggest that integration of visual feature information may occur in tasks other than object identification if we look hard enough. We think, however, that the domain of such tasks is likely to be quite restricted. The phenomenon of motion detection from size change seems likely to be real, and although not of obvious ecological benefit, may be related to a system that is not turned off during saccades. We suspect, however, that it is related to the collicular-cerebellar-cortical pathways related to visual attention and eye movements and not to the visual system dealing with pattern recognition (Ungerleider, 1985; Ungerleider & Mishkin, 1985; Wurtz, Goldberg, & Robinson, 1980, 1982). Aside from whatever computations are related to that system, however, we see no compelling reason why the visual system would need such a visual feature integration process.

First, we feel that if such an integration process exists, it would be likely to be "automatic," because it would be relatively low level. That is, it seems implausible that some sort of executive would be making decisions about turning such a mechanism on or off depending on the task demands. That is, if the process does not operate in object identification or in integrating point information to achieve a unified percept, then it is unlikely to operate for any perceptual act.

Second, upon much reflection, it is not clear what ecologically important tasks would be markedly enhanced by integration of visual information from successive fixations. We have already discussed why it does not make sense for object identification. Let us discuss briefly why it may not make sense for another class of tasks: integration of detailed foveal information acquired from two successive fixations.

Palmer and Ames' (1989) line length judgment task was an exemplar of this kind of task. But what real-world task would this relate to? Why would such accurate relative size judgments be of any value? One possibility is that such detailed information about line segments is needed in tasks like texture judgment. Thus, perhaps the details of the texture in one location could be related to the details of texture in another location on the next fixation. But why? One use of relative texture information is to determine if the two areas are part of the same surface. However, if the perceiver has reason to believe that two locations are on different surfaces, the strategy of first fixating one region and then the other and comparing details of the feature information seems nonoptimal. A better strategy would be to attempt to fixate the region where the discontinuity is likely to be and process the textural difference on a single fixation. (Although we have made the argument in detail for texture based on line segments, a similar argument can be made for other visual features such as brightness, hue, and dot density.)

Another class of tasks that suggests itself is integration of local line segment or edge information to form more global computations. One example would be if an object occludes an edge, the perceiver may use the information that the pieces of the occluded edge are co-linear in order to help determine that they are indeed part of the same edge, and thus to "parse" the scene correctly (e.g., Waltz, 1975). Perhaps this integration of edge information is related to the Kanisza illusory contour phenomena discussed earlier. However, we see no compelling reason that the visual system uses or needs such precise alignment of information. First, there is a well-known illusion (the Poggendorf illusion) that suggests that such judgments are not made well. Second, we suspect that if two edges are judged to be approximately co-linear (which can be done on a single fixation), that is probably good enough for the parsing procedure.

More generally, it is not clear that very precise global integration of any kind is done on details from individual fixations. The examples from elementary perception texts are legion: tuning forks with three prongs and two prongs, impossible "twisted" figures, and Escher drawings such as the endlessly ascending staircase and the circle of endlessly flowing water with a waterfall in it. These all suggest that detailed visual information from each fixation is not integrated with detailed information from succeeding fixations. Instead, an attempt is made to integrate detail on each fixation. If two pieces of detail are too far apart and/or or too small for both to be perceived on a single fixation, then all that can be integrated with the current information is the memory of the detail seen on the prior fixation (analogous to a lexical representation). Because the geometric absurdities of the above examples can be tolerated by the visual system, it appears that the integration of these memories is quite tolerant of mismatches between the parts extracted on successive fixations.

The above analysis may turn out to be wrong and some global information may be integrated across fixations. For example, the illusory contours in the Kanisza figure may be formed from information acquired on separate fixations. If so, however, the above analysis indicates that some hard thinking is needed to understand why the visual system would have such a computation in it.

Acknowledgments. Preparation of this chapter was supported by National Science Foundation grant BNS 86-09336 and National Institutes of Health grant HD26765. We thank Susan Boyce and Robin Morris for their helpful comments.

References

Alpern, M. (1962). Muscular mechanisms. In H. Davson (Ed.), *The Eye* (Vol. 3). New York: Academic Press.

Balota, D.A., Pollatsek, A., & Rayner, K. (1985). The interaction of contextual constraints and parafoveal visual information in reading. *Cognitive Psychology*, *17*, 364–390.

Balota, D.A., & Rayner, K. (1983). Parafoveal visual information and semantic contextual constraints. *Journal of Experimental Psychology: Human Perception and Performance*, *9*, 726–738.

Biederman, I., Mezzanotte, R.J., & Rabinowitz, J.C. (1982). Scene perception: detecting and judging objects undergoing relational violations. *Cognitive Psychology*, *14*, 143–177.

Bouma, H. (1973). Visual interference in the parafoveal recognition of initial and final letters of words. *Vision Research*, *13*, 767–782.

Bridgeman, B., & Mayer, M. (1983). Failure to integrate visual information from successive fixations. *Bulletin of the Psychonomic Society*, *21*, 285–286.

Davidson, M.L., Fox, M.J., & Dick, A.O. (1973). The effect of eye movements and backward masking on perceptual location. *Perception & Psychophysics*, *14*, 110–116.

DenBuurman, R., Boersma, T., & Gerrisen, J.F. (1981). Eye movements and the perceptual span in reading. *Reading Research Quarterly*, *16*, 227–235.

Di Lollo, V. (1977). On the spatio-temporal interactions of brief visual displays. In R.H. Day & G.V. Stanley (Eds.), *Studies in perception* (pp. 39–55) Perth: University of Western Australia Press.

Ehrlich, S.F., & Rayner, K. (1981). Contextual effects on word perception and eye movements during reading. *Journal of Verbal Learning and Verbal Behavior*, *20*, 641–655.

Estes, W.K., Allmeyer, D.H., & Reder, S.M. (1976). Serial position functions for letter identification at brief and extended exposure durations. *Perception & Psychophysics*, *19*, 1–15.

Feldman, J.A. (1985). Four frames suffice: A provisional model of vision and space. *Behavioral and Brain Sciences*, *8*, 265–289.

Henderson, J.M., Pollatsek, A., & Rayner, K. (1987). The effects of foveal priming and extrafoveal preview on object identification. *Journal of Experimental Psychology: Human Perception and Performance*, *13*, 449–463.

Henderson, J.M., Pollatsek, A., & Rayner, K. (1989). Covert attention and extrafoveal information use during object identification. *Perception & Psychophysics*, *45*, 196–208.

Ikeda, M., & Saida, S. (1978). Span of recognition in reading. *Vision Research*, *18*, 83–88.

Inhoff, A.W. (1989). Lexical access during eye fixations in sentence reading: Are word access codes used to integrate lexical information across interword fixations? *Journal of Memory and Language*, *28*, 444–461.

Irwin, D.E., Brown, J.S., & Sun, J-S. (1988). Visual masking and visual integration across saccadic eye movements. *Journal of Experimental Psychology: General*, *117*, 276–287.

Irwin, D.E., Yantis, S., & Jonides, J. (1983). Evidence against visual integration across saccadic eye movements. *Perception & Psychophysics*, *34*, 49–57.

Irwin, D.E., Zacks, J.L., & Brown, J.S. (1989). Visual memory and the perception of a stable visual environment. *Perception & Psychophysics*, *47*, 35–46.

Jonides, J., Irwin, D.E., & Yantis, S. (1982). Integrating visual information from successive fixations. *Science*, *215*, 192–194.

Jonides, J., Irwin, D.E., & Yantis, S. (1983). Failure to integrate information from successive fixations. *Science*, *222*, 188.

Lima, S.D. (1987). Morphological analysis in sentence reading. *Journal of Memory and Language*, *26*, 84–99.

Loftus, G.R., & Mackworth, N.H. (1978). Cognitive determinants of fixation location during picture viewing. *Journal of Experimental Psychology: Human Perception & Performance*, *4*, 565–572.

Mackworth, N.H. (1965). Visual noise causes tunnel vision. *Psychonomic Science*, *3*, 67–68.

Marr, D. (1982) *Vision: A computational investigation into the human representation and processing of visual information*. San Francisco: W.H. Freeman.

Matin, E. (1974). Saccadic suppression: A review and an analysis. *Psychological Bulletin, 81*, 899–917.

McClelland, J.L., & O'Regan, J.K. (1981). Expectations increase the benefit derived from parafoveal visual information in reading words aloud. *Journal of Experimental Psychology: Human Perception and Performance, 7*, 634–644.

McClelland, J.L., & Rumelhart, D.E. (1981). An interactive activation model of context effects in letter perception: Part 1. An account of basic findings. *Psychological Review, 88*, 375–407.

McConkie, G.W., & Rayner, K. (1975). The span of the effective stimulus during a fixation in reading. *Perception & Psychophysics, 17*, 578–586.

McConkie, G.W., & Rayner, K. (1976a). Identifying the span of the effective stimulus in reading: Literature review and theories of reading. In H. Singer & R.B. Ruddell (Eds.), *Theoretical models and processes in reading*. Newark, DE: International Reading Association.

McConkie, G.W., & Rayner, K. (1976b). Asymmetry of the perceptual span in reading. *Bulletin of the Psychonomic Society, 8*, 365–368.

McConkie, G.W., Underwood, N.R., Zola, D., & Wolverton, G.S. (1985). Some temporal characteristics of processing during reading. *Journal of Experimental Psychology: Human Perception and Performance, 11*, 168–186.

McConkie, G.W., & Zola, D. (1979). Is visual information integrated across successive fixations in reading? *Perception & Psychophysics, 25*, 221–224.

McConkie, G.W., Zola, D., & Wolverton, G.S. (1980, April). *How precise is eye guidance?* Paper presented at the annual meeting of the American Educational Research Association, Boston, MA.

Morrison, R.E., & Rayner, K. (1981). Saccade size in reading depends upon character spaces and not visual angle. *Perception & Psychophysics, 30*, 395–396.

Nelson, W.W., & Loftus, G.R. (1980). The functional visual field during picture viewing. *Journal of Experimental Psychology: Human Learning and Memory, 6*, 391–399.

O'Regan, J.K. (1981). The convenient viewing position hypothesis. In D.F. Fisher, R.A. Monty, & J.W. Senders (Eds.), *Eye movements: Cognition and visual perception*. Hillsdale, NJ: Erlbaum.

O'Regan, J.K., & Levy-Schoen, A. (1983). Integrating visual information from successive fixations: Does trans-saccadic fusion exist? *Vision Research, 23*, 765–768.

Paap, K.R., Newsome, S.L., McDonald, J.E., & Schvaneveldt, R.W. (1982). An activation-verification model for letter and word recognition: The word superiority effect. *Psychological Review, 89*, 573–594.

Palmer, J., & Ames, C.T. (1989). Measuring the effect of multiple eye fixations on size and shape discrimination. *Investigative Ophthalmology and Visual Science (Supplement), 30*, 159.

Parker, R.E. (1978). Picture processing during recognition. *Journal of Experimental Psychology: Human Perception and Performance, 4*, 284–293.

Pirenne, M.H. (1967). *Vision and the eye* (2nd ed.). London: Chapman and Hall.

Pollatsek, A., Bolozky, S., Well, A.D., & Rayner K. (1981). Asymmetries in the perceptual span for Israeli readers. *Brain and Language*, *14*, 174–180.

Pollatsek, A., Lesch, M., Morris, R.K., & Rayner, K. (1992). Phonological codes are used in integrating information across saccades in word identification and reading. *Journal of Experimental Psychology: Human Perception and Performance*, *18*, 148–162.

Pollatsek, A., Rayner, K., & Balota, D.A. (1986). Inferences about eye movement control from the perceptual span in reading. *Perception & Psychophysics*, *40*, 123–130.

Pollatsek, A., Rayner, K., & Collins, W.E. (1984). Integrating pictorial information across eye movements. *Journal of Experimental Psychology: General*, *113*, 426–442.

Pollatsek, A., Rayner, K., & Henderson, J.M. (1990). Role of spatial location in integration of pictorial information across saccades. *Journal of Experimental Psychology: Human Perception and Performance*, *16*, 199–210.

Rayner, K. (1975). The perceptual span and peripheral cues in reading. *Cognitive Psychology*, *7*, 65–81.

Rayner, K. (1978a). Eye movements in reading and information processing. *Psychological Bulletin*, *85*, 618–660.

Rayner, K. (1978b). Foveal and parafoveal cues in reading. In J. Requin (Ed.), *Attention and performance VII*. Hillsdale, NJ: Erlbaum.

Rayner, K., Balota, D.A., & Pollatsek, A. (1986). Against parafoveal semantic preprocessing during eye fixations in reading. *Canadian Journal of Psychology*, *40*, 473–483.

Rayner, K., & Bertera, J.H. (1979). Reading without a fovea. *Science*, *206*, 468–469.

Rayner, K., Inhoff, A.W., Morrison, R., Slowiaczek, M.L., & Bertera, J.H. (1981). Masking of foveal and parafoveal vision during eye fixations in reading. *Journal of Experimental Psychology: Human Perception and Performance*, *7*, 167–179.

Rayner, K., McConkie, G.W., & Ehrlich, S.F. (1978). Eye movements and integrating information across fixations. *Journal of Experimental Psychology: Human Perception and Performance*, *4*, 529–544.

Rayner, K., McConkie, G.W., & Zola, D. (1980). Integrating information across eye movements. *Cognitive Psychology*, *12*, 206–226.

Rayner, K., & Pollatsek, A. (1983). Is visual information integrated across saccades? *Perception & Psychophysics*, *34*, 39–48.

Rayner, K., Well, A.D., & Pollatsek, A. (1980). Asymmetry of the effective visual field in reading. *Perception & Psychophysics*, *27*, 537–544.

Rayner, K., Well, A.D., Pollatsek, A., & Bertera, J.H. (1982). The availability of useful information to the right of fixation in reading. *Perception & Psychophysics*, *31*, 537–550.

Saida, S., & Ikeda, M. (1979). Useful visual field size for pattern perception. *Perception & Psychophysics*, *25*, 119–125.

Trehub, A. (1977). Neuronal models for cognitive processes: Networks for learning, perception, and imagination. *Journal of Theoretical Biology*, *65*, 141–169.

Ungerleider, L.G. (1985). The corticocortical pathways for object recognition and spatial perception. In C.G. Chagas (Ed.), *Pattern recognition mechanisms*. Rome: Pontificiae Academiae Scientiarum Scripta Varia.

Ungerleider, L.G., & Mishkin, M. (1985). Two cortical visual systems. In D.J. Ingle, M.A. Goodale, & R.J.W. Mansfield (Eds.), *Analysis of visual behavior.* Cambridge, MA: MIT Press.

Van der Heijden, A.H.C., Bridgeman, B., & Mewhort, D.J.K. (1986). Is stimulus persistence affected by eye movements? A critique of Davidson, Fox, and Dick (1973). *Psychological Research, 48,* 179–181.

Waltz, D. (1975). Understanding line drawings of scenes with shadows. In P.H. Winston (Ed.), *The Psychology of computer vision.* New York: McGraw-Hill.

Wolf, W., Hauske, G., & Lupp, U. (1978). How presaccadic gratings modify post-saccadic modulation transfer function. *Vision Research, 18,* 1173–1179.

Wolf, W., Hauske, G., & Lupp, U. (1980). Interaction of pre- and post-saccadic patterns having the same coordinates in space. *Vision Research, 20,* 117–125.

Wurtz, R.H., Goldberg M.E., & Robinson, D.L. (1980). Behavioral modulation of visual responses in the monkey: Stimulus selection for attention and movement. In J.M. Sprague & A.N. Epstein (Eds.), *Progress in psychobiology and physiological psychology (Vol. 9)* New York: Academic Press.

Wurtz, R.H., Goldberg, M.E., & Robinson, D.L. (1982). Brain mechanisms of visual attention. *Scientific American, 246,* 124–135.

11
The Matter and Mechanisms of Integration

Donald L. Fisher

The visual world appears phenomenally as a stable, connected whole. Yet it is served up in a piecemeal fashion, one visual snapshot at a time. This has led quite naturally to the hypothesis that a spatially coherent picture of the whole is constructed from separate snapshots by aligning the snapshots spatiotopically and then integrating the information from the separate snapshots at each spatial location (e.g., Jonides, Irwin, & Yantis, 1982; McConkie & Rayner, 1976; Trehub, 1977). If the above "snapshot" hypothesis is true, then one should find the following: Specifically, suppose that on fixation n information is presented in the periphery at a given spatiotopic location and on fixation $n+1$ the eye foveates the (possibly different) information presented at the same spatiotopic location. Then, the information presented in the periphery on fixation n (the previewed information) ought to have an influence on the processing of the information presented to the fovea on fixation $n+1$ (the target information). This follows because the spatiotopic co-ordinates of the peripheral (previewed) and subsequent foveal (target) information are identical and therefore by hypothesis this information is integrated.

In the various chapters in this section, an attempt has been made to explore the influence of previewed information on subsequent target processing. Not too surprisingly, various investigators find strong evidence that the previewed information influences target processing. However, there has been an almost total rejection of the original (snapshot) explanation of why it is that information in the periphery has the influence that it does on subsequent foveal processing.

In the following brief discussion of the chapters presented in this section, I first want to review a selected subset of those experiments run by the investigators that have led them to reject the naive "snapshot" hypothesis described above. I then want to discuss the work by these investigators that suggests what exactly it is that is being integrated across fixations (the matter of integration) and how it is that this integration occurs (the mechanism of integration). Finally, I want to put the more speculative comments by the various investigators about the matter and mechanisms of integration into a somewhat broader context.

Three of the chapters (Hayhoe, Lachter, and Moeller; Irwin; and Pollatsek and Rayner) neatly fit into the above format because they all focus on the same general issues. The fourth chapter (Prinz, Nattkemper, and Ullmann) focuses on a related issue, in particular, the degree to which information gathered in a fixation influences the temporal and spatial parameters of successive saccades. The integration of the material in that chapter into the existing format occurs best at the end of the discussion. There, it can be made clear just how closely linked the two sets of topics really are.

The Snapshot Hypothesis

Three sets of experiments stand out as critical in the evaluation of the snapshot hypothesis. The first set is exemplified by the work of Irwin, Zacks, and Brown (1990). They presented to subjects in the periphery a subset of dots randomly selected from a matrix of r rows and c columns. When subjects moved their eyes to the parafovea, all dots that had been presented were removed and all dots but one that had not been presented were now displayed. Thus a total of $rc - 1$ dots were presented across fixations. Subjects were asked to indicate the location of the missing dot. If the form of each snapshot that gets integrated is low-level (raw or nearly raw) sensory data and if spatiotopic integration is occurring, then the task should be an easy one. In fact, Irwin et al. found no evidence that spatiotopic integration of raw sensory data could occur (also see Rayner & Pollatsek, 1983).

The above set of experiments strongly suggests that the snapshot hypothesis in its entirety fails. In the second set of experiments, a more detailed test was made of the assumption that the matter of integration is low-level stimulus information. These experiments are exemplified by the work of Rayner, McConkie, and Zola (1980). They presented a word in the parafovea to subjects. Subjects then moved their eyes to the word. The word either remained the same across fixations or was changed in various ways. Specifically, a change in the case of the word was made in one condition (e.g., the word "apple" appeared in the parafovea on one fixation and the word "APPLE" appeared in the fovea on the subsequent fixation). A change of the identity of the word was made in another condition (e.g., the word "apple" appeared in the parafovea and the word "fruit" appeared in fovea). Rayner et al. found that subjects benefited just as much from a parafoveal preview when the word was of a different case as they did when it was of the same case.

In the third set of experiments a more detailed test was made of the assumption that spatiotopic coordinates serve as the basis for integrating information across saccades. These experiments are nicely exemplified by the work of Rayner, McConkie, and Ehrlich (1978). They asked whether the preview benefit would occur if the spatiotopic coordinates of the information to be integrated were not identical. Specifically, unlike the condition described above, Rayner et al. required subjects to maintain fixation. A word was presented first in the parafovea followed by the presentation in the fovea of either an identical word or a word that had been changed in one of several ways. Interestingly, they found that the preview benefit when the spatiotopic coordinates of successive presentations of a stimulus were not kept constant was about as large as it was when the spatiotopic coordinates of the word were kept constant across fixations.

The Matter and Mechanisms of Integration Reconsidered

Given the continuing failure to find evidence for the snapshot hypothesis, the focus of recent research has shifted away from the direct testing of this hypothesis and toward the testing of alternative hypotheses. The various alternatives have been proposed as answers to three related questions that follow from the failure of the snapshot hypothesis. Specifically, one set of studies has attempted to determine why it is that parafoveal or peripheral information has a demonstrable effect if the snapshot hypothesis is no longer tenable. Another set of studies has attempted to determine under what circumstances, if any, one can find evidence of the retinotopic integration across saccades of raw, uncoded information. And a final set of studies has attempted to determine under what circumstances, if any, one can find evidence of spatiotopic integration across saccades of higher level, abstract information.

Word and Picture Integration

As noted above, a word presented in the parafovea can prime the processing of that word when it is foveated. The case change results demonstrate that something at a higher level than visual features is responsible for the integration. One obvious candidate is the word. Interestingly, the preview benefit remains almost as large when the word that appears in the parafovea matches the fixated word on only the first two or three letters as when it is identical to the fixated word. A second possible candidate is the meaning of the word. However, Rayner, Balota, and Pollatsek (1986) have failed to find any preview benefit when the previewed word is related semantically to the target word.

In a related series of experiments (e.g., Pollatsek, Rayner, & Henderson, 1990), an attempt has been made to determine why a preview benefit exists for pictures. As with words, there is no evidence that spatiotopic integration is required because changes in the size of the previewed and target information do not alter the preview benefit. Furthermore, and again as with words, there is no evidence for semantic facilitation. For example, no benefit is obtained when a baseball is the previewed information and a baseball cap is the target information. Interestingly, there does appear to be some evidence for facilitation based on shapes. For example, when a carrot is the previewed information it benefits the subsequent processing of a baseball bat presented as the target. This is consistent with the finding that one picture of a dog presented as the previewed information does *not* benefit a second, different picture of a dog presented as the target.

Pollatsek and Rayner (this volume) outline a model consistent with the results from the studies of word and picture integration. First, consider the results from studies of word integration. Like McClelland and Rumelhart (1981), Pollatsek and Rayner assume that the net result of presenting a stimulus word parafoveally is that the feature, letter, and word detectors specific to the stimulus word are activated. When subjects then fixate the identical stimulus word in the same case all units remain primed and thus there is a large preview benefit. When subjects fixate an identical stimulus word in a different case (or a different spatiotopic location) the word unit remains primed and there is still facilitation. And when subjects fixate words that are identical only in the first two letters, this serves as enough of an input to the already primed word unit to generate a preview benefit.

Next, consider the results from the studies of picture integration. Specifically, consider the result that requires a slight twist on the explanations offered above. This is the finding that when a picture that appears as the previewed information is visually similar (but semantically unrelated) to the picture that appears as the target, there is still a strong preview benefit. Pollatsek and Rayner seem to be suggesting that the information from the elementary feature detectors is coded on some higher dimensions of form. Because the dimensions of form may overlap for similarly shaped objects, priming can occur and with it a preview benefit.

Retinotopic Integration

No evidence exists for the spatiotopic integration of low-level information across saccades (e.g., Irwin, Yantis, & Jonides, 1983). However, the question of whether information can be integrated retinotopically across saccades has until recently remained an open one.

Irwin et al. (1990) now have information that such an integration can be performed. Specifically, they presented *foveally* a subset of dots randomly selected from a matrix. This presentation either occurred just before or long before the saccade. After the saccade, subjects were presented *foveally* the remaining dots minus one. In this case, if the two subsets of dots can be integrated retinotopically, then they reconstitute the full matrix (minus one) of dots. In fact, Irwin et al. found that retinotopic integration occurs when the first frame is presented almost immediately before the second frame (in particular, when the interframe interval averaged 67 ms), but not when the first frame is presented long before the second frame (on average 246 ms).

Spatiotopic Integration

Although it appears that low-level information cannot be integrated spatiotopically across saccades, it is not necessarily the case that higher level information cannot be so integrated. Indeed, one of the experiments reported in this section suggests that spatiotopic integration does occur when the information being integrated is at a relatively high level.

Briefly, Hayhoe, Lachter, and Feldman (1991) presented three dots to subjects. The subjects were then asked to indicate whether the three dots did or did not form a right triangle. The three dots were presented in several conditions. First, in the referenced simultaneous condition, all three dots were presented at once and for a brief period of time. The central fixation point to which the subject was attending remained visible throughout (and served as a possible reference point). Eye movements were precluded because the dots were flashed so briefly. Second, in the referenced successive position, the three dots were presented one at a time and, again, very briefly. The interval of time between the presentation of successive dots was varied across trials. Subjects had to move their eyes to the anticipated location of a new dot as soon as the current dot disappeared. The central fixation point remained visible throughout. Third, in the unreferenced successive condition the fixation point was removed as soon as the trial began. Otherwise, the third condition was identical to the second.

Hayhoe et al. (1991) found that subjects were about as good in the referenced simultaneous condition as they were in the referenced successive condition. Subjects performed most poorly in the unreferenced successive condition. This indicates that subjects are able spatiotopically to integrate material across successive fixations with little decrement as long as a reference point remains constant throughout. Furthermore, the fact that subjects performed about as well when the interval separating successive presentations of the dots was 800 ms as they did when the interval separating successive presentations of the dot was 200 ms suggests that the memory involved was not the low-level one typical of visible persistence but rather the higher level memories Irwin (this volume) refers to as information persistence or short-term visual store.

The Snapshot Hypothesis Reconsidered

Research and theory have moved away from the snapshot hypothesis. Given the weight of the evidence against this hypothesis, various investigators have gone back to rethink the original and (at the time) compelling arguments that led the field to embrace the hypothesis. This rethinking has convinced various investigators that the snapshot hypothesis is a much more implausible one than originally had been assumed. At the same time, in the course of exploring alternatives to the snapshot hypothesis several investigators have come upon results that appear to be explainable most easily in terms of the original hypothesis. Below, I consider the new arguments against the snapshot hypothesis and the recent experimental evidence that suggests that in certain very limited cases subjects may indeed integrate spatiotopically the information across successive saccades.

The Case Against Spatiotopic Integration of Low-Level Information

Irwin is perhaps the most controversial in the stand he appears to be moving toward on the question of the spatiotopic integration of low-level information. Specifically, he suggests that the only information that remains from one saccade to the next is whatever high-level abstract description of the world gets encoded in visual short-term memory. Pollatsek and Rayner (this volume) are somewhat more cautious. They suggest that there is some evidence consistent with the existence of the spatiotopic integration of low-level information. Nevertheless, this is now the exception to the rule rather than the rule itself.

Interestingly, what Pollatsek and Rayner have done is to rethink why it is that one might expect to find the spatiotopic integration of low-level information. And when they do such, the neurological, psychological, and ecological reasons against such a process appear to be overwhelming. I will consider only two of those put forward because they exemplify the larger, more complete set. First, information that appears in the parafovea is less clear than information that appears in the fovea. Some mechanism for weighting the fuzzy and distinct sets of information would be required. And second, an object may not be scaled in the parafovea exactly as it is in the fovea. Such changes in scale would need to be removed before the parafoveal information could be made of use. In short, there are several major obstacles that stand in the way of a simple implementation of the ideas upon which the snapshot hypothesis is based.

The Case For Spatiotopic Integration of Low-Level Information

Despite the above set of arguments that make the spatiotopic integration of low-level information implausible, Pollatsek and Rayner (this volume) find some evidence that such an integration may occur. For example, when a target picture is made noticeably larger (smaller) in size than a previewed picture the picture appears to loom (recede). It is difficult to understand why this perceptual effect would occur if the only information stored across saccades were at a very high, abstract level. Furthermore, it is doubtful that such an effect would occur if the spatial coordinates were changed across saccades. Of course, these intuitions would need to be tested empirically.

Although Pollatsek and Rayner (this volume) find no good ecological reason for such an effect, I would argue that such an effect is an evolutionarily desirable one. Specifically, individuals need at times to know whether an object in the parafovea or periphery is moving forward or backward with respect to them and need to know this very quickly (today, as a pedestrian trying to avoid any oncoming and unexpected traffic; yesterday, as a hunter trying to avoid any oncoming and unexpected ferocious carnivores). More generally, it would appear evolutionarily desirable in certain situations to be able to predict on the basis of successive fixations the motion along any one of the three Euclidean axes and the three rotational axes.

Visual Search and Integration

I conclude this chapter by discussing briefly the work reported by Prinz, Nattkemper, and Ullmann (this volume) and then relating this work to the current status of the research on integration described above. To begin, consider the primary focus of the research reported by Prinz et al. They set out to determine whether the movement of the eyes in a visual search task was controlled globally or locally. Prinz et al. define control as global if the temporal (fixation duration) and spatial (saccade length) parameters of eye movements are set at the beginning of the search. They define control as local if the temporal and spatial parameters are sensitive to the context and can be changed in the middle of a visual search. Prinz et al. differentiate between two types of local control, direct and indirect (see also Rayner & Pollatsek, 1981). The local control is direct if the eye movement parameters on one fixation can be influenced by the material foveated on the fixation. The local control is indirect if the eye movement parameters on one fixation are influenced sometime after the fixation.

Prinz et al. conclude that control of the eye movement parameters is a direct, local one. One study illustrates well the arguments they use to arrive at this conclusion. Briefly, subjects had to search one row at a time for a target D or Z in a background of nine nontarget letters. Eye movements were recorded and when a subject reached the end of one row, this row was removed and a new row appeared directly beneath the old row. The first four or five rows were at one level of complexity and the remaining rows at a second (usually different) level. Three levels of complexity were used. In the least complex, the density of letters was such that three different letters were contained in any adjacent set of six positions. In the moderately complex, four different letters appeared in any adjacent six positions and in the most complex six different letters appeared in each of the six adjacent positions. Of interest was the effect on the eye movement parameters of the change in complexity between the early and later parts of the search.

The results were rather striking. Saccade amplitude responded immediately to changes in complexity. Specifically, when the second set of rows was less complex than the first, the amplitude of the initial saccade on the first row from the second, less complex set was significantly larger than it was on the same row in the control condition (i.e., in the condition with no change in complexity). And when the second set of rows was more complex than the first, the amplitude of the initial saccade on the first row from the second, more complex set was significantly shorter than it was on the same row in the control condition. Fixation duration did not respond as dramatically to changes in complexity. Specifically, the first fixation duration either remained the same (with decreases in complexity) or increased slightly (with increases in complexity). However, this is to be expected given that some time must presumably be spent computing the change in complexity.

The relation of the above work to the work on visual integration might at first appear remote at best. Note that unlike the previous studies, the research reported by Prinz et al. (this volume) requires that subjects *not* be exposed to material in the parafovea that subsequently appears in the fovea. Specifically, when subjects first encounter a line of text whose complexity has been altered, this line will not have been visible previously in the parafovea. However, this does not mean that had the line been visible it would not have exerted an influence. In fact, in related work described by Prinz et al. in their chapter, there is evidence of just such an influence. Subjects were required to search a line of text for a target D or Z in a background of letter distractors (W, T, N, M, H, K, V, F, X, and L). The duration of the fixation immediately preceding the fixation of the target was longer than the average fixation (see also Rayner & Fisher, 1987). Furthermore, the length of the fixation was correlated with the size of the saccade to the target. Finally, the duration of the fixation was clearly dependent on the identity of the target (fast when the target was a D; slow when the target was a Z). All of this suggests that the identity and location of the target is being processed on the fixation immediately preceding the acquisition of the target.

If the identity and location of the target is being processed in a task such as this, then moving the target should create problems. For example, suppose that the target X was embedded in a string of letters presented in the periphery at one location and then shifted left (or right) one letter during the saccade to the target. Thus, for example, the string YWXZ might appear in the periphery and then changed during the saccade to YXWZ. If no spatiotopic integration is occurring, then the benefit that comes from previewing the target should be just as large in the above condition as a condition in which there is no movement of the location of the X in the periphery during the saccade to it. However, if spatiotopic (or relative spatiotopic integration) is occurring, then there should be some degradation when the location of the X is changed across saccades. It is my guess based on preliminary work (with Pollatsek and Rayner) that there would be such a degradation.

Given the failure to fine the spatiotopic integration of low-level material, it appears unlikely in this case that the information that gets integrated is the raw, sensory data. Rather, this information would appear to be coded in some more abstract form, perhaps at the letter level. The obvious candidate for the level of this memory is informational persistence (Irwin, this volume). What is surprising (assuming the preliminary results to be true for the moment) is that the relative spatial positions of the letters in the string matter. Given the model proposed by Pollatsek and Rayner (this volume), one would not have expected this. However, the model can easily be extended by essentially creating for each spatial location a separate letter identification network. Even so, one still has to assume for the modified model that these strings of letters are aligned spatiotopically across saccades.

Conclusion

There is now a great deal of experimental evidence to suggest that subjects do not integrate across saccades low-level information appearing at the same spatial location. In addition to this experimental evidence, the various investigators have argued that there exist good neurological, psychological, and ecological reasons for finding suspect the original snapshot hypothesis.

I have taken issue with only one of the arguments against spatiotopic integration raised by the investigators. Specifically, I have argued that there do exist ecologically valid tasks that require (or would benefit from) the integration across saccades of low-level information at the same spatial location. Such tasks include ones where it is important to detect in as short a time as possible changes in the location, orientation, size, or shape of an object. Of course, even were one to accept the ecological validity of tasks requiring the spatiotopic integration of low-level information, the actual implementation of a system that could perform such an integration still remains problematic for the various reasons noted by the investigators. However, I should note in this regard that the spatiotopic integration required to detect "ecologically significant" changes in position, orientation, size, or shape would probably not be affected by the problems inherent in the limitations imposed on the perceptual and optical hardware.

I have also noted that evidence would appear to exist for the spatio-topic integration of information that resides at an intermediate level of memory which Irwin (this volume) refers to as informational persistence. The arguments against the plausibility of finding neural machinery that can integrate low-level information would not appear to apply to the integration of information at the intermediate level, because such information has already been coded.

Finally, I should comment briefly on why it is that the experiments to date have failed for the most part to find convincing evidence of the spatiotopic integration of low-level (and intermediate-level) information if indeed such integration occurs. The simple answer follows more or less immediately from the above discussion. Specifically, the tasks used in the experimental tests of spatiotopic integration have for the most part not been ecologically valid as I have defined it. The one exception is the experiment on looming reported by Pollatsek and Rayner (this volume). And here there do appear to be effects that can most easily be explained only by assuming that subjects can integrate across saccades low-level information at the same spatial location.

Acknowledgment. The author was supported during the writing of this article by Indiana University (Department of Psychology and the Institute for the Study of Human Capabilities).

References

Hayhoe, M.M., Lachter, J., & Feldman, J.A. (1991). Integration of form across saccadic eye movements. *Perception*, *20*, 393–402.

Irwin, D.E. (1991). Information integration across saccadic eye movements. *Cognitive Psychology*, *23*, 420–456.

Irwin, D.E., Yantis, S., & Jonides, J. (1983). Evidence against visual integration across saccadic eye movements. *Perception and Psychophysics*, *34*, 49–57.

Irwin, D.E., Zacks, J.L., & Brown, J.S. (1990). Visual memory and the perception of a stable visual environment. *Perception & Psychophysics*, *47*, 35–46.

Jonides, J., Irwin, D.E., & Yantis, S. (1982). Integrating visual information from successive fixations. *Science*, *215*, 192–194.

McClelland, J.L., & Rumelhart, D.E. (1981). An interactive activation model of context effects in letter perception: Part I. An account of basic findings. *Psychological Review*, *88*, 375–407.

McConkie, G.W., & Rayner, K. (1976). Identifying the span of the effective stimulus in reading: Literature review and theories of reading. In H. Singer & R.B. Ruddell (Eds.), *Theoretical models and processes of reading* (pp. 137–162). Newark, DE: International Reading Association.

Pollatsek, A., Rayner, K., & Henderson, J.M. (1990). Role of spatial location in the integration of pictorial information across saccades. *Journal of Experimental Psychology: Human Perception and Performance, 16*, 199–210.

Rayner, K., Balota, D.A., & Pollatsek, A. (1986). Against parafoveal semantic preprocessing during eye fixations in reading. *Canadian Journal of Psychology, 40*, 473–483.

Rayner, K., & Fisher, D.L. (1987). Letter processing during eye fixations in visual search. *Perception and Psychophysics, 42*, 87–100.

Rayner, K., McConkie, G.W., & Ehrlich, S.F. (1978). Eye movements and integrating information across fixations. *Journal of Experimental Psychology: Human Perception and Performance, 4*, 529–544.

Rayner, K., & Pollatsek, A. (1981). Eye movement control during reading: Evidence for object control. *Quarterly Journal of Experimental Psychology, 33A*, 351–373

Rayner, K., & Pollatsek, A. (1983). Is visual information integrated across saccades? *Perception and Psychophysics, 34*, 39–48.

Rayner, K., McConkie, G.W., & Zola, D. (1980). Integrating information across eye movements. *Cognitive Psychology, 12*, 206–226.

Trehub, A. (1977). Neuronal models for cognitive processes: Networks for learning, perception, and imagination. *Journal of Theoretical Biology, 65*, 141–169.

12
Effects of Visual Degradation on Eye-Fixation Durations, Perceptual Processing, and Long-Term Visual Memory

GEOFFREY R. LOFTUS, LEAH KAUFMAN,
TAKEHIKO NISHIMOTO, and ERIC RUTHRUFF

We have all had the experience of processing visual stimuli that are *degraded* in one form or another. Examples of such situations include trying to decipher a photocopy of a photocopy, looking at slides or movies while the room lights are still on, and searching for an object in the dark. It seems more difficult to process these degraded stimuli relative to their undegraded or *clean* counterparts. Why is this? In this chapter, we will address two questions regarding the effects of visual degradation on cognitive processing: How does degradation affect initial perceptual process? and How does degradation affect the memory representation that presumably results from perceptual and subsequent processes?

Prologue: Visual Degradation and Eye Fixations

This research began about 6 years ago with a simple question: Does degrading a picture by lowering its contrast affect eye fixation durations on the picture? Loftus (1985, Experiment 5) reported an experiment to address this question. Observers viewed a series of complex, naturalistic color pictures at 1.5 sec apiece with the intent of subsequently being able to recognize them. Eye fixations were recorded during viewing.

Each picture was shown at one of four contrasts. Contrast control was achieved by manipulating stimulus luminance against a uniform adapting field. Because the pictures contained different shadings and different colors, it is not possible to quantitatively characterize the degree of contrast reduction. Roughly speaking, however, contrast in a typical area in a typical picture varied from about 60% in the highest contrast condition to about 20% in the lowest contrast condition.

Figure 12.1 shows the results of this experiment. Here fixation duration is plotted against contrast level, with different curves for the first, second, and third fixations on the picture. It is clear that decreasing contrast leads

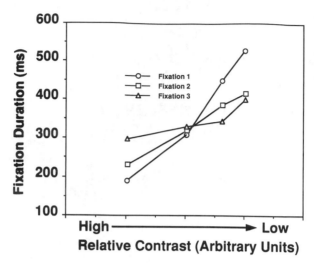

FIGURE 12.1. Fixation duration as a function of stimulus contrast. Different curves represent the first three fixations on the picture.

to increased fixation duration. This effect is most pronounced in the first fixation on the picture.[1]

The explanation that Loftus provided for this finding as is follows: It is reasonable to suppose that a fixation lasts until some criterion amount of information has been acquired from the fixation's location. With lower contrast, perceptual processing slows, which, in turn, causes information to be acquired more slowly. Accordingly, with lower contrast, longer fixations are needed to acquire the same information. This hypothesis led to the first of the two questions that we will be addressing in this chapter: Does stimulus contrast initial perceptual processing?

General Issues

In this section we will describe research designed to investigate the effects of degradation (generally achieved by manipulating stimulus contrast) on perception and memory.

---

[1] The location of the first fixation was controlled by a prestimulus fixation point, and was thus invariant across the contrast conditions. Locations of subsequent fixations, which were not controlled, may depend on contrast condition. Accordingly, the curve corresponding to the initial fixation is the only one guaranteed to be free of confounding, and should be taken the most seriously.

Questions

As noted earlier, we address two major questions. First, does degradation affect initial perceptual processes? In particular, does degradation cause a slowing of visual information acquisition from visual stimuli? Second, does degradation affect the long term-memory representation? In particular, is there some long term degradational effect apart from that mediated by variation in initial perceptual processes?

Methodology

All experiments use similar methodology: An experiment consisted of a series of trials. On each trial, some visual stimulus was presented. In general, stimulus duration and degree of degradation were jointly manipulated in a factorial design. Memory for the pictures was assessed using some form of memory test. The test could be either immediate (in which case it presumably reflected the output of initial perceptual processes) or it could be a long-term recognition test (in which case it was presumably based on a long-term memory representation).

The major data in this paradigm assume the form of a curve relating performance to stimulus duration. This curve, referred to as a performance curve, reflects the degree of processing over time, beginning at stimulus onset. As we will see, comparison of performance curves for different degradation levels allows evaluation of specific hypotheses about the degradation effect.

Effects of Degradation on Initial Perceptual Processes: Investigations of the Slowdown Hypothesis

In this section we describe a simple hypotheses called the *slowdown hypothesis*, which is that degradation slows the rate of perceptual processing by some constant factor. Within certain boundary conditions, the slowdown hypothesis has successfully characterized effects on visual memory of stimulus luminance (Loftus, 1985), stimulus priming (Reinitz, Wright, & Loftus, 1989), attentional locus (Reinitz, 1990), and observer age (Loftus, Truax, & Nelson, 1986).

Two Experiments to Investigate Two Stimulus Types

We will demonstrate that the slowdown hypothesis holds for two quite different stimulus types: one very simple, and the other very complex.

The stimuli in the first experiment were simple, consisting of four black digits on a white background. On each trial, the digits were presented at one of four contrasts[2] ranging from 0.207 to 0.053. There were six stimulus durations within each contrast level for a total of 24 conditions. The observer's task, following each stimulus presentation, was to report as many of the four digits as possible in their correct positions.

Before presenting the results of this experiment we describe the predictions of the slowdown hypothesis, which is illustrated in Figure 12.2. Suppose that we have two conditions, a clean and a degraded condition, and that perceptual processing is slowed by some factor s in the degraded condition relative to the clean condition. It would then require s times as much time to acquire a given amount of information and, accordingly, achieve any given performance level in the degraded relative to the clean condition[3]. This is illustrated in Figure 12.2a for $s = 2$. We refer to this prediction as the *equal-ratio-divergence prediction*.

To evaluate this prediction, it is convenient to plot performance as a function of duration on a log scale, as in Figure 12.2b, rather than on a linear scale as in Figure 12.2a[4]. The reason for this is that equal ratios on a linear scale translate into equal distances on a corresponding logarithmic scale. Therefore, the equal-ratio-divergence prediction becomes: clean and degraded performance curves should be horizontally parallel when plotted on a log-duration scale. If this prediction is confirmed, the horizontal distance (in log units) may be measured and exponentiated to acquire an estimate of s, the slowdown factor.

Figure 12.3 shows the results–performance curves on a log-duration axis for two observers[5]. The equal-ratio-divergence prediction is confirmed: for both observers the curves are approximately horizontally parallel[6].

---

[2] Contrast was defined to be the ratio of maximum minus minimum luminance to maximum plus minimum luminance.

[3] There is an implicit model here, that is described more fully by Loftus and Hogden (1988). The model states that there is a one-to-one correspondence between "amount of perceptual processing" and "amount of information," and similarly, there is a monotonic relationship between "amount of information" and observed memory performance.

[4] There is always some awkwardness in labeling a log scale. In some cases (e.g., in Figure 12.2b) we wish to emphasize the logarithmic units. In such instances, the axis units are linearly spaced natural log units, and the axis is labeled "ln ms." In other cases (e.g., Figure 12.3) we wish to emphasize the original scale units. In these instances, the axis units are logarithmically spaced original units and the axis is labeled "ms, ln scale."

[5] In Figure 12.3, as in all data figures, the error bars represent standard errors.

[6] In describing these data, Loftus and Ruthruff (1992) take a somewhat different tack. It turns out that the performance curves on original linear time axes can be described essentially perfectly by the exponential equation

$$P = 1.0 - e^{-(d-L)/c}$$

Figure 12.4 summarizes the contrast effect. Here we have plotted the reciprocal of the slowdown factor (scaled as a proportion of the highest contrast slowdown, which is defined to be 1.0) as a function of contrast for the two Figure 12.3 observers, plus on additional observer (KG)[7]. The best-fitting linear functions are drawn through the data points for each observer.

The interpretation of these functions is as follows: The slowdown factor may be interpreted as the relative duration required to achieve any given performance level. For example, suppose that in the highest contrast condition a duration of 1 (arbitrary time unit) is required to reach some particular performance level. In a contrast condition characterized by a slowdown factor of s, s time units would be required to achieve the same performance level.

Now consider an analogue of Bloch's law in which there is a perfect trade-off between contrast c and the duration s required to achieve the performance level. The form of this law would be

$$c \times s = k_1$$

or,

$$1/s = c/k_1 = k_2$$

where k_1 and $k_2 = 1/k_1$ are constants. The implication of this Bloch's-like law is thus that the reciprocal of the slowdown rate is linearly related to contrast with a zero intercept[8]. The Figure 12.4 linear fits are quite good, although the intercepts are not quite zero. Loftus and Ruthruff (1992) discuss the implications of this finding.

We have thus demonstrated the validity of the slowdown hypothesis when simple digit strings are used as stimuli. We next demonstrate its applicability to complex naturalistic pictures of the sort used in the eye-movement experiment described above. Such pictures were shown to subjects in one of two contrast conditions that we term *clean* and *degraded*. Again, contrast cannot be defined precisely with naturalistic pictures, but generally, a typical area in a typical picture ranged from approximately 60% contrast in the clean condition to approximately 40%

---

where P is performance, d is stimulus duration, and L and c are free parameters. The parameter L represents the duration at which performance departs from chance, and the parameter c is the exponential time constant (both L and c are in units of ms). For all observers in this experiment, contrast affected *both* c and L, but in approximately the same ratio, which is what leads to the horizontally parallel curves of Figure 12.3.

[7] KG's curve was arrived at in a somewhat complicated manner, and is described in detail by Loftus and Ruthruff (1992).

[8] Note that k_1 and k_2 are determined by the choice of time units and the particular criterion performance level. Accordingly, they are quite arbitrary.

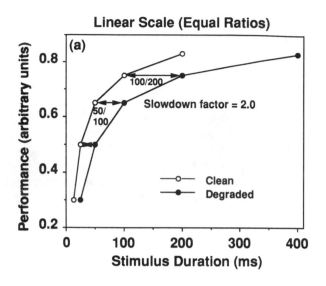

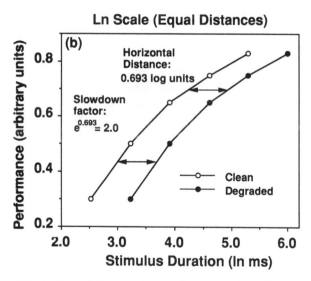

FIGURE 12.2. Illustration of the equal-ratio-divergence hypothesis for a slowdown factor of 2.0.

contrast in the degraded condition. There were six stimulus durations within each contrast condition for a total of 12 study conditions.

To assess immediate memory, subjects provided a *rating* after each stimulus presentation. This rating reflected the subject's subjective probability that he or she would subsequently recognize the picture in a long-term recognition test. The rating scale ranged from 1 ("definitely *would not* recognize the picture") to 4 ("definitely *would* recognize the picture").

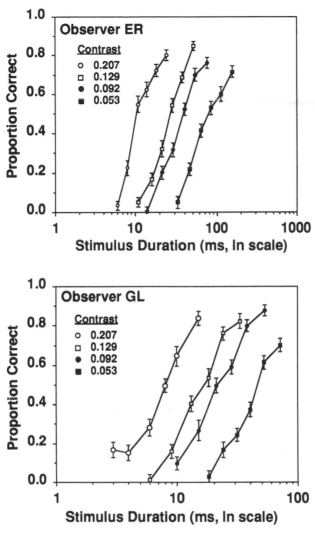

FIGURE 12.3. Results of the digit experiment: for each of two observers, the curves represent proportion of correctly recalled digits as functions of exposure duration. In each panel, separate curves represent the four contrast levels.

Figure 12.5 presents mean rating as a function of stimulus duration (again on a log scale). The curves are horizontally parallel, separated by 0.3 log units, which corresponds to a slowdown factor of 1.35.

Conclusions About the Slowdown Hypothesis

We have seen that for two quite different stimulus types the slowdown hypothesis was confirmed essentially perfectly: the duration required to

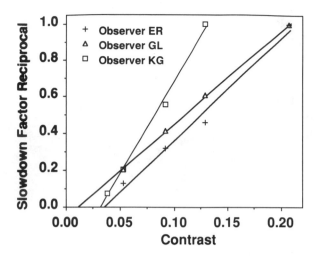

FIGURE 12.4. Results of the digit experiment: reciprocal of the slowdown factor (scaled as a proportion of the highest contrast slowdown, defined to be 1.0) as functions of stimulus contrast. Separate curves represent three separate observers.

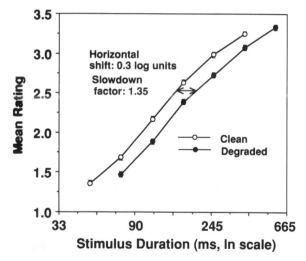

FIGURE 12.5. Results of rating experiment: mean rating as functions of stimulus duration. Separate curves represent clean and degraded pictures.

achieve any given performance level was greater by a constant factor for degraded stimuli relative to clean stimuli.

It should be noted that, as discussed by others (e.g., Loftus, Johnson & Shimamura, 1985; Reinitz et al., 1989), because our conclusions issue from horizontal comparisons, they are invariant in two important ways. First, they are invariant over any dependent variable that is monotonically related to the one actually used, e.g., they would apply to log proportion correct (cf. Schweickert, 1985) as well as to proportion correct. Second, they are invariant over any theoretical construct, e.g., "amount of information" assumed to be monotonically related to performance. Both forms of horizontal invariance occur because any two durations that produce equal performance in one scale will also produce equal performance in any monotonically transformed scale.

The stimulus complexity inherent in naturalistic pictures rendered it impossible to quantitatively characterize the contrast effect for these stimuli. With digits, however, contrast was precisely defined, and here the contrast effect was quite lawful. There was almost a perfect trade-off, analogous to Bloch's law, between stimulus duration and stimulus contrast.

Effect of Degradation on the Long-Term Memory Representation: Investigations of the Single-Dimension Hypothesis

So far we have seen a simple effect of degradation on initial perceptual processes. Normally, however, we are concerned with more than just perception of a visual stimulus. In particular, we can think of perception as being the first in a series of processing stages that ultimately result in a picture's long-term memory representation. To what degree does visual degradation affect this whole process?

The Single-Dimension Hypothesis

We couch this question in the form of what we will call the *single-dimension hypothesis*, which is that duration and degradation affect the same dimension of the memory representation.

IMPLICATIONS OF THE SINGLE-DIMENSION HYPOTHESIS

According to the single-dimension hypothesis, stimulus duration and stimulus degradation both affect initial perceptual processing *only*. Perceptual processing combines duration and degradation into an early memory representation. This representation, termed R_E, is some function P, of duration and degradation. The important idea is that R_E is assumed to be a *single number on a unidimensional scale*. The early representation, R_E is the input to conceptual processing (cf. Intraub, 1984; Loftus,

Hanna, & Lester, 1988; Potter, 1976). The result of conceptual processing is C ($\mathbf{R_E}$), a long-term memory representation.[9]

Notice that if the single-dimension hypothesis is correct, information about a stimulus's degradational state is lost at an early processing stage. For example, if $\mathbf{R_E}$ were a particular number, like 30, the system would have lost the information about whether this number resulted from a short, clean stimulus of from a longer, degraded stimulus. Informally the hypothesis is that degradation and duration operate in "equal currency." Thus, the hypothesis's implication is that degradation's only effect is to slow perceptual processes. Information about a stimulus's degradational state is not included anywhere in the memory representation.

OTHER INSTANTIATIONS OF THE SINGLE-DIMENSION HYPOTHESIS

The single-dimension hypothesis has been suggested (under various names) by other researchers. Three examples serve to illustrate.

Sternberg (1967) suggested two hypotheses for the effect of test-stimulus degradation on short-term memory scanning. By the first hypothesis—a form of the single-dimension hypothesis—a degraded test stimulus is "cleaned up" during an initial processing stage; accordingly, the test-stimulus representation that is used in the scanning/comparison stage is identical to the representation that accrues from a clean test stimulus (clean and degraded scanning rates are thus the same as well). By the second hypothesis, a degraded test stimulus simply engenders a degraded memory representation that then slows down scanning rate. Sternberg found evidence for the single-dimension hypothesis for practiced observers, but not for unpracticed observers.

McClelland (1979) analyzed data reported by Pachella and Fisher (1969) on the effects of stimulus luminance on speed-accuracy tradeoff curves. Pachella and Fisher reported that lowering luminance produced a rightward shift of the curve without affecting its shape. McClelland showed how, within the context of his cascade model, such a shift could be accounted for by assuming luminance to affect the rate of a "light-analysis process" whose operation is early and fast relative to other (e.g., decision) processes. However, this effect (essentially) occurs only during this fast, initial process. Once luminance has had its effect, the operations of subsequent processes are unchanged.

Sperling (1986) proposed that perceptual ("signal") information acquired from a visual stimulus traverses a limited-capacity serial channel enroute to short-term memory. In Sperling's theory, degrading a picture

---

[9] It should be noted that the dimension along which R_E falls need not be the *only* dimension of the early memory representation. Accordingly, conceptual processing, represented by the function C, may operate on more than R_E. It is only R_E, however, that is affected by duration and degradation.

decreases the amount of signal relative to the amount of noise that occupies the channel. Accordingly, the signal transfer rate is slowed; it takes longer for a given amount of degraded signal information compared to clean signal information to accumulate in short-term memory. The contents of short-term memory (and all subsequent memory repositories), however, contain only accumulated signal information; information is not recorded about the original signal-to-noise ratio in the serial channel. This constitutes a version of the single-dimension hypothesis (and of the slowdown hypothesis as well).

REMARK

Validity of the single-dimension hypothesis does not require validity of the slowdown hypothesis. Rather, the slowdown hypothesis implies a particular (multiplicative) form of the perceptual function **P** that combines duration and degradation.

An Initial Test of the Single-Dimension Hypothesis

The first experiment to test the single-dimension hypothesis is actually the very same complex-picture/ratings experiment that we have just described. Our above description of the ratings experiment was incompletely. As we described, pictures were indeed shown, one by one, and a "recognition-probability rating" was obtained after each presentation. However, this series of presentations also constituted the study phase of a study-phase/test-phase, old/new recognition memory procedure.

To connect the single-dimension hypothesis with data, we make the weak assumptions that (a) rating performance is some monotonic function, M_{Rt} of the early memory representation, and that (b) recognition performance is a separate monotonic function, M_{Rg} of the long-term memory representation. With these assumptions, we can then make the fundamental prediction: *two duration/degradation conditions that are equal in terms of rating should also be equal in terms of recognition.* Briefly, the reason for this prediction is as follows: If there are two duration/degradation conditions that produce equal ratings, then these conditions must have produced equal early representations, R_E. This, in turn, means that the long-term memory representation for these two conditions must be the same and therefore they must produce equal recognition performance (for elaboration see Bamber, 1979).

We tested this prediction using what Bamber (1979) refers to as a *state-trace graph*. The results are shown in Figure 12.6 wherein recognition performance is plotted as a function of rating performance, with one data point for each of the 12 study conditions. The open circles represent the six clean conditions and the closed circles represent the six degraded conditions. Note that, except for the top right-hand data points, the open

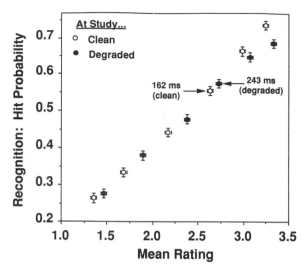

FIGURE 12.6. State-trace plot. Recognition performance as functions of rating performance. Different symbols represent clean and degraded study conditions.

and closed circles fall essentially all along the same line. We assert that this finding constitutes confirmation of the single-dimension hypothesis.

Bamber (1979) provides a formal of why this is so. To see why it is so informally, consider the two data points indicated in Figure 12.6 that correspond to the 162-ms clean condition and the 243-ms degraded condition. Note that these two data points are almost, but not quite, on top of one another.

Suppose they *were* on top of one another. In this case we would have found two degradation/duration conditions, equal in terms of rating performance, that were also equal in terms of recognition performance. This, as described earlier, is exactly the prediction of the single-dimension hypothesis.

Now suppose that we had run the "perfect experiment" in which we had tested performance at all possible stimulus durations (between, say, 0 and 500 ms) rather than just the six durations within each degradation condition that we actually used. If this were true, the state-trace graph would consist of two continuous functions: one of open circles (all squished together) and the other of closed circles (similarly squished). These two functions would be identical (fall on top of one another) if and only if any two duration/degradation conditions that were equal in terms of rating were also equal in terms of recognition, as predicted by the single-dimension hypothesis.

Returning to our actual, "imperfect" experiment, the curves corresponding to the open and the closed data points in Figure 12.6 constitute *estimates* of these perfect-experiment functions. These estimated functions lie largely on top of one another, thereby confirming the single-dimension hypothesis.

There is a notable departure from this confirmation: the two functions start to diverge in the top right-hand corner of the Figure 12.6 state-trace plot. These points correspond to the longest exposure durations, where more than one eye fixation may have occurred. If more than one eye fixation occurred, the curves would not be strictly comparable, because any eye fixation after the first (whose location was controlled by a fixation point) may be in systematically different locations for the clean versus degraded conditions. Essentially what we have shown is that the single-dimension hypothesis is confirmed as long as stimulus duration is sufficiently short that only one fixation on the picture is probably occurring.

Objects and Actions

The next test of the single-dimension hypothesis took a somewhat different tack.[10] Instead of having two dependent variables (as we had ratings and recognition in the previous experiment) we had two types of stimuli, termed *objects* and *actions*, which, although perceptually similar, differed greatly in their distinguishability from one another. Objects were pictures of single objects (e.g., a chair, a lamp, etc.), whereas actions depicted a baseball pitcher in different phases in his windup and pitch. These two types of stimuli were used in an old/new recognition experiment.

Both types of pictures were simple black line drawings on a white background. However, the objects were very dissimilar to one another, whereas the actions were very similar to one another. Preliminary pilot work indicated that recognition performance was substantially higher for the objects than it was for the actions.

During the study phase of this experiment, half of each stimulus type were shown *clean* whereas the other half were *degraded* by superimposing dim, random noise over them. Within each of the four conditions defined by a factorial combination of object/action and degraded/clean, there were five stimulus durations. These durations differed for the four conditions so as to produce approximately equal performance ranges. The durations were quite different for objects and actions: the longest clean and degraded object durations were 800 and 2,000 ms, whereas the longest clean and degraded action durations were 15 and 21 sec.

Recall that the single-dimension hypothesis states that degradation has its effect only once, on initial perceptual processes. This means that,

---

[10] This experiment was conceived, run, and analyzed by Takehiko Nishimoto.

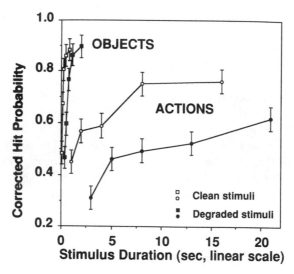

FIGURE 12.7. Results of the action/object experiment. Hit probability (corrected for false-alarm probability) as functions of stimulus duration. Separate curves represent objects (right curves) and actions (left curves) and clean and degraded study conditions (open and closed symbols).

assuming the slowdown hypotheses to be correct, the slowdown factor should be the same for objects and actions, and the memory representations of the pictures should be the same up to the time of recognition. At this point, some monotonic function M_A should operate on the long-term memory representation to produce recognition performance for actions, whereas a separate monotonic function, M_O should operate on the memory representation of objects to produce object performance.

Figure 12.7 shows the results. Here, hit probability (corrected for false-alarm probability) is shown as a function of stimulus duration on a linear scale. Several (qualitatively unsurprising) effects are evident: longer stimulus durations lead to higher performance, clean pictures are recognized better than degraded pictures, and objects are recognized better than actions. Figure 12.7 dramatically indicates the vast processing-rate difference between objects and actions: it takes an order of magnitude more time to achieve a given recognition-performance level for the actions relative to the objects. In addition, the asymptote for object performance appears close to 1.0, whereas the action-performance asymptote appears to be considerably below 1.0. In short, recognition memory performance is dramatically different for the two stimulus types.

Figure 12.8 (left panel) shows the Figure 12.7 data replotted on a log-duration scale. Now a good deal of lawfulness becomes apparent. First, for both objects and actions, the curves are approximately horizontally

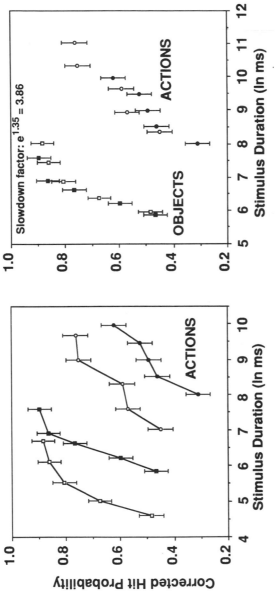

FIGURE 12.8. Results of the action/object experiment 4. Right panel: Figure 12.11 data on a log-duration abscissa. Left panel: The two clean curves have been shifted right by equal amounts (1.35 log units) relative to the two degraded curves.

parallel, indicating confirmation of the slowdown hypothesis. Second, the degree of horizontal separation is approximately the same for the two type of stimuli. The right-hand panel of Figure 12.8 shows clean-object and clean-action performance curves both shifted right by 1.35 log units relative to their degraded counterparts. Both object and action curves now line up essentially perfectly, which indicates that the slowdown factor (approximately $e^{1.35} = 3.86$) is the same for both types of stimuli.

These results allow two noteworthy conclusions. First, the slowdown hypothesis continues to be true for a very long time (up to 21 seconds!) following stimulus onset for these simple stimuli. This time, of course, vastly exceeds the duration of a single eye fixation. We conclude that for these stimuli, perceptual processing is slowed by a constant factor not only within a single eye fixation but, remarkably, across a series of perhaps 40 to 80 eye fixations.

Confirmation of the slowdown hypothesis allows a test of the single-dimension hypothesis. In particular, because the slowdown rate was approximately the same for both stimulus types, the single-dimension hypothesis is confirmed. Our second conclusion, therefore, is that for these stimuli, degradation affects cognitive processing only once by its slowing-down effect on initial perceptual processes.

We noted that in the rating/recognition experiment, the single-dimension hypothesis broke down at durations beyond about 300 ms. Yet with these action/object stimuli, the single-state hypothesis (and the slowdown hypothesis as well) is confirmed for much longer times. We conjecture that processing of these simple line drawings is more temporally homogeneous than is processing of complex scenes.

Degrading Stimuli at Study and Test

Recall the the single-dimension hypothesis implies that no information about a stimulus's degradational state is stored as part of the memory representation. Although degrading a stimulus can, by this hypothesis, affect the memory representation, it can do so only by influencing initial perceptual processing; degradation leaves no trace of itself later on. As we have seen, this hypothesis has thus far been confirmed in two experiments.

But the hypothesis carries with it a surprising prediction. Suppose that we were to do an experiment in which we presented stimuli degraded or clean at study and then presented them similarly degraded or clean, in an old/new recognition test. The single-dimension hypothesis implies that there is no advantage of a stimulus being in the same degradational state at study and test. This is contrary to the prediction of any kind of encoding-specificity hypothesis (e.g., Tulving, 1974, 1983). It is also contrary to findings by Dallett, Wilcox, 'Andrea (1968), who showed normal or degraded pictures at study and/or test, and reported a recognition-test

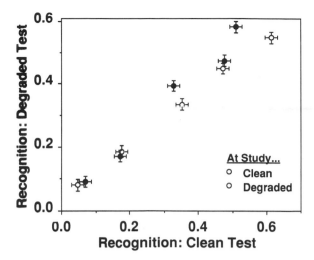

FIGURE 12.9. State-trace plot. Degraded-at-test recognition performance as functions of clean-at-test recognition performance. Different symbols represent clean and degraded study conditions.

advantage to being in the same state at study and test. This finding makes sense; a test picture presented in the same degradational state at test as it had been in at study should engender a closer memory match than a picture presented in dissimilar study and test states.

Accordingly, the single-state hypothesis's prediction is a counterintuitive one. We tested the prediction by repeating the rating/recognition experiment. As in the rating/recogntion experiment, half the stimuli were degraded at study and the other half were clean. However, in the present experiment, degradational state was also manipulated at the time of test: half the test stimuli were degraded and the other half were clean. This leads to a 2 × 2 design in which pictures were either clean or degraded at study and also were either clean or degraded at test. Within each of these four cells, pictures were shown at one of five study durations.

The prediction of the single-dimension hypothesis is based on logic analogous to that used in the rating/recognition experiment. Again, there are two dependant variables: clean recognition performance and degraded recognition performance. The prediction is that any two study-duration/ study-degradation conditions that produce the same degraded recognition performance should also produce the same clean recognition performance.

Figure 12.9 shows the state-trace plot for these data. Here, degraded recognition performance is plotted as a function of clean recognition performance. There is some noisiness in the data that precludes us from drawing strong conclusions from them. It appears, however, that the clean and degraded study curves fall approximately on top of one another, thereby providing weak support for the single-dimension hypothesis.

Noisiness Banished: Replication with New Stimuli

The results that we have just described were somewhat surprising; confirmation of the single-dimension hypothesis is inconsistent with any model implying an advantage to being in the same degradational state at study and test. Unfortunately, as noted, the data were somewhat noisy. Accordingly, we set out to replicate them for the simple purpose of increasing experimental power. The only change we made for this replication was to assemble an entirely new set of slides. This was accomplished by photographing scenes (farmland, beaches, yards, streets, and house groupings) around the Seattle area. Given this apparently minor change we had expected the replication results to be at least qualitatively the same as the original results. This did not happen.

The major replication results are shown in Figure 12.10, wherein ratings, clean-at-test recognition performance, and degraded-at-test recognition performance are shown as functions of log duration. Surprisingly, for the first time, the slowdown hypothesis is disconfirmed: the clean and degraded curves diverge even on a logarithmic scale. This effect, seen most plainly in the rating data (top panel), implies that degrading a picture at study is doing more than simply slowing down perceptual processing. Informally, we can say that degradation in this experiment has a qualitative rather than a quantitative effect.

As noted earlier, confirmation of the slowdown hypothesis is not necessary to test the single-dimension hypothesis. However, it can be seen that the separation between clean-at-study and degraded-at-study curves is much less when the test stimuli are degraded (Figure 12.10 bottom panel) than when test stimuli are clean (Figure 12.10, middle panel).

This result can be seen more clearly in Figure 12.11, a state-trace plot. The clean-at-study function is clearly separated from the degraded-at-study function. When two duration/study-degradation conditions show the same clean-test performance, the degraded-at-study conditions enjoy a benefit on a degraded relative to a clean test and vice versa. A convenient way to construe the relationship of these functions is that the degraded-at-study function is above the clean-at-study function (i.e., it is "better" from the perspective of the vertical, or degraded-test axis). However, the clean-at-study function is to the right of the degraded-at-study function, i.e., it is better from the perspective of the horizontal, or clean-test axis.

In short, the data shown in Figure 12.11 indicate that there is a recognition-performance advantage to being in the same degradational state in study and test. This confirms any sort of encoding-specificity

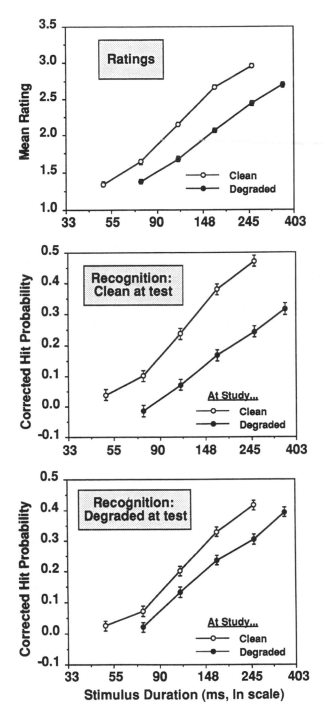

FIGURE 12.10. Replication results. Top panel: rating as functions of stimulus duration. Middle and bottom panels: hit probability (corrected for false-alarm probability) as functions of stimulus duration for pictures shown clean at test (middle panel) and degraded at test (bottom panel). In each panel, separate curves represent clean and degraded study conditions.

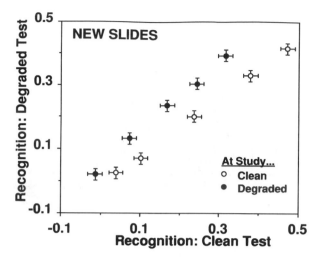

FIGURE 12.11. Replication results: state-trace plot. Degraded-at-test recognition performance is plotted as functions of clean-at-test recognition performance. Different symbols represent clean and degraded study conditions.

hypothesis, and also constitutes a replication of the Dallett et al. (1968) data.

What is Different about Original and New Stimuli?

There is, of course, a discrepancy between the replication results and all previous results. In particular, the slowdown hypothesis and the single-dimension hypothesis were both disconfirmed in the replication. This failure to replicate is most dramatic when the last two experiments are compared, which were identical except for the stimuli used. Using the original stimuli we concluded that degradational information is not stored as part of the memory representation whereas using new stimuli we concluded that degradational information *is* stored as part of the memory representation. There is a great deal of power in all experiments; thus the key to the difference must lie in the difference between the two stimulus sets.

We observed informally that the new slides seem darker and have more contrast than the original slides, which seemed to make the degrading manipulation (imposition of the adapting field) more noticeable for the new stimuli. This led to the hypothesis that degradational information is stored as part of a picture's memory representation to the degree that the picture's degradational state is noticed and actively encoded at the time of study.

To test the validity of our informal observation (and, accordingly, of the resultant "noticeability hypothesis"), we showed groups of subjects all the original stimuli and all the new stimuli. For each stimulus set, half the stimuli were clean and half were degraded. The subjects' task was to report whether each stimulus was clean or degraded.

The results of this experiment were quite clear: whereas the ability to detect degradation was quite high for both stimulus sets, it was about 12% higher for the replication stimuli relative to the original stimuli.[11]

This finding is consistent with the following explanation of the difference between the original and the replication slides. First, the results represent an upper limit on a subjects' ability to detect degradation. When the subjects are not instructed to detect degradation (as was the case in all previous experiments) it is likely that they actually notice the degradation a much smaller percentage of the time. In particular, it is possible that they almost never detect degradation in the original stimuli, whereas they may occasionally detect degradation in the new stimuli. If degradation detection always engendered explicit storage of this degradational information as part of the memory representation, this would account for the discrepancy between the two stimulus sets.

Conclusions

The original questions addressed in this chapter were, To what extent does visual degradation affect initial perceptual processes? and To what extent does visual degradation affect the ultimate memory representation?

Degradation Effects on Perceptual Processes

We have demonstrated that visual degradation almost always has a profound effect on initial perceptual process. In one form or another, this result is shown in all the experiments that we have reported. In most cases, the effect is quite specific, and conforms to the slowdown hypothesis: a given degree of degradation can be characterized as slowing initial perceptual processing by some constant factor.

In the one experiment where degradation could be defined quantitatively (the digit-recall experiment) the relation between contrast and slowdown was quite lawful; there was almost a perfect tradeoff between contrast and duration required to achieve any given performance level. Another noteworthy effect was shown in the object/action experiment, wherein the slowdown effect continued to operate for a very long time following stimulus onset.

---

[11] The hit probability is higher and the false-alarm probability is lower for the new relative to the original stimuli. Accordingly, our conclusion is unaffected by our correction-for-guessing procedure.

Degradation Effects in Long-Term Memory

In many situations, the degradational effect on perceptual processes appears to be degradation's *only* effect on picture processing. In three of the experiments, we confirmed the single-dimension hypothesis, which states, essentially, that degradational information is not stored as part of the memory representation; the information about the degradational state of the stimulus is lost during initial perceptual processing.

However, in the penultimate (replication) experiment we discovered that it is possible for degradational information to be stored as part of the memory representation. And finally, the results of our last (degradation-detection) experiment suggest that this may happen when the storage of such information is a conscious, deliberate process.

Degradation and Eye Fixations

We began this chapter by recalling an old finding: eye-fixation durations are increased when the fixated stimuli are degraded relative to when they are clean. Given the newer results that we have described here, we are now in a position to be a bit more specific about the nature of this effect. We note two possibilities, each of which provides testable predications about future eye-movement experiments.

The Slowdown Effect and Fixation Duration

We have seen that acqustion of perceptual information is slowed for degraded relative to clean stimuli. One simple hypothesis (noted at the outset of this chapter) is that eye fixations are "designed" to acquire some criterion amount of information. Such a hypothesis makes a very specific prediction: if one measured the slowdown rate (as we described above) and simultaneously measured eye fixations, then eye-fixation duration would be increase with degradation by a factor equal to the slowdown rate.

The Unidimensional Effect and Fixation Pattern

We have seen that in some instances, degradational information does not appear to be stored as part of the memory representation, whereas in other instances it does. The latter situation must entail qualitatively different information-acquisition processes for different degradational levels, whereas the former situation may entail qualitatively identical (albeit quantitatively slower) processing. Given the supposition that qualitatively same or different encoding processes might be reflected in corresponding same or different eye-fixation patterns, we would expect to see different eye fixation patterns associated with different degradational levels when degradational information is stored in memory, but similar patterns at different degradational levels when degradational information is not stored in memory.

Acknowledgments. This research was supported by an NIMH grant to Geoffrey Loftus. We thank Janeen Duncan, Christine Greenmun, and Natasha Slesnick for helping to collect the data in several of the experiments that we reported.

References

Bamber, D. (1979). State trace analysis: A method of testing simple theories of causation. *Journal of Mathematical Psychology, 19,* 137–181.

Dallett, K., Wilcox, S.G., & d'Andrea, L. (1968). Picture memory experiments. *Journal of Experimental Psychology, 76,* 312–320.

Intraub, H. (1984). Conceptual masking: The effects of subsequent visual events on memory for pictures. *Journal of Experimental Psychology: Learning, Memory and Cognition, 10,* 115–125.

Loftus, G.R. (1985). Picture perception: Effects of luminance level on available information and information-extraction rate. *Journal of Experimental Psychology: General, 114,* 342–356.

Loftus, G.R., Hanna, A., & Lester, L. (1988). Conceptual masking: How one picture steals attention from another picture. *Cognitive Psychology, 20,* 237–282.

Loftus, G.R., & Hogden, J. (1988) Picture perception: Information extraction and phenomenological persistence. In G.H. Bower (Ed.), *The Psychology of learning and motivation (Vol. 22).* New York: Academic Press.

Loftus, G.R., Johnson, C.A., & Shimamura, A.P. (1985). How much is an icon worth? *Journal of Experimental Psychology: Human Perception and Performance, 11,* 1–13.

Loftus, G.R., & Ruthruff, E. (1992). Effects of stimulus contrast on perception of simple digit stimuli: Data and a model. (submitted manuscript)

Loftus, G.R., Truax, P.E., & Nelson, W.W. (1986). Age-related differences in visual information processing: Quantitative or qualitative? In C. Schooler & K.W. Schaie (Eds.), *Cognitive functioning and social structures over the life course.*

McClelland, J.L. (1979). On the time relations of mental processes: An examination of systems of processes in cascade. *Psychological Review, 86,* 287–330.

Pachella, R.C., & Fisher, D.F. (1969). Effect of stimulus degradation and similarity on the trade-off between speed and accuracy in absolute judgements. *Journal of Experimental Psychology, 81,* 1–9.

Potter, M.C. (1976). Short-term conceptual memory for pictures. *Journal of Experimental Psychology: Human Learning and Memory, 2,* 509–522.

Reinitz, M.T. (1990). Effects of spatially directed attention on visual encoding. *Perception and Psychophysics, 47,* 497–505.

Reinitz, M.T., Wright, E., & Loftus, G.R. (1989). The effects of semantic priming on visual encoding of pictures. *Journal of Experimental Psychology: General, 118,* 280–297.

Schweickert, R. (1985). Separable effects of factors on speed and accuracy: Memory scanning, lexical decision, and choice tasks. *Psychological Bulletin*, *97*, 530–546.

Sperling, G. (1986). A signal-to-noise theory of the effects of luminance on picture memory: Commentary on Loftus. *Journal of Experimental Psychology: General*, *115*, 189–192.

Sternberg, S. (1967). Two operations in character recognition: Some evidence from reaction-time measurements. *Perception and Psychophysics 2*, 43–53.

Tulving, E. (1974). Cue-dependent forgetting. *American Scientist*, *62*, 74–82.

Tulving, E. (1983). *Elements of episodic memory*. London: Clarendon Press/ Oxford University Press.

13
An Exploration of the Effects of Scene Context on Object Identification

SUSAN J. BOYCE and ALEXANDER POLLATSEK

A major question in visual cognition is whether the identification of objects is merely the result of a bottom-up perceptual analysis or whether it is highly dependent on real-world knowledge stored in memory as an aid to perceptual processes. An important part of this question is whether the context of the real-world "scene" in which the object is placed influences the identification of the object, and if so, how. However, there is significant disagreement among researchers in the area as to what has been discovered. This is due in part to different theoretical orientations and in part to disagreement as to what paradigm or paradigms are adequate for studying object identification. As a result, we will briefly review some of the literature in order to place our research in sufficient context.

Does Scene Context Influence Object Identification?

The statement that an object that is viewed in a "natural" context is easier to process than an object that is viewed in an "unnatural" context is probably uncontroversial. What is at issue is whether a natural context is facilitating the actual identification of an object or some later stage of processing, such as integrating an identified object into a mental model of the scene being viewed. Central to this theoretical issue is the question of how to empirically assess object recognition in scene perception, or in other words, what paradigms are legitimate for studying object recognition.

We would like to distinguish between two aspects of a paradigm: (a) what the subject's basic task is and (b) the dependent variable used to assess object identification. Although the former to some extent determines what the latter will be, we think it is useful to distinguish between them. In this section, we will concentrate on the former aspect and, for the most part, delay our critical discussion of dependent variables until the end. Our general position is that no paradigm will be perfect. Thus, to whatever extent there is converging evidence from several paradigms, we will have something of substance. Moreover, if there are discrepancies between paradigms to be resolved, the better we understand the differences, the clearer the picture we will have.

Object Recognition Paradigms

THE MEMORY TASK

One of the major paradigms for studying scene context effects is to have a subject view a scene with the instruction that there will be a later memory test (usually a recognition memory test minutes after the original viewing of the scene). To obtain a reasonably pure measure of object recognition, the primary dependent variable usually chosen (Friedman, 1979; Loftus & Mackworth, 1978) is the time that the eyes fixate on an object of interest. The key finding is that subjects fixate longer on an object that does not belong in a scene (e.g., a bathtub in a living room) than on a object that does belong (e.g., a sofa in a living room). This difference in fixation times has been interpreted by these experimenters as reflecting a difference in encoding times for the objects being fixated. To simplify further discussion (following Biederman, Mezzanotte, & Rabinowitz, 1982) we will refer to objects that do not belong as objects in "violation" (of the scene) and objects that do belong as "normal" objects.

Although we will argue below that fixation time on an object is a good measure of on-line processing, we believe that the memory task imposed on the subjects severely compromises the use of the fixation time measure in these experiments. That is, the memory task imposed induces the subjects to "memorize" the scene, which probably includes not only identifying the component objects, but also relating the objects to each other, so as to remember which objects are in which scene, the relative locations of the objects, or whatever information the subject thinks is going to be tested later. Thus, a priori, a fixation is likely to register not only object identification time but all of these other processes. Moreover, these other integration and memory processes are likely to take longer if an object does not belong in a scene that if it does. This analysis is reinforced by the observation that fixation times on objects in these paradigms are quite long (e.g., in Friedman, 1979, mean first fixation times are over 400 ms and subsequent fixations on objects are almost as long) and are not plausibly reflecting only the time to identify an object.

THE TARGET SEARCH (SAME-DIFFERENT) TASK

The other paradigms that have been used try to avoid the above criticism. The target search paradigm (Biederman, 1972; Biederman et al., 1982) assesses object identification by asking the subject whether an object (identified by a verbal label) is present in a scene. The name of a target object (e.g., "sofa") is presented as a precue, followed by a brief presentation of a scene that may or may not contain the target object. Simultaneous with the offset of the scene, a "pattern mask" is presented with a superimposed cue that indicates the location of an object (which may or may not be the target object), and the subject decides if the target object was present in the scene. Although both accuracy of identification and response time have been reported in this paradigm, the accuracy data are more central because response times are often hard to interpret when there are appreciable numbers of errors.

The primary finding has been that an object in violation is identified less accurately than a normal object. A particularly interesting aspect of this research is that Biederman et al. (1982) constructed several types of "violations." In addition to the violation discussed above (and the one most commonly studied), where the target object is in the "wrong" scene, there were also violations in which objects were in the right scene but in the wrong place (e.g., a sofa floating in the air or a fire hydrant on top of a mailbox). Biederman et al. found that some of these positional violations produced as great a "cost" in identification accuracy as when the target object was in the wrong scene. We will return to discuss the fuller implications of this finding later, but briefly it indicates that "scene context" contains geometric as well as semantic information that operates on the identification of objects.

We note three potential concerns about this paradigm. The first is that, a priori, the task might allow the subject to process the object too "shallowly." That is, in order to perform above chance, the subject merely has to know that the visual features in the target location were more likely to belong to the target object (e.g., sofa) than to one of the distractor objects used in the experiment. Because the distractor items were rarely visually similar to the target objects, it is conceivable that extracting a few features would be enough to make the discrimination. However, for the most part, the positive results obtained above argue against this concern because context is less likely to influence a task that is too shallow, not more likely.

The other two concerns relate to the fact that context effects are studied in a situation where the objects are poorly seen (because they are briefly presented extrafoveally, and are followed by a pattern mask). The first is that the degraded nature of the stimulus input might mean that the influence of context is not perceptual, but rather a memorial process, possibly including conscious decision strategies (see De Graef, Christiaens, & d'Ydewalle, 1990, for a thorough discussion of this point.) Although these are reasonable concerns here, we think that the decision times being on the order of a second makes it reasonably likely that perceptual processes are being studied. Instead, our primary concern with this paradigm is one of generalizability. That is, it may be that scene context is utilized mainly in situations where the perceptual information is of poor quality (such as with peripherally and/or briefly presented objects), but utilized little in normal scene viewing (where the eyes are free to fixate any object of interest).

THE NAMING TASK

A third potential paradigm for studying object identification in scene context is object naming. However, prior to the research we report below, it was only employed with pairs of objects (Henderson, Pollatsek, & Rayner, 1987). In this paradigm, subjects first fixated a "prime" object while the target object was presented parafoveally (5° to 10° from fixation). They were instructed to move their eyes to the target object (eye movement latencies were under 300 ms) and name it. The key finding was that a target object was named more quickly when preceded by a semantically related prime than when preceded by a semantically unrelated prime. Of course, this finding is not directly relevant to whether scene context affects object identification because the context for the target object was not a scene but a single object. We will describe below how we have applied this paradigm to study objects in scenes. The two potential weaknesses of this paradigm are (a) that the method indicating which object is to be named severely changes the ecological validity of the task, and (b) naming latency is not an appropriate measure of object identification time. We should add that the primary concern for naming as a task is that it is too "deep" (i.e., it taps stages of processing beyond object identification); if it were too shallow, one would fail to observe context effects (which is not the case).

THE OBJECT-DECISION TASK

De Graef et al. (1990; see also De Graef, this volume) employed the object decision task of Kroll and Potter (1984) to investigate scene perception. In their experiment, a subject inspects a scene containing objects and "non-objects" (representations of three-dimensional solids that are in fact not identifiable objects). The subject's task is to hit a button every time a non-object is detected. Of interest, however, is fixation time on an object, which presumably reflects the time it takes to decide that the figure is indeed an object, and is unsullied by a manual response or by a memory requirement. Fixation times on objects that belonged in the scene were compared to objects that were in violation (as with Biederman et al., 1982, some were in violation by being in the wrong scene and others by being in the wrong place in the scene). The principal finding was that for the first half of the fixations on the scene (about 10), there was no context effect, with context effects developing only after the scene had been observed for several seconds.

This negative finding thus raises a challenge for the other research, which indicates that scene context effects on object recognition are immediate and perhaps automatic. We will discuss this issue in more detail at the end of this chapter, but it is possible that the object decision task used in these experiments is too "shallow." That is, if the non-objects are fairly discriminable from objects, it may be possible for the subjects to have decided that a figure was not a non-object before actually identifying what object it in fact was. We note that the fixation times in this task are quite a bit shorter than in the memory tasks described above, so that long fixation times are not necessary in scene viewing. The fact that they are quite short, of course, is consistent with the hypothesis that processing in this task is fairly shallow.

How Does Context Work?

The above discussion indicates that it is not a foregone conclusion that scene context affects object recognition, or at least that it affects object recognition in all circumstances. For the moment, however, we will assume that such context effects occur at least some of the time, and highlight a few major issues about the nature of scene context effects.

SCHEMAS VERSUS OBJECT-TO-OBJECT PRIMING

The earlier work on scene context was inspired by schema theories, in which scene context was thought to operate through a "schema" of the scene being activated, which in turn helped to activate the identification of objects that are part of the schema. A major problem with such theories is that they are not very well defined either in how schemas are constructed or in how schemas facilitate object recognition. We will take as the defining characteristic of schema theories that they posit that something more is going on than in a standard "spreading activation" explanation of how one stimulus "primes" the identification of another.

In the spreading activation model, nodes in memory (representing the various objects in the scene) are activated to varying degrees based on the quality and amount of featural information in the visual display that support identification of those objects. As these object nodes are activated, excitation flows from an object node to all "related" object nodes. Thus, if a typical scene contains many objects related to a target object, these objects would be expected—through spread of excitation—to facilitate identification of the target. (The previously cited naming experiment of Henderson et al., 1987, was an attempt to demonstrate the plausibility of a spreading activation account of context effects in scenes.) We will take as a defining characteristic of spreading activation models that the nodes that are the locus of priming are "sister" nodes, in the sense that there is no hierarchical relation between them. We also take as another defining characteristic that these nodes are conceptual in that they represent something like an episodic or semantic memory representation, and that the strength of the priming is defined by something like the semantic relationship between nodes or the episodic co-occurrence of the nodes.

We see three possible ways in which one might want to distinguish schema theory from the above. The first is that there is a node for the "schema" that is special in some sense and works differently than a node for an individual object. The second is that a schema for the scene contains spatial (or other types of geometric) information as well as semantic information. (Clearly, the effect of positional violations reported by Biederman et al., 1982, argues for schema theory using this distinction.) The third is that the degree of facilitation produced is not easily predicted by the degree of association between the schema and the object (as would be expected in a standard priming relationship) but by other variables that might pertain to schema relationships.

Except for the Biederman et al. (1982) positional violation effect mentioned above, there is little evidence to argue against an object-to-object priming explanation of scene context effects. Where successive fixations are employed, objects fixated on prior fixations could be priming objects seen on later fixations. In tachistoscopic experiments, objects are often placed near fixation, so that these centrally seen objects could be the primary influence on the target objects that are less central (rather than the scene, per se). Another aspect of the Biederman et al. experiment argues against object-to-object priming, albeit weakly. They found that the identification of an object that belongs in a scene was not affected by the presence of a single "violator" object in the scene. However, because the single violator object was extrafoveal and small, it is not clear how much of an effect one would expect it to have.

THE TIME COURSE OF CONTEXT EXTRACTION AND USE

Another important question is when context effects occur. The experiments using briefly presented scenes apparently demonstrate that the use of context is early and relatively automatic. In contrast, the object decision task of De Graef et al. (1990) apparently demonstrates that context effects occur only after several seconds. As mentioned earlier, a concern about the brief presentation method is that context may be important only when the visual information is degraded because it is hard to see. As a result, it would be good to demonstrate context effects in a paradigm in which this is not a problem. Another possibility is that scene context information is extracted rapidly (as one would infer from Biederman et al., 1982) but that viewers quickly narrow their attention to single objects to be identified. One version of such a model has been termed the "zoom hypothesis" (Eriksen & Yeh, 1985), wherein the subject's attention is set on "wide angle" on the first fixation to extract the global scene information; on subsequent fixations, however, it is set to "telephoto" to identify individual objects in the scene.

Current Research

Rationale

The work we have done (Boyce, 1989; Boyce, Pollatsek, & Rayner, 1989) has attempted to clarify some of these issues. One focus has been methodological: to assess object identification in a paradigm that is reasonably close to normal scene viewing but in which the experimenter has good control over the information flow. To this end, we have invented a "wiggle" paradigm (a version of the naming paradigm). The subject initially fixates in the center of the screen and a scene is presented; 75 ms later, a single target object "wiggles" (i.e., moves 1° and then quickly moves back to its original location), which induces the subject to fixate it. The subject names the target object and, because identification accuracy is close to 100%, naming latency is the primary dependent variable. The purpose of the wiggle is to draw the subject's attention and eyes to the target object, and the 75 ms delay is provided to allow the subject to process the scene globally before attention is drawn to the target object. The task is quite natural from the subjects' standpoint; the eyes are automatically drawn to the target object and there is no confusion about which object is to be named.

We feel that this task is quite an attractive one for studying object identification in scenes. First, in normal scene viewing, an object of interest will typically be fixated; thus this paradigm examines the effect of scene context on object identification in a situation that comes reasonably close to object identification in "real" scene viewing. This is in contrast to the tachistoscopic studies, where the target object is extrafoveal and briefly presented. Of course, the wiggle paradigm is not completely natural, because the information flow in most natural viewing situations is usually directed more endogenously, with the choice of the object to be fixated next usually determined by perceptual aspects such as its saliency or by cognitive decisions about which object needs to be identified. However, we should add that the paradigm is reasonably natural; objects in scenes (especially those that are animate) often capture the viewer's attention and eye fixations by motion. Second, the paradigm offers good control over what the subject has viewed because the subject fixates only in two locations: the first in the center of the screen and the second on the target object. Third, the measure used (naming latency) is at least a reasonable measure of object identification.

A second aim of our research was to attempt to demonstrate that scene context effects were due to more than object-to-object priming. In particular, we attempted to assess the influence of "global" scene information as opposed to "local" object information. Accordingly, the scenes were conceptualized as "backgrounds" with objects in them. The backgrounds were constructed so that they would not be easily recognizable from processing any local region (areas of 2° to 3° across). Thus, we felt that if the background had an effect on object identification, we could argue that something more interesting was occurring than the simplest version of object-to-object priming. In addition, the scenes were constructed so that there was virtually no information (either from the background or from any of the objects) in the foveal region. The construction of the scenes in this manner allowed us to factorially manipulate global scene information and local object information.

A third aim of our research was to assess the time course of scene context effects, and in particular, to test the zoom hypothesis using display changes contingent on where the subject was fixating. We will describe the technique in more detail below, but the essence is that we presented scene context information either on the first fixation, when the center of the scene was fixated, or on the second fixation, when the target object was fixated (or on neither or both fixations).

Primary Results

THE BASIC STIMULUS COMPARISON

Our original research with these materials (Boyce et al., 1989) employed the tachistoscopic paradigm of Biederman, primarily because we wanted to start with an established paradigm using new materials. In all the experiments we will describe, the basic comparison was between a target object in a *consistent background* and the same target object in an *inconsistent background*. To achieve this, a set of five target objects (consistent with each other) was placed either in a "consistent background" (i.e., a scene in which the objects belonged, such as a set of "street objects" in a "street background") or in an inconsistent background (i.e., a scene in which the objects did not belong, such as a set of "street objects" in a "swimming pool background"). (The backgrounds were paired so that the pool objects also appeared in a street background.)

For both consistent and inconsistent backgrounds, the objects were in "normal" places; that is, they were not violating any geometric or physical laws in either scene (Figure 13.1). In order to achieve this, however, the objects could not be put in the same locations in the consistent and inconsistent scenes. Thus, control "scenes" (whose background had no semantic content) were constructed for both the consistent and inconsistent background scenes, for which the location of the target

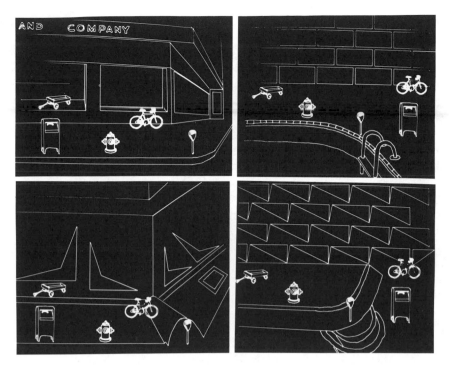

FIGURE 13.1. Examples of four types of displays used in our experiments. The top left panel is the consistent background condition and the bottom left panel is its nonsense control. The top right panel is the inconsistent background condition and the bottom right panel is its nonsense control. These four backgrounds also were matched with a set of "pool objects." The panels are photographs of the actual displays. Reprinted with permission from Boyce, Pollatsek, and Rayner (1989). Copyright by the American Psychological Association.

objects was matched. In some experiments, the control scenes were the *nonsense backgrounds* depicted in Figure 13.1, which were distortions of the meaningful backgrounds that had approximately the same complexity and three-dimensional geometric character as the meaningful backgrounds, but had no readily identifiable meaning. In other experiments, the control backgrounds were either (a) *no background* (i.e., just consisting of the set of five potential target objects in a blank field); or (b) grids (i.e., the set of target objects was superimposed on a background that looked like coarse graph paper).

RESULTS FROM THE TACHISTOSCOPIC EXPERIMENTS

The basic findings of the studies were quite clear. First, we replicated Biederman's finding that identification accuracy of a target object was higher in a consistent scene than in an inconsistent scene (the difference in accuracy was about 10%). This finding indicated that the background had an effect independent of the other objects in the scene, because target objects were always with their "friends" (e.g., "pool objects" were always with other "pool objects"—see Figure 13.1). In a second experiment, we determined that the context effect was *only* due to the background. In this experiment, the relatedness of the cohort objects to the target object and the relatedness of the background to the target object were factorially varied; the relatedness of the cohort objects had no effect on object identification, whereas the relatedness of the background had the same effect as in the prior experiment.

An aspect of these data that was a bit more problematic was the assessment of whether "good" (consistent) backgrounds facilitated object identification or "bad" (inconsistent) backgrounds inhibited identification, or both. As with all assessments of facilitation and inhibition, the answer depends on the baseline chosen to be "neutral." Compared to the no-background controls in Experiment 1, bad backgrounds inhibited but good backgrounds did not facilitate. However, compared to the nonsense background controls in Experiment 3, good backgrounds facilitated but bad backgrounds did not inhibit. We interpreted this pattern as indicating that there is a "cost" in processing a background. This cost is probably due to the fact that scenes with backgrounds are visually more complex than scenes without backgrounds. However, aside from this cost of visual complexity, the presence of a consistent scene background facilitates object identification, whereas inconsistent and nonsense scene backgrounds do not inhibit object recognition. For the stimuli we chose, the cost of processing a background was apparently approximately equal to the facilitation from the consistent background. (The pattern of facilitation and inhibition in the naming studies reported below supports a similar interpretation.)

RESULTS FROM THE WIGGLE PARADIGM

We first assessed whether the background consistency effect could be obtained in the wiggle paradigm (Boyce & Pollatsek, 1992). If it could (to recapitulate our earlier argument), then the effects of scene context on object identification are not limited to situations in which the target object is poorly seen. The principal finding was that a background consistency effect was obtained: target objects in consistent backgrounds were named about 50 ms faster than those in the inconsistent backgrounds, whereas there was no difference between the two control conditions (here again nonsense controls were used—see Figure 13.1).

Also of interest was the time course of information extraction in scenes. That is, in the above paradigm (as in normal scene viewing), the background is continually present. However, one does not know when the viewer is actually extracting and employing the background information to facilitate object identification. If the "zoom hypothesis" discussed earlier is true, then subjects are supposed to "zoom" in quickly (within about 100 ms) and attend only to a significant object. If so, then one would expect that background information present on the first fixation (where the center of the scene is fixated) should have a significant effect on target naming, whereas background information present on the second fixation (when the target object is fixated) should have little or no effect on target naming time.

We did two experiments in which the presence of background information was varied contingent on the position of the eye: meaningful background information was present either on the first fixation, the second fixation, neither fixation, or both fixations. In all cases, both the set of objects and their locations were the same on both fixations. (Because the target objects remained unchanged, it was never the case that a consistent background changed to an inconsistent background or vice versa.) Unfortunately, the first experiment employing display changes produced a strange and uninterpretable set of data. This experiment used the nonsense backgrounds as controls, and the data can be characterized as indicating that the control conditions appeared to acquire the properties of the backgrounds that they were paired with. Thus, although there was still a difference between the consistent and inconsistent background conditions, there was an approximately equal difference between the matched control conditions. We are still unclear as to why or how this happened.

A second experiment was run that was identical to the above, except that new control conditions were employed in which the backgrounds were the grids mentioned earlier. With these control backgrounds, the pattern of data was straightforward. The presence of the background on each fixation had an effect, although the context effect was slightly bigger on the first fixation in the center of the display than on the second fixation on the target. Thus, it appeared that the zoom hypothesis was wrong and that subjects utilized scene background information fairly continually throughout the trial.

Discussion

Converging Evidence for Scene Context Effects on Object Identification

Our first major result is that a scene background affects both (a) the probability of identifying a target object in a single brief presentation and (b) the time to name a target object when it is fixated and clearly seen on a second fixation. Thus, we have converging evidence that context effects on object identification appear early in scene perception and are not limited to situations in which the visual information on which the object identification must be based is degraded due to brief, extrafoveal, and masked presentation.

We earlier raised two major concerns about the "wiggle" paradigm. The first was that the unnaturalness of the cuing device would disrupt normal scene processing. This concern, however, was relevant if we had failed to get a context effect. Forcing the subject to direct attention quickly to an object should, if anything, minimize context effects. The concern that is harder to argue against is that object naming is a contaminated measure of object identification and hence that the context effects observed were not on identification but on a later process tapped by naming. Because there is little conclusive evidence at present that can be marshaled for naming latency (or any other measure) as a relatively pure measure of object identification, we have to rely largely on plausibility arguments. We would like to argue that naming latency (more properly, naming onset latency) is at least reasonable and as good as any other measure.

We begin by noting that naming time has been generally accepted as the measure of word identification time least tainted by postidentification stages of processing (see Rayner & Pollatsek, 1989, for a fuller discussion of this issue). The force of this argument is weakened, however, by the evidence (e.g., Potter & Faulconer, 1975) that object naming times are longer than word naming times (relative to semantic classification); this suggests that context effects in object naming may reflect postlexical influences more than word naming times. However, there are two comparisons that indicate that naming time reveals the same pattern of context effects as another measure.

First, there are the data of the present chapter. Using the same stimuli, context effects were observed using naming latency in the wiggle paradigm and probability of correct identification in the target search paradigm using brief exposures. (Because the measures were so different, it is difficult to estimate if the sizes of the effects were similar.)

Second, a similar pattern of object-to-object priming was observed using naming latency and eye fixation times. As mentioned earlier, Henderson et al. (1987) obtained about a 15-ms priming effect when semantically related prime and target objects were seen on successive fixations and the target object was named. Henderson et al. (1987) and Henderson (1988) assessed priming using fixation durations as the dependent variable; the subject's task was to fixate four objects in turn and then to decide if a target label presented immediately afterward (e.g., "dog") matched one of the four objects just presented. Priming was defined as the difference between the duration of the first fixation on an object when the prior fixation was on a semantically related object and the first fixation duration on the object when the prior fixation was on a related object. Subjects were encouraged not to memorize the objects;

as a result, the first fixation times on target objects were reasonably short (about 300 ms) when they could be seen in extrafoveal vision prior to fixation.

The priming effect using this paradigm was different in the two experiments. In Henderson et al. (1987), the priming effect was 30 to 40 ms (somewhat larger than the 10 to 20 ms effect observed in naming), whereas in Henderson (1988), it was about 20 ms. (The latter effect was not significant.) Although there is unfortunately some inconsistency in the data, the conclusion that emerges is that there is at least as big a priming effect observed in the first fixation duration data as in the naming data. Thus, there is nothing in the data to suggest that naming latency is more likely to pick up postlexical effects of context than is fixation duration.

This brings us to the object decision task discussed earlier (De Graef et al., 1990; see also De Graef, this volume). In their experiment, fixation times on objects were not influenced by scene context until the scene had been viewed for several seconds. This contrasts with our data and others that indicated that scene context can quickly influence object recognition. One possible resolution of the discrepancy is to posit that only the effects observed in the object decision task are on object recognition and the effects observed in other tasks are on postrecognition stages of processing. We find this hypothesis implausible, however. It is clear from the present experiments that the gist of a scene can be apprehended in a matter of 50 to 100 ms and can influence some aspects of processing very rapidly. Because later fixation durations in the object decision task were influenced by context, the hypothesis would force one to concede that scene context does influence object identification (but only after a few seconds). We see no plausible reason why it should take the scene context so long to affect object identification, given that it can do so in principle. An alternative explanation that we discuss below is that something about the object decision task discouraged subjects from processing scene context as rapidly as in other tasks.

More than Object-to-Object Priming?

Our second major result, which was the focus of the brief exposure experiments, was that the background of a scene was the sole cause of the context effect; the consistency of four other objects in the scene had no effect on the accuracy of identifying the target object. This finding extends Biederman's earlier result that a single inconsistent target object had no effect on target detection accuracy. These results rule out the object-to-object priming hypothesis as a sufficient explanation of scene context effects if "object" is taken to mean a relatively local piece of information in the display.

Two arguments could be raised in defense of the object-to-object priming hypothesis. The first is that we did not give it a fair test, as the priming objects were extrafoveal and relatively small, and hence their contributions to context would be expected to be weak. We are now testing this hypothesis further (using the wiggle paradigm) by having the subject's first fixation on a scene be on a priming object. The second argument is that the object-to-object priming mechanism works if the scene background is construed as a single large object that is identified by whatever mysterious process objects are identified. We have no strong objection to this latter argument, but note two potential problems for an object-to-object priming account.

The first is that the context effect *in naming* is much bigger for scene backgrounds (about 50 to 70 ms) than for object-to-object priming (10 to 20 ms). However, it is hard to argue for a qualitative distinction from a quantitative difference. The second problem is that there was little relation between the rated strength of how predictable the object was in the scene and the size of the facilitation effect: in the brief presentation paradigm, the correlation was about zero, whereas in the wiggle paradigm, it was about .2. A standard priming model should predict that the strength of relation (in some sense) should predict the amount of facilitation by the "related prime." One could argue that the predictability ratings are inappropriate measures of strength of relationship; this argument is made reasonably plausible because they were generated from a verbal label for the scene rather than the scene itself.

We suspect, however, that there is a deeper reason for these low correlations. What seems important is not the conditional probability of an object in a background (for example, a suitcase is not particularly likely to be in a bedroom scene). Instead, it would seem that a suitcase is reasonably probable given a bedroom scene and given a rough physical description of the object. On a process level, this suggests that the facilitation of object recognition by scene context is fairly interactive: evidence from a rough description of the object feeds to the scene node, which in turn feeds back to the object detector. One class of models that seems fairly natural here would be "verification" models, whereby a candidate set of objects is identified in a first processing stage, and then a final selection is made by a verification stage that allows interaction with context.

Such an explanation would be neutral to the question of whether the scene node were merely like an object node or had some special "schema" properties. In fact, we think that the only strong evidence in favor of a schema view is Biederman et al.'s (1982) finding that an object that belongs in a scene but is in the wrong place is less likely to be identified than an object in the right place. However, we think there might be an attentional explanation for such an effect. In their experiments, the subject sees the cue of the object name followed by the scene. A cursory analysis of the scene background might allow attention to be drawn to places that the named object might be or, more plausibly, away from locations (such as the sky) that are quite unlikely (although the display is too brief for the subject's eyes to move to the location). One test of the attentional hypothesis would be to study locational violations using the wiggle paradigm. Because the wiggle directs attention to the target object, if locational violations still affect the identification of target objects, one can ascribe it to a "deeper" effect of scene context.

The Time Course of Context Effects

Our third major finding was that scene context effects occur early in the processing of scenes; scene context extracted on the initial fixation influences object processing on the second fixation even when the scene context is no longer present. However, our data indicated that an extreme form of the "zoom" hypothesis is not true; scene context that appeared only on the second fixation had an effect on naming even though the subject was fixating the object to be named and had his or her attention drawn to that object prior to the fixation. This is in spite of the fact that our wiggle task should encourage the subject to ignore scene context on the second fixation because the task is merely to name the target word. One could argue, however, that the zoom hypothesis makes little ecological sense, because in normal scene viewing, the task is not only to identify objects, but to integrate them into a coherent percept. Such a process should require continual maintenance of some representation of the context.

We are left with the perplexing question of why De Graef et al. (1990) only found context effects late in viewing a scene. One possibility is that use of scene context—though it is natural and potentially quite rapid—is not automatic, and something about their task induced subjects not to use context whereas something about our tasks induced them to use it. In designing our wiggle task, in fact, we delayed the wiggle by 75 ms in order to give subjects a chance to process a scene globally before having their attention drawn to a particular object. Perhaps there is something about the object decision task—either its "nonsemantic" level of decision or that an important component is finding non-objects—that discourages subjects from encoding and/or using the scene information. The cost-benefit analyses on our data indicated that the scene background was not processed for free; there was cost to encoding it compared to processing a blank array or a grid. A similar conclusion emerges from a study by Malcus, Klatsky, Bennett, Genarelli, and Biederman (1983), which used a variant of the brief presentation procedure in which the location of the target object is cued before the picture appears. They found that scene background was not used (i.e., no difference between meaningful and distorted scenes) if the subjects were told not to use it and to attend only to the target, indicating that use of context is not obligatory. In addition, they found no difference in the coherent scene condition between when the subject was told to use the background and when they were told to ignore it, indicating (as we found), that the facilitative effects of meaningful scenes are only relative to meaningless backgrounds and not relative to when the background is not processed. Clearly, our discussion here is speculative and more research is needed to determine the circumstances under which scene context information is used in object identification and the extent to which its use is under subject control.

References

Biederman, I. (1972). Perceiving real-world scenes. *Science, 177*, 77–80.

Biederman, I., Mezzanotte, R.J., & Rabinowitz, J.C. (1982). Scene perception: Detecting and judging objects undergoing violation. *Cognitive Psychology, 14*, 143–177.

Boyce, S.J. (1989). *The identification of objects in scenes: The role of scene backgrounds in object naming.* PhD Thesis: University of Massachusetts, Amherst.

Boyce, S.J., & Pollatsek, A. (1992). The identification of objects in scenes: The role of scene background in object naming. *Journal of Experimental Psychology: Learning, Memory and Cognition, 18*,

Boyce, S.J., Pollatsek, A., & Rayner, K. (1989). Role of background information on object identification. *Journal of Experimental Psychology: Human Perception and Performance, 15*, 556–566.

De Graef, P., Christiaens, D., & d'Ydewalle, G. (1990). Perceptual effects of scene context on object identification. *Psychological Research, 52*, 317–329.

Eriksen, C.W., & Yeh, Y. (1985). Allocation of attention in the visual field. *Journal of Experimental Psychology: Human Perception and Performance, 11*, 583–597.

Friedman, A. (1979). Framing pictures: The role of knowledge in automatized encoding and memory from gist. *Journal of Experimental Psychology: General, 3*, 316–355.

Henderson, J.M. (1988). *Visual attention and the extraction of extrafoveal information during eye fixations.* PhD Thesis, University of Massachusetts.

Henderson, J.M., Pollatsek, A., & Rayner, K. (1987). The effects of foveal priming and extrafoveal preview on object identification. *Journal of Experimental Psychology: Human Perception and Performance, 3*, 449–463.

Kroll, J.F., & Potter, M.C. (1984). Recognizing words, pictures and concepts: A comparison of lexical, object and reality decisions. *Journal of Verbal Learning and Verbal Behavior, 23*, 39–66.

Loftus, G.R., & Mackworth, N.H. (1978). Cognitive determinants of fixation location during picture viewing. *Journal of Experimental Psychology: Human Perception and Performance, 4*, 565–572.

Malcus, L., Klatsky, G., Bennett, R.J., Genarelli, E., & Biederman, I. (1983). *Focused attention in scene perception: Evidence against automatic processing of scene backgrounds.* Paper presented at the 54th Annual Meeting of the Eastern Psychological Association, Philadelphia.

Potter, M.C., & Faulconer, B.A. (1975). Time to understand pictures and words. *Nature, 253*, 437–438.

Rayner, K., & Pollatsek, A. (1989). *The Psychology of reading.* Englewood Cliffs: Prentice Hall.

14
Scene-Context Effects and Models of Real-World Perception

PETER DE GRAEF

Most prominent models of visual object recognition (e.g., Biederman, 1987; Marr, 1982) view the apprehension of a particular object in an image as exclusively based on a data-driven preconceptual recovery of the object's structural features (e.g., geons, contour-segments, etc.) from the image. These accounts of an object-limited mapping between pattern and object meet most central demands plausible models of human object perception should meet. They offer speed, resistance to noise in the image and differences in object orientation, applicability to a wide variety of objects without losing discriminatory power, and so on. However, they do neglect one typical characteristic of everyday human object perception: objects are virtually always encountered in the context of a scene.

Often this has been taken to merely pose an additional problem of image segmentation and body-finding that needs to be solved prior to the actual process of object recognition (e.g., Waltz, 1975), which then is assumed to be identical for all objects whether appearing in isolation or in a full scene. More recently, however, evidence is accumulating in support of the position that for objects in natural, real-world scenes the pattern of light reflected by the object itself may not be the sole source of object-diagnostic information used in human object recognition.

In fact, a number of studies by Biederman and colleagues (Biederman, 1981; Biederman, Mezzanotte, & Rabinowitz, 1982; Biederman, Mezzanotte, Rabinowitz, Francolini, & Plude, 1981; Klatsky, Teitelbaum, Mezzanotte, & Biederman, 1981) appear to indicate that this pattern information may only be of secondary importance. In Biederman's studies, subjects are asked to verify whether a prenamed object was present at a cued position in a very briefly presented scene. Speed and accuracy of responses in this *speeded target verification* task are assumed to directly reflect the perceptibility of the object at the cued position. Guided by this rationale, results obtained with the speeded target verification paradigm have fostered the claim that an object's perceptibility is strongly affected by the degree to which its spatial and semantic relations to its context conform to what they typically are in the real world. Specifically, it was

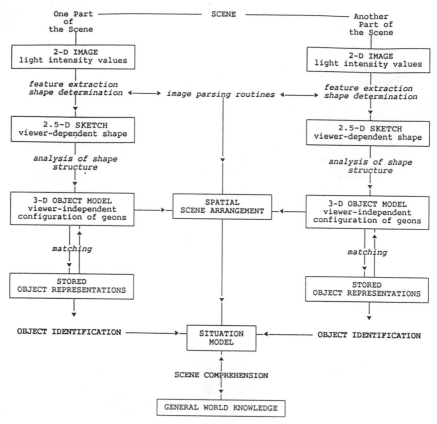

FIGURE 14.1. An object-based view on real-world perception.

found that target verification was slower and less accurate when the cued object (a) inappropriately floated, (b) appeared in an unlikely scene, (c) had an inappropriate size, or (d) was in an inappropriate position. These effects of Support, Probability, Size, and Position violations were observed for cued objects both in foveal and extrafoveal vision. Consequently, there seems to be good reason to defend the position that contextual information is not only a mandatory and integral part of the effective stimulus (Tiberghien, 1986) for object recognition, but also is sufficiently diagnostic to reliably steer this process even in the absence of detailed object pattern information. Recently, this position has been reaffirmed by Boyce, Pollatsek, and Rayner (1989). Using the same paradigm, they found that verification of extrafoveally presented objects was affected by the semantic consistency between the objects and the background of the scene they appeared in.

In combination with reports of a chronological precedence of global scene characterization over individual object recognition (e.g., Antes,

Penland, & Metzger, 1981; Loftus, Nelson, & Kallman, 1983; Metzger & Antes, 1983), these findings appear to have two important implications for the currently dominant data-driven models of visual object recognition. First, they raise the question of whether object recognition under everyday circumstances can indeed be viewed as a completely modular process, limited to a structural analysis of the pattern reflected by the object. Second, they caution against the assumption implicit in much vision research, that bottom-up models of individual object recognition constitute the core of more general models of scene perception. In Figure 14.1, I have attempted to outline this *object-based* view on real-world perception using the computational framework proposed by Marr (1982). As can be seen in this figure, a scene only becomes meaningful by virtue of the identification of the various objects in it, and the semantic interpretation of the spatial relations that hold between these objects. In other words, this view holds that scene comprehension is the result of the construction of an ad hoc "situation model" (cf. Van Dijk & Kintsch, 1983) which interfaces the specific scene that is being viewed with general world knowledge. The research mentioned above, however, suggests that more holistic scene characteristics may constitute a separate unit of perceptual analysis and representation, which is at least as important and fundamental as that formed by the individual object.

In view of these considerations, several authors (Antes & Penland, 1981; Biederman, 1981; Friedman, 1979) have postulated scene-specific *schemas* or *frames* as the central notion in models of everyday object and scene perception. Figure 14.2 offers an outline of the resulting *schema-driven* view on real-world perception.

This theory holds that activation of a scene schema (i.e., a prototypical representation of the contents and spatial relations characteristic for a particular scene) mandatorily precedes identification of individual shapes and the completion of a full three-dimensional (3-D) parse of the scene. This is because such activation is based on low-resolution image information that can be processed extrafoveally and with unfocused attention (Metzger & Antes, 1983). In addition, it does not need to be analyzed up to a full 3-D level in order to allow access to a stored representation (Biederman et al., 1982). Both scene backgrounds (Boyce et al., 1989) and certain spatial configurations of prominent geons of scene-diagnostic objects (Biederman, 1988) have been argued to provide such information.

Following this rapid schema activation, it is assumed that individual object identification as well as the apprehension of interobject relations in the scene will be driven by the schema. It should be noted, however, that there is still debate as to how precisely the schema influences these processes. I indicated this in Figure 14.2 by outlining two different hypothetical influence routes (represented with broken lines).

The strongest position (e.g., Antes & Penland, 1981; Friedman, 1979) clearly is that schema activation makes it possible to directly achieve

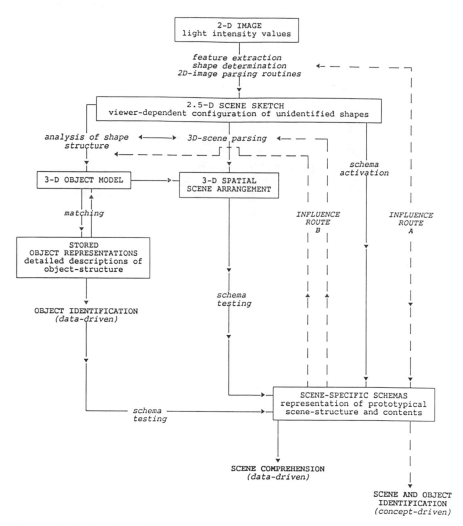

FIGURE 14.2. A schema-driven view on real-world perception.

identification of schema-consistent objects or object configurations by checking the image for the presence of gross 2-D and 2.5-D characteristics specified in the schema (*influence route* A in Figure 14.2). Overall shape, color, texture, dimensionality, aspect ratio, relative size, and position of image regions have all been suggested as relevant input for this concept-driven and resource-inexpensive mode of image interpretation. Schema-inconsistent or isolated objects, on the other hand, are identified on the basis of a data-driven and resource-expensive computation of a 3-D object model from the image, which is then compared to a detailed structural representation at the individual object level (left-hand side of Figure 14.2). Similarly, schema-inconsistent object configurations will have to be anchored in an image-driven 3-D scene parse before they can be tested against existing schemas in order to determine whether they should be marked as a deviation from an old scene or as an exemplar of an entirely novel scene.

More moderate than this postulation of two qualitatively different routes to recognition, is the view (e.g., Riseman & Hanson, 1987) that scene schemas are used as a basis for generating hypotheses about the pattern tests and image segmentations that are most likely to result in the construction of a 3-D model that is consistent both in terms of its internal structure and in terms of its relations to the rest of the scene. In this sense (*influence route B* in Figure 14.2), schema-influences do not alter the basis of visual recognition from data-driven pattern analysis to concept-driven pattern detection, but rather focus the image analysis system by constraining its search space.

Although this schema-driven alternative to the object-based view appears to be commonly accepted, I think its validity still needs to be questioned, both on theoretical and on empirical grounds. The central theoretical problem is clearly illustrated in the views on how scene-specific schemas are supposedly activated during the first glance at a scene. Antes, Mann, and Penland (1981) argued that such activation is the result of the rapid identification of one or more scene-diagnostic objects in the scene. They based this conclusion on the finding that the quality of global thematic scene characterizations significantly deteriorates when scene-diagnostic objects are either removed from the scene or replaced by "shapemates" (i.e., undetailed volumes with the same overall shape). Biederman (1981, 1988), however, argues against this route to schema activation and precisely claims that particular spatial configurations of these shapemates enable access to the appropriate schema. The main piece of evidence cited to support this claim is Mezzanotte's (1981) finding that intact target objects placed in a scene constructed entirely with shapemates, are more difficult to verify when they violate their normal spatial and semantic relations to that scene. Finally, Boyce et al. (1989) assign a crucial role to scene backgrounds, on the basis of their observation that target verification is facilitated when the object is placed in a consistent background rather than in a nonsense background. On the one hand, this questions the exclusive importance of shapemate configurations in schema activation because the target was accompanied by the same set of objects (the target's *cohort*) in the same positions in both background conditions. On the other hand, it suggests that individual objects play no part at all in schema activation because neither target-cohort consistency nor cohort-background consistency had an effect on target verification.

This lack of a consensus on the modalities of rapid schema activation exemplifies the major theoretical flaw in present schema-driven views on real-world perception, i.e., the *deus ex machina* fashion in which a scene-specific unit of perceptual analysis and representation is being postulated and the total absence of a coherent theory of scene recognition. Such a theory should answer questions about what defines a scene and distinguishes it from another scene, how tolerant recognition is with respect to deviations from these scene-diagnostic features and how this tolerance can be economically represented, how scene features can be extracted from images, what the representational format and contents of scene schemas need to be in order to be matched successfully with image information, how these representations have been learned, etc. It is clear, however, that answering these questions is a nontrivial enterprise which makes it very worthwhile to scrutinize the empirical necessity for doing away with the object-based view in favor of a schema-driven account.

The first, and best documented, finding that has been questioned as a valid basis for the schema-driven account, is the *Probability Violation Effect* (PVE), i.e., the decrease in ease of object identification when the object is presented in a scene it is unlikely to occur in (e.g., Antes & Penland, 1981; Loftus & Mackworth, 1978). The reason for this questioning, is that a number of studies established very similar effects on the ease with which isolated objects were identified (Carr, McCauley, Sperber, & Parmelee, 1982; Henderson, Pollatsek, & Rayner, 1987; Huttenlocher & Kubicek, 1983; Kroll & Potter, 1984). Specifically, it was found that the prior presentation of a semantically related object reduced object identification times, which was interpreted as evidence for an automatic spreading of activation between individual object representations. To the extent that semantically related objects also tend to appear in the same real-world scenes, one could therefore argue that interobject priming rather than schema mediation is at the basis of the PVE. In this view, the PVE does not necessitate adoption of the complex model outlined in Figure 14.2 because it can be completely accounted for by the mere addition of an activation link between stored object representations in Figure 14.1.

However, it could be argued that there appear to be constraints on the interobject priming process that may invalidate it as an explanation of the PVE. Based on the Henderson et al. (1987) studies, I examined three such constraints (De Graef, 1990).

The first constraint I examined was the limitation of priming to strictly *semantically* related objects. Although it is not an unreasonable assumption that these objects also tend to appear in the same scenes, one can undoubtedly present an impressive list of semantically unrelated objects that are also likely to appear in the same scenes (e.g., a toilet and a razor in a bathroom, a fireplace and a television in a living room, etc.). Given the robustness of the Probability Violation Effect across different studies and sets of stimuli, this could be taken to imply that priming cannot be the basic mechanism underlying the effect. However, using arrays of visually isolated objects I found evidence for priming between objects that were strictly selected on the basis of their *episodic* relatedness, i.e., their likelihood of appearing in the same scene. Specifically, foveating an episodically related object was found to produce a significant 46-ms reduction in the first fixation duration for the next object, relative to situations in which unrelated or no objects at all were fixated first. To the extent that first fixation duration reflects object identification time (e.g., Friedman, 1979; Henderson, Pollatsek, & Rayner, 1989; Loftus & Mackworth, 1978), this finding supports the hypothesis that interobject priming could indeed explain the Probability Violation Effect in full scenes.

The second constraint I examined was the limitation of priming effects to *controlled* processing of the primed object or *target*. In all studies cited above, the priming effect was measured contingent upon foveation of the target in order to name or memorize it. Advocates of the schema-driven view, however, have also reported the Probability Violation Effect for very briefly presented objects at extrafoveal and a priori uncertain locations in complex scenes (e.g., Biederman, 1981; Boyce et al., 1989). To determine whether priming could account for this phenomenon, I presented subjects with 150-ms masked exposures of arrays of isolated objects. Subjects were instructed to fixate in the center of the display, in preparation for a forced-choice object recognition task following each trial. In this manner, priming effects on *automatic* target processing could be examined by analyzing recognition performance for peripherally located targets as a function of the information in the display's center, i.e., a target-related object, a target-unrelated object, or no object at all. This analysis revealed similar performances in the latter two cases and a significantly worse, chance-level performance in the related prime condition. Although this finding was demonstrated to confirm the existence of an episodic priming mechanism, it also revealed that such a mechanism could not facilitate preattentive perceptual processing of objects. Consequently, if such processing is indeed reflected in the accuracy with which extrafoveal objects are verified in briefly presented scenes, then the Biederman (1981) and Boyce et al. (1989) studies show that priming is insufficient to fully explain the Probability Violation Effect in scene perception.

A similar conclusion was reached with respect to the third constraint, i.e., the limitation of priming effects to situations in which the *prime* itself has been subjected to *controlled* processing. While examining the two previous constraints, I also investigated whether the size of any episodic priming effects varied as a function of the number of nonattended target-related objects in the display. This analysis revealed no significant effects of target-display consistency on either first fixation durations (controlled target processing) or performance in the forced-choice task (automatic target processing). This finding confirms the Henderson, Pollatsek, and

Rayner (1987, 1988) conclusion that priming is strictly conditional upon the relation between the target and the object fixated just prior to it. It suggests that *automatic* prime processing cannot affect the perception of related objects, which leads to the prediction that facilitation of probable object identification in scenes should be preceded by a period of selective attention to another probable object. This prediction, however, runs counter to reports of a Probability Violation Effect for targets presented in foveal vision throughout a 100-ms scene exposure (Klatsky et al., 1981), as well as for targets placed in extrafoveal vision during 150 ms exposures of scenes from which foveal objects had been systematically removed (Boyce et al., 1989). Again, the priming explanation of the Probability Violation Effect in scenes is questioned, provided one can assume that the results of these studies reflect an impact on perceptual object processing.

In fact, the validity of this assumption can safely be regarded as the crucial issue in examining the empirical necessity for adopting a schema-driven view on real-world perception. Indeed, the strongest evidence for this approach stems *exclusively* from studies that use the previously described speeded target verification task. Specifically, I am referring to the reports by Biederman and colleagues that performance in this task decreases when the objects at the cued position inappropriately defy gravity, or appear in unlikely sizes or positions relative to the rest of the scene. This finding suggests that the spatial structure inherent in real-world scenes provides a contextual definition of a set of relational object features (i.e., support, position, and size) that, from the very first scene fixation on, is taken into account during object perception. Clearly, the object-based view would be inadequate to deal with this phenomenon, and could not be made to do so by simply adding unlabeled interobject activation links as was proposed in order to deal with the Probability Violation Effect. Rather, the schema-driven model, centered around the notion of an integrated representation of the typical contents and spatial layout of a particular object-context configuration, would be the most appropriate framework to explain these *Spatial Violation Effects*.

However, De Graef, Christiaens, and d'Ydewalle (1990) have cautioned against this conclusion based on the argument that response speed and accuracy in the speeded target verification task may not measure the perceptibility of the object at the cued position, but rather may reflect the subject's degree of uncertainty in postperceptually deciding whether this object was indeed the prenamed target. I will not repeat the precise rationale of our argument, but its main thrust is that the brief and extrafoveal presentation of the cued object rarely provides detailed image information about its structural features, and that subjects therefore will often have to resort to educated guesses about its identity. For this purpose they can draw upon image cues for global thematic scene identity (e.g., texture or color regions, background information such as fork and

FIGURE 14.3. Stimulus example containing three non-objects (right-front, middle, and left-rear) in addition to a Position violation (dump truck) and a Support violation (bulldozer).

arrow vertices formed by adjoining walls) and on information about gross spatial properties of the cued object (e.g., the proportion of the scene's visual angle occupied by the object, its distance to the scene's ground plane, its nearness and position relative to other scene components). Based on a comparison between this information and their a priori knowledge about the prenamed target object, subjects can generate post-perceptual guesses that can be demonstrated (De Graef et al., 1990) to lead to the exact response patterns that previously have been interpreted as reflecting Probability and Spatial Violation Effects on object perceptibility.

Because this argument obviously challenges the entire empirical basis for the schema-driven model of real-world perception, De Graef et al. (1990) attempted to test the model's validity with a less disputable paradigm for measuring the context sensitivity of object perception. Specifically, our approach involved the presentation of line drawings of realistic scenes in which selected target-objects appeared in either a normal or an inappropriate relation to the rest of the scene. The scenes also included a variable number of "non-objects," a notion we gratefully borrowed from Kroll and Potter (1984) and by which we refer to figures that resemble objects in terms of size range and the presence of a clear and closed part-structure, but which are completely meaningless otherwise. An example of our stimuli is provided in Figure 14.3. Our subjects' task was to freely explore the scenes in order to count the number of non-objects. During this scene exploration, we recorded fixation times for the target-objects that the subjects incidentally fixated in their search for non-objects.

This paradigm has two main advantages. First, it presents a task in which subjects only have to scan the scene and determine if any object-like entities they come across correspond to a known object. The absence of viewing constraints or mnemonic requirements in this "object decision task" is quite important because it means that subjects are not encouraged to deliberately capitalize upon context in order to either compensate for a lack of image information on structural object features or to facilitate memory trace formation (Schank, 1982). Consequently, any context effects observed in this task can be considered to be mandatory rather than elicited. Second, the registration of eye movements under these conditions provides an unobtrusive, on-line measure of object perceptibility. Specifically, for each object fixated in the course of scene exploration, first fixation duration can be determined as a measure of object identification time.

With this paradigm, we examined three main questions. First, could we replicate the Probability and Spatial Violation Effects? To test this, we compared fixation times for objects undergoing relational viola-tions (Violation conditions) to those for the same objects appearing in a normal relation to their context (Base condition). Second, would these effects appear from the very first scene fixation on, as predicted by the schema-driven model of real-world perception? This was investigated by analyzing differences in fixation times for the normal and violated objects as a function of the ordinal position of their first fixation in the entire fixation sequence recorded for the scene they appeared in. Third, what is the precise role of contextual information in object perception? Specifi-cally, does it directly influence the ease with which an object is appre-hended in an image? Or does it serve as a framework for testing the plausibility of the output of a modular, strictly data-driven analysis of structural object features? Although the former view can be con-ceptualized in a number of ways (De Graef et al., 1990), all these accounts imply that a facilitory component will be present in the context effect. This is in contrast to the "plausibility-checking view," which holds that context is merely used to endorse or reject the output of the object-encoding process and consequently predicts that the only effect of context will be to delay or inhibit conclusive object identification in the case of relational inconsistencies. To test which of these views is most appro-priate, we included a condition in which objects appeared out of scene context (i.e., in an array of visually isolated objects) and compared object fixation times in this Isolation condition to those in the Base condition.

An overview of the results relevant to the first two questions can be found in Table 14.1, which presents the mean first fixation durations

TABLE 14.1. Mean first fixation durations (FFD) (in ms) as a function of violation and fixation moment. Means adjusted for differences in object camouflage and size are presented in parentheses.

Fixation moment	Base	Probability	Violation Position	Size	Support
Early FFD	193	193	203	200	191
	(195)	(192)	(201)	(203)	(188)
Late FFD	203	248	246	213	239
	(204)	(247)	(249)	(213)	(237)

(FFD) for the Base and the Violation conditions, as a function of the moment in scene exploration at which the target object was fixated for the first time. "Early" and "Late" Fixation Moments were distinguished by determining ordinal fixation number for each first fixation on a target, and using the median of this distribution as the cutoff point. As can be seen in this table, an analysis of Base-Violation differences did reveal longer fixation times for objects violating Probability, Position, and Size, but only when these objects were fixated at later stages of scene exploration. As can be seen in a comparison of adjusted condition means (in parentheses), these effects remained unchanged when incidental differences in physical object characteristics with a possible effect on object perceptibility (i.e., object camouflage and absolute object size) were filtered out in an analysis of covariance.

With respect to our third research question, the pattern of results in Table 14.1 seems to indicate that the observed Violation effects reflect pure inhibition rather than a lack of facilitation. This is suggested by the fact that their late appearance is entirely due to an increase of fixation times for the violated objects, whereas fixation times for normal objects do not decrease. There is, however, one consideration that cautions against this conclusion. Specifically, studies examining the overall evolution in fixation durations during the exploration of pictorial stimuli all report considerable fixation duration increases over time. Only data reported by Loftus (1983) and the Base-condition data in the present experiment reveal no such tendency. Interestingly, both these exceptions were observed using pictures of realistic scenes whereas all other studies used stimuli such as the Thematic Apperception Test (TAT) cards (Antes, 1974) and abstract paintings (Locher & Nodine, 1987). Consequently, the reason for the discrepancy in findings may very well be that coherent real-world scenes provide stronger contextual constraints on individual scene-component identification. This suggests that the absence of a significant fixation duration increase in the Base condition may perhaps be the result of two counteracting processes, i.e., a general tendency for fixation times to increase during picture exploration and a gradually developing contextual facilitation of object identification. By the same token, the fixation duration increase in the Probability, Position, and Support conditions may (at least partly) reflect a lack of facilitation normally produced by good context, rather than pure inhibition by bad context.

Although this hypothesis obviously calls for further systematic investigation, it was supported in an analysis of Base-Isolation differences as a function of Fixation Moment. Specifically, this analysis showed that object fixation times in the isolation condition significantly increased as a function of time spent in exploring the arrays, leading to first fixation durations that were significantly longer than those in the Base condition.

Clearly, our results are at odds with the immediate context effects observed in the speeded target verification paradigm. One possible explanation for this discrepancy is that we have failed to probe the perceptual processes reflected in the speeded target verification results.

This explanation was originally proposed by Biederman et al. (1982), who argued that object fixation times are unlikely to reflect object encoding because they are much longer than the exposure durations typically required to achieve high levels of object recognition accuracy in tachistoscopic studies. One problem with this argument is that estimating the precise time-difference between these two measures is nearly impossible as it is highly dependent upon the methodology involved in obtaining the measures. This certainly is the case for the fixation time measure as demonstrated by the fact that an older and coarser eye movement recording methodology used by Friedman (1979) yielded first fixation durations that were up to 400 ms longer than ours. In addition, the method-dependency problem also holds for the exposure duration measure. Biederman and Ju (1988), for instance, report a number of experiments that show that object recognition accuracy at a given exposure duration clearly varies as a function of task, the presence of a mask, speed-accuracy trade-offs, etc. The fatal flaw, however, in the fixation time versus exposure duration argument, is of course that it fails to acknowledge the fact that only a portion of the fixation time is actually used for visual encoding. That this may correspond to a time period that falls well within the range of the 50 to 150 ms exposure durations used in tachistoscopic studies, has been nicely demonstrated in foveal masking studies of reading processes (Rayner, Inhoff, Morrison, Slowiazcek, & Bertera, 1981).

Another antifixation argument advanced by Biederman et al. (1982) is that violation effects on object fixation times are far too large to reflect increased encoding difficulties, but rather show a greater interest for "odd" objects. Again, basing the argument on absolute effect size is quite problematic because the Probability Violation Effect Biederman et al. refer to (Friedman, 1979) is about six times larger than the one we found. In addition, we did examine our data for a possible reflection of increased interest for violated objects. Specifically, due to the within-subjects nature of our experiment we were able to analyze object fixation times as a function of the number of times subjects had seen them violating normal object-context relations. Obviously, if longer fixation times for violated objects were due to greater interest, one would expect these fixation times to decrease as more violations were encountered and their interest value decreased. Our analyses showed that such an effect was indeed present for gaze durations (i.e., the total sum of successive fixations on an object), but *not* for first fixation durations. Furthermore, it should be noted that our controls for confounding influences of physical object characteristics showed a large effect of object camouflage on first fixation durations, which clearly is a desirable feature for a measure that is supposed to tap into visual processing. In this context, it is interesting to note that response speed and accuracy in the speeded target verification studies by Biederman and colleagues were completely unaffected by a manipulation (i.e., the "Interposition Violation") in which the cued object's featural structure was thoroughly disrupted by letting its background pass through it.

In view of these considerations, I feel rather confident about the validity of our paradigm and suggest that the observed discrepancy in results may be explained by reversing the argument. Do responses obtained with the speeded target verification paradigm reflect mandatory perceptual effects of context, or do they probe a deliberate, post-perceptual use of low-resolution image information as cues for making inferences about global scene and individual object identity? In this view, the speeded target verification results appear to be most relevant for developing algorithms to constrain the search space of man-made pattern recognition systems with a relatively limited capacity for data-driven image analysis. In models of human perception, however, these results do not necessitate the postulation of an immediately operating scene-encompassing mechanism for image interpretation, which mandatorily drives further object and scene identification. Instead, the perceptual impact of contextual information seems to develop only gradually, which suggests that it requires data-driven encoding of local scene components and the spatial relations between them.

Integrating the above arguments and findings, I think the framework outlined in Figure 14.4 may be most appropriate to capture the present status of research on scene-context effects and its implications for accounts of real-world perception. In essence, a data-driven view on real-world perception is proposed that preserves most of the main features of the object-based model. The outcome of object encoding and scene parsing is entered in a situational model of the viewed scene, which serves as a fluid interface between the image and general world knowledge. Parallel to its gradual definition, this model will start to influence further image processing. Our data suggest that this influence may be on

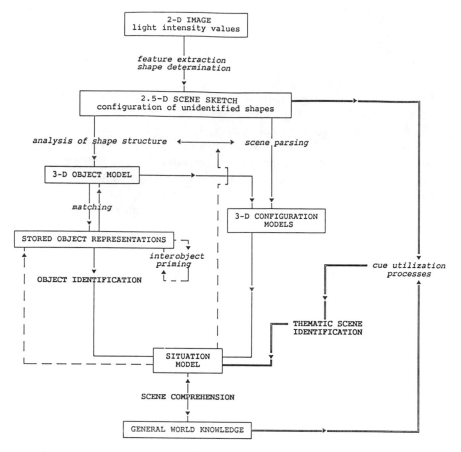

FIGURE 14.4. Scene-context effects in a data-driven view on real-world perception.

the actual encoding of the image, but much remains to be determined with respect to the exact locus of impact. Hence, the interrupted lines that represent hypothetical routes and mechanisms that may underlie the observed effects of Probability, Support, and Position violations. Although a separate scene-level of perceptual processing is considered unnecessary in the framework, the double lines on the right-hand side of Figure 14.3 were added to represent a non-perceptual explanation of the scene-context effects reported in the speeded target verification studies. Specifically, it is assumed that these results are produced by active utilization of low-resolution image cues, allowing for a thematic scene identification that will guide or completely replace the data-driven development of an ad hoc situation model.

Obviously, this proposal requires further development and will have to be amended in the face of new data. In fact, other chapters in the present volume (Boyce & Pollatsek; Henderson) already contain urgent calls for such development in their confirmation of our suspicion (De Graef et al., 1990) that differences in attentional distribution may mediate the presence of immediate and delayed components in the effects of context on perception. The presented view on scene-context effects is merely a step toward identifying the constraints that explain the ease with which we perceive our environment in spite of the tremendous computational complexities involved in even the simplest image interpretation tasks.

Acknowledgment. The writing of this chapter was supported by the Belgian government through agreement RFO/A1/04 of the Incentive Program for Fundamental Research in Artificial Intelligence.

References

Antes, J.R. (1974). The time course of picture viewing. *Journal of Experimental Psychology, 3*, 62–70.

Antes, J.R., Mann, S.M., & Penland, J.G. (1981). *Local precedence in picture naming: The importance of obligatory objects.* Paper presented at the 1981 meeting of the Psychonomic Society.

Antes, J.R., & Penland, J.G. (1981). Picture context effects on eye movement patterns. In D.F. Fischer, R.A. Monty, & J.W. Senders (Eds.), *Eye movements: Cognition and visual perception* (pp. 157–170). Hillsdale, NJ: Erlbaum.

Antes, J.R., Penland, J.G., & Metzger, R.L. (1981). Processing global information in briefly presented pictures. *Psychological Research, 43*, 277–292.

Biederman, I. (1981). On the semantics of a glance at a scene. In M. Kubovy & J.R. Pomerantz (Eds.), *Perceptual organization.* Hillsdale, NJ: Erlbaum.

Biederman, I. (1987). Recognition-by-components: A theory of human image understanding. *Psychological Review, 94*, 115–147.

Biederman, I. (1988). Aspects and extensions of a theory of human image understanding. In Z.W. Pylyshyn (Ed.), *Computational processes in human vision: An interdisciplinary approach* (pp. 370–428). Norwood, NJ: Ablex.

Biederman, I., & Ju, G. (1988). Surface versus edge-based determinants of visual recognition. *Cognitive Psychology, 20*, 38–64.

Biederman, I., Mezzanotte, R.J., & Rabinowitz, J.C. (1982). Scene perception: Detecting and judging objects undergoing relational violations. *Cognitive Psychology, 14*, 143–177.

Biederman, I., Mezzanotte, R.J., Rabinowitz, J.C., Francolini, C.M., & Plude, D. (1981). Detecting the unexpected in photointerpretation. *Human Factors, 23*, 153–164.

Boyce, S.J., Pollatsek, A., & Rayner, K. (1989). Effects of background information on object identification. *Journal of Experimental Psychology: Human Perception and Performance, 15*, 556–566.

Carr, T.H., McCauley, C., Sperber, R.D., & Parmelee, C.M. (1982). Words, pictures and priming: On semantic activation, conscious identification, and the automaticity of information processing. *Journal of Experimental Psychology: Human Perception and Performance, 8,* 757–777.

De Graef, P. (1990). *Episodic priming and object probability effects.* Unpublished master's thesis, Department of Psychology, University of Massachusetts, Amherst.

De Graef, P., Christiaens, D., & d'Ydewalle, G. (1990). Perceptual effects of scene context on object identification. *Psychological Research, 52,* 317–329.

Friedman, A. (1979). Framing pictures: The role of knowledge in automatized encoding and memory for gist. *Journal of Experimental Psychology: General, 108,* 316–355.

Henderson, J.M., Pollatsek, A., & Rayner, K. (1987). Effects of foveal priming and extrafoveal preview on object identification. *Journal of Experimental Psychology: Human Perception and Performance, 13,* 449–463.

Henderson, J.M., Pollatsek, A., & Rayner, K. (1988). *Extrafoveal information use during object identification.* Unpublished manuscript.

Henderson, J.M., Pollatsek, A., & Rayner, K. (1989). Covert visual attention and extrafoveal information use during object identification, *Perception and Psychophysics, 45,* 196–208.

Huttenlocher, J., & Kubicek, L.F. (1983). The source of relatedness effects on naming latency. *Journal of Experimental Psychology: Learning, Memory and Cognition, 9,* 486–496.

Klatsky, G.J., Teitelbaum, R.C., Mezzanotte, R.J., & Biederman, I. (1981). Mandatory processing of the background in the detection of objects in scenes. *Proceedings of the Human Factors Society, 25,* 272–276.

Kroll, J.F., & Potter, M.C. (1984). Recognizing words, pictures and concepts: A comparison of lexical, object and reality decisions. *Journal of Verbal Learning and Verbal Behavior, 23,* 39–66.

Locher, P.J., & Nodine, C.F. (1987). Symmetry catches the eye. In J.K. O'Regan & A. Lévy-Schoen (Eds.), *Eye movements: From physiology to cognition* (pp. 353–361). North-Holland: Elsevier.

Loftus, G.R. (1983). Eye fixations on text and scenes. In K. Rayner (Ed.), *Eye movements in reading* (pp. 359–376). New York: Academic Press.

Loftus, G.R., & Mackworth, N.H. (1978). Cognitive determinants of fixation location during picture viewing. *Journal of Experimental Psychology: Human Perception and Performance, 4,* 565–572.

Loftus, G.R., Nelson, W.W., & Kallman, H.J. (1983). Differential acquisition rates for different types of information from pictures. *Quarterly Journal of Experimental Psychology, 35A,* 187–198.

Marr, D. (1982). *Vision: A computational investigation into the human representation and processing of visual information.* San Francisco: Freeman.

Metzger, R.L., & Antes, J.R. (1983). The nature of processing early in picture perception. *Psychological Research, 45,* 267–274.

Mezzanotte, R.J. (1981). *Accessing visual schemata: Mechanisms invoking world knowledge in the identification of objects in scenes.* Unpublished doctoral dissertation, Department of Psychology, State University of New York at Buffalo.

Rayner, K., Inhoff, A.W., Morrison, R.E., Slowiaczek, M.L., & Bertera, J.H. (1981). Masking of foveal and parafoveal vision during eye fixations in reading. *Journal of Experimental Psychology: Human Perception and Performance, 7,* 167–179.

Riseman, E.M., & Hanson, A.R. (1987). A methodology for the development of general knowledge-based vision systems. In M. Arbib & A. Hanson (Eds.), *Vision, brain and cooperative computation* (pp. 285–328). Cambridge: M.I.T. Press.

Schank, R. (1982). *Dynamic memory. A theory of reminding and learning in computers and people*. Cambridge: Cambridge University Press.

Tiberghien, G. (1986). Context and cognition: Introduction. *Cahiers de Psychologie Cognitive*, 6, 105–119.

Van Dijk, T., & Kintsch, W. (1983). *Strategies of discourse comprehension*. New York: Academic Press.

Waltz, D. (1975). Understanding line drawings of scenes with shadows. In P.H. Winston (Ed.), *The psychology of computer vision*. New York: McGraw-Hill.

15
Visual Attention and Eye Movement Control During Reading and Picture Viewing

JOHN M. HENDERSON

Experimental psychologists have known for some time that it is possible to allocate visual-spatial attention to one region of the visual field even as we maintain eye fixation on another region. As William James stated it, ". . . we may attend to an object on the periphery of the visual field and yet not accommodate the eye for it" (James, 1890/1950, p. 437). At the same time, experimental psychologists have also known that during the course of a complex visual task such as reading or picture viewing, our eyes move from one location to another at an average rate of 3 to 5 times per second (e.g., Rayner, 1978; Tinker, 1939; Yarbus, 1967). The question therefore arises how these covert and overt changes in processing focus are related. This is the question addressed in the present chapter.

As a rough first pass, there are at least three ways in which covert changes in the locus of visual attention and overt movements of the eyes might be related. First, it could be that when the eyes are free to move, attention is always directed toward the stimulus at the point of fixation. On this view, although it might be the case that attention can be allocated away from the point of fixation under appropriate experimental conditions, this finding would be explained away as of no functional significance in natural visual tasks. At the other extreme, it might be that covert shifts of visual attention and overt shifts of the eyes are completely decoupled in complex visual tasks, so that there is little relationship between the point of fixation and the focus of visual attention. Finally, in contrast to either of these two positions, it could be that during complex visual tasks there is a functional relationship between the allocation of visual attention and overt movements of the eyes. In this chapter, I will present a review of the evidence suggesting that this last position may well be correct.

Before moving on, a definition is in order. Throughout this chapter, I will define *visual attention* as the selective use of information from one region of the visual field at the expense of other regions of the visual field.

Relationship Between Eye Movements and Attention

In this section I will review the evidence supporting the position that covert shifts of attention and overt movements of the eyes are functionally related. This review will not be exhaustive; instead, I will concentrate on studies that have examined attentional processes under conditions where the eyes were free to move and eye movements were monitored. Most of these studies have employed the *contingent display change technique* (McConkie & Rayner, 1975), in which the stimulus is changed as a function of eye position. In the typical experimental setup for this type of study, the subject is seated before a computer monitor on which stimuli are presented. The subject's eye movements are recorded while he or she views the display. Because the display monitor and the eye tracker are both interfaced with the same computer, the display shown to the subject can be changed contingent on characteristics of the subject's eye movements.

Some of the earliest studies using the contingent display change technique involved presenting a reader with a line of text in which a window moved along with the subject's eyes. In this *moving window* paradigm, the text within the moving window is normal, whereas text beyond the window is mutilated in some way. For example, each letter space in the text beyond the window might be replaced by the letter *x*. The logic of the paradigm is that if text normally used during the course of a fixation is beyond the window region, then the reading process should be disrupted in some way. On the other hand, if some region of text is beyond the window, but reading is not disrupted, then that text is presumably not normally used.

One of the most robust effects to emerge from studies using the moving window paradigm in reading is that the *perceptual span*, or region from which useful information is acquired during an eye fixation, is asymmetric rather than symmetric around the point of fixation. The maximum perceptual span has been found to be about three to four character spaces to the left of the fixated character and up to 15 character spaces to the right of the fixated character (e.g., McConkie & Rayner, 1975, 1976; Rayner, Well, & Pollatsek, 1980; Underwood & McConkie, 1985). Thus, the perceptual span generally encompasses the entire word under fixation, and one to two words to the right of the fixated word (Rayner & Pollatsek, 1987).

The fact that the perceptual span is asymmetric around the point of fixation strongly indicates that the perceptual span in reading is not determined by acuity factors alone. An obvious explanation for the asymmetry is that attentional factors contribute to the perceptual span, limiting information use from the left side and facilitating information use from the right. However, before accepting this explanation, several other possibilities must be ruled out.

One possible nonattentional explanation for the asymmetry of the perceptual span in reading is that it is due to lateralization of function in the cerebral hemispheres. Because language is left hemisphere dominant in about 80% of the population, and because the left hemisphere is more directly connected to retinal receptor cells receiving input from the right visual field, perhaps there is a cortical processing advantage for text in the right visual field. One study indicating that this explanation is incorrect was conducted by Pollatsek, Bolozky, Well, and Rayner (1981). In this study, bilinguals who could read both English and Hebrew were tested in the moving window paradigm. Hebrew is a language that, in contrast to English, is read from right to left. Pollatsek et al. found that when these bilinguals were reading English, their perceptual spans were asymmetric to the right, as found in the earlier studies. However, when these same subjects read Hebrew, then their perceptual spans reversed so that they were asymmetric to the left. This is exactly the result one would expect if the perceptual span is attentionally constrained. At the same time, this result is inconsistent with the view that the rightward asymmetry normally seen with English readers is due to hemispheric factors.

A second possible explanation for the asymmetry of the perceptual span is that it is intrinsic to the reading process rather than due to a dynamic allocation of visual attention. In other words, it could be that part of learning to become a fluent reader involves developing a perceptual module for reading in which the disposition to use information from a particular region of text is automatized or hard-wired. This explanation would suggest that the bilingual readers in the Pollatsek et al. (1981) study had developed two reading modules and were switching between them when they switched languages.

A recent study by Inhoff, Pollatsek, Posner, and Rayner (1989) argues against the notion that the asymmetry is fixed within the reading system. In this study, native readers of English were asked to read text presented in several backward formats (e.g., words facing forward but ordered right-to-left; letters within words and words ordered right-to-left), so that the subjects were required to read right-to-left. Clearly, these subjects would have had very little, if any, experience reading in this manner, and therefore would not have had a chance to develop any automatized systems devoted to reading right-to-left. Yet, in this study the perceptual span was again found to be asymmetric in the direction that the text was being read.

In sum, the studies that have used the moving window paradigm to explore the acquisition and use of visual information from text during reading show that the perceptual span is asymmetric in the direction the eyes are generally moving. This effect is not due to having learned to read in a particular direction, but instead appears to be dynamically adapted to the reading situation encountered. These findings are consistent with the view that the perceptual span is determined by the allocation of visual attention during each eye fixation. More particularly, it appears that visual attention is allocated to the region of the visual field toward which the eyes are moving. The finding that the perceptual span is not determined by acuity factors alone suggests that the term *perceptual span* is somewhat of a misnomer. Instead, the term *attentional span* would seem more appropriate.

The Sequential Attention Model

The studies reviewed in the previous section examining the attentional span in reading indicate that visual attention is generally allocated to that region of text toward which the eyes are moving. One interpretation of this finding is that there is a functional relationship between the covert allocation of visual attention and overt movements of the eyes. In this section I want to outline a particular model of this relationship. The model is based on both empirical evidence and on a consideration of recent theorizing in the cognitive control of eye movements during reading. Following presentation of the model, I will review further experimental work that bears on various aspects of the model.

Basic Assumptions

The sequential attention model contains five basic assumptions (Henderson, 1988; Henderson & Ferreira, 1990; Henderson, Pollatsek, & Rayner, 1989). First, at the beginning of each new eye fixation visual attention is allocated to the stimulus at the center of fixation. In reading, the attended stimulus is likely to be the word (McConkie & Zola, 1987), though in the case of longer words it may be just one part of the word. In scene perception, it would presumably be at the level of the object. Second, attention is reallocated to a new stimulus when the foveal stimulus is "understood." The simplest interpretation of "understood" here is that attention is reallocated when the foveal stimulus is identified (Rayner & Balota, 1989; Rayner & Pollatsek, 1987). However, attention could be reallocated when activation from the foveal stimulus reaches a critical threshold prior to recognition, or alternatively could be reallocated when a process following identification such as syntactic parsing (in reading) or semantic interpretation (in reading and scene perception) is imminent or completed. Third, the reallocation of attention is coincident with two aspects of eye movement programming: (a) when attention is reallocated, the system begins to program the motor movements necessary to bring the eyes to a new location, and (b) the new locus of attention is taken to be the location toward which the eyes should be moved. Fourth, the reallocation of attention to a new location gates higher level analysis at that new location. Finally, the eyes follow the shift of attention to the attended location following the eye movement programming latency.

Secondary Assumptions

Several aspects of the sequential attention model require further elaboration. First, the model suggests a "rubber-band" view of the relationship between attention allocation and eye movement control. At a particular point in time attention is reallocated away from the fovea and to a new location; the eyes then catch up with attention after the eye movement motor commands have been programmed and executed. This aspect of the model would seem to offer a simple account of where the eyes go from one fixation to the next: they go to the location that is currently being attended. However, this begs the question of what region will be attended next. I will assume that the location to which attention is allocated is determined on the basis of relatively low-level stimulus attributes. In particular, I make the following assumptions: First, a preattentive map of likely stimulus locations is made available to the attention allocation system. Second, stimulus locations are weighted so that attention is allocated to the stimulus location with the largest weight. Koch and Ullman (1985) discuss a neurophysiologically plausible model of the allocation of attention based on a location weighting scheme similar to this. In reading, the largest weight can generally be assigned to the stimulus location immediately to the right of the point of fixation (except under conditions when higher level language processes require a regression back to a previously read region of text). In scene perception, the situation is less constrained, but a fairly simple process could assign weights on the basis of a salience measure automatically derived from low-level analysis (Mahoney & Ullman, 1988).

The motor programming aspect of the model derives from Morrison's earlier work on the cognitive control of eye movements in reading (Morrison, 1984; see also McConkie, 1979). In accordance with Morrison, I assume that it is possible to have several eye movement programs simultaneously active. This *parallel programming* occurs when a decision is made to abort a partially programmed movement and instead to make a different movement (Becker & Jurgens, 1979). The eye movement behavior observed following parallel programming of two saccades will depend on when programming of the second movement begins. For example, if the signal to begin a new program arrives when the first program is not too far along then the first program can simply be canceled, with a possible cost in saccade latency (Hogaboam, 1983; Pollatsek, Rayner, & Balota, 1986). In this case, the target of the original saccade would be skipped (but would have been parafoveally processed, Fisher & Shebilske, 1985). If the new signal arrives a bit later, then the two programs may overlap, and the eye movement will be determined by a combination of the two programs. In this case, the eyes may land between the two target positions. Finally, if computation of the first program is well along when the signal arrives to construct a different program, then the first program may be executed. In this case, the eyes will land at the first target location, but the fixation may be brief because the program to move the eyes to the second location is already partially computed.

When would parallel eye movement programs be active according to the sequential attention model? Recall that programming of an eye movement begins when attention shifts away from the fovea. Suppose that after some amount of time, attention shifts again to a second extrafoveal location prior to an eye movement to the first extrafoveal location. This could happen if, for example, the stimulus at the first extrafoveal location were easily recognized. Because a shift of attention initiates eye movement programming, and because the locus of attention is taken to be the target of the program, the shift of attention to a second extrafoveal location will cause a second program to be readied prior to execution of the first. The type of parallel programming, of the three types outlined above, that then occurred would depend on how soon after the first attentional shift the second shift occurred.

Tests of the Model

In this section I will review research that bears on various aspects of the sequential attention model as it was outlined above.

Generality

The sequential attention model is meant to provide an account of the relationship between the allocation of visual attention and movements of the eyes. This relationship is assumed to be a fundamental aspect of visual cognition. However, the studies reviewed above primarily dealt with eye movements and attention during reading. The first question to be addressed, therefore, is whether the sequential attention model generalizes beyond reading.

To explore how eye movements and the allocation of attention are related in a task other than reading, Henderson et al. (1989) had subjects view displays composed of four line drawings of objects positioned at the corners of an imaginary square surrounding the fixation point. The subject's task was to view each of the four objects in a prescribed sequence in order to prepare for an immediate probe memory test (e.g., "Was there a tree in the display?"). To determine which object or objects were being attended on each fixation, a variation of the moving window paradigm was employed. In the *full-display* condition, all four objects were continuously displayed throughout the trial. At the other extreme, in the *one-object* condition, only the object currently being fixated was displayed; all other objects were replaced with a pattern mask. In the *one+next* condition, the object currently at the point of fixation and the object about to be fixated next in the prescribed sequence were displayed, and in the *one+last* condition, the object currently at the point of fixation and the object just fixated were displayed. Finally, in the *zoom* condition all objects were initially displayed, but once the subject moved his or her eyes to the first object, the trial proceeded as in the one-object condition.

The logic of this experiment was similar to that of the moving window studies in reading. If information that is normally used during picture viewing is outside of the window, then viewing behavior should be disrupted in comparison to the full-display condition. On the other hand, if information that is not normally used is beyond the window, then no disruption should be observed. The prediction of the sequential attention model is that eye movement behavior in the one+next condition should be similar to the full-display condition, because in both cases the information normally attended is available (the object at fixation and the object about to be fixated), and because information normally acquired preattentively (e.g., information about where potential objects are) is still available due to the location of the pattern masks. On the other hand, eye movement behavior should be disrupted in the one-object, one+last, and zoom conditions because the object about to be fixated is not available for processing.

These predictions were supported. The full and one+next conditions were statistically equivalent for both the first fixation and gaze duration measures. In addition, the one, one+last, and zoom conditions were disrupted in comparison to the full-display condition, and the former three did not differ among themselves. The finding that information is used primarily from the object currently fixated and the object about to be fixated suggests that the asymmetric attentional span is not unique to reading. The fact that the same result was found for the object at the second location, which was fixated following a vertical eye movement, suggests that the asymmetry of the attentional span is not unique to horizontal eye movements. Finally, even though eye movements were changing direction after each object was fixated, the object about to be fixated next was generally the only extrafoveal object processed during a given fixation. This strongly suggests that attention is allocated dynamically during each fixation to the location to be fixated next. Thus, it appears that the sequential attention model generalizes beyond reading to a situation involving the identification of pictures of objects.

Necessity of Attending to the Target Location

The question arises whether it is *necessary* that attention precede an eye movement to the target location of the movement. As Klein (1980) pointed out, there are actually two independent sides to this question. First, in order to reorient attention, must an eye movement program to the attended location be initiated? Second, is an attentional shift necessary to initiate eye movement programming? Note that the sequential attention model is neutral about the first question. For the second question, the sequential attention model posits an affirmative answer. According to the model, if the eyes are going to move to a particular location, then attention must be oriented to that location in order to provide target-location parameters. Is there any evidence for this view? Shepard, Findlay, and Hockey (1986) conducted an experiment in which a target stimulus was more likely to appear at a location on one side of the fixation point, whereas the subject was required to make an eye movement to a location on the opposite side. Shepard et al. found that subjects could strategically allocate attention to the more likely location unless they were about to make an eye movement. When an eye movement was imminent, then attention was allocated only to the location that was the target of the saccade. Thus, it appears that prior to an eye movement, attention must be allocated to the location about to be fixated.

Specificity of the Attended Location

The sequential attention model clearly predicts that the focus of attention prior to an eye movement will be the *specific* location toward which the eyes will move. However, although the studies discussed above are consistent with this view, they are also consistent with the hypothesis that attention spreads out from the foveal location in the general direction of the next eye movement rather than to that specific location. For example, in the reading studies, the asymmetric perceptual span could be due to attention spreading from the fixated word to all words in the attended hemifield. This position receives some support from the suggestion that attention can only be allocated to a hemifield or at best a visual quadrant (Hughes & Zimba, 1985, 1987), though this view has recently come under attack (Henderson, 1991; Klein & McCormick, 1989). In the case of the Shepard et al. (1986) study, it could be that although subjects were unable to attend to a location in the hemifield opposite to that into which they were about to saccade, they still might be able to attend to different regions in the same hemifield. Similarly, in the Henderson et al. (1989) object study, there is no way to determine whether attention was directed to the specific location about to be fixated or more generally in the direction of the next eye movement.

I have recently conducted a study to test if attention is allocated to the specific location about to be fixated (Henderson, 1990). In this study, which is depicted in Figure 15.1, the subject began each trial looking at a fixation cross. Two preview letter strings were then presented to the right of the subject's point of fixation. In the *move* condition, the subject was

Experimental paradigm

1. Fixate:

+

.

2. Preview Appears:

| near: | + brand | csboe |

.

| far: | + csboe | brand |

.

| control: | + csboe | csboe |

.

3. Name Target Word:

move: +   brand

--------------> .

no move: brand

FIGURE 15.1. An illustration of the experimental paradigm used by Henderson (1990) to examine the allocation of attention prior to a saccadic eye movement. The subject began each trial fixating a central cross. Two letter strings then appeared to the right of fixation, with a preview of the target word appearing close to the fixation point (near), far from the fixation point (far), or not at all (control). The subject then either executed an eye movement to the far letter string (move) and named the word that appeared there, or maintained fixation (no move) and named the word that appeared at that location.

asked to execute an eye movement to the location of the letter string furthest to the right as soon as the letter strings appeared. The contingent display change technique was employed so that during the saccade the two letter strings could be replaced by a single target word positioned at the location of the letter string toward which the eyes were moving. The subject's task was to name the target word as quickly as possible once the eyes had landed. In order to examine the location from which information was acquired prior to the eye movement, three *preview conditions* were employed. In the *near-preview* condition, the letter string closest to the initial point of fixation provided a preview of the target (i.e., was the same as the target word), and the letter string further from the point of fixation but at the location toward which the eyes were about to move did not provide a preview of the target (i.e., was an unpronounceable nonsense string). In the *far-preview* condition, the letter string positions were reversed so that the preview of the target word occupied the location toward which the eyes would be moving and the nonsense string occupied the closer location. In the *control* condition, the same nonsense

Preview Benefit

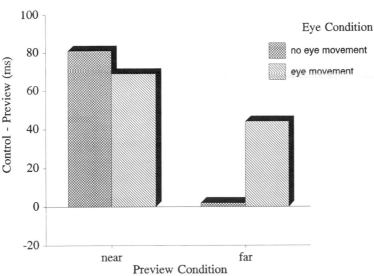

FIGURE 15.2. The results from Henderson (1990). When the preview appeared at the far location, more benefit was derived when the eyes were moving to that location compared with when the eyes remained stationary. In contrast, when the preview appeared at the near location, less preview benefit was derived when the eye moving to the far location compared with when the eyes remained stationary.

letter string occupied both locations. In the second eye behavior condition, termed the *no-move* condition, the subject was to maintain fixation on the central location throughout the trial. The same three preview conditions then occurred extrafoveally, but the target word appeared at the fixation location after a 200-ms presentation of the preview (the average saccade latency in the eye movement condition). Again, the subject was to name the target word as quickly as possible after it appeared foveally.

Two predictions can be made from the sequential attention model. First, in the move condition attention should shift to the location about to be fixated (the far location) and information at that specific location should be used to begin identifying the stimulus located there. Therefore, a greater *preview benefit* (control condition minus preview condition) should be observed for the far location (control minus far preview) in the move condition compared to the no-move condition. This prediction follows because in the no-move condition there is no reason for the subject to attend the far location over the near location. Second, a greater preview benefit should *not* be observed for the near location (control minus near preview) in the move condition compared to the no-move condition, because attention is allocated specifically to the location toward which the eyes are about to move. If, on the other hand, attention is allocated generally in the direction that the eyes will move, then both the near- and far-preview conditions should show a greater preview benefit in the move condition compared to the no-move condition.

The results of the experiment are shown in Figure 15.2. First, consider the far-preview condition. When the eyes were not moving (no-move condition), no preview benefit was derived from a preview of the target word at the far location in comparison to the control condition. On the other hand, when the eyes were about to move to the far location (move condition), significant preview benefit was derived from a preview of the target at that location. These data are consistent with the view that attention precedes an eye movement to the location toward which the eyes are about to move. Consider now the near-preview condition. The amount of preview benefit derived when the eyes were moving to the far location was statistically *less* than the amount derived when the eyes remained stationary. The finding that the preview benefit at the near location was reduced in the move compared to the no-move condition is clearly inconsistent with the view that attention spreads out from the fixation location in the direction that the eyes are about to move. Instead, these data suggest that attention moves away from the fixation point prior to the saccade. Because the near word is closer to the fixation point, when attention is directed away in the move condition, the preview benefit derived from the near location is reduced.

In sum, the results of this experiment strongly suggest that attention is allocated to the specific location toward which the eyes are about to move, and not in the general direction that the eyes are about to move. Thus, these results support the sequential attention model.

Foveal Load and the Perceptual Span

A third prediction of the sequential attention model is that variations in the difficulty of the foveal stimulus should not affect the amount of preview benefit derived from the extrafoveal stimulus about to be fixated next. This prediction follows because attention does not shift away from the foveal stimulus until foveal processing reaches a criterion level of completion. The eyes then follow the reallocation of attention to an extrafoveal location by a constant amount of time. Therefore, if the foveal stimulus is more difficult, attention should remain on that stimulus for a greater amount of time. This predicts longer fixation durations on more difficult stimuli, a ubiquitous finding (see Just & Carpenter, 1987; Rayner & Pollatsek, 1989). However, because the preview benefit derived from an extrafoveal location is a function of the programming latency (the amount of time attention is focused on the extrafoveal stimulus before the eyes get there), and because this latency does not

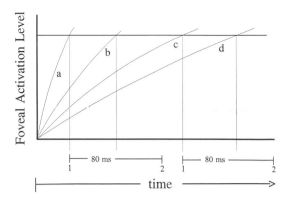

FIGURE 15.3. An illustration of the sequential attention model. The activation of the foveal stimulus is plotted against time since the beginning of the fixation. Curves (*a*) through (*d*) illustrate activation functions for progressively more difficult foveal stimuli. The horizontal line indicates the attention-shift criterion; the point in time when an activation crosses this criterion indicates when attention will shift to a new location. Along the time axis, point (*1*) indicates when attention shifts and point (*2*) indicates when the eyes begin moving, given the saccadic programming requires 80 ms (an arbitrarily chosen value). Note that for both an easy stimulus (function *a*) and a more difficult stimulus (function *c*), the latency between the shift of attention and movement of the eyes is a constant 80 ms.

change as a function of foveal load, there should be no effect of foveal load on the obtained preview benefit. Figure 15.3 illustrates this aspect of the model graphically.

READING

Although the sequential attention model clearly predicts that foveal load should not affect extrafoveal information acquisition, there are several studies that seem to indicate that foveal load may affect the perceptual span in reading. Using the moving window paradigm, Rayner (1986) found that the perceptual span for beginning readers was considerably smaller than for skilled readers. In addition, he also found that the perceptual span was smaller for skilled readers when they were reading more difficult text. One explanation for these results is that in the cases of beginning readers and skilled readers with difficult text, the reader was allocating more attention to the foveal word and therefore had less attention left over to devote to the extrafoveal words. Similarly, in the backward-reading study described above, Inhoff et al. (1989) found that the perceptual span was smaller when readers were forced to read words that were printed right to left. Here again, it could be that because the right-to-left words required more capacity to identify, there was less attention available for acquiring information from extrafoveal words.

Although the above studies are suggestive, they both suffer from a potential confound that makes them difficult to interpret. Specifically, in both studies foveal and extrafoveal difficulty covaried. For example, the relatively undeveloped word decoding skills of the beginning readers in the Rayner (1986) study would make both foveal and extrafoveal word processing more difficult. Similarly, in the Inhoff et al. (1989) study both the foveal and the extrafoveal words were printed right to left and were therefore more difficult. There is a evidence that extrafoveal difficulty directly affects the perceptual span during reading (e.g., Balota, Pollatsek, & Rayner, 1985; Inhoff & Rayner, 1986). Therefore, it is difficult to know whether the reduction in the perceptual span found in the Rayner (1986) and Inhoff et al. (1989) studies was due to increased foveal load or instead was caused by increased extrafoveal difficulty.

In order to test more directly the effect of foveal load on the perceptual span in reading, Henderson and Ferreira (1990) conducted a study in which foveal load and extrafoveal preview information were independently manipulated. While their eye movements were recorded, subjects read simple sentences such as

(1a) Mary bought a chest despite the high price.
(1b) Mary bought a trunk despite the high price.

These experiments employed the *boundary technique* (Rayner, 1975), a variant of the contingent display change technique in which only a single letter string changes as a function of eye position. For example, consider the sentence "Mary bought a chest despite the high price." In this example, the boundary was placed between the penultimate and final letters of the word *chest*, designated word n. Either a *same preview* ("despite") or a *different preview* ("zqdloyv") of word $n+1$ ("despite") was displayed as long as the eye position was to the left of the boundary.[1] When the eyes crossed the boundary, the preview was replaced by the target word ("despite"). Because the boundary was generally crossed during a saccade from word n to word $n+1$, vision was suppressed and the subjects were not consciously aware that display changes were taking place. The preview benefit derived from word $n+1$ could be assessed by comparing fixation times once the eyes landed on $n+1$ as a function of preview condition (preview benefit equals fixation time on word $n+1$ following a different preview minus fixation time following a same preview).

---

[1] One other preview condition was also employed, in which the first three letters of the preview were the same as the target word, but the final letters were different. The results from this condition were virtually identical to those in the same preview condition.

In addition to manipulating the type of preview available for word $n+1$, we also manipulated the difficulty of word n. In the *lexical difficulty* manipulation, word n was either easy or difficult depending on the frequency of the word, as assessed by the Kucera and Francis (1967) norms. The words were matched in length and roughly similar in meaning. For example, in sentences (1a) and (1b) above, "chest" and "trunk" were the high- and low-frequency versions of word n. Previous studies have shown that low-frequency words are more difficult to process (Becker & Killion, 1977; Morton, 1969) and therefore receive longer fixations during reading (Inhoff, 1984; Inhoff & Rayner, 1986; Just & Carpenter, 1980; Rayner & Duffy, 1986). If foveal load affects the amount of information acquired from an extrafoveal word, then the preview benefit observed for word $n+1$ should be reduced when word n is lower in frequency.

If it were found that lexical frequency did affect the preview benefit derived from an extrafoveal word, then we would have some evidence that foveal load affects the perceptual span. However, it could be the case that foveal lexical frequency would affect preview benefit because both lexical frequency and preview benefit are lexical phenomena. We would thus not have evidence that foveal load in general affects the perceptual span, but only that foveal load at the lexical level decreases lexical processing of the extrafoveal word. To determine if foveal load at a non-lexical level would affect preview benefit, we also employed a *syntactic difficulty* manipulation, as shown in the following sentences:

(2a) She warned that Harry bought small gifts.
(2b) She warned Harry bought small gifts.

The preview of word $n+1$ ("small" in sentence 2) was again manipulated by showing either a same or different preview, as described above. The difficulty of word n, however, depended on the syntactic structure of the sentence. In both the easy (2a) and difficult (2b) conditions, the sentences contained an embedded sentential complement. In the easy condition, the overt complementizer "that" was included in the sentence. In the difficult condition, the complementizer was absent. It has been shown that in such sentences, there is a bias on the part of the reader to take the first noun of the embedded complement as the direct object of the verb when the complementizer is absent (Ferreira & Henderson, 1990; Frazier & Rayner, 1982; Rayner & Frazier, 1987). When the verb of the embedded complement is then encountered, the sentence must be reanalyzed so that the analysis is consistent with the complement reading. Thus, processing difficulty (and reading times) are increased on the embedded verb when the complementizer is absent. If foveal load induced by syntactic difficulty affects the perceptual span, then the preview benefit observed for word $n+1$ should be reduced when word n is syntactically more difficult. Note that with the syntactic difficulty manipulation word n does not change as a function of difficulty; in the example in sentence (2), "bought" is word n in both the easy and difficult conditions.

There were two main results of this study. First, there was a clear effect of foveal load on word n for both the lexical and syntactic difficulty manipulations, as expected. Second, when word n was easy, there was a clear preview benefit: fixation times were shorter when the preview of word $n+1$ was the same compared to when it was different from the target word. On the other hand, when word n was difficult, the preview benefit disappeared. This was found even though in the difficult condition, fixation time on word n was longer, thus potentially affording more time for acquiring information from word $n+1$. Thus these data support the hypothesis that foveal load affects the amount of information acquired from an extrafoveal location prior to an eye movement to that location. The finding that foveal load decreased extrafoveal information acquisition in the syntactic case as well as the lexical case suggests that the reduced use of extrafoveal information is not simply due to interference within the lexicon.

PICTURE VIEWING

Similar results to those just described have also been observed in a picture-viewing study (Henderson, 1988). In that study, subjects viewed arrays of pictures of four objects as described above. Foveal difficulty was manipulated via the semantic similarity of the foveal object (object n) to the object viewed at the immediately prior location. We have found in previous experiments that encoding difficulty and therefore fixation time is affected by this manipulation (Henderson, 1992; Henderson, Pollatsek, & Rayner, 1987). In addition, availability of preview information from the next object ($n+1$) was manipulated: either the *same* object or a *blob* control consisting of meaningless line segments were presented as the extrafoveal preview. The difference in fixation times on object $n+1$ as a function of preview condition was again taken as the measure of preview benefit. Gaze durations on object n were 367 ms in the easy (semantically related) condition and 404 ms in the difficult (semantically unrelated) condition. Most important were the data from object $n+1$. Encoding time (as assessed by first fixation durations) for object $n+1$ was less facilitated by a preview of that object when object n was difficult (23 ms) compared with when object n was relatively easy (80 ms). Thus, these data mirror with objects the essential results of the Henderson and Ferreira (1990) study.

The finding that foveal processing difficulty affects the benefit derived from the extrafoveal stimulus about to be fixated clearly presents a problem for the sequential attention model as originally proposed. In the next section, I will explore several ways in which the model might be modified to account for these results.

Revisions to the Sequential Attention Model

The finding that foveal difficulty affects the preview benefit derived from the extrafoveal stimulus about to be fixated is clearly at odds with the sequential attention model. The model specifies that attention does not shift to the extrafoveal stimulus until the criterion level of processing is reached; as was shown in Figure 15.3, delaying when the criterion is reached affects fixation time on the foveal stimulus but should not decrease the time that attention is focused on the extrafoveal stimulus prior to the eye movement.

At this point, one possible solution would be to abandon the sequential attention model. However, given that the model is able to offer a simple account of many aspects of both the cognitive control of eye movements in complex tasks (Morrison, 1984; Rayner & Pollatsek, 1989) and the acquisition of extrafoveal information during eye fixations (Henderson et al., 1989; Henderson & Ferreira, 1990), it would seem reasonable to attempt to revise it in order to accommodate the foveal load effect.

Revision 1: Parallel Allocation of Attention

One intuitively appealing way to account for the effect of foveal load on the acquisition of extrafoveal information would be to hypothesize that attention is allocated in parallel to both the foveal stimulus and the stimulus about to be fixated next. There are several ways that this might work. The simplest version would suggest that attention be thought of as an elongated spotlight asymmetrically stretching from the foveal stimulus to the stimulus about to be fixated. However, this version would predict that a spatially intermediate stimulus between the currently fixated stimulus and the stimulus about to be fixated next should be attended. This did not happen in the Henderson (1990) study described above. A slightly more sophisticated view would suggest that attention is discretely split between the fixated stimulus and the stimulus about to be fixated. This view could account for the finding that spatially intermediate stimuli were not attended. To account for the effect of foveal load, the hypothesis would be that attention is shared between the foveal and extrafoveal stimuli, so that when one stimulus is more difficult, attention must be diverted from the other.

There are at least three potential problems with this parallel attention hypothesis. First, abandoning the sequential assumption loses much of the explanatory power of the model in accounting for eye movement control. In the original Morrison (1984) conception, the decision of when to move the eyes was based on a simple monitoring of processing success at the attended foveal location. The programming decision would be far more difficult if two locations were being attended simultaneously. In fact, abandoning the sequential assumption undermines the basic reason that the sequential attention model is able to parsimoniously account for eye movement control, because it is the signal to shift attention away from the fovea that initiates eye movement programming. Second, most theorists studying visual attention have concluded that attention cannot easily be split between two spatially noncontiguous locations (e.g., Eriksen & Yeh, 1985; Posner, Snyder, & Davidson, 1980). Therefore, proposing such a split would require the assumption that the visual attention system operates differently when it is linked with the eye movement system.

Finally, and perhaps most problematically, the parallel allocation assumption predicts that an increase in *extrafoveal* difficulty should decrease *foveal* information acquisition. However, an examination of previous experiments provides no support for this prediction. I will present here a few illustrative examples. Consider again the Henderson (1988) study described above, in which four objects were viewed successively in two preview conditions. Subjects began each trial fixated in the center of the array of objects. They then made a saccade to the first object, and subsequently to each object in turn. When the first object was fixated, either that object and an extrafoveal blob, or that object and the next object became visible on the screen. If it were the case that attention is shared between the foveal and extrafoveal objects, then processing time (and therefore fixation durations) on the foveal object should be increased when two objects were displayed. Contrary to this prediction, first fixation durations were 232 and 236 ms in the blob and two-object conditions. The equivalent gaze durations were 579 and 584 ms. Thus, there was no difference in processing time on the foveal object as a function of the availability of the extrafoveal object. Similar examples come from reading studies. For example, consider again the Henderson and Ferreira (1990) foveal load study. In this study, the parafoveal preview was either a word or a nonsense letter string. If more attention were being expended on the preview when it was a word, then foveal processing on word n should have been increased when word $n+1$ was a word. This did not happen. Mean first fixation durations were 230 and 232 ms when the preview was a word and a nonsense letter string; respectively, in the lexical difficulty experiment, and 215 and 214 ms in the syntactic difficulty experiment. The equivalent gaze durations were 257 and 262 ms in the lexical difficulty experiment and 236 and 243 ms in the syntactic difficulty experiment. Finally, Blanchard, Pollatsek, and Rayner (1989) alternated the size of the window from fixation to fixation in a moving window study. Thus, on some fixations the foveal word and the next word were displayed, and on some fixations only the foveal word was displayed. They found that the availability of parafoveal word information had no effect on the duration of the current fixation. Again, if attention were shared between the foveal and parafoveal words in reading, then the availability of the parafoveal word should have increased processing time for the foveal word.

In sum, it would appear that a model of the relation between visual attention and eye movements based on the parallel allocation of attention is not viable.

Revision 2: Fixation Cutoff Assumption

Henderson (1988; Henderson & Ferreira, 1990) proposed a modification to the sequential attention model that enables it to account for the effects of foveal load on the acquisition of extrafoveal information while expanding the model's ability to account for eye movement behavior observed in reading and picture viewing. The general notion is that the eye movement control system has a predisposition to keeping the eyes moving. Presumably, it is adaptive to continuously sample new areas of the visual field. It would be maladaptive to fixate a stimulus indefinitely, even if processing were still continuing (e.g., in attempting to identify a camouflaged animal). Therefore, although I assume that the eye movement system is usually driven by successful completion (or impending completion) of foveal processing, if success is not achieved in a certain amount of time, fixation of that stimulus will be terminated.

Evidence for the notion of a fixation cutoff derives from studies varying foveal stimulus onset during reading (Morrison, 1984; Rayner & Pollatsek, 1981). In these studies, subjects read a line of text while their eye movements were recorded. At the beginning of a new fixation, the onset of the stimulus was delayed. For example, the stimulus might not be displayed until 50 ms after the eyes had landed at a new position. The main results were that for relatively short onset delays, fixation duration on a stimulus increased by an amount of time roughly equal to the duration of the delay. These results suggest that the duration of a fixation is controlled by visual characteristics of the stimulus during that fixation. More importantly for our purposes here, however, was the finding that as the onset delay increased, the probability that the eyes would move off of a word location prior to the word's appearance increased. For example, in the Morrison (1984) study the eyes left the word prior to its onset 70% of the time when the onset delay was 350 ms. These anticipatory saccades occurred even when the duration of the onset delay was blocked. Presumably, in the blocked conditions the subject knew that the best strategy would be to wait out the delay. Thus, it appears that the eye movement system keeps the eyes moving even when comprehension would be better served by waiting.

An illustration of the sequential attention model including the fixation cutoff assumption is shown in Figure 15.4. The fixation cutoff occurs at some point in time following the beginning of a fixation. In order for the system to generate an eye movement by the fixation cutoff, a *program-*

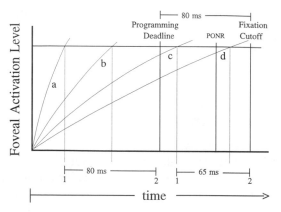

FIGURE 15.4. An illustration of the sequential attention model modified to include a fixation cutoff. This figure is to be interpreted in the same way as Figure 15.3. The fixation cutoff indicates the maximum fixation duration that the system is willing to tolerate. The programming deadline indicates the point in time when saccadic programming must begin in order to meet the fixation cutoff. The point of no return (PONR) indicates the last point in time when a saccadic program can be modified. When the foveal stimulus is easy (functions *a* and *b*), the latency between the shift of attention and initiation of the eye movement is 80 ms. When the foveal stimulus is more difficult, the attention-shift criterion is not reached prior to the programming deadline (function *c* and *d*). If the attention-shift criterion is reached soon afterward, attention will shift and the program will be modified, but the time between the attentional shift and the eye movement will be reduced (function *c*). Finally, if the shift criterion is not reached by the PONR, then the foveal stimulus will be refixated.

ming deadline must be set up that occurs *x* ms prior to the deadline, where *x* is equal to the average programming latency. In the illustration, I arbitrarily assume that the programming latency has a mean of 80 ms (with some unspecified variance), so that the programming deadline occurs 80 ms prior to the cutoff. When the foveal stimulus is relatively easy to process, the attention shift criterion will be reached prior to the programming deadline (as shown in curves *a* and *b*). In this case, the model will perform as originally outlined (see Figure 15.3).

When the foveal stimulus is more difficult, then the attention shift criterion will not be reached prior to the programming deadline (curves *c* and *d*). In this case, programming will begin at the programming deadline, even though attention has not yet shifted to the next stimulus. If the criterion is then reached soon after the programming deadline has passed, attention will shift to the new location prior to the eye movement. Attention will then be allocated to the extrafoveal stimulus for less than the full programming latency, so the preview benefit will be reduced.

The above account weakens a basic assumption of the sequential attention model in that it allows a decoupling between initiation of eye movement programming and the shift of attention. Recall that in the original formulation, initiation of programming and reorienting of attention were simultaneous events. The modified model accounts for the reduced preview benefit found with a difficult foveal stimulus by proposing that eye movement programming can sometimes begin prior to the attentional shift. This raises the question, however, of how an eye movement can be programmed to a new location when attention has not yet shifted; recall that according to the model, the attended location is to be taken as the target of the saccade. One answer falls straightforwardly out of the model: when the programming deadline is reached and programming begins, the current focus of attention is still taken to be the target location. Because attention is focused on the foveal stimulus, the programming system will take the current fixation location as the target for the programmed movement. If foveal processing then reaches the criterion level soon after the programming deadline (curve *c*), then the program may be modified so that the new location is taken as the target. This is essentially the same parallel programming mechanism that was used to explain word-skipping behavior in reading (Morrison, 1984; Rayner & Pollatsek, 1989). This view leads to several interesting predictions concerning eye movement behavior in reading and scene perception. In particular, the parallel activation of several programs (one to the foveal stimulus and one to the next stimulus) that might occur when the programming deadline is reached prior to the attention shift criterion could lead to a brief refixation on the foveal stimulus followed by a saccade to the next stimulus, or a saccade to a location between the foveal and extrafoveal stimuli (see Becker & Jurgens, 1979). Both of these types of behavior are often observed (e.g., McConkie, Kerr, Reddix, & Zola, 1988). Finally, if the attention shift criterion is not reached prior to some point of no return for the programming system (curve *d*), then it will not be possible to modify the program to the foveal stimulus. In this case, the foveal stimulus would be immediately refixated and the cycle would begin again. Consecutive fixations on a stimulus are quite common in eye movement records. Often these refixations occur on slightly different parts of the foveal stimulus, for example on a different character in a word (Just & Carpenter, 1987; Rayner & Pollatsek, 1989) or a different part of an object (Henderson, 1992). This could be explained by noise in the programming system or by slight shifts in the center of the focus of attention within the stimulus.

Summary of the Modified Sequential Attention Model

According to the modified sequential attention model, at the beginning of each eye fixation visual attention is allocated to the stimulus at the center of fixation. When foveal processing reaches a preset criterion level of completion, attention shifts to a new location and eye movement programming is initiated that will bring the eyes to that location. The eyes then move to the new location following the eye movement programming latency. Because attention precedes the eyes to the new location by an amount of time equal to the programming latency, some attentive extra-foveal processing will take place. The amount of preview benefit derived from an extrafoveal stimulus will be a function of the programming latency (the amount of time that attention is focused on the extrafoveal stimulus before the eyes fixate that stimulus). If foveal processing is easy, then attention will precede the eyes by the full programming latency, and the preview benefit will be maximal. If foveal processing is difficult, eye movement programming may begin prior to a shift of attention. If atten-tion then shifts before the program is complete, the amount of attentive extrafoveal processing prior to the eye movement will be reduced, and so will the preview benefit.

Conclusion

In this chapter I have reviewed the evidence concerning the relationship between covert allocation of visual attention and overt orienting of the eyes. I have argued that the evidence favors the view that there is a functional link between the allocation of visual attention and the direction of gaze of the eyes. Finally, I have presented a particular model of how and why visual attention and eye movements might be related. This model draws on and integrates work concerning both the acquisition of visual information and the cognitive control of eye movements during complex visual tasks.

Acknowledgment. Preparation of this chapter was supported by the Izaac Walton Killam Memorial Fund for Advanced Studies and the Natural Sciences and Engineering Research Council of Canada (OGP-41792).

References

Balota, D.A., Pollatsek, A., & Rayner, K. (1985). The interaction of contextual constraints and parafoveal visual information in reading. *Cognitive Psychology, 17,* 364–390.

Becker, W., & Jurgens, R. (1979). An analysis of the saccadic system by means of double-step stimuli. *Vision Research, 19,* 967–983.

Becker, C.A., & Killion, T.H. (1977). Interaction of visual and cognitive effects in word recognition. *Journal of Experimental Psychology: Human Perception and Performance, 3,* 389–401.

Blanchard, H.E., Pollatsek, A., & Rayner, K. (1989). Parafoveal processing during eye fixations in reading. *Perception & Psychophysics, 46,* 85–94.

Eriksen, C.W., & Yeh, Y. (1985). Allocation of attention in the visual field. *Journal of Experimental Psychology: Human Perception and Performance*, *11*, 583–597.

Ferreira, F., & Henderson, J.M. (1990). The use of verb information in syntactic parsing: Evidence from eye movements and word-by-word self-paced reading. *Journal of Experimental Psychology: Learning, Memory, and Cognition*, *16*, 555–569.

Fisher, D.F., & Shebilske, W.L. (1985). There is more that meets the eye than the eyemind assumption. In R. Groner, G.W. McConkie, & C. Menz (Eds.), *Eye movements and human information processing*. North Holland: Elsevier.

Frazier, L., & Rayner, K. (1982). Making and correcting errors during sentence comprehension: Eye movements in the analysis of structurally ambiguous sentences. *Cognitive Psychology*, *14*, 178–210.

Henderson, J.M. (1988). *Visual attention and the acquisition of extrafoveal information during eye fixations*. Unpublished doctoral dissertation, University of Massachusetts, Amherst, MA.

Henderson, J.M. (1990). *The allocation of visual-spatial attention prior to a saccadic eye movement*. Poster presented at the Annual Meeting of the Psychonomic Society, New Orleans.

Henderson, J.M. (1992). Eye movement control during visual object processing: Effects of initial fixation position and semantic constraint. *Canadian Journal of Psychology*, (in press).

Henderson, J.M. (1991). Stimulus discrimination following covert attentional orienting to an exogenous cue. *Journal of Experimental Psychology: Human Perception and Performance*, *17*, 91–106.

Henderson, J.M., & Ferreira, F. (1990). Effects of foveal processing difficulty on the perceptual span in reading: Implications for attention and eye movement control. *Journal of Experimental Psychology: Learning, Memory, and Cognition*, *16*, 417–429.

Henderson, J.M., Pollatsek, A., & Rayner, K. (1987). Effects of foveal priming and extrafoveal preview on object identification. *Journal of Experimental Psychology: Human Perception and Performance*, *13*, 449–463.

Henderson, J.M., Pollatsek, A., & Rayner, K. (1989). Covert visual attention and extrafoveal information use during object identification. *Perception & Psychophysics*, *45*, 196–208.

Hogaboam, T.W. (1983). Reading patterns in eye movement data. In K. Rayner (Ed.), *Eye movements in reading: Perceptual and language processes*. New York: Academic Press.

Hughes, H.C., & Zimba, L.D. (1985). Spatial maps of directed visual attention. *Journal of Experimental Psychology: Human Perception and Performance*, *11*, 409–430.

Hughes, H.C., & Zimba, L.D. (1987). Natural boundaries for the spread of directed visual attention. *Neuropsychologia*, *2*, 5–18.

Inhoff, A.W. (1984). Two stages of word processing during eye fixations in reading. *Journal of Verbal Learning and Verbal Behavior*, *23*, 612–624.

Inhoff, A.W., Pollatsek, A., Posner, M.I., & Rayner, K. (1989). Covert attention and eye movements in reading. *Quarterly Journal of Experimental Psychology*, *41A*, 63–89.

Inhoff, A.W., & Rayner, K. (1986). Parafoveal word processing during eye fixations in reading: Effects of word frequency. *Perception & Psychophysics*, *40*, 431–439.

James, W. (1890/1950). *The principles of psychology* (Vol. 1). New York: Dover.

Just, M.A., & Carpenter, P.A. (1980). A theory of reading: From eye fixations to comprehension. *Psychological Review*, *87*, 329–354.

Just, M.A., & Carpenter, P.A. (1987). *The psychology of reading and language comprehension*. Newton, MA: Allyn and Bacon.

Klein, R. (1980). Does oculomotor readiness mediate cognitive control of attention? In R.S. Nickerson (Ed.), *Attention and performance VIII* (pp. 259–276). Hillsdale, NJ: Erlbaum.

Klein, R., & McCormick, P. (1989). Covert visual orienting: Hemifield activation can be mimicked by zoom lens and midlocation placement strategies. *Acta Psychologica*, *770*, 235–250.

Koch, C., & Ullman, S. (1985). Shifts in selective visual attention: towards the underlying neural circuitry. *Human Neurobiology*, *4*, 219–227.

Kucera, H., & Francis, W.N. (1967). *Computational analysis of present-day American English*. Providence, RI: Brown University Press.

Mahoney, J.V., & Ullman, S. (1988). Image chunking defining spatial building blocks for scene analysis. In Z. Pylyshyn (Ed.), *Computational processes in human vision: An interdisciplinary perspective*. Norwood, NJ: Ablex.

McConkie, G.W. (1979). On the role and control of eye movements in reading. In P.A. Kolers, M.E. Wrolstad, & H. Bouma (Eds.), *Processing of visible language* (Vol. 1, pp. 37–48). New York: Plenum Press.

McConkie, G.W., Kerr, P., Reddix, M.D., & Zola, D. (1988). Eye movement control during reading: I. The location of initial eye fixations in words. *Vision Research*, *28*, 1107–1118.

McConkie, G.W., & Rayner, K. (1975). The span of the effective stimulus during a fixation in reading. *Perception & Psychophysics*, *17*, 578–586.

McConkie, G.W., & Rayner, K. (1976). Asymmetry of the perceptual span in reading. *Bulletin of the Psychonomic Society*, *8*, 365–368.

McConkie, G.W., & Zola, D. (1987). Visual attention during eye fixations in reading. *Attention and Performance XII* (pp. 385–401). London: Erlbaum.

Morrison, R.E. (1984). Manipulation of stimulus onset delay in reading: Evidence for parallel programming of saccades. *Journal of Experimental Psychology: Human Perception and Performance*, *10*, 667–682.

Morton, J. (1969). Interaction of information in word recognition. *Psychological Review*, *76*, 165–178.

Pollatsek, A., Bolozky, S., Well, A.D., & Rayner, K. (1981). Asymmetries in the perceptual span for Israeli reader. *Brain and Language*, *14*, 174–180.

Pollatsek, A., Rayner, K., & Balota, D.A. (1986). Inferences about eye movement control from the perceptual span in reading. *Perception & Psychophysics*, *40*, 123–130.

Posner, M.I., Snyder, C.R.R., & Davidson, B.J. (1980). Attention and the detection of signals. *Journal of Experimental Psychology: General, 109*, 160–174.

Rayner, K. (1975). The perceptual span and peripheral cues in reading. *Cognitive Psychology*, *7*, 65–81.

Rayner, K. (1978). Eye movements in reading and information processing. *Psychological Bulletin*, *85*, 618–660.

Rayner, K. (1986). Eye movements and the perceptual span in beginning and skilled readers. *Journal of Experimental Child Psychology*, *41*, 211–236.

Rayner, K., & Balota, D.A. (1989). Parafoveal preview and lexical access during eye fixations in reading In W. Marslen-Wilson (Ed.), *Lexical representation and process*. Cambridge, MA: MIT Press.

Rayner, K., & Duffy, S.A. (1986). Lexical complexity and fixation times in reading: Effects of word frequency, verb complexity, and lexical ambiguity. *Memory & Cognition*, *14*, 191–201.

Rayner, K., & Frazier, L. (1987). Parsing temporarily ambiguous complements. *Quarterly Journal of Experimental Psychology*, *39A*, 657–673.

Rayner, K., & Pollatsek, A. (1981). Eye movement control during reading: Evidence for direct control. *Quarterly Journal of Experimental Psychology*, *33A*, 351–373.

Rayner, K., & Pollatsek, A. (1987). Eye movements in reading: A tutorial review. *Attention and Performance XII* (pp. 327–362). London: Erlbaum.

Rayner, K., & Pollatsek, A. (1989). *The psychology of reading*. Englewood Cliffs, NJ: Prentice Hall.

Rayner, K., Well, A.D., & Pollatsek, A. (1980). Asymmetry of the effective visual field in reading. *Perception & Psychophysics*, *27*, 537–544.

Shepard, M., Findlay, J.M., & Hockey, R.J. (1986). The relationship between eye movements and spatial attention. *Quarterly Journal of Experimental Psychology*, *38A*, 475–491.

Tinker, M.A. (1939). Reliability and validity of eye-movement measures of reading. *Journal of Experimental Psychology*, *19*, 732–746.

Underwood, N.R., & McConkie, G.W. (1985). Perceptual span for letter distinctions during reading. *Reading Research Quarterly*, *20*, 153–162.

Yarbus, A.L. (1967). *Eye movements and vision*. New York: Plenum Press.

16
Making a Scene: The Debate about Context Effects for Scenes and Sentences

JUDITH F. KROLL

The chapters in this section address a variety of problems that arise in considering the processes that mediate scene perception and comprehension: What is the effect of viewing degraded presentations? How does scene context influence the perception and identification of individual objects? And what is the relation between eye movements and visual attention?

If there is a common ground among the wide range of theoretical issues raised in these chapters, I would argue that it is a focus on two important and interrelated issues. The first is the nature of the representations that emerge over time as a scene is viewed and the role of context in constraining these representations. The second concerns the best methods for measuring the representation of objects in scenes before and after the context has had some effect. Eye movement methodology appears to be a sensitive tool for addressing these issues because it provides a means to sample the changes in the available information over time and because it also seems to be sensitive to both perceptual and conceptual factors in scene understanding. Thus, context effects, if they are present, should be observed, at least in some of the eye movement measures. However, disagreement exists even among those who utilize eye movement methods as to which aspect of the eye movement record best reflects the unique contributions of perceptual and conceptual activity.

The effects of context in constraining the representations available for further processing is also not a problem that is unique to scene understanding nor to the use of eye movements as a dependent measure. Many of the same phenomena have been observed for reading text and understanding pictured material, and many of the same methodological concerns are being raised within eye movement research that have been the topic of intense scrutiny among researchers using reaction time methods.

In this chapter I would like to briefly examine these issues. In particular, I would like to consider some of the parallels in eye movement and reaction time research in attempting to determine if context influences the initial perception of objects in scenes and words in sentences or postaccess processes that later determine the goodness of fit of those objects or words to the overall meaning of the context. A question that arises in examining these parallels is whether the context effects that have been observed for scenes are indeed unique to pictured scenes or whether they reflect higher level conceptual processes that may also account for context effects in other domains such as sentence processing. Because I will focus on context effects, my comments will be directed to the issues raised by the two chapters in this section on that topic (Boyce & Pollatsek, and De Graef).

The Locus of Scene Context Effects on Object Identification

A critical issue in research on scene comprehension is to determine if, and at what level of analysis, context influences the recognition of component objects within the scene. According to schema theory, high-level contextual information influences the perception and memory of objects that are consistent or inconsistent with the scene (Biederman, 1972; Friedman, 1979; Loftus & Mackworth, 1978; Pezdek et al., 1988). Although there is some argument in the literature about the effect of consistency on object memory (e.g., Brewer & Treyens, 1981, claim that schema-consistent objects are remembered better than schema-inconsistent objects, whereas Pezdek, Whetstone, Reynolds, Askari, & Dougherty, 1989, have recently argued the opposite), there is general agreement that coherent scene context produces a benefit in initial perception and comprehension of objects in scenes (e.g., Antes, 1974; Biederman, 1972; Biederman, Mezzanotte, & Rabinowitz, 1982).

Two chapters in this section, Boyce and Pollatsek, and De Graef, presented data that lead to different conclusions about the locus of scene context effects on object identification. Clearly, some assumptions made in either or both of these studies will require revision if we are to accommodate the contradictory results. In both chapters the authors acknowledged that some measures provide better tools than others in determining the locus of context effects. For example, Boyce and Pollatsek argued that fixation times that are measured as a subject views a scene freely may be a contaminated measure of context effects on object identification because fixation times may include processes that extend beyond identification per se. Similarly, De Graef argued that research based on reaction times and accuracy measured following brief glimpses of scenes may be a contaminated measure of context effects because there may be postperceptual decision processes that encourage subjects to make educated guesses about the identity of target objects.

So far, so good. We all would agree, I think, that it is essential to use appropriately sensitive measures if we hope to determine whether scene context influences the earliest phases of object identification or whether the output of initial identication processes interact with the scene context in a later comprehension stage. However, at this point, these two studies made different choices about how to proceed. Boyce and Pollatsek introduced a wiggled object in the scene. Subjects fixated the wiggled object and named it. The measure was then the naming latency for the object. They found that the type of scene background had a significant effect on naming latency even when the scene background was only present on the first or second fixation. This result suggests that higher level context is conceptually available early in scene processing.

De Graef used a version of the object decision task (Kroll & Potter, 1984) in which pictures of real and unfamiliar but possible objects are presented. In De Graef's version of object decision, subjects counted the number of non-objects they saw while their eye movements were monitored. The effects of scene context were manipulated by using Biederman et al.'s (1982) classification for object violations within scenes. Scene violation can be introduced by having objects float in the air, appear in the wrong size or place, or by having an unlikely object appear in the scene. The striking result in the De Graef study was that the type of scene violation had an effect on performance measures that reflected later processes but not early ones; the mean first fixations that were identified as early were not influenced by the presence of scene disturbances.

These two studies, then, using different procedures for assessing the influence of scene context, came to different conclusions about the locus of scene context effects. One possible way to reconcile the results of the two studies would be to argue that the effects that Boyce and Pollatsek identified were primarily facilitation attributable to helpful scene context, whereas the failure to obtain violation effects in the De Graef study reflected the failure to observe inhibitory processes during early stages of scene understanding. It would make good sense to find that context effects at early stages of processing reflect facilitation but not inhibition. De Graef also included an out-of-context condition that allows us to determine if this inhibitory explanation is correct for his data. For early fixations, there was virtually no difference between coherent baseline scene contexts and isolated presentations. However, later fixations showed a clear facilitation for the baseline contexts compared to the isolated condition, suggesting that both facilitatory and inhibitory processes were operative at the later stage of processing.

Because the context effects were defined in different ways in these two studies, it is possible that the early facilitatory component that Boyce and Pollatsek appeared to obtain was simply not reflected in the violation continuum that De Graef used. In particular, the continuum of violations may reflect something that is more similar to the syntax rather than the semantics of a scene and, like syntactic effects on word identification, may influence later stages of processing.

An alternative explanation for the facilitatory effects of scene context was suggested by Henderson, Pollatsek, and Rayner (1987). They proposed that some of the apparent facilitation thought to be attributable to the action of scene context on object identification may really be due to object-to-object priming resulting from the fact that semantically related objects often appear together in the same scene. Many previous experiments on object identification have shown that it is possible to obtain semantic priming effects from one object to another in the absence of scene context (Bajo, 1988; Huttenlocher & Kubicek, 1983; Kroll & Potter, 1984; Lupker, 1988; Sperber, McCauley, Ragain, & Weil, 1979) so it is at least feasible that this type of process might operate within scene context as well.

Are Scene Context Effects Unique?

The issue of whether scene context effects can be reduced to priming between related objects is very reminiscent of recent debates concerning the effects of sentence context on lexical access (e.g., Duffy, Henderson, & Morris, 1989; Kroll, 1990; Masson, 1986; O'Seaghdha, 1989; Simpson, Peterson, Casteel, & Burgess, 1989). Despite the many differences between the research on scene and sentence context, including the fact that many of the recent sentence context studies have been performed using reaction time methods (but see Morris, this volume), there is a fundamental analogy in the logic that has been applied to sort out the problem of identifying context effects. The theoretical issues surrounding sentence context effects have become quite focused because those effects have been viewed as providing essential evidence regarding lexical modularity. If sentence context actually facilitates lexical access for a target word, then it would be difficult to argue that lexical entries are accessed in an independent module. Thus, recent studies have attempted to carefully determine whether the effects of sentence context on lexical access are effects of genuine facilitation in lexical retrieval, or whether they reflect postaccess integration or decision mechanisms. One suggestion that has been taken very seriously in this analysis is that sentence context effects can really be reduced to lexical priming between related or associated words that happen to appear within the context. The lexical priming hypothesis is very appealing to those who wish to preserve a strong version of lexical modularity because the context effects would arise from interactions within the lexical module (e.g., Forster, 1981). One analogy, then, is that the lexical priming explanation is to the sentence context effect what the object priming alternative is to the scene context effect. In both cases, there has been an attempt to reinterpret the effects of higher level context in terms that are modality-specific and

Hierarchical Model of Representation

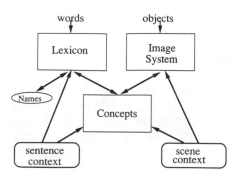

FIGURE 16.1. A hierarchical model of representation.

potentially consistent with the modularity view. Although there are different interpretations of the available evidence, I think it is fair to say that in the sentence context work there is very little support for the lexical priming hypothesis. It will remain to be seen whether any portion of the scene context effects can be explained at the level of object-to-object priming.

Another analogy between the research on scene and sentence context concerns the logic of using naming and lexical or object decision tasks as a way of minimizing the contribution of postaccess or postidentification processes. In work on lexical access, the comparison between naming and lexical decision has been taken to reflect more direct measures of lexical access, in the case of naming, and a combination of lexical access in addition to more complex decision processes, in the case of lexical decision. Thus, lexical decision has been judged by many researchers to be an inappropriate task to use if one wishes to assess the early effects of context.

The analogous arguments cannot be made in comparing picture naming and object decision. For one thing, picture naming requires concept retrieval whereas word naming does not (e.g., Potter & Faulconer, 1975). Thus, we would expect picture naming, which is a relatively slow process compared to word naming, to be influenced by context. Figure 16.1 shows a hierarchical model of representation for word and picture processing that resembles a class of models that include a common conceptual representation for both modalities (e.g., Potter, 1979). The gist of the model is that there are two levels of representation, one that represents surface forms and maintains specific, if abstract, properties of the input, and a deeper level that represents concepts in amodal form. At the surface level, words and pictures correspond to distinct lexical or image representations. At the deeper level, words and pictures correspond to the same conceptual representation. The model can be used to illustrate the problem in relying on picture naming as a way of determining the locus of context effects in object recognition. According to this conceptualization, when pictures are named at least three representations are involved: the image representation must be accessed and used to activate the appropriate meaning units in conceptual memory, and once the meaning of the picture is determined, the appropriate lexical units must be activated before a name can be produced. Depending on the timing of the presentation, picture naming may be influenced by context at the stage of accessing image information, at the stage of retrieving the concept, or even at the stage of identifying the single name that best corresponds to the activated concept.

The timing of the interaction between the context and the processing of the picture will also determine whether context facilitates picture naming or produces interference (e.g., La Heij, Dirkx, & Kramer, 1990; Levelt et al., 1991). The facilitatory effects are most likely attributable to the first two stages we have identified, access to images and concepts, whereas the interference effects, similar to other results on Stroop-type tasks and on tip-of-the-tongue states, are most likely due to inhibitory processes in using concepts to retrieve names. For example, Kroll and Smith (1989) reported that pictures were named more slowly when all the pictures in a given list were drawn from the same semantic category. Although visual similarity among same-category objects might be thought to be responsible for the interference, similar results were obtained when fluent bilinguals were asked to translate from one language to another (Kroll & Curley, 1988, and see La Heij, de Bruyn, et al., 1990, for a similar set of parallels in Stroop-type interference for picture naming and translation) suggesting that the locus of the interference in the picture naming task is probably not at the level of image representations. It is thus unclear if picture naming can be used as an uncontaminated task in the way that word naming has been used, unless a set of converging operations are included to isolate the subprocesses within picture naming that are affected by the manipulation of context.

An advantage of using the object decision task to assess the effects of context on object identification is that it does not require access to the picture's name. However, object decision is also influenced by conceptual-level processing. Kroll (1990) reported similar context effects for words in lexical decision and for pictures in object decision when the word and picture targets completed a sentence in a meaningful way. However, because decision processing is likely to be similar for lexical and object decision, it is also likely that the same postaccess mechanisms that have been proposed for lexical decision (e.g., Balota & Chumbley, 1984; Seidenberg, Waters, Sanders, & Langer, 1984) are present in object decision. Thus, object decision may include a subprocess that involves checking the conceptual integrity of the target and context and may, therefore, be less than an ideal task for evaluating the early effects of context.

Each of the context studies in this section need to be interpreted in light of these comments. The advantage of combining naming and object decision tasks with eye movement methods is that the eye movement measures provide converging sources of evidence for categorizing different processing functions as early or late. Although there is also debate within the eye movement literature about how to interpret the locus of effects observed for first durations versus gaze durations, the two sets of converging sources of evidence may ultimately provide a sensitive tool for addressing the context problem.

Conclusions

In this chapter I have discussed some of the controversies surrounding the way in which different studies have attempted to determine at what point in processing context influences object recognition. One of the common problems in this research is to develop a set of tools that will allow us to uniquely locate the interaction of context with object recognition over time. A consequence of the difficulty in isolating these object context effects is that it is not clear to what extent they are specific to objects at all; similar context effects have been reported for words in sentence context and for pictures embedded in sentence contexts (e.g., Potter, Kroll, Yachzel, Carpenter, & Sherman, 1986). Indeed, Henderson (this volume), in addressing the relations between attention and eye movements, made the point that similar results regarding the control of eye movements and the perceptual span have been observed in research on both reading and picture understanding.

At first glance it may be dispiriting to have focused on the parallels between research on scene and sentence context because the comparison suggested that many of our methods are sensitive to higher order factors common to both modalities. However, greater attention to these similarities may allow us to develop more sensitive converging methodology for isolating these components of the context effect that are form-specific. It seems fairly obvious that the glue that holds a scene together is fundamentally of different stuff than the glue than holds a sentence together. Very little of what we know about scene context effects at present, however, has really told us much about the nature of that glue. If our ultimate goal is to map out the representations that are specific to perceptual input and to understand the relation of those representations to higher level concepts, then it is essential that we identify the genuine similarities and differences among these two fundamental systems. Applying eye movement methods to this problem in conjunction with traditional paradigms is one of the most promising approaches.

Acknowledgment. The writing of this chapter was supported in part by grant MH44246 from the National Institute of Mental Health.

References

Antes, J.R. (1974). The time course of picture viewing. *Journal of Experimental Psychology*, *103*, 62–70.

Bajo, M.T. (1988). Semantic facilitation with pictures and words. *Journal of Experimental Psychology: Learning, Memory, and Cognition*, *14*, 579–589.

Balota, D.A., & Chumbley, J.I. (1984). Are lexical decisions a good measure of lexical access? The role of word frequency in the neglected decision stage. *Journal of Experimental Psychology: Human Perception and Performance*, *10*, 340–357.

Biederman, I. (1972). Perceiving real-world scenes. *Science*, *177*, 77–80.

Biederman, I., Mezzanotte, R.J., & Rabinowitz, J.C. (1982). Scene perception: Detecting and judging objects undergoing relational violations. *Cognitive Psychology*, *14*, 143–177.

Brewer, W.F., & Treyens, J.C. (1981). Role of schemata in memory for places. *Cognitive Psychology*, *13*, 207–230.

Duffy, S.A., Henderson, J.M., & Morris, R.K. (1989). The semantic facilitation of lexical access during sentence processing. *Journal of Experimental Psychology: Learning, Memory, and Cognition*, *15*, 791–801.

Forster, K.I. (1981). Priming and the effects of sentence and lexical contexts on naming time: Evidence for autonomous lexical processing. *Quarterly Journal of Experimental Psychology*, *33A*, 465–496.

Friedman, A. (1979). Framing pictures: The role of knowledge in automatized encoding and memory for gist. *Journal of Experimental Psychology: General*, *108*, 316–355.

Henderson, J.M., Pollatsek, A., & Rayner, K. (1987). Effects of foveal priming and extrafoveal preview on object identification. *Journal of Experimental Psychology: Human Perception and Performance*, *13*, 449–463.

Huttenlocher, J., & Kubicek, L.F. (1983). The source of relatedness effects on naming latency. *Journal of Experimental Psychology: Learning, Memory, and Cognition*, *9*, 486–496.

Kroll, J.F. (1990). Recognizing words and pictures in sentence context: A test of lexical modularity. *Journal of Experimental Psychology: Learning, Memory, and Cognition*, *16*, 747–759.

Kroll, J.F., & Curley, J. (1988). Lexical memory in novice bilinguals: The role of concepts in retrieving second language words. In M. Gruneberg, P. Morris, & R. Sykes (Eds.), *Practical Aspects of Memory, Vol. 2.* London: John Wiley & Sons.

Kroll, J.F., & Potter, M.C. (1984). Recognizing words, pictures, and concepts: A comparison of lexical, object, and reality decisions. *Journal of Verbal Learning and Verbal Behavior*, *23*, 39–66.

Kroll, J.F. & Smith, J. (1989). *Naming pictures and words in categories.* Poster presented at the First Annual Meeting of the American Psychological Society, Alexandria, VA.

La Heij, W., de Bruyn, E., Elens, E., Hartsuiker, R., Helaha, D., & van Schelven, L. (1990). Orthographic facilitation and categorical interference in a word-translation variant of the Stroop task. *Canadian Journal of Psychology*, *44*, 76–83.

La Heij, W., Dirkx, J., & Kramer, P. (1990). Categorical interference and associative priming in picture naming. *British Journal of Psychology*, *81*, 511–525.

Levelt, W.J.M., Schreifers, H., Vorberg, D., Meyer, A.S., Pechmann, T., & Havinga, J. (1991). The time course of lexical access in speech production: A study of picture naming. *Psychological Review*, *98*, 122–142.

Loftus, G.R., & Mackworth, N.H. (1978). Cognitive determinants of fixation location during picture viewing. *Journal of Experimental Psychology: Human Perception and Performance*, *4*, 565–576.

Lupker, S.J. (1988). Picture naming: An investigation of the nature of categorical priming. *Journal of Experimental Psychology: Learning, Memory, and Cognition*, *14*, 444–455.

Masson, M.E.J. (1986). Comprehension of rapidly presented sentences: The mind is quicker than the eye. *Journal of Memory and Language*, *25*, 588–604.

O'Seaghdha, P. (1989). The dependence of lexical relatedness effects on syntactic connectedness. *Journal of Experimental Psychology: Learning, Memory, & Cognition*, *15*, 73–87.

Pezdek, K., Maki, R., Valencia-Laver, D., Whetstone, T., Stoeckert, J., & Dougherty, T. (1988). Picture memory: Recognizing added and deleted details. *Journal of Experimental Psychology: Learning, Memory, and Cognition*, *14*, 468–476.

Pezdek, K., Whetstone, T., Reynolds, K., Askari, N., & Dougherty, T. (1989). Memory for real-world scenes: The role of consistency with schema expectation. *Journal of Experimental Psychology: Learning, Memory, and Cognition*, *15*, 587–595.

Potter, M.C. (1979). Mundane symbolism: The relations among objects, names, and ideas. In N.R. Smith & M.B. Franklin (Eds.), *Symbolic functioning in childhood*. Hillsdale, NJ: Erlbaum.

Potter, M.C., & Faulconer, B.A. (1975). Time to understand pictures and words. *Nature (London)*, *253*, 437–438.

Potter, M.C., Kroll, J.F., Yachzel, B., Carpenter, E., & Sherman, J. (1986). Pictures in sentences: Understanding without words. *Journal of Experimental Psychology: General*, *115*, 281–294.

Seidenberg, M.S., Waters, G.S., Sanders, M., & Langer, P. (1984). Pre- and postlexical loci of contextual effects on word recognition. *Memory & Cognition*, *12*, 315–328.

Simpson, G.B., Peterson, R.R., Casteel, M.A., & Burgess, C. (1989). Lexical and sentence context effects in word recognition. *Journal of Experimental Psychology: Learning, Memory, and Cognition*, *15*, 88–97.

Sperber, R.D., McCauley, C., Ragain, R.D., & Weil, C.M. (1979). Semantic priming effects on picture and word processing. *Memory & Cognition*, *5*, 339–345.

17
Perception and Cognition in Reading: Where is the Meeting Point?

GEORGE W. MCCONKIE, MICHAEL D. REDDIX, and
DAVID ZOLA

It has been common in the history of psychology to think of reading as involving two sets of processes, one that makes visual information available (perceptual processes) and the other that makes use of that information in support of the language processes involved in reading (cognitive processes). Interactive theories of reading (Rumelhart, 1977) have questioned the usefulness of such a distinction, suggesting that each processing activity occurs in the environment of, and can be subject to influences from, all other processing taking place. Recent work, however, has suggested the existence of different processing modules that are not directly influenced by the products of some other processing activities (Fodor, 1983; Frazier & Fodor, 1978). In particular, it has been proposed that the visual processes that make information available are not influenced by higher level processes (Forster, 1979; Stanovich, 1980). This chapter presents some data from a study we have conducted that supports the utility of maintaining a distinction in theories of reading between perceptual processes that make visually-provided information available and cognitive processes that use this information for the purposes of the task at hand.

The work to be presented uses a modification of the Frequency of Effects analysis that we have found useful in exploring effects observed in eye movement data (McConkie, Zola, & Wolverton, 1985). This analysis was developed to discriminate between the frequency with which an experimental manipulation produces an effect on the durations of fixations, and the size of that effect when it occurs. We begin by briefly describing the Frequency of Effects analysis, and then use a modification of that analysis to explore effects that are produced in the eye movement data when the eyes land on a pseudoword during reading. Finally, we use the results of this analysis to discuss the distinction between perceptual and cognitive processes and to consider where the meeting point might be between these two sets of processes; that is, to what level of coding do the perceptual processes automatically take text input, or, from another perspective, what is the nature of the visually provided data base that is available to the cognitive processes.

Frequency of Effects Analysis

In research involving eye movement monitoring, the investigator often examines the effect that an experimental manipulation produces on a particular set of eye fixations, perhaps the initial fixation on particular words in the text, or the first fixation after display changes take place. This is typically done by conducting a statistical test to determine if the mean fixation duration in an experimental condition is significantly different from (usually greater than) the mean fixation duration in a control condition. If these means differ by 20 ms, we conclude that the experimental manipulation increased the fixation duration by 20 ms.

Although the conclusion that the mean fixation duration was increased by 20 ms is technically correct, it is important to recognize that such an increase could result from many different patterns of effects. For example, it is possible that only 20% of the fixations were actually affected, and that the size of the effect, when it occurred, was 100 ms, with the rest of the fixations having no effect at all. For an example of such a case, see McConkie, Underwood, Wolverton, and Zola (1988). Such differences in interpretation of the data can have quite different theoretical implications.

McConkie, Zola, and Wolverton (1985) proposed a method for distinguishing between the frequency with which an experimental manipulation produces an effect on the durations of a set of eye fixations, and the size of that effect when it occurs. This method is referred to as the *Frequency of Effects analysis*. In its simplest form, the model on which this analysis is based consists of three assumptions:

1. The frequency distribution of fixation durations that is obtained in the control condition is the same as would have been obtained in the experimental condition, had it not been for the experimental manipulation.
2. A certain proportion, P, of the fixations in the experimental condition, randomly selected from the entire distribution, were actually affected by the experimental manipulation.
3. All affected fixations were increased in their duration by e ms.

Assumption 1 is an expedient, given the lack of a well-established theory that specifies the shape of frequency distributions of fixation durations in the normal reading condition (however, see Harris, Hainline, Abramov, Lemerise, & Camenzuli, 1988, and Suppes, 1990, for proposals concerning the shapes of these distributions). Assumptions 2 and 3 define the simplest possible model in which effects might occur on only a subset of the eye fixations. P is a parameter representing the proportion of fixations on which an effect was produced and e is a parameter representing the size of that effect when it occurred. In this simple version of the model, these parameters are assumed to apply equally to the entire distribution and to the fixations that would normally terminate during each time interval within the distribution, because the values of the parameters do not vary with time. Finally, a corollary to the above assumptions is that $1 - P$ fixations have an effect size of zero.

The Frequency of Effects analysis consists of the process of making estimates of the parameters in this model. These estimates are made through iterative processes similar to those employed in nonlinear regression, except that they must be carried out by operating on a table (the vectors of frequencies in the frequency distributions from the control and experimental conditions) rather than having the model fully specified in the form of equations. An initial guess is selected for the value of each parameter. Then a new frequency distribution is produced by operating on the values of the frequency distribution obtained from the control condition. Conceptually, this is done by adding e ms to the durations of a proportion P of the fixations in each time band in the control condition frequency distribution. The new distribution that is produced in this manner becomes an estimate of the distribution that would have been obtained had the experimental condition actually increased the fixation duration of P fixations by e ms, with the current values for these parameters. This new distribution is then compared to the distribution actually obtained in the experimental condition by summing the squared differences between the frequencies (or proportions) in corresponding time bands, or by making a chi-square comparison. New values for P and e are then selected and the process is repeated, yielding a new error measure. This process continues until values for the two parameters are found that minimize the error measure. These values are then taken as the estimates of the parameters, thus yielding an estimate of the frequency with which the experimental manipulation produced an effect, and the size of that effect when it occurred.

An Experiment: Measuring Onset Latency for One Component of Processing

An experiment was conducted to investigate processing-time issues during reading. It was designed to measure the amount of time that elapses from the beginning of an eye fixation on a word until different aspects of the information provided by that word come into play in the ongoing processing. In this study, selected words in a large section of text from a contemporary novel were replaced with errors of different types. On the average, there was an error of some type about once in every three lines. One of the error types used was a pseudoword, made by rearranging the letters of the original word into a sequence that was pronounceable and had the appearance of an English word, but that was not in the dictionary. We were interested to know how much time would pass from the onset of the first fixation on such an error until changes in the eye movement data could be observed, serving as evidence that the distinction between real words and pseudowords had come into play in the ongoing processing.

From eye movement data obtained while college students read the experimental materials, we identified the first fixation on each of the critical word locations when it contained a pseudoword (experimental condition) or the original word (control condition). We rejected all cases where a prior fixation had been located within six letter positions to the left of the critical word, or had previously been to the right of the word. This resulted in a set of initial fixations on the critical word location, but where that location had not been previously fixated, and where the closest fixation was far enough away that very little if any information useful for the identification of its contents had been previously obtained. From 36 subjects encountering each type of stimulus 51 times, a set of about 500 such fixations was obtained in each condition. The frequency distributions of the durations of these initial fixations on the word were compiled separately for each condition. The mean fixation duration for the pseudoword condition (244 ms) was significantly greater than that for the control condition (220 ms).

A comparison of the frequency distributions of fixation durations from the two conditions indicated that they were very similar to one another for the first 140 ms of the fixation, after which the distribution for the experimental condition dropped below that of the control condition. Thus, it appears that the initial fixation on a word must continue for more than 140 ms in order to be long enough for a pseudoword to produce an effect on the duration of that fixation. This is similar to the amount of time required to observe effects from orthographically irregular letter strings (McConkie, Underwood, Zola, & Wolverton, 1985). For fixations of 140 ms or longer, in at least some cases the following saccade was delayed, resulting in longer fixation durations.

Note that this analysis ignores completely what takes place after the first fixation on a word. Thus, the data include cases in which there is a single fixation on the critical word, as well as cases where there are multiple fixations. For current purposes, attention is limited strictly to the effect of a pseudoword on the onset time of the saccade that terminates the first fixation on that word. The data indicate that the effects of a pseudoword on processing can begin about 140 to 160 ms after the onset of a fixation on that word.

An Extension of the Frequency of Effects Model

To determine the frequency with which the presence of a pseudoword increased the durations of fixations in the experimental condition, a modification of the frequency of effects analysis was used. In applying this analysis to the data, three additional parameters were added to the model. The first was a floor parameter, f, below which no fixation duration effects are observed. That is, the duration of any fixation terminating prior to f ms is unaffected by the pseudoword. This does not necessarily mean that the errors were not perceived on these fixations. Indeed, it is quite likely that the next fixation will be longer than normal (McConkie, Underwood, Zola, & Wolverton, 1985). However, in these cases the initial fixation on the pseudoword was terminated before the effects of that error could influence the onset time of the following saccade.

The other two new parameters were increment values that were applied to the P and e parameters, indicating the amount of change in these parameters for each 20-ms increase in the fixation duration. These are referred to as the ΔP and Δe parameters. These new parameters make it possible to detect a linear change in the values of P and e across the fixation, and can take on either a positive or negative value, indicating an increase or a decrease in these values over time.

The modified Frequency of Effects Model was applied to the frequency distribution for fixation durations from the control condition to produce a distribution similar to that found in the experimental distribution as a way of estimating the parameters for the experimental condition.

Results of Model Fitting

The modified Frequency of Effects Model fit the data from the pseudoword condition very well, as can be seen in Figure 17.1. This figure presents the fixation duration frequency distributions from the experimental and control conditions together with the distribution that resulted from the optimal fit of the model. The model-produced distribution even mimics the irregularities in the experimental condition distribution, suggesting that these are real phenomena, and not just sampling irregularities. Estimates for the two Δ parameters are very near zero, providing no evidence for a linear change in parameter values across the fixation. Estimates for the other parameters are: $f = 140$ ms, $P = .32$, and $e = 28$ ms.

It is important to point out that there is an alternative model that does not fit the data. This is the model that assumes that all fixations that have not been terminated by 140 ms show a fixation duration increase at

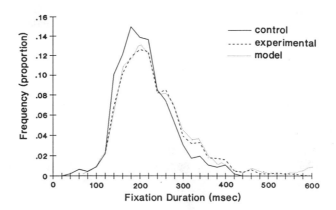

FIGURE 17.1. Frequency distributions of the durations of eye fixations for the initial fixations on selected words and pseudowords. Also presented is the predicted frequency distribution for the experimental condition, as computed from the frequency of effects model. Intervals are 20 ms, labeled from the lower boundary.

about that point in time. This type of model predicts a large dip in the frequency distribution in the 140 to 159 ms time interval that does not occur in the pseudoword condition data.

The results from the data analysis presented above suggest that an eye fixation lasting less that 140 ms is too short to show effects of processing disturbances produced by the presence of a pseudoword that is initially perceived during that fixation. This finding gives information about the speed at which word processing proceeds during eye fixations in reading. It should be noted that much of this time, perhaps 90 ms, is transmission time, getting neural signals from the retina to the visual cortex, and from the motor cortex to the ocular muscles (McConkie, Underwood, Zola, & Wolverton, 1985).

A more important point for present purposes is made by the type of model that successfully fits the data. The modified Frequency of Effects Model did not assume that at a specific time after the onset of the fixation, processing reached the point at which the distinction between real words and pseudowords produce an effect on all surviving fixations. Such an assumption would be equivalent to setting the value of P to 1.0, the value of ΔP to 0, and fitting only the remaining parameters. As indicated, this model did not produce a frequency distribution having a shape similar to that obtained in the experimental condition.

The successful model included a floor parameter indicating a fixation duration below which no effects of the pseudoword were observed on that fixation. However, for fixations longer than this minimum, the likelihood of showing an effect was constant for all following time intervals. Thus, while there was a minimum fixation duration required for an effect to occur, there was no specific point in time during the fixation at which the pseudoword typically produced its effect. Rather, the time of the effect appears to vary from fixation to fixation. Furthermore, it did not appear that there is a normal time for a pseudoword to disrupt processing, but with this effect simply being delayed on some fixations. If this were the case, the frequency of effect parameter P would have risen as fixations became longer. Instead, the ΔP parameter was very close to zero.

Time-Locked Versus Non–Time-Locked Effects

The results just described are in sharp contrast to another pattern we have observed in the frequency distributions of fixation durations obtained from several other studies. These studies have involved making changes in the text stimulus during eye fixations. For example, Blanchard, McConkie, Zola, and Wolverton (1984) masked the text for 30 ms at a certain time following the onset of an eye fixation during reading, after which the text reappeared. This type of stimulus change produces a large dip in the frequency distribution of fixation durations, beginning about 80 to 90 ms following the point of change. The change in the shape of the frequency distribution is similar to the change that would be expected if all fixations were being affected at a specific point in time, that is, if the P parameter were driven to 1.0 at that time.

We propose that these two types of results reflect two types of effects that a stimulus manipulation can produce on the reader's processing. One type of effect is time-locked to the onset of the stimulus, either to the onset of the eye fixation, at which point the stimulus begins producing its effect on the visual system, or to the time at which a change in the stimulus occurs during an eye fixation. When the effect is to delay the next saccade, this results in a sharp dip in the frequency distribution of fixation durations, because the effect is consistently occurring at the same point in time. Because there are transmission delays in the neural system, the actual time at which the processing is disrupted precedes the time at which the effect is seen in the eye movement data. This type of effect is observed when the processes being disrupted are processes that occur at a relatively fixed time and sequence after the stimulus onset. Thus, on all fixations, the point in processing at which the stimulus produces its effect is constant. The effect produced by masking the text briefly during fixations in reading is an example of a time-locked effect.

The second type of effect is a non–time-locked effect, such as that observed in initial eye fixations on pseudowords. Although a fixation must be at least of a certain duration to show an effect, the actual time at which the experimental manipulation produces its effect on processing varies from fixation to fixation. That is, the time at which this aspect of the stimulus comes into play in affecting the ongoing processing is constrained by the stimulus onset time, but is not determined by it.

The distinction just made is in harmony with a processing model having a variable utilization time (Blanchard, McConkie, Zola, & Wolverton 1984). This type of model postulates a strong distinction between processes that make information from the visible text stimulus available (that is, that *register* the stimulus information), and processes that use this information in the language processes of reading (that is, that *utilize* the visually provided information). Such a model assumes that there is some discrete time after the onset of a fixation at which visually provided information from the text becomes available for use by the higher processes, but that the time at which it is actually used in language processing is continuously variable, depending on when that information is needed. The processes involved in the registration of the stimulus information are massively parallel, automatic, and time-locked to the onset of the visual pattern on the retina. Registration essentially yields a visually provided data base from which information can be drawn by higher processes. Utilization, on the other hand, is carried out by more serial, attention-driven processes that select information from the visually provided data base at the time it is needed to advance the ongoing processing taking place.

Our proposal, then, is that briefly masking the text stimulus during fixations in reading is disruptive to the registration processes, whereas encountering a pseudoword has no effect on those processes. Rather, the stimulus information provided by the pseudoword only produces its effect when the visually provided information from that word location is selected and utilized by the ongoing language processes. Furthermore, we suggest that it may be possible to distinguish between whether a stimulus manipulation is affecting the registration or utilization processes in an ongoing task such as reading by examining its effect on the frequency distribution of fixation durations. An effective way of doing this is through the estimation of parameters in the modified Frequency of Effects model.

There is an important caveat to these suggestions. The distinction between registration and utilization processes can probably only be detected in the manner proposed above when the subjects are involved in an ongoing, resource-demanding task such as reading. In a case where individual stimuli, such as words, are presented to the subjects, it is likely that utilization processes occur in a time-locked fashion, much as the registration processes do. If there is no ongoing task, and the higher processes are simply waiting for input from the registration processes, then utilization will typically occur as soon as information needed by those processes becomes available. In such a case, the variability in utilization time will only be that associated with variability in processing complexity produced by the currently perceived stimulus materials themselves. This distinction between discrete tasks such as identification of tachistoscopically presented words and ongoing tasks such as the reading of continuous text should clarify our suggestion that the primary basis for variability in the time of utilization of visually provided information in ongoing tasks lies in variability in the time at which the higher processes are ready to make use of the information. Hence, the variability will be greatly diminished in discrete tasks.

Perception and Cognition: The Meeting Point

The distinction between registration and utilization processes naturally raises one further question. How far do the registration processes take the stimulus information? Another form of the same question is, What is the nature of the visually provided data base that is made available for use by the higher processes? At one extreme, we could assume that registration simply provides visual features, and that all further processing requires selection and attention from the strategic processes that are carrying out the task at hand, which is language processing in the case of skilled reading. At the other extreme, we could assume that the registration processes take all available information automatically through letter and word categorization and on to the arousal of lexical information, possibly even including the specification of syntactic and semantic relationships among words. In this case, the actual selection that occurs in utilization is from a data base containing rich and abstract information about word or multiword units in the text. From the perspective outlined above, this question of the nature of the visually provided data base, given a strong distinction between the registration and utilization processes, is essentially the question of where perception and cognition meet.

The results reported here give one piece of information toward the answer to this question. Letter strings that cannot be categorized as known words, but that are harmonious with English spelling regularities, do not produce a disruption of the registration processes. This suggests that the automatic processes induced by the text stimulus on the retina may not, during normal reading, produce lexical arousal. Rather, the visually provided data base contains information at a prelexical level. If this is the case, then lexical processing is induced by a request from higher processes when information is needed from a given word location, that is, when a given word location is attended.

An alternative interpretation is that, in the case of real words, the automatic processes by which registration is accomplished do result in lexical categorization and possibly in the arousal of lexical information, but encountering an unknown word does not produce a time-locked disturbance. Thus, when a pseudoword is encountered the lexical categorization and access processes are not enabled, but this does not disrupt the normal flow of time-locked processing. Only when the non–time-locked higher processes attempt to draw upon and utilize information from that word location is processing disrupted, presumably by arousing processes for dealing with unknown words, and the saccade postponed. If this second interpretation is correct, then the visually provided data base must contain information at different levels of abstraction, depending on the reader's prior experience with the stimulus. Thus, the first alternative appears to provide the simpler interpretation.

Finally, it is our hope that studies involving the manipulation of word stimuli, together with the modeling of frequency distributions of the durations of eye fixations on those words, will advance our understanding of the structure and chronology of processes involving perception and cognition during reading.

Acknowledgments. The authors wish to thank Paul Kerr for presenting the contents of this chapter at the Conference on Eye Movements in Reading and Picture Perception, University of Massachusetts, August 1990. The research was supported by grant no. OEG 0087 C1001 from OERI to the Center for the Study of Reading and grant no. MH 32884 from the National Institute of Mental Health to the senior author.

References

Blanchard, H., McConkie, G.W., Zola, D., & Wolverton, G.S. (1984). Time course of visual information utilization during fixations in reading. *Journal of Experimental Psychology: Human Perception and Performance*, *10*, 75–89.

Fodor, J.A. (1983). *Modularity of mind*. Cambridge, MA: MIT Press.

Forster, K.I. (1979). Levels of processing and the structure of the language processor. In W.E. Cooper & E. Walker (Eds.), *Sentence processing: Psycholinguistic studies presented to Merrill Garrett*. Hillsdale, NJ: Erlbaum.

Frazier, L., & Fodor, J.D. (1978). The sausage machine: a new two-stage parsing model. *Cognition*, *6*, 291–326.

Harris, C.M., Hainline, L., Abramov, I., Lemerise, E., & Camenzuli, C. (1988). The distribution of fixation durations in infants and naive adults. *Vision Research*, *28*, 419–432.

McConkie, G.W., Underwood, N.R., Wolverton, G.S., & Zola, D. (1988). Some properties of eye movement control during reading. In G. Luer, U. Lass, & J. Shallo-Hoffman (Eds.), *Eye movement research: Physiological and psychological aspects*. Toronto: C.J. Hogrefe.

McConkie, G.W., Underwood, N.R., Zola, D., & Wolverton, G.W. (1985). Some temporal characteristics of processing during reading. *Journal of Experimental Psychology: Human Perception and Performance*, *11*, 168–186.

McConkie, G.W., Zola, D., & Wolverton, G.S. (1985). Estimating frequency and size of effects due to experimental manipulations in eye movement research. In R. Groner, G.W. McConkie, & C. Menz (Eds.), *Eye movements and human information processing*. Amsterdam: North Holland.

Rumelhart, D.E. (1977). Toward an interactive model of reading. In S. Dornic (Ed.), *Attention and performance VI*. Hillsdale, NJ: Erlbaum.

Stanovich, K.E. (1980). Toward an interactive-compensatory model of individual differences in the development of reading fluency. *Reading Research Quarterly*, *16*, 32–71.

Suppes, P. (1990). Eye-movement models for arithmetic and reading performance. In E. Kowler (Ed.), *Eye movements and their role in visual and cognitive processes*. Amsterdam: Elsevier.

18
Early Lexical Effects when Fixating a Word in Reading

SARA C. SERENO

This chapter discusses the information that can be obtained when a word is first fixated in reading. This is a difficult topic for a number of reasons. Experienced readers do not jump neatly from word to word. Short words are often often skipped and longer words are usually fixated more than once. Moreover, there is uncertainty about the eye-mind span, that is, the delay between visual and cognitive processing. Nevertheless, the clever arrangement of reading materials and the use of eye-contingent displays have helped to illuminate the time course of comprehension processes in reading (McConkie & Rayner, 1975; Rayner, 1975; Rayner & Pollatsek, 1987, 1989). In this chapter, I examine research concerning lexical access processes that take place during the first fixation on a word.

The first study I discuss compares the first fixation of words fixated only once to words fixated twice. The relationship of the first to the second fixation in a refixated word is also examined. The second study investigates "fast priming" effects: In a reading context, what happens when a prime word is briefly presented at the onset of the initial fixation on a target word?

First Fixations in Refixated Words: Why are They Shorter?

The title of the first section of this chapter is intentionally ambiguous. What is the first fixation of a refixated word shorter than? Is it shorter than the first fixation of a singly fixated word? Is it shorter than the second fixation of a refixated word? Or, is it shorter than both?

To examine these questions, subjects were asked to read sentences presented one at a time on a cathode ray tube (CRT) as their eye movements were monitored by a Stanford Research Institute Dual Purkinje Eyetracker. An analysis of the data confirmed other studies showing that the first fixation of a refixated word is shorter than the fixation on a singly fixated word when variables such as word length, word frequency, preview, and context are controlled (Kliegl, Olson, & Davidson, 1983; O'Regan & Levy-Schoen, 1987; Rayner & Morris, 1992; Underwood, Clews, & Everatt, 1990; Vitu, O'Regan, & Mittau, 1990). However, I will present some data that are inconsistent with the standard explanation of this effect offered by O'Regan and his colleagues.

Table 18.1 shows results supporting the standard finding that the first fixation of a refixated word is shorter than the first fixation of a singly fixated word.[1] This effect is not surprising. The random variability of saccade amplitude from a given launch site gives rise to different landing positions on a following word. If the eyes land on a less than optimal position—so the logic goes—a second intraword fixation is quickly programmed, resulting in a shorter first fixation (O'Regan & Levy-Schoen, 1987). However, the relative durations of the first and second fixations on a refixated word are less obvious. The results of my work show that the first fixation on a refixated word is also shorter than a second fixation when textual processing constraints are minimal. I will explain these effects by a model that, in its simplest form, links lexical access to a first fixation and an attentional shift to a final fixation, whether it be a first or second fixation.

Sample stimulus materials are shown below. Target words (italicized) were either high (H) or low (L) frequency adjectives at the beginning of a sentence.

     H
(1a) The *quiet* child stared me down finally.
     L
(1b) The *gaunt* child stared me down finally.

     H   H
(2a) The *military* government promised peace.

(2b) The government promised peace.

     L   L
(3a) The *amiable* vicar preaches often.

(3b) The vicar preaches often.

Adjectives were selected as targets because they are free of syntactic or semantic closure effects that accompany the completion of an initial noun phrase. For example, in sentence 1, the reader delays closing the noun phrase until the noun "child" is read, signaling the end of the noun phrase.

---

[1] The term *refixated word* in this chapter refers specifically to a word that is fixated more than once *prior* to a saccade to another word, and thus excludes, for example, a word that is refixated via a regression from a later point in the text.

TABLE 18.1. Mean fixation duration (ms) on five- to nine-letter target words as a function of the number of fixations.

Number of fixations	Fixation	
	1st	2nd
1	251	
2	197	219

Fixation time on a modified noun in a sentence-initial noun phrase was compared to the fixation time on the identical unmodified noun (see sentences 2 and 3). Fixation time on the noun "government" or "vicar" was always longer when it was modified by an adjective. Noun modification produced a significant effect for high- and low-frequency nouns alike: modified nouns were fixated about 45 ms longer than their unmodified counterparts (see Rayner, Sereno, Morris, Schmauder, & Clifton, 1989).

By comparison, fixations on an initial adjective in a sentence are free of such effects because closure is postponed. Additionally, at the beginning of a sentence, the processing load is negligible because contextual influences are minimal. To maintain normal preview benefits, adjectives in this study were preceded by a determiner or possessive pronoun that engaged the subjects' initial fixation upon presentation of the sentence display. This procedure also established a uniform environment for the first saccade to the target word. Word frequencies of adjectives were tightly clustered within the high- and low-frequency groups. High-frequency adjectives had a mean frequency of 110 per million and low-frequency adjectives had a mean frequency of 5 per million (Francis & Kučera, 1982). Word length was matched across groups within a range of five to nine letters. In the data analysis, trials were excluded when target words were (a) initially skipped, (b) fixated more than twice, or (c) refixated with a regressive saccade from another word. Because this occurred on less than 1% of the trials, it seemed reasonable to conclude that subjects had indeed achieved word recognition during the first or first and second fixations on the target.

A standard explanation for a shorter first fixation on a refixated word compared to a word fixated only once maintains that it is a perceptual effect, resulting from a less than optimal viewing position on the target word. By this account, an early decision is made to execute an intraword saccade whenever the viewing position is deemed unsuitable. The most extreme position claims that no lexical processing is performed on the first fixation of a refixated word (O'Regan & Levy-Schoen, 1987; Vitu et al., 1990; see also O'Regan, this volume). On this view, lexical processing is postponed to the second fixation in refixated words and, consequently, accounts for its extended duration. In the case of a singly

TABLE 18.2. Mean fixation duration (ms) on low- (L) and high- (H) frequency five- to nine-letter target words as a function of the number of fixations.

Number of fixations	Frequency of target	Fixation 1st	2nd
1	L	267	
	H	235	
2	L	210	221
	H	182	217

fixated word, lexical (as well as perceptual) processing is completed during the first and only fixation, resulting in a first fixation duration that is longer than either the first or second fixation of a refixated word.

At first glance, such an account seems reasonable enough in explaining the data. Upon further consideration, however, this perceptual account of a first fixation in refixated words leads to predictions that can be tested. To confirm this view, it must be established that lexical processing is absent, or at least unprofitable, during the first fixation of a refixated word. The presence or absence of frequency effects in fixation times seems an acceptable test of whether or not lexical processing has occurred. Accordingly, differences in high- and low-frequency words should appear in the one-fixation case and in the second fixation of the two-fixation case, but *not* in the first fixation of the two-fixation case.

An analysis of the present results does not support the model of O'Regan and colleagues. Significant frequency effects were observed in the first fixation of both the one-fixation and two-fixation cases, but no effects were found in the second fixation of refixated words. These results are shown in Table 18.2. The optimal landing position interpretation suggests that (a) frequency differences should appear in the first fixation of the one-fixation case and, indeed, they do; (b) differences should not appear in the first fixation of the two-fixation case, but they do; and (c) differences should appear in the second fixation of the two-fixation case, but they do not.

These results suggest that other factors in addition to lexical access may be operative in triggering a saccade to the following word. If lexical access has been achieved on the first fixation in both cases, as suggested by the frequency effects, the question arises: Why then does the reader sometimes decide to refixate a word?

One reason may be that lexical access represents an incomplete stage of word recognition, and something more than lexical access, for example, a deeper level of word recognition, is required for a decision to move the eyes to the next word. Meanwhile, an impending deadline to make an eye movement could compel a reader to make a choice in this more or less advanced stage of word recognition. Thus, if a certain criterion for word recognition has not been met, the reader, presumably, will execute an intraword saccade to be safe.

A second reason for making another fixation on a word may in fact be related to perceptual considerations. In the present study, the landing position for the first fixation in refixated words was shifted, on average, about $1\frac{1}{2}$ character spaces to the left of the landing position of singly fixated words. It may be claimed, as before (O'Regan & Levy-Schoen, 1987), that this displacement provides a less optimal viewing position, thereby causing a problem in recognizing the word. But the fact that high- and low-frequency differences were shown to be basically equivalent in both the one-fixation and two-fixation cases argues against that inter- pretation. If processing were slowed due to a "bad" viewing position, then frequency effects should likewise be affected—but they were not. Nevertheless, it is also possible that the launch position from a given word (the location of the final fixation) could significantly affect process- ing time on a *following* word. For example, a closer launch site might increase preview benefits and improve chances for a preferred central landing position. Thus, the reader may be more apt to make an inter- mediate intraword saccade when an upcoming target is farther away. In the present study, as the distance from the launch site of word n (the adjective) to the first character of word $n + 1$ (the noun) increased, so did the fixation duration on word $n + 1$. For each added character space, fixation time on the noun increased linearly by approximately 20 ms, taking into account differences in word length and word frequency. Thus, the strategy of decreasing saccade length to the next word in order to gain a future benefit could motivate a second fixation on a word, apart from any processing difficulty associated with that word.

The second and perhaps more fundamental question that this study raises is: If lexical access has been achieved on the short first fixation in the two-fixation case, what accounts for the longer duration of the second fixation or, for that matter, the long duration of a single fixation?

I suggest that it is an obligatory attention shift, a notion that is not new in eye movement studies (see, e.g., Morrison, 1984). On this view, in both the one-fixation and two-fixation cases, additional processing time is allocated to the *final* fixation on the word. During this fixation, the critical saccade to the following word is programmed. Previous studies have indicated that the attentional span in reading is more compact than the perceptual span and more sensitive to word boundaries (see Rayner & Pollatsek, 1987). When a word is refixated, an attention shift is pre- sumably not required because the entire word already lies within the attentional field. However, when a word beyond the span of attention (the noun in this study) is the target of a saccade, the focus of attention must first be redirected and this entails a cost in programming time. Thus, fixation duration is extended in the first fixation of the one-fixation case and the second fixation of the two-fixation case even though lexical access

TABLE 18.3. Mean first fixation duration and gaze duration (ms) on low- (L) and high- (H) frequency 10- to 12-letter target words.

Target	First fixation duration	Gaze duration
L	259	464
H	263	365

Note: Gaze duration is the sum of all consecutive fixations made on a word.

is evident in the first fixation in both instances. This hypothesis assumes that, before an extraword saccade is initiated, an attentional mechanism preselects a target word or words from the parafoveal field. The attentional selection process consequently increases the duration of the last fixation on a word. Such an account provides a useful framework for understanding how information is integrated across saccades.

The results reported here were necessarily derived from a post-hoc analysis. It was not possible to determine in advance when a subject would refixate a word. Therefore, word frequencies and word lengths were recalculated for the post-hoc one-fixation and two-fixation groups to guard against possible confounding redistributions. No significant interactions between the number of fixations and word length or word frequency were found.

Finally, a sample of long words—10- to 12-letter words—was examined to see whether frequency effects appeared in first fixations. Unlike the words reported in the present study, these long words were not expected to be accessed in the course of one fixation because of perceptual constraints. This expectation was confirmed. No significant differences in the first fixations of high- and low-frequency long words were found. Frequency effects, however, were evident in subsequent fixations on the same word, indicated in the gaze duration measure (Table 18.3).

In sum, present results show that frequency differences can be found in the first fixation of refixated words as well as in the first fixation of singly fixated words under controlled conditions. The results for refixated words provide evidence against the claim that lexical access takes place only in the second fixation of these refixated words. A model in which refixations are due to attentional as well as perceptual mechanisms offers a deeper explanation.

Fast Priming During Eye Fixations

Frequency effects in first fixations raise some intriguing questions, for example: How fast can a reader access the meaning of a word? How fast can that word prime a related word? The second study that I will describe was motivated by an interest in the processing of lexically ambiguous words. Much of the research on lexical ambiguity has utilized the cross-modal priming task (Swinney, 1979; Tanenhaus, Leiman, & Seidenberg, 1979): subjects listen to a sentence and are then asked to respond to a visual probe word related to one of the meanings of an ambiguous word that occurred in the spoken sentence. The cross-modal task, however, has been challenged on methodological grounds (Glucksberg, Kreuz, & Rho, 1986; Van Petten & Kutas, 1987). The research I will now discuss represents initial work on the development of an alternative approach to examine the automatic processing of lexically ambiguous words—a paradigm using eye-contingent display changes during reading.

The eye movement technique offers several advantages in a lexical priming experiment. It has been well-documented that the processing of a word is related to its fixation time (Rayner et al., 1989). Moreover, the eye fixation measure itself, averaging about 250 ms, is much shorter than either the lexical decision or naming responses (the measures used in the cross-modal task). Such a brief response time, in fact, is inflated because the last stage of the fixation must be reserved for programming and directing the next saccade (Rayner, Slowiaczek, Clifton, & Bertera, 1983; Wurtz, Goldberg, & Robinson, 1982). The presentation of the prime in the same modality (visual) as the target also permits more accurate temporal control over the processing of prime and target, although visual masking effects must be taken into account.

Foveal placement of prime and target within a single fixation makes it possible to use fixation time on the target as a measure of fast automatic priming. A visual, semantically related word of a certain duration, immediately replaced by an overlying target (which also serves as a mask), may or may not produce priming effects on the target. One very important parameter is the stimulus onset asynchrony (SOA), that is, the time difference between onset of the prime and target (for a review, see Neely, 1991). On the one hand, if the SOA is too brief, priming will be absent because sufficient sensory information about the prime will not have been obtained. On the other hand, when primes can be reliably identified at longer SOAs, *automatic* priming effects may be obscured. Within these limits, certain constraints on the presentation of the prime are required. What are these constraints?

The first constraint on the prime is that it be brief enough to precede the deadline for programming a saccade to a following word. Otherwise, the subject's eyes will have moved beyond the target area before any meaningful measurement of fixation time on the target occurs. Also, a prime presented briefly is not as easily perceived and prevents major disruption of the fixation. A second constraint involves the control of parafoveal preview information about the prime. It has been shown that parafoveal information, that is, information about word $n + 1$ while fixating word n, can influence the later fixation duration on word $n + 1$

(see Rayner & Pollatsek, 1987, 1989). Finally, prime (and target) words must be short (e.g., four- or five-letter words). Such words are more likely to be fixated only once and more likely to be quickly accessed, and so provide the best opportunity to observe automatic priming effects.

Very few studies have examined semantic priming effects using a short SOA as well as a zero interstimulus interval—the conditions requisite for foveal priming during a single fixation in reading. In an isolated word experiment, Fischler and Goodman (1978) presented a prime word followed by a target item for lexical decision. The prime was displayed for 40 ms and was replaced immediately by a word or nonword target in the same location, masking the prime. Word primes were equally divided between "associated" and "unrelated" types. Associated primes produced a significant 41 ms facilitation. The question then is: Can priming of this sort also be achieved during an eye fixation in reading?

To investigate this question, subjects read sentences that contained a primed target. An example fixation pattern and the general sequence of events that occurred while reading a sentence in the fast priming paradigm are shown below (temporal stages are sequentially represented). Asterisks represent fixations, dashes represent saccades, and the vertical line represents a predetermined, invisible boundary.

```
        *-* ------ * -------- * ----
```
(4a) Tight quarters produce|d *gzsd* and discord.

```
               ----- *
```
(4b) Tight quarters produce|d *love* and discord.

```
             *
```
(4c) Tight quarters produce|d *hate* and discord.

```
             ---------- *
```
(4d) Tight quarters produce|d *hate* and discord.

When the eyes are to the left of the boundary (4a), a preview of random letters (*gzsd*) occupies the target position. During the saccade that crosses the boundary (4b), the preview is replaced by the prime (*love*). The duration of the prime is measured from the time the fixation begins (not from the time the boundary is crossed). Then, during the fixation (4c), the prime is replaced by the target (*hate*), which remains in place until the subject finishes reading the sentence (4d).

Eye movements were monitored with the signal from the eyetracker being sampled every millisecond by the computer. The display changes that were made, both during saccades (the change from the preview to the prime) and during fixations (the change from the prime to the target), were accomplished on average within 3 ms. Subjects were not aware of the first change that occurred during the saccade, but were often, although not always, aware of the second change from the prime to the target during the fixation. Although many subjects were conscious of this

TABLE 18.4. Mean gaze duration (ms) on the target word as a function of prime duration and prime type, Experiment 1.

Prime duration (ms)	Prime type			U − R
	I	R	U	
60	345	436	444	8
		(376)	(384)	
45	338	419	420	1
		(374)	(375)	
30	351	386	414	28
		(356)	(384)	

Note: Means in parentheses represent gaze duration minus the duration of the prime.

second display change (during the fixation), they were generally unable to identify the prime word.

Further details about the fast priming technique can be found in S.C. Sereno (1991) and Sereno and Rayner (1992). Two studies were conducted. In the first study, each noun target (e.g., *hate*) had three prime words associated with it. One of the primes (*love*) was semantically related (R) to the target and one (*rule*) was unrelated (U). In addition, there was an identical (I) condition—that is, the target (*hate*) was presented continuously from the beginning of the fixation. For each target, a subject was shown only one of the three possible primes. Based on the constraints discussed earlier and findings from previous studies (Dagenbach, Carr, & Wilhelmsen, 1989; Fischler & Goodman, 1978; Rayner, Inhoff, Morrison, Slowiaczek, & Bertera, 1981; J.A. Sereno, 1991; Warren, 1977), prime durations of 60, 45, and 30 ms were chosen.

Gaze duration on the target word was analyzed. Gaze duration represents the sum of all fixations on a word prior to an eye movement to another word. First fixation duration, on the other hand, is just that—the first fixation on a word whether it is the only fixation or the first of two or more fixations. Although both gaze and first fixation duration measures reflect the complexity of word processing, gaze duration typically yields more reliable effects. In this study, both measures were consistent, but I will focus on the gaze duration data.

Table 18.4 shows the data from the first fast priming experiment. The numbers in parentheses (in the R and U conditions) represent the gaze duration on the target minus the duration of the prime (e.g., 376 = 436 − 60). Gaze durations are thus comparable across prime durations as well as prime type.

Using this subtractive procedure, three pairwise comparisons at each level of prime duration were made: R versus U, I versus R, and I versus U. In the critical R-U comparison, there was a significant 28 ms ad-

TABLE 18.5. Mean modified gaze duration (ms) on the target word as a function of prime duration and prime type, Experiment 2.

Prime duration (ms)	Prime type			U − R
	RLS	R	U	
39	408	399	386	−13
30	389	377	408	31
21	363	376	361	−15

Note: Prime duration is subtracted from all means.

vantage for R primes at the 30-ms prime duration level. The effect of prime type, however, was not significant either at the 45- or 60-ms prime durations. I-R and I-U comparisons generally produced negative effects, almost all of which were significant. This is not surprising, though, since the presence of nonidentical primes was expected to produce some disruptive effects. These effects averaged about 35 ms. However, it is noteworthy that no disruption was apparent in the I-R comparison at the 30-ms prime duration (351 ms in the I condition, 356 ms in the R condition). Any disruption here was probably offset by the priming facilitation. One final point is that gaze durations within the I condition (345, 338, and 351 ms) were expected to be, and did turn out to be, roughly equal.

In sum, the purpose of this initial fast priming experiment was to see if priming could be obtained within the constraints of an eye movement paradigm. The study indicated that there was priming at the 30-ms prime duration condition. A second experiment was conducted (a) to determine if the R versus U priming effect at a 30-ms prime duration was replicable; (b) to bracket the effect—Would priming be seen even at a lower prime duration?; and (c) to establish a different baseline condition by replacing the I condition with a random letter string (RLS) condition. In the second experiment, R, U, and RLS primes were used. Prime durations were chosen as follows: 30 ms to replicate the first experiment, and 21 and 39 ms to bracket the effect.

Table 18.5 shows the data from the second experiment. Prime durations were subtracted from the gaze durations in *all* conditions (i.e., RLS as well as R and U). Thus, gaze durations are then comparable across prime type as well as prime duration. As before, three pairwise comparisons were made.

In the critical R-U comparison at the 30-ms prime duration, there was a significant 31 ms advantage for the R prime type. R-U comparisons at both 39 and 21 ms revealed no significant effects. Neither the RLS-R nor the RLS-U comparisons were significant at any level of prime duration. As seen in Table 18.5, gaze durations at the shortest prime duration of 21 ms were relatively short (363, 376, and 361 ms), suggesting that primes produced less disruption at this duration than at longer durations. Finally, in the RLS condition, as prime duration increased from 21 to 30 to 39 ms, so did the amount of disruption produced by RLS primes—gaze duration increased from 363 to 389 to 408 ms, respectively.

To summarize, the second experiment replicated the 30-ms priming effect. In the first experiment there was a 28 ms facilitation for targets preceded by related primes and, in the second experiment, a 31 ms facilitation. Second, the effect was bracketed. That is, priming occurred *only* at the 30-ms prime duration. Finally, the RLS condition provided a baseline that showed that disruption increased with prime duration.

With these results in hand, we can return to the question of lexical ambiguity resolution, which I mentioned at the outset as the motivation for this set of experiments. When an *ambiguous* word is presented as a prime to a target in a sentence—and the experiments described here show that reliable priming effects can be obtained at a 30-ms prime duration—either one or both of the senses of the ambiguous word prime will be activated. A biasing context is first established. If only the con- textually appropriate sense of the ambiguous prime is activated (measured by its effect on the target), a selective access account will be supported. On the other hand, if both the appropriate and inappropriate senses of the ambiguous prime are activated (again measured by their effect on the target), then a multiple or exhaustive access account will be upheld. Because of the speed, naturalness, and automaticity of eye movement responses, a test of these two accounts using this paradigm could provide important converging evidence.

In conclusion, I have discussed two approaches that examine somewhat different issues. However, they share an interest in the early stages of lexical access. They also demonstrate the versatility of using eye move- ment data and techniques to investigate on-line processes associated with word recognition and reading.

Acknowledgments. The research reported here was supported by National Science Foundation grant BNS86-09336 and National Institute of Health grant HD26765. I would like to thank Keith Rayner and Chuck Clifton for their helpful comments on this chapter.

Portions of these data were presented at the Midwestern Psychological Association meetings, Chicago, 1989, 1990 and at the Psychonomic Society meetings, New Orleans, 1990.

References

Dagenbach, D., Carr, T.H., & Wilhelmsen, A. (1989). Task-induced strategies and near-threshold priming: Conscious influences on unconscious perception. *Journal of Memory and Language, 28*, 412–443.

Fischler, I., & Goodman, G.O. (1978). Latency of associative activation in memory. *Journal of Experimental Psychology: Human Perception and Performance*, *4*, 455–470.

Francis, W.N., & Kučera, H. (1982). *Frequency analysis of English usage: Lexicon and grammar*. Boston: Houghton Mifflin.

Glucksberg, S., Kreuz, R.J., & Rho, S.H. (1986). Context can constrain lexical access: Implications for models of language comprehension. *Journal of Experimental Psychology: Learning, Memory, and Cognition*, *12*, 323–335.

Kliegl, R., Olson, R.K., & Davidson, B.J. (1983). On problems unconfounding perceptual and language processes. In K. Rayner (Ed.), *Eye movements in reading: Perceptual and language processes* (pp. 333–343). New York: Academic Press.

McConkie, G.W., & Rayner, K. (1975). The span of the effective stimulus during an eye fixation in reading. *Perception & Psychophysics*, *17*, 578–586.

Morrison, R.E. (1984). Manipulation of stimulus onset delay in reading: Evidence for parallel programming of saccades. *Journal of Experimental Psychology: Human Perception and Performance*, *10*, 667–682.

Neely, J.H. (1991). Semantic priming effects in visual word recognition: A selective review of current findings and theories. In D. Besner & G. Humphreys (Eds.), *Basic processes in reading: Visual word recognition*. Hillsdale, NJ: Erlbaum.

O'Regan, J.K., & Levy-Schoen, A. (1987). Eye movement strategy and tactics in word recognition and reading. In M. Coltheart (Ed.), *Attention and performance XII: The psychology of reading* (pp. 363–383). Hillsdale, NJ: Erlbaum.

Rayner, K. (1975). The perceptual span and peripheral cues in reading. *Cognitive Psychology*, *7*, 65–81.

Rayner, K., Inhoff, A.W., Morrison, R.E., Slowiaczek, M.L., & Bertera, J.H. (1981). Masking of foveal and parafoveal vision during eye fixations in reading. *Journal of Experimental Psychology: Human Perception and Performance*, *7*, 167–179.

Rayner, K., & Morris, R.K. (1992). Eye movement control in reading: Evidence against semantic preprocessing. *Journal of Experimental Psychology: Human Perception and Performance*, *18*, 163–172.

Rayner, K., & Pollatsek, A. (1987). Eye movements in reading: A tutorial review. In M. Coltheart (Ed.), *Attention and performance XII: The psychology of reading* (pp. 327–362). Hillsdale, NJ: Erlbaum.

Rayner, K., & Pollatsek, A. (1989). *The psychology of reading*. Englewood Cliffs, NJ: Prentice-Hall.

Rayner, K., Sereno, S.C., Morris, R.K., Schmauder, A.R., & Clifton, C., Jr. (1989). Eye movements and on-line language comprehension processes. *Language and Cognitive Processes*, *4*, SI21–49.

Rayner, K., Slowiaczek, M.L., Clifton, C., Jr., & Bertera, J.H. (1983). Latency of sequential eye movements: Implications for reading. *Human Perception and Performance*, *9*, 912–922.

Sereno, J.A. (1991). Graphemic, associative, and syntactic priming effects at a brief stimulus onset asynchrony in lexical decision and naming. *Journal of Experimental Psychology: Learning, Memory, and Cognition*, *17*, 459–477.

Sereno, S.C. (1991). *Fast priming in reading: A new eye movement paradigm.* Unpublished master's thesis, University of Massachusetts.

Sereno, S.C., & Rayner, K. (1992). Fast priming during eye fixations in reading. *Journal of Experimental Psychology: Human Perception and Performance, 18,* 173–184.

Swinney, D.A. (1979). Lexical access during sentence comprehension: (Re)consideration of context effects. *Journal of Verbal Learning and Verbal Behavior, 18,* 645–659.

Tanenhaus, M.K., Leiman, J.M., & Seidenberg, M.S. (1979). Evidence for multiple stages in the processing of ambiguous words in syntactic contexts. *Journal of Verbal Learning and Verbal Behavior, 18,* 427–440.

Underwood, G., Clews, S., & Everatt, J. (1990). How do readers know where to look next? Local information distributions influence eye fixations. *Quarterly Journal of Experimental Psychology, 42A,* 39–65.

Van Petten, C., & Kutas, M. (1987). Ambiguous words in context: An event-related potential analysis of the time course of meaning activation. *Journal of Memory and Language, 26,* 188–208.

Vitu, F., O'Regan, J.K., & Mittau, M. (1990). Optimal landing position in reading isolated words and continuous text. *Perception & Psychophysics, 47,* 583–600.

Warren, R.E. (1977). Time and the spread of activation in memory. *Journal of Experimental Psychology: Human Learning and Memory, 3,* 458–466.

Wurtz, R.H., Goldberg, M.E., & Robinson, D.L. (1982). Brain mechanisms of visual attention. *Scientific American, 246,* 124–135.

19
Sentence Context Effects on Lexical Access

ROBIN K. MORRIS

One of the most robust findings in the word recognition literature is that responses to words are faster when a word is preceded by a congruent context than when it is preceded by a neutral or incongruent context. For example, a word such as "treasure" would be recognized more quickly in the sentence "The pirate found the treasure," than in the sentence "The person liked the treasure", or worse yet, "The house was destroyed by the treasure" (e.g., Balota, Pollatsek, & Rayner, 1985; Ehrlich & Rayner, 1981; Fischler & Bloom, 1979, 1985; Foss, 1982; Schuberth, Spoehr, & Lane, 1981; Simpson, Peterson, Casteel, & Burgess, 1989; Stanovich & West, 1979). No one disputes the fact that context plays a role in the processing of individual words in a sentence.

The controversy arises when we begin to ask more specific questions about which contextual factors are influencing the construction of which representations. There are two questions at issue here: What is the locus of the context effect?, and What is the processing mechanism that accounts for it? There is widespread agreement that the structure of language can be described in terms of a number of subsystems such as morphology, syntax, and semantics, and furthermore, that these systems are fairly independent in that the rules and representations used to describe each of these systems are different. However, there are still widely divergent views about the extent to which this structural independence translates into processing independence, with modular theories of language processing at one end of the continuum and interactive theories at the other.

To illustrate the contrast between these two theoretical positions, consider a simplified model of language processing in which there are only three processing components, each corresponding to a different level of representation of the text that is being read: a lexical, a syntactic, and a message-level component. According to strongly modular theories of language processing, each component carries out its respective processing task independently of what is happening in the other components of the system. The flow of information through the system is strictly bottom-up.

317

The primary goal of the lexical module in reading is to identify the meanings of individual words in the text without benefit of information contained in (or output from) the syntactic or message-level processor. The work of the syntactic module is to parse the individual words in the sentence into their appropriate constituent units. Although this module would receive input from the lexical module, it would remain ignorant of any output from the message-level processor, and would function independently of whatever processing activity might be going on in the other components. In turn, the message-level processor constructs a discourse representation of what is read. This processor would have access to the output from the other two processors. However, there is no feedback from the message-level to either the lexical or syntactic processor (see Fodor, 1983; Forster, 1981).

Interactive models of language processing differ from modular theories in the extent to which information from different components of the language processing system is shared. The same trio of component processors (lexical, syntactic, and message-level) and the tasks assigned to each can be embodied within an interactive framework. However, according to an interactive view, the result of processing in any one component of the system may influence processing in any other level above or below it in the system (McClelland, 1987). These differences give rise to very different predictions with respect to the possible loci of context effects in word processing.

The Locus of Context Effects

For the purpose of distinguishing between the modular and interactive view, word processing can be divided into two stages. The lexical access stage is limited to the activation of lexical candidates and the codes associated with them, such as the phonemic and orthographic codes, syntactic category, and word meaning. The postaccess stage includes aspects of word processing that are generally thought to take place after access is complete, such as selection, elaboration, and integration of activated lexical representations with the context in which they occur.

The modular view predicts that word processing may be influenced by sentence context in one of two ways. First, the context in which a word is read may ease postaccess processes such as the integration of the lexical entry that has been accessed into the higher order sentence representation. That is, sentence context may influence postaccess processes. Second, the sentence context may include words that are highly related to the target word. These associations may be represented by direct links among the entries in the lexicon such that activation of one member of the pair could spread to the other, thereby facilitating access. According to this view, sentence context can influence the access stage of word processing, but only via connections among individual lexical items contained in the sentence. That is to say, sentence context effects on lexical access are the result of simple word-to-word priming embedded in a sentence frame, and not the result of priming from the integrated sentence representation.

The interactive view could account for a much broader range of context effects on lexical access, as well as effects on postaccess processes, because the flow of information among the component processors is multidirectional. According to this view, processing in the lexical component of the system could be affected by activity in any other component of the system. Higher order representations may influence access of lower order representations directly. Thus, representations in the lexical, syntactic, or message-level component could potentially facilitate lexical access.

Mechanisms That Underlie Sentence Context Effects

As the previous discussion suggests, these two models take radically different positions regarding the extent to which the components of the language processing system are independent (Forster, 1979) or interactive (McClelland, 1987). Thus, the possible processing mechanisms that could account for context effects on lexical access are quite different.

The modular theories would account for context effects on lexical access via an intralexical priming mechanism. That is, lexical representations of individual words that are strongly related have direct links within the lexicon and facilitation could occur as the result of activation spreading among these lexical items. Aside from the case of intralexical priming, the speed with which a word is accessed will not be influenced by the content of the sentence in which it is read (Tanenhaus & Lucas, 1987). This is because the internal workings of the lexical processor are impervious to the internal workings of, or the output from, any higher order processor.

In contrast, the interactive theories could account for context effects on lexical access either via intralexical priming or via a feedback mechanism. The feedback mechanism would allow for higher order knowledge to guide lower order processing. Thus, output from the syntactic or the message-level processor could feed back to influence the activation of lexical candidates directly.

Methodological Concerns

Determining the stage of word processing that is influenced by context is complicated by the difficulty in distinguishing context effects that are due to an increase in activation of a particular lexical candidate and those that are due to a change in the criterion using to select a candidate from those that have been activated. The lexical decision task is thought to be overly sensitive to effects occurring at the decision/response stage of processing (i.e., postlexical processes; Balota & Chumbley, 1984; Lorch, Balota, & Stamm, 1986; Seidenberg, Waters, Sanders, & Langer, 1984; West & Stanovich, 1982).

Naming a word is thought to be a fairly automatic response that does not involve a binary decision and is therefore less likely to be contaminated by postlexical processes (see Balota & Chumbley, 1984; Forster, 1979; Lorch et al., 1986; Seidenberg et al., 1984; Stanovich & West, 1983; Tanenhaus & Lucas, 1987; West & Stanovich, 1982). In addition, inhibitory effects have generally been thought to occur when attention processes, such as those associated with postaccess processing, or conscious prediction strategies are engaged (Neely, 1977; Posner & Snyder, 1975; Stanovich & West, 1983). However, with the use of appropriate baseline measures it is possible to discern the presence of inhibitory effects in the naming time data.

In summary, facilitation in the time to name a target word, in the absence of inhibitory effects, has come to be accepted as a relatively "pure" measure of access, whereas tasks such as lexical decision are thought to reflect postaccess processes as well as access. However, although naming time has come to be regarded as a good measure of lexical access, it has some shortcomings as a measure of reading behavior that may be of particular importance in assessing the role of sentence context in word processing.

There are a variety of presentation methods used in conjunction with the naming task. These differ in the extent to which the reader controls the rate of presentation (self-paced, rapid-serial visual presentation, or RSVP). They also differ in the amount of information that is available to the reader at any given point in time (word-by-word, phrase-by-phrase, etc., and cumulative vs. noncumulative presentation). All disrupt the normal flow of events in reading, rely on a secondary task to evaluate reading behavior, and isolate the target word from the context in some way. Any of these factors might distort the processing relations between sentence context and lexical access in reading.

Eye Movements and Language Processing

During the past 10 to 15 years considerable progress has been made in understanding the reading process through the use of eye movement monitoring techniques (see Just & Carpenter, 1987; Rayner & Pollatsek, 1989). These techniques enable researchers to observe the process of silent reading via naturalistic data and without disrupting the reading process or relying on information from secondary tasks. In addition, the eye movement record provides the researcher with an on-line record of processing activity. However, before using eye movements to study something as complex as language processing, there are a number of issues that must addressed: (a) What is the size of the perceptual span in reading? (b) How tight is the link between where the reader is looking and what information is being processed? (c) What are the best measures of word processing time, and in particular lexical access, associated with eye movement data? (See Rayner, Sereno, Morris, Schmauder, & Clifton, 1989, for a more thorough discussion of these issues.)

The Perceptual Span

Only information extracted from a very restricted area of the visual field is utilized on any given fixation, in any type of visual processing task. Knowing the size of this region and the type (or quality) of the information obtained on a given fixation in reading is important in order to infer language processing activity from the eye movement record. It would be ideal if readers fixated each and every word in turn and identified the currently fixated word, and only that word, on any given fixation. Although the situation is not quite as clear-cut and consistent as that, it is close.

The most definitive work on the perceptual span has utilized the eye contingent display change technique developed by McConkie and Rayner (1975). The primary finding is that the perceptual span in reading is quite small. Readers extract information from a region extending from the beginning of the currently fixated word (but no more than three to four character spaces to the left of fixation) to about 15 character spaces to the right of fixation, on average. However, information used to identify a word during the current fixation is generally confined to a region extending no more than five to seven character spaces to the right of fixation. That is, the word identification span is smaller than the total perceptual span. This usually means that the reader is able to identify only the currently fixated word and then must make an eye movement to the next word to take in new information. However, if two short words fall within the identification span they may both be processed in a single fixation, and as a result the second word may be skipped (not receive a direct fixation).

Even when the word to the right is not fully identified, some processing of that word is accomplished before that word is fixated. This has been termed *parafoveal preview benefit*, and most often involves the extraction of the beginning letter information about the upcoming word. Both word skipping and preview effects are natural components of the reading process and consequently to eliminate or ignore them, as some technologies designed to study reading do, is to distort the process of reading and may lead to unnatural strategies on the part of the reader, or incorrect conclusions on the part of the researcher.

The Eye-Mind Span

The eye-mind span refers to the relationship between where the eyes are looking and what the mind is processing. Again, the ideal would be a perfect relationship, in which the point of fixation was a precise indicator of what information was being processed at any given moment. However, there are two problems with claiming that fixation times on words are a pure reflection of the processes associated with comprehending that word. The first is the existence of parafoveal preview effects, which were discussed in the previous section. The second is the issue of spillover effects. That is, sometimes processing of one word spills over onto processing of the subsequent word in the text. For example, several studies that investigated the effect of word frequency on processing time have found that fixation time on low-frequency words is longer than fixation time on high-frequency words, and that processng time on the word following the low-frequency word is inflated as well (Rayner & Duffy, 1986; Rayner et al., 1989). Such effects suggest that it is important to consider the pattern of data over several different dependent measures obtained from the eye movement record, before drawing conclusions as to the cognitive processes associated with reading.

Eye Movements as a Measure of Lexical Access

What is the appropriate measure of lexical access time in the eye movement record? The most obvious candidate is the fixation time on a word. However, words are sometimes fixated once, sometimes more than once, and sometimes not at all. There is no single measure that can accurately capture all these events and measure lexical access, uncontaminated by other processes. By looking across several eye movement measures it may be possible to delineate cases in which at least the lexical access stage of word processing has been affected, if not cases in which only access has been affected.

The two most commonly used measures of word processing are *first fixation duration* and *gaze duration*; both measures include only cases in which the word was fixated (that is, a skip is not counted as a 0-ms fixation). First fixation duration on a word includes only the duration of the initial fixation on that word, regardless of the total number of fixations that were made on the word. Gaze duration is the sum of the durations of all consecutive fixations in the initial viewing of a word, before the reader moves on to another word. First fixation and gaze duration are taken to represent related processes. That is, when readers have difficulty processing a word they either maintain their initial fixation on the word, or they make a second fixation on the same word. Because it is typically the case that words that are easy to access are also easy to integrate into the text representation it is not surprising that the results obtained are usually consistent across these two measures (see Rayner et al., 1989, for a review).

Several factors throught to influence lexical processing have been investigated in eye movement studies. As a result, we know that readers look longer at low-frequency words than at high-frequency words (Inhoff, 1984; Inhoff & Rayner, 1986; Just & Carpenter, 1980; Kleigel, Olson, & Davidson, 1982; Rayner, 1977; Rayner & Duffy, 1986). In addition, fixation times on words that are highly predictable in a sentence context are shorter than on words that are less predictable (Balota et al., 1985; Ehrlich & Rayner, 1981; Inhoff, 1984; Schustack, Ehrlich, & Rayner, 1987; Zola, 1984). These results make it clear that the ease or difficulty of processing a word greatly influences the amount of time that a reader looks at that word.

Determining what stage of word processing has been affected is more difficult. Lexical factors such as word frequency have been shown to affect both first fixation and gaze duration; however, reading involves many cognitive activities in addition to lexical access: syntactic parsing, text integration, inferencing, etc. Gaze duration almost certrainly reflects some text integration processes as well as lexical access.

So where do we stand with respect to measuring sentence context effects on lexical access during reading? The naming task has the advantage that it appears to measure access uncontaminated by postaccess processes, but it also has the disadvantage of altering the task of reading and providing limited information from a task that is secondary to reading. The eye movement record provides a variety of measures obtained directly from a natural component of reading. The readers proceed through the text at their own pace, and at the same time the experimenter obtains a continuous record of reading behavior. By comparing the data obtained in these two very different tasks, it may be possible to take fuller advantage of the strengths of each of these approaches.

Converging Evidence for Lexical Access

Schustack et al. (1987) used converging evidence from eye movement data and naming time data to discriminate between effects on lexical access and effects on text integration. They found that fixation time on a target word varied as a function of distance from the previous referent and as a function of the level of constraint imposed by the verb that preceded it. To discriminate between changes in access and changes in text integration, they sought converging evidence from a naming task. Subjects in the naming time experiment read the same passages of text as were used in the eye movement experiment and named the target word when it appeared on the screen.

The logic was that because naming time is taken as a pure measure of access, the effects observed in the eye movement record that reflect an effect on lexical access should replicate in the naming data, whereas the effects that reflect an impact on text integration would not occur in the naming time data. The naming data yielded an effect of verb constraint, but not an effect of distance, suggesting that the constraint factor was influencing access of the target word, whereas the distance factor was effecting text integration. Thus, through the use of converging evidence from the naming task, they were able to specify the locus of the context effects that they observed in the eye movement data. A similar approach will be taken in the following sections, but in a somewhat different order. The primary goal is to examine cases in which context influences lexical access (substantiated with the naming task) and attempt to specify the contextual factors that are responsible for the observed effects (using converging evidence from naming and fixation time data).

Sentence Context Effects on Lexical Access

Stanovich and West (1981, 1983) provided clear evidence for sentence context effects on lexical access. In these studies subjects read a context sentence and then named the final word of the sentence aloud, as quickly as possible. In general, they found that a word was named faster when it appeared in a congruent sentence context than when it appeared in a neutral context. In addition, they found no sign of inhibition when the word was named in an incongruent context. Such a pattern of facilitation without inhibition provides convincing evidence that the locus of the observed facilitation is lexical access.

The mechanism responsible for the observed facilitation is less clear. One possibility is that the facilitation occurred via intralexical priming. However, there was no single semantic associate of the target word in the congruent context. The Stanovich and West findings leave us with two questions. First, what is the mechanism that produced the sentence context effects on lexical access? Second, will these effects generalize to a fluent silent reading task?

Evidence of Intralexical Priming in a Sentence Context

Duffy, Henderson, and Morris (1989) conducted an RSVP–naming time experiment using modified Stanovich and West materials to explore the extent to which these effects could be accounted for via intralexical priming. They noted that although the original sentence contexts contained no words that were highly associated with the target word, many of the content words were moderately related to the targets. For example, in the sentence, "The barber trimmed the *mustache*," both "barber" and "trimmed" seem modestly related to "mustache." Duffy et al. reasoned that activation coming independently from "barber" and "trimmed" might converge at "mustache." If each content item contributed a modest amount of activation to the target word then priming might occur through the accumulation of several sources of weak activation. To test this hypothesis, sentences like the following were displayed using the RSVP method, and subjects were asked to say the final word aloud as quickly as possible.

(1) The barber trimmed the mustache. (Full congruent)
(2) The person trimmed the mustache. (Subject neutral)
(3) The barber saw the mustache. (Verb neutral)
(4) The person saw the mustache. (Full neutral)

The content words of each full congruent sentence were systematically replaced with neutral words. The prediction was that there should be some facilitation observed in each of the partial content conditions, if intralexical priming was to account for the facilitation observed in the congruent context condition.

In a subsequent experiment, a short prepositional phrase was added to the end of each of these sentences, so that the target word was not the sentence final word, and subjects were asked to read them while their eye movements were recorded (Morris, 1990). The results of both experiments are presented in Table 19.1. There was clear evidence of facilitation in the full congruent condition in the naming and fixation time data. However, there was only a hint of facilitation from the partial content conditions. A closer look at the eye movement data revealed that subjects read the verb ("trimmed") in these sentences faster when it was preceded by a related subject-noun ("barber") than when it was preceded by a neutral subject-noun ("person"). It would be difficult to argue that processing time on the verb was facilitated by a higher order representa-

TABLE 19.1. Mean naming time and fixation time on a target word as a function of lexical content in sentence context.

Context condition	Naming time	First fixation duration	Gaze duration
1. Congruent	570	243	285
2. Subject neutral	587	266	328
3. Verb neutral	596	264	326
4. S-V neutral	594	261	337

Note: Condition numbers correspond to example numbers in the text.

tion of the sentence context, because it was preceded only by a single noun and function word. Although this facilitation could by no means account for all the facilitation observed in the full congruent condition, it suggests that there is some intralexical priming occurring in these sentences. But what accounts for the additional facilitation?

The Effect of Syntactic Relations on Lexical Access

If the mechanism responsible for this facilitation arises from some special property of spreading activation among combinations of items in the lexicon (see Duffy et al., 1989; Foss & Ross, 1983; Stanovich & West, 1983), it might still be possible to account for these effects without violating modularity. Such an account would have to claim that the subject-verb combination facilitated access of the target word through pathways existing within the lexicon (Forster, 1979). As a result, the facilitation effect should not be sensitive to changes in the syntactic relations among the words in the congruent sentence context. For example, the time to read "mustache" should not differ in the following two sentences from Duffy et al. (1989), because the lexical content of the two sentences is not different.

(5) While she talked to him the barber trimmed the *mustache*.
(6) While talking to the barber she trimmed the *mustache*.

An interactive model could account for a difference in the time to access "mustache" in the two conditions based upon feedback from the integrated sentence representation. That is, in the first sentence context a barber is trimming (syntactic relations preserved). Feedback from a higher order representation of this scenerio would activate lexical candidates that would be likely objects of this activity. The second sentence context is not about barbers trimming (syntactic relations disrupted), and so there is no feedback from the integrated sentence representation to the related lexical item "mustache."

As illustrated in Table 19.2, neither naming time (Duffy et al., 1989), nor fixation time measures (Morris, 1990) show an effect of syntactic relations on the processing time on the target word. Although this result is consistent with the modular model, it is not necessarily inconsistent

TABLE 19.2. Mean naming time and fixation time on a target word as a function of syntactic relations among lexical items in sentence context.

Context condition	Naming time	First fixation duration	Gaze duration
5. Syntactic relations preserved	566	264	296
6. Syntactic relations disrupted	572	265	297

with the interactive model. Although the integrated sentence representation up to the target word in sentence 2 no longer specifically represents the "barber" as the agent of "trimmed," it does portray a barbershop/ hair-trimming scenerio. Thus, it is possible that the facilitation observed in either case could be attributed to a feedback mechanism.

So the question remains unanswered: What is the source of the facilitation of lexical access for the word *mustache* in the sentence "The barber trimmed the mustache"? Is it the result of combinatory activation from the intralexical priming mechanism, as the modular model would suggest? Or, is it the result of activation from the integrated sentence representation feeding back to the lexical representation, as the interactive model would have it?

Evidence of Message-Level Effects on Lexical Access

Evidence of message-level representations influencing the access of lexical representations would violate the autonomy of the lexical processor, as proposed by the modular theory of language processing. Under a modular view, the information within each processing component is encapsulated, with each component operating independently. Thus, the lexical processor is impervious to information from elsewhere in the processing system. Within such a view, activation from the subject-noun "barber" might spread to the verb "trimmed" via intralexical connections. This combination might differentially focus the spread of activation to other lexical representations associated with the pair of items, rather than to all items associated with either 'barber" or "trimmed" alone. Under such a model, the facilitation of access of the lexical entry for "mustache" should be sensitive to the inclusion of other words in the context that (in combination with trimmed) would activate a different set of lexical candidates. For example, the word "gardener" in combination with "trimmed" might activate lexical items associated with a lawn, rather than hair. However, it should not matter how these items are connected in the message-level representation because the lexical processor is not privy to this information.

The interactive theory of language processing could also account for the previous findings via an intralexical priming mechanism, or it could account for the facilitation with a feedback meachanism. With the feedback mechanism the integrated sentence representation could feed back activation to related entries in the lexicon. According to this interpretation, the way in which the lexical items are linked by the syntactic structure of the sentence in which they occur could have a profound influence on which lexical candidates are activated. Consider the following set of sentences:

TABLE 19.3. Mean naming time and fixation time on a target word as a function of the message-level sentence context.

Context condition	First fixation duration	Gaze duration
7. Barber-trimming	262	309
8. Gardener-trimming	279	342
Neutral control	280	347

(7) The gardener watched as the barber trimmed the mustache in the morning.
(8) The gardener who watched the barber trimmed the mustache in the morning.

The lexical content of the two sentences is the same. Thus, the modular model would predict that there would be no difference in the time to access "mustache" between these two cases. However, the message-level representation of the two sentences up until the word "mustache" is encountered is quite different. The first sentence is about a barber trimming something, whereas the second sentence is about a gardener trimming. If message-level representations are influencing the time to access "mustache", fixation time on "mustache" should be shorter in the first sentence than in the second, and in fact that was the case (Table 19.3). Furthermore, there was no difference between fixation time on "mustache" in the second sentence and in a neutral control sentence. Thus, we have evidence of shorter processing time on "mustache" that appears to be due to activation from the message-level representation of the sentence context, and we have no sign of inhibition from the misleading context. Processing time in the region immediately following the target word was longer in the misleading context, suggesting that "mustache" was more difficult to integrate into the sentence representation.

Conclusions

The research presented here replicates the very common finding that words are processed more rapidly in a congruent sentence context than in a neutral or incongruent context. In addition, I have tried to specify the locus of these effects and the mechanisms by which they operate, and to compare those findings to the predictions made by two contrasting theories of the language processing system. The discussion has focused on those cases in which there is evidence that the sentence in which a word was read influenced lexical access. I have presented evidence of facilitation arising from intralexical priming and evidence of facilitation feeding back from the message-level representation of the context to the target word; there is no evidence of facilitation of lexical access due to the specific syntactic relations among the lexical items in the sentence context.

Where does this leave us with respect to the two theories of language processing?

The intralexical facilitation, and the lack of facilitation from the specific syntactic relations among lexical items in the sentence are both pieces of evidence that are consistent with a simple three component modular model of the language processing system in which representations of related words are linked in the lexicon and information flows through the system in a strictly bottom-up direction. Such a model cannot account for the activation feeding back from higher order representations to activate lexical representations.

The interactive model can account for the intralexical priming and the message-level feedback. However, it did not make clear predictions about the role of syntactic relations. It could have accounted for facilitation that was dependent on syntactic relations just as well as it could account for the result that was obtained.

Perhaps the more interesting way of assessing these findings is to ask what is similar about the two cases in which facilitation of lexical access was observed, and what is different about the case in which there was no facilitation. Tanenhaus and Lucas (1987) have suggested that what differentiates potential sources of contextual facilitation for lexical access from sources that influence postaccess processes is the extent to which the relation between the context and word is mediated by stored representations. That is, concepts that are activated as a part of accessing stored representations such as scripts, or schemas, might well activate a limited set of words associated with that concept.

Such a framework would fit well with the evidence we have discussed. For example, the sentence fragment "The barber trimmed the" might activate a barbershop or haircutting script stored in memory, and that script would, in turn, activate a limited set of related words. Assuming that "mustache" was a member of that limited set, such a model would predict facilitation in the access of "mustache." It is important to note that we are not talking about contexts that predict the target word, which may set up an expectation that would have to be discarded when the target word is encountered. In fact, the sentence contexts used in these studies do not yield accurate predictions of the target word when presented in a cloze task (see Duffy et al., 1989), and there was no sign of the inhibition that would be expected if such a decision strategy was invoked.

The sentence "The gardener who watched the barber trimmed the mustache" may activate that subset of stored representations related to hedge trimming, or gardening, and would not activate "mustache." However, the lexical processor would still produce a set of lexical candidates via activation from the visual input. No computations were executed, no wrong decisions made. So there may be little cost associated with the mismatch between the higher order representations and the individual lexical item that was encountered. In the other sentence of that pair, the barber was trimming and so the higher order representation would activate a subset of related items and access of mustache would be facilitated.

In the case of relations between context and word that involve rules (i.e., relations that must be computed) rather than activation of stored representations, the potential benefit of activation of a set of lexical candidates seems less likely. Facilitation from such computations to all stored representations that are consistent with the computation would in many cases be quite large. In addition, such computations take more time and resources than the spread of activation among a limited set of stored representations arising from the perceptual input.

The manipulation of syntactic relations that was described in an earlier section of this chapter demonstrated that when the lexical content of the context was held constant, the manipulation of the computational combinations did not affect access time on the target word. It is important to note that this manipulation did not involve syntactic anomaly, which would produce a mismatch between the computation and the lexical item that was actually read. The inhibition observed in such cases suggests that there is a response bias occurring at some stage in that situation.

In summary, it seems that the language processing system may be best described as some sort of hybrid of the two theoretical positions that we started from. My inclination would not be to abandon the modular view, but rather to embellish it with interactive capabilities that are precisely defined and necessitated by the evidence obtained from well-controlled empirical work.

Acknowledgments. The author was supported at various times during the preparation of this manuscript by grant HD26765 from the National Institutes of Health awarded to Keith Rayner at the University of Massachusetts, Amherst, MA, and by a National Institute of Mental Health Pre-Doctoral Traineeship, grant MH16745. In addition, the author received partial support from NIH Biomedical Research Support grant S07 RR07160.

References

Balota, D.A., & Chumbley, J.I. (1984). Are lexical decisions a good measure of access? The role of word frequency in the neglected decision stage. *Journal of Experimental Psychology: Human Perception & Performance, 10,* 340–357.

Balota, D.A., Pollatsek. A., & Rayner, K. (1985). The interaction of contextual constraints and parafoveal visual information in reading. *Cognitive Psychology, 17,* 364–390.

Duffy, S.A., Henderson, J.M., & Morris, R.K. (1989). The semantic facilitation of lexical access during sentence processing. *Journal of Experimental Psychology: Learning, Memory & Cognition, 15*, 791–801.

Ehrlich, S.F., & Rayner, K. (1981). Contextual effects on word perception and eye movements during reading. *Journal of Verbal Learning and Verbal Behavior, 20*, 641–655.

Fischler, I., & Bloom, P.A. (1979). Automatic and attentional processes in the effects of sentence context on word recognition. *Journal of Verbal Learning and Verbal Behavior, 18*, 1–20.

Fischler, I., & Bloom, P.A. (1985). Effects of constraint and validity of sentence context on lexical decisions. *Memory & Cognition, 13*, 128–139.

Fodor, J.A. (1983). *The modularity of mind.* Cambridge, MA: MIT Press.

Forster, K.I. (1979). Levels of processing and the structure of the language processor. In W.E. Cooper & E. Walker (Eds.), *Sentence processing: Psycholinguistic studies presented to Merrill Garrett* (pp. 27–85). Hillsdale, NJ: Erlbaum.

Forster, K.I. (1981). Priming and the effects on sentence and lexical contexts on naming time: Evidence for autonomous lexical processing. *Quarterly Journal of Experimental Psychology, 33A*, 465–495.

Foss, D.J. (1982). A discourse on semantic priming. *Cognitive Psychology, 14*, 590–607.

Foss, D.J., & Ross, J.R. (1983). Great expectations: Context effects during sentence processing. In G.B. Flores d'Arcais & R.J. Jarvella (Eds.), *The process of language understanding* (pp. 169–191). Chichester: Wiley.

Inhoff, A.W. (1984). Two stages of word processing during eye fixations in the reading of prose. *Journal of Verbal Learning and Verbal Behavior, 23*, 612–624.

Inhoff, A.W., & Rayner, K. (1986). Parafoveal word processing during eye fixations in reading: Effects of word frequency. *Perception & Psychophysics, 40*, 431–439.

Just, M.A., & Carpenter, P.A. (1980). A theory of reading: from eye fixations to comprehension. *Psychological Review, 87*, 329–354.

Just, M.A., & Carpenter, P.A. (1987). *The psychology of reading and language comprehension.* Newton, MA: Allyn and Bacon.

Kleigel, R., Olson, R.K., & Davidson, B.J. (1982). Regression analyses as a tool for studying reading processes: Comments on Just and Carpenter's fixation theory. *Memory & Cognition, 10*, 287–296.

Lorch, R.F., Jr., Balota, D.A., & Stamm, E.G. (1986). Locus of inhibition effects in the priming of lexical decisions: pre- or postlexical access? *Memory & Cognition, 14*, 95–103.

McClelland, J.L. (1987). The case for interactionism in language processing. In M. Coltheart (Ed.), *Attention and performance XII: The psychology of reading* (pp. 3–36). London: Erlbaum.

McConkie G.W., &Rayner, K. (1975). The span of the effective stimulus during a fixation in reading. *Perception & Psychophysics, 17*, 578–586.

Morris, R.K. (1990). *Lexical access in reading: The role of sentence context.* Unpublished doctoral dissertation, University of Massachusetts, Amherst.

Neely, J.H. (1977). Semantic priming and retrieval from lexical memory: Roles of spreading activation and limited capacity attention. *Journal of Experimental Psychology: General, 106*, 226–254.

Posner M.I., & Snyder, C.R.R. (1975). Attention and cognitive control. In R. Solso (Ed.), *Information, processing and cognition: The Loyola symposium* (pp. 55–86). Hillsdale, NJ: Erlbaum.

Rayner, K. (1977). Visual attention in reading: Eye movements reflect cognitive processes. *Memory & Cognition, 4,* 443–448.

Rayner, K., & Duffy, S.A. (1986). Lexical complexity and fixation times in reading: Effects of word frequency, verb complexity, and lexical ambiguity. *Memory & Cognition, 14,* 191–201.

Rayner, K., & Pollatsek, A. (1989). *The psychology of reading.* New Jersey: Prentice Hall.

Rayner, K., Sereno, S.C., Morris, R.K., Schmauder, A.R., & Clifton, C.E. (1989). Eye movements and on-line comprehension processes. *Language and Cognitive Processes, 4,* 21–50.

Schuberth, R.E., Spoehr, K.T., & Lane, D.M. (1981). Effects of stimulus and contextual information on the lexical decision process. *Memory & Cognition, 9,* 68–77.

Schustack, M., Ehrlich, S., & Rayner, K. (1987). The complexity of contextual facilitation in reading: Local and global influences. *Journal of Memory and Language, 26,* 322–340.

Seidenberg, M.S., Waters, G.S., Sanders, M., & Langer, P. (1984). Pre- and postlexical loci of contextual effects on word recognition. *Memory & Cognition, 12,* 315–328.

Simpson, G.B., Peterson, R.R., Casteel, M.A., & Burgess, C. (1989). Lexical and sentence context effects in word recognition. *Journal of Experimental Psychology: Learning, Memory & Cognition, 15,* 88–97.

Stanovich, K.E., & West, R.F. (1979). Mechanisms of sentence context effects in reading: Automatic activation and conscious attention. *Memory & Cognition, 7,* 77–85.

Stanovich, K.E., & West, R.F. (1981). The effect of sentence context on ongoing word recognition: Tests of a two-process theory. *Journal of Experimental Psychology: Human Perception & Performance, 7,* 658–672.

Stanovich, K.E., & West, R.F. (1983). On priming by a sentence context. *Journal of Experimental Psychology: General, 112,* 1–36.

Tanenhaus, M.K., & Lucas, M.M. (1987). Context effects in lexical processing. *Cognition, 25,* 213–234.

West, R.F., & Stanovich, K.E. (1982). Source of inhibition in experiments of the effect of sentence context on word recognition. *Journal of Experimental Psychology: Learning, Memory & Cognition, 25,* 385–399.

Zola, D. (1984). Redundancy and word perception in reading. *Perception & Psychophysics, 36,* 277–284.

20
Optimal Viewing Position in Words and the Strategy-Tactics Theory of Eye Movements in Reading

J. KEVIN O'REGAN

The Perceptual Span Control Hypothesis

Work on eye movements in reading received a considerable new impetus starting in about 1975, when several research groups began using computers to control eye movement experiments "on-line" (McConkie & Rayner, 1975; O'Regan, 1979; Reder, 1973). The idea of a "moving window" allowing only a limited amount of text to be visible around the instantaneous eye position was an appealing technique that allowed researchers to measure the size of the "perceptual span," that is, the zone around the fixation point from which different kinds of information is gathered. My own feeling at that time, and I believe also the feeling of other workers, was that the most reasonable thing that the eye might be doing in reading would be to adjust its saccades so that from moment to moment, the edges of successive perceptual spans would just touch, or overlap by a fixed amount. In that way, at moments when the text is easy to predict, or the words easy to recognize, the eye would be able to make larger saccades than when the eye was moving into less predictable or more difficult territory. This view of reading could be called the "perceptual span control" hypothesis (Jacobs & O'Regan, 1987). The perceptual span control hypothesis is at the root of a very large body of research in which perceptual span is measured by making perturbations in the information available in parafoveal vision (for a review see Rayner & Pollatsek, 1987): in this research, changes in eye movements are assumed to indicate changes in perceptual span. However, it has not usually been realized that this assumption can only be true to the extent that perceptual span actually directly determines eye movements.

Indeed, a series of experiments I did with my collaborators forced us to reconsider this idea. Using psychophysical methods and tachistoscopic presentation, we precisely determined the size of the region around the fixation point in which letters could be recognized out of context, in random letter strings. By changing viewing distance or interletter spacing, we could modify the size of this visual span by a few letters. We then

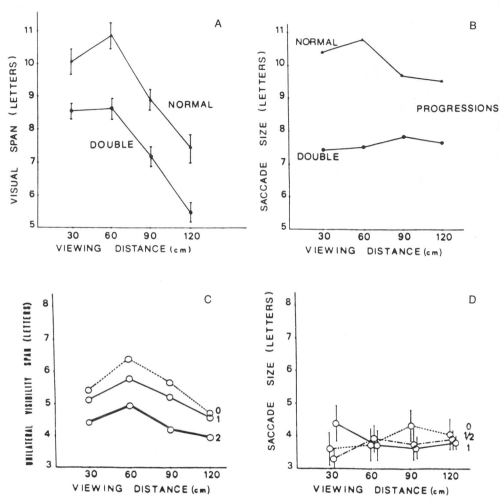

FIGURE 20.1. A. Means and error bars (showing two standard errors on each side of the mean) over four subjects, of empirically measured (unilateral) visual span, i.e., number of character spaces from the fixation point at which letters can be seen with 50% chance of being correctly reported, as a function of distance of the eye from the screen. The letters were lower case, and defined within an 8 × 8 matrix of pixels approximately 0.3 cm square. They were presented flanked on each side by a random numeral between 1 and 9. The letters were taken from a set of 10 possible letters. In the "double" condition, each letter (and numeral) contained additional white space on either side of it, so when words were written in the double typography, they appeared doubly spaced as compared to the normal condition. Reprinted, by permission, from O'Regan, Levy-Schoen, & Jacobs, 1983. B. The same as A, except a different letter set, upper case letters, and different subjects, using three degrees of spacing flanking each letter: 0 (equivalent to normal in A), 1 (equivalent to double) and 2 ("triple" spaced). Reprinted, by permission, from Lévy-Schoen, O'Regan, Jacobs, & Coëffé, 1984).

reasoned that if the subjects subsequently read texts printed with the same typography at the same viewing distances or with the same inter-letter spacing, then under the perceptual span control hypothesis, their eye saccades should vary in the same way as the visual spans had varied in the psychophysical experiment. Figure 20.1 shows the results we observed in several experiments: saccade sizes changed when perceptual span was kept constant, or did not change when perceptual span changed. In any case, saccade sizes did not behave in the way expected from the idea that they are determined directly by the size of the perceptual span.

Two other lines of research being done at that time were beginning to provide new ideas about eye movement control, and ultimately came to modify our view of eye guidance in reading, leading us to abandon perceptual span control in favor of what I call the "strategy-tactics" theory (O'Regan, 1990; O'Regan & Lévy-Schoen, 1987). One important result was Findlay's discovery of the "global effect," suggesting that it is not so easy to aim the eye where you want, when the visual field contains more than just a single target (Findlay, 1981; 1982; see also Findlay, present volume). Before addressing this, I want to consider the other important finding that led to a change in our viewpoint. It was the discovery of the "optimal viewing position" in words (previously called the "convenient viewing position" [O'Regan, 1981]).

The Optimal Viewing Position Phenomenon

If experimental conditions are arranged in such a way that when a word appears on a display screen, the subject's eyes are fixating at different letter-positions in the word, it is observed that the time it takes to name the word, or to make a lexical decision about it, or the time the eye stays on the word before moving on to other words displayed to its right, depends very strongly on the position that the eye started off fixating. There is an "optimal" viewing position, where the time it takes to recognize the word is minimal. As shown in the examples given in Figure 20.2A, when the eye's initial fixation position deviates from the optimal

←—————————————————————————————

FIGURE 20.1 (*Continued*)
C. Mean progression saccade size made by the same four subjects as in A, reading texts printed in the same typographies as in A (but using all letters of the alphabet). Saccade size is measured in letter-spaces, so in the double condition, one "letter-space" was twice as wide as in the normal condition. D. Mean progression saccade size made by the same subjects as in B, searching for the letter "B" in lines of random letters taken from the set used in B. Three spacing conditions were used: 0 and 1, corresponding to 0 and 1 in B and condition $(\frac{1}{2})$, with half as much spacing as 1.

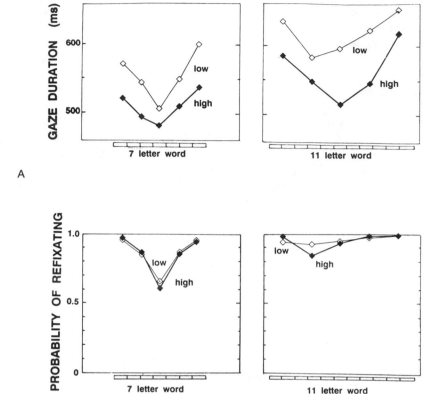

FIGURE 20.2. A. The optimal viewing position phenomenon. The curves show the total time the eye spends on a word (gaze duration) before leaving it to read the remaining words displayed on its right, plotted as a function of the eye's initial fixation position in the test word (the small rectangles on the abscissa represent letters of the word). "High" and "low" refer to words of high and low frequency in French. Each data point represents a mean over 10 subjects reading 10 words, and 50 words contribute to each curve (Latin square design). B. For the same experiment as in A, the probability of making more than one fixation in the word as a function of the position initially fixated by the eye.

position, the time it takes to recognize the word increases: indeed, the penalty for not fixating the optimum is very large, on the order of 20 ms for every letter of deviation from the optimum, even for short four- and five-letter words (O'Regan & Jacobs, 1992; O'Regan & Lévy-Schoen, 1987; O'Regan, Lévy-Schoen, Pynte, & Brugaillère, 1984; Vitu, O'Regan, & Mittau, 1990). Note that the "optimal viewing position" is not necessarily the "preferred" position where the eye actually lands; for

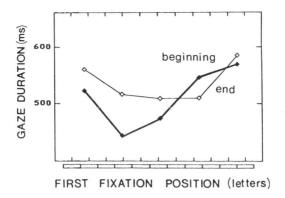

FIGURE 20.3. Optimal viewing position curves for two types of words: words selected in the French dictionary in such a way that knowing their first six letters and approximate length allowed the word to be uniquely determined ("beginning" words; examples:"coccinelle," "gladiateur"), and words such that knowing their last six letters and approximate length allowed the word to be uniquely determined ("end" words; examples: "interview," "transversal"). The words were matched for length and frequency. Each data point corresponds to 50 subjects and 2 words, with 10 words contributing to each curve in a Latin square design. Reprinted, by permission, from O'Regan & Lévy-Schoen, 1987.

reasons connected with oculomotor constraints or scanning strategies, the eye may actually tend to land elsewhere in words, and data exist on where this "preferred landing position" generally is (e.g., Dunn-Rankin, 1978; McConkie, Kerr, Reddix, Zola, 1988; Rayner, 1979).

The cause of the optimal viewing position effect is probably partly related to the dramatic falloff of visual acuity even within the fovea (McConkie, Kerr, Reddix, Zola, & Jacobs, 1989; Nazir, O'Regan, & Jacobs, 1991; O'Regan, 1983; 1989; O'Regan & Lévy-Schoen, 1987). Oculomotor factors may also contribute to the effect (Nazir, 1991). Finally, lexical structure and lexical processing also play a role: this is shown by the fact illustrated in Figure 20.3 that words with different structure can have different optimal viewing positions. For example, words whose beginnings allow their endings to be predicted have their optimal viewing positions nearer their beginnings than words whose endings allow their beginnings to be predicted (Holmes & O'Regan, 1987; O'Regan & Lévy-Schoen, 1987).

Although (with some recent exceptions, cf. Vitu, 1991a; Vitu, O'Regan, & Mittau, 1990) we have generally studied the optimal viewing position effect in situations where the word to be recognized is the first word of a sequence of words, it seems reasonable to suppose that the effect is a fundamental aspect of word recognition in general, and thus that it may also have an important role to play when the words are embedded in the body of a text, as in normal reading. To understand how the optimal

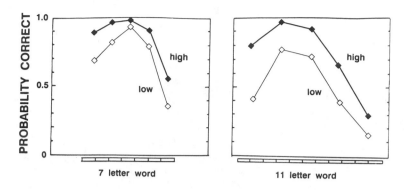

POSITION FIXATED IN WORD (letters)

FIGURE 20.4. Probability of correctly reporting words that appear at different positions with respect to the eye's fixation point. By use of a computer-controlled, eye-contingent display, the word was made to disappear if the eye attempted to move. The small rectangles on the abscissa represent the letters of the words where the eye could start fixating: "high" and "low" refer to words with high and low frequency of occurrence in French. Data points represent means over 10 words and 10 subjects. Fifty words contribute to each curve (Latin square design).

viewing position effect might influence eye movements in reading, we will look at the eye movement behavior that underlies it.

Within-Word Tactics

Are eye movements necessary to recognize words? Many people would be surprised to learn that they are, given that a century of work on tachistoscopic word recognition has not considered eye movements at all. But most of this work on word recognition has been done using short words, or, when long words were used, using presentation conditions such that the eye was fixated near the middle of the word when it appears. Under these conditions eye movements are indeed not necessary. But, as shown by the results of the experiment shown in Figure 20.4, when the eye's initial fixation position is not near the middle, words can often not be recognized if eye movements are not allowed.

What eye movements occur during word recognition? I have spent much effort attempting to understand what the eye does after it lands in a word, and I believe I am beginning to get an understanding for this. However, I have had to abandon the initially appealing idea that the eye's behavior reflects lexical processing in a moment-to-moment way. Instead, it seems that in the early stages of word recognition, lexical processing does not influence eye movements. Eye movements appear to rely on a tactic based only on rapidly available, nonlexical kinds of information. Only later, after about 200 ms, do eye movements begin to be influenced by lexical processing.

A tactic that seems to account for what is happening in the first moments of exploration of a word is schematized in Figure 20.5. If the eye does not land near a position just left of the middle of the word where the optimal viewing position generally is, it immediately moves to the other end of the word. On the other hand, if the eye lands fairly near the generally optimal viewing position, then an eye movement is triggered taking the eye out of the word. Figure 20.2B shows the probability of refixating a word as a function of the position where the eye starts off fixating in it. As predicted from the refixation tactic I am suggesting, the probability of refixating increases strongly as the eye starts off progressively further from the optimal viewing position. It is this higher probability of additional fixations occurring that is the main cause of the increased total gaze duration shown in Figure 20.2A when initial fixation positions deviate from the optimal viewing position.

For its operation, the simple visuomotor exploration tactic only requires knowledge about where the eye has landed in the word (and where the optimal viewing position generally is), and this should be available quite early, because it requires no lexical processing, only visual information about the relative position of the eye in the "blob" constituting the word. Interestingly, however, even extracting the eye's proximity to where the optimal viewing position generally is, and programming a saccade to the other side of the word, appears not to be a perfectly simple process. Figure 20.6C shows the results of an experiment in which no lexical processing was necessary at all, since the stimulus was simply a string of x's with a target "o" in the middle of it. The subject's eye started off at various positions in the string, and had to move to the central "o," and then move to another string placed to the right. The graph plots the fixation duration prior to the saccade that took the eye to the "o," as a function of where the eye was relative to the "o." Also plotted are the times the eye spent on the second fixation (on the "o") as a function of where the eye was prior to fixating it. The advantage of plotting the graphs in this way is that by summing the two times plotted at each string position, the total time spent on the string when the eye started at that string position is obtained. Although the task in this experiment is not exactly the same as what occurs in reading a word in two fixations, two fixations did occur before leaving the string. It can be seen that the closer the eye was to the middle of the string, the longer it took for a saccade to be initiated, and the less time it took for the eye to make the following saccade. It is as though a salvo of two saccades was programmed in such a way that the total time the eye spent on the string was constant, even though the time it took to initiate the first saccade increased as the eye got closer to the middle. Similar sequential programming aspects of eye

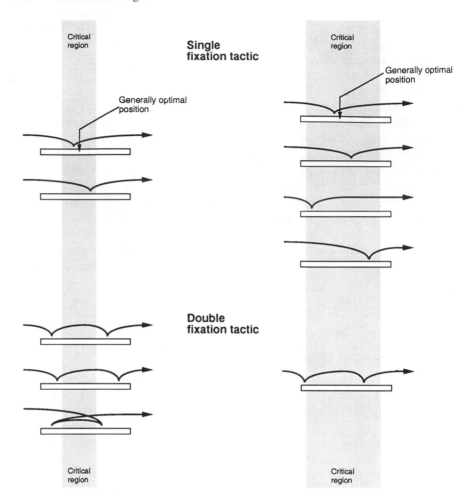

"CAREFUL" STRATEGY   "RISKY" STRATEGY

FIGURE 20.5. The eye attempts to attain the generally optimal position when it jumps into a word. However, for reasons related to oculomotor constraints, it may not land at this position. If the landing error is small enough, and the eye lands in the critical region around the aimed-for position, a single fixation is programmed in the word, and a saccade is prepared that takes the eye out of the word. However, if the eye lands outside the critical region, a saccade is immediately triggered that leads the eye to another position in the word, on the other side of the word to where the eye initially landed. Only after this second fixation in the word does the eye saccade out of the word. The figure shows an example of the operation of "careful" and "risky" scanning strategies. In the "careful" strategy, a fairly narrow critical region is defined around the position in words where the optimal viewing position generally is. In the "risky" strategy, the critical region is much larger. The durations of the individual fixations in the

movements have been illustrated in simpler tasks by Inhoff (1986) and Zingale and Kowler (1987).

The same thing seems to be happening in the exploration of words, as shown in Figure 20.6A,B. This time the peaks and troughs in the curves are not at the middle of the word, but displaced slightly toward the beginning, where the optimal viewing position generally is. However, again, as for the string experiment, there is a trade-off between the duration of the first and the second fixation. We have observed this kind of pattern for first and second fixation durations in all our experiments in which the test word is the first of a sentence or short phrase (O'Regan & Lévy-Schoen, 1987; Vitu, 1991a).

It is this trade-off between first and second fixation durations in word recognition that had initially led me astray, into thinking that lexical processing was being reflected in the eye movement behavior. I had not yet done the string experiment, and thought that the explanation for the "hump" in the first fixation curve and corresponding dip in the second fixation curve was that as the eye approaches the optimal viewing position, progressively more lexical processing can be done on the first fixation, and correspondingly less on the second. But, as suggested by the experiment on letter strings, the effect seems to have a purely visuomotor component. This can also be seen by looking at what happens with high- and low-frequency words, or with words whose information is at their beginnings or endings (Figure 20.6A,B). The first fixation when two occur is not at all sensitive to lexical factors. Only the second fixation differs according to the frequency or lexical structure of words (see also Sereno's chapter in the present volume).

Another aspect of within-word exploration data that is compatible with the idea that the first stages of this exploration are visually rather than lexically guided concerns the probability of making more than one

---

← _____

FIGURE 20.5 (*Continued*)

single and double fixation tactics are of interest. In the single fixation tactic, the single fixation is of comparatively long duration (300 ms or more). This is long enough for lexical influences to make themselves felt. On the other hand, in the first moments of the double fixation tactic, the durations of the fixations are determined purely by visual factors. When the first fixation is far from the generally optimal position it is very short (about 100 to 150 ms). The closer the first fixation comes to the generally optimal position, the longer it will be, reaching approximately 250 ms. The duration of the second fixation in the double fixation tactic is inversely proportional to the duration of the first fixation: when the first fixation is short the second is long and vice versa. This may be because a salvo of two fixations is programmed in such a way that the sum of their durations is approximately constant. The duration of the second fixation in the double fixation tactic can be influenced by lexical factors, whereas the first fixation occurs too early and is too short for this to be the case.

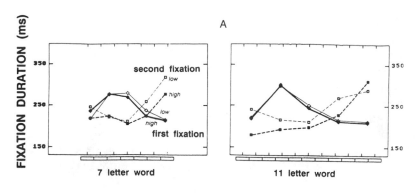

FIRST FIXATION POSITION (letters)

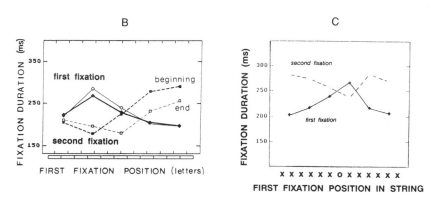

FIGURE 20.6. A. Subset of the data of the experiment described in Figure 20.2 when exactly two fixations were made: Fixation duration as a function of the position of the first fixation, that is, the position of the eye at the moment the word appeared. The second fixation durations (dotted lines) are plotted at the abscissa positions where the corresponding first fixation (solid lines) occurred. In this way, the total time spent on the word as a function of the position that the eye initially fixated can be read off by summing the data points aligned vertically at that position in the word. The thick lines (solid or dotted) correspond to high-frequency words, the thin lines (solid or dotted) to low-frequency words. Adapted with permission from O'Regan & Lévy-Schoen, 1987. B. First and second fixation durations in the subset of the data of the "Beginning-End" experiment (Figure 20.3) in which exactly two fixations occurred, plotted in the same way as in A. Reprinted, by permission, from O'Regan & Lévy-Schoen, 1987. C. Data from an experiment in which the eye started off at different positions in a string consisting of an "o" flanked on each side by six x's, and had to saccade to the "o" before saccading out of the string. The fixation duration at the initial fixation point ("first fixation" curve) and at the "o" ("second fixation" curve) are plotted in the same way as for A and B.

fixation. If, as I am suggesting, the early stages of within-word tactics are determined purely by visual and not by lexical factors, then the decision of whether additional fixations are to be made can only depend on visual, and not on lexical factors. Thus, even though low-frequency words take longer to recognize than high-frequency words (see Figure 20.2A), this difference, according to my theory, cannot be reflected in differences in the probability of making additional fixations in the word, and can only be due to later aspects of the oculomotor behavior. Figure 20.2B confirms this: the probability of refixating a word is independent of its frequency. The longer total gaze duration needed for low-frequency words comes not from higher refixation probability, but from the second of two fixations being longer.

A final question about within-word tactics concerns what happens when the eye lands sufficiently near the generally optimal viewing position, and only a single fixation is made. What determines the duration of this fixation? Oculomotor factors might intervene that make it harder or easier to aim for the next word depending on where in the currently fixated word the eye is fixating. We have some suggestion of such a purely oculomotor effect from results in which we used a simple task where the eye started off fixating a target letter at different positions in a string of k's, and then saccaded out of the string to an adjacent string. There was an indication that durations were shorter when the eye was leaving one or other end of the string (Nazir, 1991). However, an important point concerns the effect of linguistic processing on the duration of single fixations. In one view, it could be supposed that when the eye lands near the generally optimal position, it waits for lexical processing to attain some predetermined stage, and then the saccade leading to the next word is triggered. An alternative view is that the saccade to the next word might be triggered immediately, without waiting for lexical processing to have time to influence its duration. I have data from two experiments on this issue. In one experiment, the word to be recognized appeared under the eye, and the eye then moved off to a word on the right that had to be compared with the first word. When single fixations occurred on the first word in this experiment, the fixations were of comparatively long duration; 300 to 400 ms. I observed that they were sensitive to word frequency, with the single fixations being longer on low-frequency words. The second experiment I will mention in greater detail later (Vitu, 1991a). In this experiment, the eye executed a series of saccades before landing in the test word. When single fixations occurred, they were of rather shorter duration (250 to 350 ms) than in the word comparison experiment, and they were not sensitive to word frequency (except when prior linguistic context was strong, or parafoveal processing was possible; see below).

In summary, the data on within-word tactics are consistent with the idea that two processes are occurring simultaneously during word recognition. The eye is being jockeyed around by a visually based tactic that says: If you land too far from the generally optimal viewing position, immediately move to the other side of the word; if you land near the generally optimal position, then saccade out of the word. In the first stages of this tactic, fixation durations are determined purely by visuomotor factors; in particular, it seems that it takes less time for the eye to decide to refixate when it is far from the generally optimal viewing position than when it is close to it. While the oculomotor stages of the refixation tactic are taking place, lexical processing is occurring on the basis of the information being gathered. However, this lexical processing cannot influence the eye movements until later, either on the second of two fixations when two occur, or at the end of a long duration single fixation, when such a single fixation occurs.

Normal Reading

The strength of the optimal viewing position phenomenon in isolated words suggests that in normal reading it may also be advantageous to fixate near the optimal viewing position of words. After all, if the phenomenon applies to normal reading, then landing only, say, two to three letters from the optimal viewing position would give rise to 40 to 60 ms of additional gaze duration on the word, which is a considerable, 20 to 30% increase compared to the 250- to 300-ms gaze durations normally observed on words during reading.

However, it is not known to what extent normal reading is mediated by the same processes as those underlying the reading of isolated words. When the eye is fixated in a word that is surrounded by other words, the notion of optimal viewing position may have to be extended to the whole group of words. Parafoveal preprocessing of words as well as the facilitating action of contextual constraints may also modify the optimal viewing position phenomenon as compared to what occurs in isolated words. We are currently investigating these possibilities. However, as a first step, and in order to have a working hypothesis that can be tested, we wanted to verify to what extent one can espouse the extreme position according to which at least some kinds of careful reading occur in a word-by-word fashion, with each word having its optimal viewing position as in our isolated word experiments.

If we try to imagine what might be happening in such a form of word-by-word reading, two problems arise if the eye is to attain the optimal viewing position at every saccade. The first problem concerns knowing where the optimal viewing position is. As we have seen, the optimal viewing position is in different positions in different words, so the eye cannot know in advance where this position will be in a particular word. The best it can do is saccade to where the optimal viewing position generally is in words for the language being read, i.e. in English and French, just left of the middle of words. I propose this as the first part of the "strategy-tactics" hypothesis—Strategy: when leaving a word, attempt to saccade to just left of the middle of the next word.

The second problem concerns getting accurately to this aimed-for position. Whereas aiming the eye accurately is not difficult when the target is the only thing visible in the visual field, it is now known that when other nontarget elements are present, the eye tends to saccade to a position determined by a kind of cortically weighted center of gravity of the global visual configuration (Coëffé, 1987; Findlay, 1987; Vitu, 1991b). We have shown (Coëffé & O'Regan, 1987) that accuracy depends on the prior fixation duration: in conditions similar to text reading, only when the fixation duration prior to the saccade is of more than about 600 ms, is the oculomotor system capable of bringing the primary saccade to a position within a letter or two from the target. This is considerably longer than the durations normally observed in reading. It seems, therefore, that in reading the eye cannot hope to accurately attain the optimal viewing position. Within-word correction tactics such as those we observed for isolated words must therefore be used. In addition to the general strategy, therefore, I postulate the existence of within-word correction tactics: when the eye is too far from the aimed-for position, immediately make a refixation to the other side of the word. (This tactic would be similar to the one that we postulated for isolated words, that is, based only on visual information.) When the eye lands sufficiently near the aimed-for position, it moves to the next word.

Testing the Strategy-Tactics Theory

As a first step toward testing this "strategy-tactics" hypothesis, we did an experiment to compare within-word refixation tactics in isolated words and normal reading (Vitu, O'Regan, & Mittau, 1990). Under the "strategy-tactics" hypothesis, refixation tactics should be similar in isolated words and in normal reading, because an optimal viewing position effect is assumed to exist in normal reading as it does in isolated words.

In the experiment, within-word refixation tactics were analyzed for a set of test words of different length and frequency both when these words occurred as the first word of short phrases, or embedded within short 20-line stories. As shown in Figure 20.7A, the probability of refixating the test words was overall much smaller in the texts. However, the optimal viewing position phenomenon did continue to exist in the texts, because refixation probability was not constant across the words, but had a definite minimum. Interestingly, the penalty for not fixating the optimal position was considerably smaller than for isolated words, and the minimum was further left than when the words were presented in isolation. For gaze

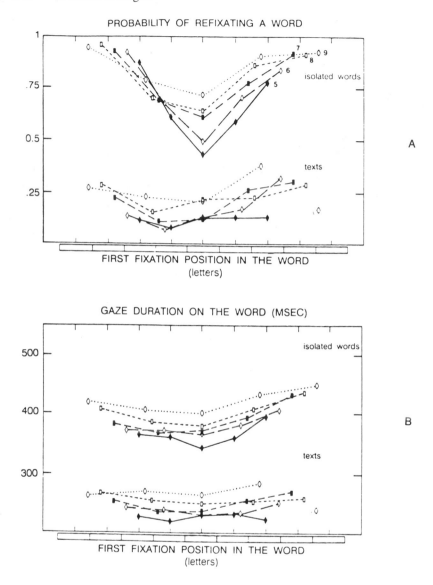

FIGURE 20.7. Data from an experiment comparing the optimal viewing position phenomenon in isolated words and in normal reading. A. Probability of refixating a word. B. Gaze duration on the word, as a function of the position in the word that the eye started fixating; data for the isolated word condition and the normal text reading condition are shown, and involved the same set of words of length five to nine letters. For nine-letter words, the data point for the fifth zone (in parentheses) corresponds to a case in which only 4% of the fixations occurred. Reprinted, by permission, from Vitu, O'Regan, & Mittau, 1990.

duration the effect was also much weaker in normal reading than in isolated words.

It might be thought that because the optimal viewing position phenomenon is so weak in normal reading, it has no relevance under normal circumstances. But exactly the opposite is true. The fact that the effect is so weak in normal reading, whereas in isolated words it is so strong, tells us that something very special is happening in normal reading—if we can determine what causes the effect to be so weak, this should give us a vital clue about what the special thing is that happens in normal reading.

One possible explanation for the weakening of the optimal viewing position phenomenon in normal reading might be that because of contextual constraints, the need to refixate a word when its optimal viewing position is not properly fixated would be diminished in normal reading. The refixation tactic used in isolated word reading could be modified so that it only comes into play with high probability when the eye is considerably further from the generally optimal viewing position than is the case for isolated words. In fact, different correction tactics could be adopted by readers depending on the degree of risk they could accept that words will not be identifiable from a single fixation. The riskiest tactic would be to make no correction tactics at all. In that case, only the general strategy of moving from word to word would be operating (see the examples of "careful" and "risky" strategies in Figure 20.5).

The leftward shift of the optimal viewing position in normal reading is a peculiar effect: one would have expected that parafoveal preprocessing of words would make it less important to fixate near their beginnings, because some information about them will have been gathered prior to their direct fixation. The optimal viewing position would therefore be expected to shift rightward rather than leftward. (Note that under the strategy-tactics theory this shift would have to be the result of a change in the general aiming strategy, not in moment-to-moment adjustment of saccade parameters as a function of parafoveal processing.) To further investigate both the weakening and the leftward shift of the optimal viewing position in normal reading, we did an experiment in which the same test words were presented either in predictable or neutral context, and either with or without the possibility of being parafoveally previewed (Vitu, 1991a). We were surprised to find that although context and parafoveal preview had global effects on the refixation probabilities (and gaze durations), making the time spent on words overall shorter, the penalties for not fixating the optimal viewing position did not weaken. Also, the minima of the optimal viewing position curves remained fairly central as found in isolated words, and did not either shift rightward, as expected from the idea that parafoveal preprocessing makes fixating the beginning of words less useful, or leftward, as found using the same words in normal reading.

In this experiment we had used a presentation paradigm that was not normal reading, but in which we had attempted to simulate normal reading conditions: the subject read the beginning of a sentence, which served as context, then moved the eyes back to the left of the screen to successively fixate two asterisks a few letters apart, then landed on the test word (which may or may not have been visible in the parafovea beforehand), and then continued with the rest of the sentence. However, the sentences were not related to one another, and a calibration check preceded each sentence. These conditions may not have generated the "riskier" scanning strategy and tactics that may be adopted in normal reading, and this may be the explanation why our optimal viewing position curves were more similar to those for reading isolated words than to those for normal reading. However, if this is true, it shows the importance of the strategy and tactics adopted by the reader, over and above context and peripheral preprocessing, in explaining reading behavior.

I turn now to another prediction of the strategy-tactics hypothesis that should be verified in the reading data. Because refixation tactics in words are assumed to be determined purely by visual information, in particular by the distance the eye lands from the generally optimal position, we should observe no dependence of refixation probabilities on linguistic factors. When data for high- and low-frequency words are separated in our reading experiment (Vitu et al., 1990) the refixation curves become rather noisy. Nevertheless, there is a suggestion that, contrary to the prediction, low-frequency words tend to be more often refixated than high-frequency words. Certainly, when all initial fixation positions are pooled, a significant effect appears.

This finding suggests that the strategy-tactics theory may be too extreme a stance to take. It may be that in reading, linguistic and contextual constraints are sufficiently strong that eye movements can sometimes be affected by ongoing processing even in the early stages of word recognition. If this is the case, then we can go back to the experiment we did in which the strength of the preceding context and parafoveal preprocessing was manipulated, and check that when context and parafoveal preprocessing are weak, refixation probabilities are independent of word frequency, but that they become dependent on word frequency when context and preprocessing are strong. This is exactly what we found (Vitu, 1991a).

Similar points can be made about fixation durations in the cases when single- and two-fixation tactics occur. Under the extreme version of the strategy-tactics theory, in reading, the duration of the first fixation when two are made should be independent of linguistic factors, and these should only play a role on the second fixation. The duration of single fixations should also only reflect linguistic factors if the fixations are rather long. Unfortunately, our data in the reading experiment become too sparse when they are divided up by frequency, and so we are not sure what happens. But in the reading-like experiment (Vitu, 1991a) where we manipulated context and parafoveal proprocessing, we observed that when there is neither context nor preprocessing, then both first fixations, when two occur, and single fixations, are not dependent on word frequency. Word frequency only influences the duration of the second fixation when two occur. However, when either parafoveal processing and/or context are available, first fixation of two and single fixations are slightly affected. In all cases the main portion of the effect of word frequency on gaze duration comes from its influence on the duration of the second fixation when two occur.

THE-Skipping

Up until this point I have only looked at the question of whether the within-word refixation tactics observed in normal reading conform to the predictions of the strategy-tactics theory. It will now be interesting to consider the word-to-word strategy component of the theory. With this component, I have assumed that the position the eye aims for cannot be determined by linguistic factors, and must only depend on the physical layout of the upcoming text material in parafoveal vision. This extreme hypothesis is exactly the opposite of the hypothesis that I had attempted to defend in an article published in 1980 (O'Regan, 1980). I had done an experiment in which saccade sizes were compared going toward the word THE and going toward a three-letter verb like HAD, WAS, ATE, etc. I had kept the preceding physical and linguistic context identical in order to make sure visuomotor factors could not cause the results, and had found that saccades were larger going toward the article than going toward verbs. I had attributed this difference to the ability of parafoveal linguistic processing to influence saccade size, contrary to what I would predict today from "strategy-tactics." This study is often cited, because the idea that the word THE can be "skipped" apparently appealed to many researchers. However, it should be noted that the word THE was never actually "skipped." Instead, what happened was that saccade sizes were slightly larger (one to two letters) going toward the word THE. Perhaps the effect could be accommodated in the strategy-tactics theory if we assumed that in context, and when fixation durations are particularly long or several occur on a word, there is sufficient time for linguistic information from the parafovea to accumulate and influence saccades.

The data from my earlier experiment are no longer available, and I did not at the time analyze them with this possibility in mind. I have therefore recently started to repeat the experiment in a French version. I used 10 sentence frames that could contain, in their middles, either an article or a verb, with everything before and after this critical location remaining identical, except for the last few words of the sentence. I measured saccade sizes leaving each position of the sentences, for 22 subjects (at

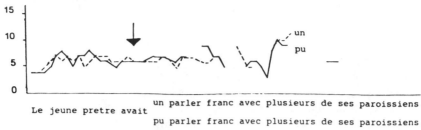

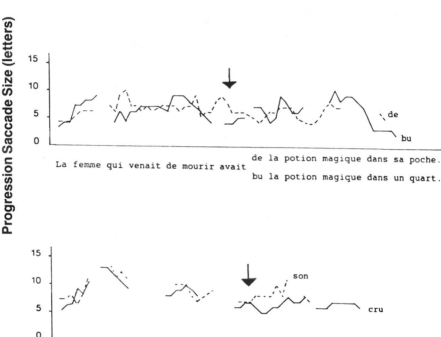

FIGURE 20.8. Progression saccade size for saccades leaving each letter of the sentences shown on the abscissa. Each data point is a median over saccades made by 22 subjects leaving that letter and the two adjacent letters. The solid curves correspond to sentences containing the verb, the dashed curves to sentences containing the article. Gaps in the curves are places where there were fewer than six saccades contributing to the data. The arrows show the critical location where differences in saccade sizes should occur if the eye is making use of parafoveal information about word identity to aim saccades. The top sentence is an example where no differences appeared. Seven out of ten of the sentences in this experiment gave data like this. The middle sentence is an example where a difference did appear in the critical region. However, this may have been noise, because similar differences appeared in other regions (see saccades leaving the word "qui" at the beginning of the sentence). The third sentence is the only sentence where the difference did appear to be significant.

present). Of the 10 sentences, 7 showed strictly similar saccade sizes approaching the critical region where there could be either the article or the verb. The top curve in Figure 20.8 shows an example. For three sentences there was a suggestion of larger saccades going toward the article, but judging from the variability of the curves (see the middle example) the difference may just be noise. The bottom case is the only case among the 10 sentence types where what looks like a reliable difference did occur in saccade size preceding the article or verb.

I conclude that THE-skipping is the exception not the rule (occurring here in only 1 out of 10 sentences), and that in the exceptional case when it occurs, it is rather weak, amounting to only a one to two letter difference. Of interest now is the question of whether this difference is due to cases where the fixation prior to the saccade was of longer than average duration. However, dividing the data into two classes in this way substantially increases variability, and with only 22 subjects I am presently unable to conclude.

Conclusion

I hope to have shown that the optimal viewing position phenomenon in words is a rich source of new ideas for understanding eye movement guidance in reading. I have presented an extreme hypothesis based on the idea that in reading the eye might be trying to get to the optimal viewing position, but cannot generally do so because it does not know where it is in advance, and because even if it did know, it would not be able to get there accurately. The hypothesis also involves the important idea that in the early stages of exploration of a word, lexical processing has not attained a stage where it can influence eye movement behavior. As a result of these constraints, the eye is obliged to adopt a general strategy of moving from place to place in the text, guided by purely visual cues such as the spaces between words. A plausible scheme for "careful, word-by-word reading" would be as follows: Strategy: move to just left of the middle of successive words. Tactics: when the eye falls somewhere else, refixate the word; when it lands near this position, move to the next word. Fixation durations in this scheme would be mainly determined by visuomotor constraints, with a trade-off between the first and second fixation durations when two are made in the word. Linguistic factors would influence only the second of two fixations in a word, and the duration of single fixations when these are long.

A scheme for "riskier" reading would be as follow: Strategy: move from word to word, aiming for near left of the middle of the next word. Tactics: none, i.e., do not refixate when the aimed-for position is not attained. Under this scheme, fixation durations would only reflect the visuomotor constraints involved in aiming each successive saccade. Of course, when comprehension fails, the strategy would be interrupted, and the more careful, word-by-word scheme would replace it. Because the zone of difficulty will most likely have been overshot by the ongoing strategy, a regression would then be necessary to bring it back to the sentence region that posed a problem.

Work in the eye movement literature over the last decades has not been oriented toward testing the strategy-tactics hypothesis, and the predictions it makes about how fixation durations should depend on within-word eye position and linguistic factors. I have reviewed what data there is in O'Regan (1990) and have come to the conclusion that nothing so far contradicts the hypothesis. The recent experimental results that we have obtained in attempting to test the theory have also up to now been compatible with it. However, it seems that its most extreme version may be false: it may be that when linguistic context is strong and parafoveal preprocessing can be done, linguistic processing can slightly influence fixation durations and (much more rarely) saccade sizes, particularly in the later stages of word exploration. Nevertheless, the fact that the influence of linguistic variables on eye movements in reading is weak is compatible with the theory.

An aspect of the theory that would be interesting to pursue is the possibility that, depending on their attitude toward the text, readers may be able to adopt strategies and tactics involving different degrees of risk. It is common knowledge that a reader can choose to read faster or slower, and the theory suggests predictions about how the optimal viewing position phenomenon and reading behavior might be modified in these conditions. The possibility also exists that some portion of differences in reading ability might be related to a reader's knowledge of where the optimal viewing position in words of the language generally is, and in the efficiency of his or her choice of exploration strategy.

References

Coëffé, C. (1987). Two ways of improving saccade accuracy. In J.K. O'Regan & A. Lévy-Schoen (Eds.), *Eye movements: from physiology to cognition* (pp. 105–113). Amsterdam: North Holland.

Coëffé, C., & O'Regan, J.K. (1987). Reducing the influence of non-target stimuli on saccade accuracy: predictability and latency effects. *Vision Research, 27,* 227–240.

Dunn-Rankin, P. (1978). The visual characteristics of words. *Scientific American, 238,* 122–130.

Findlay, J.M. (1981). Local and global influences on saccadic eye movements. In: D.F. Fisher, R.A. Monty, J.W. Senders (Eds.), *Eye movements: Cognition and visual perception* (pp. 171–180). Hillsdale, NJ: Erlbaum.

Findlay, J.M. (1982). Global visual processing for saccadic eye movements. *Vision Research, 21,* 347–354.

Findlay, J.M. (1987). Visual computation and saccadic eye movements: a theoretical perspective. *Spatial Vision*, 2, 175–189.

Holmes, V.M., & O'Regan, J.K. (1987). Decomposing French words. In J.K. O'Regan & A. Lévy-Schoen (Eds.), *Eye movements: from physiology to cognition* (pp. 459–466). Amsterdam: North Holland.

Inhoff, A.W. (1986). Preparing sequences of saccades under choice reaction conditions: effects of sequence length and context. *Acta Psychologica*, 61, 211–228.

Jacobs, A.M., & O'Regan, J.K. (1987). Spatial and/or temporal adjustments of scanning behavior to visibility changes. *Acta Psychologica*, 65, 133–146.

Lévy-Schoen, A., O'Regan, J.K., Jacobs, A.M., & Coeffé, C. (1984). The relation between visibility span and eye movements in various scanning tasks. In A.G. Gale & F. Johnson (Eds.), *Theoretical and applied aspects of eye movement research* (pp. 133–142). Amsterdam: North Holland.

McConkie, G.W., Kerr, P.W., Reddix, M.D., & Zola, D. (1988). Eye movement control during reading: I. The location of initial eye fixations on words. *Vision Research*, 28, 1107–1118.

McConkie, G.W., Kerr, P.W., Reddix, M.D., Zola, D., & Jacobs, A.M. (1989) Eye movement control during reading: II: Frequency of refixating a word. *Perception and Psychophysics*, 46, 245–253.

McConkie, G.W., & Rayner, K. (1975). The span of the effective stimulus during a fixation in reading. *Perception and Psychophysics*, 17, 578–586.

Nazir, T.A. (1991). On refixations in letter strings: the influence of the oculomotor system. *Perception and Psychophysics*, 49, 373–389.

Nazir, T.A., O'Regan, J.K., & Jacobs, A.M. (1991). On words and their letters. *Bulletin of the Psychonomics Society*, 29, 171–174.

O'Regan, J.K. (1979). Eye guidance in reading: evidence for the linguistic control hypothesis. *Perception and Psychophysics*, 25(6), 501–509.

O'Regan, J.K. (1980). The control of saccade size and fixation duration in reading: the limits of linguistic control. *Perception and Psychophysics*, 28, 112–117.

O'Regan, J.K. (1981). The convenient viewing position hypothesis. In: D.F. Fisher, R.A. Monty, & J.W. Senders (Eds.), *Eye movements: Cognition and visual perception* (pp. 289–298). Hillsdale, NS: L. Erlbaum.

O'Regan, J.K. (1983). Elementary perceptual and eye movement control processes in reading. In K. Rayner (Ed.), *Eye movements in reading: perceptual and language processes* (pp. 121–139). New York: Academic Press.

O'Regan, J.K. (1989). Visual acuity, lexical structure, and eye movements in word recognition. In B.A.G. Elsendoorn & H. Bouma, (Eds.) *Working models of human perception* (pp. 261–292). London: Academic Press.

O'Regan, J.K. (1990). Eye movements and reading. In E. Kowler (Ed.), *Eye movements and their role in visual and cognitive processes* (Vol. 4 of Reviews of Oculomotor Research, pp. 395–453). Amsterdam: Elsevier.

O'Regan, J.K., & Jacobs, A.M. (1992). The optimal viewing position effect in word recognition: A challenge to current theory. *Journal of Experimental Psychology, Human Perception and Performance*, 18(1), 185–197.

O'Regan, J.K., & Lévy-Schoen, A. (1987). Eye movement strategy and tactics in word recognition and reading. In M. Coltheart (Ed.); *Attention and performance XII: The psychology of reading* (pp. 363–383). Hillsdale, NJ: Erlbaum.

O'Regan, J.K., Lévy-Schoen, A., & Jacobs, A. (1983). The effect of visibility on eye movement parameters in reading. *Perception and Psychophysics, 34*, 457–464.

O'Regan, J.K., Lévy-Schoen, A., Pynte, J., & Brugaillère, (1984). Convenient fixation location within isolated words of different length and structure. *Journal of Experimental Psychology: Human Perception and Performance, 10*(2), 250–257.

Rayner, K. (1979). Eye guidance in reading: Fixation locations within words. *Perception, 8*, 21–30.

Rayner, K., & Pollatsek, A. (1987). Eye movements in reading: A tutorial review. In M. Coltheart (Ed.), *Attention and performance XII: The psychology of reading* (pp 327–362). Hillsdale, NJ: Erlbaum.

Reder, S.M. (1973). On-line monitoring of eye position signals in contingent and noncontingent paradigms. *Behavior Research Methods and Instrumentation, 5*, 218–227.

Vitu, F. (1991a). The influence of parafoveal preprocessing and linguistic context on the optimal landing position effect. *Perception and Psychophysics, 50*, 58–75.

Vitu, F. (1991b). The existence of a center of gravity effect during reading. *Vision Research, 31*, 1289–1313.

Vitu, F., O'Regan, J.K., & Mittau, M. (1990). Optimal landing position in reading isolated words and continuous text. *Perception and Psychophysics, 47*, 583–600.

Zingale, C.M., & Kowler, E. (1987). Planning sequences of saccades. *Vision Research, 27*, 1327–1341.

21
Integrating Text Across Fixations in Reading and Copytyping

ALBRECHT WERNER INHOFF, GREGORY BOHEMIER, and
DEBORAH BRIIHL

Visual acuity decreases sharply from the center of the fovea toward the periphery so that high-acuity vision occurs only in a relatively small retinal area, consisting of the fovea and the immediately adjacent para-fovea. Although the area of high-acuity vision is relatively small, it can be greatly expanded via the execution of eye movements. A visual area that is outside the range of high-acuity vision at one point in time may be analyzed via high-acuity vision, after an eye movement (saccade) to the area of interest has been executed. The goal of the present chapter is to examine the integration of text across saccades (i.e., successive fixations) and oculomotor control. Two tasks, reading for comprehension and the copytyping of text, will be considered. Relatively little work has been done in the study of oculomotor control during copytyping and its description will be sketchy.

The studies discussed below are based on research using the moving window technique introduced by McConkie and Rayner (1975). In these experiments, eye movements are used to control the visual display on-line. During each fixation, readers view legible text within a predefined spatial region of text (the window) with mutilated text outside this region; the window is moved in synchrony with the eyes to maintain control over readers' visual viewing conditions (Pollatsek & Rayner, this volume). Most studies use the cumulated viewing time on a word, called gaze duration, as the dependent measure (e.g., Just & Carpenter, 1980). Following Inhoff (1984), more recent studies frequently discriminate between gaze durations and the duration of the first fixation on a word.

The Range of Effective Vision in Reading

Skilled readers obtain effective visual information up to approximately 15 character spaces to the right of fixation (McConkie & Rayner, 1975; Rayner, 1975; Rayner & Bertera, 1979; Rayner, Inhoff, Morrison, Slowiaczek, & Bertera, 1981). These effects are found in several variables including the size of interword saccades and fixation durations on words. In general, nearly all effective visual information is obtained from the directly fixated word and the next word in the text (e.g., Balota, Pollatsek, & Rayner, 1985; Blanchard, Pollatsek, & Rayner, 1989; Inhoff, 1989a, 1989b, 1990; Inhoff, Pollatsek, Posner, & Rayner, 1989; Lima, 1987; Lima & Inhoff, 1985; McConkie & Rayner, 1975; Rayner, 1975; Rayner et al. 1981; Rayner, Well, Pollatsek, & Bertera, 1982). Following the convention of earlier studies, we will use the term *foveal word* to refer to the directly fixated word and the term *parafoveal word* to refer to the spatially adjacent next word in the text.

In the majority of instances the parafoveally available word is the recipient of a fixation, presumably because it was not identified prior to the decision to move the eyes to its location. Comparisons of reading conditions that either afford a (pre)view of the parafoveal word prior to its fixation or deny such previews showed that prior preview decreases subsequent first fixation durations and gaze durations on words (this will be referred to as the *parafoveal preview effect*), indicating that parafoveally obtained word or letter information is stored across interword saccades and integrated with subsequently obtained word information.

Effects of Retinal Acuity

It appears plausible to assume that the visual resolution of a parafoveal preview determines its usefulness during the integration of visual information across fixations. Visual search studies, in which subjects are required to detect individual target letters within a continuous line of "distractor" letters, showed that small increases in the retinal eccentricity of target letters decreased identification accuracy (Rayner & Fisher, 1987a, 1987b). Yet, counter to the visual search data, small changes in the retinal eccentricity of parafoveally available words seem to have negligible effects on the magnitude of parafoveal preview benefits during sentence reading (Inhoff, 1987, 1989a, 1990). In the experiments, subjects read sentences that were written either in a standard left-to-right direction, or in a reversed right-to-left direction; e.g., the sentence

(1) Everyone finally went shopping

was read in a standard left-to-right direction (as in sentence 1) or in a reversed right-to-left direction:

(2) shopping went finally Everyone

Preview of the initial letters of a word, e.g., "shoXXXXX" when "went" was fixated, was thus near the point of fixation when reading left to right and relatively far from fixation when reading right to left. Nevertheless, beginning letter previews yielded nearly equivalent preview benefits for both reading directions. Consistent with earlier work (see Rayner & Pollatsek, 1987, 1989, for summaries), we also observed larger preview benefits from previews of a word's beginning letters than from its final letters; this occurred even when beginning and ending letter previews were equidistant to the fixated word (Inhoff, 1987, 1989a, 1990). Taken together, these results indicate that small variations in the retinal eccentricity of parafoveally available words do not affect parafoveal preview benefits.

It is possible that changes in reading direction affect word fixation strategies, which could account for the lack of eccentricity effects. During normal left-to-right reading, readers tend to fixate slightly to the left of the word center (Inhoff, 1989a; O'Regan, 1979, 1983; Rayner, 1979). For instance, in sample sentence (1), the second letter "e" and the letter "r" of "Everyone" should be the most likely recipients of the word's initial fixation. When this is the case, the adjacent parafoveal word begins seven and six character spaces, respectively, to the right of the fixated letter. During reversed right-to-left reading, readers may fixate the beginning letters of words, e.g., the letters "E" or "v" of "Everyone", in which case the preview occurs eight or nine character spaces, respectively, to the left of the fixated letter. Differences in the retinal eccentricity of parafoveal previews in the normal and reversed reading conditions could thus be small, hence similar parafoveal preview effects in the normal and reversed reading conditions.

However, the outcome of a recent analysis (Inhoff & Tousman, 1990) directly rejects the possibility that retinal eccentricity is the primary determiner of parafoveal preview effects. In the study, parafoveal preview benefits were examined as a function of the size of the saccade to the parafoveal word. When the interword saccade was small, parafoveal previews were near the location of the following fixation; when interword saccades were large, parafoveal previews were relatively far from the location of the following fixation. Saccade size affected the duration of the following fixation with longer fixation durations following long saccades than short saccades. Yet, shorter saccades did not yield larger parafoveal preview benefits. As can be seen in Figure 21.1, preview benefits were even somewhat smaller after short saccades. Consistent with this finding, Inhoff and Rayner (1986) obtained larger preview benefits from parafoveally available high-frequency words than from low-frequency words (when first fixations were analyzed), irrespective of the size of the saccade to high- and low-frequency parafoveal words.

Small variations in the retinal eccentricity of parafoveal previews thus cannot account for the use of parafoveal information and the integration of text across fixations. Instead, the acquisition and use of parafoveal information in reading may be subject to task demands: as the *linguistic* processing of text becomes more difficult, less useful information is obtained from the parafovea (Henderson & Ferreira, 1990; Inhoff et al.,

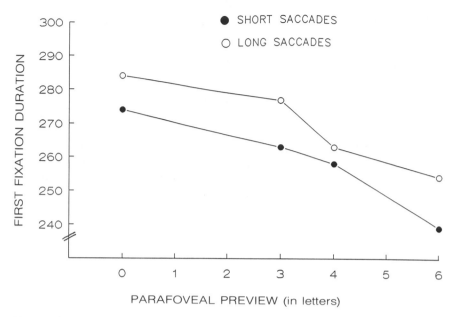

FIGURE 21.1. First fixation durations on six-letter target words as a function of saccade size and prior parafoveal preview.

1989). This is not to deny that the visibility of text affects its encoding (see below). Instead, we propose that readers seek—and generally obtain—some type of useful information from parafoveal words, irrespective of small variations in the eccentricity of previewed parafoveal words.

The Range of Effective Vision in Copytyping

To determine the perceptual span in copytyping, we (Inhoff & Wang, in press) asked eight skilled typists to copy short paragraphs of text under different viewing conditions. Across different blocks of trials, typists viewed the directly fixated letter and 8 letters of text to its left plus either 1, 3, 5, 7, 9, or 11 characters of text to the right of the fixated letter. The results showed that typists' fixation position was, on average, three character spaces ahead of the executed key-press. Using the size of inter-word saccades as dependent measure, the results also showed asymptotic saccade size values when seven or more character spaces of text were available to the right of *fixation* and asymptotic inter–key-press times and gaze durations when three or more character spaces of text were visible.

The range of effective vision, used to control saccade size and gaze duration, is thus considerably smaller in copytyping than in reading. Given that the same perceptual and retinal acuity limitations apply to the visual encoding of text during reading and copytyping, these results indicate again that the perceptual span is not solely a function of retinal acuity limitations. As suggested by the reading studies, task demands appear to determine the range of effective vision. During copytyping, the relatively time-consuming translation of encoded letters and words into manual movement sequences appears to constrain the acquisition and use of visual information.

The Representation of Parafoveally Obtained Information in Reading

Earlier work indicated that readers integrate relatively abstract information across saccades (McConkie & Zola, 1979; Rayner, McConkie, & Zola, 1980). Rayner et al. (1980) suggested that previews activate abstract *letter* units corresponding to the parafoveal word's beginning letters. These representations facilitate recognition during the word's subsequent fixation. However, more recent results indicated, first, that readers obtain useful information from all letters of the parafoveal word and, second, that parafoveally obtained word information is represented in a lexical format.

Evidence showing that all letters of the parafoveal word contribute to the preview effect has taken two forms. First, preview of complete parafoveal words yields substantially larger preview benefits than preview of the words' beginning letters alone (e.g., Inhoff, 1989a, 1989b, 1990). Second, ending letters of parafoveal words yield a significant preview benefit when they can be discriminated from uninformative beginning letters (Inhoff, 1989a).

Evidence showing that a lexical format is used has taken several forms. For instance, the cumulated preview benefit from a six-letter target words' beginning and ending trigram is considerably smaller than the preview benefit from the intact six-letter preview (Inhoff, 1989a, 1990), presumably because the complete six-letter preview offers some lexical information that cannot be gleaned from separate trigram previews. Other results corroborate this view. Preview of a high-frequency word yields a larger preview benefit than a length-matched low-frequency word (Inhoff & Rayner, 1986). Similarly, the usefulness of a parafoveal preview is a function of the predictability of the parafoveally available word with larger preview benefits for high-predictable words than for length-matched low-predictable words (Balota et al., 1985).

Taken together, these results converge in showing that readers use a lexical format to integrate text across fixations. In the following discussion, we will refer to this account as the *lexical text integration hypothesis*.

If parafoveal previews are used to activate lexical representations, then it may be possible that lexically significant subword units play a special role in the use of parafoveal previews. Taft and Forster (1976; Forster, 1976; Taft, 1979) suggested that readers use specific word-initial subword units, called *lexical access codes*, to search and activate lexical representations. According to this view, the word recognition process begins with the parsing of a word's initial letters into a letter sequence that corresponds to an access code; the code is then used to activate all lexical entries sharing the code. Lexical search is then applied to the set of activated entries to identify the fixated word. If this process was used to identify words, then parafoveally obtained information may be used to identify the access code prior to the word's fixation.

Two studies examined the role of morphologically defined subword units. In one of these studies, Lima (1987) used parafoveal previews that revealed either the beginning morpheme, e.g., "re" of "revive", or the beginning pseudomorpheme, e.g., "re" of "relish", of parafoveal words prior to fixation (the remaining letters of the parafoveal word were masked). The results showed equivalent preview benefits from prefixes and pseudoprefixes, indicating that the morphological status contributed little to the magnitude of preview benefits. In a second study, Inhoff (1989b) examined whether readers use the word's beginning morpheme to access lexical representations. Six-letter target words containing 2 three-letter morphemes (e.g., "cowboy") and 2 three-letter pseudomorphemes (e.g., "carpet") were embedded in declarative sentences. Different parafoveal preview conditions were used that revealed either no useful information about the parafoveal target word, the target's initial three letters, its initial four letters, or all six letters of the target prior to subsequent target fixation. Upon its fixation, the complete target was visible. The results showed virtually equivalent preview benefits from morphemes and from pseudomorphemes, again indicating that the morphemic status of the word's initial trigram contributed little to the parafoveal preview benefit. Other word access codes, such as Taft's basic orthographic syllabic structure (BOSS) also received little empirical support (Inhoff, 1989b).

Furthermore, lexical constraints, imposed by the parafoveal word's initial letters, do not affect the parafoveal preview benefit. Parafoveal previews in Lima and Inhoff's (1985) study consisted of trigrams that either strongly or loosely constrained the number of compatible word candidates. For instance, the high-constraint letter sequence "dwa" agrees with relatively few word candidates, the low-constraint letter sequence "roo" agrees with a large number of word candidates. Again, lexical constraint, imposed by a partial-word segment, did not affect the magnitude of the parafoveal preview benefit. Rather than integrating information from lexically significant subword units across fixations, readers appear to use lexical information conveyed by all letters of the parafoveally available word.

Effects of Retinal Acuity Revisited

When words of five or more letters are to be read, readers tend to fixate slightly to the left of the word center (O'Regan, 1983; Rayner, 1979). The preference for these positions is maintained, even when the prior parafoveal preview of a to-be-fixated word reveals only its length (e.g., a string of Xs that matches the word in length) but no useful linguistic information (Inhoff, 1989a). The positioning of the eyes near the center of words provides an "optimal" intraword fixation location as it triggers the lowest number of intraword refixations (McConkie, Kerr, Redix, Zola, & Jacobs, 1989; Vitu, O'Regan, & Mittau, 1990), yields the shortest gaze durations (O'Regan, Levy-Schoen, Pynte, & Brugailliere, 1984; Vitu et al., 1990; see also O'Regan, this volume), and word naming latencies (O'Regan, 1983). In general, these effects of the optimal viewing location are attributed to effects of retinal acuity, which affords the highest mean acuity per letter when fixations are placed near the center of words.

Notice that this explanation rests on the assumption that small variations in retinal eccentricity affect the processing of directly fixated words. This appears at odds with the claim made previously in this chapter (see The Range of Effective Vision in Reading) that small variations in the retinal eccentricity of parafoveally available words do not affect the processing of these stimuli. Superficially, it appears that the processing of the directly fixated word should be less subject to effects of retinal eccentricity than the processing of the adjacent parafoveal word, given that all letters of the directly fixated word generally enjoy a higher visual acuity than any of the letters of the parafoveal word. Nevertheless, we will argue that a visual acuity account of the optimal viewing position effect is essentially correct.

This account appears plausible if we assume that the processing of directly fixated foveal words and yet-to-be-fixated parafoveal words is subject to different goals. According to our view, readers identify the directly fixated word and interpret the word within its linguistic context; furthermore, during word fixation, some episodic tagging of the word appears to occur (e.g., determine that the fixated word was read within a specific context, occupied a specific line/page position, etc.). If gaze durations reflect the time needed for the completion of visual, lexical, syntactic, and postlexical (episodic tagging) processes, then variations in the visual analysis of a fixated word should directly affect the word's gaze duration.

Readers may pursue a different goal during the processing of parafoveally coded words. Information from these words appears to be used to direct the saccade to the right and to select or activate a set of lexical descriptions that is compatible with parafoveally coded information.

Saccade programming and the lexical activation/selection process could occur relatively fast. Small variations in eccentricity and/or the temporal availability of parafoveal previews could then have little or no effect. Consistent with this view, Henderson and Ferreira (1990) obtained larger parafoveal preview benefits when high-frequency words were fixated than when low-frequency words were fixated, even though less time was available for parafoveal word processing when high-frequency words were fixated.

Oculomotor Control in Reading

Saccades intervene between the acquisition and subsequent use of para-foveal word information and some discussion has been focused on the movement control mode that determines the timing and positioning of saccades. We will discriminate between two programming models: *early* and *late* saccade programming. Within the framework of both types of saccade programming models, we will further ask if the oculomotor system uses the same types of information to determine the size of saccades and to determine the duration of individual fixations.

Early saccade programming models assume that the decision when and where to move the eyes is made during the initial phase of a fixation in reading. This view has been espoused by a large number of reading researchers (Inhoff, 1989a; Inhoff & Rayner, 1986; Morrison, 1984; Pollatsek & Rayner, 1982; Pollatsek, Rayner, & Balota, 1986; Rayner, Slowiaczek, Clifton, & Bertera; 1983). Late programming models assume that subjects first complete the processing of the directly fixated word and then determine the location of the next fixation (Henderson & Ferreira, 1990; Just & Carpenter, 1980).

One recent finding provided major support for a late model of saccade programming. As indicated before, Henderson and Ferreira (1990), found that the usefulness of parafoveal previews was a function of the processing difficulty of the directly fixated word. According to the "late" model of saccade programming, visuospatial attention is shifted to the parafoveal after the processing of the fixated word has been completed. These attention shifts trigger saccade programming and saccade execution. Fixation of difficult text delays the shifting of attention to the parafoveal word information and the corresponding saccade execution.

However, the programming of a saccade need not be identical with saccade execution. Specifically, readers may *program* a saccade relatively early in a fixation; after some interval, this program may be *committed to action*; after yet another interval, e.g., when the linguistic processing of the fixated word has been completed, the movement may be *executed*. Research on manual movement programming and movement execution has shown, for instance, that movement planning can precede movement execution by a variable amount of time (Rosenbaum, Inhoff, & Gordon, 1984) and that movement execution occurs relatively late in the sequence of processing stages (Osman, Kornblum, & Meyer, 1990). Similar movement planning processes may apply to oculomotor control (Abrams, this volume). According to this view, readers could have planned the eye movement to the parafoveal word relatively early in Henderson and Ferreira's (1990) study, but executed these movements only after the processing of the fixated word had been completed.

Other data appear incompatible with late models of saccade programming. Morris, Rayner, and Pollatsek (1990) showed that readers obtain useful information from parafoveally available word previews *throughout* fixation durations. Furthermore, the size of the saccade seemed to be determined relatively early in a fixation. Similarly, Pollatsek and Rayner (1982) showed that word boundary (word length) information was coded within the initial 50 ms of a fixation. As word length is the primary determiner of saccade size (see Rayner & Pollatsek, 1987), these data support an early saccade programming model.

To determine if the same sources of information control fixation durations and saccade programming, Rayner and McConkie (1976) applied a correlational analyses to fixation durations and saccade size. The results showed no significant correlation between the two components of oculomotor behavior, which led to the view that autonomous processes support fixation durations and saccades.

More recent findings argue, however, against strict autonomy. Pollatsek and Rayner (1982) found that the availability of word length information affected fixation durations and saccade size. Furthermore, large saccades are followed by longer fixation durations than short saccades (Inhoff & Rayner, 1986; Pollatsek et al., 1986). The same type(s) of information thus can affect specification of saccade size and of fixation durations.

One way to accommodate these discrepant findings is to assume that fixation durations and saccade size are constrained by the same types of information under some conditions but not under other conditions. Following Inhoff and Rayner (1986) and Pollatsek et al. (1986), Inhoff (1989a) proposed a time-locked model of saccade control that rests on the following assumptions: (a) the decision of where to send the eyes is made relatively early in a fixation; (b) all sources of parafoveally available information are consulted until the saccade program is committed to action; (c) parafoveal word information can be obtained after the saccade program has been committed to action, until the eye movement is executed.

Results of Inhoff's (1989a) study are consistent with the model. The experiments determined how parafoveal previews affected first fixation durations and saccade size to a six-letter parafoveal word under three different parafoveal viewing conditions, which revealed either its beginning trigram, its ending trigram, or all six letters (the foveal word and text to its left were always visible). When contrasted with a no-preview condition, first fixation durations were significantly shorter and saccades significantly larger when the complete parafoveal word had been visible. However, when beginning and ending trigram previews were available, preview benefits were evident in the subsequent first fixation durations on previewed words but not in size of the saccade to these words. Apparently, readers obtained useful information from the parafoveal word after the oculomotor program had been committed to action. This information affected subsequent fixation durations but not saccade size.

Oculomotor control during *copytyping* shows several similarities to oculomotor control during reading, even though the range of effective vision is considerably smaller in this task. Interword saccades are particularly sensitive to word length during copytyping (Inhoff & Wang, in press) and, as previously indicated, during reading (Inhoff, 1989a; Morris et al., 1990; O'Regan, 1980; Pollatsek & Rayner, 1982). Analogously, gaze durations, are sensitive to lexical and postlexical processes during copytyping (Inhoff & Wang, in press) and reading (see Rayner & Pollatsek, 1987, 1989 for summaries). Furthermore, it appears that useful information is obtained farther into the periphery when effects of parafoveal previews on saccade size are considered than when effects of previews on gaze durations are considered, irrespective of whether a copytyping task (Inhoff & Wang, in press) or a reading task (e.g., Rayner et al., 1981) is used. It is unclear, however, whether the time-locked model of saccade control also applies to saccade programming during copytyping.

Saccade Preprogramming During Reading

The "early" time-locked model of saccade computation, as outlined above, assumes that each saccade is computed during the immediately preceding fixation. However, there are exceptions to this case and readers may program more than one saccade during some fixations (Morrison, 1984). How can the time-locked model of saccade programming account for the programming of more than one saccade during a fixation? As indicated before, the model assumes that the size of the saccade to the parafoveal word is determined early in a fixation. At a later point in time, this motor program is committed to action. Under some circumstance, e.g., when a short and highly familiar word is parafoveally available, word recognition may occur after the initial saccade programming has been completed, but before the computed saccade has been committed to action. In this case, readers may program a second (corrective) saccade farther into the periphery and either cancel the previously determined saccade or execute the previously programmed saccade, fixate for a very short amount of time, and then saccade to the corrected fixation location. Still, even after a second (corrective) saccade has been computed and the first saccade has been canceled, some interval will elapse before the corrected saccade is actually launched. Within this interval, readers may again obtain some useful parafoveal information that may affect the subsequent fixation duration.

Summary

The usefulness of parafoveal previews appears to be task dependent. During reading, effective information is obtained from *all* letters of the parafoveal word and small variations in the visual acuity of the para-foveally available stimulus do not appear to affect its usefulness. Para-foveally obtained information appears to activate lexical representations that may facilitate lexical and postlexical processes during the previewed word's subsequent fixation.

The initial programming of a saccade to a parafoveal word appears to be based on (low-level) word length information. This type of parafoveal information is available relatively early. However, some time may elapse before the computed saccade is committed to action and before a committed saccade is executed. During the interval between the initial saccade planning and its commitment to action, a second saccade may be planned. During the interval between commitment to action and movement execution, some useful information may be obtained from the to-be-fixated word affecting subsequent fixation duration on the previewed word without affecting saccade size to the word.

References

Balota, D.A., Pollatsek, A., & Rayner, K. (1985). The interaction of contextual constraints and parafoveal visual information in reading. *Cognitive Psychology*, *17*, 364–390.

Blanchard, H.E., Pollatsek, A., & Rayner, K. (1989). The acquisition of parafoveal word information in reading. *Perception & Psychophysics*, *46*, 85–94.

Forster, K.I. (1976). Accessing the mental lexicon. In R.J. Wales & E.W. Walker (Eds.), *New approaches to language mechanisms* (pp. 257–287). Amsterdam: North Holland.

Henderson, J.M., & Ferreira, F. (1990). The effect of foveal processing difficulty on the perceptual span in reading: Implications for attention and eye movement control. *Journal of Experimental Psychology: Learning, Memory, and Cognition*, *16*, 417–429.

Inhoff, A.W. (1984). Two stages of word processing during eye fixations in the reading of prose. *Journal of Verbal learning and Verbal Behavior*, *23*, 612–624.

Inhoff, A.W. (1987). Parafoveal processing of words during eye fixations in reading: Effects of visual salience and word structure. In M. Coltheart (Ed.), *Attention and performance, XII*, (pp. 403–417). Hillsdale, NJ: Lawrence Erlbaum.

Inhoff, A.W. (1989a). Parafoveal processing of words and saccade computation during eye fixations in reading. *Journal of Experimental Psychology: Human Perception and Performance, 15*, 544–555.

Inhoff, A.W. (1989b). Lexical access during eye fixations in reading: Are word access codes used to integrate lexical information across interword fixations? *Journal of Memory and Language, 28*, 444–461.

Inhoff, A.W. (1990). Integrating information across eye fixations in reading. *Acta Psychologica, 73*, 281–297.

Inhoff, A.W., Pollatsek, A., Posner, M.I., & Rayner, K. (1989). Covert attention and eye movements during reading. *Quarterly Journal of Experimental Psychology, 41a*, 63–89.

Inhoff, A.W., & Rayner, K. (1986). Parafoveal word processing during eye fixations in reading: Effects of word frequency. *Perception & Psychophysics, 40*, 431–440.

Inhoff, A.W., & Tousman, S. (1990). Lexical integration across saccades in reading. *Psychological Research, 330*–337.

Inhoff, A.W. & Wang, J. (in press), Visual encoding of text, manual movement planning, and eye-hand coordination during copytyping. *Journal of Experimental Psychology: Human Perception and Performance.*

Just, M., & Carpenter, P.A. (1980). A theory of reading: From eye fixations to comprehension. *Psychological Review, 87*, 329–354.

Lima, S.D. (1987). Morphological analysis in sentence reading. *Journal of Memory and Language, 26*, 84–99.

Lima, S.D., & Inhoff, A.W. (1985). Lexical access during eye fixations in reading: Effects of word initial letter sequence. *Journal of Experimental Psychology: Human Perception and Performance, 13*, 272–285.

McConkie, G.W., Kerr, P.W., Redix, M.D., Zola, D., & Jacobs, A.M. (1989). Eye movement control during reading: II. Frequency of refixating a word. *Perception & Psychophysics, 46*, 245–253.

McConkie, G.W., & Rayner, K. (1975). The span of the effective stimulus during a fixation in reading. *Perception & Psychophysics, 17*, 578–586.

McConkie, G.W., & Zola, D. (1979). Is visual information integrated across successive fixations in reading? *Perception & Psychophysics, 25*, 221–224.

Morris, R.K., Rayner, K., & Pollatsek, A. (1990). Eye movement guidance in reading: The role of parafoveal letter and space information. *Journal of Experimental Psychology: Human Perception and Performance, 16*, 268–281.

Morrison, R.E. (1984). Manipulation of stimulus onset delay in reading: Evidence for parallel programming of saccades. *Journal of Experimental Psychology: Human Perception and Performance, 10*, 667–682.

O'Regan, J.K. (1979). Eye guidance in reading: Evidence for the linguistic control hypothesis. *Perception & Psychophysics, 25*, 501–509.

O'Regan, J.K. (1980). Control of saccade size and fixation duration in reading: The limits of linguistic control. *Perception & Psychophysics, 28*, 501–509.

O'Regan, J.K. (1983). Elementary perception and eye movement control processes in reading. In K. Rayner (Ed.), *Eye movements in reading: Perceptual and linguistic processes* (pp. 121–140). New York: Academic Press.

O'Regan, J.K. Levy-Schoen, A., Pynte, J., & Brugailliere, B. (1984). Convenient fixation location within isolated words of different length and structure. *Journal of Experimental Psychology: Human Perception and Performance, 10,* 250–257.

Osman, A., Kornblum, S., & Meyer, D.E. (1990). Does motor programming necessitate response execution? *Journal of Experimental Psychology: Human Perception and Performance, 16,* 183–198.

Pollatsek, A., & Rayner, K. (1982). Eye movement control in reading: The role of word boundaries. *Journal of Experimental Psychology: Human Perception and Performance, 8,* 817–833.

Pollatsek, A., Rayner, K., & Balota, D.A. (1986). Inferences about eye movement control from the perceptual span in reading. *Perception & Psychophysics, 40,* 123–130.

Rayner, K. (1975). The perceptual span and peripheral cues in reading. *Cognitive Psychology, 7,* 65–81.

Rayner, K. (1979). Eye guidance in reading: Fixation locations within words. *Perception, 8,* 21–30.

Rayner, K., & Bertera, J.B. (1979). Reading without a fovea. *Science, 206,* 468–469.

Rayner, K., & Fisher, D.L. (1987a). Letter processing during eye fixations in visual search. *Perception & Psychophysics, 42,* 87–100.

Rayner, K., & Fisher, D.L. (1987b). Eye movements and the perceptual span during visual search. In J.K. O'Regan & A. Levy-Schoen (Eds.), *Eye movements: From physiology to cognition* (pp. 293–302). Amsterdam: North-Holland.

Rayner, K., Inhoff, A.W., Morrison, R.E., Slowiaczek, M.L., & Bertera, J.B. (1981). Masking of foveal and parafoveal vision during eye fixations in reading. *Journal of Experimental Psychology: Human Perception and Performance, 7,* 167–179.

Rayner, K., & McConkie, G.W. (1976). What guides a reader's eye movements. *Vision Research, 16,* 829–837.

Rayner, K., McConkie, G.W., & Zola, D. (1980). Integrating information across eye movements. *Cognitive Psychology, 12,* 206–226.

Rayner, K., & Pollatsek, A. (1987). Eye movements in reading: A tutorial review. In M. Coltheart, (Ed). *Attention and performance, XII.* London: Erlbaum.

Rayner, K., & Pollatsek, A. (1989). *The psychology of reading.* Englewood Cliffs, NJ: Prentice Hall.

Rayner, K., Slowiaczek, M.L., Clifton, C.E., & Bertera, J.B. (1983). Latency of sequential eye movements; implications for reading. *Journal of Experimental Psychology: Human Perception and Performance, 9,* 912–922.

Rayner, K., Well, A.D., Pollatsek, A., & Bertera, J.B. (1982). The availability of useful information to the right of fixation in reading. *Perception & Psychophysics, 31,* 537–550.

Rosenbaum, D.A., Inhoff, A.W., & Gordon, A.M. (1984). Choosing between movement sequences: A hierarchical editor model. *Journal of Experimental Psychology: General, 113,* 372–393.

Taft, M. (1979). Lexical access via an orthographic code: The basic orthographic syllable structure (BOSS). *Journal of Verbal Learning and Verbal Behavior, 18,* 21–39.

Taft, M., & Forster, K.I. (1976). Lexical storage and retrieval of polymorphemic and polysyllabic words. *Journal of Verbal Learning and Verbal Behavior*, *15*, 607–620.

Vitu, F., O'Regan, J.K., & Mittau, M. (1990). Optimal landing position in reading isolated words and continuous text. *Perception & Psychophysics*, *47*, 583–600.

22
Eye Movements and Reading Processes

A. RENÉ SCHMAUDER

Researchers investigating eye movements during reading often follow a strategy of letting theoretical considerations tell us what locations in text to focus on in analyzing the eye movement record. We attempt to draw conclusions about processing at these locations by considering results obtained with several different measures. Some of the measures we use are first fixation duration, gaze duration, probability of fixating a target word, number of fixations on a target word, length of saccades off a target word, and spillover effects (effects on words following a target word). We have argued in several places (Rayner & Pollatsek, 1987, 1989; Rayner, Sereno, Morris, Schmauder, & Clifton, 1989; Schmauder, 1991) that this strategy, as well as use of multiple paradigms to test a constant stimulus set, provides researchers with converging evidence and yields a more complete picture of cognitive processes operative during reading than that obtainable using either a single measure or a single paradigm.

This strategy of looking for converging evidence will prove profitable in considering what the five chapters in this section of the book tell us about eye movements during normal reading. This chapter is organized in five sections: comments on the optimal viewing position; comments on lexical access and refixations; issues in eye movement control; eye movements and message–level processing; and consideration of the frequency of effects analysis. I will begin with comments on O'Regan and colleagues' work on the optimal viewing position in words and in text and on Sereno's work on first fixations of refixated words (words that receive more than one fixation before another word is fixated).[1]

---

[1] Note that in this chapter, as in Sereno's chapter, the term *refixated word* refers to those words that are fixated more than once before a subject fixates some other (preceding or following) word. Here the term does not refer to words that are fixated a second time as a result of a regression after a subject has fixated some other word.

The Optimal Viewing Position

O'Regan (this volume; 1990) found a consistent optimal viewing position in words read in isolation, such that the probability of refixating a word was least when the first fixation on the refixated word was near or at this optimal viewing position.[2] This effect occurred, to a much lesser degree, in words read as part of a continuous text (Vitu, O'Regan, & Mittau, 1990). Vitu et al. (1990) noted that not only was the optimal viewing position effect reduced for words in text versus words in isolation, but also the optimal viewing position shifted slightly to the left of center of words presented in text, occurring quite near the preferred viewing location. The preferred viewing location is between the beginning and the middle of a word (Rayner, 1979) but to the left of the optimal viewing position in words presented in isolation (O'Regan, this volume; 1990).

Vitu et al. (1990) considered whether the parafoveal preview phenomenon provided an explanation for the leftward shift of the optimal viewing position in words presented in text versus words presented in isolation. Parafoveal preview is the partial processing of the word (word $n+1$) to the right of the currently fixated word (word n), which occurs before word $n+1$ is fixated directly (see Rayner & Pollatsek, 1989, for an overview). Parafoveal preview of words to the right of fixation is enabled in part by a condition in which the perceptual span extends beyond the end of the currently fixated word. Types of information identified in the parafovea and integrated across saccades during reading include partial abstract letter information (Balota, Pollatsek, & Rayner, 1985; Henderson & Ferreira, 1990; Rayner, McConkie, & Zola, 1980; but cf. Inhoff, 1989b) and phonological codes (Pollatsek, Lesch, Morris, & Rayner, 1992; cf. Rayner et al., 1980).

Vitu et al. (1990) argued that parafoveal preview did not account for the leftward shift of the optimal viewing position, using, in part, a post-hoc analysis of the influence on slopes of refixation probability curves of the distance (near or far) of the previous fixation from the current fixation. They argued that if parafoveal preview reduced the need to process the initial letters of words further by directly fixating them, one would expect the optimal viewing position to shift to the right, a prediction in direct conflict with the observed results. This reasoning and failure of the distance of a previous fixation to influence the slope of refixation probability curves led Vitu et al. to say they had no explanation for the left shift of the optimal viewing position in words read in text.

---

[2] O'Regan (this volume; 1990) uses the term *optimal viewing position*, whereas Vitu et al. (1990) refer to the *optimal landing position*. O'Regan (1981) called this the *convenient viewing position*. These terms appear to refer to the same phenomenon. I will use *optimal viewing position* throughout, consistent with O'Regan's chapter.

In fact, contrary to Vitu et al.'s (1990) supposition, there is no reason to expect that parafoveal preview of a word (word $n+1$) to the right of the currently fixated word ever would exert an influence on the *location* of the optimal viewing position in word $n+1$. Several theories of eye-movement control are compatible with the following course of events on two successive fixations (Morris, Rayner, & Pollatsek, 1990; Pollatsek & Rayner, 1982): On fixation n, the location to which the next saccade will bring the eye is calculated. Further, this location is calculated relatively early during fixation n, earlier than abstract letter information obtained via parafoveal preview from word $n+1$ (the word to the right of fixation n) becomes available. Therefore, information obtained by parafoveal preview will influence only the duration of a fixation on word $n+1$, not the location of the fixation on word $n+1$. A similar suggestion is made in Inhoff et al.'s chapter, and results mentioned by O'Regan in his chapter support this claim.

I should explain why the optimal viewing position is to the left of center of words in text (versus words in isolation). A model similar to Morrison's (1984) model of eye-movement control proposes that attention is directed to the right of a fixation preceding an eye movement to a new fixation location. It is likely that covert attention shifts preceding eye movements are directed further to the right during reading of text than they are while subjects are processing words in isolation. Coupling the existence of rightward attention shifts with the asymmetry of the perceptual span to the right—letter information is available no more than three to four spaces to the left of fixation and at least six to ten letter spaces to the right of fixation (see Rayner & Pollatsek, 1989, for an overview)—leads to predictions relevant to the optimal viewing position phenomenon.

The asymmetry of the perceptual span suggests that the most productive fixation location in most short-to-medium length words will be somewhere between the beginning and middle of such words. From a position between the beginning and middle of the word, letter information both to the left and to the right of fixation is available for processing, increasing the likelihood that substantial processing can be accomplished on this fixation. Add to this the fact that covert attention shifts to the right during text reading probably increase the ease of processing text outside the fovea, and we have an account of the leftward shift of the optimal viewing position during reading of text as opposed to reading words in isolation. In the text case, the perceptual span asymmetry and covert attention shifts mean that fixating further to the left will not jeopardize processing of the fixated word. When a word is presented in isolation, covert attention shifts may not be directed as far to the right as they are during text processing, because the subject is aware that there is no word to the right of the currently fixated word.

Note that this explanation does not imply, as Vitu et al. (1990) claim, that parafoveal preview across word boundaries should lead to a rightward shift of the optimal viewing position. Parafoveal processing across word boundaries presents a different set of problems than processing of a single word during a fixation on that word. The present account of the leftward shift of the optimal viewing position in words presented in text does not apply directly to processing across word boundaries. Also note that many factors may influence the actual fixation locations observed, factors like the overall difficulty of the text, word frequency and length, and morphology. Researchers are far from understanding how these factors influence eye movements during reading.

Lexical Access and Refixations

The optimal viewing position is a central part of O'Regan's strategy-tactics theory of eye movement control. The strategy-tactics theory explains within- and between-word eye movements in terms of perceptual constraints, providing a mechanistic, visuomotor explanation of refixation. O'Regan (this volume; 1990) proposed that according to the strategy-tactics theory, saccades are directed to a position just left of word center in order to maximize the likelihood of landing at the optimal viewing position. When the eye lands close to or at the optimal viewing position, the next saccade position will be in the next word, i.e., a word initially fixated sufficiently close to the optimal viewing position will not be refixated prior to moving on to subsequent words in the text. An initial fixation that does not fall sufficiently close to the optimal viewing position will be followed by a refixation at the opposite side of the word. Refixation probability effects cited by O'Regan (1990) support this position.

Sereno's results (this volume) show that frequency effects were evident in first fixations of multiply fixated words but absent from second fixations and contradict predictions made by a strong interpretation of the strategy-tactics theory. The predictions are that lexical effects such as frequency effects should not occur on first fixations of multiply fixated words, although they will be evident in second fixations of such words (O'Regan & Levy-Schoen, 1987; Vitu et al., 1990). Sereno found that lexical processing occurred during first fixations of some refixated words, and that this lexical processing was productive in that frequency information was extracted. Moreover, first fixations that displayed frequency effects sometimes were of durations less than 200 ms, indicating lexical factors have an earlier impact on eye movements than O'Regan (this volume) implied. Sereno's results support a model according to which refixations are made for attentional rather than perceptual reasons. Further revision of the strategy-tactics theory is required to explain text processing and to accommodate the role of attention in eye-movement control.

The need for revision of the strategy-tactics theory is supported further by McConkie, Kerr, Reddix, Zola, and Jacobs' (1989) finding that high-frequency, four-letter words sometimes were refixated following initial fixation at the words' centers. They suggested it was highly unlikely that refixation occurred because sufficient visual information was not obtained on the initial fixation on such words. Further work needs to be done to determine why such short, high-frequency words *are* refixated and to expand existing theories of eye movement control (like Morrison's, 1984, model) to explain the full range of refixation phenomena. However, it will continue to be profitable to contrast predictions made by a modified Morrison model, for example, with those made by future versions of the strategy-tactics theory.

Eye-Movement Control

Inhoff et al. (this volume) raised several interesting suggestions about eye movement control. They cited evidence in support of the lexical text integration hypothesis, the hypothesis that integration of text across fixations utilizes "lexical units" (Inhoff, 1989a, 1989b, 1990). Further, Inhoff et al. (this volume) proposed an early, time-locked model of saccade control, according to which saccade target location is calculated early in a fixation, and some parafoveally available information is used prior to completion of the fixation. Parafoveal information that becomes available later in the fixation influences the duration of the next fixation (not its location), and this parafoveal information sometimes is consulted during preprogramming of a second saccade. Finally, Inhoff et al. suggested that this time-locked model of saccade control entails conditions under which first fixations do not reflect visual and/or linguistic processes, occasions on which two saccades are simultaneously preplanned and a very short fixation intervenes. The time-locked model of saccade control is exactly the kind of expansion to Morrison's (1984) theory that we need.

Another implication of the early, time-locked model of saccade control is that we need to consider further the duration of first fixations, because it is possible, as O'Regan proposed in his chapter, that first fixations reflect primarily perceptual processes. Additionally, we must consider the impact of processing load on first fixation times. Sereno (this volume) found frequency effects on first fixations with durations between 180 ms and 200 ms in adjectives modifying sentence-initial noun phrases. Because the target adjectives occurred at the start of the experimental sentences, processing of target words was not contaminated by semantic and pragmatic factors that influence construction of a final sentence representation. More than word position in a sentence or discourse influences when lexical information impacts fixation times. Topic shifts and plausibility, for instance, may cause variation in when and how lexical information is used by the language processor. We are far from understanding these phenomena.

Eye Movements and Message-Level Processing

Morris's results (this volume) pose a major challenge to strictly modular models of language processing, which posit the lexicon is encapsulated and lexical access is not influenced by message-level representations. Her case against strictly modular models is strengthened by the fact that message-level processing seems to impact both first fixation times and gaze durations: typically, first fixations have been taken to be less influenced by semantic information than are gaze durations.

Consider a question raised by Patrick Carroll with respect to Morris's results: What type of information is message-level information? There are at least two possibilities. First, perhaps readers calculate truth conditions or belief states as they process written input and as a result construct a representation such as the following:

(1) It is true that the gardener trimmed the mustache.

If this is the information that influences lexical access, the distinction between knowledge of the situation being discussed and knowledge about words is called into question.

A second possibility is that message-level information is topic or focus (in the technical sense used by linguists). The lexicon may be subject to activation from a variety of sources, and one such source may be focus. That is, perhaps the state of the lexicon is influenced by what one is talking about. If focus is the sort of message-level information that influences lexical processing, Morris's results can be explained as follows. Consider the barber-trimming sentence:

(2) The gardener watched as the barber trimmed the mustache. . . .

Here, "barber" is in focus, and it enters into a priming relation with "trimmed," yielding facilitation compared to the neutral control condition. In the gardener-trimming sentence:

(3) The gardener who watched the barber trimmed the mustache . . .

"gardener" is focused, "barber" is defocused, and intralexically, a different sense of "trimmed" is selected (that is, a different sense than the sense compatible with "barber"), resulting in interference.

This two-stage model is slightly inelegant, but it makes at least the following prediction. Consider the sentence:

(4) The gardener who watched the barber trim the mustache stood up quickly and left the room.[3]

---

[3] Example provided by Charles Clifton, Jr.

If only focus influences the lexicon, no facilitation should obtain in this sentence, because the gardener is in focus, not the barber. That is, this sentence should resemble Morris's results from the gardener-trimming condition, in which no facilitation occurred in sentences such as sentence 3. If message-level factors involving the content of the message influence the lexicon, one would again expect facilitation on "mustache" in "The gardener who watched the barber trim the mustache stood up quickly and left the room."

As Morris suggested in her conclusion, her results indicated that strictly modular models of the language processing system may be untenable. But the data do not require that we adopt a completely interactive model just yet. Morris's results are compatible with a weak modular model according to which information from the message level sometimes filters back to the lexical or syntactic modules before these lower level modules have completed their operations. On this weak modular view, information sometimes, although not always, arrives at lower level modules in time to influence either selection among multiple alternative analyses calculated strictly from the bottom up or revision of a single analysis that turns out to be incompatible with the higher, message-level analysis (see Frazier, 1990, for a similar proposal). Intralexical priming, as evidenced by faster reading times for verbs preceded by related nouns than for verbs preceded by neutral nouns (Morris, this volume), indicates operation of early, within-lexical-module processes. Message-level information may influence stages of processing subsequent to this intramodular spread of activation. In short, researchers need to investigate the operation of the language processor further if we are to discover what message-level information looks like and how message-level information interacts with information used at different stages of processing.

Frequency of Effects Analysis

McConkie, Reddix, & Zola's results (their chapter in this volume) suggest that researchers should draw conclusions from the eye movement record by consulting information in addition to that provided by the measures I mentioned earlier (first fixation time, gaze durations, etc.). Analyses of the entire distribution of fixation durations, such as the frequency of effects analysis, may enable researchers to determine more accurately the effects of experimental manipulations.

The relevant results are that the modified frequency of effects model applied to McConkie et al.'s pseudoword condition suggested that a 28-ms disruption began at 140-ms fixation duration, exhibited as a drop in the frequency distribution for the pseudoword condition compared to the control condition. The model also indicated that only 32% of fixations were influenced in the pseudoword condition. McConkie et al. posited that this pattern of effects is characteristic of a non–time-locked effect; the pseudoword effect did not appear at the same point in every fixation it influenced but rather produced its effect at a time that varied from fixation to fixation. They contrasted this non–time-locked effect with a time-locked effect like that induced by masking text during a fixation.

I suggest we consider an alternative account of the differences claimed to indicate that there are two types of effects. McConkie et al. (this volume) referred to Blanchard, McConkie, Zola, and Wolverton's (1984) experiments in which text was masked for 30 ms at either 50, 80, or 120 ms after the onset of fixation. This manipulation caused a dip in the frequency distribution of fixations at a point starting 80 to 90 ms after occurrence of the mask. So the dip in the frequency distribution occurred anywhere from 160 to 240 ms into the fixations on which the mask occurred. Without examining the actual frequency distribution of fixations from the relevant experiment, it is not clear how many fixations were affected by the mask. But it is possible that there were quite a few fixations within the affected range, and McConkie et al. report that the mask influenced roughly 100% of the fixations between 160 and 240 ms. In comparison, the pseudoword effect only influenced 32% of fixations at a point starting at 140 ms fixation duration, already a low point in the distribution. Possibly the pseudoword effect influenced too few fixations to appear as a dip in the distribution. There may be no difference in kind between the effects of a mask and a pseudoword at all; both effects may be equally time-locked.

Conclusion

I have raised questions about some of the research presented by McConkie et al., Sereno, Morris, Inhoff et al., and O'Regan. Nonetheless, I think each researcher is following just the right strategy. They reported conclusions based on data gathered with several measures and across paradigms. It is important to determine where in words the eye lands, what information is acquired on a fixation, and how quickly information is acquired. We need to know precisely what kinds of high-level information influence quick acquisition of information during fixations. And it is imperative that we develop new ways of extracting even more information from our eyetracking data than we have managed to glean so far. I find especially promising the development of approaches such as McConkie and colleagues' strategy of looking at the distribution of fixation times and Sereno's development of the fast-priming technique. Although the theories proposed by O'Regan, Inhoff et al., McConkie et al., Sereno, and Morris are not perfect, each researcher is bringing us closer to an accurate and complete picture of the processes reflected in eye movements during reading.

Acknowledgments. Preparation of this chapter was supported in part by National Institutes of Health grant HD-07327 to the University of Massachusetts and by a Mount Holyoke College Alumnae Fellowship to A. René Schmauder. Correspondence regarding this chapter may be addressed to A. René Schmauder, Department of Psychology, Tobin Hall, University of Massachusetts, Amherst, MA 01003. The author thanks Charles Clifton, Jr. and Keith Rayner for comments on an earlier version of this chapter.

References

Balota, D.A., Pollatsek, A., & Rayner, K. (1985). The interaction of contextual constraints and parafoveal visual information in reading. *Cognitive Psychology*, *17*, 364–390.

Blanchard, H.E., McConkie, G.W., Zola, D., & Wolverton, G.S. (1984). Time course of visual information utilization during fixations in reading. *Journal of Experimental Psychology: Human Perception and Performance*, *10*, 75–89.

Frazier, L. (1990). Exploring the architecture of the language-processing system. In G.T. Altmann (Ed.), *Cognitive models of speech processing: Psycholinguistic and computational perspectives* (pp. 409–433). Cambridge, MA: MIT Press.

Henderson, J.M., & Ferreira, F. (1990). Effects of foveal processing difficulty on the perceptual span in reading: Implications for attention and eye movement control. *Journal of Experimental Psychology: Learning, Memory, and Cognition*, *16*, 417–429.

Inhoff, A.W. (1989a). Parafoveal processing of words and saccade computation during eye fixations in reading. *Journal of Experimental Psychology: Human Perception and Performance*, *15*, 544–555.

Inhoff, A.W. (1989b). Lexical access during eye fixations in reading: Are word access codes used to integrate lexical information across interword fixations? *Journal of Memory and Language*, *28*, 444–461.

Inhoff, A.W. (1990). Integrating information across eye fixations in reading. *Acta Psychologica*, *73*, 281–297.

McConkie, G.W., Kerr, P.W., Reddix, M.D., Zola, D., & Jacobs, A.M. (1989). Eye movement control during reading: II. Frequency of refixating a word. *Perception and Psychophysics*, *17*, 578–586.

Morris, R.K., Rayner, K., & Pollatsek, A. (1990). Eye movement guidance in reading: The role of parafoveal letter and space information. *Journal of Experimental Psychology: Human Perception and Performance*, *16*, 268–281.

Morrison, R.E. (1984). Manipulation of stimulus onset delay in reading: Evidence for parallel programming of saccades. *Journal of Experimental Psychology: Human Perception and Performance*, *10*, 667–682.

O'Regan, J.K. (1990). Eye movements and reading. In E. Kowler (Ed.), *Eye movements and their role in visual and cognitive processes*. Vol. 4 of Reviews of Oculomotor Research. Amsterdam: Elsevier.

O'Regan, J.K. (1981). The convenient viewing position hypothesis. In D.F. Fisher, R.A. Monty, & J.W. Senders (Eds.), *Eye Movements: Cognition and visual perception*. Hillsdale, NJ: Erlbaum.

O'Regan, J.K., & Levy-Schoen, A. (1987). Eye movement strategy and tactics in word recognition and reading. In M. Coltheart (Ed.), *Attention and performance XII: The psychology of reading* (pp. 363–383). Hillsdale, NJ: Erlbaum.

Pollatsek, A., Lesch, M., Morris, R.K., & Rayner, K. (1992). Phonological codes are used in the integration of information across saccades in word identification and reading. *Journal of Experimental Psychology: Human Perception and Performance, 18,* 148–162.

Pollatsek, A., & Rayner, K. (1982). Eye movement control in reading: The role of word boundaries. *Journal of Experimental Psychology: Human Perception and Performance, 8,* 817–833.

Rayner, K. (1979). Eye guidance in reading: Fixation locations within words. *Perception, 8,* 21–30.

Rayner, K., McConkie, G.W., & Zola, D. (1980). Integrating information across eye movements. *Cognitive Psychology, 12,* 206–226.

Rayner, K., & Pollatsek, A. (1987). Eye movements in reading: A tutorial review. In M. Coltheart (Ed.), *Attention and performance XII: The psychology of reading* (pp. 327–362). Hillsdale, NJ: Erlbaum.

Rayner, K., & Pollatsek, A. (1989). *The psychology of reading.* Englewood Cliffs, NJ: Prentice Hall.

Rayner, K., Sereno, S.C., Morris, R.K., Schmauder, A.R., & Clifton, C. (1989). Eye movements and on-line language comprehension processes. *Language and Cognitive Processes, 4,* SI 21–49.

Schmauder, A.R. (1991). Argument structure frames: A lexical complexity metric? *Journal of Experimental Psychology: Learning, Memory, and Cognition, 17,* 49–65.

Vitu, F., O'Regan, J.K., & Mittau, M. (1990). Optimal landing position in reading isolated words and continuous text. *Perception and Psychophysics, 47,* 583–600.

23
The Spatial Coding Hypothesis

ALAN KENNEDY

This chapter explores the consequences for the reader of the fact that the printed page (or screen display) is itself a physical object, capable of being inspected at will. Printed text differs in this respect from speech, where the stimulus must be processed in real-time and can only be "reinspected" in a metaphorical sense—for example, by calling on a form of auditory short-term memory. The organization of the the chapter takes the form of a brief review of the notion of spatial representation; perceptual processes in reading; the definition of coordinate systems; spatial manipulations and reading—in particular, the fact that reading appears to be possible without a spatial representation of text; and the possible function of the "spatial code" to the reader. The chapter concludes with a summary of some recent experimental work on spatialization that suggests that the spatially extended text may, in some circumstances, bestow two advantages on the skilled reader: (a) aiding the computation of syntactic relationships, by providing an important cue to word order; and (b) facilitating the processes of reanalysis, by providing the necessary spatial information to control reinspection.

Spatial Representation

A fundamental issue in visual perception concerns the mechanism that translates a succession of retinal "images" into a stable, spatially extended, visual world. There have been numerous attempts to deal with this question since the time of Lotze (1886). It is easy to see what the problem is: while the brain has access to retinal signals and hence, probably, to retinal locations, movements of the eyes, head, and body make this information an unreliable guide both to spatial location and visual direction. Most attempts to solve the problem do so by an appeal to mapping operations between different coordinate systems, or "frames" (Feldman, 1985; Swanston, Wade, & Day, 1987). The only alternative would appear to be the Gibsonian proposition that, in some way, "the visual system knows where the eye is looking only by virtue of what it is looking at" (Kolers, 1983). Although this is, in many ways, an appealing proposition, it will not be further considered here because, in the context of reading, it is very difficult to know what it might mean. Although the number of frames and their interdependence is a lively research topic, it is the initial step, mapping the retinal (framework) to some spatial framework, which represents the most intractable problem. Unfortunately, the analogy between the retina and a 2-D array of detectors, which has proved so fruitful in computational approaches to vision (Marr, 1982) is less helpful here than may appear at first sight. In fact, to pose the question as a computational problem, where, for example, edges must be identified in an array, is to miss the point that the retinal surface itself can only be treated in this way (in effect, as a 2-D object) within a co-ordinate system, with the consequent danger that the solution is smuggled in as one of the premises. It is not the purpose of this chapter to add to this theoretical controversy. Rather, the aim is to raise some issues in visual integration and spatial coding that appear to be peculiar to the task of reading.

Perceptual Processes in Reading

Programming Saccades

Reading makes almost exclusive use of the saccadic system. Indeed, in the reading literature, discussion of visual or spatial integration is often couched in terms of "trans-saccadic" effects (Breitmeyer, 1983; Rayner & Pollatsek, 1983). In the real world, some changes in retinal image occur as a result of saccades, but far more result from unplanned shifts in the position of the head and body, in drifts of the eye, and through the use of pursuit eye movements (Haber, 1985). It is worth asking, therefore, whether saccades are controlled by a form of "dead-reckoning" navigation, that is, coded as displacements from the current eye position, or are directed to specific spatial locations. In general the evidence supports the notion of spatial control (Mays & Sparks, 1980), but it should be stressed that this conclusion leaves open the question as to whether information surviving the saccade is integrated in a specifically spatial framework (Davidson, Fox, & Dick, 1973; Irwin, Brown, & Sun, 1988). It is necessary to make a clear distinction between the level at which information might be integrated (e.g., ranging from a point-to-point visual code to a completely abstract representation) and the role, if any, that spatial location might play in the process. In fact, studies comparing picture perception and reading suggest quite different conclusions. There is evidence that when looking at pictures some strictly visual information may be integrated over saccades, although no positional information survives (Pollatsek and Rayner, this volume). On the other hand, data from studies of reading suggest that trans-saccadic integration is carried out exclusively at an abstract level (see Rayner & Pollatsek, 1989, for a review). That is, it is information on the identity of letters, rather than their form, that is preserved from one saccade to the next. Unfortunately, however, there is no conclusive direct evidence either way that strictly spatial information is coded. In the next section some indirect evidence on the question is presented.

Scanpaths

In the perception of objects in the world it is doubtful if the viewer makes use of, or even has access to, information on the temporal order of fixations. The distribution of eye movements over objects and pictures of objects appears to be unconstrained by anything other than figural properties. (The evidence for the contrary view, implicit in Noton & Stark, 1971, is not strong.) That is, there is no canonical scanpath for a particular object, no "right way" of looking at it. The internal representation of the visual world appears to be glued together from a set of snapshots in which the temporal and the spatial are effectively decoupled. However, it is not possible to consider the printed page as simply another visual object, available for inspection. At least in the case of an alphabetic script, written words and word elements are also clues to speech, and the act of reading, in part, can be seen as the recovery of this speech-like representation. From this perspective, the substrate of written text has a necessary temporal order. Because words can be inspected in a succession of discrete fixations in any order, the "integration" question now re-emerges. How is the spatial order, necessary for comprehension, recovered from this unconstrained temporal sequence? It is at this point that a spatially coded memory representation that will survive the saccade may play a role. Only if the text can be coded as a stable visual object, so the claim goes, can the reader be free to inspect it at will. The alternative proposition (implicit, for example, in the "immediacy" hypothesis of Just & Carpenter, 1980) is that, in general, the uptake of information by the reader will match, in temporal sequence, the written order of words. Obviously, this is an empirical question, but the occurrence of reinspections and other nonsystematic sequences of fixations makes the hypothesis appear vulnerable. The contrast between these positions (a reader knowing both "what" and "where," versus a reader with access only to "what") is the principal theoretical issue raised in this chapter.

Coordinate Systems

A dissociation between location and content may be demonstrated in experimental studies of "illusory conjunctions" (Treisman, 1988) showing, for example, that under some conditions of presentation a word may be accurately identified but inaccurately localized. However, it is important to note that, at one level in such a task, accurate spatial information is preserved. That is, the particular configuration of letters comprising a word does not itself fragment. What might be termed local spatial information (that is, local to the "frame" defined by the boundary of the word) is not disrupted. Any disturbance takes place in a coordinate system defined by the boundaries of the screen, which can encompass the display of several words. Interestingly, dissociation of letters within words (or letter migration) can be demonstrated when the word boundary defines the relevant spatial frame (Davidson, et al., 1973; Irwin et al., 1988). Taken together, these observations are consistent with the claims of Swanston et al. (1985) whose data suggest that eye movement control in reading takes place in what they refer to as a "patterncentric" co-ordinate system. Obviously, the page (or screen) exists as an object in a geocentrically defined space, but for the reader, eye movement control cannot take place in this coordinate system. Rather, it must depend on the extraction and representation of relational information in the pattern projected on the retina. Elements with common relational motion within the geocentric representation of the visual world will be employed to define local "frames of reference." The claim here is that it is the page, or screen, boundary that defines this local frame. As Mackay (1973) suggested in another context, the page may come to serve as a "stable map"—a memory that may be addressed directly through its spatial coordinates. It is important to note, in the context of the present discussion, that there are important circumstances where this mapping of word position within a local frame can break down. Relative changes in word position within a *screen* boundary (as distinct from a printed page) are not only possible, but quite frequent. For example, if a word appears within a visual frame such as a "window" it may have one location with respect to the local visual frame of reference (the window), and another with respect to the screen and the environment. Work has begun, in collaboration with Mike Swanston in Dundee and Joel Pynte in Aix-en-Provence, to examine the interesting situation in which a window itself moves with respect to the screen boundary. In this case, the geocentric position of a word may change under conditions where it is physically stationary.

In summary, it may be argued that integration of information by the reader follows inspection by means of a succession of planned fixations, in a local frame of reference. It is this spatial knowledge that allows for the recovery of a temporally coded event. That is, only by knowing where words lie can the reader be completely freed from the requirements to inspect them in a strictly controlled order. Clearly, this is a strong hypothesis and before going on to consider evidence in its support it is necessary to examine in some detail the apparently contrary data from studies in which readers are called on to process text under conditions where differential spatial information is not present.

Reading and the Spatial Code

Word-Objects

In the discussion that follows, it should be stressed that the primary concern is with relationships between words. It is recognized that the printed word itself can be thought of as a visual object and that this spatial knowledge may play an essential disambiguating role *within* the word (e.g., in distinguishing "was" from "saw"). Nonetheless, it is not unreasonable to consider the "primitive object level" in reading to be the word (McConkie & Zola, 1987). Three lines of evidence can be recruited in support of this view: (a) Letters within words appear to be processed in parallel (Slowiaczek & Rayner, 1987); thus, for each fixation, "letter sequence" may be directly available as spatial information and not derived from some additional temporal scan. (b) Although words cannot be recovered from streams of letters presented successively at speed in a single physical location (Kolers & Lewis, 1972), sentence recognition under similar presentation conditions, i.e., rapid-serial visual presentation (RSVP) is possible (Forster, 1970; Kanwisher, 1987). (c) Saccade end-point in normal reading is determined by a combination of two parameters: the distance from the to-be-fixated word and its length (McConkie, Kerr, Reddix, & Zola, 1988). In other words, a primary variable in between-word eye movement control is the sequence of "objects" defined by interword spaces in text.

Reading from a Single Location

The fact that reading is possible under conditions where individual words or phrases appear in foveal vision in a single physical location (Bouma & de Voogd, 1974; Juola, Ward, & McNamara, 1982; Monk, 1985) appears to contradict the suggestion that spatial information is necessary for comprehension. The first observation to make on these findings, however, is that "line-stepped" or "nonspatialized" presentation modes actually solve what would be, under normal circumstances, a crucial problem for the reader. The procedure itself permits temporal order to become an experimental given and not something to be derived from a spatially unconstrained succession of fixations. Consequently, it would be unwise, on the basis of such evidence, to arrive at the immediate conclusion that readers *normally* do not have access to spatial information when directing eye movements over text. There is, in fact, at least one important source of evidence concerning the effective control of refixations that argues against such a conclusion. Saccades are frequently launched to some previously inspected target location well outside the immediate span of attention. There are severe constraints on the degree to which such reinspecting saccades could be controlled by the physical identification of the remote target. The acuity function of the eye (Anstis, 1974) reveals a remarkably steep relationship between distance from the current viewing position, in character positions, and visibility (see O'Regan, 1990, for further discussion of this point). This is consistent with well-established data on the size of the perceptual span in reading (Rayner, 1975): effective visual information (that is, enough to permit identification of a word) is only available from within a restricted local region around the current fixation point. But if physical identification of the intended target is not possible, how, if not by the use of spatially coded information, can accurate saccades to such targets be executed at all? One possible source of control would be an algorithm based on time (i.e., an instruction like "saccade *n* words back"). This would provide an adequate, if crude, ranging mechanism if "back" is taken to mean, invariably, "left on the current line." But although this has become almost a matter of definition in traditional psycholinguistic experiments, where materials are frequently presented on a single line, it is clearly not typical of normal reading, and would lead to the prediction of spectacular errors under conditions where a temporal "back" would need to be decoded as a spatial "go right." There is no evidence that errors of this kind occur. Thus, more formally, the proposal that readers do not code for place carries with it a clear prediction that the endpoint error of reinspecting saccades in reading should be large and should correlate positively with their extent (Monk, 1985). The data do not support this proposition: not only is the obtained correlation effectively zero, but large reinspecting saccades are generally accurately located, if this is taken to mean hitting the intended target word (Kennedy & Murray, 1987).

The Tokens of Spatial Representation

It is difficult to decouple visual direction and attention. Indeed, to do so would undermine one important definition of attention itself. Thus, given that we might go along with the notion of a "spatially addressed" memory, it is necessary to ask what its contents might be? That is, what precisely, do the pointers in this coding system point to? In the context of reading, this is a highly pertinent question, because it focuses on an apparent paradox. The spatially coded page allows the reader a method of reanalysis, via reinspection, and there is a considerable body of evidence that such reinspection may be highly selective. For example, a pronominal anaphor may trigger a saccade back to a possible antecedent. Similarly, ambiguity at a lexical, syntactic, or pragmatic level may trigger systematic reexamination of portions of previously read text. It is at this point that the paradox becomes apparent. Why, in relatively short sentences, that can be readily understood if spoken, should the reader look at the same word twice (Kennedy, 1983)? Two broad altenatives present themselves as possible answers to this question. (a) It may be that the positional code directs the eyes to a particular token—a string of letters defined visually. Because we are dealing with reinspection, this is, essentially, a second visual access to the lexicon; by the time the event occurs, the original access processes have been completed and have given way to subsequent processes of thematic integration. Perhaps, if alternative interpretations at a lexical level are called for, it may be relatively difficult to derive them on the basis of a memory record. The most efficient route will be via visual access to the lexicon, and this demands looking again. Once a particular thematic representation has been established, it cannot easily be revised without further visual input, and the mandatory processes of lexical access, being stimulus-driven, require a stimulus input. Some support for this idea can be derived from the dramatic demonstration of "repetition blindness" by Kanwisher (1987). Her interpretation of this effect is that visual inspection of a word (or "token") instantiates a "type" representation. Additional occurrences of the same token under RSVP presentation conditions are not discriminated and, as a result, the observer does not see them. (b) An alternative account involves considering attentional mechanisms directly. The literature is replete with evidence that cognitive activity may have locative aspects, either incidentally or essentially. Perhaps the most global summary of all these studies is to be found in the notion of a "mental model" (Johnson-Laird, 1983; see also Hegarty, this volume). From this perspective, reinspection in reading would not be considered as to the word, but to the point in space where certain cognitive operations took place (the metaphor is perhaps not altogether accidental). Clearly, for the reader, the primary cognitive operation involves deriving a word's referent. Consequently, reinspection will fall at the place where the word is (or was), but it would be incorrect to see the word itself as the target. In fact, there is evidence that readers do remember the location of key text items (Christie & Just, 1976; Zechmeister & McKillop, 1972) and may direct attention to those positions, regardless of whether the text remains visible or not (Baccino, Pynte, & Kennedy, 1990; Kennedy, 1983).

Spatial Cues to Word Order: Reanalysis and Reinspection

If these claims regarding reinspection are correct, an important gloss is placed on the proposition that unimpaired reading from a single location is even possible. It may be for straightforward text, but if reinspection becomes necessary for comprehension (for example, to resolve a temporary ambiguity), then a decrement in performance is clearly predicted. The evidence we have obtained up to the present generally confirms this prediction: disrupting the reader's ability to assign words to distinct spatial locations leads to performance decrements, if the text is sufficiently complex (Kennedy & Murray, 1984; Pynte, Kennedy, Murray, & Courrieu, 1988). Put very generally, our data suggest that, following "nonspatialized" (i.e., single-location) presentation, readers are less able to carry out efficient reanalysis. At one level, this outcome may appear fairly straightforward; obviously, a nonspatialized presentation will deprive the reader of the coordinates with which to direct accurate reinspecting saccades. But another, more subtle, interpretation of the data can be offered. It is possible that seeing all the words of a sentence in the same place may exact not one, but two, penalties. Not only will later reinspection be affected, but the reader may be deprived, *at the time of presentation*, of information that is essential for comprehension. The reason for thinking this, is that word order is a crucial cue to syntax and knowing what comes next is significantly aided by the powerful cue of spatial adjacency. That is, for the fluent reader "what comes next" and "what is adjacent to" may be interdependent concepts. The question of when syntactic decisions are made—and the units of this decision-making—is a notoriously contentious issue and certainly not one that can be reviewed here, but our data do offer one important gloss on the question, to the degree that spatial extension may lower the cost of syntactic reanalysis.

The crucial example derives from the evidence suggesting that parsing errors are more easily corrected if potential "points of return" are coded (e.g., Frazier & Rayner, 1982). Clearly, whether or not a reader can safely adopt a single initial syntactic analysis when faced with ambiguity depends on the cost of reanalysis and this cost may be too high if the operations call for computations over a speech-based record. In this case, the hearer, as distinct from the reader, may play safe and engage in a

```
Spatialised:                                    Non-Spatialised:



t1: The                                              The

t2:      old                                         old

t3:          man                                     man

t4:              walked                              walked

t5: The old man walked home.   The old man walked home.
```

FIGURE 23.1. Spatialized and nonspatialized presentation modes.

degree of parallel representation. In contrast, this cost can be greatly reduced if the reader has access to a form of representation that can capitalize on the stability and permanence of spatially extended text. In fact, an intimate link between the mechanisms that control visual inspection and the cognitive processes of reanalysis has been assumed in the literature without a complete understanding of what, in psychological terms, such a link involves (Kennedy, Murray, Jennings, & Reid, 1989). At a linguistic level, it is entirely consistent (even self-evident) that subjects should direct eye movements back to where an incorrect attachment has been made. However, psychologically, this phenomenon itself demands explanation. It is necessary to ask what representations the reader has maintained to allow selective reinspection to occur.

Syntactic Operations and Spatial Coding

The work to be reported here makes use of a technique developed in collaboration with Joel Pynte and Wayne Murray. This technique facilitates the examination of the effects of spatialization at the time of initial reading and the later effects on rereading. The work set out to examine the proposition that the most likely locus of on-line effects of spatialization would be on syntactic operations, because these are dependent on the extraction of order information (Pynte et al., 1988).

The experimental procedure involves a form of self-paced reading. Two conditions are contrasted. In the first, successive words appear on a display singly, in the same physical location. For obvious reasons, this is referred to as a nonspatialized presentation mode. In the second (spatialized) condition, words appear singly and successively in appropriate locations across the display (i.e., as a "sequential" or "moving window" presentation). In both conditions, readers only have access to one word at a time, but in one case there is additional differential spatial information available. The two presentation modes are illustrated in Figure 23.1, where t1 to t5 represent successive time intervals. The task is in one important respect different from earlier studies of self-paced reading. In both conditions, the final word appears together with all the previously presented text in a spatially extended format. To achieve this it is necessary to display items in the nonspatialized mode "in register" on the right of the display.

Clearly, the two tasks impose somewhat different demands on the reader and not all of these relate directly to display format. For example, in the nonspatialized condition, only intraword saccades can occur up to the point where the whole sentence is displayed, whereas in the spatialized condition, not only must interword saccades be executed, but their programming may be delayed until the appearance of each successive word. In this sense, both tasks are only approximations to normal reading and the discovery of main effects of spatialization in the initial word-by-word reading phase would be relatively uninteresting. However, interactions between linguistic or other task variables and presentation mode do permit conclusions to be drawn with respect to the effects of spatialization. In addition, the task has the advantage that, in the "whole sentence" presentation phase stimulus conditions are identical and the obtained effects of spatialization here must reflect the prior presentation mode.

Experimental Results

READING TIMES

The first study to be discussed looked at the effects of spatialization on the performance of a reading task involving the detection of a syntactic anomaly. This question was approached using a task involving a direct syntactic judgment. Sentences such as the following were constructed:

(1) The busy executive lost his *expensive watch* near the smart night club.
(2) The man took his eldest *daughter through* the quiet old city park.

Both sentences types contained 12 words. The pair of words (words 6 and 7) shown italicized was presented in reverse order in the self-paced presentation phase, but in their correct order in the whole-sentence presentation. The principal manipulation in the experiment concerned the consequence, for the reader, of the reversal that occurred in the initial presentation of the experimental items. In sentence 1 the change to ". . . lost his watch expensive . . ." represents a relatively shallow syntactic violation, involving a reversal low in the sentence structure (adjective–noun). In contrast, the change in 2—". . . his eldest through daughter . . ." —is a violation involving a boundary relatively high in the sentence structure between a main clause and a prepositional attachment.

Subjects were asked to read the material, word by word, then to read the whole sentence and decide whether any words had been changed in the successive presentations. They were asked to make this decision regardless of any changes in word order they may notice. The experimental sentences were buffered with numerous fillers containing instances of changes both to word order and to content. The content changes invariably involved replacing a single word with a close synonym. No content changes were made to experimental sentences (i.e., all demanded a "yes" response). The aim of the study was to examine the effects of a spatialized presentation mode in the two successive phases: first, at the time of initial presentation, by an analysis of Inter-Response Times (IRTs), and second, while rereading, by an analysis of Sentence Reading Times and Errors.

TABLE 23.1. Mean interresponse times (ms) for the word defining the syntactic violation (word 2) and the preceding and following word (Experiment 1).

	Word position		
	Word 1	Word 2	Word 3
Spatialized			
Low reversal	377	404	414
Nonreversal	386	392	399
High reversal	380	410	436
Nonreversal	366	386	382
Nonspatialized			
Low reversal	361	379	408
Nonreversal	360	380	357
High reversal	352	373	402
Nonreversal	363	363	370

The first question to be directed at the results concerns on-line sensitivity to the syntactic word-order manipulation. It should be noted that the earliest point at which the violation caused by the reversal could be detected by subjects differs for the two structures. For the High Reversals, the anomaly is evident at once and should be reflected in changes in IRT in the region of word 6. For Low Reversals, it is detectable one word later. The mean IRT for the relevant three critical words in each structure (e.g., in terms of the example sentences above, "watch expensive near" and "though daughter the") are shown in Table 23.1. Overall, IRTs for the reversed structures are significantly slower than for their equivalent unreversed versions. More importantly from the perspective of the present discussion, there is a significant[1] interaction between Reversal Type (High or Low), Word Position, and Spatialization. The appropriate comparison for each reversed structure is the pattern of response in its equivalent unreversed version. These analyses reveal significant interactions between Word Position and Reversal *only* under conditions of Spatialized presentation. Examination of the data in Table 23.1 show immediate sensitivity to syntactic violation on encountering Word 2 in the Spatialized presentation mode (indexed by an interaction between Reversal and Position over Words 1 and 2). This relative increase in IRT spills over into Word Position 3. No such immediate effects is found in the Nonspatialized condition and the effect apparent on Word 3 is not, in fact, statistically reliable and arises from the data of one or two subjects who responded relatively very slowly.

---

[1] "Significant" in the discussion of the data that follow should be taken to mean a significance level at or beyond $p < .05$ in both subject (F1) and item (F2) analyses.

TABLE 23.2. Mean sentence reading times (ms) and percentage errors (Experiment 1).

	Spatialized		Nonspatialized	
	RT	% Error	RT	% Error
Low reversal	2,570	15.6	2,430	13.5
Low OK	2,560	6.3	2,390	5.2
High reversal	2,420	26.0	2,410	20.8
High OK	2,460	7.3	2,320	8.3

Table 23.2 shows the Reading Times and errors in the whole sentence presentation phase. No significant effects or interactions with spatialization are present in the Reading Time data, but there are significantly more errors overall following Spatialized presentation. It must be borne in mind that an error in the present task can most easily be interpreted as reflecting detection of the word-order reversal, leading to an increase in false negatives. The data are, therefore, quite consistent with the interpretation that a Spatialized presentation mode increases subjects' sensitivity to word order.

EYE MOVEMENTS

The data from the first experiment suggest that Spatialization has systematic effects both on-line (as indexed by IRT) and on later comprehension. However, the IRT data can, at best, be considered as only indicative. Measures of Reading Time (either IRTs or Whole Sentence RTs) are extraordinarily difficult to interpret. They are frequently very variable and often mask interactions between different components of the pattern of eye movements that form their substrate. At the extreme, for example, it is possible to find highly significant trade-offs between the number and duration of fixations, which more global measures will fail to detect (Kennedy & Murray, 1986; Pynte et al., 1988). Clearly, what is needed is a fine-grained analysis of the eye movement behavior as subjects reinspect the sentence following presentation under the two word-by-word conditions. The second study achieved this, with a replication[2] of the first, measuring eye movements during both presentation phases. The same materials and design were employed.

Although the primary focus of the study is the pattern of eye movements in the final whole sentence presentation phase, it is interesting to compare IRTs in the two studies. Table 23.3 gives the relevant data.

---

[2] The study reported was part of a larger experiment in which conditions of illumination and screen refresh rate were manipulated. The results discussed here are restricted to consideration of the effects of spatialization.

TABLE 23.3. Mean interresponse times (ms) for the word defining the syntactic violation (word 2) and the preceding and following word (Experiment 2).

	Word position		
	Word 1	Word 2	Word 3
Spatialized			
Low reversal	543	587	628
Nonreversal	567	575	569
High reversal	581	632	673
Nonreversal	560	590	573
Nonspatialized			
Low reversal	694	724	712
Nonreversal	693	710	717
High reversal	666	719	772
Nonreversal	689	672	696

There is a striking overall increase in IRT, compared to Experiment 1, which may, in large measure, be attributed to the changed task demands (the subject's head is restrained by means of a bite-bar, frequent calibration trials probably induce a more careful reading style, and the contrast of the display used was considerably lower than in the first study [see Footnote 2]). Again, the critical comparison in each presentation mode relates to performance in the reversed and unreversed versions of the two structures. For the High Reversal sentences, a similar pattern of IRT is evident in both Spatialized and Nonspatialized conditions, although subjects are significantly faster in the Spatialized mode. The Low Reversal structures, in contrast, show significantly different patterns in the two Modes. In Spatialized presentation, performance on the reversed and unreversed versions differs, with an increase in IRT spilling over from Word 2 to Word 3. In Nonspatialized presentation, the pattern of IRTs for reversed and unreversed versions is very similar. The data differ, however, from the results of Experiment 1, in that subjects appear to detect the anomaly in the High-Reversal structures under both presentation conditions, whereas the Low-Reversal anomaly goes unnoticed under conditions of Nonspatialized presentation (it will be recalled that a few very slow subjects in Experiment 1 in fact showed this pattern of response). Possibly the more extreme violation is evident, even in Nonspatialized presentation, when the overall response rate is comparatively slow.

Table 23.4 shows the Reading Times and errors in the whole sentence presentation phase. In contrast to Experiment 1, there is a strong effect of Spatialization: subjects were significantly slower to read the sentence and make a response following Nonspatialized presentation. As in Experiment 1 there was an overall tendency to make more errors following spatialized presentation, again suggesting a greater sensitivity to syntactic violation in this condition.

TABLE 23.4. Mean sentence reading times (ms) and percentage errors (Experiment 2).

| | Spatialized | | Nonspatialized | |
	RT	% Error	RT	% Error
Low reversal	3,463	28.5	4,003	25.4
Nonreversal	3,273	13.2	3,699	8.6
High reversal	3,396	25.0	3,991	22.7
Nonreversal	3,221	10.2	3,670	9.4

TABLE 23.5. Number of landings (per sentence on the initial (first three) and final (last three) words following the first saccade into the sentence (Experiment 2).

	Spatialized	Nonspatialized
Initial	5.06	0.62
Final	4.85	1.60

The analyses of eye movement data concentrated on the pattern of reinspection over the sentence following the final button-press (i.e., in the whole sentence display phase). The data provide very clear evidence that Nonspatialized presentation induces a different (and less efficient) pattern of rereading. The number of fixations made before the critical region was initially fixated shows a strong interaction between Presentation Mode and Reversal. For reversed structures, the difference was highly significant (5.96 fixations following Spatialized presentation and 6.31 following Nonspatialized). There was no difference for nonreversed structures (6.52 and 6.54). In addition, subjects are more likely, following Spatialized presentation, to direct their initial inspection to the critical region (Words 5 and 6 for High Reversals, and 6 and 7 for Low). This increased selectivity confirms the earlier findings of Pynte, et al. (1988). Taken overall, these patterns of reinspection strongly suggest faster and more efficient identification of the critical region when the displayed sentence has been preceded by a Spatialized presentation.

The *distributions* of reinspecting saccades were analyzed by counting the number of "landings" at each word position following the first saccade after the final button-press, which brought about the display of the whole sentence. The data, collapsed over the initial and final three words, for the two presentation conditions are shown in Table 23.5. There is a significant interaction: a landing near the beginning of the displayed sentence is more likely following Spatialized presentation, whereas, in contrast, a short saccade toward the end of the sentence is more likely following a Nonspatialized display. In fact, this difference arises from a quite profound difference in reading *strategy*. Non-

TABLE 23.6. Number of changes in direction (per sentence) in the whole sentence display (Experiment 2).

	Spatialized	Nonspatialized
Low reversal	1.63	2.60
Nonreversal	0.19	0.19
High reversal	0.27	0.31
Nonreversal	0.29	0.42

spatialized presentation induces many more backtracks and changes in direction during inspection of the sentence. (See Murray & Kennedy, 1988, for a description of similar strategic differences in reading style.) The data in Table 23.6 mirror the pattern of IRTs, suggesting that Low Reversal sentences did indeed represent a problem postponed for subjects in the Nonspatialized condition and that they dealt with this by executing more rereads in the Whole Sentence phase. The difference in Table 23.6 between Spatialized and Nonspatialized conditions is significant.

Subjects made significantly more fixations overall following Nonspatialized presentation (12.3 vs. 11.3 per sentence) and shorter saccades (8.6 vs. 9.6 character positions). This latter measure *excluded* the class of small corrective saccades (less than or equal to three character positions) because the incidence of these showed strong effects of prior presentation mode with significantly more following Nonspatialized presentation (1.50 vs. 1.03 per sentence). It is important to note, however, that this difference arises solely from a significant tendency to execute more small *within-word* saccades moving in a left-to-right direction (0.021 vs. 0.038 per word). The number of right-to-left corrections did not differ (0.022 vs. 0.025).

Conclusion

This is a report of work in progress and any conclusions must be considered provisional. However, the data do show important consequences for the reader of having access to differential spatial information. The effects occur at three levels. First, the results from both experiments support the contention that a Nonspatialized presentation mode renders the reader less sensitive to syntactic violations. The obtained interactions with level of violation suggest that whether or not impairments are observed in single-location self-paced presentation modes may depend on the complexity of the materials being processed and on the reader's strategy (at least insofar as reading speed reflects this). Second, Nonspatialized presentation induces very marked differences in the pattern of later reinspection of a sentence, with more fixations, shorter saccades, and a greater tendency to reread. Finally, there are clear within-word effects, suggesting that Nonspatialized presentation leads to an increase in nonoptimal landing position and a consequential increase in corrective saccades. These results have clear implications for text processing under conditions where spatial coding is disrupted. There are two obvious candidates for further investigation: text editing, in which various dynamic techniques (e.g., paging, scrolling, insertion, and formatting) serve to destroy relative spatial information; and operations within windows, where the relevant spatial frame becomes ambiguous.

Acknowledgment. The work reported in this chapter has been supported by grants from the Medical Research Council (grant no. G9006692N in collaboration with Wayne S. Murray) and travel grants from the Royal Society and the British Council. Thanks are due to Elizabeth Kennedy, Wayne Murray, Joel Pynte, and Nick Wade for helpful comments on the issues raised.

References

Anstis, S.M. (1974). A chart demonstrating variations in acuity with retinal position. *Vision Research*, *14*, 589–592.

Baccino, T., Pynte, J., & Kennedy, A. (1990). *Spatial coding of word position in text during mouse operations.* Paper presented at the Fourth Conference of the European Society for Cognitive Psychology, Como, Italy.

Bouma, H., & de Voogd, A.H. (1974). On the control of eye saccades in reading. *Vision Research*, *14*, 273–284.

Breitmeyer, B.G. (1983). Sensory masking, persistence, and enhancement in visual exploration and reading. In K. Rayner (Ed.), *Eye movements in reading: Perceptual and language processes*. New York: Academic Press.

Christie, J., & Just, M.A. (1975). Remembering the location and content of sentences in a prose passage. *Journal of Educational Psychology*, *68*, 702–710.

Davidson, M.L., Fox, M.J., & Dick, A.O. (1973). Effect of eye movements on backward masking and perceived location. *Perception and Psychophysics*, *14*, 110–116.

Feldman, J.A. (1985). Four frames suffice: A provisional model of vision and space. *Behavioral and Brain Sciences*, *8*, 265–289.

Forster, K.I. (1970). Visual perception of rapidly presented word sequences of varying complexity. *Perception and Psychophysics*, *8*, 215–221.

Frazier, L., & Rayner, K. (1982). Making and correcting errors during sentence comprehension. Eye movements in the analysis of structurally ambiguous sentences. *Cognitive Psychology*, *14*, 178–210.

Haber, R.N. (1985). Three frames suffice: Drop the retinotopic frame. Commentary on Feldman's "Four Frames suffice. A provisional model of vision and space." *Behavioral and Brain Sciences*, *8*, 295–296.

Irwin, D.E., Brown, J.S., & Sun J-S. (1988). Visual masking and visual integration across saccadic eye movements. *Journal of Experimental Psychology: General, 117*, 276–287.

Johnson-Laird, P.N. (1983). *Mental models*. Cambridge: Cambridge University Press.

Juola, J.F., Ward, N.J., & McNamara, T. (1982) Visual search and reading of rapid serial presentations of letter strings, words and text. *Journal of Experimental Psychology: General, 111*, 208–227.

Just, M.A., & Carpenter, P.A. (1980). A theory of reading: From eye fixations to comprehension. *Psychological Review, 87*, 329–354.

Kanwisher, N.G. (1987). Repetition blindness: Type recognition without token individuation. *Cognition, 27*, 117–143.

Kennedy, A. (1983). On looking into space. In K. Rayner (Ed.), *Eye movements in reading: Perceptual and language processes*. New York: Academic Press.

Kennedy, A., & Murray, W.S. (1984). Inspection times for words in syntactically ambiguous sentences under three presentation conditions. *Journal of Experimental Psychology: Human Perception and Performance, 10*, 833–849.

Kennedy, A., & Murray, W.S. (1986). The components of reading time: Eye movement patterns of good and poor readers. In J.K. O'Regan & A. Levy-Schoen (Eds.), *Proceedings of Third European Conference on Eye Movements*. Amsterdam: Elsivier.

Kennedy, A., & Murray, W.S. (1987). Spatial coordinates and reading: Comments on Monk (1985). *Quarterly Journal of Experimental Psychology, 39A*, 649–656.

Kennedy, A., Murray, W.S., Jennings, F., & Reid, C. (1989). Parsing complements: Comments on the generality of the principle of minimal attachment. *Language and Cognitive Processes, 4*, 51–76.

Kolers, P.A. (1983). Locations and contents. In K. Rayner (Ed.), *Eye movements in reading: Perceptual and language processes*. New York: Academic Press.

Kolers, P.A., & Lewis, C.L. (1972). Visual perception of rapidly presented words. *Acta Psychologica, 36*, 112–124.

Lotze, H. (1886). *Outline of psychology*. G.T. Ladd (Ed. and Trans.). Boston: Ginn.

Mackay, D.M. (1973). Visual stability and voluntary eye movements. In R. Jung (Ed.) *Handbook of Sensory Physiology*. Vol. 7. Springer: Berlin.

Marr, D. (1982). *Vision: A computational investigation into the human representation and processing of visual information*. San Francisco: Freeman.

Mays, L.E., & Sparks, D.L. (1980). Saccades are spatially, not retinocentrically, coded. *Science, 208*, 1163–1165.

McConkie, G.W., Kerr, P.W., Reddix, M.D., & Zola, D. (1988). Eye movement control during reading: I. The location of initial fixations on words. *Vision Research, 28*, 1107–1118.

McConkie, G.W., & Zola, D. (1987). Visual attention during eye fixations while reading. In M. Coltheart (Ed.), *Attention and performance XII: The psychology of reading*. Hillsdale NJ: Erlbaum.

Monk, A.F. (1985). Theoretical note: Coordinate systems in visual word recognition. *Quarterly Journal of Experimental Psychology, 37A*, 613–626.

Murray, W.S., & Kennedy, A. (1988). Spatial coding in the processing of anaphor by good and poor readers: Evidence from eye movement analyses. *Quarterly Journal of Experimental Psychology*, *40A*, 693–718.

Noton, D., & Stark, L. (1971). Scanpaths in saccadic eye movements while viewing and recognizing patterns. *Vision Research*, *11*, 929–942.

O'Regan, J.K. (1990). Eye movements and reading. In E. Kowler (Ed.), *Eye movements and their role in visual and cognitive processes*. Amsterdam: Elsevier.

Pynte, J., Kennedy, A., Murray, W.S., & Courrieu, P. (1988). The effects of spatialization on the processing of ambiguous pronominal reference. In G. Luer, U. Lass, & J. Shallo-Hoffman (Eds.), *Eye movement research: Physiological and psychological aspects*. Gottingen: Hogrefe.

Rayner, K. (1975). The perceptual span and peripheral cues in reading. *Cognitive Psychology*, *7*, 65–81.

Rayner, K., & Pollatsek, A. (1983). Is visual information integrated across saccades? *Perception and Psychophysics*, *34*, 39–48.

Rayner, K., & Pollatsek, A. (1989). *The psychology of reading*. Englewood Cliffs, NJ: Prentice Hall.

Slowiaczek, M.L., & Rayner, K. (1987). Sequential masking during eye fixations in reading. *Bulletin of the Psychonomic Society*, *25*, 175–178.

Swanston, M.T., Wade, N.J., & Day, R.H. (1987). The representation of uniform motion in vision. *Perception*, *16*, 143–159.

Treisman, A. (1988). Features and objects: The fourteenth Bartlett Memorial Lecture. *Quarterly Journal of Experimental Psychology*, *40A*, 201–237.

Zechmeister, E.B., & McKillop, J. (1972). Recall of place on the page. *Journal of Educational Psychology*, *63*, 446–453.

24
Tracing the Course of Sentence Comprehension: How Lexical Information is Used

CHARLES CLIFTON, JR.

There are several reasons why the study of sentence comprehension has become interesting again. Since its earliest days, psycholinguistics was concerned with how people use their knowledge of grammar to construct representations of sentences (Fodor, Bever, & Garrett, 1974; Miller, 1962). This concern has not changed. However, the theoretical and methodological tools for addressing it have improved dramatically. The theories that were entertained two decades ago relied on inappropriate grammatical analyses (as, for example, the derivational theory of complexity relied on transformations) or placed unrealistic demands on the cognitive processor (e.g., analysis by synthesis theories) (cf. Fodor et al., 1974). Most of the available techniques focused on the products of comprehension (Fillenbaum, 1970). The few on-line measures that were used failed to disentangle the results of processes occurring at several different stages of comprehension (Gough, 1965). In the last decade, however, explicit, controversial theories that illuminate the fine-grained details of parsing have been proposed (Abney, 1989; Altmann & Steedman, 1988; Fodor, 1983; Forster, 1979; Frazier, 1978; Kimball, 1973; Marslen-Wilson & Tyler, 1987; Pritchett, 1988; Tanenhaus & Carlson, 1989; cf. Tanenhaus, 1988, for a good overview). Linguistic theory has changed in ways that make it much more consistent with psychological theorizing (Chomsky, 1981; Frazier, 1988). Finally, and critically, techniques for addressing questions of real-time processing have been developed.

Measurement of where the eyes look during reading, and how long fixations are held, has proven to be one of the most illuminating techniques (Frazier, 1987; Frazier & Rayner, 1982; Just & Carpenter, 1980; Rayner & Pollatsek, 1989). The technique provides enough temporal resolution to reflect the automatic, quick-acting processes that many current theories invoke to explain parsing. It also permits the experimenter to examine the entire pattern of a variety of measures that can be obtained in an experiment. These measures include first fixation duration (the duration of the first fixation made in a target region, e.g., a word), first pass time (the sum of the fixation durations in a region prior to an eye movement out of that region; referred to as "gaze duration" when the region is a single word), and total reading time (the sum of all fixations made in a region). The pattern of effects observed in these different measures is informative, in that the measures may be differentially sensitive to distinct processes (see Rayner, Sereno, Morris, Schmauder, & Clifton, 1989, for further discussion).

This chapter describes two lines of research that examine the contribution that different sources of knowledge make to sentence comprehension. Each tries to disentangle contributions made by a reader's knowledge of possible syntactic structures from contributions made by semantic knowledge. In one case, the semantic knowledge specifies the possible arguments that the head of a phrase can take (Clifton, Speer, & Abney, 1991). In the other case, the semantic knowledge concerns the probable thematic roles that a phrase can play in a sentence (Clifton, in preparation; Stowe, 1989). In both cases, I will argue that the eye-tracking record provides evidence that the initial structural analysis of a sentence is built by a specialized syntactic processing module, initially operating with little or no guidance from other processing systems, including systems for processing the forms of semantic knowledge investigated here (Ferreira & Clifton, 1986; Frazier, 1985, 1987, 1990b; Rayner, Carlson, & Frazier, 1983).

Processing Argument Structure

The central theoretical claim behind the research presented here derives from Frazier's (1987) analysis of parsing strategies. Frazier argued that the human sentence parsing mechanism uses knowledge of possible syntactic structures, encoded as phrase structure rules, to build an initial analysis of a sentence as it is read. The mechanism parses a string of words into its phrasal constituents and specifies their structural relationships. The resulting analysis can be represented as a labeled tree structure. The parser builds a single analysis at a time, initially accepting the first analysis that becomes available. The rationale for this "first available analysis" principle derives from the widely recognized nature of human short-term memory: a limited amount of unstructured material can be held in memory, but much more material can be retained when appropriately structured. Parsing imposes structure on incoming words; quick parsing imposes it quickly, before information is lost.

The first available analysis principle motivates the two parsing strategies that have received the most experimental attention:

1. *Minimal attachment*: attach each incoming lexical item into the existing structure adding the smallest possible number of new nodes.
2. *Late closure*: when grammatically permissible, attach incoming lexical items into the phrase currently being processed.

Minimal attachment satisfies the first available analysis principle because each new node requires the application of a new rule, which presumably adds processing time. Late closure satisfies it because the phrase currently being processed is the first phrase available for further elaboration. Both strategies assume that the initial attachment of a word into a sentence structure is based on a limited amount of information, specifically, the lexical category (part of speech) of the word and the phrase structure rules that refer to that part of speech. Initial analysis is not affected by meaning or context or information specific to a particular lexical item, such as its most frequent or even its possible grammatical usages.

Early evidence for these claims was provided by Rayner et al. (1983). They used eye-tracking measurement to demonstrate that temporarily ambiguous sentences that were eventually disambiguated so that they were consistent with the minimal attachment strategy were read more quickly than sentences that proved to be inconsistent with the strategy. This was true whether syntactic information or semantic plausibility provided the disambiguation. In one experiment, their subjects read sentences like 1a and 1b. In the former the prepositional phrase "with binoculars" most plausibly modifies the verb "see."

(1a) *Minimal attachment*: The spy saw the cop with binoculars but the cop didn't see him.
(1b) *Nonminimal attachment*: The spy saw the cop with a revolver but the cop didn't see him.

In the latter, the prepositional phrase "with a revolver" most plausibly modifies the noun phrase "the cop." Sentence 1a is consistent with the minimal attachment strategy, because (under the syntactic analysis Rayner et al. assumed) attaching a prepositional phrase as a modifier of a verb requires one less syntactic node than attaching it as modifier of a noun phrase. Sentence 1b, a "nonminimal attachment" sentence, is inconsistent with the strategy.

Eye fixation durations were longer in the disambiguating region (the object of the prepositional phrase) for nonminimal attachment sentences than for minimal attachment sentences. The straightforward interpretation of these results is that the prepositional phrase is initially analyzed as a modifier of the verb (minimal attachment), but that this analysis must be discarded when it is realized that semantic factors require the prepositional phrase to modify the noun.

This interpretation has been challenged. Taraban and McClelland (1988, 1990) suggested that although the conclusions of Rayner et al. (1983) held for their materials, it was possible to construct materials whose semantic bias was sufficient to result in an initial parsing preference for nonminimal attachment. Taraban and McClelland showed that such nonminimal attachment sentences were read faster than their minimal attachment versions. However, the self-paced reading technique

Taraban and McClelland used may not have had the temporal resolution needed to detect a brief minimal attachment advantage. Abney (1989) advanced a different objection to Rayner et al.'s interpretation. In addition to criticizing the syntactic analysis on which they based their predictions (but cf. Frazier, 1990a), he proposed that the actual principle that resolves temporary ambiguities is a preference for analyzing a phrase as an *argument* rather than an *adjunct*.

For present purposes, an argument can be taken to be a phrase that is a syntactic sister of the *head* of the phrase that contains it.[1] An adjunct is attached higher in the syntactic tree, and is a sister of some projection of the head of the phrase. An intuitive grasp of the distinction can be gained by thinking of an argument as a phrase whose role is lexically specified by the head of the phrase containing it (as, for example, "put" specifies a noun phrase object and a prepositional phrase location). Adjuncts are phrases that need not be specified by particular heads of phrases, but can be "adjoined" to all phrases of a given type.

In many minimal attachment items that have been used, the temporarily ambiguous phrase (e.g., the prepositional phrase in sentence 1) can be taken as an argument of the verb, whereas in all or nearly all the nonminimal attachment items, the temporarily ambiguous phrase is an adjunct of the noun. Thus, a preference to analyze a phrase initially as an argument leads in most cases to quicker comprehension of sentences in which the prepositional phrase modifies the verb than in which it modifies the noun.

However, as Abney (1989) pointed out, it is possible to construct cases in which a preference for arguments over adjuncts should result in easier processing for noun modification ("nonminimal attachment") than for verb modification ("minimal attachment") sentences. Consider the following sentence:

(2) The man expressed his interest in the car.

The prepositional phrase is (ambiguously) an argument of the noun or an adjunct of the verb. Intuition suggests that it is quickly and perhaps immediately taken to modify the noun, "interest," and not the verb, "expressed."

The experiments reported by Clifton et al. (1991) were designed to see if this intuition is supported by the eye-tracking record. We constructed 16 sets of four sentences each; one set is shown in Table 24.1. In this table, the potential argument assigner appears in capital letters, and the prepositional phrase whose attachment site is in question is italicized. The first two forms are minimal attachment sentences, in that considerations of plausibility force the prepositional phrase to modify the verb. The

---

[1] "Sister of x" means "immediately dominated by the same node as x."

TABLE 24.1. Sample sentences from Clifton, Speer, and Abney (1991).

MINIMAL ATTACHMENT, ARGUMENT
The saleswoman tried to INTEREST the man *in a wallet* during the storewide sale at
    Steigers.
MINIMAL ATTACHMENT, NONARGUMENT
The man expressed his INTEREST *in a hurry* during the storewide sale at Steigers.
NONMINIMAL ATTACHMENT, ARGUMENT
The man expressed his INTEREST *in a wallet* during the storewide sale at Steigers.
NONMINIMAL ATTACHMENT, NONARGUMENT
The salesman tried to INTEREST the man *in his fifties* during the storewide sale at Steigers.

second two forms are nonminimal attachment sentences in which the prepositional phrase must modify the object noun. Orthogonally, the first and third forms are argument attachment sentences in which the prepositional phrase serves as an argument of the head of the phrase that includes it. In the second and fourth forms, the prepositional phrase is an adjunct of the phrase. If initial parsing decisions follow the minimal attachment strategy, and are guided solely by phrase structure rules and knowledge about part of speech, then the first two forms should be read more quickly than the last two. If, on the other hand, initial parsing decisions reflect a preference for arguments over adjuncts, then the first and third sentences should show less disruption in reading than the second and fourth.

Thirty-two subjects read the 16 sentences, four in each form shown in Table 24.1 (counterbalanced over items), while their eye movements were measured using an SRI eye tracker (see Clifton et al., 1991; for procedural details). A variety of eye movement measures were computed for each of several regions: the noun phrase preceding the ambiguously attached prepositional phrase, the prepositional phrase itself, and a region of a few words that immediately followed the prepositional phrase (common to all four forms of a sentence). The *first pass* measure is the sum of all fixation durations made in a region, from the time the region was entered to when it was first exited. The *total time* measure is the sum of all fixation durations in a region, including rereadings of that region. Both measures were divided by the number of characters in the region, to provide a millisecond per character measure (Figure 24.1).

The results were straightforward. In the prepositional phrase region, first-pass reading times were significantly[2] faster for verb attachment than for noun attachment sentences, 30.8 versus 35.4 ms/character, supporting the predictions of the minimal attachment analysis. However, in this same

---

[2] All results reported were significant beyond the .05 level in analyses permitting generalization to subjects and to items, unless otherwise indicated.

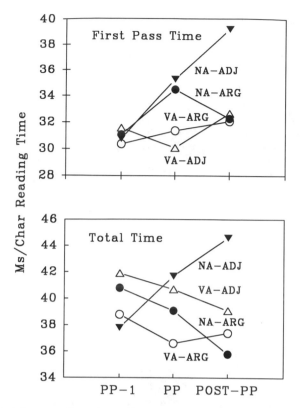

Figure 24.1. Mean reading times (first-pass and total times) for Experiment 1. Reprinted, by permission, from Clifton, Speer, & Abney, *Journal of Memory and Language*, 1991.

region, total reading times were faster for argument attachment sentences than for adjunct attachment sentences, 37.9 versus 41.2 ms/character. The difference between verb and noun attachment in total reading time was nonsignificant. In the region following the prepositional phrase, the first pass measure did not yield statistically significant effects, but total reading times showed disruption for adjunct phrases in general.

The simplest interpretation of the data is that there is an initial preference to attach a prepositional phrase as a modifier of a verb rather than of a noun (perhaps specifically an argument). When the object of the preposition indicates the implausibility of such an analysis, reading is disrupted. A preference for arguments over adjuncts appears slightly later, in the region following the prepositional phrase and in regressions into the prepositional phrase region. A sentence with a phrase that is the argument of a noun is read quite easily, because the preference for arguments over adjuncts guides the revision of the initial verb phrase attachment. A sentence with a noun phrase adjunct is read with difficulty, because the initial verb attachment analysis must be rejected but argument structure provides no guidance to replacing it.

This analysis illustrates the power of eye-tracking data to illuminate the details of the parsing process. As Clifton et al. (1991) detail, the data do not actually require acceptance of the minimal attachment strategy. Abney's (1989) claims for argument priority could be maintained, if other reasons are advanced for initially preferring attachment of a phrase to a verb rather than to a noun (e.g., in the present data, the fact that the verb appears earlier in the sentence than the noun does). Further, eye-tracking data are not the only possible data for analyzing parsing. Clifton et al. report another study using self-paced reading procedures that also points to an early preference for verb attachment followed by a later preference for argument attachment (cf. Ferreira & Henderson, 1990, for a similar pattern of results concerning verb subcategorization preferences). Nonetheless, the eye movement data certainly do strongly suggest that a sentence is initially analyzed in the way that was predicted by the minimal attachment strategy, and that other factors, such as argument status, operate at a later point in parsing.

Processing Thematic Structure

Argument status can be viewed as semantic information, and the conclusion that it is not used initially in parsing suggests that semantic information is not used to guide an initial parse. However, argument status is not the only potentially relevant type of semantic information. One particularly interesting possibility is that thematic role information may guide initial parsing decisions (Stowe, 1989).

Thematic roles, for present purposes, can be viewed as lexically specified semantic relationships between a lexical item and its arguments. A simple example is

(3) John gave a book to Bill.

Here, "John" is the agent, the intentional agent responsible for the action; "book" is the theme, the object that undergoes the action; and "Bill" is the recipient. Some verbs (ergative verbs, such as *break*, *stop*, *open*, *dry*) provide multiple thematic role possibilities. Their subject can be agent and their object theme, as in sentences 4a and 5a, or their subject can be theme, as in the objectless 4b and 5b:

(4a) The police stopped the driver.
(4b) The truck stopped.
(5a) The truck stopped the driver.
(5b) The police stopped.

TABLE 24.2. Example of sentences used in Experiment 2 (and by Stowe, 1989).

(| indicates division into regions for purposes of data analysis)
ANIMATE, DISAMBIGUATING ADVERBIAL PHRASE
a) While his friend| was cooking| in the kitchen| the meat| was sitting| on the table.|
ANIMATE, NO DISAMBIGUATING ADVERBIAL PHRASE
b) While his friend| was cooking| the meat| was sitting| on the table.|
INANIMATE, DISAMBIGUATING ADVERBIAL PHRASE
c) While his dinner| was cooking| in the kitchen| the meat| was sitting| on the table.|
INANIMATE, NO DISAMBIGUATING ADVERBIAL PHRASE
d) While his dinner| was cooking| the meat| was sitting| on the table.|

In 4, the thematically preferred relations are expressed, whereas in 5, the thematically unpreferred relations are expressed. That is, an animate subject, such as "police," is preferentially taken as an agent, whereas an inanimate subject, such as "truck," is preferentially taken as theme.

Stowe (1989) raised the following question: When faced with a decision about how to relate two phrases such as "the police" and "stopped," does the processor take into account the thematic role possibilities and preferences, or does it just relate them syntactically (as subject and verb, in the present case)? Stowe considered several different answers to the question, and provided data that suggested an affirmative answer to the first option. She used a self-paced reading task in which readers judged the acceptability of a sentence in a word-by-word fashion, indicating when a sentence becomes ungrammatical (if it does). In one experiment, she used sentences like those in Table 24.2. Here, the noun phrase, "the meat," is temporarily ambiguous in its position after the verb. It could be the direct object and theme of the verb "was cooking," or it could be the subject of the next clause. The late closure strategy entails a preference for the former analysis. Such a choice, however, is disconfirmed by the next phrase, "was sitting." This phrase triggers a syntactic reanalysis, which should disrupt reading. No such disruption should be observed if the sentence had an adverbial phrase ("in the kitchen") after the verb, preventing "the meat" from being analyzed as direct object of "was cooking" in the first place.

Stowe found that reading time was dramatically slowed in the disambiguating verb phrase "was sitting" for sentences that were temporarily ambiguous, as compared to sentences with the disambiguating adverbial phrase after the first verb. However, this effect was observed only for sentences with animate subjects. Reading time for the disambiguating verb was slower than 1,400 ms/word for sentences like (b) in Table 24.2, compared to approximately 800 ms/word for sentences like (a). No such difference appeared when the subject was inanimate ("his dinner"). Reading times for the disambiguating verbs in sentences like (c) and (d) of Table 24.2 were also approximately 800 ms/character. Readers may have used their knowledge that "dinner" is more likely to be the theme than the agent of an ergative verb to guide their initial analysis of the sentences. If the sentence subject fills the theme role of the verb, and if parsing is guided by thematic information, no postverbal theme should be expected. The postverbal noun phrase should be taken initially as the subject of the matrix sentence[3], and no disruption should be observed when the following verb phrase is read.

Just as in the case of argument structure, one can ask when thematic role information is consulted in the course of parsing a sentence. Stowe's (1989) reading times were very slow, on the order of 750 ms/word before the disambiguating region. Further, her word-by-word grammaticality judgment task could well have disrupted normal processing. Eye movement methodology can, in principle, avoid both these problems, allowing a finer-grained analysis of sentence comprehension processes during normal reading.

Three eye movement experiments (Experiments 2, 3, and 4) were conducted to see whether Stowe's results actually indicated an initial or a delayed contribution of thematic role information to parsing. In Experiment 2, 24 subjects read Stowe's 16 sentences, embedded in a total of 80 sentences. The difference in first pass time and total time (ms/character) between the temporarily ambiguous (no adverbial phrase) and unambiguous forms is shown in Figure 24.2. The *total time* data were consistent with what Stowe observed. Reading times on the disambiguating verb phrase ("was sitting") were particularly long for sentences with an animate subject and no disambiguating adverbial phrase (although statistical significance was marginal; interaction $p < .06$). A similar, and significant, effect was seen on the noun phrase before the disambiguating region, presumably because of the high frequency of regressive eye movements out of the disambiguating region.

A different conclusion is suggested by analysis of *first-pass* times. Table 24.3 presents an analysis of reading in the disambiguating region, using a procedure in which the left boundary of the region is repositioned to the left, character by character, up to four characters, if no fixations otherwise occur in the region. First-pass reading time in this region was slow, and a relatively large number of first-pass fixations were made in it, when the sentence was temporarily ambiguous. This held true for both animate and inanimate sentence subjects.

The contrast between first-pass and total time data suggests that Stowe's results may not have reflected initial decisions made in parsing.

---

[3] The fact that the sentence begins with an initial subordinate clause entails that a matrix sentence occurs later. Thus, taking the postverbal noun phrase as subject of a new sentence rather than as object of the first verb does not violate minimal attachment.

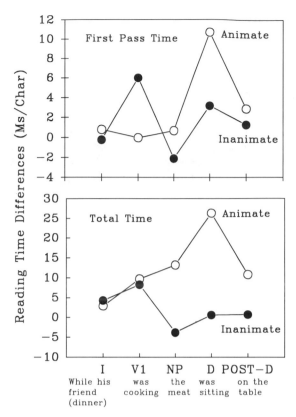

FIGURE 24.2. Differences in reading time (mean ms/character, first-pass and total times) between temporarily ambiguous and unambiguous sentences, Experiment 2.

Rather, thematic role possibilities and preferences may have affected only later stages in processing, in which the structural analyses proposed on the basis of purely syntactic factors are evaluated thematically (Ferreira & Clifton, 1986; Frazier, 1990b; Rayner et al., 1983).[4]

---

[4] Two aspects of the data warrant comment. First, reading times appear to be particularly long in the region of the first verb for ambiguous inanimate subject sentences. However, the relevant interaction was thoroughly nonsignificant, and all hint of the interaction disappeared when the data were rescored with the right-hand boundary of this region moved left by four characters. The effect, if real, may have been due to subjects occasionally fixating near the end of the verb and obtaining preview information from the next region. Second, the fact that reading times for postverbal noun phrases following inanimate subjects were not slow will be seen to be incongruent with the finding that they were slow in the next two experiments. The reason for this inconsistency across experiments is not apparent, but it may have something to do with the generally slow reading times in Experiment 2.

TABLE 24.3. First-pass duration and mean number of first-pass fixations in disambiguating region, expanded if necessary (Experiment 2).

Condition	Gaze duration	Number of fixations
Animate/disambiguated	414	1.2
Animate/ambiguous	518	1.5
Inanimate/disambiguated	441	1.1
Inanimate/ambiguous	516	1.4

TABLE 24.4. Example of sentences used in Experiments 3 and 4.

Experiment 3
ANIMATE, DISAMBIGUATING COMMA
a) Before the police stopped, the moon had risen over the ocean.
ANIMATE, NO DISAMBIGUATING COMMA
b) Before the police stopped the moon had risen over the ocean.
INANIMATE, DISAMBIGUATING COMMA
c) Before the truck stopped, the moon had risen over the ocean.
INANIMATE, NO DISAMBIGUATING COMMA
d) Before the truck stopped the moon had risen over the ocean.

Experiment 4
ANIMATE, DISAMBIGUATING COMMA
e) Before the police stopped, the Datsun disappeared into the night.
ANIMATE, NO DISAMBIGUATING COMMA
f) Before the police stopped the Datsun disappeared into the night.
INANIMATE, DISAMBIGUATING COMMA
g) Before the truck stopped, the Datsun disappeared into the night.
INANIMATE, NO DISAMBIGUATING COMMA
h) Before the truck stopped the Datsun disappeared into the night.

However, one factor makes both Stowe's results and the present data hard to interpret. Although the postverbal nouns were always plausible objects when the subject was animate, many were implausible when the subject was inanimate (e.g., "the doors opened the shop," "the car turned the lights," "his dinner was cooking the meat," "the report returned the memo"). Forty-seven University of Massachusetts students rated Stowe's sentences (among others) on a seven-point plausibility rating scale. Each saw half the sentences with an animate subject, and half with an inanimate subject. The mean plausibility rating was 6.09 (7.0 maximum plausibility) for sentences with animate subjects, but only 2.95 for sentences with inanimate subjects. The sheer implausibility of the relationships, rather than effects of animacy on thematic role preferences, may have been the source of the differences between sentences with animate and inanimate subjects that were observed in the total reading time data.

Two additional experiments were conducted to control the role of plausibility. In one (Experiment 3), the postverbal noun phrase was made

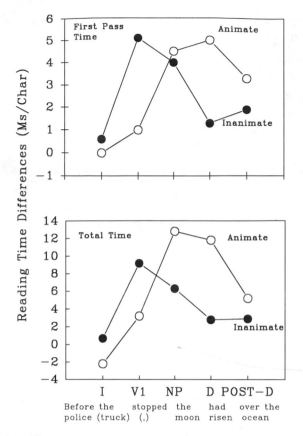

FIGURE 24.3. Differences in reading time (mean ms/character, first-pass and total times) between temporarily ambiguous and unambiguous sentences, Experiment 3.

anomalous as object for *all* sentences. In the other (Experiment 4), the postverbal noun phrase was made acceptable as object for all sentences, regardless of animacy. Efforts were taken to make the noun phrases as plausible as possible in this latter experiment, but it proved impossible to make them as plausible for inanimate as for animate subject sentences.

Examples of the sentences appear in Table 24.4. Most of the 16 sentences used in Experiments 3 and 4 contained the ergative verbs used in Experiment 2. The unambiguous controls were made unambiguous by including a comma rather than an adverbial phrase before the postverbal noun phrase. Forty subjects read the sentences of Experiment 3, and 24 read the sentences of Experiment 4.

The data for Experiments 3 and 4 appear in Figures 24.3 and 24.4, respectively. In each case, the first pass and total times present much the same picture. The differences between the first pass and total time

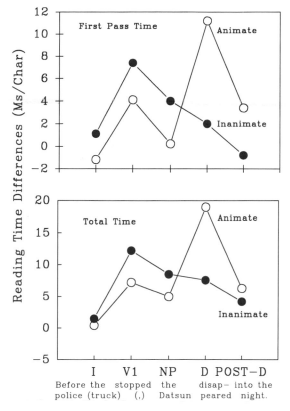

FIGURE 24.4. Differences in reading time (mean ms/character, first-pass and total times) between temporarily ambiguous and unambiguous sentences, Experiment 4.

measures that were seen in Experiment 2 appear as differences among regions in Experiments 3 and 4. The reasons for this difference are unclear. The Experiments 3 and 4 subjects read more quickly than the Experiment 2 subjects. First pass reading times in the region of the first verb and the following noun phrase averaged 32.2 ms/character in Experiment 3 and 30.5 in Experiment 4, as compared to 41.7 in Experiment 2. Further, the Experiments 3 and 4 subjects made fewer regressive eye movements; 12.5% of the sentences used in Experiment 3 showed regressions out of the disambiguating region and 6.5% in Experiment 3, as compared with 17% in Experiment 2. The difference cannot be traced to subject population differences, because most subjects in all experiments were graduate students or other members of the University of Massachusetts community who were typically quite experienced with eye-tracking procedures. In any event, because of the similarity between the first pass and total time measures in Experiments 3 and 4, only the first pass time data will be discussed here.

First consider Experiment 3. The data from the disambiguating region (the verb that follows the postverbal noun) were generally compatible with the results reported by Stowe (1989) and observed in Experiment 2 total reading times. First pass times were selectively slowed in the animate subject/no comma condition—37.2 ms/character in this condition versus 33.5 in the other three conditions. Although this interaction did not reach satisfactory levels of significance, it was significant for both the total time measure and a measure of the duration of the very first fixation made in the disambiguating region.

Although no evidence of disruption in reading sentences with inanimate subjects appeared in the disambiguating region, substantial disruption appeared in the previous region, particularly in the first-pass time measure. First pass times were longer for ambiguous (no comma) than for unambiguous sentences in this region, 32.3 versus 28.1 ms/character. There was no sign of an interaction with animacy.

It appears that readers did initially analyze the postverbal noun phrase as object of the verb, even for ergative verbs with inanimate subjects. They then very quickly considered the plausibility of the analysis, and rejected it as implausible, causing some disruption of reading. If the subject was inanimate, thematic role preferences then guided reanalysis, facilitating interpretation of the first noun phrase as theme rather than as agent. If the subject was animate, thematic role preferences provided no attractive alternative, resulting in a long-lasting disruption of reading. In neither case, however, did thematic role preferences block the initial object analysis of the postverbal noun phrase. If animacy-based thematic role preferences had blocked this analysis (as the comma seems to have done), then no disruption should have been seen while reading the noun phrase.

Consider now Experiment 4. It was intended to provide postverbal noun phrases that were uniformly plausible as objects of the verb, but otherwise to be as similar as possible to Experiment 3. Unfortunately, it proved impossible to achieve full uniformity of plausibility. The 47 University of Massachusetts students who rated the plausibility of Stowe's sentences also rated the simple sentences that expressed the relation among subject, verb, and noun phrase object of the sentences used in Experiment 4. The mean plausibility (7 = highly plausible) of the sentences with animate subjects was 5.51, whereas it was 4.51 for sentences with inanimate subjects.

This difference in plausibility apparently affected the data that appear in Figure 24.4. The disambiguating region showed the familiar selective reading problems for ambiguous (no comma) sentences with animate subjects. The postverbal noun phrase region showed fairly clear signs of exactly the opposite result: slow reading times for ambiguous sentences with inanimate subjects (but only at the .10 level of significance). This pattern of results suggests that the postverbal noun phrase was initially analyzed as object. When the initial subject was animate, this analysis was maintained until the disambiguating verb occurred. However, when the subject was inanimate, the analysis was questioned and corrected during the reading of the postverbal noun phrase. The marginal plausibility of the object analysis, or animacy-based thematic role preferences, or both, could have triggered this reanalysis.

There are peculiarities in the data that make this simple story seem slightly inadequate. The most notable peculiarity is the large difference in times to read the verbs of inanimate subject sentences with and without a disambiguating comma. This difference was due in Experiment 3 (where it was most notable) to fast reading times in the inanimate subject/ disambiguating comma condition (30.8 ms/character) compared to the other conditions (34.4 to 35.9 ms/character). It also appeared in Experiment 4, for at least partly similar reasons (28.8 ms/character reading time for inanimate/comma, 31.4 ms/character for animate/comma, but 35.2 and 36.2 ms/character for the two no-comma conditions). The effects may reflect differences in the ease of interpreting the comma itself. The comma implies that there will be no direct object, and thus that the subject must be theme. Deciding that an inanimate subject is theme might be easier than deciding that an inanimate subject is. Some evidence for this suggestion is provided by an analysis in which the right-hand boundary of the verb phrase region (which is terminated by the comma, if one is present) is moved left by three spaces. The remaining fixations in the verb phrase region were less likely to have provided useful information about the comma. In fact, they showed no sign of the difference between animate and inanimate subject conditions noted in Figures 24.3 and 24.4.

Conclusions

Two lines of research have been described. Both used eye-tracking methodology to explore the detailed time course of when phrase structure, argument structure, and thematic role information are used in sentence comprehension. In both cases, the eye movement record provided evidence that initial decisions about the structural analysis of sentences were made based solely on phrase structure considerations, following the minimal attachment and late closure strategies. The other forms of information had substantial effects on sentence comprehension, but the effects appeared later in the eye movement record. Knowledge of argument structure and thematic role preferences seem to have been used to evaluate and correct analyses that were initially constructed with appeal to phrase structure information.

Puzzles remain, of course. "Early" versus "late" comprehension processes do not appear at rigidly fixed points in the eye movement record. The contrast between initial and later processes appeared as a difference between first-pass and total reading times in some of the experiments reported here, but as differences between earlier and later regions of the sentences in others. This inconsistency is not yet understood. It may be due to procedural differences in the present experiments (e.g., the different unambiguous controls that were used in Experiment 2 vs. Experiments 3 and 4), although the mechanism that caused the differences is not clear.

Even with these interpretive ambiguities, the present experiments make it clear that the eye movement record provides a rich and detailed set of data that can support strong conclusions about the reading process. As Rayner et al. (1989) argued, it is not possible to make inferences mechanically from particular eye movement effects to particular cognitive processes. It will be necessary, for the foreseeable future, to interpret an entire pattern of data in a cautious manner, not to search for specific signals, in order to understand a complex process. Doing so in the case of the present experiments has suggested a clear substantive conclusion: It appears that the initial structural analysis that is assigned to words in a sentence as they are read is determined by globally applicable rules of syntax. Information specific to particular lexical items, including argument structure information and thematic role information, seems to be used slightly later, to evaluate and correct the initial syntactic analysis.

Acknowledgments. The research reported here was supported by grant HD 18708 from NIH to Charles Clifton and Lyn Frazier. The author would like to express his appreciation to René Schmauder for her comments on an earlier version of this chapter, and to Sara Sereno for pointing out a vast number of infelicities and errors, some of which he corrected.

References

Abney, S. (1989). A computational model of human parsing. *Journal of Psycholinguistic Research*, *18*, 129–144.

Altmann, G., Steedman, M. (1988). Interaction with context during human sentence processing. *Cognition*, *30*, 191–238.

Chomsky, N. (1981). *Lectures on government and binding*. Cambridge, MA: MIT Press.

Clifton, C. Jr. (in preparation). The role of thematic roles in sentence parsing.

Clifton, C. Jr., Speer, S., & Abney, S. (1991). Parsing arguments: Phrase structure and argument structure as determinants of initial parsing decisions. *Journal of Memory and Language*, *30*, 251–271.

Ferreira, F., & Clifton, C. Jr. (1986). The independence of syntactic processing. *Journal of Memory and Language*, *25*, 348–368.

Ferreira, F., & Henderson, J. (1990). The use of verb information in syntactic parsing: A comparison of evidence from eye movements and segment-by-segment self-paced reading. *Journal of Experimental Psychology: Learning, Memory, and Cognition*, *16*, 555–568.

Fillenbaum, S. (1970). On the use of memorial techniques to assess syntactic structures. *Psychological Bulletin*, *73*, 231–237.

Fodor, J.A. (1983). *Modularity of mind*. Cambridge, MA: MIT Press.

Fodor, J.A., Bever, T., & Garrett, M.F. (1974). *The psychology of language*. New York: McGraw-Hill.

Forster, K.I. (1979). Levels of processing and the structure of the language processor. In W.E. Cooper & E.C.T. Walker (Eds.), *Sentence processing* (pp. 27–86). Hillsdale, NJ: Erlbaum.

Frazier, L. (1978). *On comprehending sentences: Syntactic parsing strategies*. Unpublished doctoral dissertation, University of Connecticut.

Frazier, L. (1985). *Modularity and the representational hypothesis*. *Proceedings of NELS 12*. Amherst, Ma: Graduate Linguistic Students Association.

Frazier, L. (1987). Sentence processing: A tutorial review. In M. Coltheart (Ed.), *Attention and performance XII* (pp. 559–586). Hillsdale, NJ: Erlbaum.

Frazier, L. (1988). Grammar and language processing. In F.J. Newmeyer (Ed.), *Linguistics: The Cambridge survey*. *Vol II: Linguistic theory: Extensions and implications* (pp. 15–34). Cambridge: Cambridge University Press.

Frazier, L. (1990a). Parsing modifiers: Special purpose routines in the HSPM? In D. Balota, G.B. Flores D'Arcais, & K. Rayner (Eds.), *Comprehension processes in reading*. Hillsdale, NJ: Erlbaum.

Frazier, L. (1990b). Exploring the architecture of the language-processing system. In G. Altmann (Ed.), *Cognitive models of speech processing* (pp. 409–433). Cambridge, MA: MIT Press.

Frazier, L., & Rayner, K. (1982). Making and correcting errors during sentence comprehension: Eye movements in the analysis of structurally ambiguous sentences. *Cognitive Psychology*, *14*, 178–210.

Gough, P.B. (1965). Grammatical transformations and speed of understanding. *Journal of Verbal Learning and Verbal Behavior*, *4*, 107–111.

Just, M.A., & Carpenter, P. (1980). A theory of reading: From eye fixations to comprehension. *Psychological Review*, *85*, 109–130.

Kimball, J. (1973). Seven principles of surface structure parsing in natural language. *Cognition*, *2*, 15–47.

Marslen-Wilson, W.D., & Tyler, L.K. (1987). Against modularity. In J. Garfield (Ed.), *Modularity in knowledge representation and natural language understanding*. Cambridge, MA: MIT Press.

Miller, G.A. (1962). Some psychological studies of grammar. *American Psychologist*, *17*, 748–762.

Pritchett, B.L. (1988). Garden path phenomena and the grammatical basis of language processing. *Language*, *64*, 539–576.

Rayner, K., Carlson, M., & Frazier, L. (1983). The interaction of syntax and semantics during sentence processing: Eye movements in the analysis of semantically biased sentences. *Journal of Verbal Learning and Verbal Behavior*, *22*, 358–374.

Rayner, K., & Pollatsek, A. (1989). *The psychology of reading*. Englewood Cliffs, NJ: Prentice-Hall.

Rayner, K., Sereno, S., Morris, R., Schmauder, R., & Clifton, C. Jr. (1989). Eye movements and on-line language comprehension processes. *Language and Cognitive Processes*, *4*, SI 21–50.

Stowe, L. (1989). Thematic structures and sentence comprehension. In G.N. Carlson & M.K. Tanenhaus (Eds.), *Linguistic structure in language processing*. Dordrecht: Kluwer Academic Publishers.

Tanenhaus, M. (1988). Psycholinguistics: An overview. In F.J. Newmeyer (Ed.), *Linguistics: The Cambridge survey. Vol III: Language: Psychological and biological aspects* (pp. 1–37). Cambridge: Cambridge University Press.

Tanenhaus, M.K., & Carlson, G.N. (1989). Lexical structure and language comprehension. In W. Marslen-Wilson (Ed.), *Lexical representation and process* (pp. 529–562). Cambridge, MA: MIT.

Taraban, R., & McClelland, J.R. (1988). Constitutent attachment and thematic role assignment in sentence processing: Influences of content-based expectations. *Journal of Memory and Language*, *27*, 597–632.

Taraban, R., & McClelland, J.L. (1990). Parsing and comprehension: A multiple-constraint view. In D. Balota, G.B. Flores d'Arcais, & K. Rayner (Eds.), *Comprehension processes in reading*. Hillsdale, NJ: Erlbaum.

25
Attention Allocation with Overlapping Sound, Image, and Text

GÉRY D'YDEWALLE and INGRID GIELEN

In daily life people are often confronted with more than one source of information at a time, as, for example, when watching television. A television program has at least two channels of information: a visual one (the image) and an auditory one (the sound). In some countries most of the television programs are imported from abroad and subtitled in the native language. The subtitles, then, are a third source of information. Characteristically, each of these three sources of information are partly redundant: they do not contradict but rather supplement one another, or express the same content in a different form.

If one applies earlier theories on attention (Broadbent, 1958; Treisman, 1968) to research on audiovisual broadcasts, some implications are straightforward: at any given time, only one among the audio and visual inputs is fully analyzed; moreover, it takes time to switch inputs. If one accepts some parallel processing or multiple-resource allocations, more flexibility within the human system is assumed to occur. Conventional research on attention, however, has mainly been focused on simple stimulus presentations with no information redundancy between input channels. As pointed out above, there is considerable information overlap in film and television presentations. As most film and television research does not address attention and processing issues, the main purpose of our studies was to look at the dynamics of attention in this complex information situation.

As the main question is how a person is able to divide and shift his or her attention in such a complex situation, the eye movement patterns in between the image and the subtitles were measured with the use of the pupil center–corneal reflection method in almost all experiments to be reported here. From the eye registrations, three values were examined: the time devoted to the subtitles, the time devoted to the image, and the latency time (i.e., the time necessary to shift from the image to the subtitle when the latter appears). Although it is thus possible to determine what someone is looking at in the image or the subtitle, a different technique is required to determine how a person registers sound at the same time, or how the person shifts attention from the visual image to the soundtracks. Below, we will propose a variant of the double-task technique to infer the sound processing.

Prior to our work, very little research had been done in connection with subtitles. The few studies that did exist focused mainly on improving television programs for the hearing impaired (Baker, 1981; Nederlandse Omroep Stichting, 1977). New ground was broken by a study of the Belgian Radio and Television (BRT; Muylaert, Nootens, Poesmans, & Pugh, 1983), which sparked our research on the viewing of subtitled programs with a more theoretical basis.

Is There Really Reading of Subtitles?

In a study reported by d'Ydewalle, Van Rensbergen, and Pollet (1987) an attempt was first made to gain a better insight into the presentation time of subtitles. The conventional, standard presentation time of subtitles is based on the 6-second rule, which means that a subtitle of two lines (double subtitle) with a total of 64 characters and spaces (which equals the maximum number allowed) is shown for 6 seconds. The presentation time of a shorter subtitle is inferred from this rule and from the number of characters (and spaces) of the subtitle. To our knowledge, the rule is applied in all countries that use subtitles, although no one seems to know why. It is strange that the presentation time of subtitles should be determined by the number of characters, for research on reading (for a review, see Rayner & Pollatsek, 1989) has shown that words are not read letter by letter, and that some words, like articles, are mostly not fixated at all. In some of the experiments to be reported here, we will speed up or slow down the presentation of the subtitles by using also a 2-, 4- and 8-second rule.

The subjects were shown a television series in which the subtitles were presented following the 4-, 6-, or 8-seconds rule. The task was to immediately judge whether the presentation time was too short, sufficient, or too long. The findings partly corroborated the efficiency of the "intuitive" presentation rule: the best combination turned out to be the double subtitle presented for 6 seconds. It is clear that such a presentation time may be preferred by the subjects because they are used to seeing subtitles at that duration. Another finding was that a single subtitle (a subtitle of one line) is always experienced as quicker, regardless of the presentation time. We will discuss the difference between single and double subtitles after reviewing more data showing a difference in processing them.

In another experiment (d'Ydewalle et al., 1987) we manipulated the time rule (2- 4-, and 6-seconds rule) and varied the availability of the sound track (sound, no sound, and knowledge of the language used in the soundtrack). In the conditions with knowledge of the language, the subjects had an excellent command of the language used (German) as they all were advanced students of German. In the condition without sound, the subjects had to fully rely on the subtitles as no other information was available apart from the image. In the condition with knowledge of the language, the subjects did not need the subtitles to understand the story; accordingly, we definitely expected less reading of the subtitles.

A first important observation is that the subtitles are read, despite the fact that the subjects alternate between viewing the image and viewing the subtitles. No differences were found for the conditions with and without sound. This is an unexpected finding as the assumption was that in the condition without sound the subjects would proportionally devote more time to the subtitles in order to understand the movie. Equally surprising is the finding that, with a normal presentation time (6-second rule), no difference occurred between the subjects who knew the language used and those who did not. It seems more logical not to read the subtitles (or at least only partly) if one understands the language used; looking at the subtitles always causes a partial loss of the visual information, as it is impossible to look at both the subtitles and the image at the same time.

The findings gave rise to two closely related hypotheses. The first hypothesis states that reading the subtitles is a more or less automatically initiated behavior due to long-standing experience with a television environment almost always involving subtitles (automaticity hypothesis). Subtitles are such a familiar phenomenon that one simply cannot escape reading them. In small language communities, all foreign television programs are subtitled and one is taught to follow these subtitles from childhood.

The second hypothesis states that it takes less time and it is more efficient to read the subtitles than to listen to the soundtrack (efficiency hypothesis). Usually the subtitles can be read before the actors have spoken them. Moreover, the subtitles can be reread, whereas the soundtrack can be listened to only once.

English Viewers with English Subtitles, Dutch Viewers with Dutch Subtitles

One way to test the hypotheses on the nature of the underlying processes in reading subtitles is to confront persons without subtitle experience with this source of information. d'Ydewalle, Praet, Verfaillie, and Van Rensbergen (1991) showed an American film with English subtitles to American students. These American students do not have much experience with subtitles as in the United States mostly American television programs are shown and foreign programs are usually dubbed. If these subjects read the subtitles, their reading behavior cannot be attributed to a habit created by long-standing experience.

The results indicated that the American students devoted as much time to the subtitles and showed a similar pattern of attention shift as the subjects in previous studies. As such, the results corroborate the efficiency hypothesis. Even subjects who do not have a long-standing experience with subtitles read them. Proportionally the subjects devoted somewhat more time to the subtitles when sound was absent, but this difference was only marginally significant. The results pointed to a preference for subtitles in both situations (with and without sound).

In the second experiment of d'Ydewalle et al. (1991), Dutch-speaking students were shown a Dutch film with Dutch subtitles. The two most important conditions were again sound and no sound. The analysis showed that in the condition without sound somewhat more time was devoted to the subtitles than in the condition with sound. However, in both conditions at least one third of the time was given to the subtitles. Apparently these subjects preferred the subtitles as well.

The Dynamics of the Content: Film Versus News Broadcast

I. Gielen (1988) investigated the influence of two factors on the processing of subtitles, namely knowledge of the language used, and types of information in the image. In contrast with d'Ydewalle et al. (1987), I. Gielen (1988) did not manipulate the knowledge of the subjects but, instead, the language used in the soundtrack was varied. This was done because the conclusion that knowledge of the language did not have an influence could be explained by the fact that the subjects with knowledge of the foreign language preferred their mother tongue, which was used in the subtitles. The choice of the mother tongue seems a logical one, no matter how thorough one's knowledge of the foreign language and regardless of the type of information channel.

The second factor, the type of information presented in the image, is a new one that up to now had not been investigated. Previous studies all used a segment from a film or a television series. I. Gielen (1988) used not only a segment from a film, but also a news broadcast. These television programs differ in several respects. First, one is not used to watching a news broadcast with subtitles, whereas 90% of the films shown on Dutch television networks are foreign and subtitled in Dutch. Second, the type, quantity, and succession of information are different for each television program. A film represents entertainment, deals with only one story with a beginning and an end, and features a number of reappearing characters. The images are often more attractive than the dialogue, and the pace is, in general, rather slow. A news broadcast, on the other hand, is meant to inform the viewers of what is going on in the world at large. The text is often far more important than are the images; it is almost a "spoken newspaper." A news broadcast provides a great deal of concrete information in a very short period of time. Moreover, the different news items within a news broadcast do not relate to one another.

The subjects were divided among four conditions: a Dutch film, a German film, a Dutch news broadcast, and a German news broadcast, all provided with Dutch subtitles. The results were as follows. The subjects devoted proportionally more time to the subtitles in the case of a foreign soundtrack as well as in the case of a news broadcast. Also, the latency time from image to subtitle in these conditions was significantly shorter. The results suggest that the subjects have a greater need for subtitles in these conditions, as they start to look at the subtitles at a faster pace and read them for longer periods. Likewise, the analyses of each television program separately indicated the influence of the language used and of the images seen during the presentation of the subtitles. During the news broadcast, for instance, more time was devoted to visual reports and speakers in the foreign language than to other images. These differences between the language used, the type of television program, and the images again make the efficiency hypothesis more plausible. This does not mean, however, that there are no automatic processes involved in the processing of subtitles; subtitles were still read even when they were not really necessary.

Are Sound and Subtitles Processed Simultaneously?

d'Ydewalle et al. (in 1991) pointed out that reading the subtitles does not necessarily imply a failure to process the sound at the same time. Most of the films that are shown on the Dutch-speaking networks are in English or French, two languages that most of the Dutch-speaking people are at least familiar with. As such, it is perfectly possible that part of the soundtrack is processed as well. This is incidentally suggested by spontaneous reports from the subjects that the translation in the subtitle did not fully agree with the spoken dialogue, in cases where such a mismatch had occurred. To find out to what extent the soundtrack is processed, Sohl (1989) used a double-task technique. Apart from watching a television program, the subjects had to react to flashing lights as fast as possible. The reaction time to the flashing lights was taken as a measurement for the amount of processing done with the first task, which was the viewing of a television program. The flashing lights were given at specific moments: subtitle and speaker(s) present, no subtitle, and neither subtitle nor speaker(s) present. The slowest reaction times were obtained whenever both a speaker and a subtitle were present, which demonstrates that the subjects did make an effort to follow the speech. More detailed internal analyses also confirmed that the subjects were processing the soundtrack.

Foveal and Peripheral Processing of Subtitles

The previous studies suggest that a television viewer is able to process information from the subtitles while watching the image right above. This led M. Gielen (1988) to investigate the parafoveal and peripheral processing of subtitles. Various conditions were built in to force the subjects, in different ways, to absorb information from the subtitles in a foveal or extrafoveal way, using a variant of the moving window technique (McConkie & Rayner, 1975). The dependent variables that were to measure the influence on the reading behavior, consisted of the average viewing time of the subtitle and the performance on a recognition task. It was expected that the more the areas containing important image information approached the area of the subtitles, the less time they would spend looking at the subtitles. However, the findings did not point in this direction. The main reason was that the subjects were strongly inclined to look into the area close above the area of the subtitles. This area seems to be the main focus of visual attention when people watch television. This suggests the strategy used by the television viewer: close to the subtitled area, viewers are able to grasp the most important events on the screen and have a quick look at the subtitles whenever these are shown.

Incidental Learning of Subtitles

M. Gielen (1988) also examined the nature of the information that is processed from the subtitles. To this end, a considerable number of subjects were shown a 10-minute segment from a German television series with Dutch subtitles. Afterward they were given an unexpected recognition task concerning the subtitles. The task consisted of multiple-choice questions, each with four possible answers, one being the subtitle presented in the movie, three others being distractors: one distractor used the words of the subtitle but in a different sentence structure, another distractor used the same sentence structure with different words, and the third distractor was totally unrelated. The results showed that the correct subtitle was chosen in 97% of the cases. In a control study the same segment was shown to other subjects, this time without subtitles. Here, 43% of the subtitles that should have been shown were correctly identified. For the subjects receiving the subtitled movie, the order of preference of the alternatives may reflect the nature of the information that is processed from the subtitles. The second choice is the distractor with the same words but a different sentence structure. Then comes the distractors with different words and similar sentence structures. The distractors with differences in both words and sentence structure are rarely selected. These findings suggest that the subjects gather detailed information from the subtitles.

Subtitle Reading by Children and Older People

d'Ydewalle and Van Rensbergen (1989) described two experiments with children in primary school. These experiments were set up to see from which age onward the subtitles are read, as well as to examine if the pattern of attention shift resembles that of adults. In the first experiment, children in the second, fourth, and sixth grades were shown the English cartoon "Popeye" or "Garfield" with subtitles. The children in the fourth and sixth grade watched both cartoons in exactly the same way as adults. This was not the case for the second-grade children: a different pattern was found for each film.

Therefore, in the second experiment all the children were shown both cartoons in a different order: half of them watched "Popeye" first and then "Garfield," the other half of them vice versa. Once again, the fourth- and sixth-grade children watched the cartoons like adults. This was also the case for the second-grade children for both cartoons, but only if they watched "Garfield" first. The analyses furthermore suggest that second-grade pupils did not systematically read the subtitles of "Popeye," unless it was preceded by "Garfield." This was also apparent from latencies: for "Popeye" it was almost 1 second (which is extremely long in comparison with the preceding studies where an average value of approximately 300 ms is usually obtained). Most probably they glanced only once in a while at some words in the subtitles.

On the basis of these experiments with children from primary school, d'Ydewalle and Van Rensbergen (1989) reach the following conclusions: The attention pattern of fourth- and sixth-grade children strongly resembles the pattern found in adults. The acquired habit of reading the subtitles is not yet fully developed in second-grade children. When both cartoons are shown, the eye movement pattern is transferred from one film to the other. "Garfield" alone or as the first cartoon elicited a pattern very similar to that of the adults. When "Popeye" was shown alone or as the first cartoon, the children did not show any reading behavior. "Popeye" is a cartoon that suits their age, with plenty of action and the dialogue is of minor importance. As a result, they will not read the subtitles. In "Garfield," however, the dialogue is an important factor in following the story line. Here, not surprisingly, the second-grade children were much more inclined to read the subtitles.

At the moment, Praet, Van Rensbergen, and d'Ydewalle (in preparation) are working on a follow-up study that concentrates on children from the first grade through the beginning of the second grade of primary school. The analyses suggest that reading behavior is absent at the end of the first grade but emerges very quickly at the beginning of the second grade (in the second week).

In a research survey, Tonla Briquet (1979) found that elderly people complain more about subtitles than other age groups. d'Ydewalle, Warlop, and Van Rensbergen (1989) tried to discover if the complaints by older people manifest themselves in their eye movement pattern. Two experiments were conducted, of which only the first will be discussed. In this experiment, a number of younger (average age of 20 years) and older (average age of 61 years) subjects were shown a fragment from an English series. The results show that the younger people look longer at the double subtitle than the older people, and even more so when the subtitle becomes longer.

d'Ydewalle et al. (1989) explained this observation as follows. If one assumes that younger people read faster than older people and therefore finish reading earlier, then it is possible that younger people start rereading the subtitles and, as such, linger longer in the subtitles. This age-related difference does not occur with single subtitles because in that case nobody has extra time at his/her disposal (d'Ydewalle et al., 1987). On the other hand, watching a subtitled television program requires the continual integration of image, subtitles, and sound. Reading the subtitles probably demands a higher processing capacity than watching the image, which was already suggested in our studies with the double-task technique (Sohl, 1989; see above). Moreover, if the aging process involves a decrease of the total available processing capacity (Craik & Rabinowitz, 1984), it is likely that older people tend to integrate the information when looking at the image rather than when looking at the subtitles. That is why older people will return to the image as quickly as possible after having read the subtitle. A number of further analyses of the numerical data and the screening of the video recordings of the experiments confirmed this explanation.

The most important conclusion of both experiments is that older people show a different viewing behavior. They seem to have greater difficulties with reading subtitles than do younger adults. However, age-related differences should not necessarily be interpreted as a deficit in older people; the differences in age can also be attributed to different viewing strategies.

The Processing of Subtitles by Deaf People

Not only normal hearing people but also deaf people seem to prefer reading the subtitles to other available channels of information. Verfaillie and d'Ydewalle (1987) investigated the preference of modality, and the understanding of a message in relation to this preference, in people who are deaf from birth and received an oral education. Three different sources of information were presented: subtitles, sign language, and lip reading. To find out which modality was preferred, the eye movements of the subjects were measured while they were watching a spoken television story. All subjects were shown stories in four different modalities: (a) speaker, sign interpreter, and subtitles at the same time; (b) subtitles and sign interpreter; (c) subtitles and speaker; and (d) speaker and sign interpreter. The effect of the preference of modality on the general understanding of the message was assessed by a number of detailed "true/ false" questions, which were posed by the speaker, the sign language, and the subtitles at the same time, as well by some general written questions about the story that were asked after viewing each story.

The results showed a strong preference for the subtitles. When enough time was left after reading the subtitles, the subjects looked at other parts of the screen, preferring signs to lip reading. When no subtitles were shown, the subjects preferred sign language. The subjects showed better results in the general written questions when they were presented with subtitles as compared to without. Apparently they were not able to follow the story line with the help of sign language or lip reading only. In the detailed "true/false" questions the subjects scored higher when the subtitles were available in the story, but then only when sign language was absent. Apparently the sign language negatively affected the reading of the subtitles while watching the story.

Verfaillie and d'Ydewalle (1987) explained the preference for subtitles with the early deaf as follows. If the subjects follow the sign language, they are not able to look at other parts of the screen for fear of losing part of the message. Moreover, the subtitle remains visible on the screen long enough for them to have a second look at certain words. Another explanation is that the subtitles elicit quasi-automatic reading behavior. The explanations strongly agree with the interpretations of the processing of subtitles in people with normal hearing capacity. The viewing behavior of the early deaf with an oral tradition and people with normal hearing capacity appears to be based on the same underlying cognitive processes.

Processing Differences with Single and Double Subtitles

An important factor in the research of viewing behavior with subtitled programs is the number of lines that the subtitle consists of: one or two. In nearly all experiments, differences have been noted in connection with this factor. In general, double subtitles are looked at longer and, in some cases, the latency to go to the subtitles was also longer. Therefore, conclusions regarding experimental manipulations must often be qualified depending upon the number of lines dealt with.

d'Ydewalle et al. (1991) gave two explanations for the differences observed in single and double subtitles. A first explanation is related to the observation that latencies are sometimes longer for a double subtitle than for a single one. The investigators believe that the subjects prefer to look at the image and therefore do not spend much time reading the subtitles. Moreover, the subjects seem to know that a single subtitle appears for a shorter period of time than does a double (see 6-second rule, above). Some evidence for this has been found. The analysis of the questionnaire data in d'Ydewalle et al. (1987) shows that the subjects are able to distinguish between subtitles on the basis of their presentation time. In addition, the single subtitle is always experienced as faster (too fast?) than a double one. This is why the subjects want to look at a subtitle faster in case it is a single one. In case of a double subtitle they subjectively (and objectively) dispose of more time and so they will take their time to look at the subtitle. This "length-expectation" hypothesis suggests that the subjects decide how quickly they will look at the subtitle on the basis of the length and therefore the presentation time of the subtitle. This explanation presupposes that the subjects are able to grasp the length and shape of the subtitle while looking at the image, i.e., peripherally. Some evidence for this was found in the second experiment of d'Ydewalle et al. (1989). The average latencies demonstrate that youngsters are able to distinguish between different types of subtitles while looking at the image.

The second explanation answers the observation that proportionally more time is devoted to a double subtitle than to a single one. A double subtitle would cause more lateral interference than would a single. It is possible that a double subtitle makes it more difficult to start right away with the first word on the first line. A double subtitle, moreover, requires a return sweep from the end of the first line to the beginning of the second. These various forms of interferences between the two lines of a double subtitle increase the chances of more corrective eye movements and thus of more time devoted to the double subtitle.

Praet, Verfaillie, De Graef, Van Rensbergen, and d'Ydewalle (1990) further examined this lateral interference. In their study, the subjects were only shown the subtitles as text on screen, i.e., without sound or image. To discover the effect of lateral interference, the spacing between the lines of the subtitle was manipulated. The general conclusion was that no lateral interference takes place. On the contrary, evidence was found that double subtitles are read more quickly. Double subtitles have more semantic and syntactic complexity, whereas single subtitles are often short statements or even exclamations. The semantic and syntactic structures of double subtitles, then, probably greatly enhance their processing as they cause more redundancy of information within the sentence. Striking in this respect is the comparison of the reading times of subtitles without images, in this study, with the reading times of the same subtitles with images in a previous setup. Double subtitles accompanied by images were read slower than single subtitles; opposite results were reached without the images. The lack of images places in the foreground the syntactically and semantically more complex structure of double subtitles, which results in a redundancy of information and an increased reading facilitation. The image, on the other hand, supplies more redundant information in comparison with single subtitles, so that the latter can be read more quickly; double subtitles contain more information than is already present in the image. Praet et al. (1990) concluded that redundancy of information facilitates the processing of subtitles.

Conclusion

When people watch television, the distribution of attention between different channels of information turns out to be an effortless process. Viewers seem to have developed a strategy that allows them to process these channels without problems and in which reading the subtitles occupies a major place. This pattern of attention is developed in childhood and, because of long-standing experience, it is largely based on automatic processes. Some observations, however, indicate that the reading of subtitles should not be considered as a totally automatically elicited type of behavior: Television viewers seem to be able to smoothly distribute their attention between the image and the subtitles as a function of their own interest, the information in the image, and the need for subtitles.

Acknowledgments. The investigation was partially financed by a Concerted Research Action (G.O.A.) of the Belgian Ministry for Research Policy and by a F.C.F.O. project of the Flemish Ministry of Education. We would like to thank Caroline Praet, Johan Van Rensbergen, and Karl Verfaillie for their comments on earlier drafts of this chapter. A slightly different version of the text appeared in the 1989 Proceedings of the Greek Psychological Association.

References

Baker, R.G. (1981). *Guidelines for the subtitling of television programmes for the deaf and hard of hearing.* Southampton, UK: Southampton University.

Broadbent, D.E. (1958). *Perception and communication.* Oxford: Pergamon Press.

Craik, F.I.M., & Rabinowitz, J.C. (1984). Age differences in the use and acquisition of visual information: A tutorial review. In H. Bouma & D.G.

Bouwhuis (Eds.), *Attention and performance. Vol. X: Control of language processes* (pp. 471–499). London: Erlbaum.

d'Ydewalle, G., Praet, C., Verfaillie, K., & Van Rensbergen, J. (1991). Choosing between redundant information channels: Speech and text. *Communication Research, 18*, 650–666.

d'Ydewalle, G., & Van Rensbergen, J. (1989). Developmental studies of text-picture interaction in the perception of animated cartoons with text. In H. Mandl & J.R. Levin (Eds.), *Knowledge acquisition from text and pictures* (pp. 223–248). Amsterdam: Elsevier Science Publishers B.V. (North–Holland).

d'Ydewalle, G., Van Rensbergen, J., & Pollet, J. (1987). Reading a message when the same message is available auditorily in another language: The case of subtitling. In J.K. O'Regan & A. Lévy-Schoen (Eds.), *Eye movements: From physiology to cognition* (pp. 313–321). Amsterdam: Elsevier Science Publishers B.V. (North–Holland).

d'Ydewalle, G., Warlop, L., & Van Rensbergen, J. (1989). Differences between young and older adults in the division of attention over different sources of TV information. *Medienpsychologie: Zeitschrift für Individual- und Massenkommunikation, 1*, 42–57.

Gielen, I. (1988). *Het verwerken van ondertitels in functie van de taalkennis van de klankband en typen van informatie in het beeld* [The processing of subtitles in function of the knowledge of the language used in the soundtrack and types of information on the screen]. Unpublished thesis, University of Leuven, Leuven.

Gielen, M. (1988). *Perceptie en ondertitels: De parafoveale en perifere informatieverwerking van ondertitels* [Perception and subtitles: Parafoveal and peripheral processing of subtitles]. Unpublished thesis, University of Leuven, Leuven.

McConkie, G.W., & Rayner, K. (1975). The span of effective stimulus during a fixation in reading. *Perception & Psychophysics, 17*, 578–586.

Muylaert, W., Nootens, J., Poesmans, D., & Pugh, A.K. (1983). Design and utilisation of subtitles on foreign language television programmes. In P.H. Nelde (Ed.), *Theorie, Methoden und Modelle der Kontaktlinguistik* (pp. 201–214). Bonn: Dummler.

Nederlandse Omroep Stichting (1977). *De behoeften van doven en slechthorenden aan ondertiteling van Nederlandstalige televisieprogramma's* [The need of deaf and hard of hearing people for subtitled Dutch television programs]. (Research Rep. No. R77.194). Hilversum, the Netherlands.

Praet, C., Verfaillie, K., De Graef, P., Van Rensbergen, J., & d'Ydewalle, G. (1990). A one line text is not half a two line text. In R. Groner, G. d'Ydewalle, & R. Parham (Eds.), *From eye to mind: Information acquisition in perception, search, and reading* (pp. 205–213). Amsterdam: Elsevier Science Publishers B.V. (North–Holland).

Rayner, K., & Pollatsek, A. (1989). *The psychology of reading*. Englewood Cliffs, NJ: Prentice-Hall.

Sohl, G. (1989). *Het verwerken van de vreemdtalige gesproken tekst in een ondertiteld TV-programma* [Processing a foreign spoken text in a subtitled television program]. Unpublished thesis, University of Leuven, Leuven.

Tonla Briquet, G. (1979). *Investigation into the subtitling of film and TV*. Unpublished thesis, Brussels: Higher Governments Institute for translators and interpreters.

Treisman, A. (1968). Strategies and models of selective attention. *Psychological Review*, *84*, 127–190.

Verfaillie, K., & d'Ydewalle, G. (1987). *Modality preference and message comprehension in deaf youngsters watching TV*. (Psychological Reports No. 70). Leuven: University of Leuven, Laboratory of Experimental Psychology.

26
The Mechanics of Comprehension and Comprehension of Mechanics

MARY HEGARTY

When people solve mechanical problems, such as troubleshooting, designing, or understanding the operation of mechanical systems, they typically operate on visual displays of these systems—either the machine itself or a schematic diagram of the machine. If the display is central to their problem-solving process, we can assume that their eye fixations on the display indicate the information that they are processing at each stage of the problem-solving process (Just & Carpenter, 1976). Given this assumption, eye-fixation data has provided important insight into cognitive tasks such as mental rotation (Just & Carpenter, 1976, 1985), sentence-picture verification (Just & Carpenter, 1976) and visual analogies (Carpenter, Just, & Shell, 1990). This chapter presents research in which eye-fixation data was used to study a more complex cognitive task, the task of understanding a mechanical system.

A central component of mechanical understanding is knowledge of how the different components of a machine interact dynamically to achieve the function of the machine. This depends on the possible states of the machine components and the configuration of these components. The pulley system presented in Figure 26.1 is a typical machine, made up of components that are free to move in certain ways, but which constrain each others' movements. For example, the movement of the lower pulley in Figure 26.1, is constrained by its spatial relations to the upper and lower ropes. This chapter provides an account of how people learn to understand a simple machine such as a pulley system by processing texts and diagrams.

Understanding the text presented in Figure 26.1 is a complex comprehension process. The inputs to this comprehension process include the text, the diagram, and the reader's prior knowledge. The text on the left begins by identifying the basic components of the system—two pulleys, two ropes, and a crate. Then it describes the configuration of these components, i.e., their spatial relations to one other. Finally it describes how the components move when the pulley system is in operation. The diagram on the right provides another description of the system con-

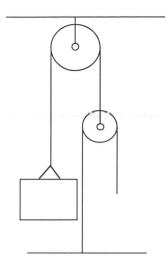

This pulley system consists of two pulleys, two ropes and a crate. The upper pulley is attached to the ceiling. The upper rope passes over this pulley and is attached to the crate at one end and the lower pulley at the other. The lower rope is attached to the floor at one end, passes over the lower pulley and is free at the other end. When the free end of the lower rope is pulled, the rope moves over the lower pulley, pulling down on this pulley and the rope from which it is suspended. This causes the upper rope to move over the upper pulley and to pull up the crate.

FIGURE 26.1. Example of a text and diagram read by subjects in the experiments described in this chapter.

figuration, this time in a spatial medium. It provides a representation of the static system but no information about motion. The reader's prior knowledge includes both knowledge of mechanical systems and strategies that he or she might have developed for reading technical texts accompanied by diagrams.

The output of the comprehension process is a representation of how the different components of the machine interact spatially and dynamically to achieve its function. This type of understanding is often called a mental model of a mechanical system (Gentner & Stevens, 1983; Hegarty, Just, & Morrison, 1988; Kieras & Bovair, 1984).

Constructing a mental model of a mechanical system from text and diagrams involves three types of cognitive processes:

1. processes for reading the text
2. processes for inspecting the diagram, and
3. processes for coordinating the intake of information from the text and diagram.

The research described in this chapter investigates the nature of these processes and of their outcomes. The first section of the chapter concerns the quality of mental models acquired by people when they read text alone, inspect diagrams alone, and read text accompanied by diagrams. The second section describes how people coordinate the processes of reading text and inspecting diagrams when both media are present. The third section focuses on the processing of diagrams, describing how people infer the kinematics (motion) of the components of a machine from the static representation of the machine provided in a diagram. This research illuminates both the comprehension process and the nature of mechanical understanding itself.

Mental Models Acquired from Texts, Diagrams, and Texts Accompanied by Diagrams

This section discusses the inputs and the outputs of the comprehension process, describing an experiment in which I investigated the quality of the mental models that people acquire when they study text alone, diagrams alone, and text accompanied by diagrams describing a mechanical system (Hegarty & Just, 1991).

The quality of the mental models that people construct from a diagram alone will depend on their ability to infer the system kinematics from the static view of the system presented in the diagram. It is possible that subjects accomplish this task by constructing a mental image of the diagram and "mentally animating" that image to infer the system kinematics. However, such a process would surely be constrained by people's ability to transform mental images (Just & Carpenter, 1985; Kosslyn, 1980) and by limitations of spatial working memory (Baddeley & Lieberman, 1978).

The quality of the mental models that people construct from the text alone will depend on their ability to construct a referential representation of the configuration and kinematics of the pulley system from the verbal description of the system in the text. A comparison of the quality of mental models constructed from both text and diagrams, and from either of these media alone, provides information regarding the importance of each of the media for comprehension. For example, if there is no difference in the mental models of subjects who read text alone and subjects who read text accompanied by diagrams, we can assume that diagrams are not necessary for constructing a mental model of a mechanical system.

In this experiment, subjects were presented with either text alone, diagrams alone, or text accompanied by diagrams describing a number of pulley systems. All subjects were instructed that their task was to understand the pulley system so that they would be able to explain to someone else how it worked. Their mechanical ability was measured using a standardized test (Bennett, 1969). The quality of their mental models of the pulley systems was assessed by their answers to comprehension questions and their ability to draw the configuration of the pulley systems when the text and/or diagrams were no longer present. The comprehension questions assessed both static and kinematic models of the pulley systems. An example of a question about static characteristics is, "Name all the objects that touch the lower pulley," whereas a question about kinematics is, "How does the lower pulley move when the rope is pulled?" Many of these comprehension questions could not be answered directly by propositions expressed in the text (the text base in Kintsch & Van Dijk's, 1978, scheme) and depended on whether the subject had constructed a representation of the referent of the text (a situation model).

Subjects' comprehension scores and drawings indicated that the quality of their mental models depended on the medium that they studied (text, diagrams, or both) and on their mechanical ability. Readers had better comprehension if they studied the text and the diagram than if they studied either medium alone. Furthermore, the effects of medium and ability were greater in the case of questions about kinematics than in the case of questions about configuration. In general, subjects had lower scores on comprehension questions about the kinematics of the system, but these scores were particularly low (<20% correct answers) for low-ability subjects who received the text or diagram alone.

These results suggest that the subjects needed to process both text and diagrams in order to construct a complete and accurate mental model of a pulley system. It is interesting that although subjects with high mechanical ability had better comprehension of all displays than subjects with low ability, they were not able to construct a complete representation of the pulley systems from either medium alone. Thus, greater mechanical knowledge could not compensate completely for the absence of the text or diagram.

Finally, although there were few differences in comprehension between subjects who received the text alone and subjects who received the diagram alone, subjects who received the diagram spent much less time constructing their representations of the pulley systems. This result suggests that subjects' final representations are more like the diagrammatic representation than the text representation, supporting the view that an image-like representation of the pulley system is crucial to understanding.

Coordinating the Intake of Information from a Text and Diagram

Because readers clearly benefit from the information in both the text and diagram when they attempt to understand mechanical systems, it is meaningful to ask how they coordinate the processes of reading text and inspecting diagrams when they are presented with both media. This section describes a series of experiments (Hegarty, 1988; Hegarty & Just, 1989; Hegarty & Just, 1991) in which readers' eye fixations were tracked as they read text and diagrams in order to understand this coordination process.

In this series of experiments, subjects were presented with text and diagrams describing pulley systems, such as the example in Figure 26.1.

Episode 1   Components Fixated

Text Read

This pulley system consists of
two pulleys, two ropes and a crate

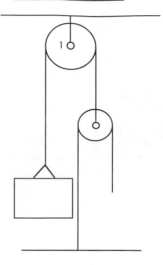

Episode 2   Components Fixated

Text Read:

The upper pulley us attached to
the ceiling. The upper rope passes
over this pulley,

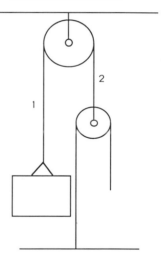

FIGURE 26.2. Protocol of a subject reading a text and diagram describing a
mechanical system. At each stage of the comprehension process, the text that the
subject read is shown on the left side of the figure and the location and order of
the subject's gazes on the diagram is shown on the right side of the figure.

They were instructed to read the descriptions to understand how the
pulley systems worked. Their comprehension was assessed by comprehension questions as described above. Their mechanical ability was
measured using the Bennett Mechanical Comprehension Test. I will first
present a protocol showing a typical sequence of eye fixations on the text

<u>Episode 3</u>

<u>Components Fixated</u>

<u>Text Read</u>

The upper rope passes over this
pulley and is attached to the crate
at one end and the lower pulley at
the other. The lower rope is attached
to the floor at one end, passes over
the lower pulley, and is free at the
other end.

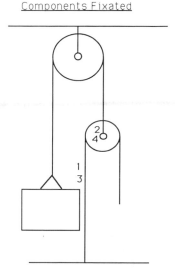

<u>Episode 4</u>

<u>Components Fixated</u>

<u>Text Read:</u>

When the free end of the rope is
pulled, the rope moves over the
lower pulley, pulling down on this
pulley and the rope from which it
is suspended. This causes the
upper rope to move over the
upper pulley and to pull up the
crate.

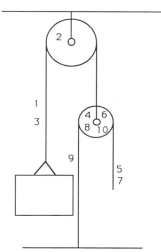

FIGURE 26.2. *Continued*

and diagram, then discuss the general characteristics of the reading protocols, and finally discuss the individual differences in comprehension.

A Typical Reading Protocol

Figure 26.2 presents an example of the sequence of one subject's eye
fixations as she studied the text and diagram in Figure 26.1. This protocol

can be divided into four episodes. During each of these episodes, the subject first reads a section of the text and then inspects one or more components in the diagram. During the first episode, the subject reads the sentences describing the components of the pulley system and the connection of the upper pulley to the ceiling and inspects the upper pulley. In the next episode she goes on to read the sentence describing the configuration of the upper rope and inspects this upper rope in the diagram. In the third episode she reads about the configuration of the lower rope and pulley, and inspects these components in the diagram. Finally, she reads the last two sentences, describing the system kinematics. During this episode she spends more time inspecting the diagram and inspects it more extensively, first fixating the upper rope and pulley, and then repeatedly fixating the lower components in the system.

This eye-fixation protocol suggests that the subject's mental model of the pulley system is constructed incrementally. At each increment she starts by reading a section of the text and then inspects the referent of that section of text in the diagram, suggesting that the order of construction of parts of the representation is largely directed by the text. It appears that this subject first constructs a static representation of the pulley system in increments, and then operates on this static representation to construct a kinematic representation of the pulley system. At each stage of this process, constructing a representation of a section of text is accompanied by eye fixations on the referent of that section of text, and this is particularly true when the text described the kinematics of the pulley system.

General Characteristics of Subjects' Eye Fixations

What features of this protocol are typical? One general characteristic is that subjects' construction of the representation is largely text directed. Subjects tend to inspect the diagram at the ends of sentences and clauses (approximately 80% of their diagram inspections). Thus, they attempt to fully interpret a sentence or clause before they inspect its referent in the diagram.

However, readers do not inspect the diagram after every clause. They inspect the diagram about once every three clauses read. It is interesting to speculate why they inspect the diagram after some clauses and not others. One possibility is that subjects inspect the diagram only after reading particularly difficult clauses, i.e., clauses that cannot be easily translated to a spatial representation. Another possibility is that subjects construct initial representations of each clause as they read the text and store these representations in a temporary buffer until the buffer becomes full, when they then check it against the diagram.

To assess which of these processes best accounts for subjects' behavior, we examined the correspondence between the components fixated during a given diagram inspection and the text read prior to that diagram inspection. If subjects inspect the diagram only to construct the representation of difficult clauses, they should always inspect the referent of the most recently read clause of the text, i.e., the one that caused difficulty. On the other hand, if subjects are buffering a representation of three or more clauses before constructing the final representation of these clauses, their diagram inspections could be on the referents of any clause in the most recently read section of text. Approximately 40% of subjects' fixations on the diagram were referents of the most recently read clause but a further 36% of their inspections were related to the second and third most recently read clauses. Each of these proportions was significantly greater than the proportion of eye fixations that would have been related to recent text if the subjects were inspecting the diagram randomly.

These results suggest that subjects construct an initial representation of individual clauses of text that they later check against the diagram. Future research will focus on specifying the stages of construction of the representation more precisely. One possibility is that subjects attempt to fully construct the representation of each clause as they read it, and inspect the diagram to periodically check this representation. However, it is also possible that subjects' diagram inspections play a more central role in the comprehension process, e.g., in converting a text-based representation to a spatial representation, or in integrating the representations of individual clauses of text (Hegarty & Just, 1989).

Another general characteristic of subjects' protocols is that their final inspections of the diagram tend to be longer and more global, whereas their diagram inspections during the reading of the text are shorter and focused on one or two components that the subjects has just read about. There are two possible explanations for these different types of diagram inspections. One possibility is that their final inspection of the diagram is longer because it includes a final check that they have fully understood the pulley system. Another possible explanation for these longer diagram inspections is that information about the system kinematics always came at the end of the text in the descriptions that subjects read. Inspection of the diagram is central to the process of imagining motion (Hegarty, in press). This process is described more fully in the final section of this chapter.

In summary, subjects' eye fixations as they read text accompanied by diagrams indicate that the comprehension process is largely text directed. The diagram is inspected to check or to construct the representation of information recently read in the text, and diagram inspection appears to be more central to representing certain types of information, in particular information about the kinematics of the system.

Individual Differences

The study of individual differences in text-and-diagram processing provides further insight into this comprehension process. We have examined how people with different levels of spatial and mechanical ability process text and diagrams as they attempt to construct mental models of machines.

One of the most striking differences between high- and low-ability individuals is that low-ability individuals inspect the diagram more often and read fewer clauses between diagram inspections. This result is consistent with the preliminary model of text-and-diagram processing described above. This model proposes that people construct a preliminary representation of the mechanical system as they read the text and inspect the diagram to check this representation and possibly to convert it to a visual-spatial representation. The low-ability individuals in my sample were low in both spatial and mechanical ability. Thus, we might expect them to have more difficulty constructing spatial representations from text alone, which would cause them to look at the diagram more often. Second, because low-ability readers were probably less familiar with the mechanical domain, reading the text would be more effortful for these readers, so that their ability to store the representations of previous clauses in working memory would be impaired (Carpenter & Just, 1989; Daneman & Carpenter, 1980).

A second difference between high- and low-ability individuals is that low-ability individuals are less able to compensate for difficulty in understanding the text by extracting information from the diagram. Two experiments investigated how subjects processed the text and diagram when the text was more difficult to understand. In one experiment, the static configuration of the mechanical system was not described in the text, so that the diagram was the only source of this information (Hegarty & Just, 1989). High-ability individuals compensated by spending more time inspecting the diagram, whereas low-ability subjects spent less time inspecting the diagram than when they read a text that included information about configuration. When information is missing from the text, high-ability subjects can use their prior knowledge of the domain to direct their processing of the diagram. For example, they might have used the knowledge that the configuration of components in a mechanical system constrains the kinematics so that understanding system configuration is preliminary to understanding kinematics. On the other hand, low-ability subjects are primarily directed by the text in processing the diagram.

In another experiment, I varied the order of information in the text, so that one text was more cohesive than the other (Hegarty, 1988). In the cohesive text, clauses describing the same component of the pulley system (e.g., the upper rope) were presented consecutively. In the noncohesive text, clauses describing different system components were presented in a scrambled order so that clauses describing the same component were not usually presented consecutively. Inspecting the diagram should be a particularly adaptive strategy for constructing an integrated representation of a pulley system in this situation, because each component of the pulley system is depicted in only one location in the diagram.

High-ability subjects who read the noncohesive text spent more time inspecting the diagram than high-ability subjects who read the cohesive text, and the comprehension scores of both groups indicated that they had constructed complete and accurate mental models of the pulley systems. In contrast, low-ability subjects who read the noncohesive text spent less time inspecting the diagram and had lower comprehension scores than their low-ability counterparts who read the cohesive text. Again low-ability individuals were unable to compensate for problems in the text by using the information in the diagram.

In summary, studies of individual differences in text-and-diagram processing point to the importance of domain knowledge as an input to the comprehension process. There are a number of ways in which domain knowledge might influence comprehension. Familiarity with the domain might be necessary to extract information from the diagram because it includes knowledge of the conventions embodied in diagrammatic representations. It may allow readers to make inferences beyond the information presented in the diagram. Finally, background knowledge of the domain might be necessary for comprehension monitoring, e.g., detecting that the information in the text is not sufficient for understanding the mechanical system.

Inferring Motion from Static Diagrams

This section focuses on diagram processing, and particularly on how people infer the kinematics of a mechanical system from a static diagram of the system. The studies presented above suggest that representing the kinematics of a mechanical system is a difficult process. When subjects attempt to understand a mechanical system from text or diagrams alone, they gain very little understanding of the system kinematics. When subjects attempt to understand a mechanical system from both text and diagrams, they spend more time inspecting the diagram after reading clauses describing the system kinematics.

In the final experiment that I will describe, I investigated how subjects determine the movement of a component of a mechanical system from a static display of the system. Consider the pulley system presented in Figure 26.3. The movement of the different components of this system can be described as a causal chain of events that occurs when the rope is pulled. When the rope is pulled, it moves over the upper pulley, causing the upper pulley to rotate clockwise and under the middle pulley, causing the middle pulley to rise and to rotate counterclockwise, etc. However, the movements of the different components do not follow each

Static Relation

The lower pulley is attached to
the weight

Kinematic Relation

(When the rope is pulled,)

The lower rope moves to the
right under the lower pulley

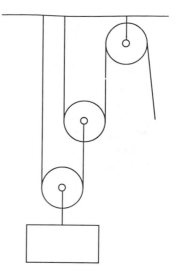

FIGURE 26.3. Example of a diagram of a pulley system and sentences describing static and kinematic attributes of components of the pulley system that subjects were asked to verify.

other in sequence as the causal description might suggest. Instead, all of the components move at once.

How do people infer the movement of a part of a system from a static diagram? Do they trace through the causal chain of events in the system, or can they "mentally animate" all parts of the system at once and then zoom in on the component in question in their mental representation? Theoretical accounts of this process in the artificial intelligence literature suggest that people's knowledge of mechanical systems consists of causal rules stating the relations between system components, so that the process of inferring motion involves making a chain of inferences through the causal chain of events in the device (de Kleer & Brown, 1984; Forbus, 1984). This view is supported by studies showing that people who are instructed about the causal chain of events in a device are better able to solve problems about the device (Mayer, 1989) and to operate the device (Kieras & Bovair, 1984).

Recently Spoehr and Horvath (1989) studied the process of inferring system behavior more directly, by measuring subjects' reaction times while they determined the state of a component of an electrical circuit. They found that the time to determine the state of the component was a function of the causal complexity of the device. This data is consistent with both serial and parallel models of inferring system behavior. In a more complex system, the chain of inferences to determine the state of a component would be longer. However, if all components of the system are animated at once and this is a capacity-limited process, then the more components in the system, the more time it would take to animate it.

I studied subjects reaction times and eye fixations as they attempted to determine the motion of components at different positions in the causal chain of events in a pulley system (Hegarty, in press). If people determine the motion of a system component by making a chain of inferences from the input of the system to that component, then it should take less time to determine the motion of components earlier in the causal chain of events. On the other hand, if people mentally animate all components of the system at once and then zoom in on the component in question, it should take the same amount of time to determine the motion of all components.

In this experiment, subjects were given a sentence-picture verification task. They were presented with a static diagram of a pulley system and a sentence describing the motion of a component of a pulley system and asked to respond whether the sentence was true or false of the depicted system. Sentences describing static attributes of the same components were included as a control. (Examples of static and kinematic statements are given in Figure 26.3.) The main independent measure was the location of the component in the chain of events in the pulley system. There were three groups of components: components near the beginning of the causal chain (e.g., the upper pulley in Figure 26.3), components near the middle of the causal chain (e.g., the middle pulley), and components near the end of the causal chain (e.g., the lower pulley).

The dependent measures were errors, reaction times, and eye fixations. If subjects determine the motion of a component by making a chain of inferences from the input of the system to the component in question, then they should take more time to verify statements about the motion of components later in the causal chain of events. They might also make more errors verifying these statements, depending on the difficulty of the task. Finally, we should observe them fixating earlier components in the causal chain of events as they determine the motion of components later in that chain of events.

For sentences stating static attributes of system components, there should be no difference in reaction times or errors for statements about components in different locations. When verifying static statements, subjects should fixate only the referents of the sentence.

The error rate on the task was low ($<10\%$). However, the majority of errors were made on kinematic statements describing events later in the kinematic chain of events (i.e., at the middle or end of the causal chain), indicating that the task was more difficult when it involved inferring the motion of a system component and when that component was later in the causal chain.

The reaction times showed a similar pattern. Reaction times for the verification of kinematic statements were longer than reaction times for

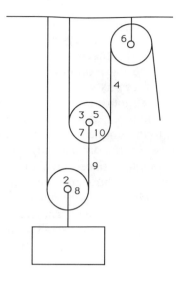

1

The lower rope moves to the
right under the lower pulley

Gaze	Object Fixated	Gaze Duration
1	text	4343 milliseconds
2	lower pulley	418
3	middle pulley	284
4	right upper rope	501
5	middle pulley	368
6	upper pulley	835
7	middle pulley	484
8	lower pulley	267
9	right lower rope	1153
10	middle pulley	935

FIGURE 26.4. Protocol of a subject verifying a statement about the motion of a component of a pulley system. The numbers indicate the location and order of the subject's gazes on the display.

the verification of static statements, reflecting the additional step of determining motion from the static diagram. Furthermore, reaction time for the verification of kinematic statements increased with the distance of the referent from the beginning of the causal chain of events in the pulley system. In contrast, reaction times for the verification of static statements did not vary with the position of the referent. These results support the view that when people attempt to determine how a component of a pulley system moves, they make a chain of inferences following the chain of causality in the system.

Analysis of the eye-fixation data allowed reaction time to be broken down into (a) time spent fixating the text, (b) time spent fixating the diagram depiction of the referent of the text, (c) time spent fixating the diagram depiction of components occurring before the referent in the causal chain of events, and (d) time spent fixating all other parts of the display. The additional time spent verifying kinematic statements was largely time spent fixating the diagram, indicating that diagram inspection was central to the mental animation process.

To verify static statements, subjects primarily fixated the diagram depiction of the referent of the statement. To verify kinematic statements, they fixated the depiction of both the referent and components that occur before the referent in the kinematic chain. Thus the eye-fixation data also provided support for the view that subjects determine the motion of a component by first determining the motion of components earlier in the causal chain of events in the system.

Greater insight into the mental animation process can be gained by examining the sequence of subjects' eye fixations on the text and diagram as they determine the motion of a component of a pulley system. Figure 26.4 shows a typical protocol of a subject verifying a statement about the movement of a component toward the end of the chain of events in a pulley system. In the data presented here, eye fixations have been aggregated to gazes, or groups of sequential fixations on the text or components of the diagram.

Two features of this protocol are notable. First, the subject does not start by inspecting the input of the system (the pull rope), but first gazes at one of the referents of the sentence (gaze 2) and then traces back to the upper pulley, which is close to the input of the system (gazes 3 to 6) before tracing forward, i.e., in the direction of the causal chain, to the referents of the sentences. Second, the later gazes (gazes 6 to 12) are longer than the earlier gazes. One possible interpretation is that the subject begins by examining the static relations between the pulley system components (gazes 2 to 6), and the longer gazes later in the protocol reflect the process of inferring the motion of successive components from this information about static relations. Future research will be concerned with analyzing the sequence of eye fixations to develop a more precise model of the stages of the mental animation process.

In summary, reaction time and eye-fixation data suggest that people determine the motion of a pulley system component by tracing the causal chain of events from the input of the system to the motion of the component in question and that inspection of the diagram is central to this mental animation process.

Conclusion

The research presented in this chapter demonstrates the usefulness of eye fixation data for studying complex cognitive tasks. The analysis of subjects' eye fixations provides an account of the cognitive processes involved in comprehending text and diagrams, suggesting that these processes are largely directed by the text, especially for readers with little background knowledge of the domain. Furthermore, eye fixation data gives us insight into the nature of people's representations of dynamic systems, suggesting that people represent the motion in a mechanical system as a causal chain of events starting with the input of the system. The eye-fixation methodology is a promising one for the study of visual problem-solving tasks in general.

References

Baddeley, A.D., & Lieberman, K. (1978). Spatial working memory. In R. Nickerson (Ed.), *Attention and performance* (pp. 521–539). London: Academic Press.

Bennett, C.K. (1969). *Bennett mechanical comprehension test*. New York: The Psychological Corporation.

Carpenter, P.A., & Just, M.A. (1989). The role of working memory in language comprehension. In D. Klahr & K. Kotovsky (Eds.), *Complex information processing: The impact of Herbert A. Simon*. Hillsdale, NJ: Erlbaum.

Carpenter, P.A., Just, M.A., & Shell, P. (1990). What one intelligence test measures: A theoretical account of the processing in the Raven Progressive Matrices Test. *Psychological Review*, 97, 404–431.

Daneman, M., & Carpenter, P.A. (1980). Individual differences in working memory and reading. *Journal of Verbal Learning and Verbal Behavior*, 19, 450–466.

de Kleer, J., & Brown, J.S. (1984). A qualitative physics based on confluences. *Artificial Intelligence*, 24, 7–83.

Forbus, K.D. (1984). Qualitative process theory. *Artificial Intelligence*, 24, 85–168.

Gentner, D., & Stevens, A.L. (Eds.). (1983). *Mental models*. Hillsdale, NJ: Erlbaum.

Hegarty, M. (1988). *Comprehension of diagrams accompanied by text*. Unpublished doctoral dissertation, Carnegie Mellon University.

Hegarty, M. (in press). *Mental animation: Inferring motion from static displays of mechanical systems*. Journal of Experimental Psychology: Learning, Memory & Cognition.

Hegarty, M., & Just, M.A. (1989). Understanding machines from text and diagrams. In H. Mandl & J. Levin (Eds.), *Knowledge acquisition from text and picture* (pp. 171–194). Amsterdam: North Holland.

Hegarty, M. & Just, M.A. (1991). *Constructing mental models of machines from text and diagrams*. Manuscript submitted for publication.

Hegarty, M., Just, M.A., & Morrison, I.R. (1988). Mental models of mechanical systems: Individual differences in qualitative and quantitative reasoning. *Cognitive Psychology*, 20, 191–236.

Just, M.A., & Carpenter, P.A. (1976). Eye fixations and cognitive processes. *Cognitive Psychology*, 8, 441–480.

Just, M.A., & Carpenter, P.A. (1985). Cognitive coordinate systems: Accounts of mental rotation and individual differences in spatial ability. *Psychological Review*, 92, 137–172.

Kieras, D.E., & Bovair, S. (1984). The role of a mental model in learning to operate a device. *Cognitive Science, 8,* 255–273.

Kintsch W., & Van Dijk, T.A. (1978). Toward a model of text comprehension and production, *Psychological Review, 85,* 363–394.

Kosslyn, S.M. (1980). *Image and mind.* Cambridge, MA: Harvard University Press.

Mayer, R.E. (1989). Models for understanding. *Review of Educational Research, 59,* 43–64.

Spoehr, K.T., & Horvath, J.A. (1989) *Running a mental model: Evidence from reaction time studies.* Paper presented at the Conference of the Psychonomic Society, Atlanta, Georgia.

27
Visual Analysis of Cartoons: A View from the Far Side

PATRICK J. CARROLL, JASON R. YOUNG, and
MICHAEL S. GUERTIN

Analyzing humor

"To ask how humor works in a grown-up person is to ask how everything works in a grown-up person," says Marvin Minsky (1988), making the issue sound profoundly important until the depressing realization sets in that understanding humor must consequently be remarkably complicated. Some solace comes from the fact that you can insert virtually any moderately complex psychological activity into Minsky's quotation, replacing "humor," and the quotation still works. Nevertheless, Minsky is right: humor is an intricate, somewhat murky phenomenon, probably explaining why scores of deep thinkers from Plato and Aristotle through

Descartes, Hobbes, and Kant to Darwin, Dewey, and Freud have had theories of humor.

From the cognitive perspective, humor is no joke. Lurking behind all that fun we are having on our periphery, in consciousness, armies of nerd-like processes are grinding away with serious determination, dissecting percepts, parsing captions, discovering appropriate domains of world knowledge, and reconstituting everything in a snap of recognition that, oddly enough—odd *especially* from the somber cognitive perspective—makes us laugh.

It is that instant of recognition, an experience that certainly deserves to be called a change of cognitive state, that is most striking about many forms of humor. (There are also "gentle" forms of humor that carry us along into a happier state, but do so without a jolt of recognition.) The change that occurs at the point in a joke when you "get it" is especially notable in that it is marked by an unmistakable behavior: laughter or a chuckle. This behavioral marker is interesting because it communicates in two directions: it is a social act, which tells everyone around us that comprehension has taken place, and it is self-informative, letting us know that a new phase of our own understanding has been initiated.

The fact that a change of mental state takes place in some forms of humor has not gone unnoticed. "Release" theories of humor (see Keith-Spiegel, 1972) suppose that tension is built up and then released in what Berlyne (1972) calls an arousal boost-jag. The first step, the boost, requires the person to experience a degree of uncomfortable confusion. The body of the joke must build this tension. The punch line ends the puzzlement, leading to a rapid discharge of tension, the jag. This dramatic change in level of internal pressure is experienced as humor.

Cognitive approaches to humor (again, see Keith-Spiegel, 1972) are not necessarily incompatible with Release theories, but they tend to emphasize information processing issues, such as expectations and problem solving. For example, Suls's (1972) two-stage theory, like Berlyne's, claims that humor results from two successive processing steps. According to Suls, in the first stage, the perceiver builds up expectations from the body of the joke and, at the end of the stage, finds the punch line to be incompatible with these expectations. The second stage is the denouement, achieved by problem solving that eventually finds a way to reconcile the seemingly incongruous information represented in the first stage. Following the lead of Newell, Shaw, and Simon's (1958) General Problem Solver, Suls characterizes the activity of the second stage as the discovery of a rule, a logical proposition, or some other elementary unit of information, that permits processing of all aspects of the joke without internal contradiction.

Cartoon Viewing

We have recently had the opportunity to observe college students viewing single-frame, captioned cartoons. We used an eye tracker to record scan paths as cartoons were presented. Cartoons offer a special brand of humor, although they fit neatly with the two-stage theories discussed above (Suls, 1972). We will restrict our discussion of cartoons by only referring to those having a single still picture, with no dialogue balloons, and a single caption. These cartoons frequently play off apparent incompatibility between the picture and the caption. This reflects Suls's first stage of humor processing. One set of expectations arises from looking at the caption and another from reading the text. There is a dynamic tension produced by the fact that the two sets of expectations do not mesh. The second stage of processing involves the attempt to make the picture and caption compatible with one another.

Take Figure 27.2 as an example of a typical single-frame cartoon. The picture has Dennis the Menace and his family eating dinner.[1] This cartoon is shown exactly as it appeared in a newspaper, but the caption should be disconcerting for anyone familiar with the comic strip. Dennis would never say such a thing. The caption was a mistake, taken by a typesetter from another cartoon, Gary Larson's *The Far Side*. This example was chosen to freeze you, the reader, as effectively as we could, at the end of the first stage. You should feel that something is not right. The picture makes sense; it is a normal dinner scene. The caption is pretty gruesome, but it makes sense; it is something a mad taxonomist might mutter to a snake or an opossum. The actual caption intended by the cartoonist is, "If I get as big as Dad, won't my skin be too TIGHT?" Fitting this caption to the picture should allow you to maneuver your way successfully through the second stage of processing. In this second stage, you will need to make a few decisions (e.g., it is the child, Dennis, who is talking) and fill in a few inferential steps (e.g., children are small; they may not realize that skin can grow with the rest of the body). The humor comes from realizing possible assumptions of the child's logic about the world and about his or her own body, similar to endless examples documented by students of cognitive development.

In addition to our interest in humor processing, we were also interested in studying people viewing pictures. As readers of this volume are undoubtedly aware, the study of picture viewing has a long history, and contributions by Boyce and Pollatsek, De Graef, Henderson, and Hegarty, all in this volume, give reason to hope that the topic will receive

---

[1] "Dennis the Menace" has been a popular comic strip in American newspapers for decades and the characters are very familiar to American readers. The full cartoon comes from Gary Larson's book, *The Prehistory of the Far Side* (1990).

"I see your little, petrified skull . . . labeled
and resting on a shelf somewhere."

FIGURE 27.2. A single-frame cartoon.

the renewed attention it deserves. Cartoon pictures attracted us because they combine a simplicity and orderliness not found in natural scenes but with sufficient complexity that people enjoy exploring them. Furthermore, these pictures have a correct interpretation; there is something going on in a cartoon picture that must be accurately construed for the cartoon to make sense. This means that someone can view a cartoon picture, unlike an ineffable natural scene, with the goal of understanding it, just as a person might study a text with the goal of understanding it.

For our studies, we showed subjects cartoons from Gary Larson's *The Far Side*.[2] These cartoons are popular among college-educated people. Although their humor tends to be fairly broad, the relationship between the caption and the picture can be subtle and challenging. We selected 24 cartoons by having judges rate 136 candidate cartoons on a number of dimensions. We chose cartoons that were, according to the judges, funny

---

[2] "The Far Side" is a syndicated, single-frame cartoon that is very popular in newspapers in the United States. Our examples were taken from "The Far Side 1989 Off-the-Wall Calendar" by Gary Larson, which contains cartoons that have previously appeared in the newspaper.

and easy to understand. For these 24 cartoons, judges also felt that both the picture and the caption together were necessary to make the cartoon funny; neither element alone was sufficient.

Order of Presentation

Normally, when you look at a cartoon, you can decide how much time to allocate to the picture and how much time to the caption. People report different tendencies. We observed a few subjects under these typical conditions and found, consistent with introspective reports, some differences in what people look at first and what order they view pictures and captions.[3] Figure 27.3 shows an arbitrarily chosen example of the viewing pattern of a subject for one of the cartoons.

In Figure 27.3, the subject first observed the picture, making three fixations (picture fixation durations are listed in order to the left of the picture), then she looked at the caption, reading it completely. Finally, she returned to the picture, viewing both characters, the speaker and Morty the Brain, but making few unnecessary fixations.

A similar pattern of fixations, with minor variations, has been produced by the handful of subjects we have monitored under these conditions. A few tentative generalizations are possible. First, processing of the picture and the caption are relatively isolated events. Viewers do not move back and forth repeatedly between cartoon elements. Second, the picture frequently is not given a full inspection until the caption has been read. For example, one subject (not the one from Figure 27.3) never looked at the picture before looking at the caption, and she never returned to the caption after she began picture viewing. Even in Figure 27.3, only a quick and partial picture analysis precedes caption reading. These findings are consistent with results reported by Hegarty and Just (1989; see also Hegarty, this volume), showing that people looked at diagrams only after reading supporting text, and they moved to the diagrams at major syntactic and semantic boundaries.

These points about viewing patterns, although limited by being anecdotal, help explain the procedure used in our experimental studies, in which picture and caption were presented separately. We decided to simplify the task from our point of view by presenting the picture and caption separately in sequence for each cartoon. There were two experimental conditions in Experiment 1: either the picture was presented first, followed by the caption (the Picture-First condition) or the caption was presented before the picture (the Caption-First condition). The virtue of

---

[3] We have conducted a full study of viewing under these conditions, but these data are not yet available.

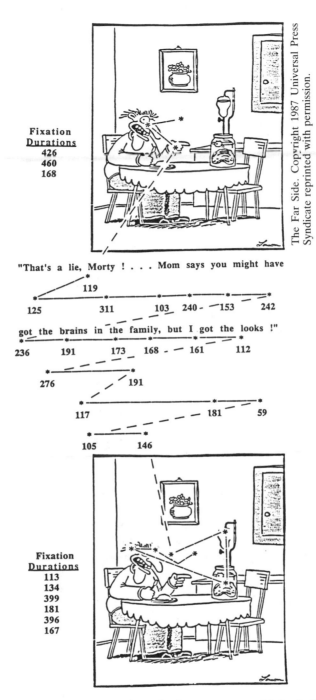

FIGURE 27.3. Scan path for one subject viewing a cartoon with both the picture and caption simultaneously visible. The picture is shown twice to indicate that the subject viewed the picture, then read the caption, and then returned to the picture. Fixation locations are marked with asterisks. For the caption, the asterisks are placed under the letter fixated, and fixation durations are marked in milliseconds below the appropriate asterisk. For the pictures, fixation durations are listed in order to the left of the picture.

this procedure is that it allows us to have subjects view cartoons in a nearly normal way and still have comparison conditions. The two presentation orders change the part of the cartoon visible when integration of caption and picture take place. When the subject views the picture in the Picture-First condition, it is not yet possible to fully understand the cartoon—to get the joke—so this processing is merely preparatory. The goal must be to commit information from the picture to memory in order to make it possible to understand the joke when the caption is shown. Picture viewing in the Caption-First condition has two things going on. Visual analysis similar to that required in the Picture-First condition certainly must occur; the attempt to integrate the picture and caption also takes place, resulting in the experience of incongruity. This same reasoning can also be applied to caption reading. In the Caption-First condition, the caption can be encoded, but the possibility of experiencing humor awaits presentation of the picture. In the Picture-First condition, the caption is encoded and integrated with a memory representation of the previously presented picture, and the stage two humor reaction can take place.

Our method in this study was to track viewers' eyes using an SRI Dual Purkinje eye tracker as they studied both pictures and captions. Subjects saw the first part of the cartoon and pressed a button when they were satisfied that they had sufficient information to go on to the second portion. This second element was presented immediately, and subjects indicated that they had gotten the joke by pressing the button again. Pressing the button terminated eye tracking for each element. Subjects were instructed to press the button as soon as they understood the joke, so button pressing on the second element roughly corresponded with the chuckle or laugh when they thought the cartoon was funny. If they did not understand the cartoon, they told the experimenter.[4]

We analyzed picture viewing much as we would analyze text processing, recording fixation times, saccade lengths, and number of fixations. Because the same picture or caption was observed in both conditions, differences in the values of these processing variables can be attributed to differences in task demands between the two conditions. Our discussion here is organized by separating picture viewing and caption reading. We start with the results of the picture viewing analyses, shown in Table 27.1.

---

[4] Less than 5% of the time, subjects reported an inability to understand a cartoon. There were strong individual differences in comprehension, with most reporting no problems, and others having difficulties with several. The most troublesome cartoon was one showing some cowboys sitting around a fire, with the caption: "Say, Simmons here just uttered a discouraging word." Apparently we have raised a generation deprived of the most fundamental knowledge of basic cowboy songs.

As can be seen in Table 27.1, total processing time did not differ between the two experimental conditions. Subjects viewed the pictures for about the same amount of time whether they had already read the caption or not. However, there were differences between the two experimental conditions. Average fixation duration was significantly longer in the Caption-First condition ($M = 289$ ms) than in the Picture-First condition ($M = 258$ ms). None of the other differences shown in Table 27.1 is statistically reliable, but it is worthwhile to note the trade-off in number of fixations and mean fixation duration. Subjects in the Caption-First condition—that is, the integration of the joke condition—make fewer and longer fixations, and their saccades are shorter. All of these factors are consistent with more careful processing. Longer fixation durations in text processing are believed to reflect deeper and more complex processing (cf. Rayner & Pollatsek, 1989, for a review of this literature). The Picture-First subjects, with shorter fixation durations, more fixations, and longer saccades show what might be considered an exploration pattern, which is a reasonable strategy (viz., be a little less careful and cover more ground) for viewing a picture that will be removed from sight before the caption is presented.

Two findings about picture viewing that are frequently cited are the fact that the first 100 ms of viewing seem to allow the viewer to determine the general structure of the scene (Biederman, 1972; Potter, 1975) and the fact that viewers seem to fixate "informative elements" of the picture (Antes, 1974; Mackworth & Morandi, 1967; Yarbus, 1967). These findings suggest that, from very early in picture viewing, the gist of the scene is understood, and higher cognitive activities can be initiated. If this is the case, we might expect that processing differences between the two experimental conditions will appear early and persist throughout picture processing. To explore this issue more thoroughly, we plotted the durations for each of the first 10 fixations.[5]

As Figure 27.4 shows, there is very little difference in processing times between the two experimental conditions for the first six fixations.[6] Thus,

---

[5] We stopped at 10 fixations because variance was rapidly increasing for each fixation. As can be seen in Table 27.1, the average number of fixations on pictures in Experiment 1 was approximately 12. Few pictures received fewer than 6 fixations, but some received many more than 12. The modal number of fixations was closer to 10 for each picture. The number of observations contributing to the means beyond 10 fixations decreased rapidly.

[6] The first fixation clearly shows a large difference in average fixation duration. It might be interesting to try to make something of this difference, but we will not do so here. One important reason for avoiding attributing importance to this difference is that the same kind of difference (though about half the magnitude) distinguished the two conditions in Experiment 2, which will be discussed later in this chapter. Unfortunately, *both* experimental conditions in Experiment 2 were equivalent to the Caption-First condition in Experiment 1. Rather than proposing

TABLE 27.1. Eye tracking measures for the picture portions of the cartoons in Experiment 1.

| | Picture viewing | |
	Picture first	Caption first
Total time (ms)	3,629	3,687
Mean fixation duration (ms)	258	289
Mean saccade length (degrees visual angle)	2.74	2.61
Mean number of fixations	12.50	12.05

Based on nine subjects each viewing 24 cartoons in the caption-first condition and nine subjects viewing 24 cartoons in the picture-first condition.

for about the first 1,600 ms, picture processing does not differ between a condition where the viewer is integrating the caption and subsequently cracking the joke (Caption First) and a condition where the viewer is inspecting the picture in anticipation of the caption (Picture First). It is also interesting that the fixation durations are relatively long (several around 300 ms) compared to reading fixation durations, which tend to average below 250 ms.

Starting with the seventh fixation, something curious happens. The average fixation time for the Picture-First condition drops quite dramatically, whereas the Caption-First condition, with all of its integration activity, continues to show the long fixation times. It is important to keep in mind that the subject terminates processing when he or she understands the joke; the processing times we are seeing here precede the laughter response.

Two Stages of Processing

Suls's theory holds that the cartoon processor should commit information from the first part of the cartoon to memory and then begin to process the second part of the cartoon. At some point while processing this second part, stage one should end with the experience of incongruity between the expectations arising from the two cartoon parts and stage two should begin with the attempt to resolve this incongruity. The results shown in Figure 27.4 are consistent with Suls's predictions. Between the sixth and seventh fixation, a change in processing seems to take place.[7] The

---

one explanation for the effect in Experiment 1 and an entirely different explanation in Experiment 2, we merely throw up our hands and mutter: "How about that!"

[7] There is nothing special about the sixth fixation or 1,600 ms. We assume that, for the cartoons we used, approximately this amount of time and inspection was needed to complete visual analysis and begin integration. For other Larson cartoons or for cartoons by another cartoonist, a different transition point might be found.

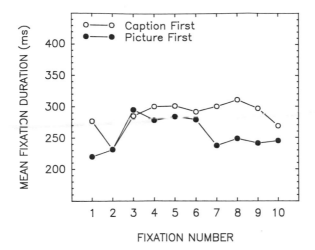

FIGURE 27.4. Mean fixation durations for the first 10 fixations on the picture portions of the cartoons in Experiment 1. Subjects in the caption-first condition had already read the captions, whereas those in the picture-first condition had not yet seen the captions. Each data point represents nine subjects each viewing 24 cartoons.

similarity in processing times for the first set of fixations suggests that the same thing is happening for both conditions. We interpret this as a period of visual analysis of the picture and identification of characters and objects in the picture. In Suls's terms, the viewer is looking for a schema that is consistent with the picture alone, independent of the caption. The difference in times after the sixth fixation indicates that something different is happening between conditions; subjects in the Caption-First condition continue to show long, deep-processing fixations, whereas subjects in the Picture-First condition show briefer fixations. This suggests to us that the Caption-First subjects are now resolving incongruities between the schemas associated with the caption and picture. This is a difficult problem-solving process, reflected in long fixation durations. Subjects in the Picture-First condition are still in stage one; they are checking their schema against details of the picture, but this is simply a double-checking process, necessitated only because the picture will not be available when the caption is presented.

According to Suls, during the first stage of humor processing, we are searching for the appropriate schema to understand the joke or cartoon. To help clarify what this means, it might be interesting to draw an analogy between cartoon processing and metaphor processing. Both kinds of stimuli, cartoons and linguistic metaphors, are creative; they avoid normal expectations while, for the sake of communication, trying to stay within the problem-solving capabilities of the reader or listener. Research

TABLE 27.2. Eye tracking measures for the caption portions of the cartoons in Experiment 1.

| | Caption reading | |
	Picture first	Caption first
Total time (ms)	3,166	4,338
Mean fixation duration (ms)	239	233
Mean saccade length (degrees visual angle)	3.07	2.64
Mean number of fixations	12.22	16.99

Based on nine subjects each viewing 24 cartoons in the caption-first condition and nine subjects viewing 24 cartoons in the picture-first condition.

has shown that, under certain circumstances, metaphors are interpreted in two stages. If only a brief metaphorical context has been provided, in the form of a sentence or two that initiates the use of a metaphor, then the processor must first interpret the linguistic information literally, and only thereafter, finding that the discourse is literal nonsense, try to find a metaphorical interpretation. If the context that creates the foundation for the metaphor is more substantial, then there is only one stage of processing, the metaphorical (Inhoff, Lima, & Carroll, 1984; Ortony, Schallert, Reynolds, & Antos, 1978). Using metaphors as a model, if we consider the cartoon to provide a brief context, then the goal of the first stage of processing is a literal representation of the cartoon elements. The caption is read without detection of plays on words. The picture is interpreted (e.g., a bunch of slugs are sitting around a table and another slug is emerging from the center of a huge cake on the table). Only after this, do we switch to "metaphor" processing (it is group of male slugs at a bachelor party, and the slug in the cake is a female). By this view, stage one involves a literal representation of the first cartoon element, and then a literal representation of the second cartoon element. Stage two involves a search for a nonliteral interpretation of the cartoon elements (e.g., unmarried human males are like slugs . . . hmmm).

The idea that a change in processing mode should be reflected in eye movement data is implicit in a broad range of literature. In one explicit statement of this view, Carroll and Slowiaczek (1987) described viewing patterns for garden-path sentences and texts containing grammatical and semantic anomalies. They claimed that there were two kinds of processing that can be observed in eye movements while people are reading extended text: "normal" processing mode, under control of an automatic lexical encoding stage and characterized by fixation durations around 250 ms and few interword regressions, and a "search-and-problem-solving" mode, in which eye movements come under control of top-down processes. This second mode of processing is characterized by longer fixations and more regressive fixations.

The two modes of eye movement behavior, and their underlying modes of processing, are roughly analogous to the two processing stages we have been discussing. In the picture viewing results, we saw elevated fixation durations, but not an increased number of fixations. We also examined caption reading results (Table 27.2). Recall that caption reading in the Caption-First condition should be entirely in stage one, whereas caption reading in the Picture-First condition should include both stage one (literal) and stage two (problem-solving) processing. As seen in Table 27.2, subjects spent much more time reading the Caption in the Caption-First condition, which is inconsistent with our predictions above. Looking at the elements of the viewing process, it is clear that the extra time is not due to increased fixation duration, but to shorter average saccade length and more fixations in the Caption-First condition. Carroll and Slowiaczek (1987) describe this as typical of a memorization pattern for single sentences (not longer texts); when we memorize we reread and, within each pass, show more regressions. They claim that number of fixations is more indicative of memorization of brief text than is a change in fixation duration.

The pattern for caption reading probably reflects a task-specific strategy; that is, subjects in the Caption-First condition may have felt compelled to memorize the caption to facilitate their comprehension of the subsequently presented drawing. This appears to have resulted in longer caption processing times in the Caption-First condition. The Picture-First subjects, on the other hand, did not need to memorize the caption; rather they simply needed to read the caption and then integrate it with their recollection of the previously encountered drawing. Why, then, did the memorization of pictures not have a similarly strong impact on response times in the Picture-First condition? It seems that the processing of pictures and sentences is different, and part of that difference is in our ability to quickly form a memory representation of these stimuli. For example, Shepard (1967) showed nearly perfect picture recognition after subjects viewed 612 pictures, each for an average of less than 6 seconds, following a 2-hour delay. Sentence memory was not as good in his experiment. Shepard's explanation for performance differences is that our capacity for assimilation and retrieval is greater for pictures than for sentences. Memorization can be seen as a strategy for compensating for memory limitations, as may occur when encoding linguistic information. Ultimately, understanding the extent of this disparity between picture memory and sentence memory remains an empirical issue.

Mismatched Captions

Our first experiment gave some support to a two-stage model of cartoon understanding. Our second experiment was inspired by the Dennis the Menace example (Figure 27.2). In this study, half of the cartoons for each subject had the wrong caption, and the other half had the correct caption. We accomplished this by incorrectly pairing half of the pictures and

TABLE 27.3. Eye tracking measures for the picture and caption portions of the cartoons in Experiment 2.

	Match	Mismatch
Picture viewing		
Total time (ms)	3,490	4,490
Mean fixation duration (ms)	300	291
Mean saccade length (degrees visual angle)	2.81	2.95
Mean number of fixations	10.44	13.73
Caption reading		
Total time (ms)	3,754	3,746
Mean fixation duration (ms)	237	226
Mean saccade length (degrees visual angle)	2.83	2.88
Mean number of fixations	14.04	14.60

Based on 20 subjects, each contributing to both match and mismatch conditions. Each subject viewed 12 cartoons in each condition.

captions used in Experiment 1. This new pairing was haphazard, except that we tried to avoid any mispaired cartoons that were inadvertently funny. Thus, the humor reaction should not mislead anyone into thinking the captions were correctly paired. All cartoons were presented in the Caption-First order. Because we have argued above that picture viewing is more informative about the stages of processing, the Caption-First condition allows us to concentrate on this cartoon element.

In Experiment 1, different subjects (9 in each group) were in the Caption-First and Picture-First conditions, each viewing all 24 cartoons in that condition. In Experiment 2, each subject ($N = 20$) served in both experimental conditions. Half of the 24 cartoons were properly matched with their captions (Match condition) and half had incorrect captions (Mismatch condition). Each cartoon was seen an equal number of times in the Match and Mismatch conditions across subjects, although for a given subject the cartoon was only seen once and in only one condition.

Table 27.3 shows the results of the second experiment. Picture viewing is the place to look for completion of stage one and initiation of stage two processing. We will not discuss caption reading, because this is identical for both conditions in Experiment 2. As Table 27.3 shows, there were no significant differences in caption reading for any of our eye movement measures. For picture viewing, there was a significant difference in total processing time between the two conditions, with picture viewing taking significantly longer on the average in the Mismatch condition, as might be expected. Average fixation durations for the two conditions are not significantly different, and they are comparable to the average fixation duration for the Caption-First condition in Experiment 1. Figure 27.5 shows fixation durations for the first 10 fixations. (Results from the

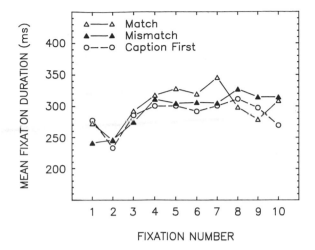

FIXATION NUMBER

FIGURE 27.5. Mean fixation durations for the first 10 fixations on the picture portions of the cartoons in Experiment 2. For comparison purposes, the caption-first condition from Experiment 1 is also plotted (open circles). The caption-first data is the same information as shown in Figure 27.4. For the match and mismatch conditions from Experiment 2, each data point represents 20 subjects each viewing 12 cartoons.

Caption-First condition in Experiment 1 are plotted here for comparison purposes.) The overlapping curves are consistent with the fact that there is no statistically reliable difference between the Match and Mismatch conditions across these first 10 fixations.[8]

If we use the explanation developed for Experiment 1, the fixation duration results are quite reasonable. We assume that stage one occurs in the Mismatch condition just as it does in the Match condition: both elements of the cartoon, picture and caption, must be literally represented and an incongruity discovered. This should take the same amount of time that it did in the first study, about 1,600 ms, or about six fixations. Stage two is marked by a maintenance of long fixation durations. This is what is shown in Figure 27.5.

The two conditions in this experiment should differ, however. Table 27.3 makes it clear where this difference lies: number of fixations. In the Mismatch condition, subjects make an average of more than three addit-

---

[8] Because some subjects would make only five or six fixations on a picture, after about the fifth fixation, a decreasing number of data points contributes to each point plotted here. This is true for Figure 27.4 as well. Beyond 10 fixations, the number declines rapidly and differentially for the two conditions. Thus, plotting beyond the first fixation uses distributions that have progressively increasing variance and a corresponding loss of stability in estimating mean performance.

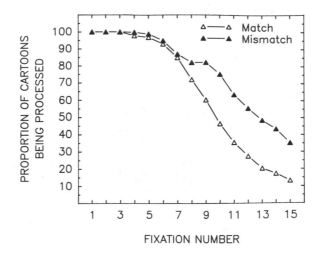

FIGURE 27.6. The relative rate with which subjects finished processing cartoons in the two conditions in Experiment 2, plotted for the first 15 possible fixations. Every cartoon received at least three fixations, and subjects tended to complete processing in the match conditions with fewer fixations than in the mismatch condition. Tracking was terminated by the subject's pressing a button to indicate that the cartoon had been understood.

ional fixations. In the Match condition—when the caption and picture belong together—processing can be terminated as the viewer understands the joke. In the Mismatch condition, the viewer must be sure to look and think long enough to be confident that there is no joke to be gotten. Stage two processing is extended.

One way to look for an extended stage two is to record the point, counted in number of fixations, when the viewer presses the button to terminate processing. In Experiment 2, the subject's response criterion was slightly different from that used in the first study. In Experiment 1, subjects merely pressed the response button when they understood the joke in the cartoon. In Experiment 2, they pressed one of two buttons. If they believed that the caption and picture belonged together, they pressed one button (the "Match" decision) and if they thought the caption and picture did not belong together, they pressed another button (a "Mismatch" decision). Subjects almost always made the correct decision.

The Match decision can be made when a person gets the cartoon's joke. The Mismatch decision must be based on a failure to find a joke, though there were relatively subtle linguistic cues in some examples. Figure 27.6 gives us an indication of the way that the two experimental conditions in Experiment 2 differed. It shows the proportion of cartoons still being processed at each of the first 15 fixations, simply pooling all data from all 20 subjects. It shows that every subject made at least three fixations on every cartoon. Only a handful of cartoons received fewer than five fixations. The slope of both lines begins to decline at six fixations, but the conditions diverge noticeably at the eighth fixation. Experiment 1 showed no difference at all between conditions using this measurement.

Two interesting points can be made from the results shown in Figure 27.6. First, the difference between the Match and Mismatch conditions is entirely in the number of fixations the viewer devotes to viewing the picture. Those fixations are relatively long (around 300 ms) in both conditions, and saccade lengths are about the same in both conditions as well. Second, if we expect that it takes about five fixations to complete stage one processing, as we found in Experiment 1, then divergence in processing at about the eighth fixation is about right: just enough time to complete stage one literal processing and begin stage two problem solving. These data are consistent with our evidence from Experiment 1.

Conclusion

We have described cartoon understanding as a two-stage process, in which the pleasure—in some way we do not fully understand—is a consequence of solving a puzzle or resolving a problem. Within the context of general eye movement issues, cartoon processing provides another example of the short distance between peripheral control of eye movements and deep processes that serve understanding. Cartoons originally intrigued us because of an analogy we drew between text processing and cartoon processing. When a person is reading extended discourse, information is encoded, stored away, and selectively retrieved as new information is encoded. For decades, psycholinguists have emphasized the constructive nature of discourse processing (e.g., Bransford & Johnson, 1972). By this claim, they assert that coherence is not inherent in the text; it must be constructed by the reader from the literal information arriving through the senses and from knowledge the reader brings to the text. This same interplay of new information and stored knowledge is required for understanding cartoons. Usually, the picture is visually simplified—at least compared to a natural-world scene—and the caption is relatively simple linguistically. Such simplicity generally means that something is left out, something is "left to the imagination." Using the Dennis the Menace example (Figure 27.2), we must add to the picture and caption considerable knowledge about children's reasoning (e.g., that they might think of growing up as being analogous to blowing up a balloon). The cartoon makes no sense if we do not add our own ideas to the information provided by the cartoonist.

A corollary of the fact that comprehension is constructive is the fact that we are active processors. This means that we must make decisions about the proper representation of incoming information, and these decisions are risky; they may successfully integrate the text or they may fail to do so. The processor must have the requisite knowledge to contribute to comprehension and must succeed in retrieving it when it is needed. The same holds true for cartoon viewing. The processor must have the knowledge necessary to interpret the cartoon and must succeed in applying the available knowledge as the cartoonist intended. The failure of the transition from the first to the second stage is the nightmare of the guy who can't tell a joke. He builds up the story and tells the punch line. An interminable 5 seconds later, he breaks the silence by retelling the punch line and explaining its logic. Everyone politely titters and leaves to check on the babysitter. Either stage one ended with no conflict or stage two petered out with no resolution.

Theories of humor processing are not very sophisticated and the data are limited, but the phenomenon itself is such a wonderful one. What inventor would ever have thought of making a machine with such a strange proclivity? Humor is automatic and conscious, cognitive and emotional, intelligent and stupid. Humor is profoundly and uniquely human.

Acknowledgments. The authors thank Brian Smith, Derrick Smith, and Scott Seraboff for their assistance in conducting this research. We also express our appreciation to Beverly A. Wright for helping produce the figures and especially for her insights and advice on earlier versions of this chapter.

References

Antes, J.R. (1974). The time course of picture viewing. *Journal of Experimental Psychology, 103*, 62–70.

Berlyne, D.E. (1972). Humor and its kin. In J.H. Goldstein and P.E. McGhee (Eds.), *The psychology of humor* (pp. 43–60). New York: Academic Press.

Biederman, I. (1972). Perceiving real-world scenes. *Science, 177*, 77–80.

Bransford, J.D., & Johnson, M.K. (1972). Contextual prerequisites for understanding: Some investigations of comprehension and recall. *Journal of Verbal Learning and Verbal Behavior, 11*, 717–726.

Carroll, P.J., & Slowiaczek, M.L. (1987). Modes and modules: Multiple paths to the language processor. In J.L. Garfield (Ed.), *Modularity in knowledge representation and natural-language understanding* (pp. 221–247). Cambridge, MA: MIT Press.

Hegarty, M., & Just, M.A. (1989). Understanding machines from text and diagrams. In H. Mandl & J.R. Levin (Eds.), *Knowledge acquisition from text and picture*. Amsterdam: North Holland.

Inhoff, A.W., Lima, S.D., & Carroll, P.J. (1984). Contextual effects on metaphor comprehension in reading. *Memory & Cognition*, *12*, 558–567.

Keith-Spiegel, P. (1972). Early conceptions of humor: Varieties and issues. In J.H. Goldstein & P.E. McGhee (Eds.), *The psychology of humor* (pp. 4–39). New York: Academic Press.

Larson, G. (1990). *The prehistory of the Far Side*. Kansas City, MI: Andrews and McMeel.

Mackworth, N.H., & Morandi, A.J. (1967). The gaze selects informative details within pictures. *Perception and Psychophysics*, *2*, 547–552.

Minsky, M. (1988). *The society of mind*. New York: Touchstone Books.

Newell, A., Shaw, R., & Simon, H. (1958). Elements of a theory of human problem solving. *Psychological Review*, *65*, 151–166.

Ortony, A., Schallert, D.L., Reynolds, R.E., & Antos, S.J. (1978). Interpreting metaphors and idioms: Some effects of context on comprehension. *Journal of Verbal Learning and Verbal Behavior*, *17*, 465–477.

Potter, M.C. (1975). Meaning in visual search. *Science*, *187*, 965–966.

Rayner, K., & Pollatsek, A. (1989). *The psychology of reading*. Englewood Cliffs, NJ: Prentice-Hall.

Shepard, R.N. (1967). Recognition memory for words, sentences, and pictures. *Journal of Verbal Learning and Verbal Behavior*, *6*, 156–163.

Suls, J.M. (1972). A two-stage model for the appreciation of jokes and cartoons: An information-processing analysis. In J.H. Goldstein & P.E. McGhee (Eds.), *The psychology of humor* (pp. 81–100). New York: Academic Press.

Yarbus, A.L. (1967). *Eye movements and vision*. New York: Plenum Press.

28
Eye Movements and Complex Comprehension Processes

SUSAN A. DUFFY

The chapters in this section focused on discovering what the eyes can tell us about the higher level processes involved in language comprehension, from the comprehension of individual sentences to the comprehension of text accompanied by pictures. In discussing these chapters I have chosen to elaborate on three themes that are common to several of them. In the process, I will raise more questions than answers, because I see these themes as ones that the field is just beginning to address.

Picture-Text Comprehension

Research within cognitive psychology on language comprehension processes has for the most part focused on the processing of linguistic information alone. In retrospect this is somewhat surprising, especially within the reading literature, because so much of what we read is accompanied by pictorial or diagrammatic information. This pairing of visual language with pictures begins with our first reading experiences in school and continues in our adult experience with magazines and newspapers, instructions for using appliances, journal articles, subtitled movies, etc. Presumably, most skilled readers are skilled at alternating between pictures and text in order to produce a mental model of the complete message. Yet we know little about this complex process. The chapters by Hegarty, by Carroll, Young and Guertin, and by d'Ydewalle and Gielen are welcome sorties into this new area of research.

Ideally, what would we want to know about the process of comprehending picture-text combinations? It seems reasonable to begin by assuming that there are two separate processing systems involved, one for analyzing the pictures and one for analyzing the language. Presumably these are two independent systems; the picture processing system cannot use the lexicon accessed by the language processor. Similarly, if there is a syntax of pictures, it is undoubtedly not the same as that of linguistic material.

Although these two systems are independent, each capable of working without the other, they cannot be working independently when processing picture-text combinations. That is, they are working toward building an integrated representation of the message. As Carroll et al. make clear, the humor is absent when one sees just the caption or picture alone. Similarly, in the Hegarty work, comprehension may fail when diagrams or text are presented alone. Thus, the systems must communicate in some way to build this integrated representation. This leads us to the question of where the points of communication occur.

Points of Communication

Some possible hypotheses come to mind, inspired by research within the reading literature. In this literature, the effect of context on lexical access is currently a hotly debated topic, with the debate centering on the extent to which lexical access is autonomous (e.g., Duffy, Henderson, & Morris, 1989). Within that literature, context is thought of as the linguistic context in which a word appears (i.e., the preceding words in the sentence). Within picture-text processing, one might expect to find cross-modality context effects in which lexical access is influenced by the pictures recently processed or in which picture recognition is influenced by the words recently read. Carroll et al. have shown that reading the caption first does influence processing of the picture, although the locus of the influence cannot be assigned at this point. One could turn the question around and ask to what extent viewing the cartoon first influenced the processing of the caption. Such influences, if influences on lexical access, would seem relevant to the modularity debates.

Another area of communication suggested by the reading literature is at the level of the search for referents for noun phrases. There is a general consensus that readers do regularly retrieve the antecedents for pronoun and noun phrase anaphora by searching the mental representation of the text that they have built during comprehension (Lesgold, Roth & Curtis, 1979; McKoon & Ratcliff, 1980; O'Brien, Duffy, & Myers, 1986). Furthermore, the search for an antecedent seems to be initiated (but not necessarily completed) immediately when an anaphoric noun phrase is encountered (Duffy & Rayner, 1990; Just & Carpenter, 1980). When a text is accompanied by pictures, the referents for various noun phrases in the text can be found in the picture. To what extent do readers search the pictures for referents for the noun phrases that they have read, and how is this search timed?

Hegarty has begun to answer these questions with her eye movement data for subjects comprehending texts accompanied by diagrams of pulley systems. She finds that subjects tend to fixate those objects in the diagram referred to by the most recently read sentences. Thus, readers are indeed searching for referents in the diagram. In contrast to the search for a linguistic antecedent, this search is not immediate. Subjects tend not to jump immediately from a noun phrase to its diagram representation. Rather subjects wait until the end of a clause or sentence to inspect the diagram. This difference in the timing of the search for a linguistic versus nonlinguistic referent must reflect some property of the comprehension system and the representations it operates on. It seems worthy of further investigation.

Control of the Eyes

A second characteristic of the operation of these two processing systems is that they must compete (or cooperate) to use the eyes. The eyes are, of course, a limited-capacity resource because they can only focus on one limited area at a time. This becomes especially apparent in the problem that d'Ydewalle and Gielen are addressing in which both language and picture information are displayed for a limited amount of time on the screen. One might ask how the two processes control the sharing of the eyes. The answer suggested by the research reported here is that the language processor is in control. In the work of d'Ydewalle and Gielen, the eyes were drawn to the subtitles when they appeared on the screen even when the subjects knew the language they were hearing. It would be interesting to know if this "magnet" effect of subtitles holds no matter what compelling events are occurring on the screen. Hegarty's work also suggests the dominance of the language processor in determining when each processor controls the eyes. She found that readers tended to break away from linguistic material at the end of a sensible linguistic boundary rather than interrupting in the middle of a linguistic unit. Furthermore, the eyes tended to look at that part of the picture that represented what had just been read. Similarly, Carroll et al. found that subjects given both picture and caption tended to delay a full inspection of the picture until fully processing the caption. Thus, it seems to be the linguistic processor that determines when the picture processor may use the eyes and what it is the eyes should look for in the picture. One might ask whether there are any circumstances in which the picture processor is in control. If there are, what principles determine the controlling process?

Regressions

Another issue that is raised in a number of ways in these chapters is the role of regressive eye movements in the comprehension process. These are the movements of the eyes in which the reader refixates information that has already been fixated. For example, in Carroll et al.'s Figure 3, the subject regresses twice to the word "brains" in the course of reading the caption of the picture. Similarly, in Hegarty's Figure 2c, the subject fixates the lower left-hand rope and then the lower pulley and then refixates the same two locations in the same order. Regressions also play a critical role in Clifton's chapter. Clifton reports two different sets of means from his data: first-pass time and total time. Total time differs from first-pass time in that it includes regressions to information in the sentence. Interestingly, the first-pass data and the total time data in some cases provide different pictures of processing difficulty. For example, in the first experiment, first-pass times reveal processing difficulties for noun attachment sentences; this difficulty is absent from the total time data which instead reflect a difficulty for adjunct attachment sentences. The reasonable conclusion is that variability in first-pass times is reflecting an early stage of processing (i.e., the syntactic processor) and variability spent in regressions is reflecting later stages of processing.

Why Regress?

Kennedy raises the intriguing question of why readers refixate information that they have already fixated. This question is especially puzzling when one considers the examples given above. In all cases it is reasonable to assume that the refixated information should be currently sitting in working memory. This is true for the majority of regressions found in eye movement data. Subjects rarely regress far. My impression from scoring this kind of data is that in most text, readers almost never regress to earlier lines; regressions, when they occur, are confined to the current line.

Kennedy suggests some possible answers. One is that readers need to access a word all over again. This makes sense for words for which initial lexical access processes have resulted in selection of the wrong meaning (Duffy, Morris, & Rayner, 1988) or syntactic processes have selected the wrong part of speech (Frazier & Rayner, 1987). There is a suggestive bit of data in a classic paper of Carpenter and Daneman (1981) that is relevant. They had subjects read aloud sentences containing homographs (e.g., "tears") while they monitored eye movements. They found that word length correlated with the initial gaze durations on the target words, but word length did not correlate with the durations of regressions to the target words. Although ideally one would like to see similar data from a more natural, silent reading task, this finding suggests that subjects are not reprocessing the word in the same way as it was initially processed.

Mental Regressions Versus Eye Regressions

In addressing the question of the role of regressions, it may be useful to view eye regressions in a broader context. Physical eye regressions can be thought of as one type of reprocessing operation. By reprocessing operation, I mean those operations initiated because the reader has a need to retrieve information that has already been processed once. Such reprocessing operations are a frequent occurrence during reading. Sometimes they are initiated to correct an error. For example, the reader must find an alternative meaning for an ambiguous word that was incorrectly interpreted. Or, the reader must find an alternative parse for part of a sentence after being garden-pathed. Sometimes these operations are initiated to reinstate information that is needed for the comprehension of what is currently being processed, as in the case of antecedent information for anaphora (McKoon & Ratcliff, 1980; O'Brien et al., 1986), or goal information that is needed to help understand why a character is currently doing what she/he is doing (Myers, 1990).

The point is that these reprocessing operations are sometimes accomplished by a physical eye regression and on other occasions they are accomplished by a mental regression alone. What distinguishes these two situations? One possibility is that an eye regression is an operation of last resort, initiated only when a mental regression fails. In this case, one would expect that all eye regressions would be preceded by a long fixation, indicating that a mental regression is being attempted. Alternatively, there may be certain kinds of situations that immediately call for a mental regression and others that immediately call for an eye regression. Each kind of regression seems to have a cost associated with it. The mental regression may be fast but there is always the risk that the needed information will not be found in the mental representation. The eye regression may ensure that the needed information is found, but it may be time-consuming both in terms of the movements of the eyes back and forth on the page and in terms of the amount of reprocessing that may be required once the needed information is located. Thus, the reader may be doing some optimizing in choosing between a mental and an eye regression.

Two factors are likely to be relevant to the choice. The first is the level of information needed. An antecedent, for example, may be available in a more appropriate representational form in the reader's mental representation of the text than it is in the information on the physical page. This may account for the scarcity of regressions in Ehrlich and Rayner's (1983) data on disambiguation of pronouns. Even in their distant condition, where the antecedent for the pronoun was far enough away to sound awkward, subjects initiated an eye regression on only 4% of the trials. Alternatively, if a process early in sentence comprehension has failed, recovery might be most easily accomplished by refixating the problem area (which should be physically close on the page) rather than trying to reprocess a string of words fading from working memory. This may account for the frequency of eye regressions in the garden-path sentences used by Frazier and Rayner (1982); subjects initiated an eye regression on an average of 43% of the sentences.

A second factor that is likely to be relevant is the distance of the targeted information. Readers seem to be more willing to make a regression to information on the current line than to information on earlier lines in a text. This may reflect the availability of a spatial representation for close information, as suggested by Kennedy. This may also reflect an increasing cost of distant eye regressions. The farther the eye regresses, the more eye movements may be needed precisely to locate the needed information and then to get the eyes back to the point from which they regressed.

Regressions for Recovery from Error

Although mental regressions are more frequently used than eye regressions to retrieve information that is at some distance in the text, within a sentence both kinds of regressions are used to recover from error. Evidence of these two kinds of recovery processes can be seen in Clifton's Experiment 1 data. Consider just the NA-ADJ sentences compared with the VA-ADJ sentences. For both of these sentences, the critical prepositional phrase has a less preferred adjunct relationship to the preceding verb or noun rather than a more preferred argument relationship. In addition, the NA-ADJ sentences are non–minimal attachment sentences for which the parser should be initially garden-pathed. Thus, for the NA-ADJ sentences, there are two potential errors to be made on the prepositional phrase that may require recovery; for the VA-ADJ there is only one.

The eye movement record suggests that the error recovery procedures differ for the two sentences. For the NA-ADJ sentences, the recovery takes place on the first pass through the region that follows the critical prepositional phrase. The time spent in regressions is comparable to the time spent on the VA-ARG sentences (which can be considered the baseline here because there should be no systematic parsing problems for these sentences). Presumably, the extremely long time spent on the post-PP region reflects a mental regression that reparses the earlier part of the sentence without needing to consult the physical record. In contrast, for the VA-ADJ sentences, there is no hint of a problem within the first-pass data, with the times as fast as those for the baseline VA-ARG sentences. The error recovery shows up in the difference between the first-pass times and the total times; this difference is largest for the VA-ADJ sentences compared with the other sentences. The inference is that error recovery is carried out through a series of eye regressions in which the critical earlier parts of the sentence are refixated. These different recovery patterns may reflect the relative timing of the discovery of the error. That is, the initial attachment error for the NA-ADJ sentences (to the verb rather than the noun) may be discovered earlier in processing than the type of attachment error for the VA-ADJ sentences (attachment as argument rather than adjunct). When an error is discovered early, it is more likely that an accurate trace of the sentence will remain in working memory.

Clifton finds the same kind of contrast when comparing the data for the last three experiments. Sometimes the error recovery emerges in the form of lengthened fixations in the late regions of the sentence; sometimes the error recovery can be seen in a series of regressive eye movements. As Clifton indicates, the puzzle is to account for these different patterns. Systematic differences in error recovery should provide more clues to the operation of the comprehension system and to the properties of the representations it uses.

Representations Available During Reading

Running through both of the themes I have discussed so far is a third issue, the issue of what mental representations are available during comprehension. The issue is raised at two levels. First, the picture-text work raises the question of what kind of final representation is produced by the joint operation of the picture and text processing systems. Is it some kind of mix of images and linguistic material, each stored in a different format, the language in some sense annotating the images? Or, alternatively, is it some modality-free representation that preserves the message distilled from the picture-text combination? Memory studies in which one tested memory for the modality in which a given piece of information was presented might at least indicate the extent to which modality-specific memories exist.

A second level of representation addressed, in Kennedy's chapter and in my discussion of error recovery procedures, is the representation at the initial, or surface level of processing during reading. Kennedy's claim is that the reader maintains a spatial memory that preserves the location of the various words on the page. Furthermore, this memory is used during the comprehension process for keeping track of word order during encoding. Some support for this kind of claim appears in Frazier and Rayner's (1982) paper on garden-path sentences. Frazier and Rayner looked at patterns of eye regressions as a way to judge whether subjects simply worked their way methodically back through the information in a sentence until they reached the misparsed information. They found that subjects most frequently regressed directly to the misparsed information. Of course, subjects could have been carrying out the word by word search mentally and only moving the eyes when the mental search ended, but the point is that subjects must have had a spatial representation of the sentence available in order accurately to direct an eye movement to the misparsed information, as Kennedy claims.

The claim is an intriguing one that leads to speculations about additional uses for this type of representation. For example, is this spatial representation also used for mental regressions that occur instead of eye regressions for recovery from error? If so, the kinds of sentences used by Frazier and Rayner (1982) or by Clifton in this volume should be more difficult to comprehend when presented in the standard rapid-serial visual presentation (RSVP) format (Kennedy's nonspatial mode), each word appearing in the same position, compared to a word by word format in which the words appear in consecutive positions across the screen (Kennedy's spatial mode).

Readers also regress (usually mentally, rarely with the eyes) to find the antecedent for a current anaphoric phrase. Does a spatial representation exist for earlier sentences as well as the current one? And is this representation used to guide the regression? Here the duration of such a spatial representation becomes relevant. The fact that eye regressions tend to be to information that is physically close might be an indication that the spatial representation that guides these regressions is short-lived. As a result, at any point in a text a spatial representation would be available for directing eye regressions or mental regressions to recently read information but not to more distant information. There is, however, some evidence that Kennedy cites (e.g., Zechmeister & McKillop, 1972) that suggests that readers do have some memory for the position of distant information on the page. One might want to speculate whether that kind of surface information, in addition to propositional or mental model information, is actually used for locating a distant anaphor that is currently needed.

Conclusions

The chapters in this section have focused on modeling the higher level processes involved in visual language comprehension. The goal is a comprehension model in which we identify the component processes, the principles by which these processes are scheduled, and the representations available to each process. It is difficult to imagine the field arriving at such a model without the benefit of the kind of eye movement data reported here. The eye movement record is currently the best record we have of moment-to-moment processing during comprehension. As we have seen from the Clifton data, if we are to understand something about real-time comprehension processes, we will frequently be misled if we depend on total time measures summed across many fixations.

Although the eyes may provide a window into the mind, it is not a perfectly clear window. For the complex comprehension tasks studied here the drawback is that the eye movement record is exceedingly complex. The challenge is to look at the kind of data that Carroll et al. present in Figure 3 and determine some reasonable way to summarize the pattern averaged across texts and subjects. It is clear that as we become more experienced at looking at eye movement data for complex comprehension tasks, we become better at cleverly "parsing" that data so that we can draw sensible inferences about the underlying comprehension processes. For example, Clifton has separated first-pass data from the later pass fixations that contribute to his total time measure. It is this kind of careful approach to the eye movement record that will allow us to establish the link between the movement of the eyes and the complex comprehension process that we are interested in understanding.

Acknowledgments. Preparation of this chapter was supported in part by National Institute of Mental Health research grants 5 R03 MH46855 to Amherst College and 1 R01 MH40029 to the University of Massachusetts and by National Institutes of Health research grant DC-0111-14 to Indiana University where the final version of the chapter was prepared.

References

Carpenter, P.A., & Daneman, M. (1981). Lexical retrieval and error recovery in reading: A model based on eye fixations. *Journal of Verbal Learning and Verbal Behavior, 20*, 137–160.

Duffy, S.A., Henderson, J.M., & Morris, R.K. (1989). Semantic facilitation of lexical access during sentence processing. *Journal of Experimental Psychology: Learning, Memory and Cognition, 15*, 791–801.

Duffy, S.A., Morris, R.K., & Rayner, K. (1988). Lexical ambiguity and fixation times in reading. *Journal of Memory and Language, 27*, 429–446.

Duffy, S.A., & Rayner, K. (1990). Eye movements and anaphor resolution: Effects of antecedent typicality and distance. *Language and Speech, 33*, 103–119.

Ehrlich, K., & Rayner, K. (1983). Pronoun assignment and semantic integration during reading: Eye movements and immediacy of processing. *Journal of Verbal Learning and Verbal Behavior, 22*, 75–87.

Frazier, L., & Rayner, K. (1982). Making and correcting errors during sentence comprehension: Eye movements in the analysis of structurally ambiguous sentences. *Cognitive Psychology, 14*, 178–210.

Frazier, L., & Rayner, K. (1987). Resolution of syntactic category ambiguities: Eye movements in parsing lexically ambiguous sentences. *Journal of Memory and Language, 26*, 505–526.

Just, M.A., & Carpenter, P.A. (1980). A theory of reading: From eye fixations to comprehension. *Psychological Review, 87*, 329–354.

Lesgold, A.M., Roth, S.F., & Curtis, M.E. (1979). Foregrounding effects in discourse comprehension. *Journal of Verbal Learning and Verbal Behavior, 18*, 291–308.

McKoon, G., & Ratcliff, R. (1980). The comprehension processes and memory structures involved in anaphoric reference. *Journal of Verbal Learning and Verbal Behavior, 19*, 668–682.

Myers, J.L. (1990). Causal relatedness and text comprehension. In D.A. Balota, G.B. Flores d'Arcais, & K. Rayner (Eds.), *Comprehension processes in reading* (pp. 361–375). Hillsdale, NJ: Erlbaum.

O'Brien, E.J., Duffy, S.A., & Myers, J.L. (1986). Anaphoric inference during reading. *Journal of Experimental Psychology: Learning, Memory and Cognition, 12*, 346–352.

Zechmeister, C.B., & McKillop, J. (1972). Recall of place on the page. *Journal of Educational Psychology, 63*, 446–453.

Index